FISHING TACKLE

FISHING TACKLE

A Collector's Guide

Graham Turner

WARD LOCK

First published in Great Britain in 1989 by
Ward Lock Limited, Artillery House, Artillery Row,
London SW1 1RT.
A Cassell Company.

British Library Cataloguing in Publication Data

Turner, Graham
Fishing tackle: a collector's guide.
1. Angling equipment
I. Title
799.1'2'028

ISBN 0–7063–6839–8

Designed and Produced exclusively for
Ward Lock Limited by
Jamesway Graphics
18/19 Hanson Close
Middleton, Manchester M24 2HD.

Printed in Italy

CONTENTS

ACKNOWLEDGEMENTS

The author wishes to express his gratitude to the people in Britain, America and other countries who have provided information, material and photographs for inclusion in this publication. Also to collectors for allowing him access to early angling books, trade catalogues, and tackle for photographs, especially Mr James Hardy for use of the Hardy Bros archives.

A debt is acknowledged to the Kentucky History Museum, Richard W Oliver Galleries and American collectors Steven Vernon, Frank Stewart and Karl White.

The author would further like to say a special thank you to the following for their generous help:–
Her Royal Highness Queen Elizabeth the Queen Mother; staff of the Lord Chamberlain's Office and Kew Palace; Mr G George at Hampton Court Palace; The British Museum; Professor Lord Adrian MD, FRS (Vice-Chancellor) University of Cambridge; Dr D W Phillipson MA, PhD, FSA Museum of Archaeology and Anthropology, Cambridge University; Mr A G Credland, Town Docks Museum, Kingston upon Hull; Patent Office; Mrs G M Getz of The State Museum of Pennsylvania and The Pennsylvania Historical and Museum Commission; Alanna Fisher, American Museum of Fly Fishing; Mr Brian M Fagan, University of California; Mr Paul F Beelitz, American Museum of Natural History; Mr I W Brown (Curator), Peabody Museum of Archaeology and Ethnology of Harvard University; The Curator, Museum of Natural History, New York; The National Museum of Zimbabwe; Mr Arun D Mazel, Natal Museum, South Africa; The Curator, B C Provincial Museum, Canada; Mr Li Helen, Beijing Liu Xum Museum, China; The Curator, Museum of China, Peking; Sinolink, London (Chinese Translations); The Hermitage Museum, Leningrad, Russia; Dr Ludek Seitl, Moravian Museum, Czechoslovakia.
Staff of the British Library, GLC Records Library and Guildhall Library in London. Librarians at reference libraries including P Baird (Birmingham), R Riding (Dundee), J Main Durham, N Armstrong, Mr Hogg, A G D White (Edinburgh), A J Shute (Exeter), J Reid (Glasgow), V Tyrrell (Hanley), A W Ball (Harrow), D Richards (Holborn), R Kirkpatrick (Kilrea), A Heap (Leeds), K Wright (Manchester), R A J Vinnicombe (Newark on Trent), A T Bryce (Perth and Kinross), V L Prowse (St Albans), J M Olive (Sheffield), D F Mann (Wick), G G Hand (York).
James G Booth, Sotheby's; David Hall, Christie's of Scotland; Mr Partridge, Provincial of Stockbridge; Phillips of Chester and Exeter; Bonhams of Chelsea; Richard A Bourne Co Inc of America; National Fishing Lure Collector's Club (NFLCC); David Beazley; Ron Blackmore; Fred Buller; Alan Clout; John Drewitt; John Essex; Dr Stephen Harrison; John Knott; John McKinley; Nick Marchant-Lane; Jamie Maxtone-Graham; Jess Miller; Dick Orton; Joseph Peters; Mr J S Sharpe, Director of Farlow's of Pall Mall; John Stevenson (assisted with the history of David Slater and threadline reels after 1910); Roger Still; George Thornton; John Turner; Antony Witherby; Bruce Dyer (Canada); Ron Gast; Clyde A Harbin; Art and Scott Kimball; Trig C Lund; Harry Macdonald (Canada); Gary L Miller; Larry Peterson; Dean A Smith; Larry Smith; Stuart Snyder.

The book represents four full years research on the part of the author, who in addition to the text, produced the photographic work except were otherwise stated. He wishes to record his grateful thanks to Mr Paul Hicks, Managing Director of Jamesway Graphics for his professionalism in producing the book in its entirety although some of the photographs had been taken from grubby old catalogues and were of doubtful quality.

A final thanks to the author's wife Christine for her support and encouragement.

THE EARLY DAYS

The earliest surviving fishing implements are the gorge, the hook and the harpoon. They all came from a time in man's history which preceded the great civilisations of Rome, Greece and China, earlier than the dawn of ancient Egypt and the neolithic period of New Stone Age Man. They were left behind by Upper Palaeolithic Man and tell us that he was using specially designed pieces of tackle in addition to nets made from natural materials together with river traps and weirs of wood and stones.

It is impossible to say which of man's hunter-fisher ancestors was the first to invent these pieces of tackle, examples of which have been found from the same early period in various parts of the world with a remarkable degree of similarity.

Harpoons were fashioned with two kinds of head, one with barbs on one side, the other barbed down both sides. Early man may have been cleverer in his construction than would first appear. The barbs were obviously introduced to better secure the prey after penetration, but the design may have been carefully chosen for the performance and passage of the harpoon. The one with barbs on both sides would take a straight passage when thrown through water whereas the harpoon with single barbs would tend to bend direction slightly. Early man may have been skilled in the use of a single barbed harpoon to achieve a degree of compensation for the angle of refraction through water.

Another type of harpoon was one with a detachable head secured to a line. When a fish had been penetrated, the harpoon head came away from the pole and it was landed by means of a line.

The gorge was a straight piece of bone, usually pointed at both ends, to which a line was attached at the centre. It was used by means of concealment in a piece of bait, which when swallowed by the fish, would be pulled to trap the gorge across the stomach or

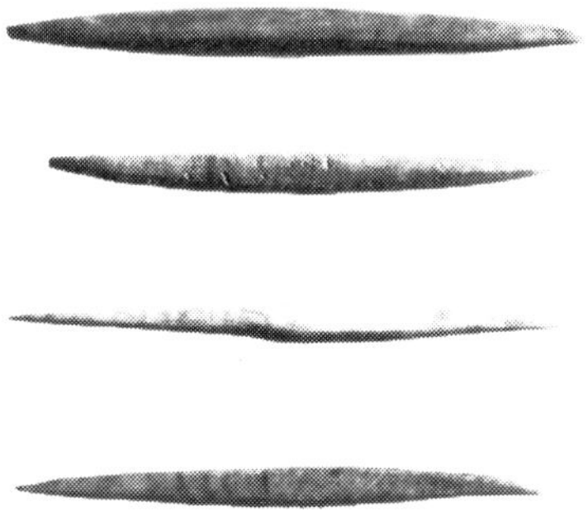

Moravian Museum

Bone gorges

gullet. The material used depended on what was readily available and could have been bone, flint, shell or wood.

Harpoons have been found at Bruniquel and La Madeleine as well as other sites in France, Britain, Spain, Switzerland and various stations throughout Europe. Bone gorges have been found at some together with other collective artefacts, all of which help us to understand the mode of life and common use of tackle by our ancestors.

There is little evidence of the hook from palaeolithic times but we can be sure it was in regular use. The principle on which the hook works is different to that of the gorge. It is based on penetration rather than simple resistance, and the transition would have been an easy step for the expert hunter-fisher. The advent of the hook did not mean that the gorge became obsolete, and it has continued to find favour with some natives up to modern times. Probably both were used and the choice depended on their success or failure to catch fish.

Hooks would have been fashioned from any number of natural materials but apart from stone, bone hooks would have been the only ones with a chance to survive. The problem is that if there is insufficient lime in the soil, the calcium in the bone is dissolved by the acids in the earth, and the bone will crumble to dust. This was described by Hans Jorgen Hurum in *History of the Fish Hook,* which also made reference to the oldest bone hook at Predmosti, Moravia in Czechoslovakia. Thanks to this author's lead, I have been able to trace what is probably the world's oldest bone hook to the Moravian Museum, who have kindly supplied a photograph and given permission for it to be illustrated. The survival of this early bone hook is due to the fact that the site contained the bones of large numbers of mammoth which were regularly killed by organised collective hunting.

Thorn has provided suitable hooks from earliest times, having a ready shaped bend and point and capable of holding. It has been used in countries from

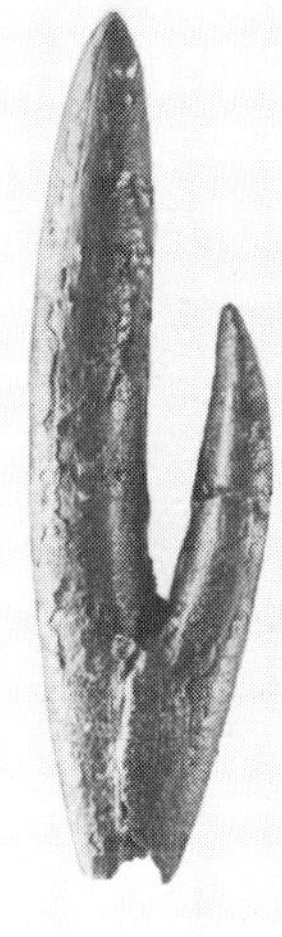

Moravian Museum

The earliest bone hook in the Moravian Museum classified as Pavlovian, a culture of Upper Palaeolithic Mammoth Hunters who lived close to Dolni Vestonice in Southern Moravia, Czechoslovakia. The radio-carbon dating is approximately 24,000 BC

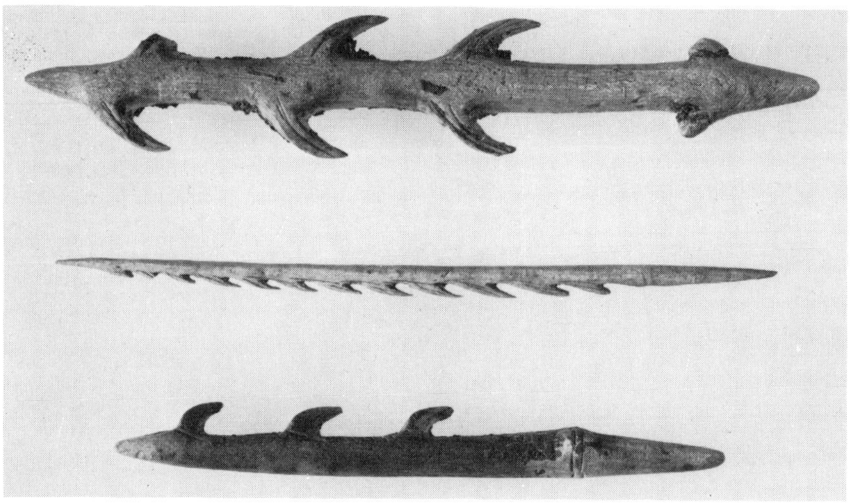

Three harpoons from Bruniquel

Europe to as far away as the Middle East, Africa and North America.

The early hunter-fisher would probably have used compound hooks, constructed by tying a shank of wood to a barb of bone, or any combination of materials. He would also have utilised the bones of animals and birds which resembled a hook shape, in a similar way to the ones used by natives of modern times.

William Radcliffe in *Fishing from the Earliest Times* gave interesting examples, one being Lancustrian Dwellers who made a hook from the upper mandible of an eagle and another race who used the upper mandible of the male of the insect *Eurycantho Latro.*

There is no evidence of the use of the rod or reel by early stone-age man, but this does not mean that he never used such devices. He probably used a piece of wood as a rod, to reach over a stretch of water where he suspected large fish were lurking, and may have used a simple object to wind his line round. The use of such pieces of tackle can only be a matter of speculation, as nothing could survive in recognisable form and no cave painting from that period has ever been found which shows a rod or winding device. However, it would seem reasonable to suppose that the method and inventiveness of the hunter-fisher was equal to that of the domesticated fisherman of succeeding civilisations.

The first recorded evidence of the rod, reel and artificial fly comes from four of the early civilisations.

The Egyptian civilisation began towards the end of the palaeolithic age and developed to neolithic farming close to the River Nile. Its people discovered the Calendar as early as 4241 BC and invented the Hieroglyphic Script which consisted of a number of pictorial symbols. The most important revelation concerning fishing, was the discovery, in Egypt, of the world's earliest recorded evidence of a fishing rod.

A small section of the scenes on the west wall of the main chamber of tomb 3 – Beni Hasan showing a fishing scene depicting the earliest pictorial record of a fishing rod c.2000 BC

Harpoon reel from tomb 3 – Beni Hasan

Along the eastern edge of the Nile Valley is a long range of cliffs, among which is the hill of Beni Hasan. It was named after a family of Arabs calling themselves Beni Hasan, meaning 'son of Hasan', who settled at the base. At this site, 39 tombs were found and excavated, one of which contained the all important fishing scene, depicting the earliest rod. Percy E Newberry in his *Archaeological Survey of Egypt, Beni Hasan* (1893) gave this information, together with illustrations. Newberry tells us that the great tombs were often decorated as befitted the exalted rank of the deceased, and tomb 3 was that of Prince Khnumhotep believed to be the early XIIth Egyptian Dynasty at about 2000BC. The fishing scene appeared on the west wall of the main chamber and clearly shows a rod and what appears to be a fixed line, landing a fish.

On the north wall of tomb 3 at Beni Hasan was another picture of a bident harpoon with the barbed heads impaled in fish. There was also a more important one of the first type of winding device and cord, thought to be a harpoon reel, and generally believed to have only been used to capture hippopotami.

I believe that the close proximity of the harpoon reel to the bident harpoon and fish, both being on the same wall, strongly suggest that it was used to assist the capture of fish. It was probably used against large species, which had the power to break the head from the shaft of a spear, and was possibly a hand version and the forerunner of the harpoon winch used in commercial fishing. There is no evidence of a winder in the form of a fishing reel used with a hook and rod, during that early period in Egypt, and we have to leave the Middle East to find the earliest record of this piece of tackle.

It is generally believed that the fishing reel did not make its appearance until the 17th century in Britain. The truth is that it was being used several hundred years earlier in China. Records show that 'spool fishing rods' were invented in the Tang Dynasty (618 AD to 907 AD), the evidence of which came from poems about fishing, in which references are found to 'fishing reel', 'running reel' or 'reel car'.

Reels were widely used in the Sung Dynasty (960 AD to 1279 AD) and it is from the North Sung period that we get the first glimpse of one in Mr T Wong's painting (1037 – ?) – *'Rowing on the Fishing Pond'.* Two more paintings from the 12th and 13th centuries and another from the

Ming Dynasty give clearer pictures of the Chinese reel.

The earliest records of Chinese fishing rods come from the Tang Dynasty in poems – *Fishing Alone* by Mr Y Han (768 AD – 824 AD) and another on fishing equipment by Mr Y M Lok (? – 881 AD).

The earliest bone fish hooks found in China were 6000 years old and unearthed from Banpo Xi'an, Shanxi Province; others found at Dachengshan, Tangshan Hebei Province were dated at 4000 years old.

Hooks made of copper, recovered from Zhengzhou, Henan Province were from the Shang Dynasty (16th century BC to 11th century BC) and according to historical records, the fishing lines of that period were often made of silk, a product known to the Chinese for five thousand years. Once again we find that the Chinese were far in advance of Europe in the use of fishing tackle materials.

The Chinese must also be credited with being the first people to devise the method of splitting cane into strips and glueing them together to eliminate the hollow centre and increase the strength. Almost three thousand years ago a book by Tchouang-Tseu (950 BC West Chou Dynasty), described the construction of glued and bound split cane rods, and another book the *History of T'chou and T'au* (345 BC East Chou Dynasty), referred to these type of rods, and suggested that they were used for carrying water by placing them across the shoulders.

The classical civilisations of Greece and Rome followed and respectively brought creative genius and stability to the world. The artificial fly was part of that creativity and was being used in both countries two thousand years ago. It is impossible to say

Museum of China, Peking

Fishing Alone on a Cold River by Y Ma. (12th to 13th century)

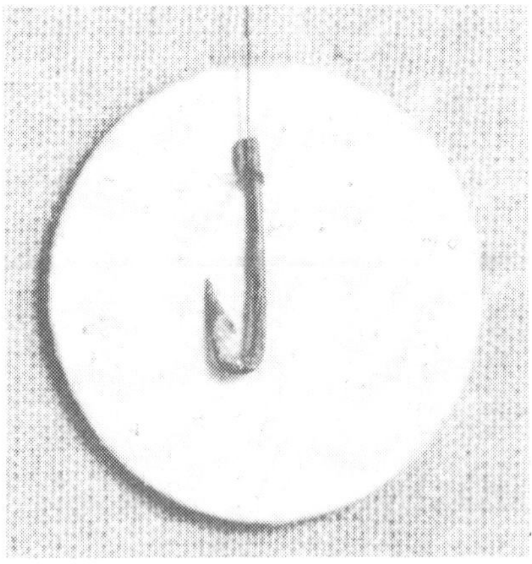

Museum of China, Peking

Left: Bone fish hook about 6000 years old unearthed from Banpo Xi'an, Shanxi Province

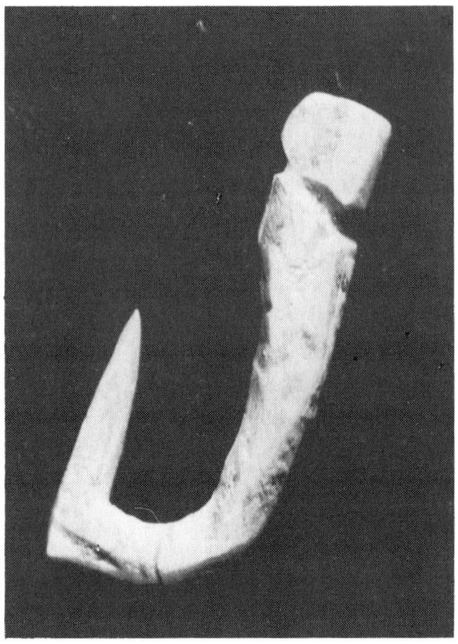

Museum of China, Peking

Bone fish hook about 4000 years old unearthed from Dachengshan, Tangshan Hebei Province

Museum of China, Peking

Painting of turtle fishing Ming Dynasty (1368 AD – 1644 AD)

Museum of China, Peking

Right: Rowing on the Fishing Pond by Mr T Wong (c.1037 AD)

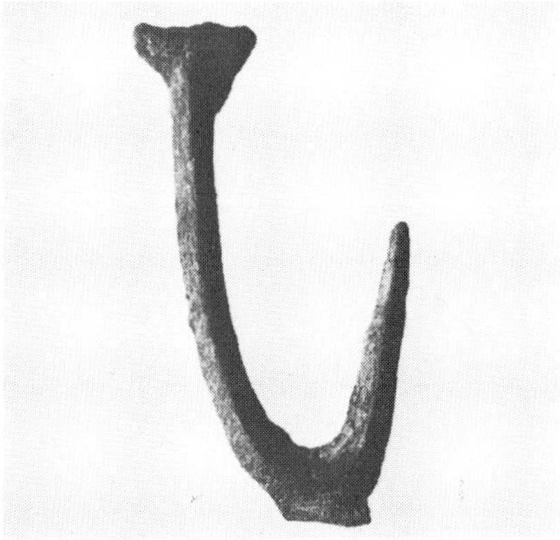

Museum of China, Peking

Copper fish hook, Shang Dynasty (16th century BC to 11th century BC) unearthed from Zhengzhou, Henan Province

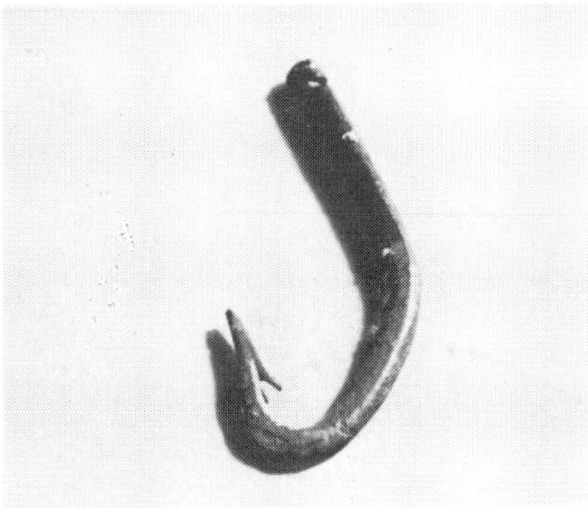

Museum of China, Peking

Copper fish hook, Xizhou Period, (approx. 11th century BC to 770 BC) unearthed from Jurong, Jiangsu Province

Museum of China, Peking

Clay fish hook mould Dongzhou Period (770 BC – 221 BC) unearthed from Houma, Shanxi Province

with certainty which country should be credited with being the first, because the evidence available from each comes from contemporary writers. One was a Roman satirist poet called Marcus Valerius Martialis (AD 40-102 AD) who is usually referred to as Martial.

He was born in Spain and went to Rome when he was about twenty years of age. His famous lines of importance were – *'Namique quis rescit Avidum vorata decipi scarum musca,'* which translated means – 'Who has not seen the scarus rise. Decoyed and killed by fraudful flies.' The other writer was a man called Aelian (80 AD to 140 AD) who was born an Italian but learned the Greek language so proficiently that he was able to write books in the language. These books became the accepted authority on the subject of natural history. He described the ecology of fish and flies and the construction of an artificial fly in the finest detail, which remarkably was one of only two recordings in fourteen hundred years, until Dame Juliana Bernes described twelve flies in *Treatyse of Fysshynge wyth an Angle* published in England in 1496.

The credit for the discovery of the Aelian text must be given to Stephen Oliver, who pointed out this important passage in his *Scenes and Recollections of Fly Fishing*, first published in 1834.

The earliest evidence of the use of a lure comes from the hooks dug out of the ruins of Pompeii and believed to be in the Museum of Naples. Historians have described the hooks as 'conico-cylindrical' and fashioned to the shape of a fish. Therefore, the ancient Pompeian fishermen used an imitation fish lure.

The full text of Aelian reads as follows:

'I have heard of a Macedonian way of catching fish and it is this: between Beroe and Thessalonica runs a river called the Astraeus and in there are fish with speckled skins; what the natives of the country call them you had better ask the Macedonians. These fish feed on a fly peculiar to the country, which hovers on the river. It is not like flies found elsewhere, nor does it resemble a wasp in appearance, nor in shape would one justly describe it as a midge or a bee, yet it has something of each of these. The natives generally call it Hippouros. These flies seek their food over the river but do not escape the observations of the fish swimming below. When the fish observes a fly on the surface, it swims quietly up, afraid to stir the water above lest it should scare away its prey; then coming up by its shadow, it opens its mouth gently and gulps down the fly, like a wolf carrying off a sheep from the fold or an eagle a goose from the farmyard; having done this it goes below the rippling water. Now, though the fishermen know of this, they do not use these flies at all for bait for fish; for if a man's hand touch them, they lose their natural colour, their wings wither and they become unfit for food for the fish. For this reason they have nothing to do with them, hating them for their bad character, but they have planned a snare for the fish, and get the better of them by their fisherman's craft.

They fasten red wool round a hook and fix on to the wool two feathers which grow under a cock's wattles and which in colour are like wax. Their rod is six feet long and their line is the same length. They then throw their snare and the fish, attracted and maddened by the colour, come straight at it, thinking from the pretty sight to get a dainty mouthful, when however it opens its jaws, it is caught by the hook, and enjoys a bitter repast, a captive.'

EARLY FISHING IMPLEMENTS FOUND IN RUSSIA

Bone fish hooks, 5.9 cm and 6.3 cm. Date 3000 BC (East Ural)

Bone harpoon, length 23 cm. Date 4000 – 3000 BC (East Ural)

Bone harpoon, length 24 cm. Date 4000 – 3000 BC (East Ural)

Stone fish, length 27.5 cm, width 6.4 cm. Date 3000 BC (East Siberia) Probably used as a net sinker

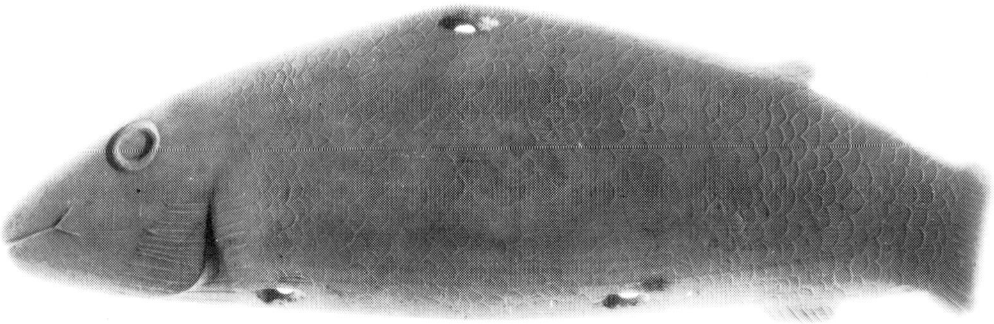

Stone fish, length 27.5 cm, width 9.3 cm. Date 3000 BC (East Siberia)

Hermitage Museum, Leningrad

EVOLUTION IN BRITAIN

Fishing has been practised in Britain from the earliest times but up to the 15th century there was no record of the methods or the tackle. Traps and nets would have been used to catch large numbers on a commercial basis, while a fisherman seeking a few fish and a bit of sport on his local waters would probably have used a rod or pole with a fixed line. The more ambitious angler, after bigger fish such as pike and salmon, may have added a loop to the end of the rod to accommodate a running line thrown on the ground, while many may not have bothered with a rod at all, and simply used a hand line. The earliest angling books are our only source of information as to the use and development of fishing tackle.

The oldest English literature on fishing was *The Colloquy of Aelfric* written by the Archbishop of Canterbury in c.995 AD, but it failed to give any information on tackle or method of fishing. There was no mention of a rod and he may have used a hand line. The only information offered was his preference for fishing with his feet on the ground and his dislike of sea fishing, saying – 'I would rather catch a fish I can kill, than one that can kill me'.

Five hundred years later the first specialist book on fishing was printed by Wynkyn de-Worde with the title *Treatyse of Fysshynge wyth an Angle* in 1496 AD. It was an additional section to the second edition of a book first produced ten years earlier by an unidentified printer at 'Seynt albons' and consisted of four separate treatises on Hawking, Hunting, the *Lynage of Coote Armuris* and the *Blasyng of Armys* together with extra associated text. In the 1486 book the name of the authoress was given to the second section on Hunting at the end of the twenty fourth page with the words 'Explicit Dam Julyans Barnes'. In the second edition, ten years later, which included the additional *Treatyse of Fysshynge wyth an Angle* the name in the colophon had been changed to read – 'Explicit dame Julyans Bernes doctryne in her boke of huntynge' and the whole reprint ended with – 'Enprynted at Weftmeftre by Wynkyn the Worde the yere of thyncarnacon of our lorde. mcccc. lxxxxvj'.

Frontispiece of Dame Juliana's book

Therefore, the printer Wynkyn de Worde made her the authoress of the treatise on Hunting and succeeding authorities attributed the whole book to her pen.

The title of the book changed in 1586 to the *Boke of St Albans, Hawking, Hunting and Fishing with the True Measures of Blowing*, Printed by Edward Allde.

There has been fierce debate throughout the centuries as to the identity and existence of Dame Juliana who fails to appear in any official records. Evidence to support her claim to being the authoress has been given by a number of writers but none have declared the source on which their information was based. Almost everything written about the lady since the beginning of the eighteenth-century is merely an echo or an extension of two early biographers. One was John Bale, Bishop of Ossory whose *Lives of the Most Eminent British Writers* was printed in Latin in 1559 and included information about Dame Juliana with the text – 'Femina illustris . . . corporis et animi dotibus abundans ac forma elegantia spectabilis' and went on to confirm that she was alive in the year 1460.

John Bale would seem to provide the strongest proof of the existence of Dame Juliana because he lived at the time of the publication of the book containing the *Treatyse of Fysshynge wyth an Angle*. He was born at Cove in Sussex in 1495, just a year before it was printed and up to the age of 40 years was a contemporary of the printer Wynkyn de Worde. There would have been every opportunity to check should he have considered there to be any question of the authenticity of the lady author, and it is difficult to think of any reason why a man of the cloth should write anything but the truth on the matter.

More information was given by William Burton who lived from c.1575 to 1645 and took a keen interest in the Dame's work. He had a copy of the first edition of 1486, and in the book wrote the following information – 'This Booke was made by the Lady Julian Berners, daughter of Sr James Berners of Berners – Roding in Essex. Knight and sister to Richard Lord Berners. She was Lady Prioress of Sopwell, a nunnery neere St. Albans in wch Abby of St. Albans this was first printed 1486. She was living 1460 according to John Bale'. Burton does not say where he obtained the new information but it was from his text that the lady's surname became better known as Berners. It has been suggested that his source may have been manuscript notes, which came into his possession, compiled by a man called Leland.

John Leland was a priest at the court of Henry VIII who was commissioned by the King to do a survey of people and real estate and was also given the power to seize manuscripts and records from abbeys and religious buildings at the time of the religious persecution. He became insane before his death in 1552 and his work was never completed. Some of his data survived and was published early in the eighteenth century but contained no reference to Dame Juliana.

The details of her background

introduced by William Burton have proved impossible to authenticate and will always remain a mystery. If she was born an aristocrat to the Berners family her name never appeared in their pedigree. Neither did she appear in the records of Sopwell Priory where she is believed to have been Prioress in 1460.

However, the records are incomplete with details of the relevant years missing and listed only Lititia Wyttenham from 1405–1426, Matilda de Flamstead 1426–1430 (died aged 80 years) and then a gap of 50 years until Joan Chappell who in 1480 was relieved of her duties because she was old and infirm. The post was only held by senior and usually elderly nuns for relatively short periods.

The source of Burton's information about Dame Juliana can only be a matter of speculation. He wrote about her in a 1486 first edition copy which was printed about 89 years before he was born. The book was a best seller in the sixteenth century and probably one of his favourites. Either he simply repeated the work of unknown past authorities or general beliefs, together with Bale's information that Dame Juliana was alive in 1460, or he conducted his own investigation. The word 'Dame' in the sixteenth century meant nothing more than 'Mrs' so he would have had no clue from the word that she came from a titled family.

It has been suggested that the Berners family name was sometimes spelt Barnes and this, together with the fact that ladies in Sopwell Priory were often from noble stock, may have encouraged the belief that there was a connection. It would seem hardly sufficient evidence alone and there may have been different reasons altogether which prompted Burton's record of Dame Juliana. What we can be sure of is that he must have believed the information to be correct by virtue of the fact that he wrote it in his own private book.

It seems unlikely that we will ever know with certainty whether William Burton was mistaken or possibly partly mistaken. It may be that Dame Juliana was indeed Prioress at Sopwell but had no connection with the Berners family in Essex which would have changed everything. If her father had not been Sir James Berners, who incidentally, was beheaded on Tower Hill in 1388, she may have been alive when the first edition was printed. The possibilities are endless and writers over two centuries have covered every aspect of the mystery.

In 1577 Holinshed wrote about

Earliest illustration of a fishing rod in Britain

Dame Juliana based on Bale's text but got the name wrong. The printer mistook the letters 'rn' for 'm' and called the authoress Julyan Bemes. Baker in his Chronicles made a worse blunder by thinking Julyan must be a man's name and wrote '. . . a gentleman of excellent gifts who wrote certain treatises of Hawking and Hunting'.

In 1700, Chauncy's *History of Heartfordshire* expanded on the family history first given by Burton, and Haslewood's *Boke of St Albans* (1810) gave the full Berner's family pedigree together with details of how the authoress spent her youth, suggesting she was probably at court and enjoyed woodland sports.

The legend of Dame Juliana came under the fiercest attack from William Blades *Boke of St Albans in Facsimile* (1881) and a revue by Edmund W. Gosse in *The Academy* on April 16th 1881 gives a wonderful summary of Blades work with the words – 'Like the people who broke up stained glass windows for the sake of the lead, Mr Blades bursts into this fairy chapel of false history, and, being infatuated with the printer of St. Albans and his types, thinks nothing of shattering this many coloured vision. Dame Juliana Berners – 'Dam Julyans Barnes', the original misprints it – becomes mere Mrs Barnes who was not an aristocrat, kept no diary, had nothing whatever to do with Sopwell, and, as Mr Blades has the cruelty to hint, possibly had very little indeed to do with the *Boke of St Albans* that has made her so famous. In all this however, as is often the case with reformers, Mr Blades goes too far.'

The words Blades used were 'What is really known of the Dame is nothing and may be summed up in the following few words. She probably lived at the beginning of the fifteenth century and she possibly compiled from existing MSS some rhymes on hunting'. He also suggested that the printer Wynkyn de Worde may have written the book, but this looks extremely unlikely when one examines the record of the man. According to Walter Shaw Sparrow in *Angling in British Art* he married an English lady called Elizabeth and rented a house from the church authorities at Westminster Abbey. Because he was a foreigner the property he rented had to be registered on November 4th 1480 in his wife's name.

He must have been a young man because it is known he lived another fifty years. In 1534 he made a will naming James Gaver and John Byddell as executors and on the 19th January 1535 this will was proved. Therefore if it is supposed that he was 74 years of age at his death he would only have been 25 years old in 1486 when the first edition of the book was printed. Hardly the age to produce a quality work on such specialised subjects practised only by the nobility. It is unlikely he possessed such literary talent because he never produced any work in the following forty-nine years.

The *Treatyse of Fysshynge wyth an Angle* symbolizes the true beginning of fishing as a sport and pastime in Britain, with the laying down of rules and ideals and a description of the tackle to be used.

It gives a grounding in basic ideas which have changed little in modern times; the ideas of sportsmanship, keeping clear of the sight of the fish, disguising the bait to imitate the natural food, not overfishing and the use of sophisticated artificial flies.

It is doubtful whether new evidence will be found to settle the arguments about Dame Juliana. She is a wonderful legendary person whose life as Prioress of Sopwell completes the picture. Her name is on the book and although one cannot prove her authorship conclusively, it is equally impossible to disprove. The only new information was found in 1883 when Messrs Satchell published the *Treatyse of Fysshynge with an Angle* from a manuscript in the possession of A Denison Esq. which differed considerably from that in the *Boke of St Albans* and a Professor Skeat was of the opinion that it could be dated earlier than 1450. The new revelation only added to the confusion and proved nothing either way.

The Treatyse tells not only about fishing but gives an insight into life in mediaeval England in the fifteenth century.

Dame Juliana is so thorough in her description of fishing tackle, that anything not mentioned must not have been invented. No reference to a reel, therefore it has not reached Britain, and she describes how one has to make all one's tackle, even the hooks, proving no fishing tackle shops or manufacturers had yet started in business. The Treatyse gives a comprehensive explanation of all aspects of fishing but the scope of this book limits reference to only the section on tackle. Fishing with an angle means fishing with a hook and she gave detailed instructions for their manufacture

TACKLE ILLUSTRATED IN DAME JULIANA'S BOOK

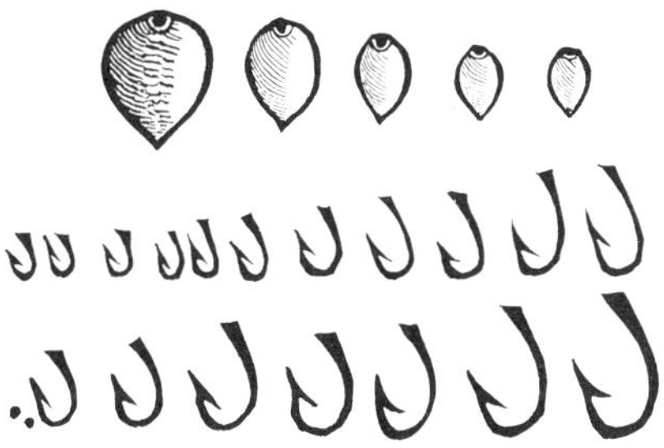

Range of hooks

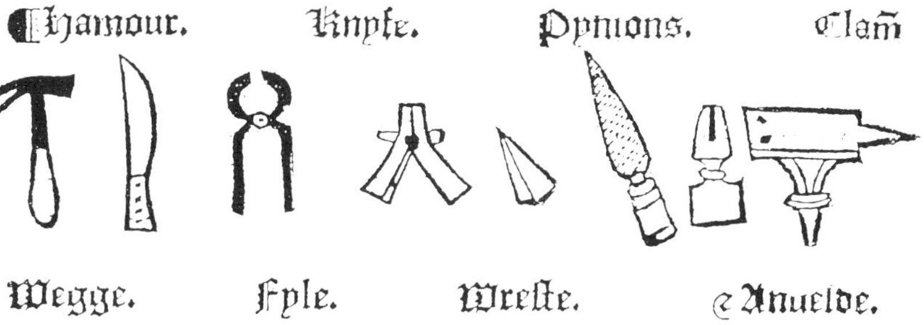

Set of tools

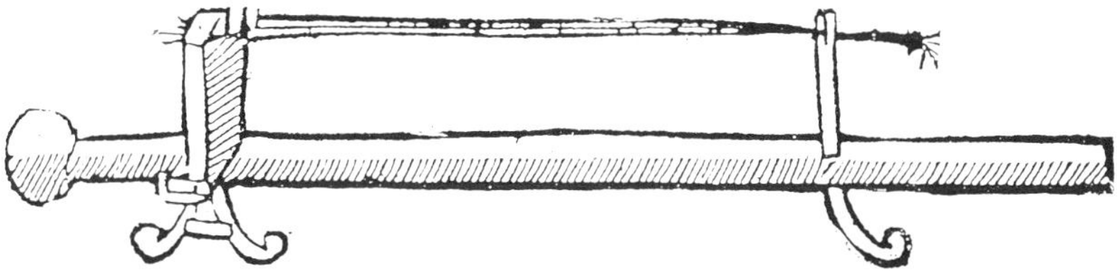

Line making equipment

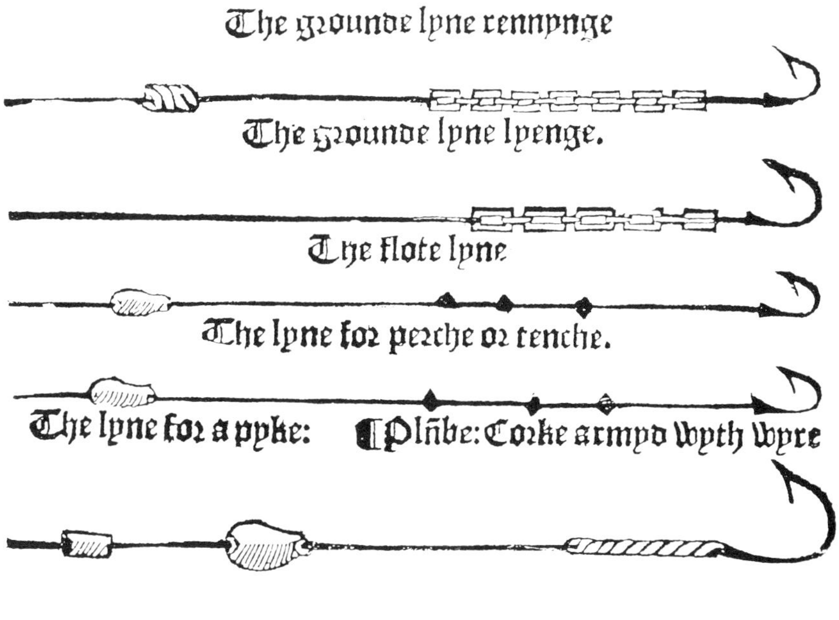

Lines set by Dame Juliana for various types of fishing

and a woodcut of eighteen various sizes. A set of eight small tools was also illustrated and included a vice, a pair of tongs, hammer, bending device, knife and file and a description of their use. Different types of square headed needles were used to make the hooks, depending on the variety of fish they were to be used against, but the method of fashioning them was the same. Each was heated red hot a number of times in the various stages of shaping and sharpening, the last stage being the flattening of the end where the eye would be on a modern hook. Finally completed, the red-hot hook was plunged into cold water to give it the correct temper. Dame Juliana told of the best way to secure the hook using silk thread, and detailed the various constructions of lines for catching various types of fish. Thickness varied from a single horse hair for minnow, two for gudgeon and young bream right up to fifteen hairs for salmon. Instruction was given on the construction of a tapered line from horse hair and even more text on the dyeing of the line according to season – green like water weeds for summer, brown for autumn and tawny for winter or spring. An illustration was given which showed how she considered lines should be set up for various types of fishing, and included a floating line, one for perch or tench and a pike line which had an additional reinforced section of wire-covered cork to combat the creature's fearsome teeth.

The most important piece of tackle she described was the 'harness' or rod. Not only did she give the first illustration of a fishing rod in English literature but also advised on the materials and method of construction. Her seventeen to eighteen foot rod was made in three pieces, a top of hazel, a middle of hazel, willow, or ash and a butt of blackthorne, crab, medlar or juniper. The butt was hollowed out by using a plumber's red-hot pointed wire, while red-hot spits were used on the ends of the two larger pieces to form sockets into which fitted the next parts.

It is interesting to note that she instructed that the wood from which the butt was to be made should first be put in an oven and then seasoned for a month. Later in the building process it was placed in the 'smoke on the roof' (roof opening for a central hearth). The use of ovens and heat treatment was to play an important part in the building of the classic rods of America four centuries later.

The practice of using live baits for pike fishing was prevalent during the middle ages and they were not limited to the use of fish. Dame Juliana was the first to suggest that if the roach or herring failed, then a frog or even a goose should be used. Izaac Walton also mentioned the use of both these creatures and adds a duck to the list. The use of live bait becomes progressively more abhorrent as creatures of a higher order are used and one can imagine the outcry today if such a method was used.

Walton's favourite live bait was the minnow and he used it in a most original way. By his very special intricate method of attaching it to the hook, which he gave in great detail, he was able to make it turn round when it was drawn through water. He must have been highly skilled because Charles Cotton witnessed that he was the best hand in England with the minnow. Sometimes, Walton could not obtain a live minnow, which led to him using the first recorded artificial lure in Britain and made for him – 'by a handsome woman, that had a fine hand, and a live Minnow lying by her; the mould or body of the Minnow was cloth, and wrought upon or over it thus with a needle; the back of it with very sad French green silk, and paler green silk towards the belly, shadowed as perfectly as you can imagine, just as you see a Minnow; the belly was wrought also with a needle, and it was a part of it white silk, and another part of it with silver thread; the tail and fins were a quill which was shaven thin, the eyes were of two little black beads, and the head was so shadowed, and all of it so curiously wrought, and so exactly dissembled, that it would beguile any sharp sighted Trout in a swift stream'.

It was sometime during the first half of the seventeenth century when the reel is believed to have first come into use in Britain and it is impossible at present to say whether it had been introduced from the East or had evolved independently. The first recording of a winding device was in 1651 in Thomas Barker's first edition of the *Art of Angling* in which he says – 'The manner of his trolling was with a hazel rod 12 foot long with a ring of wire in the top of his rod for his line to run through; within two feet of the bottom of the rod, there was a hole, to put in a wind, to turn with a barell, to gather up his line, and loose it at his pleasure'. There is

Twist engine boxes used by the early horse-hair line makers

A spike foot brass winch

Left: A spike foot brass winch

Below left: 1⅞″ diameter clamp foot winch

Below: Multiplying winch 1¾″ diameter with rim stop

Here begynnyth the treatyse of fysshynge wyth an Angle.

Salamon in his parablys sayth that a good spyryte makyth a flourynge aege / that is a fayre aege & a longe. And syth it is soo: I aske this questyon / Whiche ben the meanes & the causes that enduce a man in to a mery spyryte.: Truly to my beste dyscrecōn it semeth good dysportes & honest gamys in whom a man Joyeth wythout ony repentaunce after. Thenne folowyth it ẏ gode dysportes & honest games ben cause of mannys fayr aege & longe life. And therfore now woll I chose of foure good disportes & honeste gamys / that is to wyte: of huntynge: hawkynge: fysshynge: & foulynge. The beste to my symple dyscrecōn whyche is fysshynge: callyd Anglynge wyth a rodde: and a lyne

Left: The first illustration of a fishing rod in English literature from the first book on fishing. 'Treatyse of Fysshynge wyth an Angle' by Dame Juliana Bernes in 1496

Above and below: Ruins on the site of Sopwell Priory. The place where angling as a sport and recreation was born by the pen of Dame Juliana. The ruins are not those of the Priory but a 16th century house built by Sir Richard Lee using materials from the nearby Monastery of St Albans. His ownership was a result of a deed of gift from Henry VIII for services rendered by Lee, and some say his wife, at the time of the King's religious persecution

The River Ver which runs along the site of Sopwell Priory, possibly the fishing place and inspiration of the legendary Dame Juliana

no illustration and very little information to establish the design of the earliest wind. The word barrell may have meant bar, which suggests it could have been a simple winch. I believe it was the same one as Barker illustrated with a crude drawing in his second edition six years later, except it had a spike foot for attaching through the hole in the rod, instead of the spring clip fitting shown on the second version.

The reel must have been a recent innovation and not widely used because Izaac Walton does not mention such a device when writing the *Compleat Angler* which was first printed in 1653. In 1655, the second edition of the famous work was produced and this copy contained the following 'Note also that many used to fish for a Salmon with a ring of wire on

A brass spike foot winch, 19th century

Clamp foot multiplying winch, 19th century

the top of their rod, through which the line may run, to as great a length as is needful when he is hooked. And to that end some use a wheel, about the middle of their rod, or neer their hand, which is to be observed better by seeing one of them than by a large demonstration of words'. Walton obviously knew very little about the winch or its workings, which was beginning to make its appearance, and he cleverly keeps clear of the subject.

Barker's Delight or *The Art of Angling* (second edition) was printed in 1657 and gives new information about a winch for salmon fishing and says 'You must have your winder within two feet of the bottom, to go on your rod, made in this manner, with a spring, that you may put it as low as you please'.

This was the forerunner of a clamp foot winch, before it developed the shaped collar and tightening screw. It was developed at the same early period as the spike foot because it was more versatile. Rods at that time were all shapes, sizes and thicknesses from a variety of woods such as hickory, hazel, greenheart and bamboo cane, and surfaces were uneven. The spring clip with a pad of leather or other material inside could be firmly attached at any position. This edition also gives the first crude drawing of a winch which would not be recognised as such if there was no accompanying text.

Five years later in 1662 the second illustration of a winch is printed on the frontispiece of a book *The Experienced Angler* by Robert Venables, who was the Governor of Chester and formerly an Officer in Cromwell's army. This time a better picture is shown of a large crude winch which he says one can buy ready made.

Fishing line was made of horse-hair in the seventeenth century and the principle of its manufacture had hardly changed since the simple device of Dame Juliana. The early makers used a twist engine box which consisted of a master wheel engaging by teeth into three smaller wheels into each of which was set a hook. A strand of horse-hair was attached to each hook and the other three ends knotted together and a weight fixed to hang downwards. A spacer such as a cork or piece of wood with three holes was set half way down the centre to keep the three hairs apart. The master wheel was turned and twisted each strand equally and simultaneously causing the strand to twist together at the weighted end. The spacer was moved upwards as the full length was completed and finally the three strands were twisted together to tighten and complete the length.

By using different numbers of hairs in different lengths, the thickness could be varied and a tapered line could be constructed making a line which got finer to the hook end. If a section of twelve hair thickness was required, hairs of this number of similar thickness and lengths were selected. The weak and frayed ends were trimmed and the twelve divided into three strands of four hairs each and the twist engine joined them into one complete length. The process was repeated for all lengths of line varying the thickness from eighteen hairs down to three. Finally all the lengths were joined together by knots, similar to Dame Juliana's 'water-knots', and each one whipped. By careful selection the line could be made to taper to the thickness required.

Towards the latter part of the seventeenth century a cheaper form of line was imported called 'Indian Weed' or 'Grass' and continued to compete with horse-hair throughout the next century. It was a form of jute and although very strong was more conspicuous. To obtain the best performance it was recommended that it should be soaked in water before use.

Rods had tended to be heavy in the fifteenth century and the big tapered jointed rod described by Dame Juliana would have been used by only the more affluent fly fishermen, after salmon and trout or trolling for pike. The majority would at best have been equipped with a short one-piece tapered rod which would double for bottom fishing with a fixed line, or a loop on the end, and a large quantity of running line thrown on the ground for more ambitious sport. The rods would have been strong and sturdy but heavy particularly in wet weather.

By the middle of the seventeenth century quality of design and preparation of materials had greatly improved and cane had been introduced as an alternative. It had become fashionable to treat rods with oil and paint to both keep out the water and make them more attractive, in the same way as bowyers and fletchers had painted the English longbows and arrows at the time of the military archery period.

Evidence of this was given by Izaac Walton's words – 'a right-grown top is a choice commodity and should be preserved from the water soaking into it, which makes it in wet weather to be heavy, and fish ill favouredly and not true; also it rots quickly for want of painting, and I think a good top is worth preserving or I had not taken care to keep a top above twenty years.' He goes on to give careful instructions on the preparation and application saying – 'And as for painting your rod, which must be in oil, you must first make a size with glue and water, boiled together until the glue is dissolved, and the size of a lye-colour: then strike your size upon the wood with a bristle or a brush or a pencil, whilst it is hot; that being quite dry take White-lead and a little Red-lead and a little Coal-black, so much as all together will make an ash-colour, grind these all together with Linseed-oil; let it be thick and lay it thin upon the wood with a brush or pencil; this do for the ground of any colour to be upon the wood. For a Green take Pink and Virdigrise and grind them together in Linseed-oil, as thin as you can well grind it; then lay it smoothly on with your brush, and drive it in thin; once doing for the most part, will serve, if you lay it well and if twice, be sure your first colour be thoroughly dry before you lay on a second.'

The craftsmen of the seventeenth century took great care in selecting, seasoning and treating woods used for making fishing rods and Colonel Venables gives the fullest description in the *Experienced Angler or Angler Improved* (1662) with the following text – 'The time to provide stocks and tops is in the Autumn when the leaves are almost or altogether fallen, which is usually about the Winter Solstice, the sap being then in the root; which about the middle of January begins to ascend again and then the time is past to provide yourself with stocks and tops: you need not be so exactly curious for your stocks as your tops, though I wish you to choose the neatest Taper-grown you can for stocks, but let your tops be the most neat Rush-grown shoots you can get, straight and smooth; and if for the ground rod near or full two yards long. If for the fly of what length you please, because you must either choose them to fit the stock or the stock to fit them in the most exact proportion; neither do they need to be so very much Taper-grown as those for the ground; for if your rod be not most exactly proportionable, as well as slender, it will neither cast well, strike readily, or ply and bend equally, which will very much endanger your line. When you have fitted yourself with tops and stocks, for all must be gathered in the one season, and if any of them be crooked, bind them all together and they will keep one another straight; or lay them on some even boarded floor with a weight on the crooked parts or else bind them close to some straight staff or pole; but before you do this you must bathe (heat) them all, save the very top in a gentle fire'.

The second illustration of a reel in Britain. It appeared on the Frontispiece of Robert Venables The Experienced Angler *1662*

Although only a crude drawing, it is the first illustration of a winch in Britain. It appeared in Barker's Delight *1657*

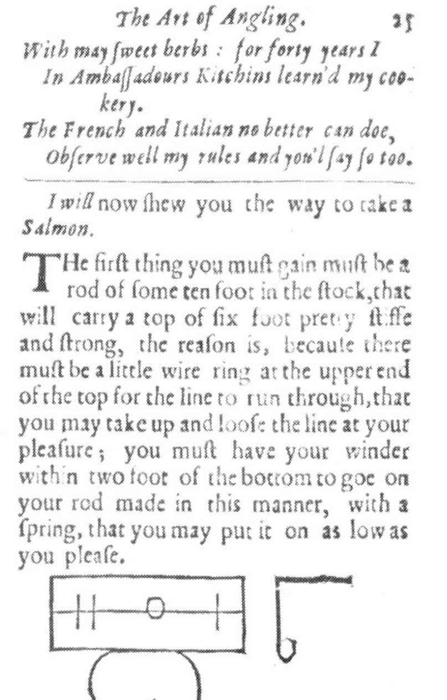

The Art of Angling. 25

With may ſweet herbs: for forty years I
In Ambaſſadours Kitchins learn'd my cookery.
The French and Italian no better can doe,
Obſerve well my rules and you'l ſay ſo too.

I will now ſhew you the way to take a *Salmon.*

THE firſt thing you muſt gain muſt be a rod of ſome ten foot in the ſtock, that will carry a top of ſix foot pretty ſtiffe and ſtrong, the reaſon is, becauſe there muſt be a little wire ring at the upper end of the top for the line to run through, that you may take up and looſe the line at your pleaſure; you muſt have your winder within two foot of the bottom to goe on your rod made in this manner, with a ſpring, that you may put it on as low as you pleaſe.

Venables recommended that rods should be kept eighteen months but preferably two years before use. His preference for a bottom rod was cane because of its length and lightness and he suggested that it should be covered with thin leather or parchment, dyed to a selected colour or simply paint applied direct to the cane which he said was the method employed by the London makers. Hazel is mentioned as making a slender rod ideal for fly fishing because it was long, light and could be managed with one hand.

LONDON TACKLE MAKERS

London was the place where the fishing tackle trade really started in Britain, as it had all the necessary market potential. There was a big population, a large section of which was relatively wealthy, and there was the River Thames fishing on the doorstep. The search for information to piece together the history of the tackle trade in London has been most rewarding.

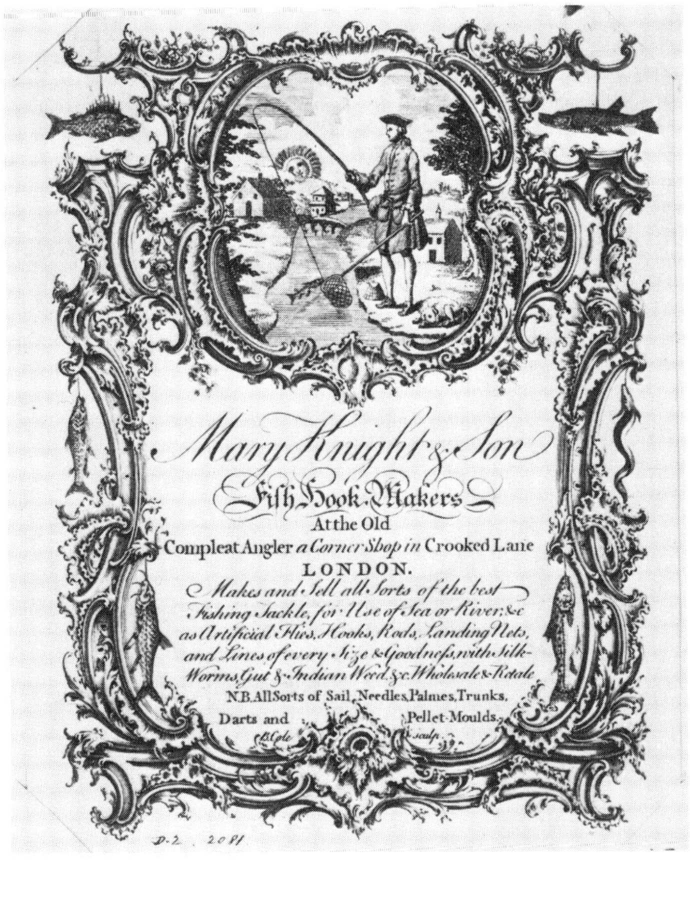
Mary Knight & Son
Fish Hook Makers
At the Old
Compleat Angler a Corner Shop in Crooked Lane
LONDON.
Makes and Sell all Sorts of the best
Fishing Tackle, for Use of Sea or River; &c
as Artificial Flies, Hooks, Rods, Landing Nets,
and Lines of every Size & Goodness, with Silk-
Worms, Gut & Indian Weed, &c. Wholesale & Retale
N.B. All Sorts of Sail, Needles, Palmes, Trunks,
Darts and Pellet-Moulds.
sculp.
D.2. 2081

It is clear from the book of Dame Juliana that there were no fishing tackle shops or manufacturers in Britain in the 15th century and the earliest tackle made and sold commercially would be as a sideline to another trade. Probably, some rods would have been made by a bowyer or fletcher whose work was long bows or arrows, and the needle makers would have quickly realised that they could make extra money by bending a few needles and selling them as fish hooks. John Denny's *Secrets Of Angling* 1613 gives the first indication that they were in production with the words: 'Then buy your hooks the finest and the best that may be had of such as use to sell'. A contemporary writer, Gervas Markham made it clear that tackle makers were in business and selling through general stores rather than specialist tackle shops at that period by recommending his reader of *Country Contentments* c.1612 to buy their rods – 'because there is a great choice of them in every haberdashers store'.

What started out as listing the few makers mentioned in the early angling books led to research in London at the Guildhall, the GLC Records Office and the British Museum, where a small collection of trade cards were discovered. They had been given by the late Sir Ambrose Heale who had a great interest in the early tackle trade and these together with the history from various sources has made it possible to give a brief outline of the early London makers and to show illustrations of advertisements which they designed and used two centuries ago.

A few makers and traders were in business as early as 1600, and by the latter part of the eighteenth century, there were flourishing tackle centres at Crooked Lane and Bell Yard, supplying the eastern and western areas of the River Thames.

The exciting discovery which the research and the early documents show is that a lot of the fishing tackle, particularly the artificial baits, which are believed

A print from a watercolour by Robert Seymour (committed suicide in 1836) which best showed the two types of fishermen and the difference in the tackle they used

to be mainly products of the 19th century, were in fact being used throughout the 18th century and possibly earlier. The shops and makers were supplying a wide range of hooks, snap-hooks,rods of every size and construction, brass winches of various designs, artificial flies and metal lures and plugs in many shapes and materials. Trolling means moving round in repetition and has been practised by fishermen in Britain for centuries. It involves trolling an actual fish such as a minnow impaled on the hooks and is mentioned by all the early writers such as Dame Juliana (1496), Barker (1651) and Col. Venables (1662) but the bait has always been assumed to be a dead or a live fish. The earliest record of an artificial fish lure in Britain was the one used by Walton, described as an artificial minnow made from cloth and silk, and its use was not confined to that of the great author as is generally believed. Walton in fact said 'And here let me tell you what many old Anglers know right well, that at some times and in some waters, a minnow is not to be got, and therefore let me tell you I have, which I will show to you – an artificial Minnow'.

Venables was also familiar with this form of bait which he mentioned in saying – 'You may also imitate the minnow, as well as a fly but it must be done by an artist with a needle'.

Throughout the eighteenth century the London tackle makers offered a wide range of artificial fish and these were probably made in the same fashion. The *Gentleman's Recreation* (1710) advised 'If you fish with the minnow or stickleback, let it not be too big; or for want of Natural Minnows use Artificial ones.' In 1726 *The Gentleman Angler* gave details of how to make one but his text was cribbed from Walton.

A hundred years later, artificial fish baits were still being hand sewn in cloth and silk and detailed advice on the construction was given by Mr G Smeeton in *The Art of Angling* c.1822, with the following – 'Make the body of yellow bees wax and the head of black dubbin and black silk, and make the body of yellow wash leather, or buff or shammy and the head of black silk. The bait takes Salmon, Trout, Grayling, Tench, Roach, Chubb, Dace, Ruff, Bream, Barble etc.'.

Therefore it would seem reasonable to believe that the many varieties of artificial fish offered as 'Fitted up' on the trade card advertisements distributed by the 18th century tackle makers were of similar design and probably very attractive and lifelike.

This would seem to be confirmed by an advertisement placed at a much later period by an Irish maker O'Shaughnessy in the Limerick Chronicle on March 8th 1848, which read – 'O'Shaughnessy has at present an unrivalled assortment of Flies suited to the various lakes and rivers of the Three Kingdoms; also the celebrated Archimedian Minnow, the Artificial Par (or

Graveling), the Loach or Colley, the Hibernice Callagh Roe. These unique baits have met with the approval of the most scientific, as well as the best practical Anglers and are the only effective ones for Salmon, Trout, Pike and other fishing. They present the exact appearance of the natural bait, and are about the same weight; all composed of one durable material and the outside appearance can be easily renewed, when discoloured from use'.

Metal lures were also in common use throughout the 18th century, and an early description is given, following the advice on the construction of an artificial minnow, in the already mentioned book of 1726, *The Gentleman Angler*. The text read – 'Another Sort Of Artificial Minnow is made of Tin and painted very naturally, which will be of great service when live minnows cannot be had, and may be bought at a Fishing Tackle Shop, but they are dear'.

In 1754 a full list of artificial baits was given by George Smith in his *Anglers Magazine* and included – Devon minnows in gold, silver and natural colours, Wagtail baits in various colours, wobblers, plug-baits, true spinners, fly-spoons – 'in modern tackle shops and ironmongers they are legion'. It is interesting to note the use of the word 'plug baits' and the inclusion of fly-spoons which are baits generally believed to be inventions of the following century. The fact that two types of shops were selling the baits shows that they were very popular and widely used.

Swivels have been in use since the 17th century and later appear on all the trade cards of the London makers. John Woolbridge in his *Systema Agriculturae* in 1681 described them as a new invention for the following use – 'If you bait with a minnow you must so place it on your hook that the minnow must run round as you draw it towards you; and to that end you must have a swivel on your line lest the running round of the minnow over twist your lines'.

In 1767 Bartho Lowe put out a trade card from the 'Golden Fish' in Drury Lane and offered among other things – 'all sorts of artificial flies and minnows, made by the ablest and best hands'. Three years later in 1770 appeared a little booklet *The True Art Of Angling* which contained the famous advertisement of Ustonson which recorded a multiplying winch but also listed 'Minnow tackle, Jack and Perch and Artificial Minnows, and all sorts of artificial baits and made upon the best hooks'. Evidence of the sale of imitation baits by Ustonson is detailed in the history of this important maker and includes the sale of artificial mice in 1792 and a wide range of artificial lures and metal baits to King George IV in 1827.

Another London maker was Henry Patten at The Saw and Crown, Middle Row, Holborn and he issued a competing trade card in 1771 offering flies, artificial minnows for trout and other sorts of artificial baits, also treble, double and single box swivels and 'fitted up' Minnow, Perch and Jack Tackle. John Doughty at the Fish And Fly at York announced in 1756 'Upon the said best hooks, makes artificial mice for pike and chevin' and later in 1786 his son Joseph, who had succeeded him in business, was selling artificial flies, frogs and mice. Mrs Tait at the 'Fishing and Fowling Tackle Warehouse' in Glasgow also issued a broadsheet in about 1780 offering a wide range of imitation baits and tackle.

A trimmer was sometimes used in conjunction with a live bait for pike fishing and was an unsavoury form of sport. It was best described by T P Lathy in *The Angler* (1820).

Up to 1750 Britain had hardly changed in a thousand years having been an agricultural country with husbandry as the occupation of the working class. Most things were made by hand with very little mechanisation, while transportation was slow, relying on the horse and the sailing ship. The rural population were poor and made only a bare living in the villages. There was very little movement of the people and the roads were in poor condition, consisting of the main roads inherited from the Romans, connected by a network of dusty tracks. Apart from having to trade at the nearest market town, there was little incentive to use the roads.

Development of fishing tackle outside London and the larger cities must have been very slow and the use of a fishing reel would have been an irrelevance to the peasant fisherman. They were still using a rod or pole with a fixed line or a ring on the end of the rod and a running line thrown on the ground. Evidence of the development and use of the reel comes from research into fishing scenes painted by artists between 1700 and 1850, and shows clearly the size of reels and the type of fishing for which they were used. Of thirty-four paintings studied, fourteen showed fishermen using winches of which twelve were approximately 2 inches to 3 inches diameter and all but one were being used on 11ft to 18ft rods and all fly fishing or trolling for pike. The other twenty

Text from *The Angler* (1820)

'A trimmer is a small cylinder of wood, about the middle, which is turned to a less diameter, is wound a good quantity of good strong pack thread, twelve or fifteen yards thereabouts. A yard thereof is allowed to hang down and is tied to the armed wire of a jack hook after a living roach hath been put on the said hook in the manner described as lay hook fishing. The trimmer thus furnished is cast upon the water to seek its fortune. If a pike takes the bait, he runs the line off the trimmer and carries both away with him to the reeds near the shore. These live baits may be attached to the body of a goose or duck and driven across a pond; or to bladders, boughs, bundles of straw, hay or flags to swim down a river whilst the angler walks at ease along the shore watching the event.'

paintings showed fishermen using shorter 6ft to 10ft rods with a fixed line, without a reel and all bottom fishing. Therefore it would seem that up to the end of the eighteenth century the winch was small in size and used by only the more affluent fly fisherman.

Fishing lines at that period had been mainly horse-hair or Indian Weed but in the early part of the nineteenth century a new form became popular for a time. It was composed of a mixture of silk and hair and was made on an adapted twist engine. Instead of having rotating hooks which had been the standard design for making hair or gut, it had tubes into which hair was fed to form a mixed line with the silk. Geo C Bainbridge's *Fly Fishers Guide* of 1828 gave the best description of twist-engines and the method of making silk-hair line.

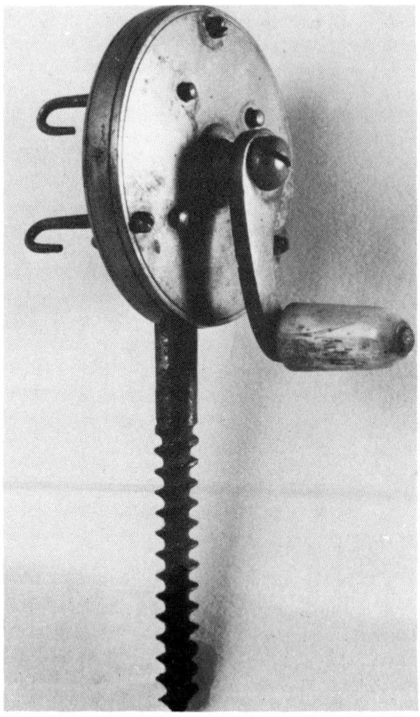

A simple form of twist engine

Trunks were blow-pipes or pipe tubes. I thank Arthur G Credland, Keeper of the Museum of Kingston-upon-Hull for information on the subject.

Apparently they were widely used in Europe in the seventeenth and eighteenth centuries. The earliest documentary evidence of their use in Europe was about 1425 in Italy. A priest from Fiesole published a book of funny stories, one of which described a king sitting in the window of his room and blowing small pellets after one of his cooks.

The first illustration of one appeared in the second half of the sixteenth century in France in manuscripts in Pietro de Crescenzis' *Treastise of Rural Economy*. It showed a figure with a five to six foot tube held to his mouth and aiming into the trees to kill birds. They were in common use in the eighteenth century in Britain and the ones sold by fishing tackle makers were probably made from bamboo, similar to rods. The first edition of *Johnson's Dictionary* (1775–6) describes Trunks as long tubes through which pellets of clay are blown.

A most informative advertisement appeared in a copy of *Land and Water* by a man named Lang of 22 Cockspur Street, London who offered – 'The walking stick blow tube . . . A very powerful and accurate weapon for destroying vermin, shooting birds etc . . . when reduced in size,

Text from *Fly Fishers Guide* (1828)

'Twisting engine is used in making reel lines free from knots and may be had at almost all tackle shops or may be made by an ingenious watch maker with very little directions. It is a small brass box containing four wheels, three of which are of small dimensions, the other is of larger size and has a handle. This instrument may be screwed into the back of a chair or other substance in such a manner that the operator may employ both hands both before and behind the engine, which bears a reduced resemblance to the wheels used by rope makers. It is necessary then to procure three balls of yellow silk, somewhat longer than the line intended to be made, and before fastening them to the respective tubes, due notice must be taken that the silk is so placed as to prevent it being untwisted by the action of the instrument; for should one of the threads be improperly placed, it will require an increased degree of labour and a neat line can never be produced.

The hairs in proportion to the thickness of the line required, must next be introduced, by means of small quills into the tube, and twisted (perhaps two or more) with each end of the silk. When the lengths are twisted in, the quills must be taken out, and the tubes again fed with hair; and so on until the whole of the silk be unwound from the balls. It is necessary to observe that the hairs should be of unequal length when introduced; otherwise, should it after the commencement, be necessary to put in two hairs at one time, the line will be clumsy and uneven'.

The author goes on to describe a simpler form of twist engine for hair or gut – 'Besides the engine before described there is another of simpler form which answers very well for short lengths, when a knot is used, and is much more easily managed, as it merely requires the silk or the hair to be fastened to the iron hooks in front and then twisted together.'

Eventually gut replaced horse-hair and hair mixed lines because of ease of manufacture and better performance.

In about 1909 a gut substitute was introduced from Japan which consisted of a silk core covered with a glue substance derived from animal fats and extracts of seaweed. It was marketed under various brand names and although strong and cheap proved too soft and inferior. In the late 1930s synthetic gut was perfected and called Nylon which was the forerunner of the modern synthetic fishing lines.

Some of the trade cards of the early fishing tackle makers include items described as 'Trunks for darts and pellets'. Also 'Pellet Moulds'. I would have expected these to be ammunition for guns and was greatly surprised to discover that

forms with a target, one of the best indoor amusements for ladies and gentlemen.'

These walking stick blow tubes looked like ordinary walking canes but through the centre ran a brass tube of about 3/8" diameter. There was usually a handle to the stick which could be removed ready for use and similarly a removable ferrule at the other end.

The pellet moulds advertised were scissor-moulds similar to the ones for casting lead bullets except there was no pouring hole. Darts were like darning needles with paper cones attached to the rear end to provide a tight fit in the tube.

These tubes must have been in regular use and reached their peak between 1760 and 1780 because John Herro was advertising them and Ustonson, who succeeded him at 48 Bell Yard continued to put them on his broadsheets.

Other makers trading in them included George Hutchinson, Bartho Lowe and Mary Knight all of whom were in business during that period.

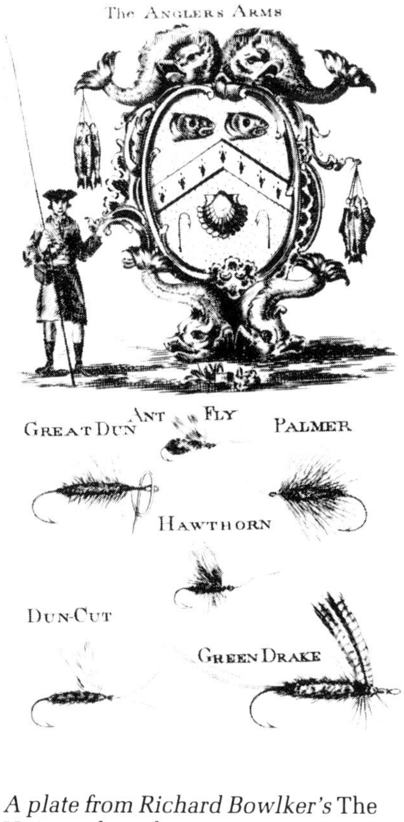

A plate from Richard Bowlker's The Universal Angler, *1766*

THE EARLY LONDON TACKLE TRADE

c.1650 – 1676 JOHN MARGRAVE, The Three Trouts, St. Paul's Churchyard

John Margrave placed an advertisement in Venables' *Experienced Angler* published in 1662, which read – 'Courtious Reader. You may be pleased to take notice that at the Three Trouts, on the north side of St Paul's Churchyard, you may be fitted with all sorts of best fishing tackle by John Margrave'.

He was still there in 1676 confirmed by Walton in the fifth edition of the *Compleat Angler*, saying he recommended a visit 'to Mr Margrave who dwells amongst the booksellers in St Paul's Churchyard'.

c.1650 – 1770s CHARLES KIRBY Harp Alley, Shoe Lane

Charles Kirby was the most important of all hook makers and was the first to perfect quality hooks.

By 1600 many shops in London were stocking fishing tackle to meet the needs of the growing number of Thames fishermen. Makers of rods and reels had sprung up and were making a living, both retailing and wholesaling their products.

Hooks in Britain at that time were rather poor quality and unreliable. The profit on hooks was so small that they had not attracted much attention, nor any new ideas in manufacture.

Charles Kirby realised the opportunity and set about finding a way to temper and produce hooks of consistent quality. He was so successful that his name became synonymous with fish hooks worldwide and the family business dominated the early market for over a century.

Walton's 1655 edition of the *Compleat Angler* gives the earliest mention of Kirby hooks saying – 'But if you will buy choice hooks, I will one day, walk with you to Charles Kirby's in Harp Alley, in Shoe Lane, who is the most exact and best hook maker that the nation affords'.

The 1681 edition of the *Angler's Vade Mecum* says that Charles Kirby is in Globe Court, Shoe Lane.

It would appear that there were three Charles Kirbys during the life of the Kirby hook business. Very little is known about the founder except a brief mention in the early angling books. More information is available on a Charles Kirby and the famous hooks in the first quarter of the eighteenth century and it would appear that this man was the grandson and the second Charles Kirby. He placed an advertisement in 1726, the first part of which reads:

> 'To all lovers of ANGLING.
> I CHARLES KIRBY son of the late Timothy Kirby and Grandson to old Charles Kirby, sole Maker of the so much admired Fish-Hooks, Master of the Grand Arcanum of Tempering Wire, to which Perfection, none but my said Ancestors and myself have arrived; do hereby certify all lovers of Angling that the right Kirby Hooks are sold by me and me only.'

There he states clearly that his grandfather was Charles Kirby but even more important is the information – 'to which Perfection none but my Ancestors and myself have arrived' which shows the involvement of his predecessors.

One of these was Timothy who was the second generation to trade in the famous Charles Kirby name until his son Charles II succeeded him.

The Kirby hooks became so famous that the marketing in London was done through a sole agent and this system sometimes led to trouble.

For a few years up to 1720 William Browne had been the agent but there must have been problems and Charles Kirby changed his outlet to Robert

WILLIAM BROWNE, at the Sign of the Fish, the lower end of Black Horse Alley, in Fleet-ftreet near Fleet-Bridge, maketh all forts of Fifhing-Rods, and all manner of the beft Fifhing-Tackle; and ftill felleth the right Kirby's Hooks, as ufual. Note, Mr. Kirbee having for Two Years laft paft received due Encouragement, has fo effectually applied himfelf to the making of curious, fine and ftrong Hooks, that thofe now made by him far exceed the Old Kirby's Hooks in all refpects. Therefore all Gentlemen and others who delight in Angling, are defired to take notice, that tho' they may meet with the Old Kirby's Hooks at other Places (they not being now valued fo much as formerly) yet the only true Kirbee's Hooks (which fo far excel them) are only to be had at William Browne's aforefaid; who likewife felleth all other forts of Fifh-Hooks. N. B. At the fame Place, all Gentlemen may be furnifh'd with the beft of Silk Worm Gut, newly come over.

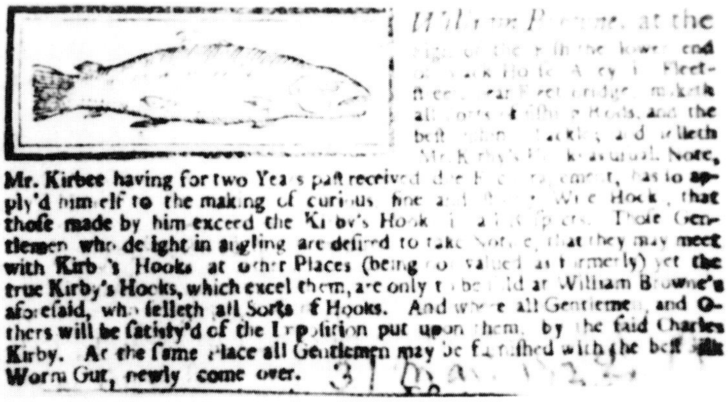

William Browne, at the Sign of the Fifh the lower end of Black Horfe Alley in Fleet-ftreet near Fleet Bridge maketh all forts of Fifhing Rods, and the beft Fifhing Tackle, and felleth Mr. Kirby's Hooks as ufual. Note, Mr. Kirbee having for two Years paft receiv'd due Encouragement, has fo apply'd himfelf to the making of curious fine and ftrong Wire Hooks, that thofe made by him exceed the Kirby's Hook in all Refpects. Thofe Gentlemen who delight in angling are defired to take Notice, that they may meet with Kirby's Hooks at other Places (being not valued as formerly) yet the true Kirby's Hooks, which excel them, are only to be fold at William Browne's aforefaid, who felleth all Sorts of Hooks. And where all Gentlemen, and Others will be fatisfy'd of the Impofition put upon them by the faid Charles Kirby. At the fame Place all Gentlemen may be furnifhed with the beft Silk Worm Gut, newly come over.

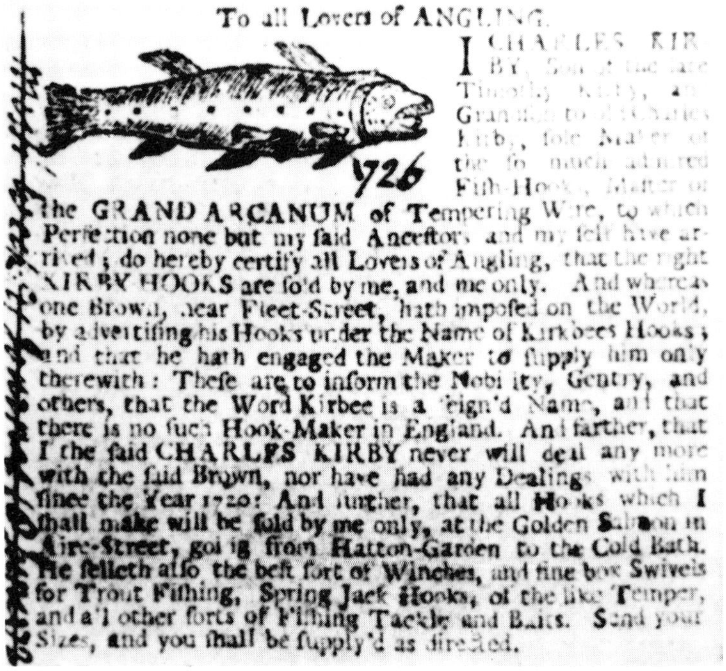

To all Lovers of ANGLING.

I CHARLES KIRBY, Son of the late Timothy Kirby, and Grandfon to old Charles Kirby, fole Maker of the fo much admired Fifh-Hooks, Mafter of the GRAND ARCANUM of Tempering Wire, to which Perfection none but my faid Anceftors and my felf have arrived; do hereby certify all Lovers of Angling, that the right KIRBY HOOKS are fold by me, and me only. And whereas one Brown, near Fleet-Street, hath impofed on the World, by advertifing his Hooks under the Name of Kirkbees Hooks; and that he hath engaged the Maker to fupply him only therewith: Thefe are to inform the Nobility, Gentry, and others, that the Word Kirbee is a feign'd Name, and that there is no fuch Hook-Maker in England. And farther, that I the faid CHARLES KIRBY never will deal any more with the faid Brown, nor have had any Dealings with him fince the Year 1720: And further, that all Hooks which I fhall make will be fold by me only, at the Golden Salmon in Aire-Street, going from Hatton-Garden to the Cold Bath. He felleth alfo the beft fort of Winches, and fine box Swivels for Trout Fifhing, Spring Jack Hooks, of the like Temper, and all other forts of Fifhing Tackle and Baits. Send your Sizes, and you fhall be fupply'd as directed.

The above are three original advertisements placed by Kirby and Browne in the 1720s

Hopkins. Browne carried on selling hooks but describing them as Kirby Hooks and after two years Kirby issued the following announcement – 'I, Charles Kirby, son of the late Timothy Kirby and Grandson of old Charles Kirby, have left off dealing with William Browne of Black Horse Alley, near Fleet Bridge, for two years past, and now have contracted and agreed with Mr. Robert Hopkins of Bell Yard, near Temple Bar at the Sign of the Salmon, and with him only: And whereas the said, William Browne, has pretended to sell Fish-hooks under the name of Kirby, these are to advertise that they are not my Hooks, but are an Imposition upon the World'.

Browne was reluctant to lose the advantages of the famous trade name, and placed his own advertisements on February 24th and March 31st 1722 which read –

'William Browne, at the Sign of the Fish, the lower end of Black Horse Alley, in Fleet Street, near Fleet Bridge, maketh all sorts of fishing Rods and the best Fishing Tackle; and selleth Mr Kirby's hooks as usual. Note – Mr Kirbee having for two years past received due Encouragement, has so apply'd himself to the making of curious fine and strong Wire Hooks, that those made by him, exceed the Kirby's Hook in all Respects. Those Gentlemen who delight in angling are desired to take Notice that they may meet with Kirby's Hooks at other places (not being valued as formerly) yet the true Kirby's Hooks, which excel them, are only sold at William Browne's, as aforesaid'.

He had invented a fictitious Mr Kirbee in order to carry on calling his hooks by the famous trade name.

Browne must have continued to trade in this manner for four years, in which time Kirby had ceased to sell through Robert Hopkins. In 1726, Kirby made his final announcement — 'And whereas one Brown, near Fleet Street, hath imposed on the World, by advertising his Hooks under the Name of Kirbee's Hooks, and that he hath engaged the Maker to supply him only therewith; These are to inform the

Nobility, Gentry and others that the Word Kirbee is a Feign'd Name and there is no such Hook-Maker in England. And farther that I the said Charles Kirby will never deal any more with the said Brown, nor have had any Dealings with him since the year 1720; And farther, that all Hooks, which I shall make, will be sold by me only, at the Golden Salmon in Aire St. going from Hatton-Gardens to the Cold Bath. He selleth also the best sort of Winches, and fine box Swivels for Trout Fishing, Spring Jack Hooks, of like Temper and all other sorts of Fishing Tackle and Baits. Send your sizes and you shall be supply'd as directed.'

Little is known of what happened after this period except that he had a son who carried on the Kirby hook family business and he was also called Charles Kirby. He carried on with the same method of supplying hooks in the London area on a franchise basis. An address at Crowthers Well Alley near Aldersgate St. is believed to have been used in 1760.

In 1768 Charles Kirby III was trading from St. Anne's Lane, Aldergate and was using Ustonson as his agent. On the 6th of May that year a large advertisement by Ustonson appeared listing all the tackle he could supply and below it appeared a second announcement by Charles Kirby III. This was the last evidence of the Kirby business which had disappeared by the time the industry moved to Redditch early in the nineteenth century. I can find no connection with the Kirby, Beard & Co Ltd who made hooks in later years.

Below is the announcement by Charles Kirby III. The last known evidence of the Kirby business

St. Anne's Lane Aldergate

TO ALL LOVERS OF ANGLING

Charles Kirby

Nephew of Thomas Kirby (lately deceased) Son of Charles Kirby and Grandson of Timothy, the original Maker of the much admired Fish-Hooks, for Temper, Strength and Smallness of Wire. Well known by the name of Kirby's Hooks. (of which I am now the only maker). To prevent all Impositions of pretending Makers and Sellers of Hooks, called Kirby Hooks do hereby declare my Engagement with –

Mr. USTONSON at No. 48, the bottom of Bell Yard, near Temple Bar, London

The old original shop, for who I make, and for no other Person.

At the above shop are made and sold all sorts of Fishing Rods and Tackle both Wholesale and Retail.

c. 1650 – 1676 JOHN HOBS

In 1657 *Barkers Delight* tells us that 'John Hobs liveth at the sign of the George, behind the mews by Charring-Cross' and describes him as 'the man for you if you would have a rod to beare and to fit neatly.'

By 1676 he had acquired the business of Charles Brandon which was confirmed by Walton's fifth edition with Piscator saying – 'Mr Margrove who dwells amongst the booksellers in St Paul's Churchyard or to Mr Hobs near to the Swan in Golding Lane.'

c.1653–1660s OLIVER FLETCHER Dean's Court St. Pauls

The First Edition Walton 1653 gives a description of two tackle shops by Piscator, the second of which is mentioned as follows – 'Or to Mr Fletcher's in the Court, which did once belong to the Dean of St. Pauls, that I told you was a good man and a good fisher; they both be honest men and will fit an angler with what tackle he wants.'.

c. 1653 – 1670s CHARLES BRANDON Golding Lane (Near to the Swan)

Walton tells us about him in the first edition of *Compleat Angler 1653* – 'I will go with you to either Charles Brandon's near to the Swan in Golding Lane etc.'

c. 1682 WILLIAM TOWNSEND Blew Ball, against Serjeants Inn, Fleet Street

He advertised in *Brooks Loyal Impartial Mercury* on August 25th 1682 – 'the best fish hooks in England are now at last sold in London; to be had, only had, at his establishment, besides other fishing tackle'.

c. 1689 – 1720s WILLIAM BROWNE Sign of the Fish, Black Horse Alley

William Browne placed an advertisement in the first edition of Cheetham's *The Angler's Vade Mecum* of 1689. He announced that he 'Maketh all Sorts of Fishing Rods, Artificial Flyes and selleth Kirbie's Hooks, the Indian weed commonly called Grass, Worms, Gentles, and all sorts of Fishing Tackle'.

By 1700 he had expanded to a second shop – 'The Golden Fish' at St. Paul's Churchyard. He was a man who believed in making bold press announcements. In the *London Gazette* of 19th April 1708, he announced that his wife had eloped and taken the best of his goods with her. Two years later on 28th March 1710, he placed a statement in the *Daily Courier* saying – 'several have reported that the said William Browne is dead – the report is false. He now liveth at the end of Black Horse Alley, near Fleet Bridge and continues to sell.'

He was one of the largest dealers in London and was agent for Kirby hooks up to about 1720 and then the relationship went sour and Kirby withdrew the franchise.

Undeterred Browne continued to use the Kirby name for his hooks until the matter finally came to a head when Charles Kirby made a public announcement naming Robert Hopkins as his agent and saying that Browne was falsely using his name to sell hooks.

Browne replied as described in

the Kirby history by inventing a Mr Kirbee to try to hold on to the valuable hook trade name. His advert inventing the mythical person was one of the first to offer Silkworm Gut.

Kirby made a final announcement saying no hook maker by the name of Kirbee had ever existed and that Browne had never sold any of his hooks since 1720 and never would again.

JOHN BROWNE The Salmon, St. Paul's Churchyard

He succeeded William and extended his activities to that of goldsmith and jeweller and incorporated the French language into the text of his advertisements.

c. 1700 – 1730 ROBERT HOPKINS The Salmon, 48 Bell Yard, Temple Bar

In 1700 he placed the following advertisement in *Angler's Vade Mecum* –

> At the Sign of the Salmon in Bell Yard, near Temple Bar, London, liveth Robert Hopkins – Who maketh all sorts of fishing rods, and all manner of the best fishing tackle with Worms, Gentles and Flyes, and also the Indian Weed commonly called Grass, – newly come over. Note he selleth Denton's Hooks of Yorkshire known to be the best Hooks that ever was made, for their strength and the fineness of the Wire now made in the best shape and approved by some of the best Anglers in England. Note these hooks are sold by me, and no other person in the Kingdom'.

He was agent for Kirby hooks from 1722 to 1725 – died about 1730.

c. 1730 – 1760s JOHN HERRO Fish & Crown, 48 Bell Yard, Temple Bar

John Herro was apprenticed to Robert Hopkins and took over the business when his employer died. He traded at that address for over thirty years and was succeeded by Onesimus Ustonson.

AT the Sign of the *Fiſh*, in the Lower End of *Black-Horſe-Alley*, at the Steps near *Fleet-Bridge*; Liveth *William Browne*, who Maketh all Sorts of Fiſhing-Rods, Artificial Flyes, and Selleth *Kerbie's* Hooks, the *Indian*-Weed, commonly called Graſs-Worms; Gentles, and all other Sorts of Fiſhing-Tackle.

British Museum

Trade card of William Browne

To all Lovers of Angling.

JOHN HERRO,

At the Fiſh *and* Crown *in* Bell-Yard, *near* Temple-Bar, *Servant to the late Mr.* HOPKINS,

MAKES all Sorts of Fiſhing Rods, and all manner of the beſt Fiſhing Tackle, Wholeſale or Retail; With the right *Denton* Hooks; the beſt Sort of Spring Snap Hooks for Pike; and all other Sort of Fiſhing Hooks.

HE alſo Maketh the beſt Sort of Artificial Flies, ſo much admired by all Gentlemen who have made uſe of them. And alſo the *Indian* Weed, commonly called Graſs; the only Thing for Trout and Carp Fiſhing, when ſoaked for Half an Hour before uſed.

HE likewiſe Selleth the fine Silk-Worm-Gut, freſh come over; It is as fine as a Hair, and as ſtrong as Six: It is uſed, and approved of by ſeveral Anglers, for Fly-fiſhing for Trout and Salmon.

AND the beſt Sort of Winches, and fine Box Swivels, for Trout and Salmon. And all Sorts of Trunks to ſhoot Darts and Pellets. Fiſhing Stools; and many other Curioſities in the Way of Angling.

British Museum

A trade card issued in 1734 by John Herro

c. 1760s – 1855 USTONSON
Fish & Crown 48 Bell Yard

From 1775 – 205 Fleet St
From 1818 – 204 Fleet St
From 1846 – 48 Bell Yard
1848 – 1855 – Ustonson & Peters
48 Bell Yard

c. 1730 – 1760s JOHN SOUCH
The Golden Salmon and Spectacles on London Bridge

He was the first maker recorded as advertising as a wholesaler and exporter, offering his goods to Newfoundland, New England, Virginia, Jamaica and Barbados or any other parts of the world. Records from 1763 list an Edward Souch trading from Crooked Lane.

c. 1732 HENRY PARKHURST
Fleet St.

c. 1744 – 1771 COLES CHILD
The Blew Bore, London Bridge

The 'Blew Bore' stood on the west end of the bridge and was leased to Coles Child for a period of 21 years on an annual rent of £7.

Child was a haberdasher who sold 'ink-horns, fountain pens, buckles, coffee mills, horn lanthorns, needles, bodkins' also – 'Cane and Hazel Fishing Rods and Lines and all sorts of Fishing Tackle'. When the properties on the Bridge were demolished in 1760, he moved to No. 123 Lower Thames Street opposite St. Magnus Church, where he was buried in 1771 and his grave marked by an inscribed tablet.

British Museum

British Museum

c. 1752 – 1760s JOHN CHESHIRE and WILLIAM BUSICK
Angler and Trout, Crooked Lane

They offered fishing tackle for sea and rivers and white chapel needles for all trades.

Needle makers records show that on the 9th January 1752, a John Kirby, was apprenticed to John Cheshire. This boy was probably a member of the famous Kirby hook making family.

British Museum

c. 1763 JOHN CHESHIRE & CO.

c. 1756 STEPHEN PENSTONE
The Fish, Drury Lane

He sold a full range of tackle including brass winches and 'Northern Hooks'. These were Denton hooks from Yetland, Yorkshire.

c. 1766/7 BARTHO LOWE,
Golden Fish, Drury Lane

Bartho Lowe was the successor to Stephen Penstone.

1760s GEORGE HUTCHINSON
The Amberley Trout, Snow Hill

His decorative trade card tells us that his business was 'Selling a variety of goods including all sorts of fishing tackle (except nets).'

c. 1763 MICHAEL MOLE
Crooked Lane

c. 1771 Mr GREGORY
Dial and Fish, The Strand

He was a clockmaker and fishing tackle manufacturer.

c. 1779 – 1800 JOHN HIGGINBOTHAM
The Golden Fish, 91 The Strand

He inserted an advertisement in Shirley's *The Angler's Museum* c. 1784, saying that he sold 'the right Kirby's and Ford's hooks so much admired for their goodness of temper.'

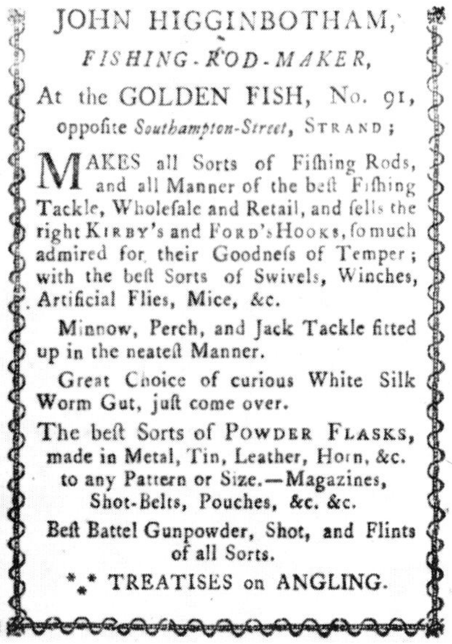
JOHN HIGGINBOTHAM,
FISHING-ROD-MAKER,
At the GOLDEN FISH, No. 91,
opposite *Southampton-Street*, STRAND;
MAKES all Sorts of Fifhing Rods, and all Manner of the beft Fifhing Tackle, Wholefale and Retail, and fells the right KIRBY's and FORD's HOOKS, fo much admired for their Goodnefs of Temper; with the beft Sorts of Swivels, Winches, Artificial Flies, Mice, &c.
Minnow, Perch, and Jack Tackle fitted up in the neateft Manner.
Great Choice of curious White Silk Worm Gut, juft come over.
The beft Sorts of POWDER FLASKS, made in Metal, Tin, Leather, Horn, &c. to any Pattern or Size.—Magazines, Shot-Belts, Pouches, &c. &c.
Beft Battel Gunpowder, Shot, and Flints of all Sorts.
** TREATISES on ANGLING.

Trade card of John Higginbotham

Trade card of the first known woman tackle dealer, Sarah Sandon

c. 1740 SARAH SANDON
Compleat Angler, Crooked Lane

The first lady recorded as running a fishing tackle business. She issued a broadsheet offering 'all sorts of best fishing tackle for use of ye sea or river'.

c. 1750s Mr KNIGHT
Compleat Angler, Crooked Lane

Followed Sarah Sandon at the Compleat Angler in Crooked Lane. The only knowledge of his existence is given on a billcard put out by his widow.

c. 1750s – 1762 MARY KNIGHT
Compleat Angler, Crooked Lane

She took over the business on the death of her husband and made her son a partner. She issued one of the most attractive trade cards which was designed by Benjamin Cole.

1763 – 1834 STONE and IVERSON

It is generally believed that Stone and Iverson immediately succeeded Mary Knight & Son in Crooked Lane because they issued the same cartouche designed by Benjamin Cole for and used by the earlier proprietress. They replaced her name with that of their own and added the words 'Successor to M Knight'. My research has found a trades list of 1763, in the Guildhall Library in London, which includes four fishing tackle makers in Crooked Lane. There is no mention of a Mary Knight but it does give a 'Henry Stone & Co.' This would suggest that Henry Stone & Co. succeeded Mary Knight & Son and

Mary Knight & Son
Fish Hook Makers
At the Old
Compleat Angler a Corner Shop in Crooked Lane
LONDON.
Makes and Sell all Sorts of the best
Fishing Tackle, for Use of Sea or River; &c
as Artificial Flies, Hooks, Rods, Landing Nets,
and Lines of every Size & Goodness, with Silk-
Worms Gut & Indian Weed, &c Wholesale & Retale
N.B. All Sorts of Sail, Needles, Palmes, Trunks,
Darts and Pellet-Moulds.
B. Cole sculp.

British Museum

would fill the gap up to 1772 when Stone had taken Iverson into partnership.

By 1790 there was a new title 'Iverson & Stone', which would suggest that Henry Stone had died and Iverson had become the senior partner with a Henry Stone Junior.

In 1794 they moved and acquired Gimber & Sons premises at 10 Crooked Lane.

By 1817 Charles Iverson must have died and his interest acquired by the Stone family as the business was registered as Henry Stone, and continued to trade with that title up to 1834.

Summary Circa Dates:
1763-1771 – Henry Stone & Co, Crooked Lane
1772-1789 – Stone & Iverson, Crooked Lane
1790-1793 – Iverson and Stone, 13 Crooked Lane
1794-1816 – Iverson and Stone, 10 Crooked Lane
1817-1831 – Henry Stone, 10 Crooked Lane
1832-1834 – Henry Stone, 67 Cannon St.

c. 1769 – 1779 JOHN BRAILSFORD Fish and Case of Knives, St. Martins Court

He sold a full range of tackle including artificial fish, frogs and insects.

c. 1771 HENRY PATTEN The Saw and Crown, Middle Row, Holborn

He was trading as early as 1756 as a razor maker and later as a cutler who also sold a wide range of fishing tackle. He issued a broadsheet in 1771 offering multiplying brass winches which was only a short time after the earliest advertisement for this item of tackle by Ustonson. Other goods offered included 'fishing rods, Kirby hooks, spring snap hooks, white and yellow gimp, the best woven hair and silk lines. Baits included flies, artificial minnows for trout and other sorts of artificial baits, treble, double and single box swivels and fitted up – Minnow, Perch and Jack Tackle.'

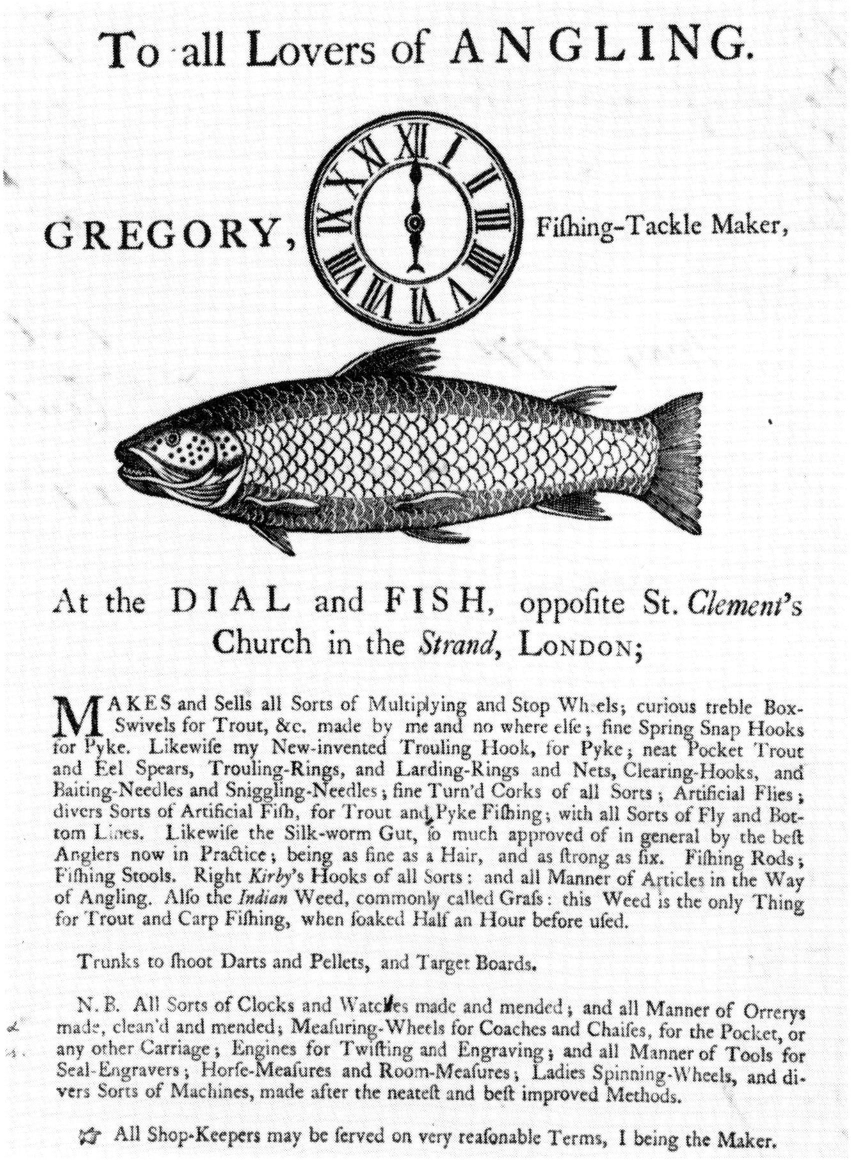
To all Lovers of ANGLING.
GREGORY, Fiſhing-Tackle Maker,
At the DIAL and FISH, oppoſite St. Clement's Church in the Strand, LONDON;
MAKES and Sells all Sorts of Multiplying and Stop Wheels; curious treble Box-Swivels for Trout, &c. made by me and no where elſe; fine Spring Snap Hooks for Pyke. Likewiſe my New-invented Trouling Hook, for Pyke; neat Pocket Trout and Eel Spears, Trouling-Rings, and Larding-Rings and Nets, Clearing-Hooks, and Baiting-Needles and Sniggling-Needles; fine Turn'd Corks of all Sorts; Artificial Flies; divers Sorts of Artificial Fiſh, for Trout and Pyke Fiſhing; with all Sorts of Fly and Bottom Lines. Likewiſe the Silk-worm Gut, ſo much approved of in general by the beſt Anglers now in Practice; being as fine as a Hair, and as ſtrong as ſix. Fiſhing Rods; Fiſhing Stools. Right Kirby's Hooks of all Sorts: and all Manner of Articles in the Way of Angling. Alſo the Indian Weed, commonly called Graſs: this Weed is the only Thing for Trout and Carp Fiſhing, when ſoaked Half an Hour before uſed.
Trunks to ſhoot Darts and Pellets, and Target Boards.
N. B. All Sorts of Clocks and Watches made and mended; and all Manner of Orrerys made, clean'd and mended; Meaſuring-Wheels for Coaches and Chaiſes, for the Pocket, or any other Carriage; Engines for Twiſting and Engraving; and all Manner of Tools for Seal-Engravers; Horſe-Meaſures and Room-Meaſures; Ladies Spinning-Wheels, and divers Sorts of Machines, made after the neateſt and beſt improved Methods.
All Shop-Keepers may be ſerved on very reaſonable Terms, I being the Maker.

British Museum

Trade card of a Mr Gregory

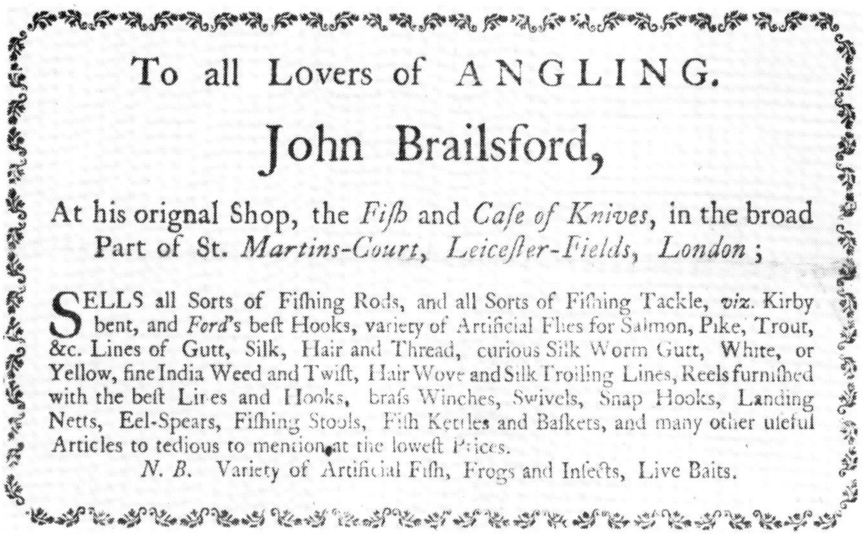
To all Lovers of ANGLING.
John Brailsford,
At his orignal Shop, the Fiſh and Caſe of Knives, in the broad Part of St. Martins-Court, Leiceſter-Fields, London;
SELLS all Sorts of Fiſhing Rods, and all Sorts of Fiſhing Tackle, viz. Kirby bent, and Ford's beſt Hooks, variety of Artificial Flies for Salmon, Pike, Trout, &c. Lines of Gutt, Silk, Hair and Thread, curious Silk Worm Gutt, White, or Yellow, fine India Weed and Twiſt, Hair Wove and Silk Troiling Lines, Reels furniſhed with the beſt Lines and Hooks, braſs Winches, Swivels, Snap Hooks, Landing Netts, Eel-Spears, Fiſhing Stools, Fiſh Kettles and Baſkets, and many other uſeful Articles to tedious to mention at the loweſt Prices.
N. B. Variety of Artificial Fiſh, Frogs and Inſects, Live Baits.

British Museum

Trade card of John Brailsford

USTONSON 1760's — 1855

USTONSON is the most important of all the early tackle makers and although various members of the family traded for almost a century, very few examples of their work have survived. Their output of marked rods and reels must have been very small and confined to custom built items for the upper class anglers while producing some unmarked tackle for the cheaper end of the market. This policy would have made it possible to maintain their image for supplying quality, together with an individual and exclusive service and was so successful that they received commissions from titled people and succeeding British Monarchs.

1760s – 1791
ONESIMUS USTONSON

The Ustonson story began in the late 1760s with the founder, a man with the unusual name of Onesimus Ustonson. He purchased an old established tackle business the 'Fish and Crown', No. 48 Bell Yard, Temple Bar, London which had enjoyed continuous trading, back to 1700 with proprietors John Herro (c. 1760 – 1730) and Robert Hopkins (c. 1730 – 1700).

Bell Yard was a busy, grimy, overcrowded area of 48 houses and shops and extended to 165 yards long. It was a well known haunt of London anglers because it not only housed the 'Fish and Crown', originally 'The Salmon' in the days of Robert Hopkins, but also the well known shops of Chavalier at No. 12 and Bowness at No. 14. Eventually the two famous families, trading next door to one another, amalgamated, and formed a number of partnerships and complicated mixed family businesses from their adjoining properties. By the 1830s a further three tackle shops had opened at numbers 2, 10, and 33.

Ustonson's shop, number 48, was situated at the bottom end of Bell Yard and on a corner next door to No. 205 Fleet Street, which was an area close to the hustle and bustle of the dusty main thoroughfare along which the horse-drawn carriages passed.

Nearby was a large stone gateway, designed by Wren, called Temple Bar which was not a City gate but a symbolic boundary between City and Court. When the Sovereign wished to pass through, a ceremony was performed in which the doors were closed and opened on the sound of a trumpet, followed by the Lord Mayor presenting a sword to the Monarch who returned it before Royalty were free to pass.

The top of Temple Bar was at times used to display the rotting heads of executed prisoners and the gruesome spectacle survived until the last head fell from its pike during a storm in 1772. That was the background to the busy, dirty, Dickensian type market place where Ustonson sold fishing

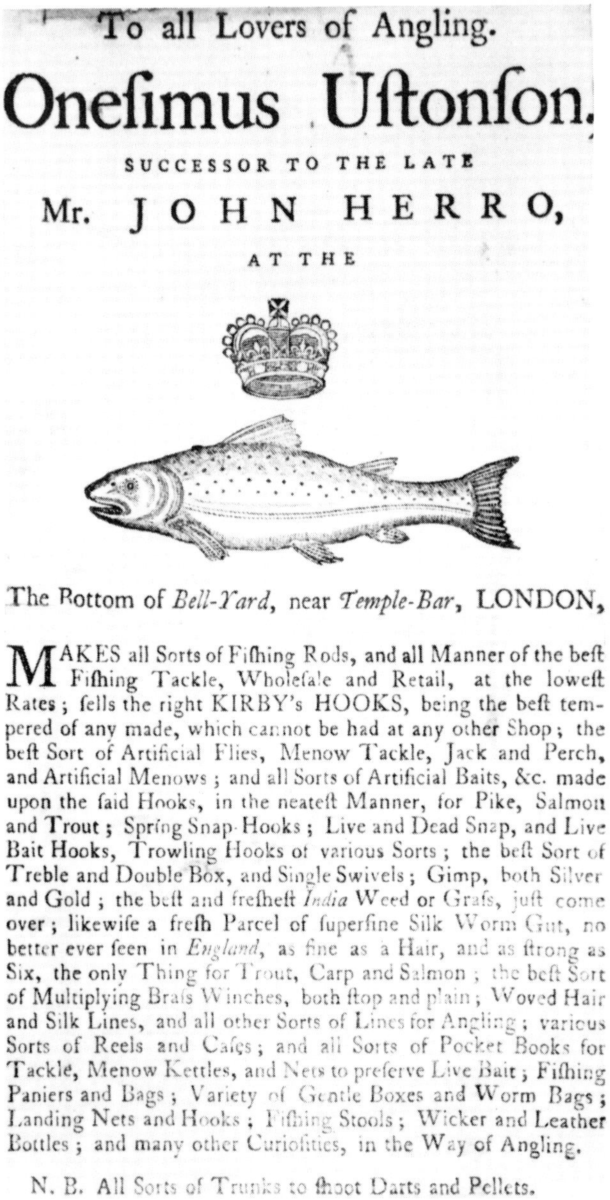

To all Lovers of Angling.
Oneſimus Uſtonſon.
SUCCESSOR TO THE LATE
Mr. JOHN HERRO,
AT THE

The Bottom of *Bell-Yard*, near *Temple-Bar*, LONDON,

MAKES all Sorts of Fiſhing Rods, and all Manner of the beſt Fiſhing Tackle, Wholeſale and Retail, at the loweſt Rates; ſells the right KIRBY's HOOKS, being the beſt tempered of any made, which cannot be had at any other Shop; the beſt Sort of Artificial Flies, Menow Tackle, Jack and Perch, and Artificial Menows; and all Sorts of Artificial Baits, &c. made upon the ſaid Hooks, in the neateſt Manner, for Pike, Salmon and Trout; Spring Snap-Hooks; Live and Dead Snap, and Live Bait Hooks, Trowling Hooks of various Sorts; the beſt Sort of Treble and Double Box, and Single Swivels; Gimp, both Silver and Gold; the beſt and freſheſt *India* Weed or Graſs, juſt come over; likewiſe a freſh Parcel of ſuperfine Silk Worm Gut, no better ever ſeen in *England*, as fine as a Hair, and as ſtrong as Six, the only Thing for Trout, Carp and Salmon; the beſt Sort of Multiplying Braſs Winches, both ſtop and plain; Woved Hair and Silk Lines, and all other Sorts of Lines for Angling; various Sorts of Reels and Caſes; and all Sorts of Pocket Books for Tackle, Menow Kettles, and Nets to preſerve Live Bait; Fiſhing Paniers and Bags; Variety of Gentle Boxes and Worm Bags; Landing Nets and Hooks; Fiſhing Stools; Wicker and Leather Bottles; and many other Curioſities, in the Way of Angling.

N. B. All Sorts of Trunks to ſhoot Darts and Pellets.

British Museum

Trade card put out in the late 1760's by Onesimus Ustonson

tackle from the 'Fish and Crown', alongside other traders in a world of poor working people through which passed the rich merchants and gentry. The earliest record of the activities of Onesimus Ustonson was in about 1768 when he put out a trade-card informing all lovers of angling that he was successor to John Herro at the 'Fish and Crown'. It gave a full list of all the tackle he sold, which included artificial flies, fish and all manner of baits also 'the best sort of multiplying brass winches both stop and plain.' This trade-card was distributed in the late 1760s and is the earliest record of a multiplying winch, pre-dating a similar one placed in the *Art of Angling* 1770, which has always been considered the earliest reference to that type of reel, and one of a number of early advertisements which proved Dr Henshall wrong in claiming the multiplying principle to be an American invention.

In 1775 he was distributing a slightly different trade-card which had dropped all mention of being successor to John Herro and he was confidently trading under his own name but from a new address at No. 205 Fleet Street.

The new premises were only next door to the 48, Bell Yard shop but the move gave him a more impressive main road frontage position and address, from where he could attract the upper class anglers of the day.

One such celebrity was The Right Honorable The Earl of Winterton, who was a very keen fisherman. He had been a customer of Bartholomew Lowe at the 'Golden Fish' in Drury Lane and on June 10th 1775 he visited Ustonson's new shop and purchased tackle amounting to £2.3s.2d which included:–

	£– s – d
6 cork trimmers – fixed complete	0 – 9 – 0
1 silk snap line – fixed complete	0 – 2 – 3
2 dead snap hooks and swivels	0 – 1 – 6
1 brass winch and strong silk line	0 – 7 – 6
2 trawing hooks, 2 needles	0 – 1 – 6
1 flat reel, 6 lines fixed, and pocket books	0 – 12 – 0
3 hair lines, 6 hooks	0 – 2 – 0
1 landing net fixed	0 – 5 – 0
1 large packing case	0 – 2 – 3
Paid for booking	0 – 0 – 2
TOTAL	£2 – 3 – 2

A detailed invoice was hand written on the back of the trade-card which carried the signature of Ustonson for the account settled on June 19th 1775. The total finally paid was £3.8s.0d and included an additional purchase.

The firm continued to trade in the founder's name from the same Fleet Street address on the corner of Bell Yard but by 1783 a son was working in the business. Proof of this comes from a Ustonson bill to Mr. Mann which was dated March 1st 1783. It shows the signature of a Thomas Onesimus Ustonson, accompanied by the words 'Rec'd The Contents in full for my Father.' This signature can be compared and shown to be a different one to that of his father, which appeared on an invoice dated 1786.

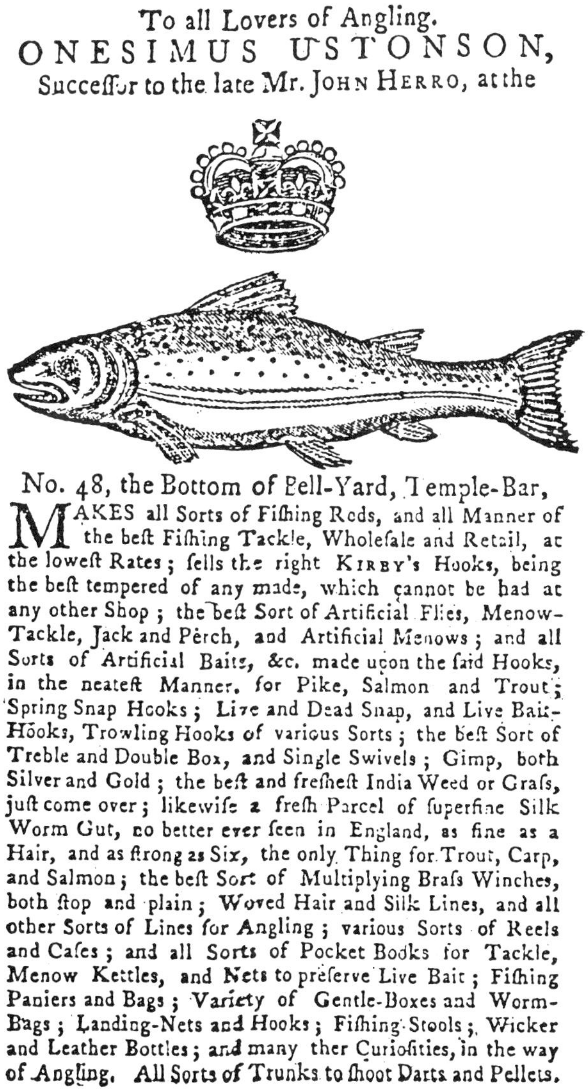

British Museum

An advertisement placed in the Art of Angling *in 1770*

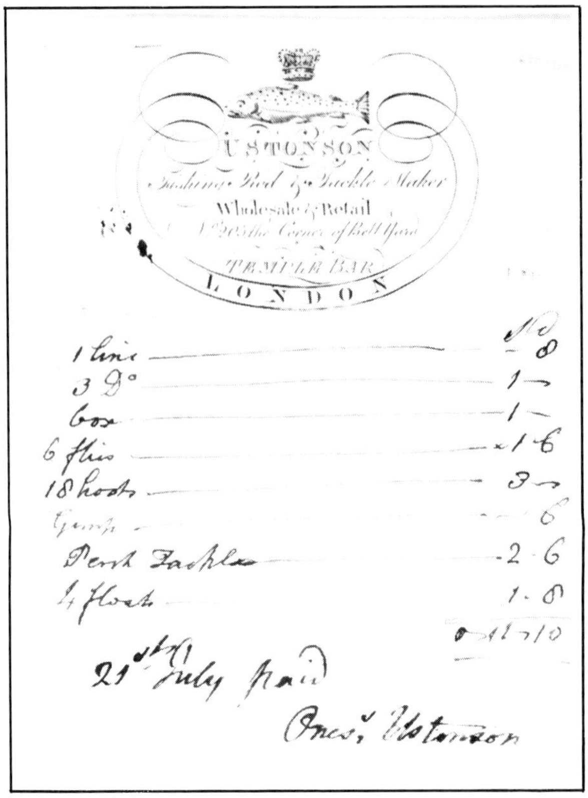

British Museum

Signature of Onesimus Ustonson, the founder, on an invoice dated 1786

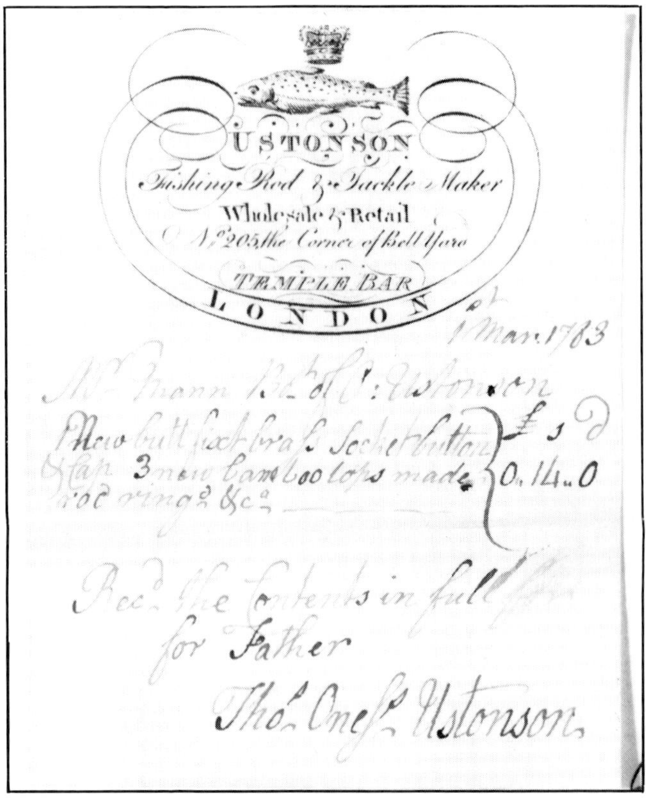

British Museum

Signature of son Thomas Onesimus Ustonson on invoice dated 1783

1792 – 1808 USTONSON & SON

In 1792 the name of the business became Ustonson & Son trading from 205 Fleet Street, and it continued in that style up to 1808. The son must have been Thomas Onesimus, who, having served his apprenticeship had become skilled, and had his name added to the title of the business. It has been possible to confirm that he was working in the firm at that time by the discovery of a bill bearing his signature and dated 1792. It is interesting to note that on the invoice was a mouse-plug priced 2/6d.

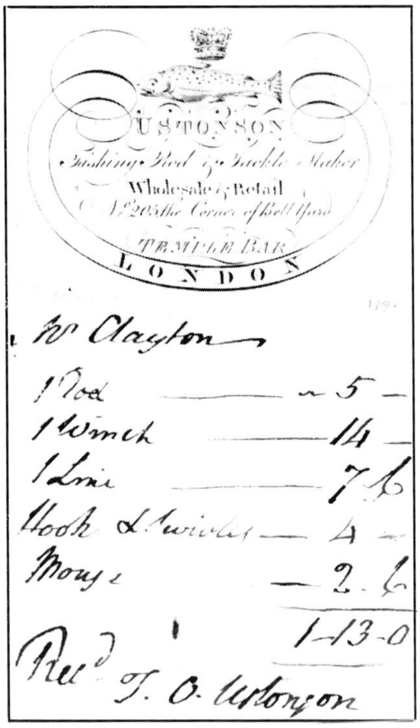

British Museum

A bill dated 1792 bearing the signature of Thomas Onesimus Ustonson

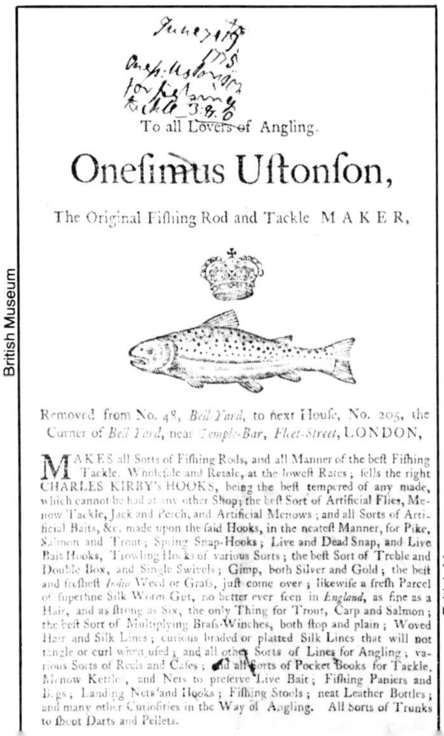

To all Lovers of Angling.

Onesimus Ustonson,

The Original Fishing Rod and Tackle MAKER,

Removed from No. 48, *Bell-Yard*, to next House, No. 205, the Corner of *Bell-Yard*, near *Temple-Bar*, *Fleet-Street*, LONDON,

MAKES all Sorts of Fishing Rods, and all Manner of the best Fishing Tackle. Wholesale and Retale, at the lowest Rates; sells the right CHARLES KIRBY's HOOKS, being the best tempered of any made, which cannot be had at any other Shop; the best Sort of Artificial Flies, Menow Tackle, Jack and Perch, and Artificial Menows; and all Sorts of Artificial Baits, &c. made upon the said Hooks, in the neatest Manner, for Pike, Salmon and Trout; Spring Snap-Hooks; Live and Dead Snap, and Live Bait Hooks, Trowling Hooks of various Sorts; the best Sort of Treble and Double Box, and Single Swivels; Gimp, both Silver and Gold; the best and freshest *India* Weed or Grass, just come over; likewise a fresh Parcel of superfine Silk Worm Gut, no better ever seen in *England*, as fine as a Hair, and as strong as Six, the only Thing for Trout, Carp and Salmon; the best Sort of Multiplying Brass-Winches, both stop and plain; Woved Hair and Silk Lines; curious braded or platted Silk Lines that will not tangle or curl when used; and all other Sorts of Lines for Angling; various Sorts of Reels and Cases; and all Sorts of Pocket Books for Tackle, Menow Kettles, and Nets to preserve Live Bait; Fishing Paniers and Bags; Landing Nets and Hooks; Fishing Stools; neat Leather Bottles; and many other Curiosities in the Way of Angling. All Sorts of Trunks to shoot Darts and Pellets.

British Museum

A trade card on the rear of which was detailed the invoice for The Right Honorable The Earl of Winterton

1809 – 1814
ONESIMUS USTONSON

In 1809 the business title reverted to Onesimus Ustonson which suggests that either the founder of the firm, Onesimus senior, or his son Thomas Onesimus had died or left the business. Trading continued with this title for another six years before the name Onesimus was removed forever.

1815 – 1821 CHARLES USTONSON 205 Fleet Street

Charles, a new member of the family and previously unknown, became head of the business in 1815. The founder Onesimus was probably dead and Charles, having worked in the business for a number of years, took charge and ran the firm until 1821. The address was changed to 204 Fleet Street in 1818.

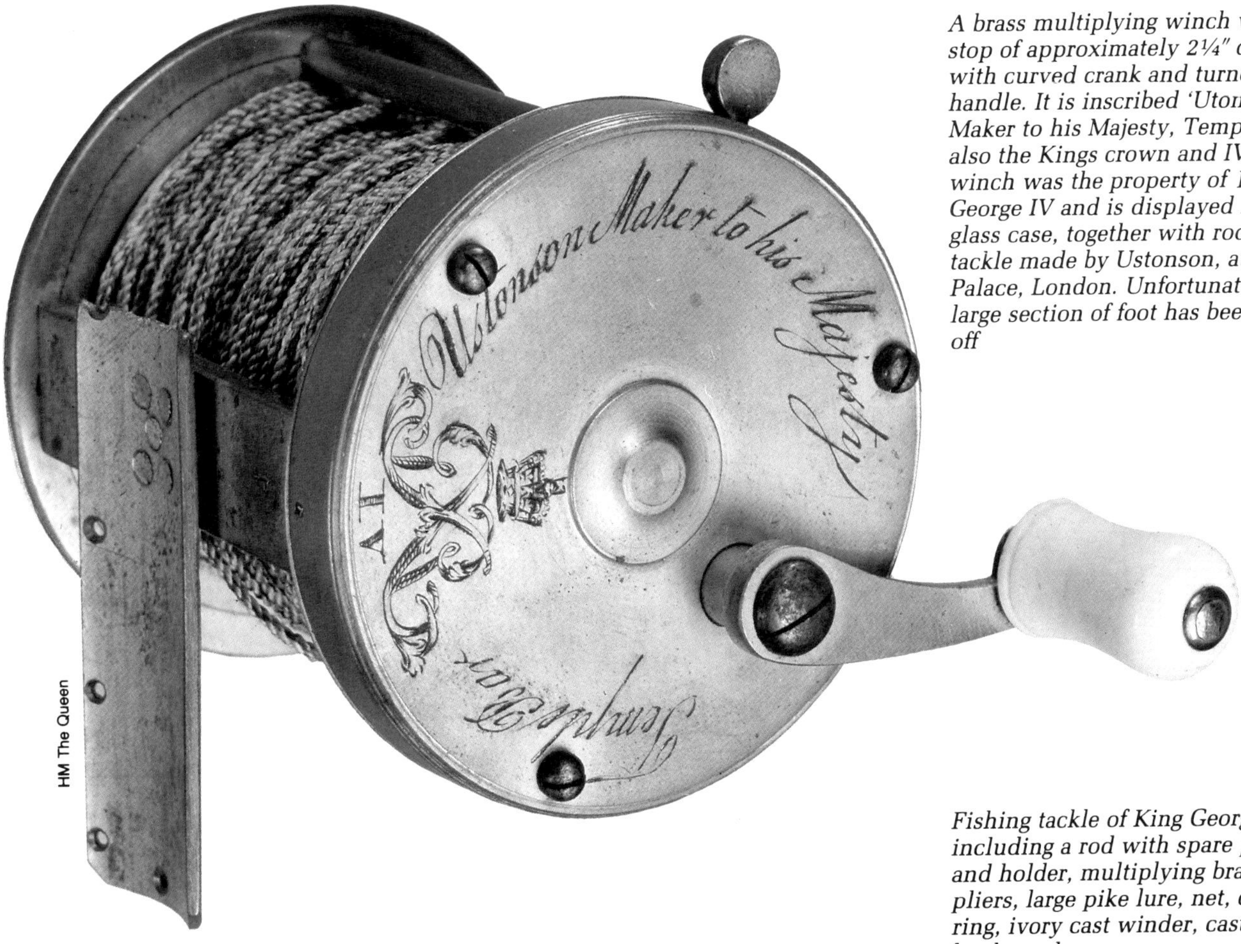

HM The Queen

A brass multiplying winch with rim stop of approximately 2¼″ diameter with curved crank and turned ivory handle. It is inscribed 'Utonson, Maker to his Majesty, Temple Bar,' also the Kings crown and IV. This winch was the property of King George IV and is displayed inside a glass case, together with rod and tackle made by Ustonson, at Kew Palace, London. Unfortunately a large section of foot has been broken off

Fishing tackle of King George IV including a rod with spare pieces and holder, multiplying brass winch, pliers, large pike lure, net, clearing ring, ivory cast winder, cast book, books and case

HM The Queen

Temple Bar, London, the area close to Bell Yard where Ustonson and many of the London tackle makers traded

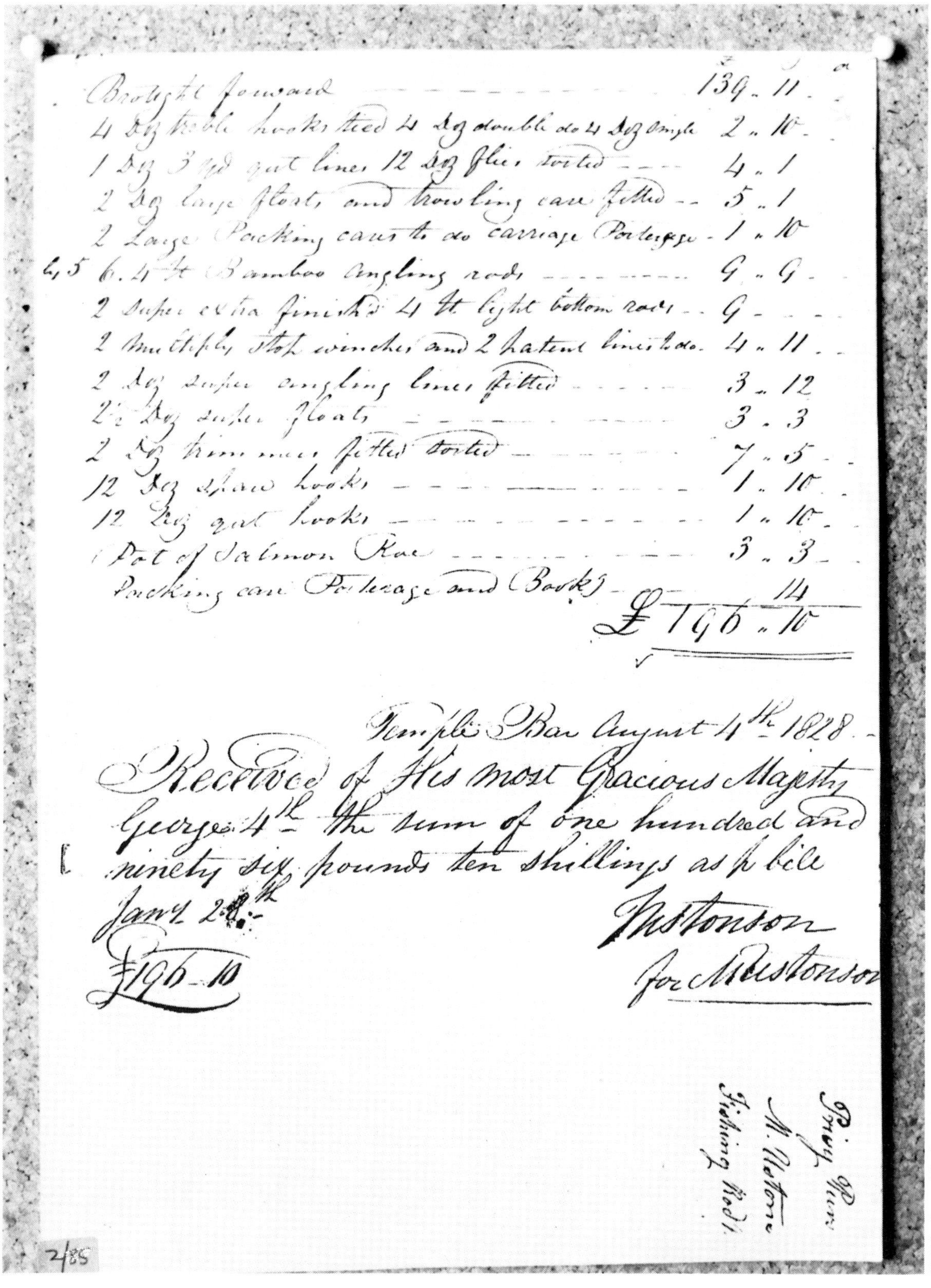
Brought forward — 139 . 11 .
4 Doz treble hooks tied 4 Doz double do 4 Doz single 2 . 10 .
1 Doz 3 Yd gut lines 12 Doz flies sorted — 4 . 1
2 Doz large floats and trowling case fitted — 5 . 1
2 Large Packing cases to do carriage Porterage — 1 . 10
6 . 4 ft Bamboo angling rods — 9 . 9 .
2 Super extra finish'd 4 ft light bottom rods — 9 . .
2 Multiply stop winches and 2 patent lines to do. 4 . 11 .
2 Doz super angling lines fitted — 3 . 12
2½ Doz super floats — 3 . 3
2 Doz trimmers fitted sorted — 7 . 5 .
12 Doz spare hooks — 1 . 10
12 Doz gut hooks — 1 . 10 .
1 Pot of Salmon Roe — 3 . 3 .
Packing case Porterage and Book — 14
£ 196 . 10

Temple Bar August 4th 1828 —
Received of His most Gracious Majesty George 4th the sum of one hundred and ninety six pounds ten shillings as p bill
Jany 28th
£196 . 10
M Ustonson
for M Ustonson

Ustonson invoice sent to King George IV in 1828

Pencil drawing of King George IV by H H Earl in 1828

As a result of information kindly supplied by Her Royal Highness Queen Elizabeth The Queen Mother, herself a skilled and knowledgeable angler, it has been possible to trace some of the tackle of King George IV to Kew Palace where it is now on display. I thank Her Royal Highness, as I do the staff of the Lord Chamberlain's Office, who arranged a series of photographs and gave permission for them to be illustrated.

Fishing tackle of King George IV. Ivory cast winder, pliers, cast book and large pike lure

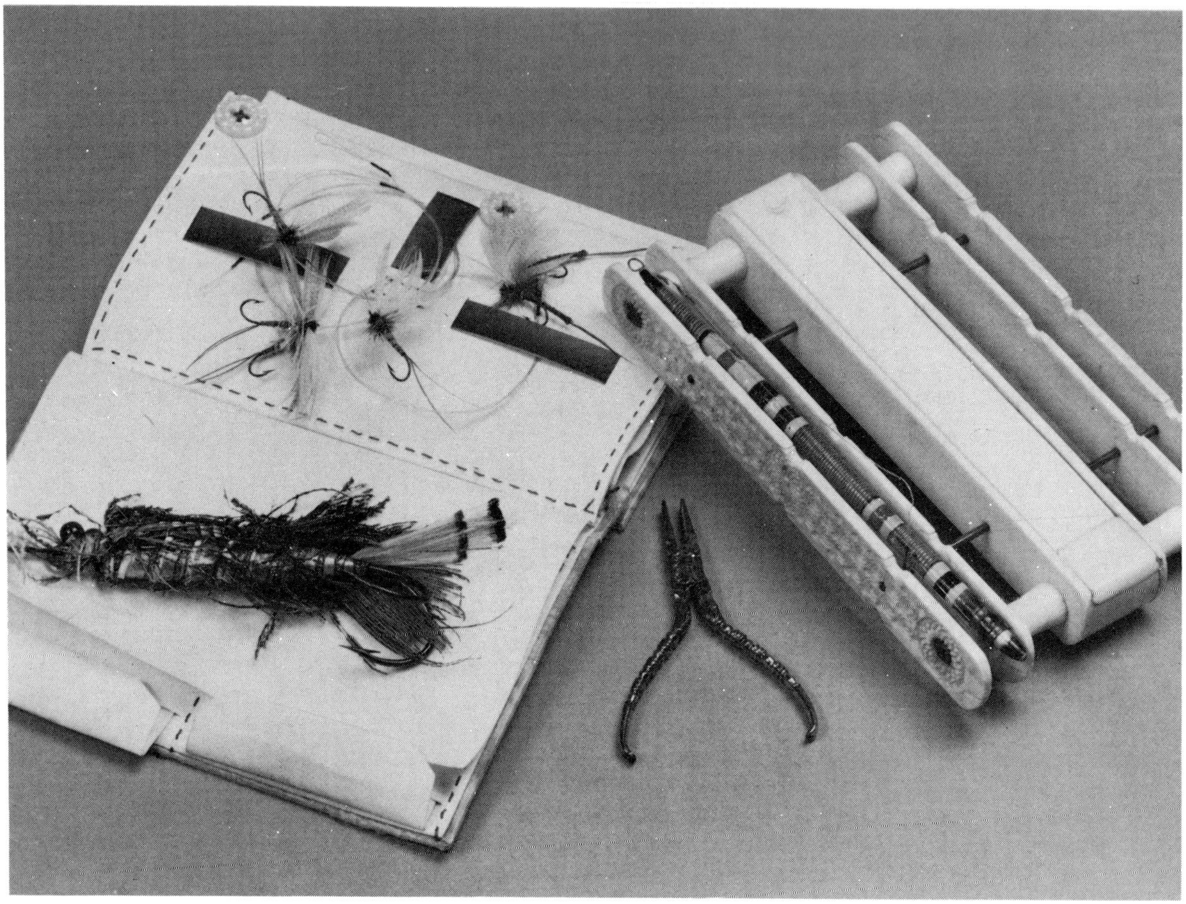

H M The Queen, The Royal Collection

Maria continued to run the business under the name of M. Ustonson from 204 Fleet Street. That address also appears to have been her home which she shared with Robert Joy and two children. A population census form returned from 204 Fleet Street showed the following people in residence:-

DATE OF CENSUS – 1841

Head of Household
Robert Joy – age 50 years
Maria, female – age 50 years
Henry, male – age 20 years
Rosetta, female – age 15 years

Also servants
Alfred Hobday – age 15 years
Rachael Bishop – age 15 years

It has not been possible to ascertain whether Maria was married to Robert Joy, which is likely, or her relationship to Henry or Rosetta, although the girl's name sounds of the same extraction and was probably her daughter.

A Henry Joy was proprietor of No. 6 Opera Arcade from 1845 – 1870 and this may have been the boy mentioned in the 1841 census but can only be speculation.

Maria guided the Ustonson business through some of its most successful years when it enjoyed the patronage of two Kings and a Queen of England, and proved a most capable successor to Onesimus and his heirs. In 1846 there was a change of business address from 204 Fleet Street, back to 48 Bell Yard and Ustonson ceased to trade independently in 1847.

1848 – 1855 USTONSON & PETERS, 48 Bell Yard

In 1847 William Peters started to make and sell fishing tackle from Ustonson's premises at 48 Bell Yard and the following year he had entered into a partnership which lasted seven years. Reels produced during that period were marked – 'Ustonson & Peters, Maker to the Queen, 48 Bell Yard, Temple Bar, London'. It was in that name that an entry of fishing tackle was made in the Great Exhibition of 1851, and described as follows:-

> USTONSON & PETERS,
> 48, BELL YARD, TEMPLE BAR
> INVENTORS & MAKERS
> Bamboo cane fly and salmon fishing-rod. Each joint is formed of three triangular parts connected together from end to end. Box of artificial angling baits, including rare specimens of flies and insects silkworm gut, taper fly line etc.

They did not win any prizes and were just another good average display among the twenty five entries from British makers. The business had come full circle, starting off as just another tackle shop at 48 Bell Yard rising to become the most prestigious tackle maker supplying the highest in the land, and finally returning to the ranks of traders from the address where it had all started almost a century earlier. The final year of the partnership was 1855, as in the following year Peters left for a new address at 71 Long Acre, where he traded until 1862 as William Peters and Son.

Ustonson brass winches are extremely rare and although it is impossible to say with certainty the number which exist today, I have knowledge of only five pure Ustonsons and two made by Ustonson and Peters, all of which are illusrated in this book in colour.

I would be pleased to receive details and photographs of any Ustonson winch or tackle which does not appear in this book but I must sound a warning about false claims which have been made in America in recent years. No winch can be considered to be an Ustonson unless it carries the markings described and illustrated, which obviously must be authentic. Only four Ustonson winches have been discovered in Britain and it poses the question of how many are still hiding in old country houses. Certainly not many, but every collector dreams of finding something of supreme importance in a small provincial auction or among early relics in the shop of an uninformed trader. My ultimate find would be an undamaged brass Ustonson winch which I consider to be the most important of all collectors reels. Such a discovery would be the epitome of Bell Yard and Crooked Lane and the London tackle shops with their trade cards.

It would be a tangible piece of the antiquity of the early makers of which Ustonson was the most important, and it seems reasonable to believe that one day a Ustonson winch will be sold for a world record price.

H M The Queen, The Royal Collection

Ustonson rod on display at Kew Palace

DEVELOPMENT OF THE ROD

Fishing rods between 1750 and 1850 continued to be made from a variety of woods including ash, hickory, lancewood and bamboo cane. It was the period of the industrial revolution when communications and travel improved and the number of anglers greatly increased and became more mobile.

Although the larger jointed rods continued to be used for fly fishing or trolling for pike and the shorter rods and poles for bottom fishing, there was a new popularity for multi-piece 'travellers rods'. These were usually made from greenheart or other wood and consisted of several pieces which fitted neatly into a small holder or bag and could be carried comfortably in the pocket. Walking stick rods were another model, but never became popular and were sold for only a short period.

In the first half of the nineteenth century the usual length of rod for trout fishing was under 12 feet and for salmon a bigger size up to 18 feet. They were tapered gradually from the butt to the tip and some were fitted with drop rings which could fold down against the wood with the exception of the end one at the tip. Although the rod could be made up of any number of pieces the greatest importance was placed on an even and correct springiness. It was undesirable to have a rod too whippy but yet not too stiff. All the writers of the period favoured a rod that could play easily and bend slightly throughout the whole length. Many rods had pieces made from different carefully selected woods and were usually fitted with a four or five inch whalebone tip. The rods were stained to whatever shade or colour was required by the trade. The connecting ends of the pieces of a rod had screw or other type metal ferrules to secure the union but many anglers still preferred to use a splice jointed rod. This design was simply a connection formed by fitting together the spliced ends of the two pieces of rod and held by a collar fitting and wrapped and fastened by a length of leather thong or other material. Many believed that a rod with the pieces connected in this way could throw a fly in a smoother manner because the spring from the hand travelled uninterrupted by ferrules. This type of rod has always found favour with some anglers particularly in the north of England and production has continued up to the present day.

Anglers have always tried to improve the top piece of their rods and all manner of woods have been used. Eventually split cane was introduced and became generally accepted, but there has always been speculation as to when it was first used on fishing rods in Britain.

I have been unable to find any new evidence of an earlier date than the ones suggested by past authorities. The book most quoted by historians as the earliest to mention split-cane for rod tops is *Practical Observations on Angling in the River Trent* by an unknown author, believed to have been published in 1801. It describes rod construction with the text – 'sections of cane are glued together after which they are tapered with planes and fine rasps; finished off with sand

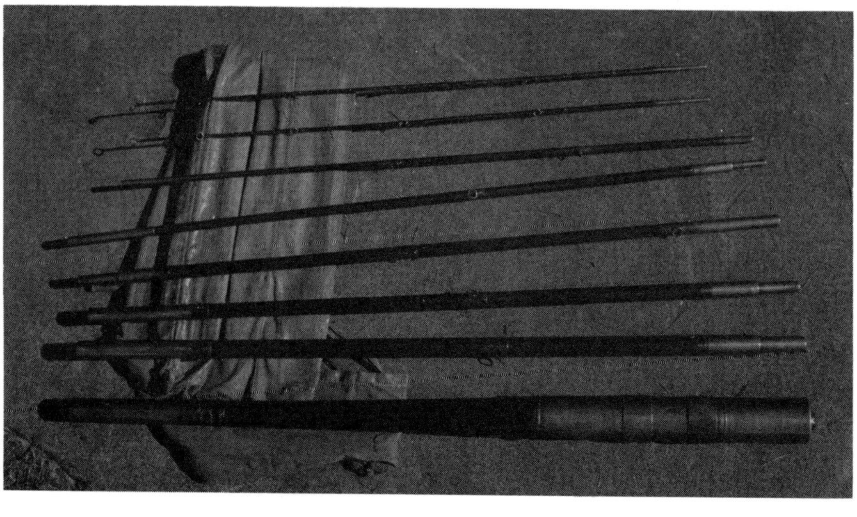

Above: Spliced ends of a spliced jointed rod

Rare travellers rod, engraved on brass butt cap 'Alfred Maker, 41 Coleman St, London.' Seven piece, wooden hollow butt, drop rings, fine rounded split cane tips which fit inside the butt, c.1822–48

paper and the joints wrapped with silk'. Further books which mention split cane for rod tops were – *Young Anglers Companion* c.1820 and *Handbook of Angling* 1847 by Fitzgibbon which discusses the use of five and six strip split cane for the top-joint of rods.

The late Courtney Williams in *Angling Diversions* suggested that Ustonson was possibly one of the earliest makers to build a split cane rod and mentions a date of about 1830. His evidence to support this view was given as information supplied by a rod maker called Irwin who repaired a split cane rod for the Earl of Craven in 1851, and confirmed that it had been in use for twenty years and was the work of Usterson (Ustonson) Temple Bar. Unfortunately the source of this information was not given. Although split cane was used on fishing rods early in the nineteenth century it would appear to be virtually unknown as

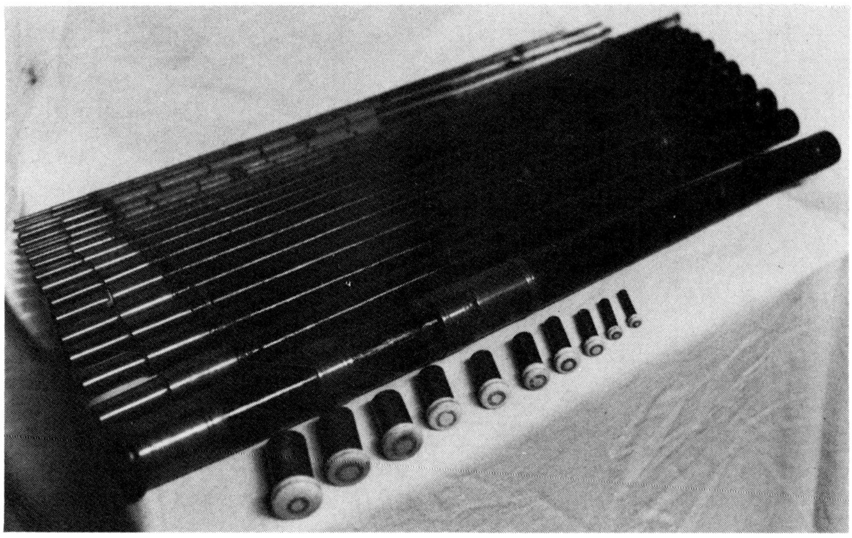

Travellers hickory rod by William Blacker, 54 Dean St, London. Eleven pieces with drop rings and brass and ivory ferrule caps c.1840s/1850s.

Below: A rare three-strip valise rod by T Aldred. It is constructed of glued-up split bamboo cane in ten pieces with a spare tip, and close whipped with drop rings, nickel silver spiggot ferrules and butt mounts. It has a hollow tapered butt which retains long and short tips. Length – 11 feet – Mid 19th century. Other tackle includes an 18th century leather pot-bellied creel, a small bellied bait can, live bait horn, a line clearing ring, a priest, a quantity of gut-eyed salmon flies and a brass clamp foot winch

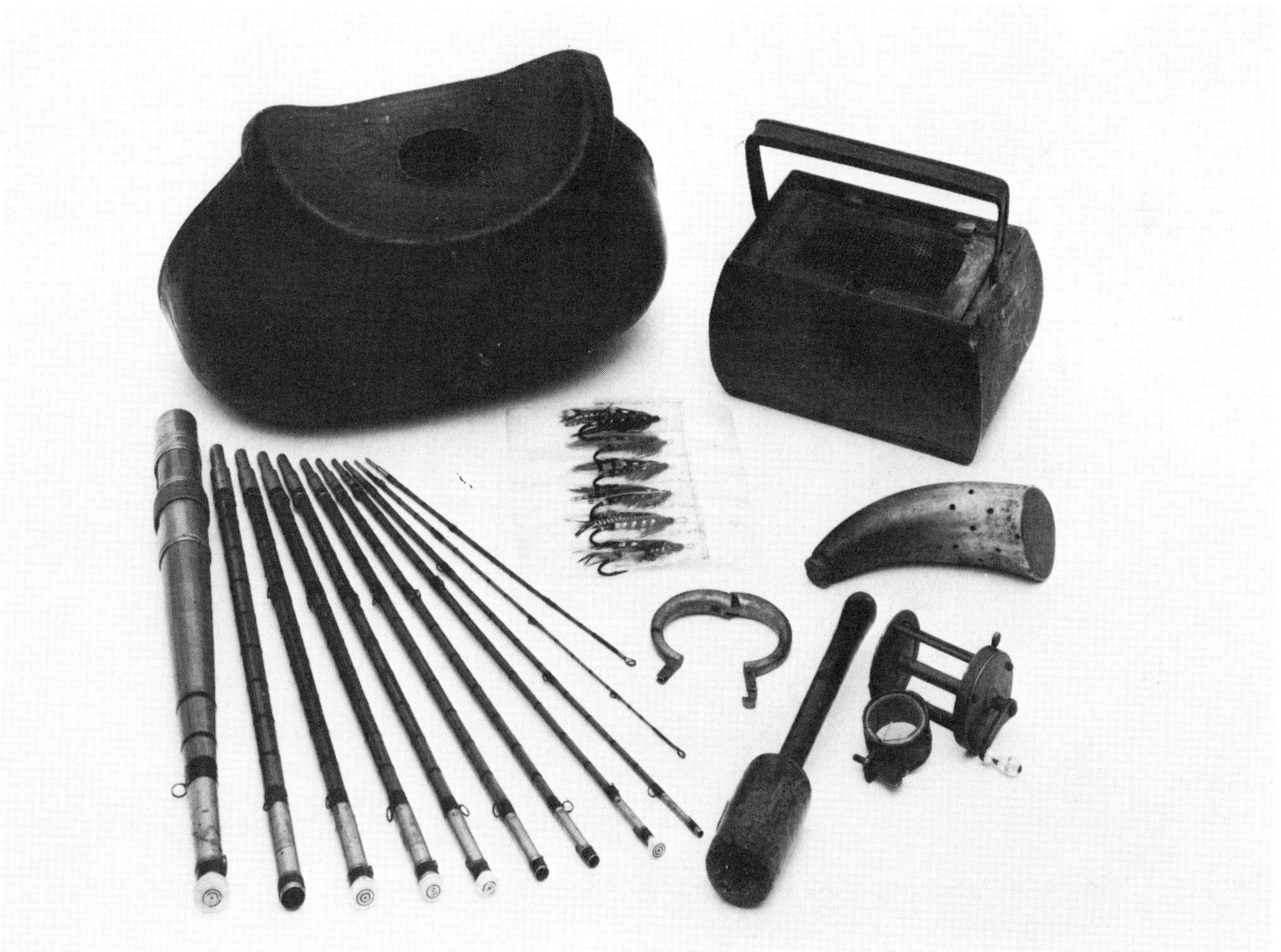

Sotheby's

demonstrated by the absence of any mention by leading anglers of the period.

It was obviously introduced and became accepted some time up to 1851 because split cane was used for tops and also complete rods by leading makers at the Great Exhibition of that year.

The firm of Ainge & Aldred was one such exhibitor and listed among their wide range of tackle were the following:

1 Hickory salmon-rod with improved screw ferrules, ornamented and chased, three glued up tops and stoppers of carved ivory, representing the heads of the salmon, grayling and trout.

2 A three piece glued up trout rod with engine-turned silver ferrules and acorn stoppers.

3 Unique three piece glued up pocket fly-rod with gilt ferrules ornamented with emeralds and rubies.

There were other rods and a wide range of tackle by this maker and a footnote below the list gave the following information. 'The wood of which fishing rods are made is in general hickory, and the top sometimes formed of lance or other wood; not infrequently two varieties of wood are combined by splicing. For convenience of carriage the rod is at times divided into four or more pieces, which are held together when in use by screws or slip joints; others are tied together by means of cord (splice jointed rods): this latter method is occasionally preferred by practical anglers. The eyes or conductors of the line are small brass rings secured to the rod by a small slip of metal and tied or wrapped with silk thread: this arrangement allows the eye to fold to the side of the rod when not in use and is a vast improvement on the old permanently projecting eye.'

Further information in the catalogue said – 'Ainge & Aldred exhibit some spliced rods of excellent construction, each joint being composed of three pieces bound together longitudinally and thereby less liable to twist or warp; whilst it retains an even spring and elasticity throughout – Prize Medal for fishing tackle and archery implements.'

J Bernard and J K Farlow were reported as exhibiting rods of similar construction with an improvement in the design of the ferrules having the lower and larger joints fitted into the upper, instead of vice versa, giving the advantage of water being less likely to enter the joints and cause swelling.

Some of the rods, reels and fishing tackle made for the Great Exhibition were designed specially decorative and the judges made comment about the added embellishments. The text read – 'The articles exhibited by C Farlow, Ainge & Aldred, J K Farlow and James Jones may all claim much credit for execution and high finish. In this respect the only distinction between their work appears to be the amount and character of the ornaments attached to it. But it should be observed that a profuse expenditure of silver and gilding in the metal work of a fishing rod, the application of precious stones to the reels and joints, the inlaying of the butts with ivory and rare woods and the use of velvet or silk, embossed and gilt in the place of leather or other more appropriate materials of which the books and cases for containing fishing tackle are more usually and properly made, cannot be considered as improvements of the articles in question.'

It is clear that three strip glued-up split cane rods were being widely made at that time and the evidence would suggest that odd makers tried split cane for the top piece of a rod as early as c.1800. However it appears to have remained almost unknown until much later and it would seem reasonable to record that it was probably in the 1830s or 1840s that it came into general use. At the present time there is no conclusive documentary evidence to show which maker was the first to make fishing rods entirely from split cane. The earliest I have seen is a ten piece valise rod by T Aldred constructed of glued-up three strip bamboo cane, dated mid-19th century. The earliest known American maker to use split cane was Samuel Phillippe, who, between 1845 and 1855, built rods with three and four strip bamboo end pieces.

According to James A Henshall in *The Book of The Black Bass* Solon, the son of Samuel Phillippe, made rods with six strip cane end pieces in 1859.

In the mid 19th century, rods made completely of split cane were not popular and the use of the construction was confined mainly to tops. London was still the centre for quality rod making and Blaine's *Encylopedia of Rural Sports* c.1858 gave details of the best manufacturers with the text:

> 'One of the best rod makers in London is Mr Blacker of 54 Dean St, Soho because he is a practical fly-fisher of great experience and takes pride in turning out perfect fly-rods. He pays his men the highest wages and will have them work according to his taste and judgement. Next to him are Mr Bond of Cannon Street who is a trustworthy tradesman, Mr Little of 15 Fetter Lane, Mr C Farlow, 221 The Strand, Mr Eaton, 6 & 7 Crooked Lane and Mr Bernard of Church Place Piccadilly. The Messrs Bowness, Bell Yard, Temple Bar are makers that we can safely recommend. We particularly caution the young angler against the purchase of cheap fly-rods. A good trout fly rod, double brazed, cannot be made to anything like perfection for less than thirty shillings; nor can a salmon rod be guaranteed good for less than four guineas. Some fly rods are now made with rent and glued bamboo which promises to be an improvement, as such tops never warp and under fair treatment cannot be broken! They are dearer than the other rods.'

The next development was the introduction of rods made completely of sections of glued-up five and six strip bamboo. Many people believe that this construction was first developed in America, the pioneers in that country being E A Green who built the first split cane rod and Charles F Murphy who built the first six strip version early in the 1860s.

What is certain is that six strip was quickly accepted as the best construction and by the 1870s the makers had perfected its use in making the finest fishing rods. Manufacture by that time was international and the supremacy enjoyed by the London makers for two centuries had gone for ever. Farlow, Hardy Bros., Allock, together with makers in the Midlands and Scotland, shared in the booming market and in America, Leonard and other classic makers produced some of the finest rods of all time.

I have attempted to compile the first list of London Fishing Tackle Makers, giving names under which they traded, addresses and the years they were in business. The information is based mainly on the classified trades directories and the data given can only be as accurate as what is recorded in these books. Unfortunately the yearly directories, listing trades in separate sections, did not begin on an annual basis until the 1830s and there is almost nothing in this form from the eighteenth century.

Another problem is that the years of inclusion of a maker were not necessarily the only years he was in business. A person could have been trading for a number of years before the name appeared in the trade directories.

The title under which a maker sold his goods could also vary from what the books record. One can find examples of a fishing reel with 'and Son' or 'Company' added to the maker's name, of which there is no mention in the trade lists.

It has been impossible to separate the tackle makers from mere retailers because the lot are listed together as Fishing Tackle Makers. Nevertheless, even with the failings mentioned, I consider the compilation of a list of London makers worthwhile in order that tackle collectors can, for the first time, enjoy reference data as is available to collectors in other fields.

ALDER, Anthony 1853
2a Cross St.

ALDRED 1851 – 1904
1851 Ainge & Aldred
126 Oxford St.
1856 – 1881 Thomas Aldred
126 Oxford St.
1882 – 1892 Thomas Aldred
258 Oxford St.
1893 – 1904 Thomas Aldred
110 Edgeware Rd.

ALFRED c.1745 – 1903
William Henry Alfred c.1822 – 1855
W.H. Alfred & Son 1856 – 1903
1822 – 1848 41 Coleman St.
1849 – 1876 54 Moorgate St.
1877 – 1903 20 Moorgate St.

ALLEN, Edward 1842 – 1853
1842 198 Oxford St.
1843 1 Duke St.
1850 – 1853 83 Regent St.

ALLPORT, Smith, John
1858 – 1867
41 Bethnal Green Rd.

Small brass multiplying reel with straight crank, locking disc and folding ivory knob. Marked 'Ainge & Aldred, 126 Oxford St., London'. Diameter 2¾"

Brass multiplying reel with raised casing, straight crank, locking disc, and folding ivory knob. Marked 'T. Aldred, 126 Oxford St. London'. Diameter 3¼"

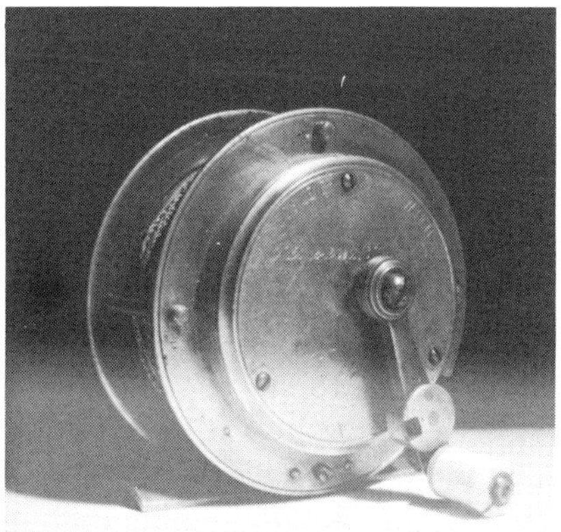

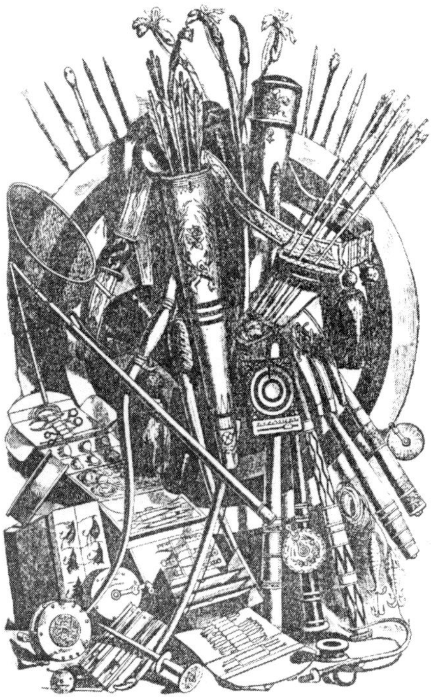

The winning exhibit of Ainge and Aldred at the Great Exhibition of 1851

ANDERSON, Archibald
1848 – 1861
1848 – 1853 13 Broad Court,
1853 – 1861 71 Long Acre

ANSTISS, Frederick William
1904 – 1921
23 First St.

ARMY & NAVY CO-OP SOC LTD
1902 – 1939
105 Victoria St

AYECHOURN, Fred c.1849
3 Exeter Change

BARNETT, Timothy 1865 – 1895
1865 – 1880 3 Goswell Terrace
1881 – 1895 26 Church St.

Army & Navy – Hercules type reel with ivorine handle and rim regulator screw Diameter 2½"

Army & Navy – Hercules type brass reel with ebonite handle – Diameter 3½"

BARTH, Benj 1836 – 1848
32 Cockspur St

BARTHOLOMEW 1822 – 1851
John Bartholomew 1822 – 1848
Mrs Sophia Bartholomew 1849 – 1851
1822 – 1835 1 Crooked Lane
1835 – 1851 4 Crooked Lane

BARTLÉET, William 1890 – 1932
1890 – 1900 53 Gresham St (successor to Henry Walker)
1901 – 1904 12 Goldsmith St.
(From 1905 William Bartleet & Son)
1905 – 1932 122 Wood St.

BATES 1910 – 1916
Charles, Bates, Bradford & Co.
1910 – 1912 16 Stockmar Rd.
1913 27 and 29 Carter Lane
1914 – 16 Bates & Co. 39 Lombard St.

A G BAYLISS & SON 1900 – 1901
4 Russia Court

BAZIN 1832 – 1853
John Bazin 1832 – 1839
James Bazin 1840 – 1853
1832 – 1844 3 Duncan Place
1845 – 1853 8 Duncan Place

BEATTIE, James c.1841
11 Compton St.

BECK, Charles 1884 – 1885
40 North St.

BERGSTROM, Christian 1832 – 1836
10 Tottenham Court Rd.
Peter C. Bergstrom – 1836

BERNARD c.1790 – 1940
A Bernard is believed to have started in 1790 but the earliest listing in the trade directories is for Timothy Bernard in 1823.
Timothy Bernard 1823 – 1825
20 Bath St.
John Bernard 1826 – 1863
John Bernard & Son 1864 – 1940
1826 – 1844 5 Church Passage
1845 – 1880 4 Church Place
1881 – 1902 5 Church Place
1903 – 1926 45 Jermyn St.
1927 – 1934 45 Pall Mall
1935 – 1936 55 & 58 Pall Mall
1937 – 1939 330 Kings Rd.
1939 – 1940 326 Kings Rd.

BERNARD, Edward 1850 – 1851
15a North Audley St.

BEW, Henry 1826 – 1839
1826 – 1835 Bartholomew Close and 19 Newgate St.
1836 – 1839 Only 19 Newgate St.

Small brass reel with ivorine handle – 'J Bernard, 45 Jermyn St., St. James Sq. London.' Diameter 2½"

Small brass reel marked 'J Bernard & Son, 5 Church Place Piccadilly'. Diameter 2¼"

BIGG, Sexton 1881 – 1885
27 Russel St.

BILLINGTON, John 1842 – 1870
93 Charlton St.
1869 – 1870 Billington & Warren

J. BIRCH & SON 1885 – 1895
13 Little Queen St.

BLACKER, William 1842 – 1857
54 Dean St. (Author of *Art of Angling* 1842)
Mrs Sarah Blacker 1858

BLIGHT, James Henry
1936 – 1939
77 Kingsland Rd.

BODEN & Co 1823 – 1839
1823 – 1824 137 Drury Lane
1832 – 1835 42 Drury Lane
1836 14 Wood St.
J. Boden, Acton & Co. 1840 – 1843
16 Maiden Lane

BOND 1795 – 1860
Thomas Bond 1795 – 1825
1795 – 1825 37 Crooked Lane, 'Salmon & Bell'
1826 Thomas Bond & Son
1834 – 1860 62 Cannon St.

BOULTON 1822 – 1836
Robert Boulton 1822 Borough Rd
George Boulton 1823 – 1825 86 Long Lane
1826 – 1836 Great Dover St.

A brass bound fishing tackle box by Bond & Son, 62 Cannon St, London – date 1834 containing two winches, a mahogany priest, leather bound cast case and carved wood cast furnisher

BOWNESS & CHEVALIER

The record of the two famous families of tackle makers and the business names and addresses they used is very complicated because they traded at times, both individually and in partnership at the same address. It is only possible to record their activities from 1817 when they first appeared in trade directories although both makers are known to have been in business at a much earlier period. Thomas Bowness is believed to have traded on his own account from 1780 at 14 Bell Yard, the 'Fish & Bell' and a Susannah Bowness in 1802 – 1804. The firm of Chevalier is believed to have started in 1737 and a Samuel Chevalier is known to have been trading in 1775.

BOWNESS
1780 Thomas Bowness
14 Bell Yard 'Fish & Bell'
1802 – 1804 Susannah Bowness
1817 – 1828 George Bowness
14 Bell Yard 'Fish & Bell'
1839 – 1875 George Bowness & Son
1839 – 1842 14 Bell Yard
1843 – 1859 12 & 14 Bell Yard
1860 – 1875 only 12 Bell Yard.
(In 1847 Ephemera mentioned Bowness in connection with a split cane rod which had been 'for many years in use')
1851 – 1882 Bowness & Bowness
230 The Strand
1866 – 1882 Chevalier, Bowness & Son 12 Bell Yard
1883 – 1895 Chevalier, Bowness & Bowness 230 The Strand

Also trading
1838 – 1860 George Bowness Jnr.
1838 – 1859 33 Bell Yard.
1860 49 King St.
1864 – 1880 Edward Bowness
1864 – 1867 17 Hanover St.
1880 65 Mortimer St.

CHEVALIER
Established in 1737
1775 Samuel Chevalier
1817 – 1825 R Chevalier
12 Bell Yard
1826 – 1853 Benjamin Chevalier
12 Bell Yard

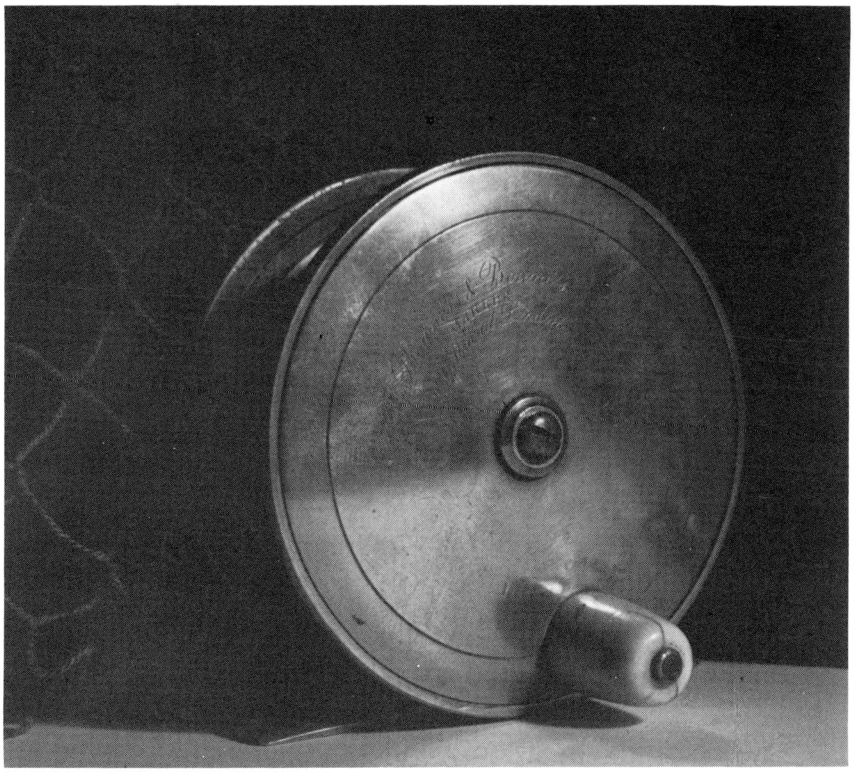

Brass plate wind marked 'Bowness & Bowness, 230 The Strand, London.' Diameter 3½"

Brass plate reel marked 'Chevalier, Bowness and Bowness, 230 The Strand, London'. Diameter 4½"

BRAILSFORD, John c.1769 – 1779
Fish & Case of Knives, St. Martin's Court

BRAIN, William 1846 – 1865
158 High Holborn & 4 Park Side
1847 – 1865 only 4 Park Rd.

BRANDER, Edward 1841 – 1856
27 Wormword St.

BRANDON, Charles
c.1653 – 1670s
Golding Lane

BREZENZER c.1911
38 Goldsmith Row

BROCAS, Letitia Jane, Mrs
1861 – 1895
1861 – 1867 25 Hart St.
1868 – 1885 4 Mill St.
1886 – 1895 5 Rochester Row

BRODIE, John c.1863
3 Old Compton St.

BROWN, Charles Junior
1881 – 1901
7 Walton St.

BROWN 1823 – 1839
Mile End Rd.
John Brown 1823 – 1825
James Brown 1826 – 1835
Sarah Brown 1836 – 1839

BROWN (SUMMERS) & Co.
c.1910
40 Whitecross St.

BROWN, William 1689 – 1720s
Sign of the Fish, Black Horse Alley

BROWN, John 1720s
The Salmon in St Paul's Churchyard

BULMER, Arthur 1882 – 1895
62 Wandsworth Rd.

BURCOMBE & LAURENCE
c.1880
10 Turner Sq.

CANVER, Robert c.1848
17 Sherrard St.

CARTER, 1853 – 1969
Alfred Carter 1853 – 1900
1853 – 1856 4 Eliza Place

The Jardine reel sold and first registered by A Carter in 1883 and improved by R Heaton Patent No 18817. It was also sold by Dale of Hanley and A W Gamage Ltd of Holborn

1856 – 1867 124 St John St. Rd.
(purchased the business of Turpin on his death.)
1868 – 1905 137 St John St. Rd.
Became Carter & Co. from 1901
1906 – 1914 371 St John St. Rd.
(from 1911 additional premises – 11 South Molton)
1915 – 1969 11 South Molton only.

CARVELL, Charles 1856 – 1867
Cambridge St.
1860 – 1867 44 Kings Rd.

CAVE, Robert 1843 – 1858
1843 – 1844 52 Oakley St.
1845 – 1846 2 Oakley St.
1847 – 1858 5 Oakley St.

CHEEK, John 1833 – 1860
1839 – 1842 52 The Strand
1843 – 1860 132 Oxford St.

CHILD, Coles c.1744 – 1771
The Blew Bore, London Bridge

CHILD, Thomas Benjamin
1832 – 1839
133 Pentonville Rd.

JOHN CHESHIRE & Co. 1763

JOHN CHESHIRE & WILLIAM BUSICK 1752 – 1760s
The Angler & Trout, Crooked Lane

CHUBB, John 1841
1 Brighton Place

CLARKE, George Henry
1927 – 1932
185 Shaftsbury Av.

CLARKE, George 1832 – 1834
43 Compton St.

CLARKE George Spencer
1856 – 1864
5 Old Ford Rd.

CLARKE, Joseph 1832 – 1880
11 St. Johns Lane
1880 6 Little Compton St.

CLARKE, P 1805 – 1818
91 The Strand
(Successor to Higginbottam)

CLERKE, Thomas c.1848
11 Compton St.

COBBETT, W c.1845
11 Evangelist Court

COGSWELL & HARRISON LTD.
1936 – 1939
168 Piccadilly

COLLINS c.1779
Ball Alley

CONWAY, William James
1853 – 1875
21 Gee St.
1875 32 Cloudesley St.

COOKSLEY, Joseph c.1836
13 Goldsmith Terrace

Trade card by J Clarke

COOPER, Godfrey Charles c.1890
131 High Holborn.

COXE, Stephen 1848 – 1849
8 Brownlowe St.

CREED, Ebenezer 1839 – 1865
33 Wilderness Row

CROFTS, William 1860 – 1875
47 Hollywell Lane

CURETON 1826 – 1869
1826 Joseph Richard Cureton
3 Old Rd., Stepney
1832 – 1835 51 Cannon St.
1836 – 1842 8 Ball Alley
1843 – 1852 48 Snowfields
1853 – 1869 114 Snowfields
Title – Mrs E Cureton from 1865

DARBY, George 1831 – 1832
32 Westbourne Terrace

DAVIES, Edmund 1839 –1890
1839 12 Lower St.
1844 – 1847 Ryders Court
1848 – 1862 Great Hall,
Hungerford Mkt.
1863 – 1874 21 King William St.
1875 – 1886 36 Russel St.
1887 – 1890 37 Hart St.

DAVIES, John 1822 – 1824
1822 – 1823 3 Duke St.
1824 45 Great James St.

DAWSON, Edward 1861 – 1867
33 Bell Yard
1867 Partnership Dawson & Bowness

DE SAXE, Charles c. 1853
420 Oxford St.

DICKS 1851 – 1870
1851 – 1852 49 Brick Lane
1853 – 1855 3 Whitmore Place
1856 – 1861 29 Whitmore Place
1862 – 1870 112 St. Johns Rd.
Mrs E Dicks – from 1864

DICKS, James 1826
10 Bell Yard

DIGGINS, Ann Mrs. 1839 – 1853
37 Gibson St.

DIXON, Hezekiah 1841 – 1853
1841 – 1847 10 Ball Alley
1848 – 1853 172 Fenchurch St.

Brass reel with curved crank & turned ivory knob, marked – 'Edward Dawson, 33 Bell Yard.' Diameter 3¼″

The hollow ash butt of a 25 ft salmon rod marked – 'Geo Eaton Maker, 6 Crooked Lane, London' with greenheart intermediate sections and lancewood top

DODGE, William 1847 – 1849
1 Commercial Place
1849 – William Dodge & Watts.

DOUGALL, James Daniel & Son
1883 – 1890
8 Bennett St.

DYSON, George 1856 – 1862
3 Minerva St.

THE EATON TACKLE MAKERS
1790 – 1951
1790 Joseph Eaton
6 Crooked Lane
By 1817 Joseph Eaton & Son
6 Crooked Lane
By 1822 Joseph & George Eaton
6 Crooked Lane
1825 George Eaton
6 Crooked Lane
1836 – 1856 George Eaton
6 & 7 Crooked Lane
1857 – 1951 Eaton & Deller
6 & 7 Crooked Lane
Mr Deller died in 1887

WIDOW EATON & SON c.1825
3 Great East Cheap
There must have been a family business break up after the death of Joseph Eaton. An advert was placed by Widow Eaton which said 'Widow Eaton & Son 3 Great

An Eaton & Deller 3¼″ brass crank wind reel with brass spherical knob, 'S' shaped crank, raised check housing, riveted foot, triple pillared cage, fixed check, engraved 'Eaton & Deller, Makers, 6 & 7 Crooked Lane, London'

East Cheap, near Crooked Lane but no connection with the shop in Crooked Lane' and goes on to explain 'in consequence of the recent death of Mr Joseph Eaton of the late firm of Joseph & George Eaton our concern is carried on as the above'. This explains the entry of the business name in the London Trade Directory in 1825.

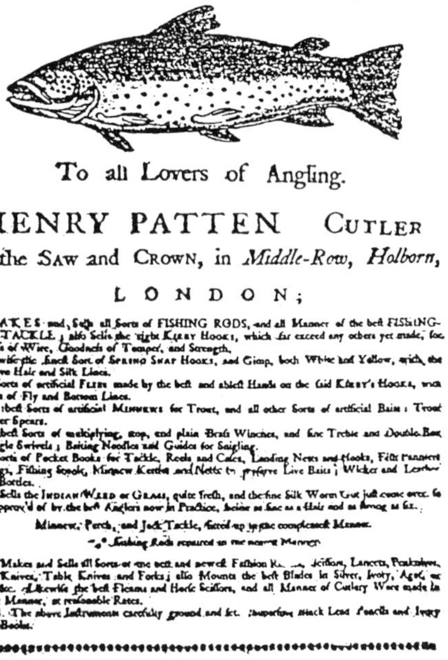

To all Lovers of Angling.
HENRY PATTEN CUTLER
At the SAW and CROWN, in *Middle-Row, Holborn,*
LONDON;
MAKES and Sells all Sorts of FISHING RODS, and all Manner of the best FISHING-TACKLE; also Sells the right KIRBY HOOKS, which far exceed any others yet made, for Fineness of Wire, Goodness of Temper, and Strength.
Likewise the finest Sort of SPRING SNAP HOOKS, and Gimp, both White and Yellow, with the best wove Hair and Silk Lines.
All Sorts of artificial FLIES made by the best and ablest Hands on the said KIRBY's HOOKS, with all Sorts of Fly and Bottom Lines.
The best Sorts of artificial MINNOWS for Trout, and all other Sorts of artificial Baits; Trout and other Spears.
The best Sorts of multiplying, stop, and plain Brass Winches, and fine Treble and Double Box and Single Swivels; Baiting Needles and Guides for Sniggling.
All Sorts of Pocket Books for Tackle, Rods and Cases, Landing Nets and Hooks, Fish Panniers and Bags, Fishing Stools, Minnow Kettles and Netts to preserve Live Baits; Wicker and Leather Dram Bottles.
Also Sells the INDIAN WEED or GRASS, quite fresh, and the fine Silk Worm Gut just come over, so much approv'd of by the best Anglers now in Practice, being as fine as a Hair and as strong as six.
Minnow, Perch, and Jack Tackle, fitted up in the completest Manner.
Fishing Rods repaired in the neatest Manner.
Also Makes and Sells all Sorts of the best and newest Fashion Knives, Scissors, Lancets, Penknives, Pocket Knives, Table Knives and Forks; also Mounts the best Blades in Silver, Ivory, Agot, or Hafts, &c. Likewise the best Fleams and Horse Scissors, and all Manner of Cutlery Ware made in the best Manner, at reasonable Rates.
N.B. The above Instruments carefully ground and set. Superfine Black Lead Pencils and Ivory Pocket Books.

Trade card of Henry Patten c.1771

EDMUNDS, William 1836 – 1877
1836 – 1867 15 East Rd
1868 – 1877 75 East Rd

EMBERRY, Mary 1817 – 1826
1817 – 1818 41 Union St.
1818 – 1826 44 Union St.

ETON, John 1842
47 High Holborn

EVANS, Charles, Alexander
1898 – 1932
78 Green St.

EVATT, Abraham 1839 – 1856
1839 – 1847 6 Warwick St.
1848 – 1855 9 Great Ryder St.
1856 2 Chorlton St.

EWINS & TURNER c.1880
23 Carter Lane

EYLE, George Alfred 1860 – 1862
15 and 16 Carnby St.

FAIRSERVICE & RICKETT
1870 – 1877
1 Charles St.

C FARLOW & Co. Ltd
1840 – Current

C Farlow – 221 The Strand
1840 – 1851
C Farlow – 191 The Strand
1852 – 1884
C Farlow & Co – 191 The Strand
1885 – 1894
C Farlow & Co Ltd –
191 The Strand 1895 – 1906

Silver with engraved plate, straight crank, locking disc and folding ivory knob. Diameter 4". Made for the Great Exhibition of 1851. Maker was John King Farlow & Co

C Farlow & Co Ltd –
191 The Strand & 10 Charles St
1907 – 1915
C Farlow & Co Ltd – 10 Charles St
1916 – 1925
C Farlow & Co Ltd – 11 Panton St
1926 – 1957
C Farlow & Co Ltd – 13 Bruton St
– 1958 – 1964 and part of the period at 23 Conduit St – c.1960
C Farlow & Co Ltd – 5b Pall Mall
1965 – current

JOHN KING FARLOW & Co
1843 – 1856
1843 – 1852 5 Crooked Lane
1853 – 1856 4 and 5 Crooked Lane

FENTON, Thomas 1845 – 1848
5 Patriot Row

FERNANDES, Marcos
1851 – 1867
1851 – 1852 24 Bury St.
1853 – 1867 2 Devonshire Sq.

FLETCHER, Joseph 1832 – 1834
3 Short St.

FORD, Thomas c.1853
79 Great Queen St.

FOSTER, J 1863 – 1867
1863 – 1867 16 Portland Terr.
1867 10 St Johns Rd.

FOXHALL, Thomas & Son
1925 – 1926
154 and 156 Drummond St.

British Museum

British Museum

Trade card of W. J. Gee & Co

FRANCIS, William c.1842
9 Sherbourne Lane

FREEMAN, John 1841 – 1843
126 Oxford St.

FULLERTON, William c.1875
53a Wells St.

GARDNER & Co
1884 – 1885
1 Flood St.

GARDNER, William 1832 – 1856
1832 – 1840 53 Noble St.
1841 – 1852 58 Noble St.
1853 – 1856 William Edward Gardner 2 Pear Tree St.
1856 36 Noble St.

GEE 1867 – 1906
William John Gee 1867 – 1884
1867 – 1879 19 St Andrew St.
1880– 1884 22 Grays Inn Rd.
1885 – 1906 William Gee Junior & Co 19 St Andrew St.

GILLETT, John 1865 – 1906
1865 – 1876 115 Fetter Lane
1877 – 1906 40 Fetter Lane

GIMBER 1777 – 1794
George Gimber 1777 – 1789
38 Crooked Lane (possibly succeeded Cheshire & Busick)
1790 – 1794 Gimber & Son, 10 Crooked Lane (succeeded by Iverson & Stone)
A partnership of Gimber & Bare is known to have traded from No. 10 Crooked Lane but not recorded in the trade directories.

GOLD, John Edwin 1866 – 1906
1866 – 1889 19 Charterhouse St.
1890 – 1906 17 Oakley St.

GOODWIN, T 1830 – 1834
7 Tottenham Court Rd.

GOULD, Alfred 1849 – 1867
1849 – 1860
36 Great Marylebone St.
1861 – 1862 132 Oxford St. (took over business of J Cheek)
1863 – 1867 268a Oxford St.

GOWLAND, William B
1856 – 1890
3 and 4 Crooked Lane

GREGORY c.1771
Dial & Trout

JOSEPH GUILDING & Co.
1876 – 1885
33 and 35 Mary Axe.

WILLIAM HALL & Co. Ltd
1900 – 1916
4 Russia Court

HANCOCK, W T c.1895
308 High Holborn (late Watson & Hancock)

HARDING 1936 – 1939
239 High Rd.

HEMENS, George William (Rods)
1884 – 1906
1884 – 1885 103 Sheperdess Walk
1886 – 1897 251 New North Rd.
1898 – 1906 62 Wadsworth Rd.

HERMAN, William George
1936 – 1939
614 Fulham Rd.

A wooden Nottingham Star Back, marked 'J. Gillet, 40 Fetter Lane, London,'. Diameter 4½"

Small brass multiplying reel by W. B. Gowland with curved crank and ivory knob. Diameter 2"

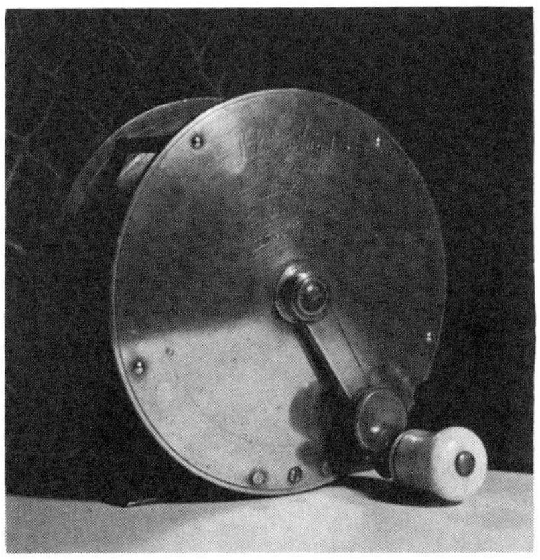

Large brass reel by W. B. Gowland with straight crank, locking disc and folding ivory knob Diameter 4½"

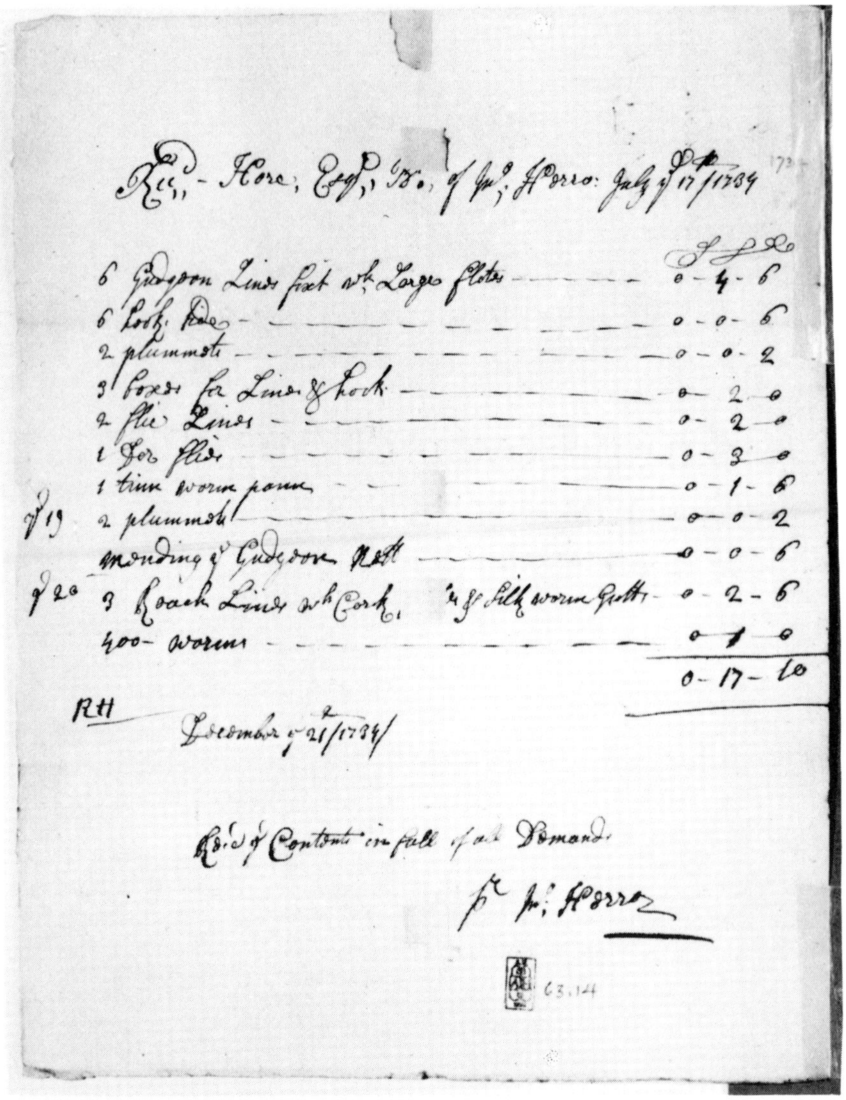

British Museum

A detailed bill of John Herro signed and dated 1734

A brass plate wind by J S Holroyd with ivorine handle and marked with the '59 Gracechurch St' address. Diameter 3"

Brass reel with serpentine crank, ivory knob and marked 'J.S. Holroyd, 19 Fish St. Hill, London'

HERRO, John 1730 – 1760s
Fish & Crown, 48 Bell Yard

HEYDON, Thomas c.1858
30 Chichester Place

HIGGINBOTHAM, John
c.1779 – 1800
The Golden Fish, 91 The Strand

HOBBS, William c.1890
63 Brindle St.

HOLLAMBY, Benjamen c.1867
24 Francis St.

HOLMES 1817 – 1864
1817 – 1818 J Holmes
123 Fetter Lane
1822 – 1824 Charles Holmes
10 Bell Yard
1822 – 1852 Charles Holmes
123 Fetter Lane
1822 – 1852 Charles Holmes & Son 123 Fetter Lane
1832 – 1849 Charles Holmes Junior 2 Sidney Alley
1853 – 1855 Mrs Rebecca Holmes
115 Fetter Lane
1856 – 1864 Holmes & Co
115 Fetter Lane

THOMAS HOLBROW & Co.
1879 – 1950
1879 – 1883 111, Jermyn St
1884 – 1892 7 Eagle Place
1893 – 1894 9 Eagle Place
– 40 Duke St
1895 – 1950 40 Duke St only

HOLROYD 1815 – 1911
1815 – 1833 John Holroyd
31 Crooked Lane
1834 – 1872 John Spear Holroyd
1873 – 1890 Edmund Adelphs Holroyd
1891 – 1904 Holroyd Bros.
1834 – 1835 65 Cannon St.
1836 – 1845 19 Fish St. Hill
1846 – 1904 59 Gracechurch St.
1905 – 1911 John Holroyd
13 Fish St. Hill

THOMAS T HOLROYD & Co.
1881 – 1895
1881 – 1883 111 Jermyn St.
1884 – 1892 7 Eagle Place
1893 – 1895 40 Duke St.
(Listed at the same address as Thomas Holbrow & Co?)

HOMER, William Frederick
1922 – 1970
105 Wood Grange Rd.
Became Homers (Fishing Tackle) Ltd. in 1963

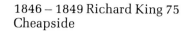

HOON, Henry 1841 – 1845
12 Lisson Grove

HOPKINS, Robert 1700 – 1730
The Salmon, 48 Bell Yard

HORSNELL, John 1841 – 1853
1841 33 Windmill St.
1842 – 1844 3 Broadway
1845 – 1853 1 Willow Walk.

HUTCHINSON, George c.1760's
The Amberley Trout, Snow Hill

HUTCHINSON & SMITH c.1847
67 Wood St and 1 Sherbourne Lane

IRWIN, Charles 1850 – 1861
8 St John's Court (c.1860/1)

IVERSON & STONE
c.1772 – c.1816
Circa Dates
1772 – 1789 – Stone & Iverson, Crooked Lane
1790 – 1793 – Iverson & Stone, 13 Crooked Lane
1794 – 1816 – Iverson & Stone, 10 Crooked Lane

JACKSON, Thomas Hunt
1849 – 1853
56 Bethnal Green

JACOBS, Abraham Richard
1831 – 1849
1831 – 1847 145 Regent St.
1848 – 1849 32 Cockspur St.
(Formerly the Benjamin Barth business).

JAMES, John & Son (Fish Hooks)
1901 – 1920
1901 – 1911 39 Cheapside
1912 – 1919 54 Aldermanbury
1920 80 Wood St.

CHARLES JOHNSON & CO.
c.1870
79 Dean St.

JONES 1839 – 1885
James Jones 1839 – 1852
1839 – 1844 8 Princess St.
1845 – 1852 111 Jermyn St.
1853 – 1855 Mrs. Maria Jones
1856 – 1868 James Jones & Co.
1869 – 1872 Miss Phoebe Mari Jones
1873 – 1884 Jones & Co.
1885 Jones & Co. 39 Duke St.

JOY, Henry 1845 – 1870
6 Opera Arcade

JUSTICE, Joseph 1839 – 1840
9 Whitmore Row

KENNING M'KIERNAN & CO.
1864 – 1870
1864 – 1865 4 Little Britain.
1866 – 1870 George Kenning

KEWELL, Charles 1864 – 1880
1864 – 1865 12 St. John St. Rd.
1866 – 1867 98 St. John St. Rd.
1868 – 1880 197 St. John St. Rd.

KEWELL & Sons 1877 – 1880
1a Conduit St.

KEWELL, William 1850 – 1851
6 Church St.

KING 1836 – 1849
James King 1836 – 1841
1842 John King 5 Crooked Lane
1846 – 1849 Richard King 75 Cheapside

KIRBY, Charles c.1650 – 1770s
Addresses included:
Harp Alley
Globe Court
Aire St.
Crowthers Well Alley
St Anne's Lane

KIRBY, Beard & Co. Ltd.
Sir Ambrose Heale carried out lengthy investigations to try to find a connection with the Kirby hook-making family. He was unable to find any evidence and my research has proved no more successful. A brief background to the early history is as follows:
1743 William Cowcher and Finch (depots at London, Gloucester, Reading).
1805 R. Cowcher and Robert Kirby (depots at London, Gloucester and Reading)
1816 Robert Kirby served in the office of a Sherriff of London.
1823 Cowcher, Kirby, Beard
1826 – 1912 Kirby Beard & Co. with departments in London, Birmingham, Redditch, Montreal & Melbourne.
1830 Kirby, Beard & Kirby – Pin and needle maker 46 Cannon St.

KITCHINGMAN, J
1817 – 1821 20 Nicholas Lane
1822 – 1826 44 Crooked Lane
1827 – 1832 44 Crooked Lane and 2 Bell Yard
1833 – 1839 – Henry Kitchingman, 61 Skinner St
1840 64 Skinner St and 1 Ship Yard
1841 – 1848 – only 64 Skinner St
The Trade directories misprint various names including KITCHINGHAM and HUTCHINGHAM

KNEVETT, Joseph 1858 – 1861
8 Rufford Row.

KNIGHT 1750's – 1760's.
Compleat Angler, Crooked Lane

KNOCK, Richard c.1853
15 Bath Place

Brass reel by J Jones with straight crank, locking disc and turned folding ivory knob. Diameter 3¾"

LAURENCE, William 1858 – 1861
33 George St.

LEADER, William 1876 – 1890
30 Upper Marylebone St.

LITTLE 1839 – 1925
Giles Little 1839 – 1874
15 Fetter Lane.
1875 – 1925 Giles Little & Co.
1886 Additional premises 63 Haymarket.
1887 – 1925 only 63 Haymarket

LORBERG 1888 – 1895
38 Kensington High St.

LOWE, Bartholomew c.1766/7
Golden Fish, Drury Lane

MACEY, Edward 1860 – 1864
1860 – 1861 19 North St.
1862 – 1864 17 North St.

MAGNIAC, Herbert c.1860s
16 Charles St.

MAIN, George 1882 – 1901
45 Jermyn St.

MARCH, William 1795 – 1843
1795 – 1816 175 The Strand
1817 – 1821 March & Son
56 Fleet St.
1822 – 1835 William March
1836 – 1839 March & Son
1840 – 1843 John March 118 Chancery Lane

MARGRAVE, John c.1650 – 1676
The Three Trouts, St Paul's Churchyard

MARTIN, John 1856 – 1870
1856 2 Upper Queens Row
1857 – 1870 4 Belvedere

MARTIN, John William
1901 – 1924
1901 – 1902 8 Seymour St.
1903 – 1915 22 Seymour St.

Trade card of J. Kitchingman
In 1817 Crooked Lane was 131 yards long and contained 47 houses

THE
Cheapest Shop in London.
J. Kitchingman,
No. 44,
CROOKED LANE,
The only Manufacturer of all sorts of
Bamboo, Fly, Bottom and Troling Rods—Spliced Bamboo and walking-stick Fly Rods; also a new invented Portable Fly Rod—Brass Multiplying and plain Wheels--Clearing and Landing Rings, Nets, &c.—All sorts of Salmon and Trout Flys to order—Artificial Fish, Minnows, Silver and Pearl—Artificial Baits of every kind, Insects, &c.—Silkworm-Gut of the finest quality, Lines, &c.—Ivory, Ebony, and Box Reels of the best sort. Original maker of Cane Floats and inventor of the compound Multiplying Wheels; also double-spliced Bamboo tops, warranted not to warp—Superior Hooks of various patterns; Portable Landing Net Handles, double Swivels and Plain—Cork Trimmers, Eel and Trout Spears, Shrimp and Minnow Nets—Tin Bait Boxes, Kettles and Baskets—Live Minnows and Gudgeons all the Year, and many other Articles too numerous to mention.
All sorts of Tackle taken in exchange, or repaired.
Holliday, Printer, 9, Robert Street, Bedford Row.

Guildhall Library

Small brass reel with straight crank, locking disc and turned folding knob marked 'G. Little & Co. Fetter Lane, London'. Diameter 2¾"

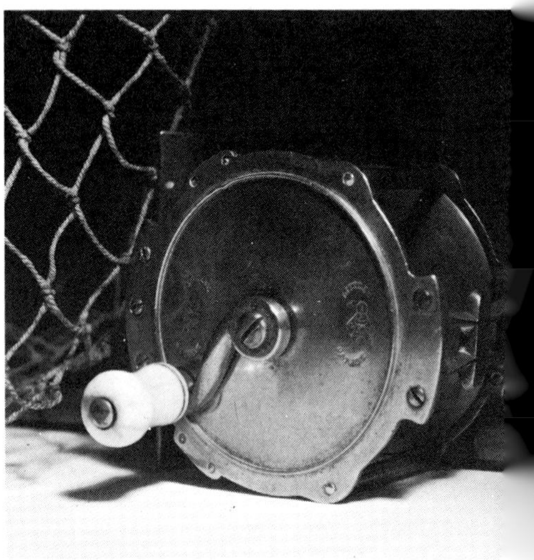

Brass external pillared reel by G Little & Co. with serpentine crank, turned ivory knob and frame foot. Diameter 3"

Hercules type brass reel marked 'G Little & Co., 63 Haymarket, London'. Diameter 3½"

1916 – 1924 J W Martin & Son (Rods) 19 Arlington St.

MASSEY, Sidney 1857 – 1858
19 North St.

McFEE, James 1836 – 1846
1836 – 1838 Tabernacle Walk
1839 – 1845 Parsonage Row
1846 208 High St.

McGOWAN, John 1857 – 1882
7 Bruton St.

METZ 1909 – 1926
Frederick Metz 1909 – 1921
185 Shaftsbury Ave.
1922 – 1926 Mrs. Minnie Metz

MEWISON, John c. 1836
7 Upper King St.

MEYERS, Barnet 1848 – 1864
1848 – 1855 18 Crutched Friars
1856 – 1864 Mill Lane & 143 Boro High St.

M'KIERNAN, James 1866 – 1870
15 St. Johns Lane

MOLE, Michael c.1763
Crooked Lane

J & T MUIRSON 1840 – 1847
7 Upper King St.

NASH, Alfred John 1856 – 1857
3 Hooper St.

NOON, Charles c.1895
116 Lower Kennington

OGDEN SMITH 1890 – 1964
6 Parkside (Traded as OGDEN SMITHS LTD)
1901 – 1903 Additional premises at 34 St Johns Hill
1904 – 1906 34 Knightsbridge
1907 – 1917 24 Knightsbridge
1918 – 1955 62 St. James St.
1960 6a White Horse St.
1963 – 1967 2 & 3 Royal Exchange

PALMER St. James St. 1779

PALMER, Thomas 1840 – 1849
1840 – 1847 69 Red Lion St.
1848 – 1849 242 Tottenham Court Rd.

PARDOW, James 1839 – 1840
96 Wood St.

PARKER, Robert 1878 – 1880
248 Holloway Rd.

PARKHURST, Henry c.1732
Fleet St.

Large brass external pillared crank handled reel by John McGowan with ebonite knob. Diameter 4½″

Silex type dual handled reel with rim regulator screw and drum release latch sold by Ogden Smiths Ltd. Diameter 4″

Brass plate wind 'Exchequer' model by Ogden Smiths Ltd with rim regulator screw and ebonite handle. Diameter 3″

PARMENTER, John c.1849
1 Whitmore Place East

PARRETT, Stephen c.1866
10 Dean St.

PARTRIDGE, George 1887 – 1895
402 Oxford St.

PATTEN, Henry c.1771
The Saw & Crown, Middle Row, Holborn

PEEK, John & Son 1896 – 1960s
40 Grays Inn Rd. (listed under dealers from 1965).

PETERS, William 1847 – 1862
48 Bell Yard.
In 1847 William Peters was trading separately from M Ustonson although using the same premises at 48 Bell Yard. The following year the two were trading in partnership.
1848 – 1855 Ustonson and Peters
1856 – 1862 William Peters and Son at a new address at 71 Long Acre.

PINCHBECK c.1779
Cockspur St.

PLUNCKNETT, John 1839 – 1851
1839 – 1846 54 Amelia St.
1847 – 1851 Mrs A Plunckett

PLUMPTON 1841 – 1844
19 Newgate St.

POLDEN, James A 1856 – 1870
1856 20 Castle St.
1857 – 1870 29 Castle St.

POOLE, William 1890 – 1939
1890 – 1894 100 Broadwall
1895 – 1906 104a Broadwall
1907 – 1915 108 Broadwall
1916 – 1939 6 Nine Elms Lane.

POTTLE, William Henry
1869 – 1870
230 Grays Inn Rd.

PRICE, Samuel 1875 – 1895
8 Seymour St.

PULLEN, David 1856 – 1885
1856 – 1884 7 Villa St.
1885 1½ Neate St.

PUTMAN, George 1865 – 1868
12 Broad Court

QUARRIER, Elizabeth Mrs
1863 – 1878
17 Little Grays Inn Lane

RAMSFORD, Maria Mrs. c.1853
4 Dean St.

READ 1876 – 1916
George Read 1876 – 1914
1876 – 1894 91 Goldsmith Row
1895 – 1916 38 Goldsmith Row
1915 – 1916 Mrs Lucy Read

REED, Joseph 1822 – 1824
14 St. Mary-At-Hill.

REDRUPP, Charles c.1880
25 Essex Rd.

REYNOLDS 1857 – 1869
1857 – 1858 S. Reynolds
1859 – 1864 Reynolds & Son.
1865 – 1867 T Reynolds & Co.
69 High Holborn
1868 – 1869 Reynolds & Johnson

RICHARDS, James 1826 – 1834
1826 – 1833 19 Bell St.
1834 26 William St. (he placed advertisements offering artificial fish & insects)

RICHARDS, John 1879 – 1885
97 Church St.

RICHARDSON, Edwin
1869 – 1890
1869 – 1887 1 Vernon Sq.
1888 – 1890 128 Church Rd.

RICHARDSON, Henry
1885 – 1890
77 Finsbury Pavement

RICHARDSON, Joseph
1890 – 1901
1890 – 1897 151 High St.
1898 – 1899 111 Judd St.
1900 – 1901 123 Euston Rd.

ROBERTS, Samuel 1849 – 1853
10 Crooked Lane.

ROBLOW, Thomas Henry
1832 – 1875
1832 – 1843
46 Upper Marylebone St.
1844 – 1875
30 Upper Marylebone St.

RODMAN, Richard 1853 – 1856
15 Hexton Old Rd.

ROSE, Thomas 1853 – 1895
98 Cleveland St.

SANDERSON, John 1848 – 1864
1848 – 1857 10 Blackfriars
1858 – 1864 9 Blackfriars

SANDON, Sarah c.1740
Compleat Angler, Crooked Lane

SHARPE, Sutton c.1790
6 New Bridge.

SHEARWOOD, Thomas c.1790
61 Ratcliffe Highway

SMITH, Ann 1832 – 1834
33 Union St.

SMITH, Thomas 1875
2 Eliza Place

SMITH, William 1841 – 1850
1841 – 1847 3 Broadway
1848 – 1850 67 Wood St and 1 Sherborne Lane

SMITH BROS, 1889 – 1895
33 Fetter Lane.

SNEATH, Charles 1822 – 1840
11 Compton St.

SOUCH, John 1730 – 1760s
The Golden Salmon & Spectacles, London Bridge

SOWERBUTTS, Thomas H
1841 – 1981
1840's 12 Duke St.
1863 – 1875 3 Blossom Terrace
1876 8 Commercial St.
1877 – 1981 151 Commercial St.
From 1884 traded as T H Sowerbutts & Son.
From 1951 traded as T H Sowerbutts & Son. Ltd.

SPARROW, Thomas Henry & Son
1894 – 1926
1894 8 Middle Row
1895 – 1900 151 Commercial St.
1901 – 1905 6 Middle Row
1906 – 1921 121 Goswell Rd.
1922 – 1926 William Sparrow, 22 Southgate Rd.

SPINKS, William c.1795
15 Crooked Lane.

STACKHOUSE, WILLIAM
c.1700s.
'Rising Sun,' 6 Little Britain

STEPHENS, Timothy 1836 – 1840
7 Tottenham Court Rd.

STEWART, John 1883 – 1885
165 Pentonville Rd.

STONE AND IVERSON and HENRY STONE 1760s – 1834
1763 – 1771 Henry Stone & Co., Crooked Lane
1772 – 1789 Stone & Iverson, Crooked Lane

Trade card of William Tanner

1790 – 1793 Iverson & Stone,
13 Crooked Lane
1794 – 1816 Iverson & Stone,
10 Crooked Lane
1817 – 1831 Henry Stone,
10 Crooked Lane
1832 – 1834 Henry Stone,
67 Cannon St

STRACHAN, James 1867 – 1868
22 Charlotte St.

TANNER c.1820 – 1840s
c.1820 – 1830s W Tanner
9 Clerkonwell Green
c.1830s – 40s J J Tanner
1 New Basinghall St.

TAYLOR, John 1822 – 1845
1822 – 1841 64 Piccadilly
1842 – 1845 75 Cheapside

TOWNSEND, William c.1682
Blew Ball, Against Serjeants Inn,
Fleet St.

TENNANT 1846 – 1885
Tenant, William Mathew
1846 – 1883
1846 – 1848 3 Broadway
1849 – 1855 54 Kingland Rd.
1856 – 1864 52 Hollywell Lane
1865 – 1885 6 Hollywell Lane
1884 – 1885 Traded as William &
Charles Tenant

TURPIN 1825 – 1861
Henry Turpin 1825 – 1855
1825 – 1846 2 Myddleton Place
1847 – 1855 124 St. Johns St. Rd.
1856 – 1861 Mrs Sarah Turpin, 4
Susannah Walk

UNSTEAD, Thomas 1887 – 1890
13 Penton St.

USTONSON 1760s – 1855
1760's – 1791 Onesimus
Ustonson, 48 Bell Yard
(From 1775 205 Fleet St.)
1792 – 1808 Ustonson & Son,
205 Fleet St.
1809 – 1814 Onesimus Ustonson,
205 Fleet St.
1815 – 1821 Charles Ustonson
(From 1818, 204 Fleet St.)
1822 – 1847 Maria Ustonson,
204 Fleet St.
1846 – 1847 48 Bell Yard
1848 – 1855 Ustonson & Peters,
48 Bell Yard

VALENTINE, Daniel 1836 – 1843
1836 – 1839 4 Corporation Lane
1840 – 1843 18 Coppice Row

VICKERS, Rebecca 1839 – 1840
14 Rood Lane

VIEWEG, Fraser Gustave
1866 – 1867
249 Old Kent Rd.

WALFORD c.1779
29 St. Johns Sq.

WALKER, Henry 1880 – 1885
53 Gresham St.

WALTON & SELLERS
1882 – 1885
14 St. Mary's Axe.

WARD, R 1832 – 1853
1832 – 1839 Robert Ward, 8
Wellington St.
1840 – 1853 Richard Ward
1849 – 1852 32 Seword St.
1853 12 Easton St.

WARREN, Stephen (Rods)
1911 – 1916
25 Southampton St.

WATSON, W 1882 – 1890
308 High Holborn (in 1890
Watson & Hancock).

WEBSTER, GEORGE c 1700s
'The Fish,' Chiswell St.

WEBSTER, J 1822 – 1824
4 Grub St.

WILLIAMS 1856 – 1932
1856 – 1860 Charles Williams
10 Prospect Place.
1866 – 1872 Frederick Thomas
Williams, 13 Broad Court.
1873 – 1921 10 Great Queen St.
1922 – 1924 22 Wellington St.
1925 – 1932 8 Little St.
Traded as F T Williams & Co.

WILLIAMS, T 1853 – 1931
1853 – 1872 26a Upper York St.
1873 – 1889 97 York St.
1890 – became Alfred Williams 87
York St.
1891 – 1929 84 York St.
1930 – 1931 266 Higher Rd.

WILLINGHAM c.1822 – 1860
1822 – 1831 E I Willingham &
Jones 91 The Strand (Successor to
Clarke late Higginbottam)
1832 – 1834 E Willingham
'Golden Salmon', 36 Maiden Lane
1856 – 1860 Henry Willingham 8
Prospect Place
1860 C Willingham 10 Prospect
Place

WILLIS, John 1832 – 1848
1832 – 1839 3 Eyre St. Hill
1840 – 1848 120 Chancery Lane

WILSON, Thomas 1905 – 1911
1 Sheldon St.

C. WRIGHT & CO. 1856 – 1877
1856 – 1861 1 Fenchurch St.
1862 – 1875 376 The Strand
1876 – 1877 29 Lime St.

WYNNE, John 1817 – 1818
256 Oxford St.

YOUNG, ALFRED 1877 – 1885
174b Oxford St.

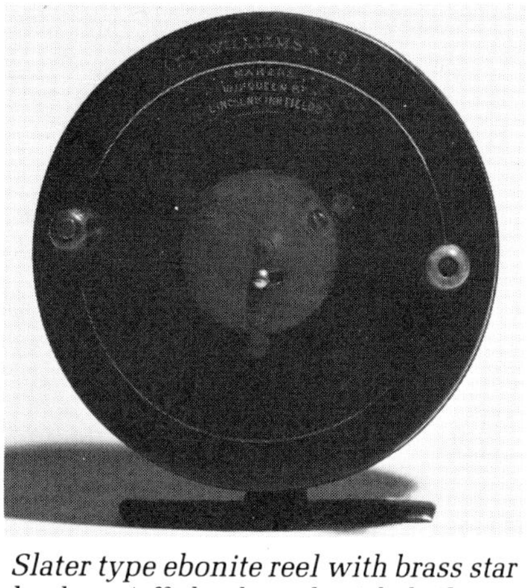

Slater type ebonite reel with brass star back, on/off check stud, nickel silver rim and drum release button inscribed – 'F T Williams & Co' etc.

Brass reel with curved crank, ivory knob and marked, 'F T Williams, 10 Great Queen St., Lincolns Inn Fields'. Diameter 3½"

FISHING TACKLE ACCESSORIES

Carved softwood cast furnisher with sub-divided centre to hold lead shot hooks etc. All retained in paper mâché case

Creeper or bait horn made from cow horn with wood base and stopper

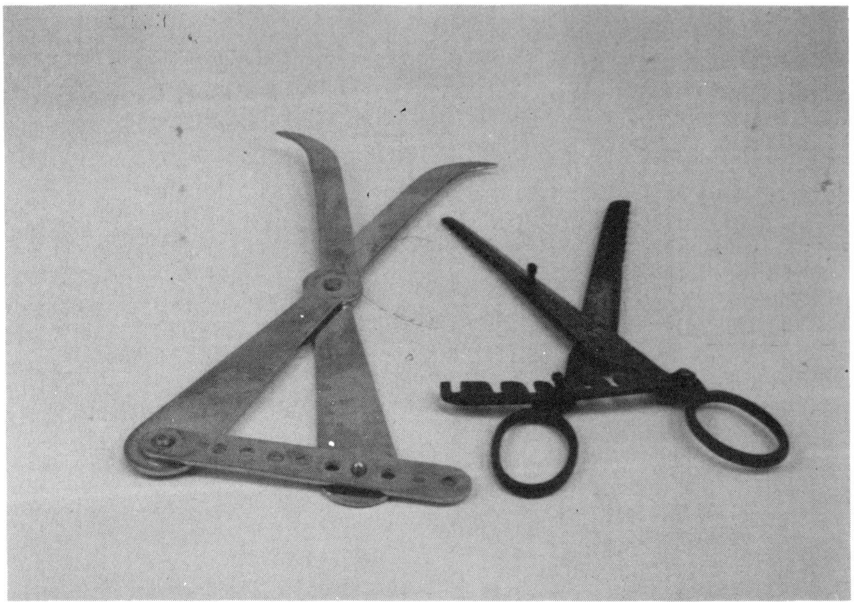

Pike gags by Allcock c.1890 and c.1910

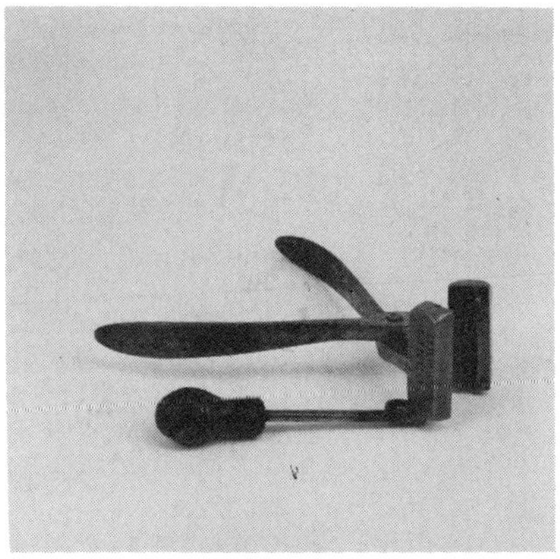

Lead minnow mold c.1870

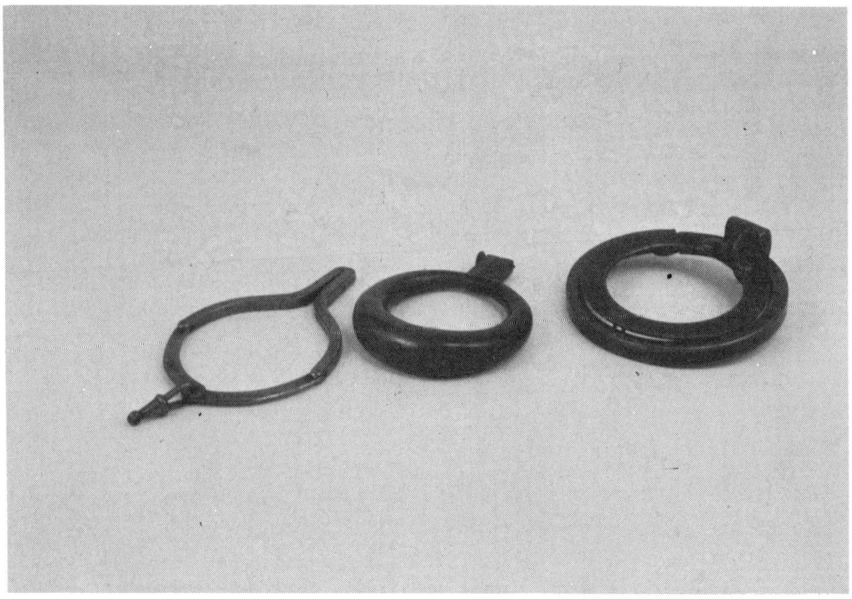

Three line clearing rings. The larger is a Hardy Bros, one unnamed and the lightweight one by Allcocks

Ron Blackmore

Bank rumner and trimmer 19th century

A 19th century brass line twister with crank handle and turned ivory knob

Ron Blackmore

Curved wooden maggot box dated 1885

Rosewood float and cast winder, bone pillars, 4 compartment centre

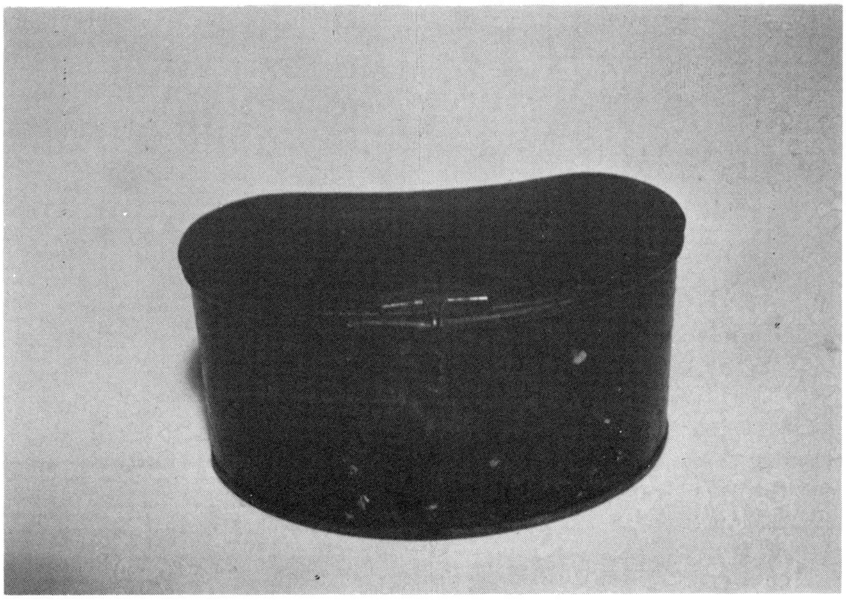

Ron Blackmore

Kidney shaped bait tin with rear belt attachment loops

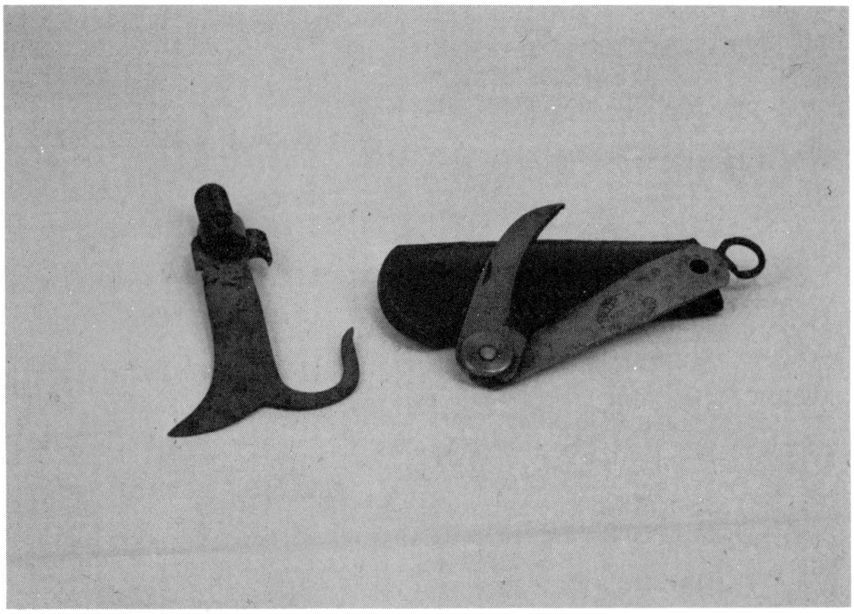

Ron Blackmore

Two fly tackle releasers. One threaded to screw into landing net and the other on a cord and directed by rod tip

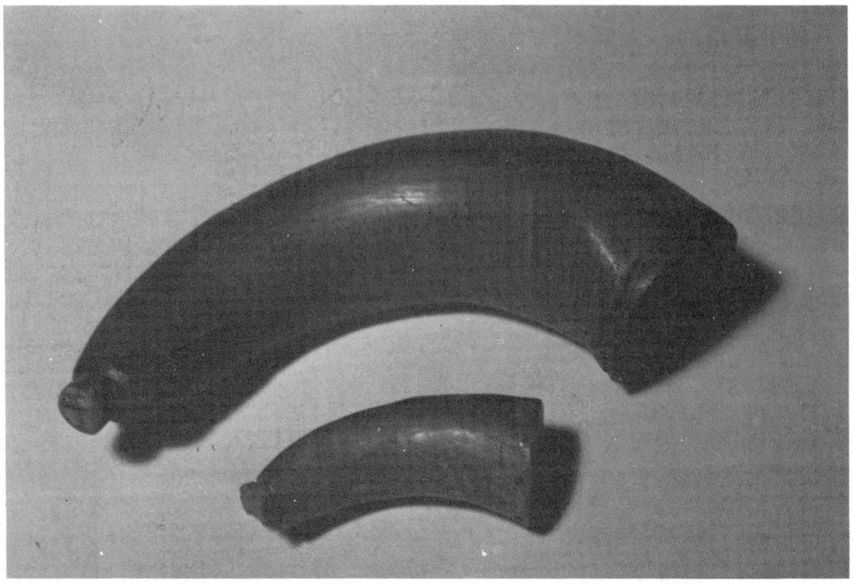

Ron Blackmore

Horn containers for bait and lead shot

Ron Blackmore

A maggot shute

Ron Blackmore

'Ryder' patent butt fitting reel. Marketed by both Foster Bros and Hardy Bros in the late 19th century

FAMILIAR NAMES

The fishing tackle market, which had been dominated by the London tackle makers, rapidly expanded to all parts of Britain from the beginning of the 19th century, leading to Redditch becoming a major centre.
Scotland soon established a large fishing tackle industry, which was not surprising considering the abundance of fresh water lochs and rivers, which offered the finest salmon fishing in the world.

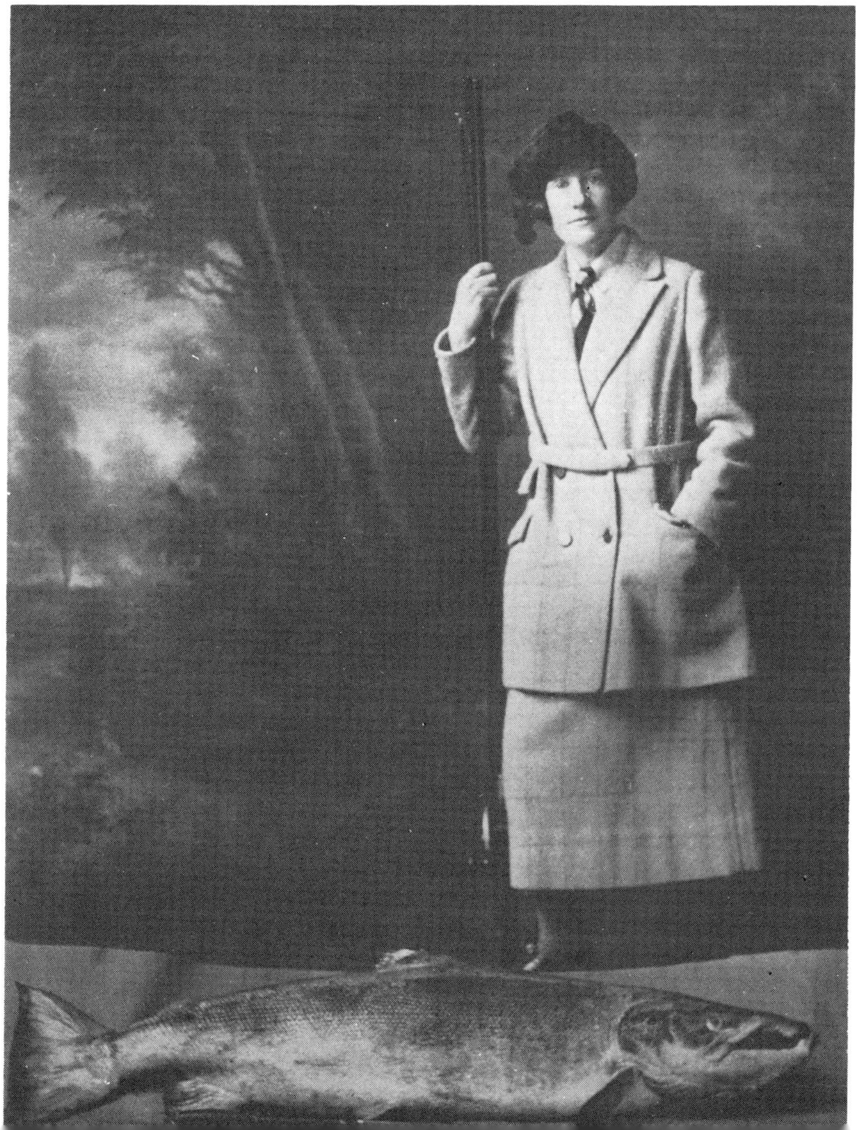

S. ALLCOCK & COMPANY

Polycarp Allcock started making fish hooks in 1803 as a result of the development of hook making as a side line to needle manufacture, to which he had been apprenticed, at a time when it was very much a cottage industry.

In 1829, a son named Samuel was born to Polycarp and when he reached the age of ten began work for his father. Even at an early age he was a very active little businessman and travelled along the cobbled roads by coach to sell his father's hooks in the towns and cities.

Samuel grew up in the small family business at the time of the industrial revolution and his travels gave him the opportunity to see the potential market for rods and other tackle.

It was Samuel who really extended the business, utilising the large numbers of people available which necessitated a new works. By 1866 this had been erected in Clive Road and the labour force had increased to thirty, having become established as hook, float and rod maker. Hook making was still done by primitive methods but Samuel introduced an early form of mechanisation for making rods and other pieces of tackle.

By 1867 Allcock's were manufacturing eyed hooks and had appointed an agent in the capital by the name of J S Holroyd of 59 Gracechurch Street, London. Samuel's early training as a salesboy stood him in good stead and he became both a shrewd buyer and a good salesman, travelling to America, Canada and Europe.

Although the Great Exhibition of 1851 included displays of split cane rods, they never became popular, probably through lack of quality. However, they came into favour when Allcock's and other manufacturers started producing them in the 1870s.

By 1879 Allcock's was one of the early makers producing the hexagonal split cane rods which had been made earlier but not on the same scale. The company's catalogue for the year 1881 offered both American and their own 'Hexagonal Built or Split Cane Rods' and the prices were £4.17.6d for a trout rod of 10′ and £12 for an 18′ salmon rod. Also offered were best quality greenheart trout rods at 23s. 0d. and 20′ salmon hickory rods for £5.5s.

By 1880 Samuel Allcock employed 400 people and was one of the largest makers of fishing tackle in the world.

In the 1890s he opened a factory at Murcia in Spain for the production of silkworm gut and the output increased to enormous proportions supplying markets all over the world. Samuel became an expert on the production of salmon sizes and make up of salmon casts. The Spanish venture was successful up to the introduction of substitutes when the factory was sold.

In 1884 Samuel Allcock took two sons-in-law into partnership whose names were A Williams and G E Leach. In 1902 a third son-in-law Shrimpton also joined the business and eventually became Chairman and Managing Director when Samuel died in 1910.

The 1914-18 war suspended production of the normal range of tackle and the Allcock works was turned over to the war effort, in common with their tackle competitors, producing large quantities of hooks for the Admiralty. When hostilities ceased there was a big demand for fishing tackle and Allcock's once more sold their range of goods both at home and abroad.

There was a marked difference in the type of people fishing in the years between the wars, to the ones in Samuel Allcock's day. Previously, the tackle had been purchased largely by people of leisure, whereas the fishermen of the later age were much more numerous and came from all walks of life. Cheap travel increased leisure and the low cost of fishing created a new popularity in angling. The Second World War again interrupted the business but the post-war years saw a continued increase in the number of anglers both at home and abroad. The success of the Allcock company lay in their ability to produce a good product at a price the volume sales part of the market could afford.

They sold over one hundred and forty reel models, often with variations of each, in their last century of trading and the task of compiling an accurate account has proved an impossible one. The only available source of information has been the limited number of Allcock's catalogues, of which only a dozen early editions

The Aerial Match of 1939 was possibly the ultimate in Aerial reels. The three versions illustrated are a right hand wind, a left hand wind and one without a line guide

have been located. They include 1865, 1871, 1882, 1887, 1897, 1901, 1907, 1912, 1915, 1921, 1925 and c.1930 and are believed to be the main ones printed by the company in the early years. The circa dates given in the illustrated listing of the reels are based on both their appearance in editions, and the intervening years when a catalogue was still being used. For example, if a model made its final appearance in the catalogue of 1907, it is recorded as finishing in 1911, which was the last year before the next known new catalogue was issued in 1912. *It is only an approximate date of when a reel model is known to have appeared in the company catalogues and not necessarily the full years of production.* My research has been greatly assisted by Mr D A Orton, the former Sales and Marketing Manager with the S Allcock Company. He kindly allowed me access to some early catalogues which he saved from the fire that burnt down Standard Works on the 5th November 1966. I thank that gentleman as I do John Turner, John McKinley, and Jamie Maxtone Graham who also allowed me to examine and take data from their collections of catalogues.

Allcock's were one of the longest running and at one time the largest tackle manufacturer in the world. The Aerial reels were the most successful products they marketed and even today they are collected and used all over the world. The Coxon Aerial is generally believed to be the finest model but the personal choice of Mr D A Orton would be the Aerial Match (No. 9053) size 4″ which was only made in 1939. It was a perfect combination of ultra-light alloy and superb engineering and unfortunately perfected at the outbreak of World War II. Production of tackle ceased and a misguided decision was taken to store all the company tools and dyes in Birmingham, which attracted some of the heaviest bombing, and everything was destroyed.

Production started up again after the war and the Allcock Aerial was reintroduced in the late 1940s. In 1965 the last model of the range appeared, a 4½″ New Match Aerial C 340 and although it was a nice reel, it had neither the quality of material or engineering of the original model of 1939. The general purpose Aerials came to an end in 1966 and the New Match Aerial in 1971.

By 1963 the Allcock company had been taken over by the Cope Allman Group who had gained control of the J W Young Company. In 1965 Cope Allman sold the Young and Allcock tackle businesses, which were trading as Top Tackle, to the Shakespeare Company, Kalamazoo, Michigan, USA. The new management merged the total production into a big spread of tackle imported principally from Japan and sold under the Norris-Shakespeare brand, a name under which all their European trading was done. The dilution of the famous British brands of Allcock and Young by so much cheaper a product line, proved disastrous, and by 1970 production of rods and reels had virtually ceased and these famous names disappeared.

Allcock trade mark

A brass reel marked 'Samuel Allcock esq., The Cedars, Redditch' with shaped pillars and milled decoration. This reel is believed to have been the property of Samuel Allcock and one which he had inscribed to hide the fact that he was not really a fisherman

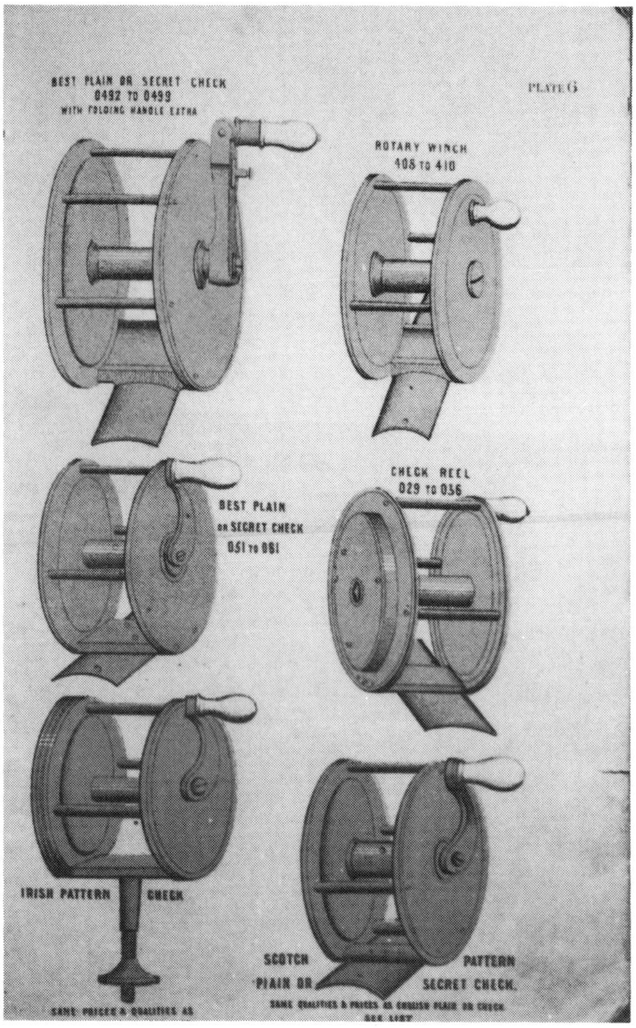

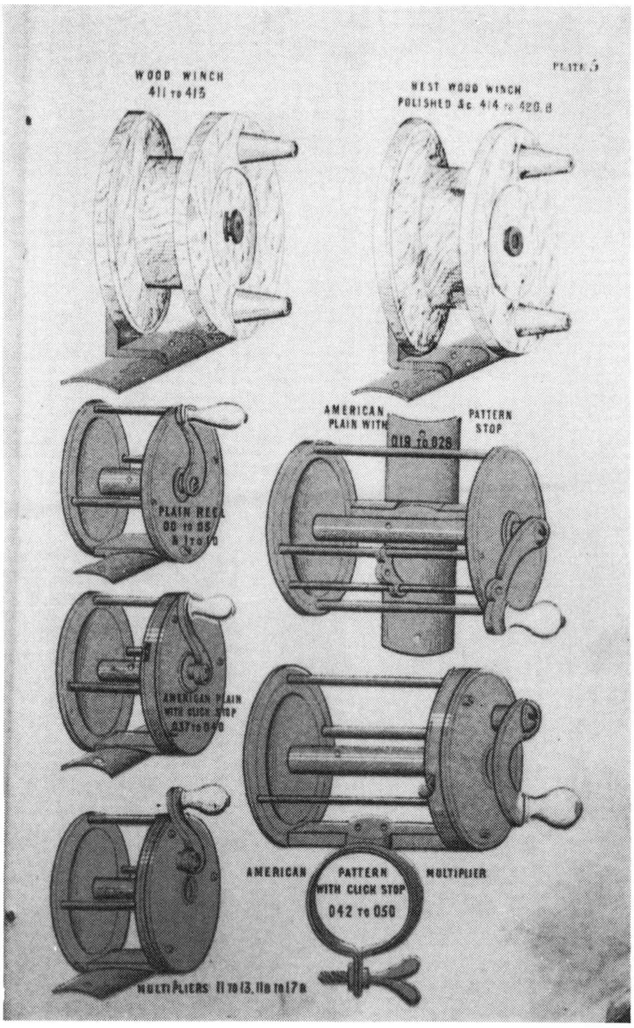

Illustrations from 1871 catalogue

Circa	Model
1865 – 1886	American Pattern Multiplier 042 – 050
	American Pattern 019 – 028
1865 – 1896	Best Plain or Secret Check 0492 – 0499
	Best Plain or Secret Check 051 – 061
	Irish Pattern
	Rotary Winch 408 – 410
	Check Click 029 – 036
	Scotch Pattern
	American Plain with Click 037 – 040
	Multipliers 11 to 13, 11B to 17B
1865	Best Wood Winch 414. From 1882 became Superior Wood Trolling Reel 414B – 422B
	Wood Winch 411
	Plain Reel 00 – 05 and 1 – 10 (evolved to 04C model)

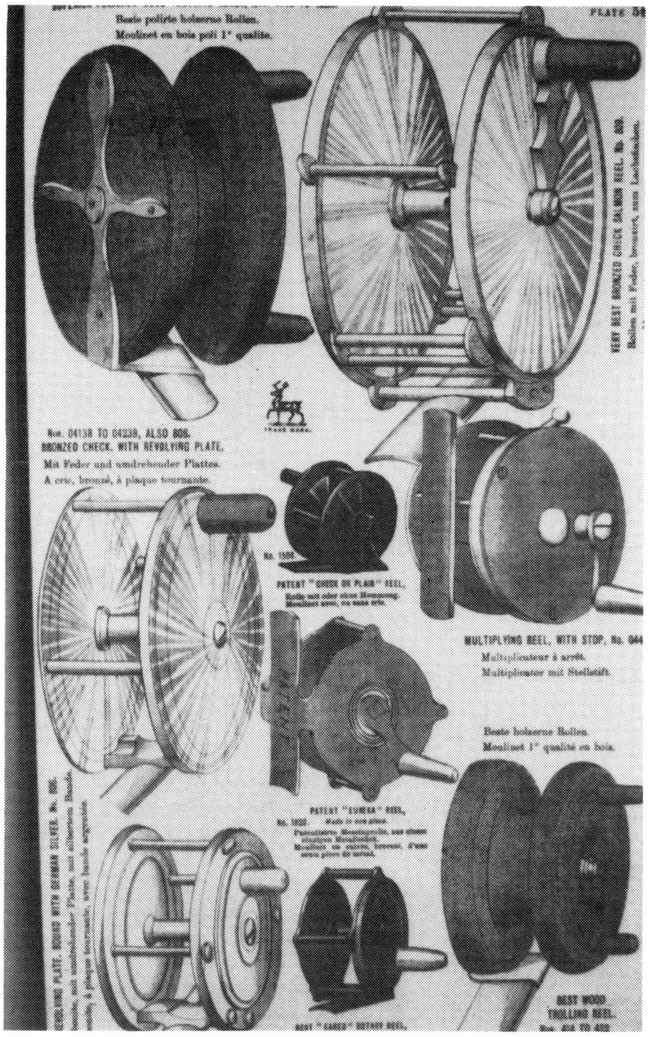

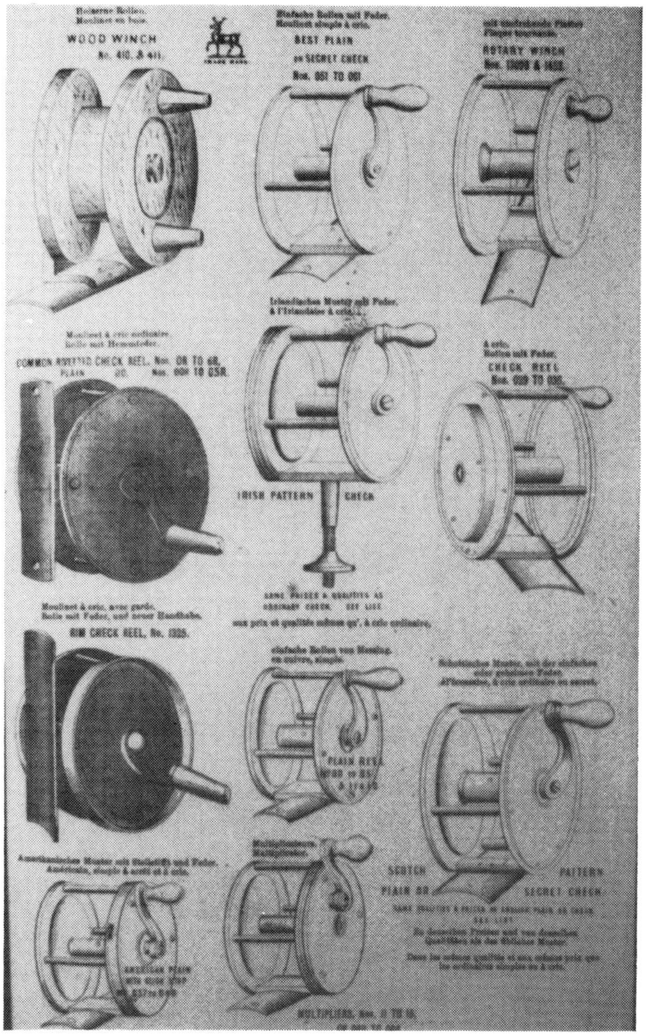

Illustration from catalogue of 1887

Circa	Model
1871 – 1896	Multiplying Reel with Stop No 044
1877 – 1914	Ebonite Revolving Plate Reel No 806
1882 – 1886	Ebonite Check Reel No 057E to 061E
	Rotary Ebonite Salmon No 0421E
	Walnut Trolling Reel 3½″ No 423
1882 – 1896	Very Best Bronzed Check Salmon 4½″ – No 809
1882 – 1911	Bronzed Check with Revolving Plate 0413B – 0423B
1882 – c.1940	Superior Polished Wood Trolling Reel 414B – 422B This wood type of reel continued in various forms of 414 series up to C1940.
1887 – 1896	Patent Check or Plain Reel No 1556
	Patent Eureka No 1820
	Common Rivetted Check Reel No 0R to 6R
	Rim Check Reel No 1325
1887 – 1914	Best Eared Rotory No 1372

All circa dates given for reels and lures are nothing more than years in which they are known to have appeared in the *few* catalogues available at the present time.

COXON ARIEL c.1896 – 1929
The Coxon Aerial was marketed in 1896 by S Allcock & Co and the original model number was 4104 described in the company sales literature simply as the 'Aerial'.

The unusual feature of the reel was the use of spokes which connected the hub to the rim of the flanges, making a much lighter reel with a greater drying capability for the line. There has been speculation and debate as to who was the actual inventor of the spoke-frame type reel and the three contenders have always been Henry Coxon, Samuel Allcock and J W Young. I believe that each of these gentlemen played a part to varying degrees in the introduction and application of the design to fishing reels, but the actual invention of the lightweight spoke support arrangement was made by two gentlemen who probably had no interest in the sport or its tackle. Their names were James Stanley and William Hillman of the Coventry Machine Co. and in 1870 they patented the first wire-spoke tension wheels which were fitted to their lightweight metal bicycles, described as velocipedes.

They gave a practical demonstration of their machines with the new type wheels by undertaking a ride of 96 miles from London to Coventry in a day. They accomplished the feat successfully with no time to spare, as their arrival at Stanley's house was marked by the Cathedral clock striking midnight. They marketed their bicycle at a price of £8 and £12 with a speed gear, and the name of their model was the 'Ariel' spelt with an 'e'.

Over twenty years later Henry Coxon, a well known fishing personality, realised that the lightweight spoke design which had been a success on the bicycle wheel would give the same lightweight advantages to a fishing reel, plus the added bonus of better line drying. In about 1894 he got Allcock & Co. interested in his idea and their reel department set about perfecting a practical model. Originally it had been conceived with the spokes attached to the centre of the bracing tubes between the flanges, but that arrangement must have proved unsatisfactory as the production model of 1896 had the spokes attached to the flange rims. This construction was confirmed by patent No 6612 which Samuel Allcock took out on March 26th 1896 showing spokes fixed to the rims.

I have no knowledge at the present time of any example of an Allcock Aerial type reel with spokes attached to the centre of the cross-tubes, and if any were produced it would probably have been only an odd prototype. An illustration block of the new Aerial must have been made in 1894 or 1895, probably by Allcock's, before they found it necessary to reposition the spoke attachments. This illustration of the reel, recognisable by letters A and B on the picture, and with the spokes incorrectly shown as attached to the centre of the cross tubes, was used in the catalogues of the 1890s and made available to other publications.

In 1896 Henry Coxon himself had a book published entitled *Modern Treatise on Practical Course Fish Angling* which contained the early Coxon Aerial illustration and text which read – 'I suggested to Messrs Allcock & Co, in practical form, the desirability of bringing out the new patent reel, the "Aerial" bearing my name. I had long felt in chub fishing, as in dace fishing, that a lighter reel, on the drum, was required, and after the exercise of considerable ingenuity and apt mechanism, on the part of the "Standard" works employees, that lightness now stands out as an accomplished fact.' This would appear to confirm that Henry Coxon was instrumental in instigating the development of the Aerial reel.

Further evidence to support Henry Coxon as the man who introduced the design to fishing reels comes from other publications of the period. On July 11th 1896 *The Fishing*

Patent drawing of spoke-tension bicycle wheel by James Stanley and William Hillman

Gazette printed a review of the Aerial reel with the following opening text 'Messrs S Allcock & Co., Standard Works, Redditch, have sent us one of their new lightweight reels, known as the "Coxon Aerial", for which they claim the following advantages'. The article contained the same early illustration with the A and B markings which appeared in Henry Coxon's book and two years later it appeared again in Alfred Jardine's *Pike and Perch* c.1898 with the same name of 'Coxon Aerial'.

In 1906 a book was published entitled *Practical Fishing for the So Called Course Fishes* in which the author J W Martin said Coxon was the inventor. Therefore it is clear that all the fishing fraternity at that time knew the reel as the Coxon Aerial and everything written about it gave the same title. The exceptions were the early Allcock catalogues which left out the word 'Coxon' and

The early illustration of the 'Coxon Aerial' with the spokes attached to the centre of the cross tubes

called the reel simply the 'Aerial'. Samuel Allcock may have intentionally made the omission, because he thought that as he had taken out a patent for the design in 1896, and his company was marketing the reel, the name 'Coxon' would be quickly forgotten. However, if that had been his hope he was disappointed, and by 1912 the Allcock company had started to use Coxon's name. They placed an advertisement that year in a paperback book entitled *The Rudiments of Angling* by William Powell-Owen which contained a new illustration of the reel with the spokes in the correct position attached to the flange rims and the name of the reel was 'Coxon Aerial'. Another appeared in the *Fishing Gazette* of December 5th 1914 which contained the following 'What an astonishing run the Aerial Reel has had to be sure. Much water – a veritable ocean – has poured itself beneath the ancient bridges of the Trent since the day Mr Coxon of Nottingham, in a moment of inspiration evolved the principle upon which the first Aerial Reel was constructed and Allcock's of Redditch turned their serious attention to the question of its wholesale distribution and manufacture.'

Therefore, there can be no doubt that it was Henry Coxon who introduced the lightweight spoke design to the construction of fishing reels and it was Samuel Allcock and the employees of his company who transformed the idea into a practical model.

It has been suggested that J W Young, the founder of J W Young & Son, should be considered as the inventor of the Aerial because he designed a superb Nottingham or centre pin reel in 1884, while he was head of reel making at Allcock & Co. I would consider such a claim fails on two counts. There is no documentary evidence to show that at the time, or within a reasonable period, J W Young considered himself to be the inventor, and he never applied for a patent to protect the idea. He did in fact make an application for patent No 3328 on February 17th 1905, which involved a spoke frame reel, but the principle idea was for an adjustable brake. It was never granted as no sealing completion fee was paid. I think it would be reasonable to say that while J W Young was an employee of S Allcock & Co. he possibly played a principal part in the development of a practical model of Coxon's spoke design but his work should be considered as an act of assistance rather than inventing or introducing a new design.

Having considered the evolution of the reel, the much harder task has been deciding what constitutes a Coxon Aerial and recording the difference from its stable companion, the Allcock Aerial. The generally accepted definition is that Aerials with an ebonite unventilated flange are Coxons and ones with a ventilated aluminium flange are Allcock Aerials, no matter whether they have wood or aluminium backs. This method of classification is not supported by the Allcock catalogues and the 1925 edition creates further confusion by including a ventilated flange variety described as an 'Improved Coxon Aerial'.

At the present time, no authority has produced an easy way of identifying all these important reels and therefore I have attempted to devise a simple form of classification. I examined the data from Allcock catalogues from 1896 to 1925 together with advertisements in other publications, and found that whenever the company called a reel 'Coxon Aerial' it invariably was described as having a wood back. The best evidence of the difference between a Coxon Aerial and an Allcock Aerial was given in the catalogue of 1915, which was the first edition to separate the two models. Included were two Coxon Aerials, No 4108 and No 4108A, and both had wood backs.

The three Allcock Aerials included two unventilated ebonite flange varieties No 5101 and No 5138 (the tiny holes for the cross tube fixtures are not considered as ventilations) and the first ventilated aluminium flange model No 7950DB. All three Allcock Aerials had aluminium backs. In the catalogue of 1925 the Coxon Aerials appeared for the last time and included No 4108A plus an additional new model No 7995. This was described as the 'Improved Coxon Aerial' which had the unusual feature of a ventilated aluminium flange and although it looked like an Allcock Aerial it had the distinguishing feature of a wood back.

Therefore the evidence from the catalogues shows that if an Aerial had a wood back it was a Coxon and if an alloy back it was an Allcock Aerial. It is generally believed that only the Coxon Aerials were made in the early years but there is evidence to show that the aluminium back model was being produced from the beginning of the Aerial range in 1896.

On November 14th 1896 *The Field* published a letter from a practical angler, Mr J P Tundley of Northwich, Cheshire, which gave testimony to the Aerial winch. At the end of the letter a footnote was included which read 'The makers (Messrs S Allcock's & Co., Standard Works, Redditch) are now making the 'Aerial' in aluminium in two sizes larger, namely 4″ and 5″ diameter, so that the drum will hold as much line as is required, either for pike or salmon fishing. The whole of the reels are being finished with a check, and this addition should be cordially welcomed.'

Coxon Aerial c.1896–1929

Sizes 3″, 3½″, 4″, 4½″. Features include a spoke frame lightweight drum with ebonite flange and the essential requirement of a 'Coxon' – a wood back

Rear elevation showing a wood back

Improved Coxon Aerial 1925–1929

Sizes 3½″, 4″. Improved Coxon Aerial with a ventilated aluminium flange and a wood back

Rear elevation showing a wood back

BRASS WINCHES

A rare multiplying brass winch with curved crank and turned ivory knob. Marked 'JJ Tanner, No.1 New Basinghall St,

Below left: A brass winch with a serpentine crank and brass knob and raised back check housing. Marked 'Eaton & Deller, Makers 6&7 Crooked Lane London'. Diameter 3¼"

Above: A large brass winch by J McGowan with raised pillars, pillar roller bar, straight crank and ebonite knob. Diameter 4¼"

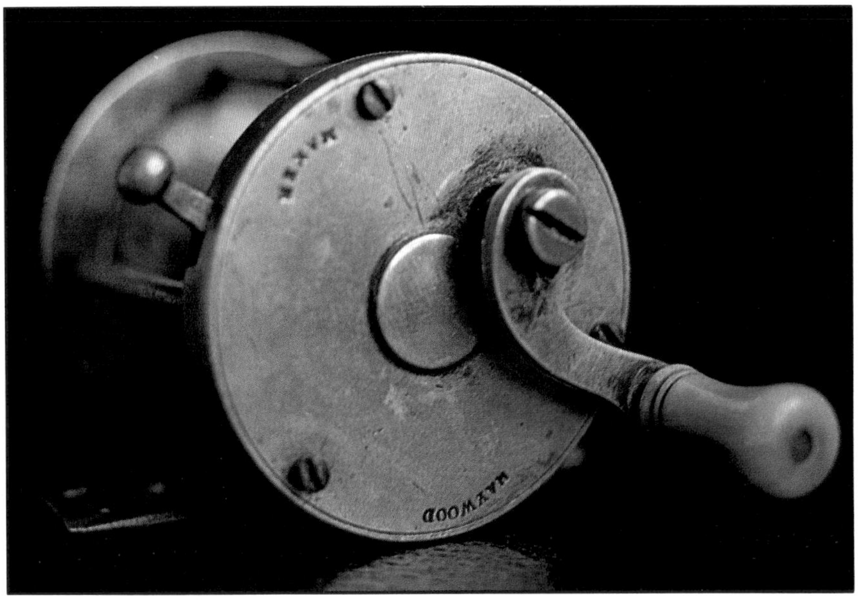

A brass multiplying winch with curved crank, turned ivory knob, perforated foot and rim lock.

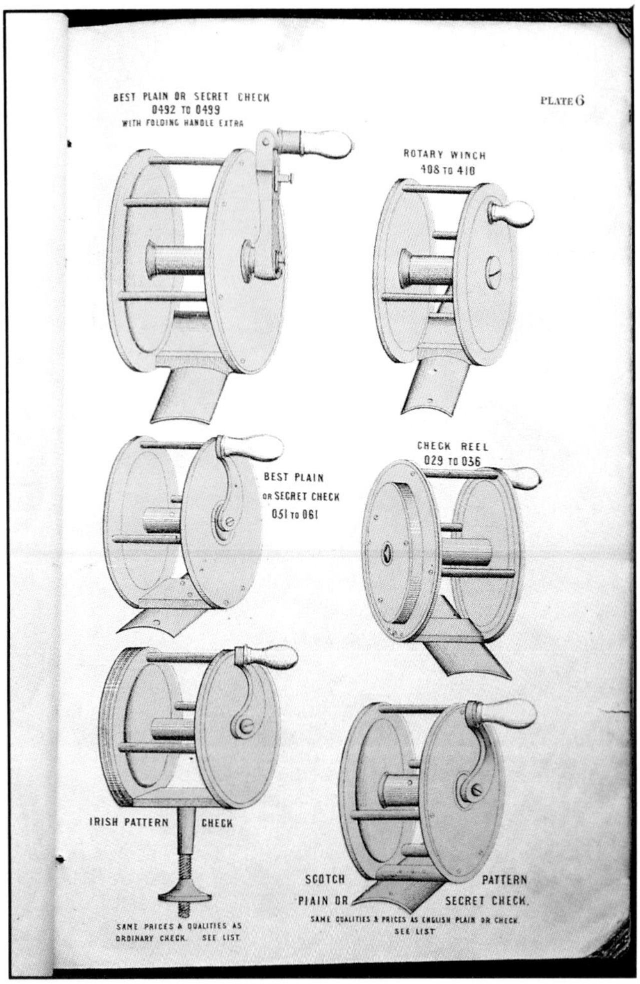
BEST PLAIN OR SECRET CHECK
0492 TO 0499
WITH FOLDING HANDLE EXTRA
PLATE 6
ROTARY WINCH
408 TO 410
BEST PLAIN
OR SECRET CHECK
051 TO 061
CHECK REEL
029 TO 036
IRISH PATTERN CHECK
SCOTCH PATTERN
PLAIN OR SECRET CHECK.
SAME PRICES & QUALITIES AS
ORDINARY CHECK. SEE LIST.
SAME QUALITIES & PRICES AS ENGLISH PLAIN OR CHECK.
SEE LIST

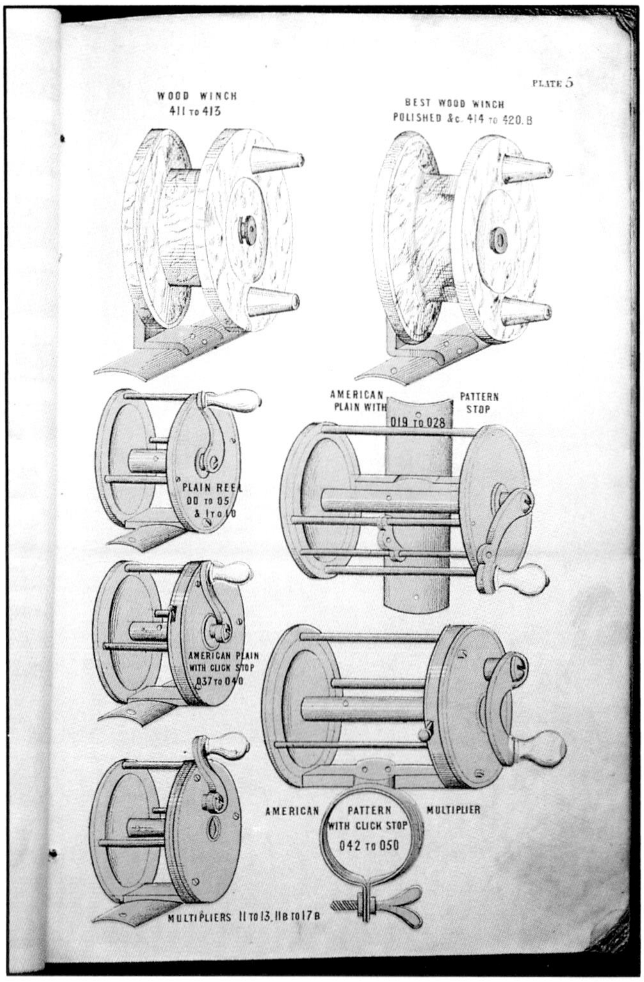
PLATE 5
WOOD WINCH
411 TO 413
BEST WOOD WINCH
POLISHED &c. 414 TO 420.B
AMERICAN PATTERN
PLAIN WITH STOP
019 TO 028
PLAIN REEL
00 TO 05
& 1 TO 10
AMERICAN PLAIN
WITH CLICK STOP
037 TO 040
AMERICAN PATTERN MULTIPLIER
WITH CLICK STOP
042 TO 050
MULTIPLIERS 11 TO 13, 11B TO 17B

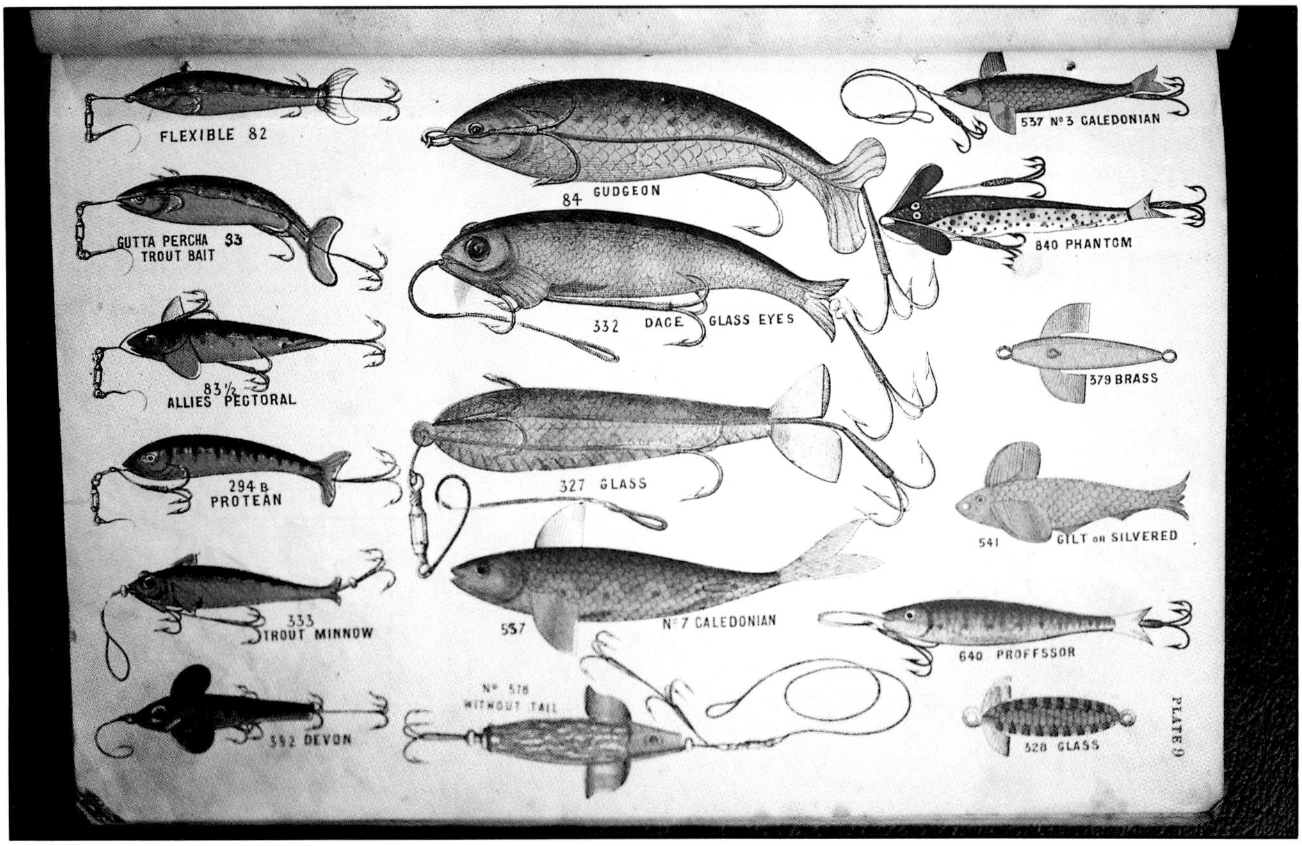
FLEXIBLE 82
84 GUDGEON
537 No 3 CALEDONIAN
GUTTA PERCHA 33
TROUT BAIT
840 PHANTOM
332 DACE GLASS EYES
83½
ALLIES PECTORAL
379 BRASS
294 B
PROTEAN
327 GLASS
541 GILT OR SILVERED
333
TROUT MINNOW
537 No 7 CALEDONIAN
640 PROFFSSOR
392 DEVON
No 578
WITHOUT TAIL
328 GLASS
PLATE 9

The illustrations on these pages have been reproduced from Messrs Allcock's catalogue dated 1871

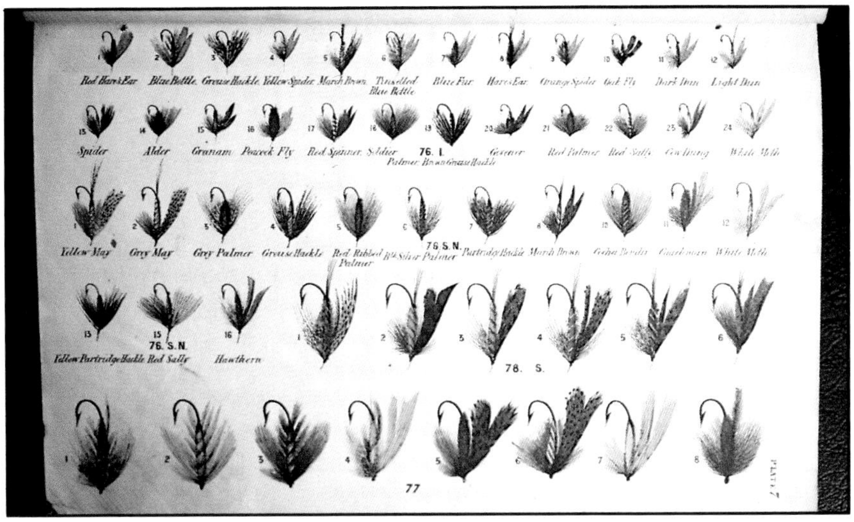

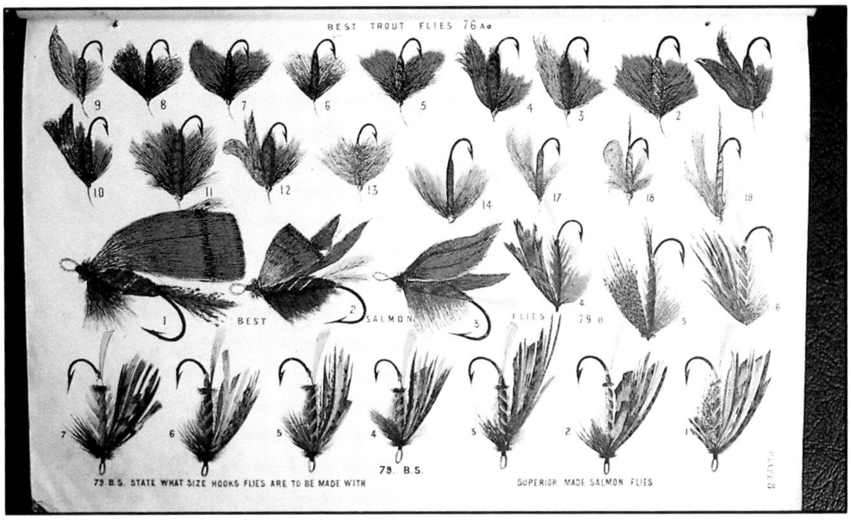

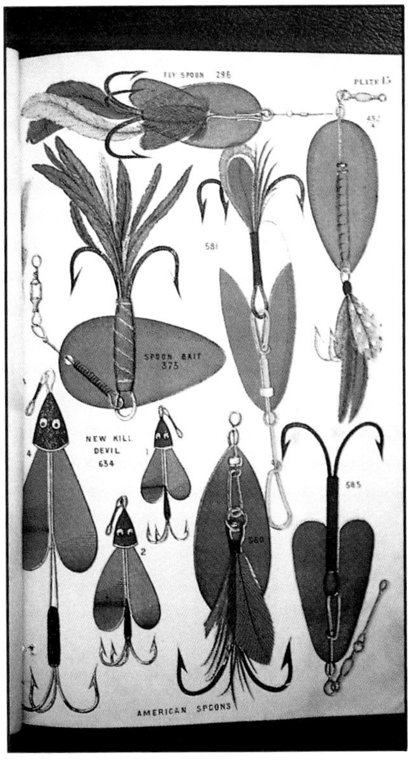

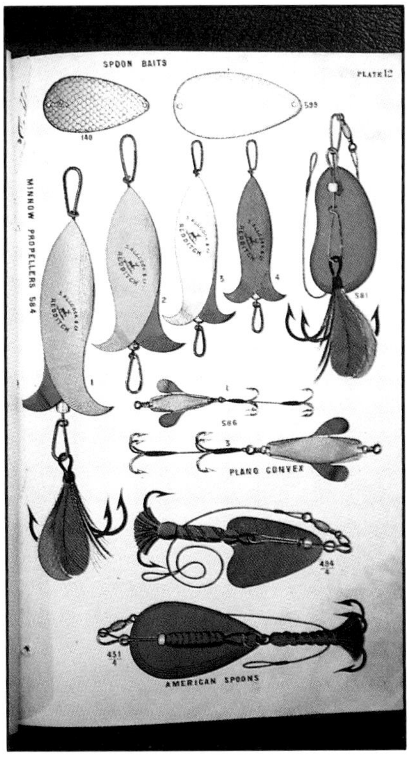

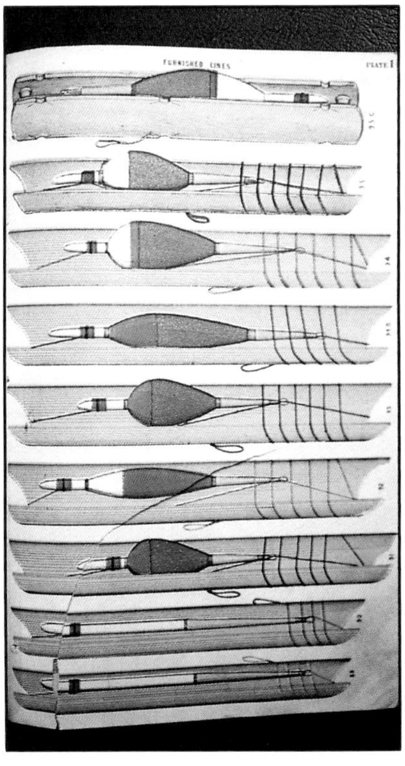

A very rare Allcock all brass multiplying reel with curved crank and ivory knob. Marked 'S Allcock'. The only example I have ever seen of a model which appeared in the earliest catalogues

An Improved Coxon Aerial of 4″ diameter and a Coxon Aerial of 3¼″ diameter

A Match Aerial (1939 Model) of 4″ diameter, an Unventilated Allcock Aerial of 3½″ diameter and a Ventilated Allcock Aerial of 4″ diameter

Unventilated Allcock Aerial
c.1896–1924

Unventilated Allcock Aerial with spoke supports, unventilated ebonite flange and metal back

Front elevation.

Back elevation

Ventilated Allcock Aerial
c.1914 – 1966

This model was introduced in c.1914 in the form of 7950 which had an optional check, regulating brake and no line guard. An additional model No 7981 was introduced in 1921 which had a line guard and continued in production in sizes 3″, 3½″, 4″, 4½″ up to 1933. After that date Model No 7950 continued in the same sizes with the option of an aluminium line guard with revolving bar for 10/– on a 3½″, 12/6d on 4″ and 16/6d on the 4½″. This model also continued to offer an optional ratchet check lever on the rim. Production ceased in 1939 but was revived after the Second World War in the 1940s. It was the most successful and longest running Allcock reel and sales continued up to c.1966.

Ventilated Allcock Aerial with usual Aerial features, all metal construction and perforated channel flange

CATALOGUE DATA ON AERIALS 1896 – 1939

Circa	Models
1896	Model No 4104 – Aerial. The illustration of this reel showed the spoke supports connected to the centre of the cross-tubes.
1907	Model No 4108 – Aerial. It was described as having a wood back and the illustration is the same as the earlier one with the spokes connected to the centre of the cross tubes. Model No 5101 – Aerial. This was described as having an aluminium back, check, line guard and deep flange. It is illustrated with the spokes connected to the flange rims.
1912	Model No 5101 and a new No 5138 Aerial with aluminium back and fitted with regulator brake for which a patent had been applied. Model No 4108 Aerial with wood back but with a new illustration with the spokes connected to the flange rims.
1914 and 1915	Five Aerial models separated into Coxon Aerials and Allcock Aerials. Model No 4108 'Coxon Aerial'. Spinning reel with wood back and illustrated with spokes to flange rims. Model No 4108A 'Coxon Aerial'. Spinning reel with wood back, optional check and regulator brake. Spokes connected to flange rims. Model No 5101 'Allcock Aerial'. Spinning reel with aluminium back, optional check, 'BP' line guard. Model No 5138 'Allcock Aerial'. Spinning reel with aluminium back, optional check, 'BP' line guard and fitted with regulating brake. Model No 7950 DB. 'Allcock Aerial.' Latest 1915 model spinning reel, aluminium finished 'dead black', optional check, regulating brake and no line guard. The illustration of this reel showed the model to be the first Aerial with a ventilated aluminium flange.

Circa	Model
In 1914 only	Model No 5100 Allock Aerial in bronzed aluminium and ebonite. Model No 5100½. Similar to No 5100 with patent regulating brake.
1921	Model No 4108A described as 'Combined Fly and Spinning reel'. Model No 7950 Aluminium back, ventilated flange and no line guard. Model No 7981 made of aluminium with ventilated flange and line guard.
1925	Model No 5138 with aluminium back and ebonite drum. All made in sizes 3″, 3½″, 4″, 4½″. The last catalogue appearance of Coxon Aerials. Model No 4108A in sizes 3″, 4″, 4½″. Model No 7995 in sizes 3½″, 4″. 'Improved Coxon Aerial' and illustrated with aluminium ventilated flange with wood back. Model No 7950 Allock Aerial with aluminium back, perforated aluminium front and back flanges, finished black in sizes 3″, 3½″, 4″, 4½″, (48/- to 57/6d each) Models 7981 and 7986. There was a new model No 7990 which appeared in 1925 described as – Allcock Aerial with lever for salmon or mahseer fishing. It had a rim lever control and was constructed extra wide.
1930	Allcock Aerial Models No 7981 (sizes 3½″, 4″, 4½″) and No 7950 (sizes 3½″, 4″, 4½″). Aerial Popular Model No 8902 which was a cheaper version and introduced in sizes 3″, 3½″, 4″, 4½″.
	Allock Aerial Sea Reel No 8916 Made of Bakelite.
1937	Allcock Aerial No 7950 (Improved Model) sizes 3½″, 4″, 4½″. Aerial Popular No 8902, sizes 3″, 3½″, 4″, 4½″.
1939	Allcock Aerial No 7950, Aerial Popular No 8902 and the only year of the Aerial Match No 9053, 4″.

28 S. ALLCOCK, & CO., Ltd., REDDITCH, ENGLAND.

The "Allcock Aerial" (Regd. Trade Mark) and "Coxon Aerial" (Regd. Trade Mark.) Spinning Reels.

(Patent No. 4776).

No. 4108. The "Coxon-Aerial" Spinning Reel, wood back, optional check.

No. 4108A. The "Coxon-Aerial" Spinning Reel, wood back, optional check, fitted with Regulating Brake.

No. 7958. The "Britannia" (1915 Mode[l]) solid wood back, ebonite fron[t] plate and flange. Regulatin[g] Brake.

No. 5138. The "Allcock-Aerial" Spinning Reel, aluminium back, optional check, "B.P." line guard, fitted with Regulating Brake.

No. 5197. Apart. The "Britannia" Sea and Spinning Reel, solid ebonite front, aluminium back, all brass fittings, dust-proof and watertight cap on front spindle, Regulating Brake, "B.P." gun-metal line guard.

No. 5101. The "Allcock-Aerial" Spinning Reel, aluminium ba[ck], optional check, with "B.[P."] gun-metal line guard.

No. 7950DB. The "Allcock-Aerial" Latest 1915 Model Spinning Reel, aluminium finished "dead-black," optional check, Regulating Brake, no line guard.

No. 5198. Apart. No. 5198. Complete.
The "Britannia" Sea and Spinning Reel, solid ebonite front, wood back lined with brass, fitted same as No. 5197 but without line guard.

Catalogue of 1915

Match Aerial No 9053 – 1939

Match Aerial of superb quality combining the finest material and engineering. Produced only in 1939. Size 4″

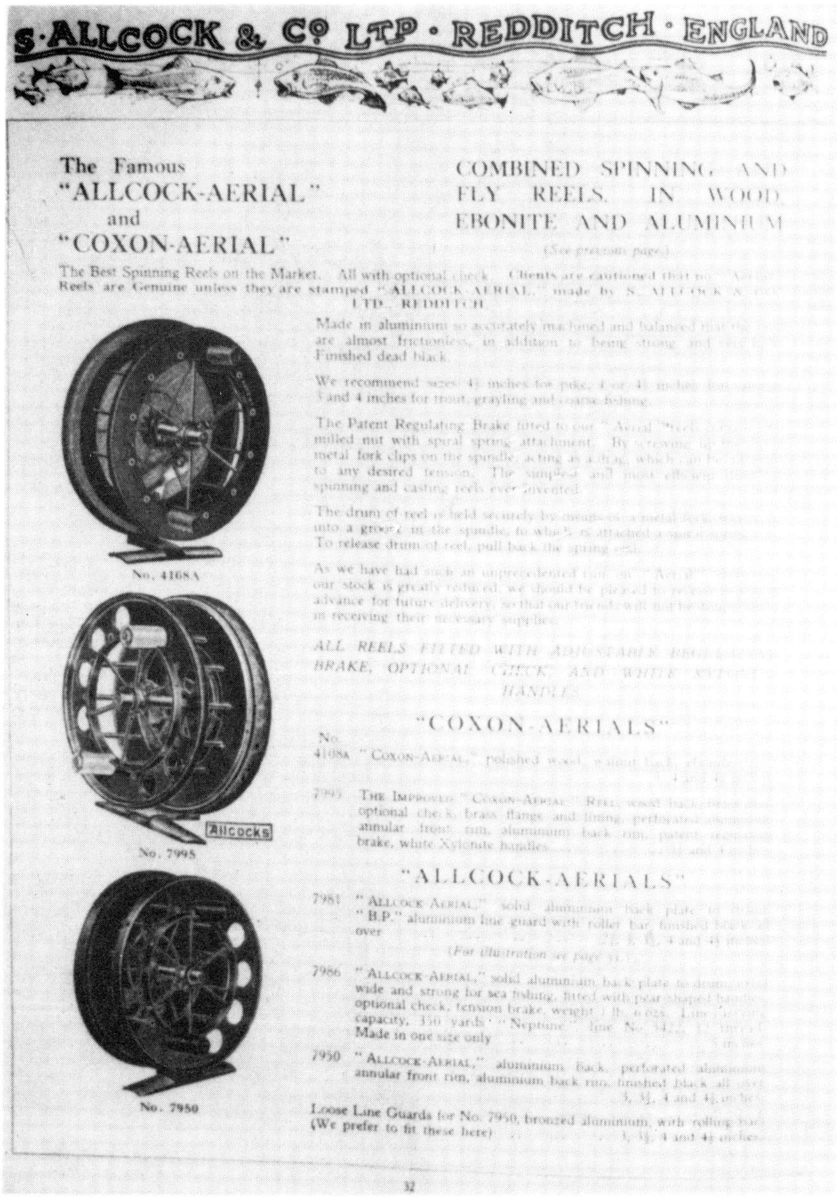

S. ALLCOCK & Co LTD · REDDITCH · ENGLAND

The Famous
"ALLCOCK-AERIAL"
and
"COXON-AERIAL"

COMBINED SPINNING AND FLY REELS IN WOOD, EBONITE AND ALUMINIUM

(See previous page.)

The Best Spinning Reels on the Market. All with optional check. Clients are cautioned that no "Aerial" Reels are Genuine unless they are stamped "ALLCOCK-AERIAL," made by S. ALLCOCK & [illegible] LTD., REDDITCH.

Made in aluminium so accurately machined and balanced that the [illegible] are almost frictionless, in addition to being strong and [illegible] Finished dead black.

We recommend sizes 4½ inches for pike, 4 or 4½ inches [illegible] 3 and 4 inches for trout, grayling and coarse fishing.

The Patent Regulating Brake fitted to our "Aerial" Reels [illegible] milled nut with spiral spring attachment. By screwing up [illegible] metal fork clips on the spindle, acting as a drag, which can be [illegible] to any desired tension. The simplest and most efficient [illegible] spinning and casting reels ever invented.

The drum of reel is held securely by means of a metal fork [illegible] into a groove in the spindle, to which is attached a [illegible] To release drum of reel, pull back the spring end.

As we have had such an unprecedented run on "Aerial" [illegible] our stock is greatly reduced, we should be pleased to receive [illegible] advance for future delivery, so that our friends will not be [illegible] in receiving their necessary supplies.

ALL REELS FITTED WITH ADJUSTABLE [illegible] BRAKE, OPTIONAL CHECK, AND WHITE XYLONITE HANDLES.

No. 4168A

"COXON-AERIALS"

No.
4168A "Coxon-Aerial," polished wood, walnut back, [illegible] 4 and 4½

7995 The Improved "Coxon-Aerial" Reel, wood back, [illegible] optional check, brass flange and lining, perforated [illegible] annular front rim, aluminium back rim, patent [illegible] brake, white Xylonite handles [illegible]

Allcocks

No. 7995

"ALLCOCK-AERIALS"

7981 "Allcock-Aerial," solid aluminium back plate [illegible] "B.P." aluminium line guard with roller bar, finished black all over 2½, 3, 3½, 4 and 4½ inches

(For illustration see page 31.)

7986 "Allcock-Aerial," solid aluminium back plate to drum [illegible] wide and strong for sea fishing, fitted with pear shaped handles, optional check, tension brake, weight 1 lb. 6 ozs. Line capacity, 350 yards "Neptune" line No. 3422 [illegible] Made in one size only [illegible]

7950 "Allcock-Aerial," aluminium back, perforated aluminium annular front rim, aluminium back rim, finished black all over 3, 3½, 4 and 4½ inches

No. 7950

Loose Line Guards for No. 7950, bronzed aluminium, with rolling bar (We prefer to fit these here) 3, 3½, 4 and 4½ inches

32

The final appearance of Coxon Aerials in the catalogue of 1925

Aerial Popular c.1927 – 1962

This model was introduced in about 1930 as a cheaper form of the Ventilated Aerial with model No 8902. It continued up to the outbreak of hostilities in 1939 and was reintroduced in the late 1940s. It continued in production up to 1961/1962.

Aerial Popular No 8902. Sizes 3″, 3½″, 4″, 4½″

Special Match C706 1955 – 1962

This was an average quality reel produced in a 4″ size

Circa	Model
1893 – 1929	Moscrop reel No 4106 (Two models offered in either gun metal 4107 or aluminium 4107A from 1912)
1893 – 1906	German Silver & Ebonite No 3154
1897 – 1906	Automatic Reel No 3486 Duplex Fly Reel No 3526 Simplex Nottingham No 3673 Boys Brass No 3481 Badminton Sea Reel No 3840
1897 – 1911	Gunmetal & Ebonite No 3180 (c.1912 named "The Summit") Special Light Reel No 3092
1901 – 1911	Wood Steel Centre No 424 Wood No 3604 with line guard
1901 – 1920	Boys Wood Reel No 409

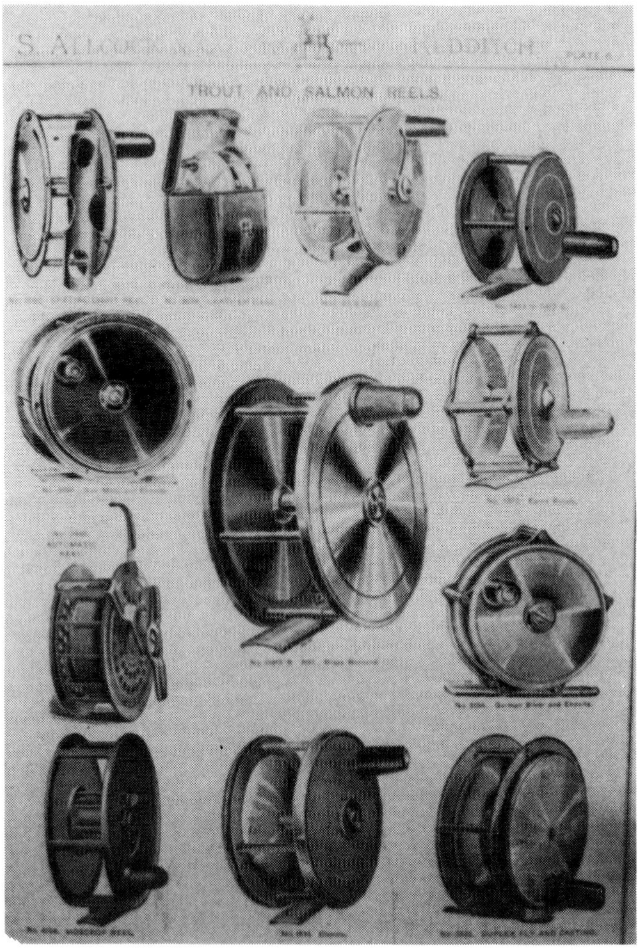

New Match Aerial C340 1965 – 1971

The last Aerial model to be produced. Size 4½". Confusion is often caused by it being wrongly catalogued as a Match Aerial.

Circa	**Model**
1907 – 1912	Mahseer Reel No 4110 and 4110½ (4110A with thumb brake in 1912)
1907 – 1911	Nottingham No 2664 Sea Reel No 5102½
1907 – 1922	Wilcock Sea Reel No 4130 – sizes 4″ to 6″
1907 – 1924	Brass Plain Reel No 4115 Multiplier with Check and Drag No 4121
1911 – 1920	The Special 1911 Model No 7932
1912 – 1920	Ebonite Tarpon No 5196. Alloy Trout and Salmon No 7945. Alloy Trout and Salmon No 7939. Silent Knight No 4129. Ingram Aluminium Centre Pin No 7926. 'Schooling' Bait Casting Reels Nos 7912, 7913, 7914 and 7924.

Circa	**Model**
1912 – 1924	Ebonite Star Back No 4124 Ebonite Centre Pin Spinning No 4123 Superior Trout and Salmon No 3092A. Became the 'Roland' Aluminium Plate Reel in 1921.
1912 – 1929	Rotory Reel No 7925. Became 'The Calgary' Trout Reel No 7930 and then 'The Luckie'.

Circa	Model
1912 – 1920	Pilot Wood Sea Reel No 7915. Britannia Sea and Spinning Reels No 5197 and 5198. Wood Sea Reels No 5147 and No 5149.
1912 – 1924	St. George Sea Reel No 7911 (Became the 'Neptune,' sizes 4″ to 8″, in 1921) SA Big Fish Reel No 7929, sizes 6″ and 8″. King Wood Sea Reel No 7923, sizes 4½″ to 7½″. Wood Sea Reels No 5143, No 5145, No 7920 (Became the 'Fowley' 4″ in 1921)
1915 – 1920	Inkford Revolving Plate No 7954. Peerless Aluminium Revolving Plate No 7963. Trevor No 7938.

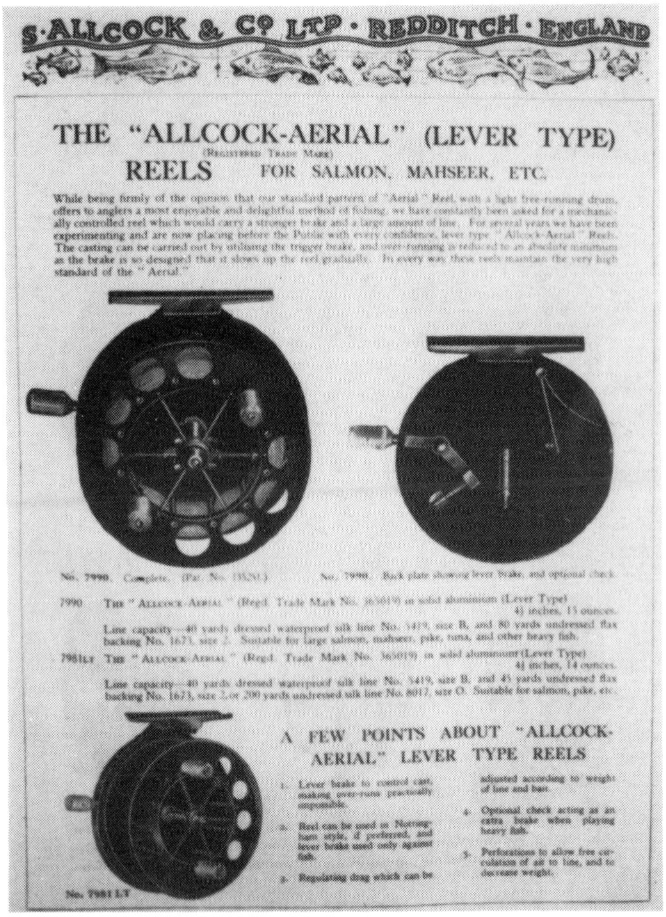

Allcock's Aerial with Lever No 7990. c.1925 – 1929
This was an Aerial with an extra wide drum and is a rare and collectable reel. Size 4½″

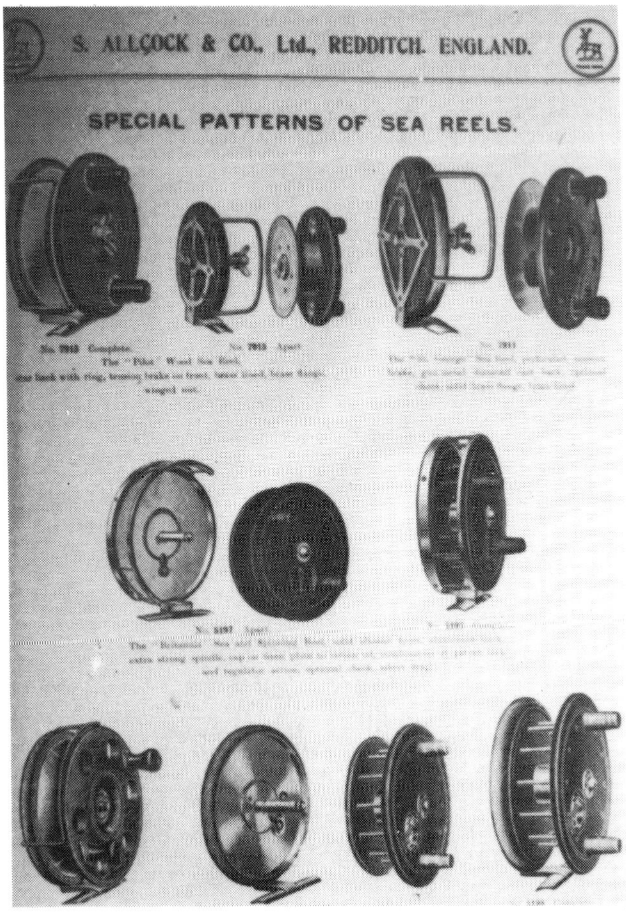

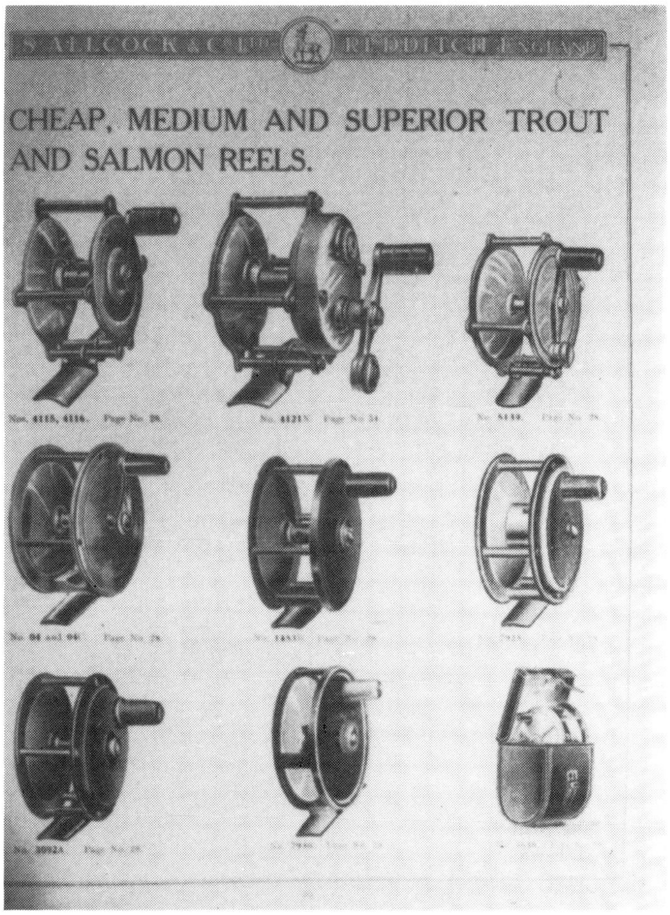

Circa	Model
1912 – 1920	Reel with Balanced Crank No 5139. Wood and Roach Spinning Reels Nos 7907, 7908, 7909, 7918/9, 7928 The Thames.
1912 – 1924	Sheffield Pattern No 4141. Plate Reel No 1453B.
1915 – 1924	Hercules Style No 3092A.
1921 – 1924	Centre Brake Reel No 7978, sizes 2¾″, 3″, 3¼″, 3½″, 4″, 4½″.

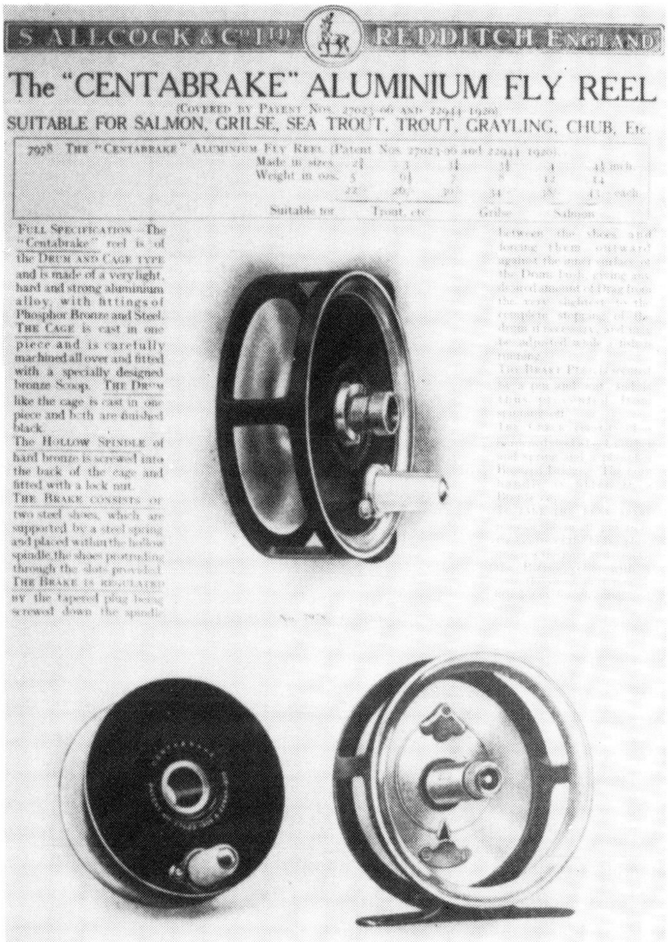

Circa	Model
1915 – 1929	Fermoy No 7941 Calgary No 7925
1922 – 1937	Scarborough No 8909
1925 – 1929	Brigald No 7992 Strathclyde No 2966 Superior Grade Aluminium No 4140
1925 – 1962	Flick Em Model 1925 Improved Flick Em No 7987 and 7987A. 1935 – 1936 Flick Em No 8936 – 4″. 1937 Flick Em No 8936 and No 8937 – 3½″, 4″. 1939 – Flick Em No 8936, also No 8937 The Swift (a cheaper version). 1947 – 1962 Flick Em No 8121 in a 4″.
1930 – 1937	Walnut No 5143½.
1930 – 1939	Ousel No 7997 – 2¾″, 3″, 4″.
1930 – 1947	Coquet No 7999 – 3″, 3½″, 4″, 4½″. In 1937 became No 8920 – 4″, 4¼″.
1930 – 1962	Argus No 5130 – 4″, 4½″, 5″, 5½″, 6″. (1930 – 1937). From 1949 – 1953. It was listed as No B170 – 4″, 4½″, 5″, 6″. The Argus model was also listed in 1961 and 1962 catalogues.
1930 – 1963	Aerialite Reels. 1930 – 1939 No 8915 – 3″, 3½″, 4″, 5″. Aerialite. 1933 – 1939 No 8929 – 3″. Aerialite Fly Reel. No 8930 – 4″. Aerialite Surf Casting Reel. No 8916 – 4″. Aerialite Sea Reel. 1933 – 1949 No 8922 – 2¾″. Better quality than Boys reels. No 8918 – 1¾″ and 2¼″. Aerialite Boys. No 8926 – 3¾″. Swimming Reel.

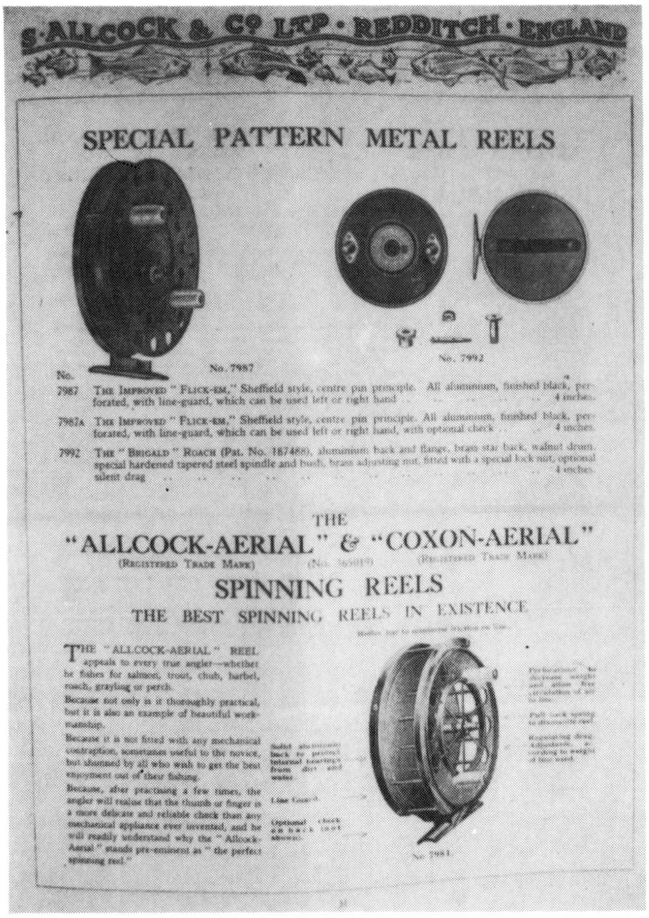

Circa	Model
	New models/numbers were introduced 1949/1950. 1949 – c.1961 No B145 – 3¼″. 1949 – 1963 No B180/B181 – 4″, 5″. 1950 – 1953 No B115 – 3″. 1950 – 1957 No B110 – 2¾″. 1950 – c.1960 No C705 – 4″. 1950 – 1963 No B120 – 3¾″. No C815 3¾″.
1930 – 1947	Trout & Salmon No 8000 3″. Became 'The Fraser' 1935 – 1947.
1930 – 1961	Marvel No 8927 – 3″, 3½″, 4″, (4½″ 1931). Became C765, 1947 – 1961. Sizes 3″, 3¼″, 3½″, 3¾″, 4″. Gilmour No 7995 – 3½″. From 1937 – 3¼″. Became C760 1947 – 1961 – 3¼″, 3½″, 3¾″.

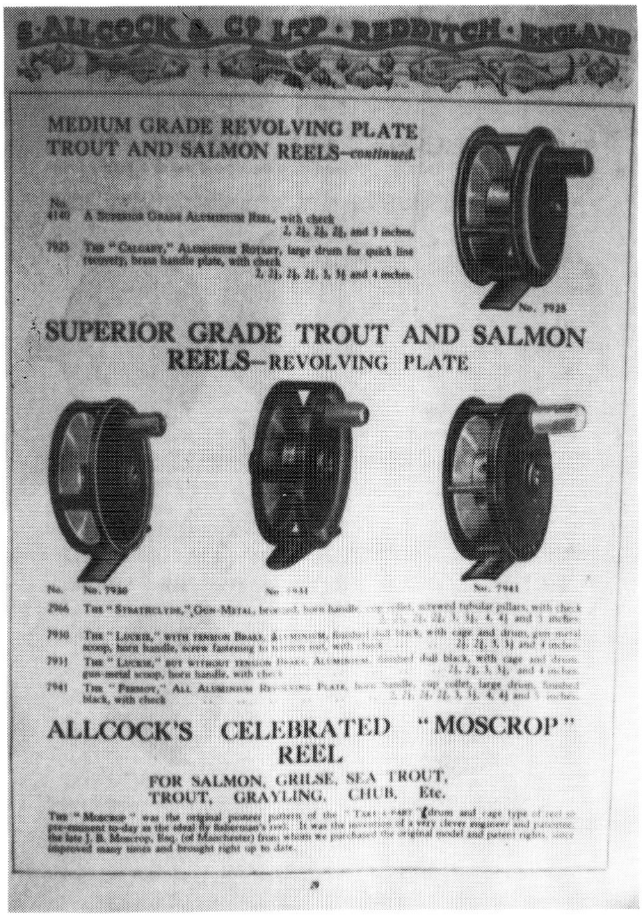

Circa	Model
1932 – 1936	Barton No 4134A – 3½″.
1932 – 1937	Facile No 8924 – 4″.
1932 – 1947	Bell Sea Reel No 8934 – 6″. Duplex No 8937. By 1937 Model No 3.
1933 – 1957	Allcock's Stanley No 8931. Became B150 from 1947 and described as 'Improved Allcock's Stanley' in 1950s.
1933 – 1962	Black Knight No 8933, 2½″, 2¾″, 3″, 3¼″.
1958 – 1962	No B265. Black Knight (heavily perforated).
1933 – 1965	Easicast No 8928 – 4″. Also 3½″ from 1935. Became Improved Easicast in 1937. In c.1947 described as Improved

Circa	Model
	Easicast No 3, No C810 – 3¾″ and in 1963 the reel number changed to B250.
1936 – 1947	Stockbridge 3⅛″, 3⅜″, 4″. Dovedale No 8943 – 3⅛″, 3⅜″.
1937	Ross No 8938 and 8939.
1937 – 1939	South African No 8921. Duches 8923. Filey. Salar No 9032 – 4″, 4½″.
1937 – 1947	Tunny Reel – a balance handle multiplier.
1937 – 1962	Felton Crosswind No 9027 and Junior Model No 9027A. In 1950 became No C790 No 2 Model and in 1955 – No C791, changing again in the 1960s to C792.
1939	Kennett No 9050 – 3½″.
1939 – 1949	Teme – 2¾″, 3″, 3¼″.
1949	Kastilite No C770.
1949 – 1956	Superb No C775. Became Silver Superb in 1951.
1949 – 1958	Viking No C805 3¾″. Also 4½″ from 1955
1949 – 1961	Duco No C780, 1955/6 – C780 and C781 Duco 'B'. 1957 only C781.
1950 – 1961	Gildex No C820. From 1955 No C821 – 2″.
1955 – 1957	Lucky Strike C701 – 4″.
1958 – 1961	Kasteasy. Allcock reels in the early 1960s were mainly imported and included – Penn – Kirkodo – Dam – Commodore – Leviatham C600 – Seymour – Windex C410 and C412 – Quick Super C184 – Record Breaker – Intrepid Surfcaster – Silver Knight – Sea Knight – Sea Boy C826 – Baymaster C830 – Delmar C833 – Beachmaster C832.

ALLCOCK LURES

The Allcock company sold a large number of lures, and the popular models, which appeared in the company catalogues are illustrated with the approximate production years listed, using the same method as for reels.

Circa	Model
1866 – 1881	Gudgeon No 84 (similar Gudgeon appeared in 1921 as No 7225).
1866	Gutta Percha Trout Bait No 83.
1866 – 1890	Trout Minnow No 333.
1866 – 1900	Dace Glass Eye No 332. (Became No 863). Flexible No 82. Protean No 294B. Glass No 327. Allies Pectoral No 83½.
1866 – 1940	Devon No 392.
1871 – 1881	Gilt and Silvered No 541. Without Tail No 578. Brass No 379.
1871 – 1886	Professor No 640.
1871 – 1900	Glass No 327 and No 328.
1871 – 1911	Phantom No 840.
1871 – 1924	Caledonian No 537.
1882 – 1886	Jointed Wriggler Bait No 999.
1882 – 1920	Nickel Plated No 930.
1882 – 1900	The Pearl No 281. Silver Plaited Bait No 731. Gilt and Plaited Bait No 732.
1882 – 1911	Cleopatra Jointed Bait No 1005.
1887 – 1900	Dace Glass Eye No 863. Acme Bait No 1119. Hollow Plaited Spinning Bait No 1144. Superior Flexible Jointed No 1080. Flat Metal Bait No 100 Flat Metal Bait No 1068.
1887 – 1900	Dace Bait No 1112.
1887 – 1911	Windsor Bee No 1115.

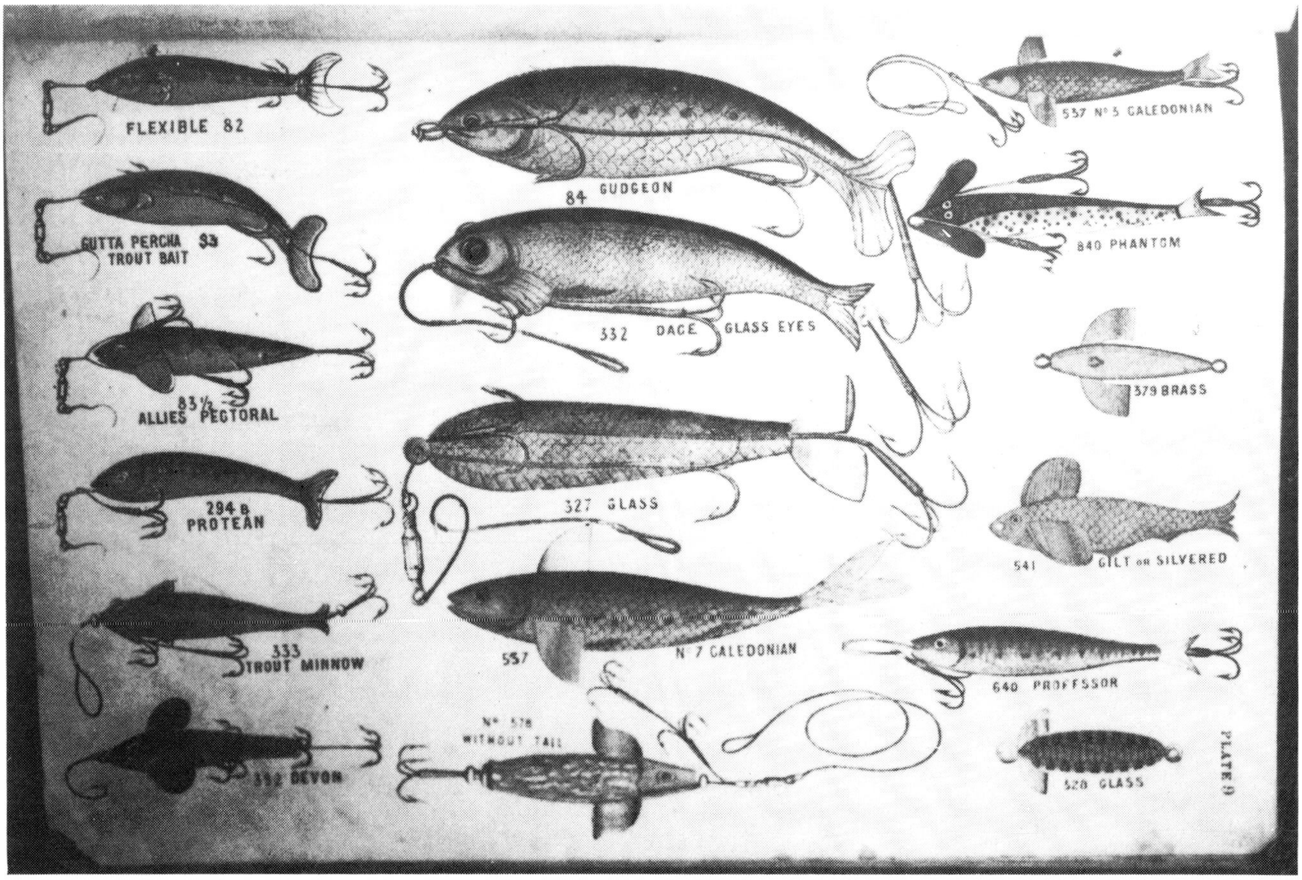

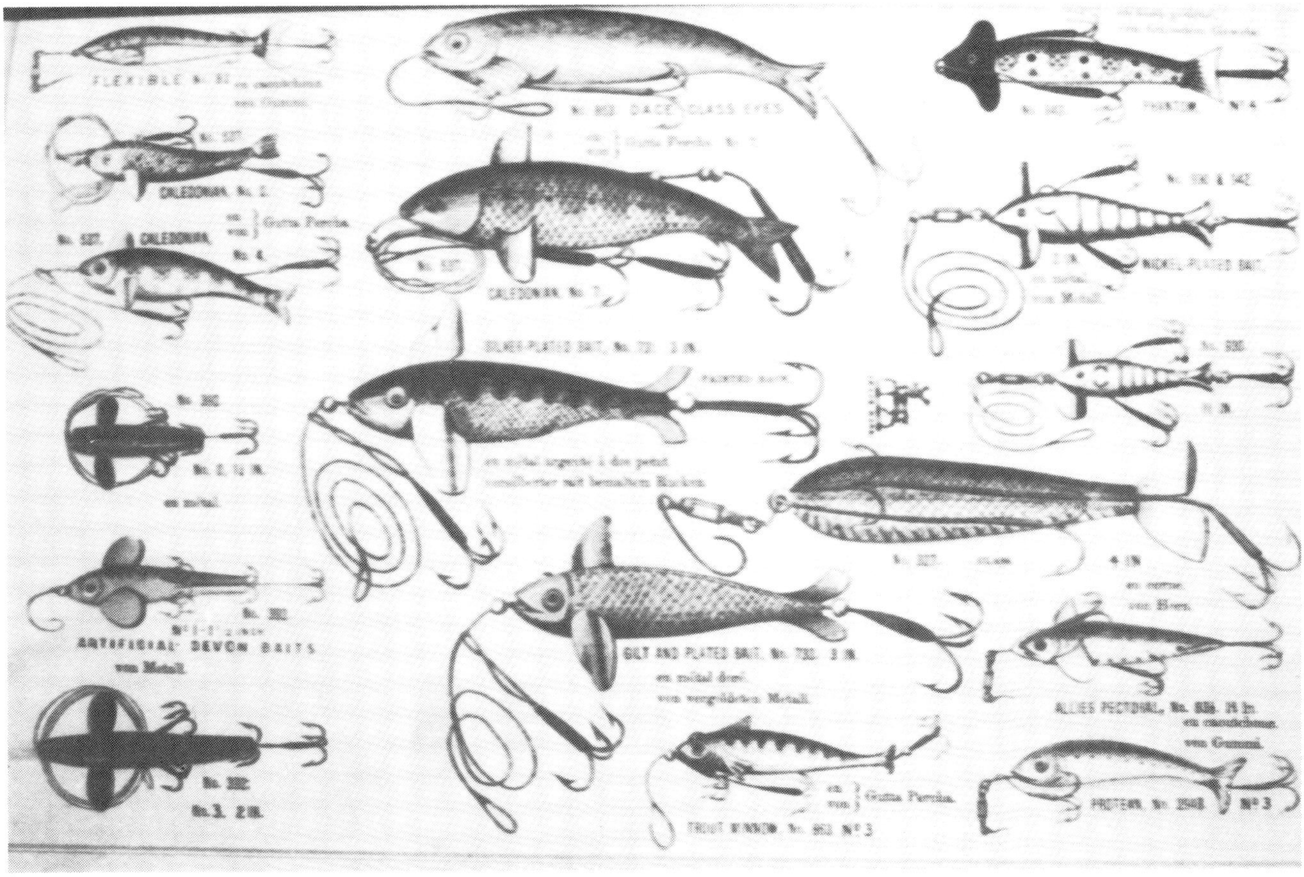
CALEDONIAN, No. 7.
SILVER-PLATED BAIT, No. 731. 3 IN.
ARTIFICIAL DEVON BAITS
GILT AND PLATED BAIT, No. 732. 3 IN.
TROUT MINNOW
NICKEL-PLATED BAIT.
PHANTOM
ALLIES PECTORAL
PROTEAN

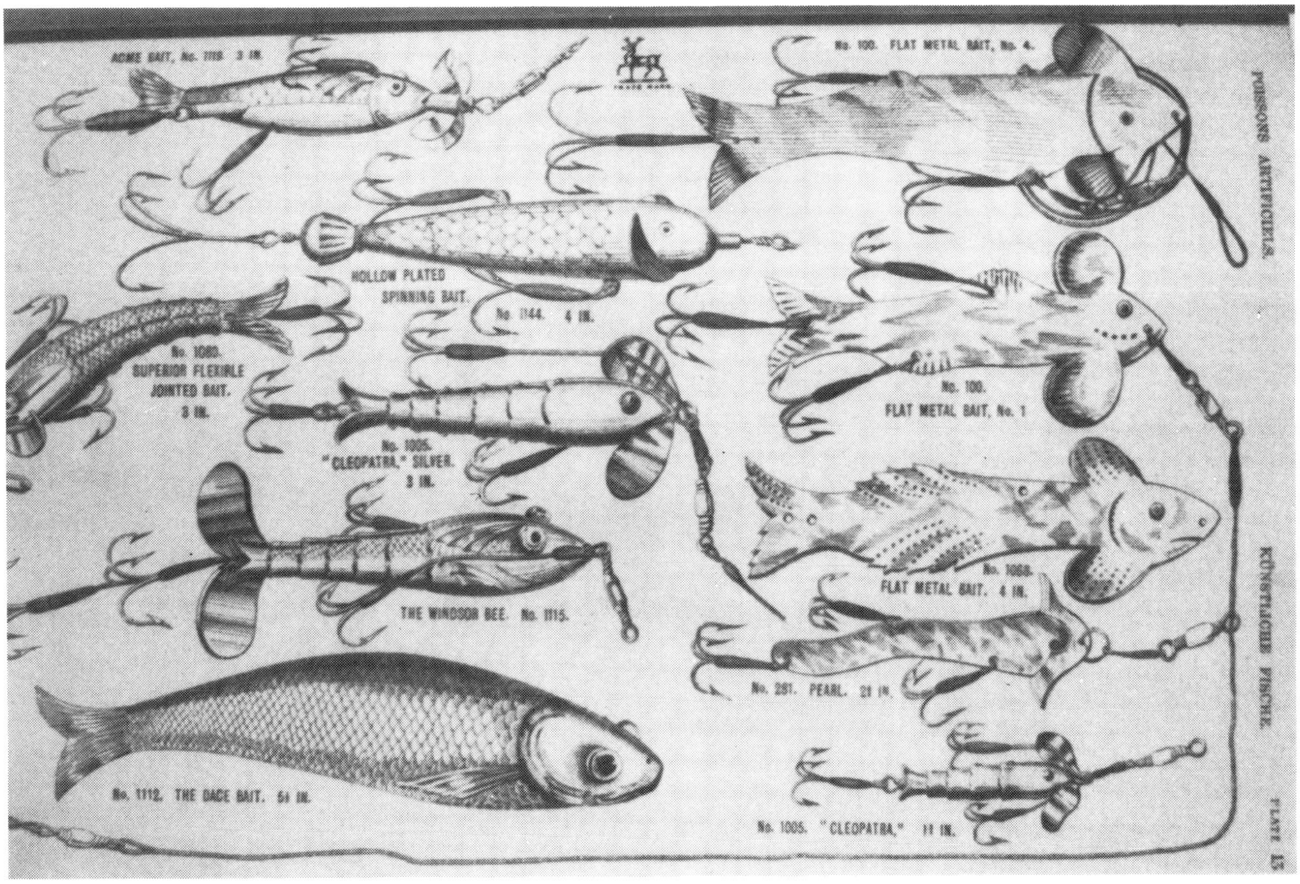
ACME BAIT, No. 778. 3 IN.
No. 100. FLAT METAL BAIT, No. 4.
POISSONS ARTIFICIELS.
HOLLOW PLATED SPINNING BAIT.
No. 1144. 4 IN.
No. 1080. SUPERIOR FLEXIBLE JOINTED BAIT. 3 IN.
No. 100. FLAT METAL BAIT, No. 1
No. 1005. "CLEOPATRA," SILVER. 3 IN.
KÜNSTLICHE FISCHE.
No. 1068. FLAT METAL BAIT. 4 IN.
THE WINDSOR BEE. No. 1115.
No. 281. PEARL. 2½ IN.
No. 1112. THE DACE BAIT. 5½ IN.
No. 1005. "CLEOPATRA," 1½ IN.
PLATE 13

Circa	Model
1901 – 1906	Transparent Quill Devon No 2667. Featherweight Devon No 3571. Swivel Tail No 2029.
1901 – 1911	Plunger No 3712. Heavy Devon No 2758.
1901 – 1920	Paragon No 732.
1901 – 1924	Kill Devel Devon No 2715.
1901 – 1930	Quill Minnow No 2041.
1907 – 1911	A.1. Phantom. Tin Baits No 575A. Geen's Spiral Bait No 2917.
1907 – 1920	Cartman No 3724. Enaka Phantom No 3782.
1907 – 1924	Whitebait Phantom No 2157.
1907 – 1939	Clipper No 1065.

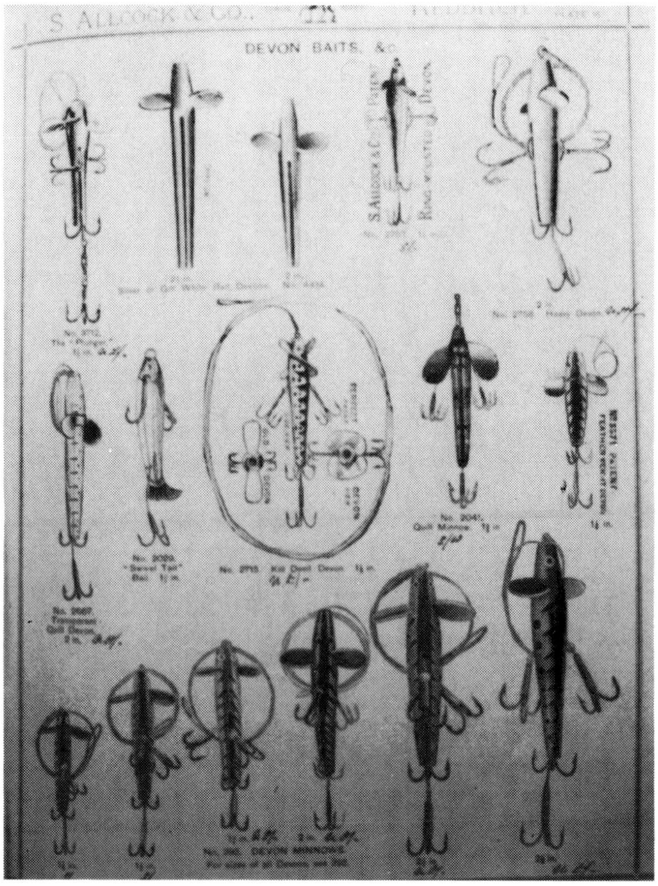

Insects 1907 – 1924
1. Locust
2. Grub
3. Caterpillar
4. Wasp
5. Grasshopper
6. Bumblebee
7. Ladybird
8. Worm
9. Housefly
10. Mayfly
11. Fernfly
12. Beetle
13. Cricket
14. Water Beetle
15. Bluebottle
16. Coch-y-Bondhu

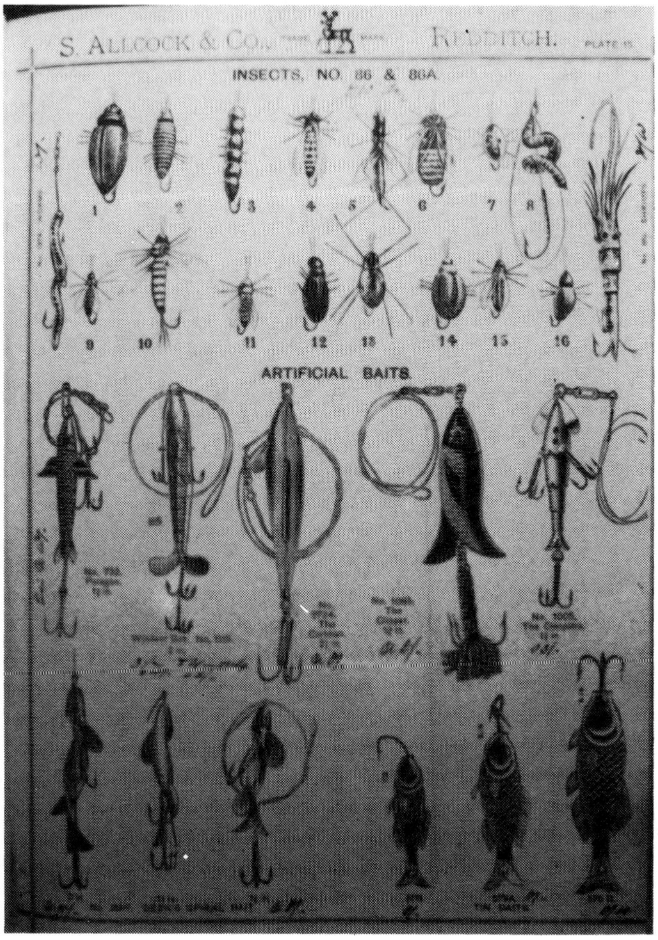

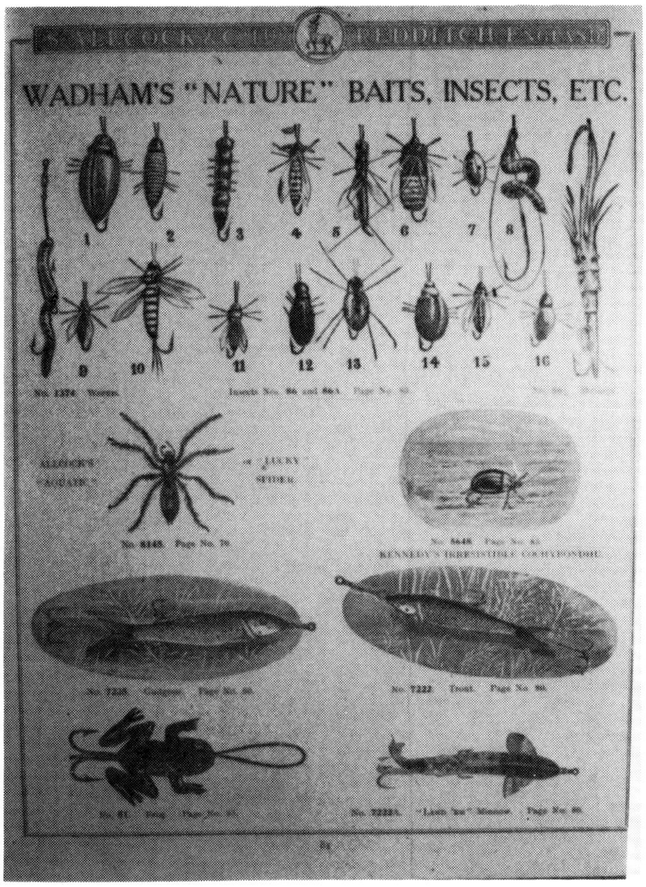

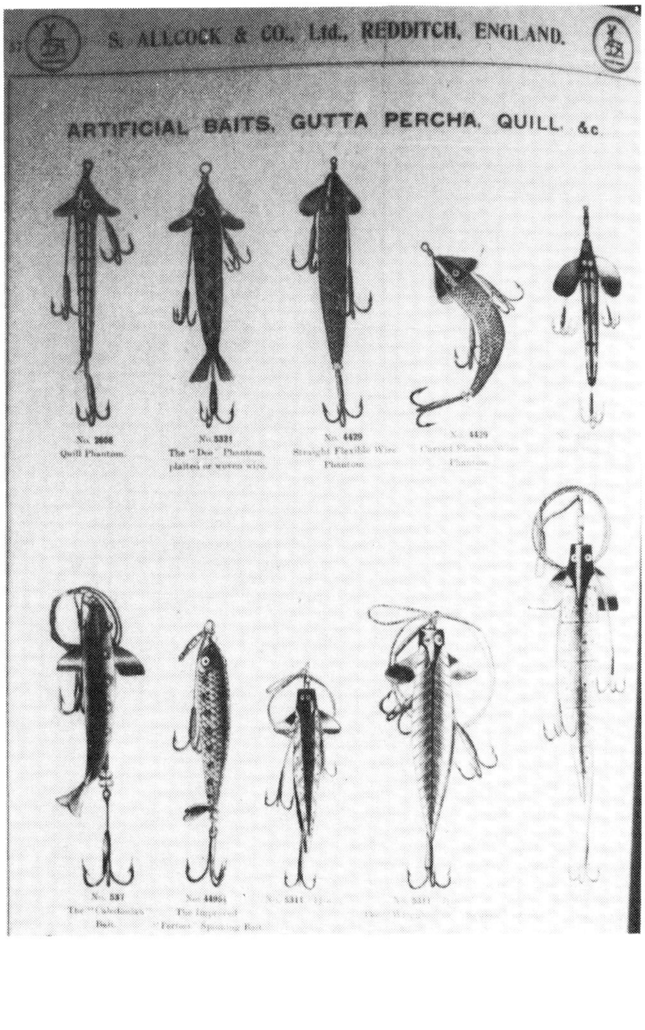

Circa	Model
1907 – 1920	Quill Phantom No 2608.
1912 – 1914	Mermaid Wooden Devon Minnow. Nos 7207 and 7209.
1912 – 1920	Improved Perfect Spinning Bait No 4495½. Dee Phantom No 5321. Straight Flexible Wire Phantom No 4429 and Curved Flexible Wire Phantom.
1912 – 1924	Frog No 81.
1912 – 1939	Wriggler or Wagtail No 5311.
1915 – 1924	Gudgeon No 7225. Trout No 7222. Land-em Minnow No 7222A. Kennedy's Irresistible Cochybondhu No 5648.
1921 – 1924	Lucky Spider No 8145.

ALLCOCK LURES OF THE 1930s

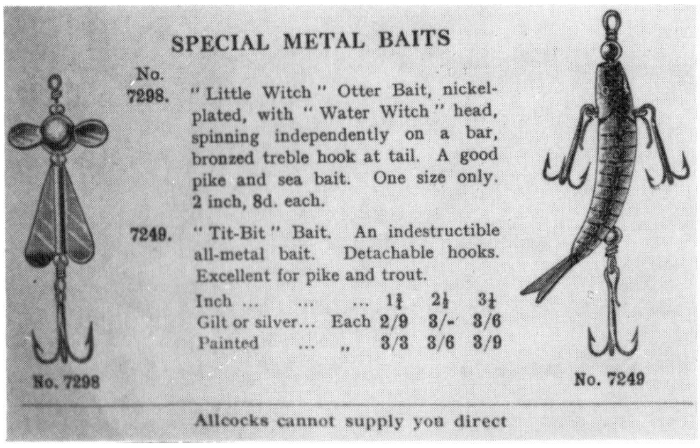

SPECIAL METAL BAITS

No. 7298. "Little Witch" Otter Bait, nickel-plated, with "Water Witch" head, spinning independently on a bar, bronzed treble hook at tail. A good pike and sea bait. One size only. 2 inch, 8d. each.

7249. "Tit-Bit" Bait. An indestructible all-metal bait. Detachable hooks. Excellent for pike and trout.

Inch	$1\frac{3}{4}$	$2\frac{1}{2}$	$3\frac{1}{4}$
Gilt or silver... Each	2/9	3/-	3/6
Painted ... „	3/3	3/6	3/9

No. 7298 No. 7249

Allcocks cannot supply you direct

Tit-Bit No 7249 1930-1939

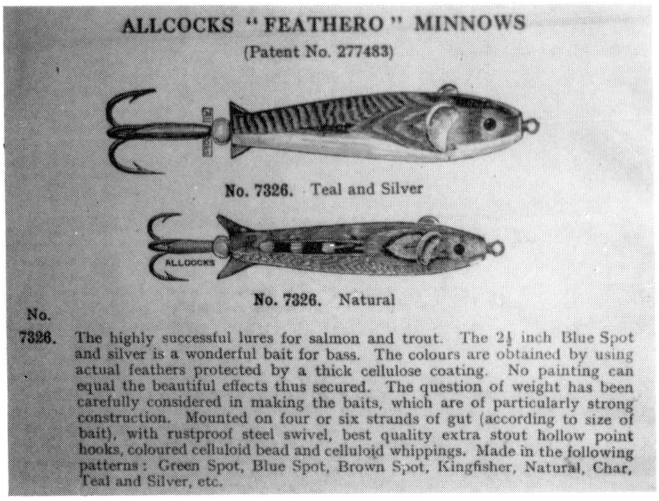

ALLCOCKS "FEATHERO" MINNOWS

(Patent No. 277483)

No. 7326. Teal and Silver

No. 7326. Natural

No. 7326. The highly successful lures for salmon and trout. The $2\frac{1}{2}$ inch Blue Spot and silver is a wonderful bait for bass. The colours are obtained by using actual feathers protected by a thick cellulose coating. No painting can equal the beautiful effects thus secured. The question of weight has been carefully considered in making the baits, which are of particularly strong construction. Mounted on four or six strands of gut (according to size of bait), with rustproof steel swivel, best quality extra stout hollow point hooks, coloured celluloid bead and celluloid whippings. Made in the following patterns: Green Spot, Blue Spot, Brown Spot, Kingfisher, Natural, Char, Teal and Silver, etc.

1933-1939

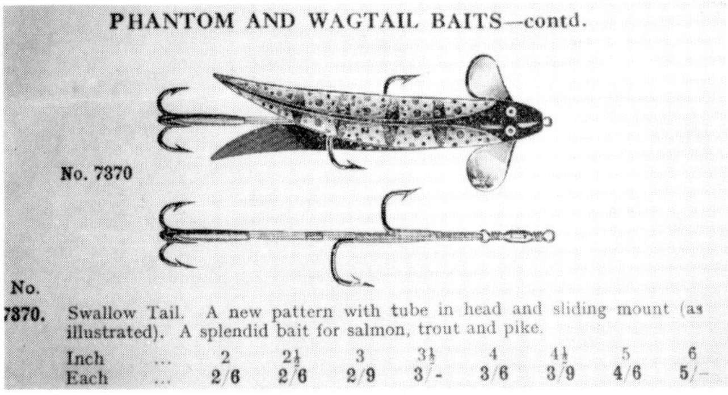

PHANTOM AND WAGTAIL BAITS—contd.

No. 7370

No. 7370. Swallow Tail. A new pattern with tube in head and sliding mount (as illustrated). A splendid bait for salmon, trout and pike.

Inch ...	2	$2\frac{1}{2}$	3	$3\frac{1}{2}$	4	$4\frac{1}{2}$	5	6
Each ...	2/6	2/6	2/9	3/-	3/6	3/9	4/6	5/-

1935-1939

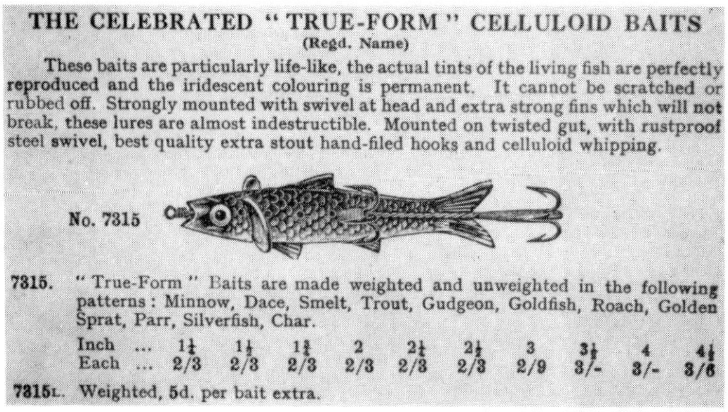

THE CELEBRATED "TRUE-FORM" CELLULOID BAITS

(Regd. Name)

These baits are particularly life-like, the actual tints of the living fish are perfectly reproduced and the iridescent colouring is permanent. It cannot be scratched or rubbed off. Strongly mounted with swivel at head and extra strong fins which will not break, these lures are almost indestructible. Mounted on twisted gut, with rustproof steel swivel, best quality extra stout hand-filed hooks and celluloid whipping.

No. 7315

7315. "True-Form" Baits are made weighted and unweighted in the following patterns: Minnow, Dace, Smelt, Trout, Gudgeon, Goldfish, Roach, Golden Sprat, Parr, Silverfish, Char.

Inch ...	$1\frac{1}{4}$	$1\frac{1}{2}$	$1\frac{3}{4}$	2	$2\frac{1}{4}$	$2\frac{1}{2}$	3	$3\frac{1}{2}$	4	$4\frac{1}{2}$
Each ...	2/3	2/3	2/3	2/3	2/3	2/3	2/9	3/-	3/-	3/6

7315L. Weighted, 5d. per bait extra.

1933-1939

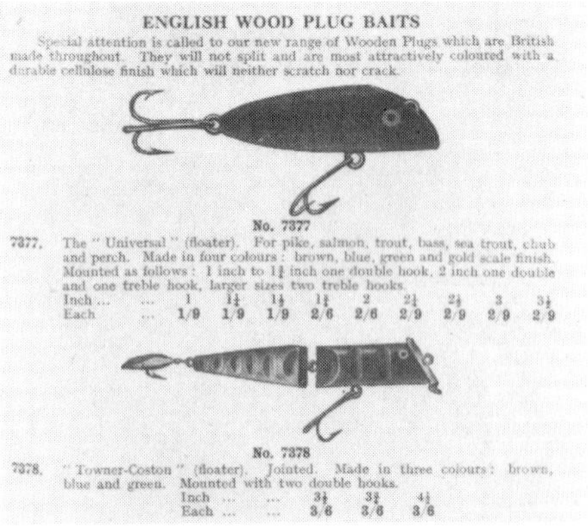

ENGLISH WOOD PLUG BAITS

Special attention is called to our new range of Wooden Plugs which are British made throughout. They will not split and are most attractively coloured with a durable cellulose finish which will neither scratch nor crack.

No. 7377

7377. The "Universal" (floater). For pike, salmon, trout, bass, sea trout, chub and perch. Made in four colours: brown, blue, green and gold scale finish. Mounted as follows: 1 inch to $1\frac{3}{4}$ inch one double hook, 2 inch one double and one treble hook, larger sizes two treble hooks.

Inch	1	$1\frac{1}{4}$	$1\frac{1}{2}$	$1\frac{3}{4}$	2	$2\frac{1}{4}$	$2\frac{1}{2}$	3	$3\frac{1}{2}$
Each ...	1/9	1/9	1/9	2/6	2/6	2/9	2/9	2/9	2/9

No. 7378

7378. "Towner-Coston" (floater). Jointed. Made in three colours: brown, blue and green. Mounted with two double hooks.

Inch	$3\frac{1}{4}$	$3\frac{3}{4}$	$4\frac{1}{2}$
Each	3/6	3/6	3/6

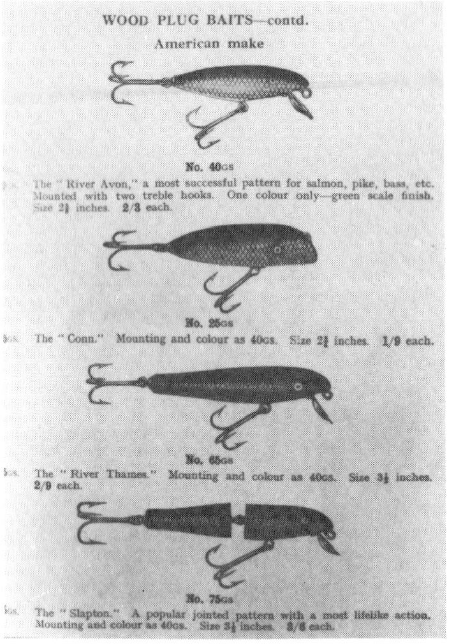

WOOD PLUG BAITS—contd.

American make

No. 40GS

The "River Avon," a most successful pattern for salmon, pike, bass, etc. Mounted with two treble hooks. One colour only—green scale finish. Size $2\frac{1}{2}$ inches. 2/3 each.

No. 25GS

The "Conn." Mounting and colour as 40GS. Size $2\frac{3}{4}$ inches. 1/9 each.

No. 65GS

The "River Thames." Mounting and colour as 40GS. Size $3\frac{1}{2}$ inches. 2/9 each.

No. 75GS

The "Slapton." A popular jointed pattern with a most lifelike action. Mounting and colour as 40GS. Size $3\frac{1}{2}$ inches. 3/6 each.

1937-1957

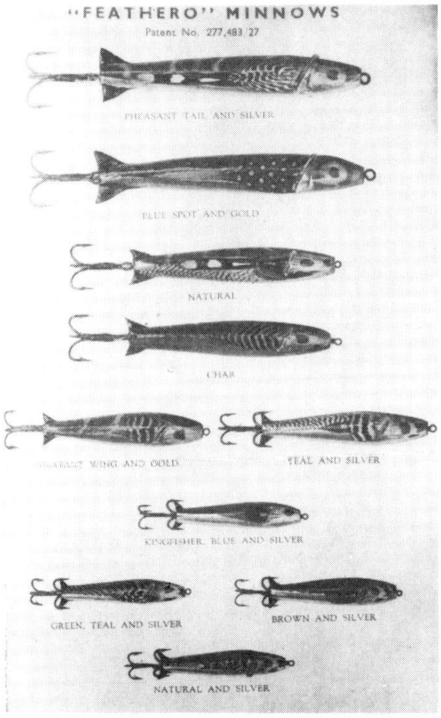

Nevison Range 1939-1960's

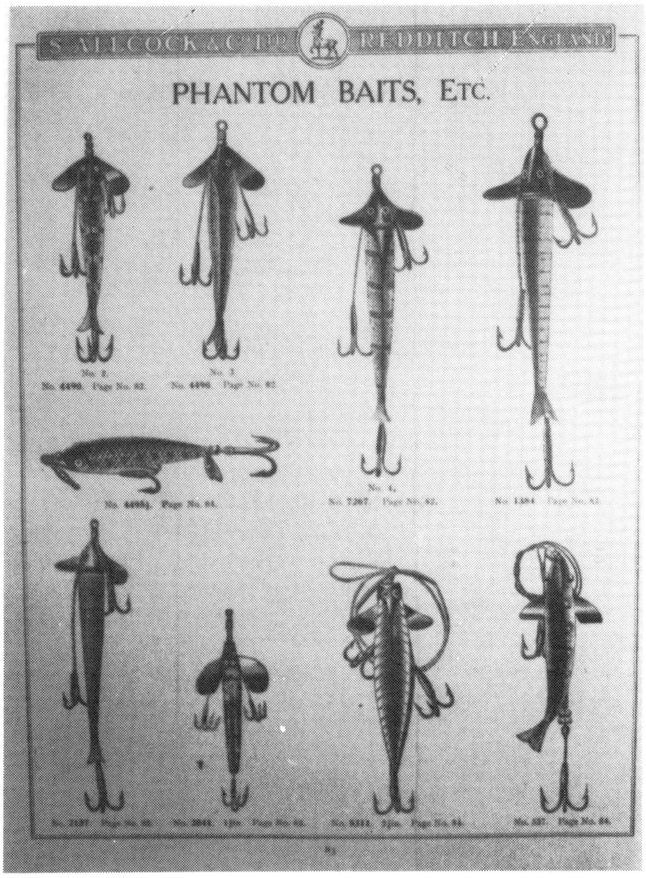

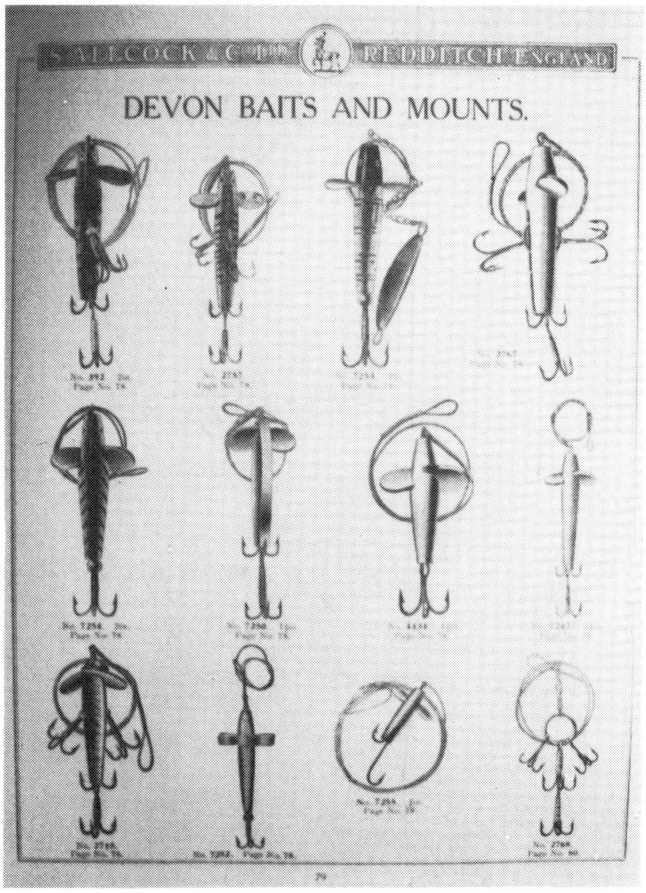

Circa	**Model**
1907 – 1924	Best Soleskin No 1384.
1907 – 1932	Silk Phantom No 4490.
1907 – 1939	Canvas Phantom No 7267. Sun Ray Slotless Devon Minnow No 7250. Wye Favorite Aluminium Slotless No 7254. Lite Waite Aluminium Slotless No 7247. Little Devon Aluminium Slotless No 7255. 'XL' Devon Aluminium Slotless No 4434. The Slotness Devon Minnows continued up to the 1960s with a different number classification.
1915 – 1924	Best Silk White Bait No 2157 Whitney Wood Devon No 7253.

ALNWICK FISHING TACKLE TRADERS

1872 – current	Hardy Bros. (see Hardy Bros. Chapter).
	Lesser known makers were listed in trade directories as follows:
c.1911 – 1940	William Henry Dingley, Climax Reel Works. W Dingley was a Hardy Bros employee who started in business on his own account and usually stamped his reels with a 'D' inside.
1914 –	Nettleship & Co., Howick St.
1921 –	Duns & Stephenson, Howick St.
1929 – 1938	J A Walker & Co., Howick St.
1938 –	Edminson Bros., Howick St.
1921 – 1968	Walker Bampton, Northern Rod & Reel Works, Hotspur Place, Alnwick.
1938 –	John Stephenson, St. Michaels Pant (A 'Pant' was a water fountain for public use).
1968 –	Douglas Bell Ltd., Bondgate House, 69-72 Bondgate.

Cummins of Bishop Auckland 1857-1960

William J Cummins started trading as a printer, bookbinder, stationer and fishing tackle maker at Fore Bondgate, and his private residence was Clarence Villas.

1865 – 1897 Traded from 53 Market Place.
1890 – 1897 Also proprietor of the *Aukland Times and Herald.* The founder must have died soon after the turn of the century, as from 1902 only his wife is listed, followed later by male members of the family, probably sons, registered at Clarence Villas. The firm continued to trade as W F Cummins but from 1902 there was a new business address at 13 Newgate St. Other listings include:

1914 Charles E Cummins – Clarence House.
1921 Charles E Cummins and Alfred P Cummins.
1954 W Cummins Ltd.
They do not appear in trade lists after 1960.

Doughty c. 1756-1801

Fish & Fly, Within Minster Gate, York. (Wholesale & Retail)

John Doughty was selling a wide range of tackle including 'Pike Wheels', lines of Indian Weed, silkworm gut and horse-hair, together with a wide range of flies, and plugs, including artificial mice. He placed an advertisement in the *York Courant* on June 22nd 1756 listing all manner of tackle and promised 'Any gentleman on sending his orders by carrier or News-Man, will have the same carefully observed, and as well used, as if he had presented himself'. It is interesting to note that his services extended to mending and mounting fans and replacing spouts and handles on teapots and mugs, showing that things must have had a much longer life than they could have expected in today's 'throw away' society.

By 1786, his son Joseph Doughty had succeeded him and had extended the fishing tackle business to the manufacture of umbrellas and the sale of toys, hygrometers, barometers, thermometers, also pen knives, powder flasks & combs. He put out an advertisement on August 1st 1786, similar to the early one of his father but also offered winches and artificial frogs as well as mice. In 1798 he was trading from Coney St, where he continued up to his death in 1801.

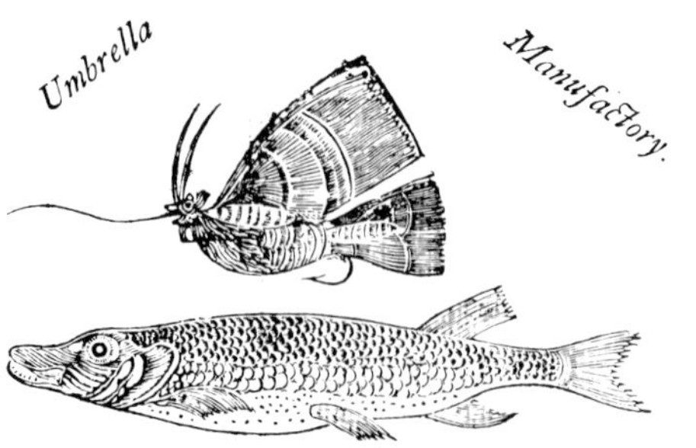

TO ALL LOVERS OF ANGLING.

JOSEPH DOUGHTY

At the FISH and FLY, within the MINSTER-GATES, YORK,

Makes all Sorts of Fiſhing Rods, and all Manner of the beſt Fiſhing Tackle, and the Right KIRBIE Hooks, ſo juſtly admired beyond others for Goodneſs of Temper and Strength. Fiſhing and Fowling Nets made to any Dimentions.

The ANGLER's COMPANION, *being an Explanation of the whole Art of Angling; wherein is ſhewn at one View the Harbours, Seaſons, and Depths for Catching all Sorts of Fiſh uſually Angled for: Alſo various Baits for each, ſo digeſted as to contain the whole of all the Treatiſes ever wrote on the Subject.*

Names	Where found.	Seaſon	Ti. to ang.	Depth from Ground	Proper Baits. Flies. No.	Paſtes No.	Worms No.	Fiſh and Inſects No. 8.
Bream	rough ſtr. river or mid pond	Apr. to Mich	S. riſe to 9 3 to S. ſet	touch ground	—	1 5	1234567	
Barbel	gravel bank in currents under bridges	Apr. to Aug.	very early or late.	ditto	—	2	2 6 7	—
Bleak	ſandy bottom deep rivers, ſhip ſterns*	May to Oct.	all day	6 inches from bottom	1 2	2	2 3 8	—
Carp	ſtill deep mud bottom pond or river	May to Aug.	S. riſe to 9 3 to S. ſet	3 inches from bottom hot weather mid. water	—	1 3 4	1 2 3 4 7	—
Chub or Chevin	ditto.	May to Dec.	ditto.	ditto.	1 2 3 4 5	2	123456789	7 8 9
Dace	ſandy bottom deep river, ſhip ſterns*	May to Oct.	all day	6 to 12 inch. from bot. and top	ditto.	3 4	12345 & 8	—
Eel	ſandy bottom deep rivers, and ponds	Mar. to Mic	day & night	ditto.	—	—	6 7 8	1 2 3 4
Gudgeon	gravel ſhoals	May to Oct.	all day	near or on ground	—	3 4	2 8	—
Pike	near clay banks	All the year	ditto.	mid water	with a ſtrong line and float and ſnaphook from those			1 2 3 4 5 6 7
Pearch	river in ſtream / pond deepeſt pt — gravel or weedy bottom	May to Aug. / Aug. to May	S. riſe to 10 2 to S. ſet / mid. day	ditto / 6 inches from bottom	2	1	3 5 7 8	1 6
Pope	deep holes in rivers	May to Oct.	all day	ditto	5	—	all	—
Roach	ſandy bottom deep river, ſhips ſterns*	May to Oct.	ditto.	6 to 12 inches	1 2 4 5	3 4	ditto	7 8 9
Salmon	deep rivers	Mar. to Sept.	6 to 9 3 to 6	mid way to the bottom	all large	—	1 5 6 7	1
Smelts	ſhips ſterns * and docks	Apr. to Oct.	all day	mid way to bottom variable	all ſmall	—	1 2 5	bits of ſmelts
Trout	purling ſtream and eddies of ſtony bottom river	Mar. to Mich	ditto.	cold wea. 6 inches to 9 hot wea. top to mid. wa.	1 2 3 4 5	—	1 2 5 to 8	1 8
Tench	mud bottom river or pond	All the year	S. riſe to 9 3 to S. ſet	cold wea. 3 in. from bot. hot wea. mid. water	—	1 3 4	134567	—
Umber or Grayling	clay bottom, ſwift ſtream	All the year	all day	cold wea. 6 to 9 inch. hot wea. top to mid. wa.	1 2 3 4 5	—	12345678	1 8

* *To fiſh at ſterns let the bait ſink two or three yards; in this a paternoſter line is commonly uſed, that is, five or ſix hooks [illegible] five inches diſtance; bait as above.*

FISH and INSECTS.

1. Minnow. 2. Gudgeon. 3. Roach. 4. Dace. 5. Smelt. 6 Yellow-Frog. 7. Snail Slit. 8. Graſshopper. 9. Waſp or Bee-grubs.

FLIES.

1. Stone-fly, found under hollow ſtones at the ſide of rivers, is of a brown colour, with yellow ſtreaks on the back and belly, has large wings, and in ſeaſon from April to July.

2. Green-drake, found among ſtones by river ſides, has a yellow body ribb'd with green, is long and ſlender, with wings like a butter-fly, his tail turns on his back, and from May to Midſummer is very good.

3. Oak-fly, found in the body of an old oak or aſh, with its head downwards, is of a brown colour, and excellent from May to September; for trout, put a cod-bait or gentle on the point, and let it ſink a few inches in clear water.

4. Palmer-fly, or worm, found on leaves of plants, is commonly called a caterpillar, and when it comes to a fly is excellent for trout.

5. Ant-fly, found in ant-hills from June to September.

PASTES.

1. Take the blood of ſheeps hearts, and mix it with honey and flower worked to a proper conſiſtence.

2. Take old cheeſe grated, a little butter ſufficient to work it, and colour it with ſaffron; in winter uſe ruſty bacon inſtead of butter.

3. Crumbs of bread chew'd or work'd with honey (or ſugar) moiſtened with gum-ivy water.

4. Bread chew'd and work'd in the hand till ſtiff. And Grains or boil'd Wheat.

Deſcription of proper WORMS *for* BAITS.

1. The Earth-bob, found in ſandy ground after ploughing; it is white, with a red head, and bigger than a gentle. Another is found in heathy ground, with a black or blue head. Keep them in an earthen veſſel well covered, and a ſufficient quantity of the mould they harbour in. They are excellent from April to November.

2. Gentles, to be had from putrid fleſh; let them lie in wheat bran a few days before uſed.

3. Flag-worms, found in the roots of flags; they are of a pale yellow colour, are longer and thinner than a gentle, and muſt be ſcoured like them.

4. Cow-turd-bob, or Clap-bait, found under a cow-turd from May to Michaelmas; it is like a gentle, but larger. Keep it in its native earth like the Earth-bob.

5. Cadis-worm, or Cod-bait, found under looſe ſtones in ſhallow rivers; they are yellow, bigger than a gentle, with a black or blue head, and are in ſeaſon from April to July. Keep them in flannel bags.

6. Lob-worm, found in gardens; it is very large, and has a red head, a ſtreak down the back, and a flat broad tail.

7. Marſh-worms, found in marſhy ground. Keep them in moſs ten days before you uſe them; their colour is a bluiſh red, and are a good bait from March to Michaelmas.

8. Brandlings, Red-worms, or Blood-worms, found in rotten dunghills and tanners bark; they are ſmall red worms, [illegible] all fiſh, have ſometimes a yellow tail, and are called [illegible] tail.

9. Beaſt-brains, and the pith of the back-bone.

N. B. Artificial Flies reſembling the Natural, may be had as above. And will direct what Tackle is proper for each Sort of Fiſhing.

PRICE THREE-PENCE.

Angler's Companion put out by Doughty

TO ALL LOVERS OF ANGLING
JOHN DOUGHTY at the Fish and Fly within Minster Gates, York, makes and sells by wholesale and retail, all sorts of fishing rods, and all manner of best fishing tackle; and makes the best sorts of fishing hooks, much admired for the finest of wire and goodness of temper; the best sort of spring snap hooks for pike; sells the right Kirby hooks and all other sorts of fishing hooks.

Upon the said best hooks makes artificial mice for pike and chevin; the best sorts of artificial flies for pike, salmon and trout; and all other sorts of artificial flies, greatly admired by all gentlemen who have made use of them; and sells Indian weed commonly called Grass, the only thing for trout and carp fishing, when soaked half an hour before used. Sells the fine silk worm gut, first come over, which is as fine as a hair and as strong as six, used and approved of by several anglers for fly fishing etc. Likewise curious hair lines, any length, without a knot, for pike and salmon angling; Pike-wheels, swivels, night-lines for live or dead baits; landing nets and hooks; fishing stools and many other curiosities in the way of angling; also trunks for shooting darts and pellets. Any gentleman, on sending his order by carrier or news-man will have the same carefully observed, and as well used, as if present himself.

N.B. At the same place fan sticks are mended and mounted; spouts and handles put on tea-pots, mugs etc and china mended after the newest and best methods.

To all Lovers of ANGLING.

JOHN DOUGHTY, at the Fiſh and Fly within the Minſter-Gates, York, makes and ſells, by Wholeſale and Retale, all Sorts of Fiſhing Rods, and all Manner of the beſt Fiſhing Tackle; and makes the beſt Sort of Fiſhing Hooks, much admired for the Fineneſs of Wire and Goodneſs of Temper; the beſt Sort of Spring Snap-Hooks for Pike; ſells the right Kirby's Hooks, and all other Sorts of Fiſhing Hooks.

Upon the ſaid beſt Hooks makes artificial Mice for Pike and Chevin; the beſt Sort of artificial Flies for Pike, Salmon, and Trout; and all other Sorts of artificial Flies, greatly admired by all Gentlemen who have made Uſe of them; and ſells the Indian Weed, commonly called Graſs, the only Thing for Trout and Carp Fiſhing, when ſoaked half an Hour before uſed.

Sells the fine Silk Worm Gut, freſh come over, which is as fine as a Hair, and as ſtrong as ſix, uſed and approved of by ſeveral Anglers for Fly-ing Fiſh, &c. Likewiſe makes curious Hair Lines, any Length, without a Knot, for Pike and Salmon Angling; Pike-Wheels, Swivels, Night-Lines for live or dead Baits; Landing Nets and Hooks; Fiſhing Stools, and many other Curioſities in the Way of Angling; alſo Trunks for ſhooting Darts and Pellets.

Any Gentleman, on ſending his Order by Carrier or News-Man, will have the ſame carefully obſerved, and as well uſed as if preſent himſelf.

N. B. At the ſame Place Fanſticks are mended and mounted; Spouts and Handles put on Tea-Pots, Mugs, &c. and China mended after the neweſt and beſt Methods.

Advertisement in York Courant 22nd June, 1756

FISHING TACKLE, WALKING STICK, and UMBRELLA MANUFACTORY.

JOSEPH DOUGHTY,

(SON and SUCCESSOR to the late Mr. JOHN DOUGHTY)

At the FISH and FLY, MINSTER-GATES, YORK,

RETURNS his ſincere Thanks to his Friends for Favours received, and humbly takes this Method to acquaint the Nobility, Gentry, and others, that he carries on the above Buſineſſes in all their Branches, where they may be ſerved with the beſt of all Sorts of Fiſhing Tackle, viz. Rods, Silk and Hair Lines, Hooks, Winches, Menow Tackle, artificial Flies, Frogs, and Mice, Indian Weed, Silk-Worm Gut, Gimp; Landing, Trammel, Drag, Caſt, and Thief Nets—Bamboo, Wanghe, Dragon, and Ratan Canes—Walking Sticks and Whips—Umbrellas of all Sorts—Fans and Fan-Mounts—Hygrometers, Barometers, and Thermometers—Toys, Powder-Flaſks, Penknives, Combs, with numerous other Articles.

☞ Orders ſent by LADIES and GENTLEMEN will be gratefully attended to and gratefully received.

FISHING TACKLE
WALKING STICK and
UMBRELLA MAKER
JOSEPH DOUGHTY
(Son and successor to the late John Doughty)
At the Fish and Fly, Minster Gates, York.

Returns his sincere thanks to his friends for favours received and humbly takes this method to acquaint the nobility, gentry and others that he carries on the above business in all their branches, where they may be served with the best of all sorts of fishing tackle. Viz – rods, silk and hair lines, hooks, winches, minnow tackle, artificial flies, frogs and mice, Indian weed, silk worm gut, gimp, landing, trammel, drag, cast and keep nets – bamboo, wanghe, dragon and ratan canes – walking sticks and whips – umbrellas of all sorts – fans and fan mounts – hygrometers, barometers, thermometers – toys, powder-flasks, penknives, combs, with numerous other articles.

Orders sent by ladies and gentlemen will be carefully attended to and gratefully received.

Advertisement in York Courant 1st August, 1786

Charles Farlow 1840 – current

Charles Farlow started his fishing tackle business in 1840 at No 221 The Strand, trading as C Farlow. In 1852 the address was changed by the local authority to No 191 The Strand from where he continued to trade in his own name.

About 1885 he changed the title of his business to C Farlow & Co, and continued in that style up to 1894 when C Farlow & Co. Ltd. was adopted. In 1895 he died and was succeeded by two sons Charles Paas and John Ambrose who became joint governing directors.

The business continued to expand and in 1907 they acquired additional premises at 10 Charles St and the following year took in Charles Fitzroy Farlow who was the grandson of the founder. This new member of the family had been to Charterhouse, qualified as an engineer, and became Works Manager and Secretary. He was very enthusiastic, visiting the Paris casting tournament and demonstrating his newly designed Billiken reel which was recorded as casting a 1½ oz bait 40 yards and ½oz bait 50 yards or over, which were respectable distances at the time.

The lease on 191 The Strand ended in 1915 and the registered office was moved to 10 Charles St. Prior to the move, the company had purchased a piece of land in Croydon in 1911 to erect a factory. It is interesting to note a Minute in the Company records on October 3rd 1911 which stated that the cost of the land and the said factory should be redeemed by an annual payment of £50. In 1919 Charles Paas Farlow died and John Ambrose Farlow became sole Governor Director and Charles F Farlow was appointed to the Board as Managing Director.

In 1925 the company took a 21 years lease on No 11 Panton St to add to the established factory at Croydon and showroom in the West End. The Farlow catalogues, which had always been small pocket editions, became more sophisticated. They included articles and illustrations in both black and white and colour, and projected a more upmarket image. By 1931 the business was doing well enough to reward the great efforts and ideas of C F Farlow by increasing his salary to £700 per annum.

In 1932 his uncle J A Farlow died and C F Farlow became Chairman. He was destined to steer the company through its most difficult years of the thirties depression followed by the Second World War. On occasions he gave financial assistance from his assets, but by 1942 the factory had used all its old stock and was hardly able to function. It was placed on full war production and was working in this way when on March 27th 1944 a double tragedy struck. Charles Fitzroy Farlow died suddenly and his son Jack was killed on active service. The death of the head of the business caused the election of two ladies to the Board. One was Mrs Virginia Ruth Farlow, Jack's widow, who joined on October 18th 1844 and the other Mrs K M Lewis, the daughter of the late C F Farlow on June 10th 1945.

Farlow's sign

By 1950 Mrs V R Farlow was Chairman and outright owner of the company, by which time the manufacture of rods had ceased in order to concentrate on marketing. An agreement had been made with Walker Bampton of Alnwick to make rods under Farlow's name. A decision to sell the business was taken in 1957 and the sale was completed on August 1st of that year. It was purchased by Messrs Westley Richards, the well known gunmakers.

Mrs Farlow continued to work in the capacity of joint Managing Director until June 1960, when she retired and severed the Farlow connection with the firm after some 120 years of continuous family trading. For the next four years Westley Richards and Holland & Holland carried on the business at C Farlow's Fishing Tackle Department at 13 Bruton St, though for a while during that period Farlow's office and retail outlet was in Conduit St.

There was another change of ownership on February 1st 1964 when it was sold to the Drayton Group of 117 Old Broad St, London. After eight months the new proprietors moved the Farlow tackle business to a better site at No 5 Pall Mall.

The year 1964/5 brought an amalgamation of Farlow's with Messrs J S Sharpe of Aberdeen, who had a long history in the manufacture of split cane and greenheart rods. The following year the combined firm was sold to Mr A R Baxter and it became a subsidiary of his family company Shawfield Street Securities Ltd. Rationalisation for reasons of proximity to motorways and general convenience resulted in the head office and wholesale department being transferred to Cheltenham, while the factory continued to operate at John St, Aberdeen. The flagship of the company was the entrance to the Royal Opera Arcade in Pall Mall, from where it has continued to trade.

"Farlow's" in 1853

TACKLE OFFERED IN FARLOWS CATALOGUE OF 1846

Rods

BOTTOM RODS
2 Joint Hazel, Tin Ferrules 5d.
3 Joint Hazel, Tin Ferrules 9d.
2 Joint with Whalebone Top 1/-
3 Joint with Whalebone Top 1/-
4 Joint Cane, Whalebone Top 2/-
5 Joint Cane, Whalebone Top 2/6d
3 Joint Hazel, Superior Butt 3/-
4 Joint Hazel, Superior Butt 4/-
5 Joint Hazel, Superior Butt 5/-

WITH TWO TOPS
5 Joint Hazel, Superior Butt 7/6d
6 Joint Hazel, Superior Butt 9/-

Bamboo from 3 Joint – 2/6d to 10/-

Hickory 4 Joint – 5/- to 20/-

TROLLING RODS
Hickory, ringed 7/- to 18/6d

Trolling Bottom 8/- to 20/-
Walking Stick Rods 2/6d to 21/-
White Cane Roach 16/- (16′) 35/- (20′)
Bamboo Pocket Rods 13/- to 40/-
Fly Rods 8/6d to 17/-
General Rods 22/- to 40/-
Salmon Rods 30/- to 80/-

Bait Kettles of Gold Fish Net each 9d
Landing nets 6d, large 9d, 1/-, small mesh 2/6d
Salmon landing nets 1/6d to 3/-

Fly tackle trolling cases, small fly cases 1/6d to 7/-
Clearing rings 2d, Brass jointed rings 2/-
Twisted engines 5/-, bank runners 1/-

Best flies dressed on Limerick bent hooks per doz. 2/-
Chub and Mayflies 3/-, Sea Trout Flies 10/-,
Salmon Flies 18/-, Artificial Frogs 1/6d,
Dace, Gudgeon 1/6d to 5/-,
Minnows 1/6d to 3/6d
Artificial Mice 2/-,
Artificial Beetles, Wasps, Hornets, Grasshoppers and Cockroaches 5/-
Pearl and Glass Minnows 2/6d

Winches

Plain		Multiplying	
1¼″	1/6d	1½″	4/6d
1½″	2/6d	1¾″	5/6d
1¾″	3/6d	2″	7/-
2″	4/-	2¼″	10/-
2¾″	5/-	2¾″	11/6d
3″	7/6d	3″	13/6d
3¼″	9/-	3¼″	16/-
3½″	10/-	3½″	20/-

Check winches are 6d each less than the Multiplying, and Multiplying and Checks are 2/- each extra.

Wooden Reels

Reels for:
one line in box wood – 4d
two line in box wood – 6d
three line in box wood – 1/-
four line in box wood – 1/-
five line in box wood – 1/3d
six line in box wood – 1/6d
Reels for:
two lines with box in centre to hold shot caps, plummet – 1/6d
four line with box in centre to hold shot caps, plummet – 2/-
six line with box in centre to hold shot caps, plummet – 2/6d

Lines

3 yards single Hair lines 3d, 4d or 6d.
3 yards with twisted top 6d
7 yards finest China Twist 4d
Hank of finest China Twist 1/-
Twisted Hair line 4d.

Silkworm Gut

Silkworm Gut per hank – 4d to 6d
Good Silkworm Gut per hank – 1/-, 1/6d, 2/-
Superior Silkworm Gut per hank – 2/6d, 3/4d, 5/-
Salmon Silkworm Gut per hank – 5/6d, 8/-

Gimp

Finest Gimp per yard 2d
Middle size per yard 3d
Stout per yard 4d
Stoutest per yard 6d

Summary of Titles, Addresses and dates

C. Farlow	221 The Strand	1840 – 1851
C. Farlow	191 The Strand	1852 – 1884
C. Farlow & Co.	191 The Strand	1885 – 1894
C. Farlow & Co. Ltd.	191 The Strand	1895 – 1906
C. Farlow & Co. Ltd.	191 The Strand & 10 Charles St.	1907 – 1915
C. Farlow & Co. Ltd.	10 Charles St.	1916 – 1925
C. Farlow & Co. Ltd.	11 Panton St.	1926 – 1957
C. Farlow & Co. Ltd	13 Bruton St.	c.1958 – 1964
	for a part of this period at 23 Conduit St.	c.1960
C. Farlow & Co. Ltd.	5b Pall Mall	1965 – current

Farlow's early 'Fish' trade mark. This was replaced by the 'Holdfast' mark in later years

Above left: Plain brass reel with curved crank and ivory handle. Diameter 3½". Marked CF221, The Strand (early address) Pre 1852
Left: All brass plate reel, 5" diameter with horn handle and 'fish' trade mark on foot. Marked, 'Chas. Farlow Maker, 191 The Strand, London'. The 1852–84 title and address
Below Left: All brass reel with straight crank, ivory handle and anti-foul rim. 4½" diameter, marked 'Chas Farlow & Co. 191 The Strand, London'. The 1885–1894 title and address
Above: Brass plate reel with ivorine handle and 'fish' trade mark on the foot, marked 'Chas. Farlow & Co. 191 The Strand, London'. The 1885–1894 title and address
Below: A brass reel with unusual brass handle and oil hole in centre of backplate. 'Fish' trade mark on foot, marked 'C. Farlow & Co. Ltd, 10 Charles St., St. James Sq. SW and 191 The Strand, London'. The 1907–1915 title and address

Farlow's Reels 1880's – 1940

The compilation of a brief record of the important Farlow reels is confined to the period up to the Second World War and the data which accompanies each one are the years in which the model is known to have appeared in company catalogues. The dates are not necessarily the full production years because it has only been possible to locate a limited numer of Farlow catalogues. It is further complicated by some reels introducing modifications and adopting new names.

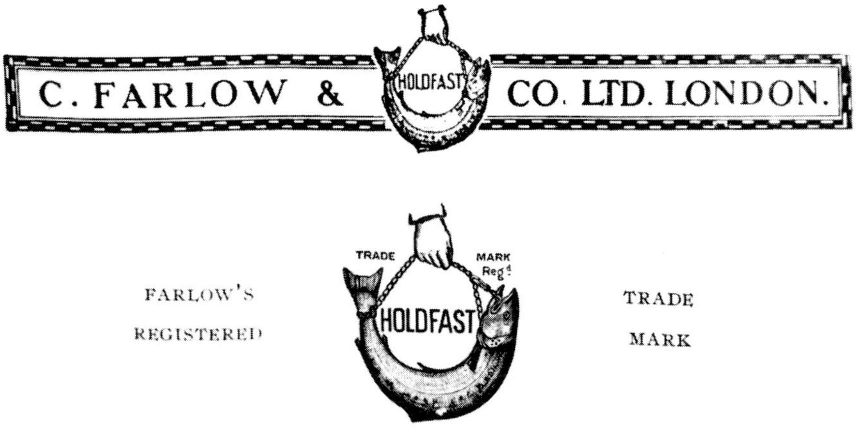

Holdfast trade mark

BEST LONDON MADE BRONZED WINCHES.

Inches	2	2¼	2½	2¾	3	3¼	3½	3¾	4	4¼	4½	4¾	5
	21/-	21/-	21/-	25/-	27/6	30/-	32/6	35/-	40/-	45/-	50/-	55/-	63/-

This Winch is made of the best possible material, each plate is well hammered to harden it before being turned, the interior mechanism is of superior quality steel, carefully tempered and adjusted, the handle is ivory and lined with hard metal, so that it works without any friction and cannot wear no matter how much it may be used, it is fixed on the revolving plate, which quite prevents the line being caught.

They have stood the test of years, and we guarantee them to be trustworthy, practical Winches.

Best London Bronzed Winch 1880s – 1909 *Sizes – 2″, 2¼″, 2½″, 2¾″, 3″, 3¼″, 3½″, 3¾″, 4″, 4¼″, 4½″, 4¾″, 5″*
Other models–London Made Bronzed (2nd quality) sizes 2″ to 4″.
Superior Bronzed 1910–14
Bronzed Winch 1907–14

Brass Check (Steel Works) c.1880s – c.1900. *Sizes 2″, 2¼″, 2½″, 2¾″, 3″, 3¼″, 3½″, 3¾″, 4″*

Farlows marketed other makers' reels including
Malloch Patent Sidecaster 1880s – 1940
Moscrop Manchester Reel 1898 – 1915
Illingworth models 1907 – 1938
Edward Vom Hofe 1912 – 1915
Allcock Aerial 1915 – 1940

Ebonite c.1891 – 1914
Sizes 2¼″, 2½″, 2¾″, 3″

Patent Lever 1880s – c.1920s
Early models had the adjustable check on handle plate. This was transferred on later reels to the rear plate

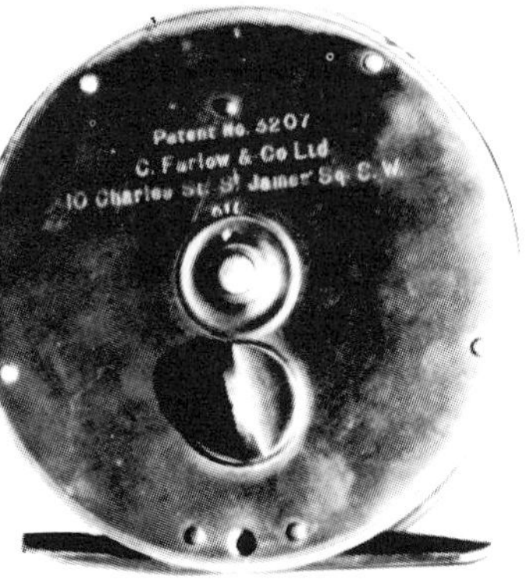

Patent Lever with check control on rear plate. Sizes 3½″, 3¾″, 4″, 4¼″, 4½″, 4¾″, 5″

Pennell Perfect Salmon c.1904 – 1905
Sizes 4″, 4¼″, 4½″

Aluminium Patent Lever c.1900 – 1914. *This reel became the 'Kelson' from 1911 – 1914 and made in sizes 4¼″, 4½″*
Sizes 3½″, 3¾″, 4″, 4¼″, 4½″

Bickerdyke Sea Reel c.1903 – 1936.
This reel started off as the New Sea Reel with Bickerdyke line guide in 1903 and became Bickerdyke Sea Reel from 1924. Sizes 4½″, 5″

Deep Sea Reel c.1904 – 1909
Sizes 4½″, 5″, 5½″

A Ventilated Aerial stamped Farlow & Co Ltd. made by S Allcock & Co.

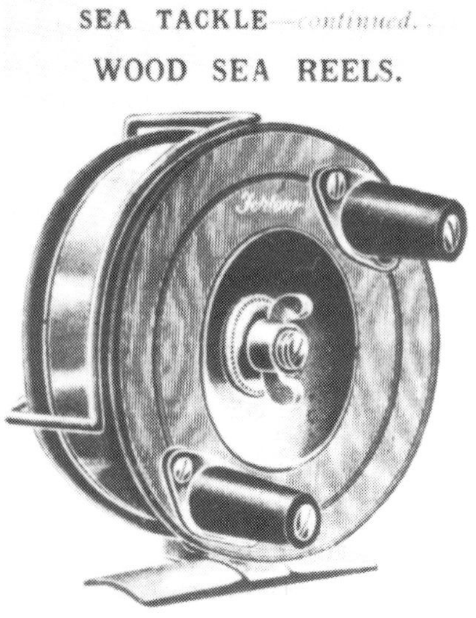

Wood Sea Reel c.1908 – 1937
Sizes 4″, 4½″, 5″, 5½″

New Dry Fly c.1907 – 1908
Sizes 2¾″, 3″, 3¼″, 3½″

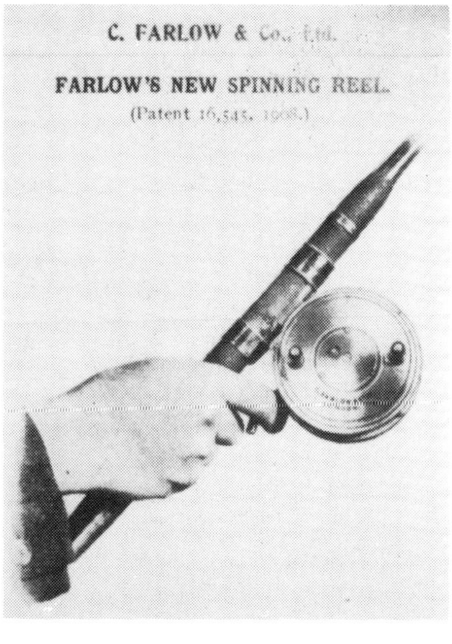

Farlight c.1909 – 1913
Size 4″. Succeeded by the Grenaby

Sun Nottingham c.1880s – 1940
Sizes 3″, 3½″, 4″, 4½″, 5″

There were two additional cheaper Nottingham models c.1888 – 1924 Nottingham with adjustable check and decribed as the 'Superior Nottingham' from c.1905 in size 3″ to 5″.
c.1889 – 1924 Nottingham without adjustable check in size 2½″ to 5″. Another model was the Combination Wood Nottingham which had all round line guard on the frame c.1924 –1929 Sizes 3″, 3½″, 4″, 4½″

Aluminium Salmon & Trout c.1909 – 1938. *Early sizes 3″, 3½″, 4″, 4½″. 1930s model 2¾″, 3″, 3½″, 4″*

Billiken c.1911 – 1940. *A very rare and collectable reel*

Patent Steel Handled c.1910 – 1913
Sizes 3″, 3½″, 4″, 4½″

Gunmetal Salmon and Trout c.1910 – 1914. *Sizes 2¼″, 2½″, 2¾″, 3″, 3¼″, 3½″, 3¾″, 4″, 4¼″, 4½″, 4¾″, 5″*

Aluminium Fly Reel c.1907 – 1929.
Sizes 2¾″, 3″, 3½″

The Heyworth c.1910 – 1940.
Early sizes 2¾", 3", 3½", 4", 4½" (In the 1920s – 3", from c.1938 – 3", 3½", 4"). The Heyworth was succeeded by the 'Silent Reel' of the 1960s

Cooper Multiplier Reel c.1910 – 1913
Sizes 3", 4½"

Inexpensive Trout Reel c.1929 – 1940
Size 2¾". Became the 'Panton' c.1930 – 1940 in sizes 2¾", 3". Also sizes 3¼", 3½" The Fly Fisher Reel

Masters c.1915.
Sizes 3½", 4", 4½"

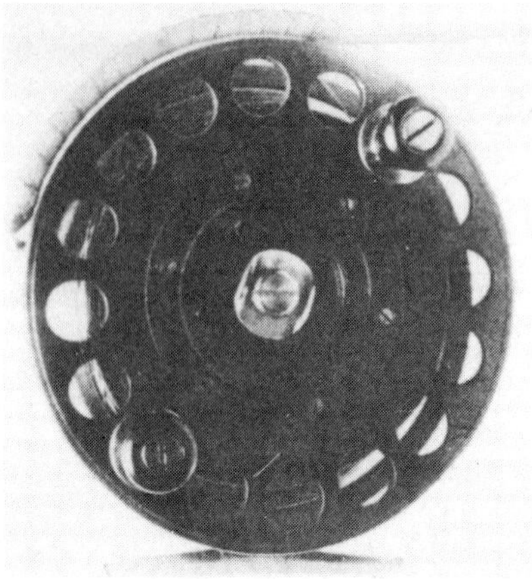

Pelican Sea Reel c.1912 – 1915
Size 6"

Grenaby Reels c.1913 – c.1966

Grenaby Unperforated 1913 – 1928
Sizes 3", 3½", 4½"

Grenaby Spinning c.1914 – 1920s
Size 4½" (1924 – 3½", 4", 4½")

Grenaby Perforated c.1929 – 1966
Sizes 3", 3½", 3⅞" (from 1938). Only a 3½" in 1960

Grenaby Salmon 4¼", 1929 – 1940
(3½", 4", 4½" in 1940")

There was also
Super Grenaby *3½", 3⅞" 1938 – 1940.*

Ballbearing Reel c.1912 – 1938
Size 4½"

Improved Light Bait Casting or Turntable Reel c.1924 – 1937
A very rare and collectable reel

Barrett c.1928 – 1940.
Sizes 4″, 4½″

Regal 1930 – 1940.
Sizes 2¾″, 3″, 3½″

Tope Sea Reel c.1923 – 1937
Size 5½″

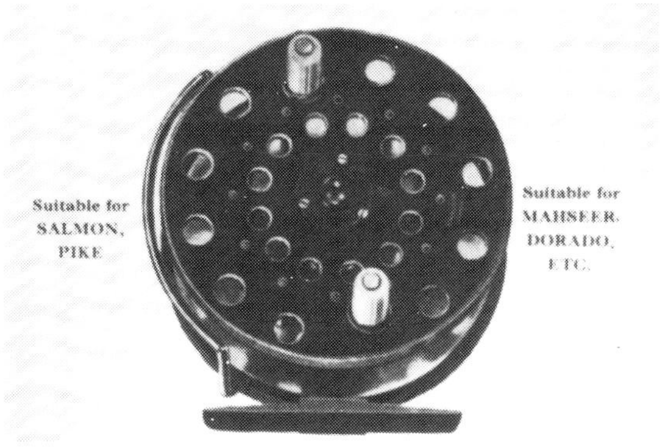

Utility c.1936 – 1940. *Size 4″*

Self-Controlled Spinning c.1936 – 1940. *Size 4″*

Other Models Included –
Live Wire 4″ c.1928 – 1938
Paramount Pike Reel 4″ c.1929
The Avon 3½″ c.1929 – 1938
The Alten 6″ c.1929 – 1940
Aurland 3½″ c.1929 – 1940
Regal Salmon 4″, 4½″ c.1937 – 1940

Four Farlow brass reels

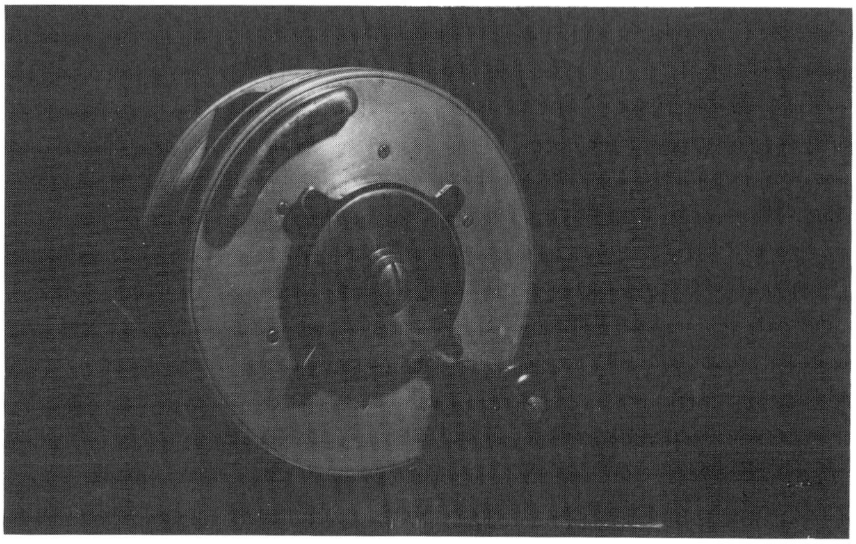

New Zealand 7″ Big Game Reel c.1936 – 1939

This was probably of the finest reel Farlow's ever made and could match any big game reel in the world. Made for only a short period and retailed at 12 guineas. It is one of the most valuable collectable sea reels.

A collection of Farlow reels

FARLOW LURES 1880s – 1940

Bells Life – 1888 – 1900
Phantoms (Brown's) – 1888 – 1908
Devon Bait – 1888 – 1910
Excelsion Devon – 1911 – 1912
Improved Devon – 1913 – 1915
Otter Bait – 1888 – 1907
Comet Bait – 1888 – 1908
Watchet Bait – 1888 – 1940 (became Improved Watchet in 1904)

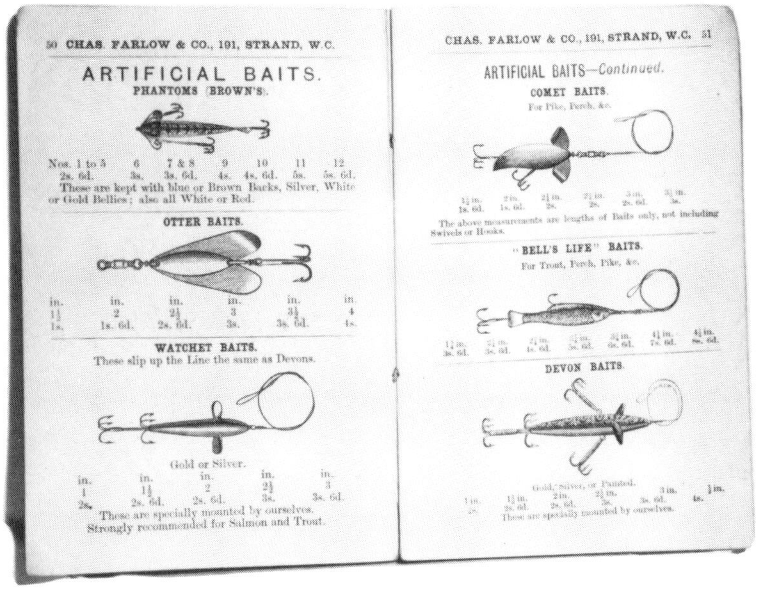

50 CHAS. FARLOW & CO., 191, STRAND, W.C.

ARTIFICIAL BAITS.

PHANTOMS (BROWN'S).

Nos. 1 to 5	6	7 & 8	9	10	11	12
2s. 6d.	3s.	3s. 6d.	4s.	4s. 6d.	5s.	5s. 6d.

These are kept with blue or Brown Backs, Silver, White or Gold Bellies; also all White or Red.

OTTER BAITS.

in.	in.	in.	in.	in.	in.
1½	2	2½	3	3½	4
1s.	1s. 6d.	2s. 6d.	3s.	3s. 6d.	4s.

WATCHET BAITS.

These slip up the Line the same as Devons.

Gold or Silver.

in.	in.	in.	in.	in.
1	1½	2	2½	3
2s.	2s. 6d.	2s. 6d.	3s.	3s. 6d.

These are specially mounted by ourselves. Strongly recommended for Salmon and Trout.

CHAS. FARLOW & CO., 191, STRAND, W.C. 51

ARTIFICIAL BAITS—*Continued.*

COMET BAITS.

For Pike, Perch, &c.

The above measurements are lengths of Baits only, not including Swivels or Hooks.

"BELL'S LIFE" BAITS.

For Trout, Perch, Pike, &c.

DEVON BAITS.

Gold, Silver, or Painted.

These are specially mounted by ourselves.

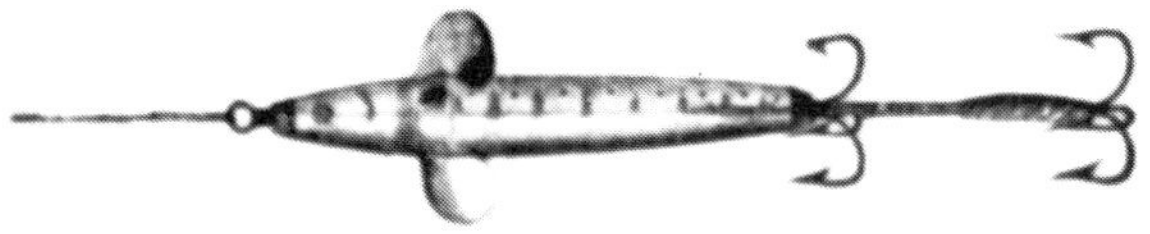

This Minnow is exceedingly light, and can be used with a Fly Rod. It has been found to be most killing in clear streams, where the water is low.

Trout size, 2s. 6d. each; Salmon, 3s. 6d. and 4s. 6d. each.

Quill Fly Minnow 1888 – 1908

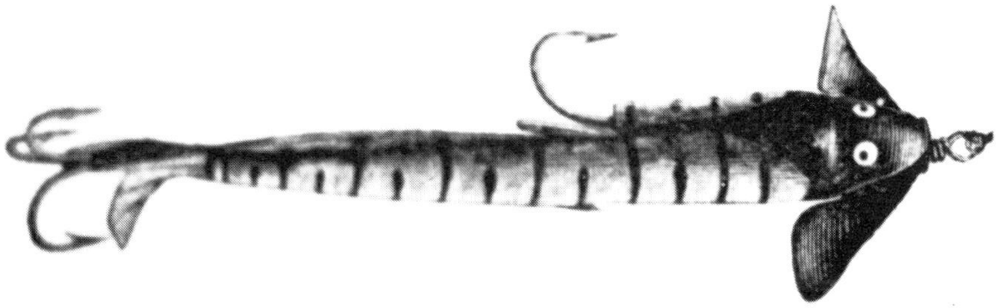

Patent Swivel Nose Phantom 1890 – 1915

Cruikshank Bait c.1891.
Sizes 2", 2¼", 2½", 3", 3¾", 4¼"

C. FARLOW & Co., Ltd., 191, STRAND, W.C. 105

ARTIFICIAL BAITS

PATENT SWIVEL NOSE PHANTOMS Brown's

The advantage of this invention will at once recommend it to all practical fishermen.

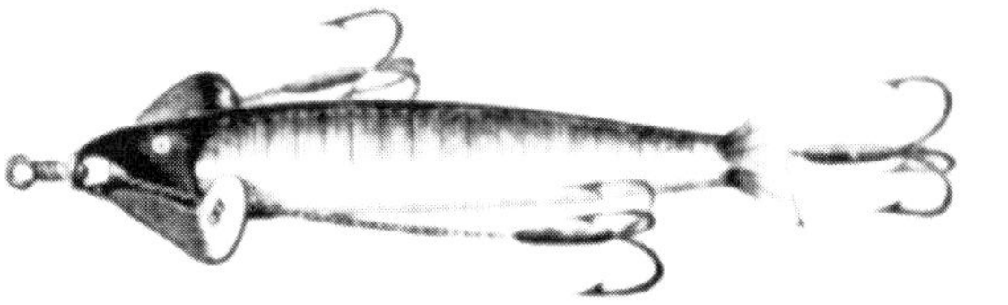

These are kept with Blue or Brown Backs, Silver, White or Gold Bellies; also all White or Red.

Phantom Devon 1895 – 1905.
Sizes 2", 2½", 3", 3½", 4", 4½", 5", 5½", 6"

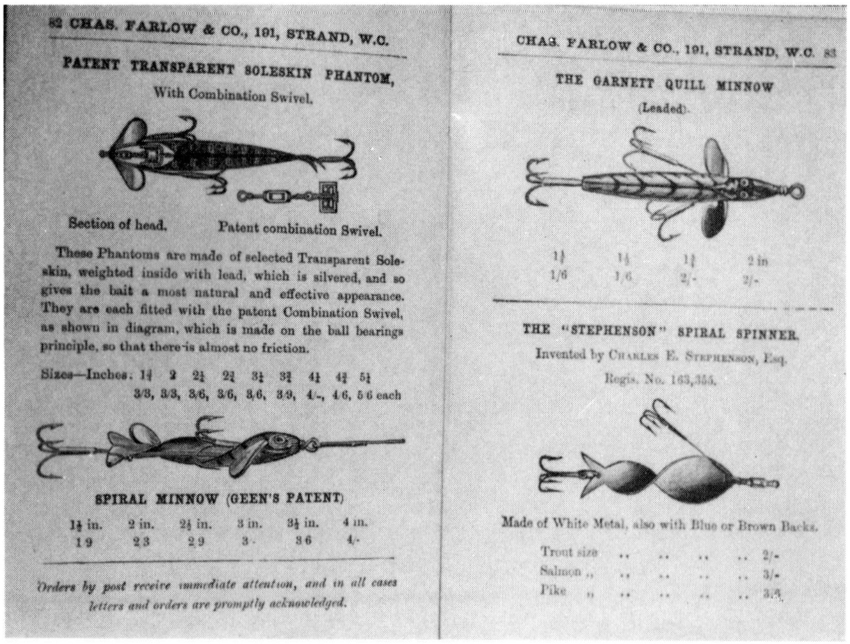
82 CHAS. FARLOW & CO., 191, STRAND, W.C.

PATENT TRANSPARENT SOLESKIN PHANTOM,
With Combination Swivel.

Section of head. Patent combination Swivel.

These Phantoms are made of selected Transparent Sole-skin, weighted inside with lead, which is silvered, and so gives the bait a most natural and effective appearance. They are each fitted with the patent Combination Swivel, as shown in diagram, which is made on the ball bearings principle, so that there is almost no friction.

Sizes—Inches.	1¾	2	2¼	2¾	3¼	3¾	4¼	4¾	5¼	
	3/3,	3/3,	3/6,	3/6,	3/6,	3/9,	4/-,	4/6,	5/6	each

SPIRAL MINNOW (GEEN'S PATENT)

1½ in.	2 in.	2½ in.	3 in.	3½ in.	4 in.
1/9	2/3	2/9	3/-	3/6	4/-

Orders by post receive immediate attention, and in all cases letters and orders are promptly acknowledged.

CHAS. FARLOW & CO., 191, STRAND, W.C. 83

THE GARNETT QUILL MINNOW
(Leaded).

1¼	1½	1¾	2 in
1/6	1/6	2/-	2/-

THE "STEPHENSON" SPIRAL SPINNER.
Invented by CHARLES E. STEPHENSON, Esq.
Regis. No. 163,355.

Made of White Metal, also with Blue or Brown Backs.

Trout size 2/-
Salmon ,, ... 3/-
Pike ,, ... 3/3

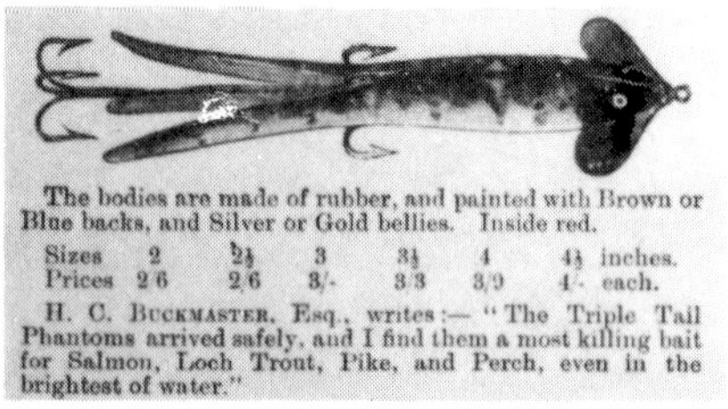
The bodies are made of rubber, and painted with Brown or Blue backs, and Silver or Gold bellies. Inside red.

Sizes	2	2½	3	3½	4	4½	inches.
Prices	2/6	2/6	3/-	3/3	3/9	4/-	each.

H. C. BUCKMASTER, Esq., writes:— "The Triple Tail Phantoms arrived safely, and I find them a most killing bait for Salmon, Loch Trout, Pike, and Perch, even in the brightest of water."

Triple Tail Phantom 1903 – 1910

Transparent Soleskin Phantom 1891 – 1915
Garnett Quill Minnow 1893 – 1900
Stevensons Spiral Spinner 1893 – 1907
Spiral Minnow 1893 – 1908

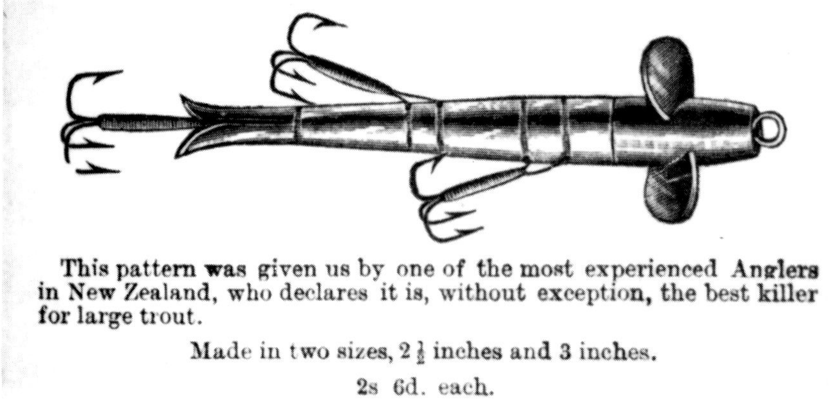
This pattern was given us by one of the most experienced Anglers in New Zealand, who declares it is, without exception, the best killer for large trout.

Made in two sizes, 2½ inches and 3 inches.

2s 6d. each.

Amberite Minnow 1900 – 1908

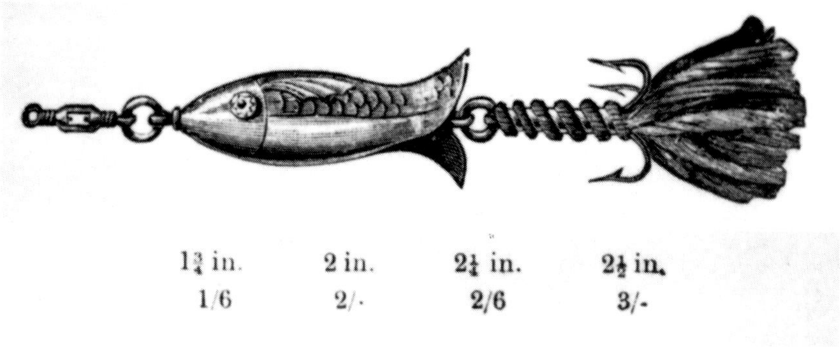

1¾ in.	2 in.	2¼ in.	2½ in.
1/6	2/-	2/6	3/-

Clipper Bait 1896 – 1908

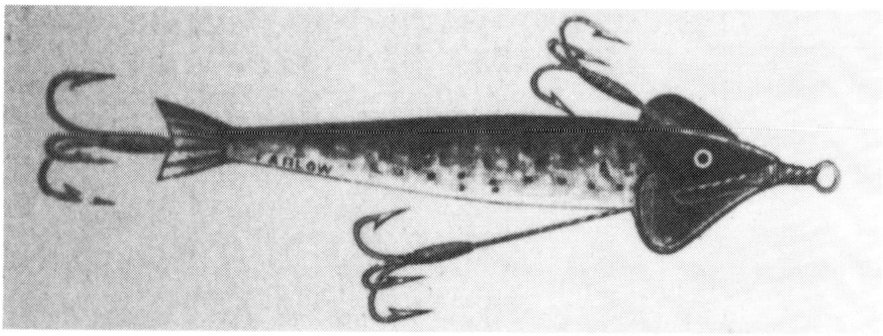

Improved Wagtail Bait 1904 – 1915
Sizes 2″, 2½″, 3″, 3½″, 4″, 4½″, 5″

Screw Tail Phantom 1907 – 1910

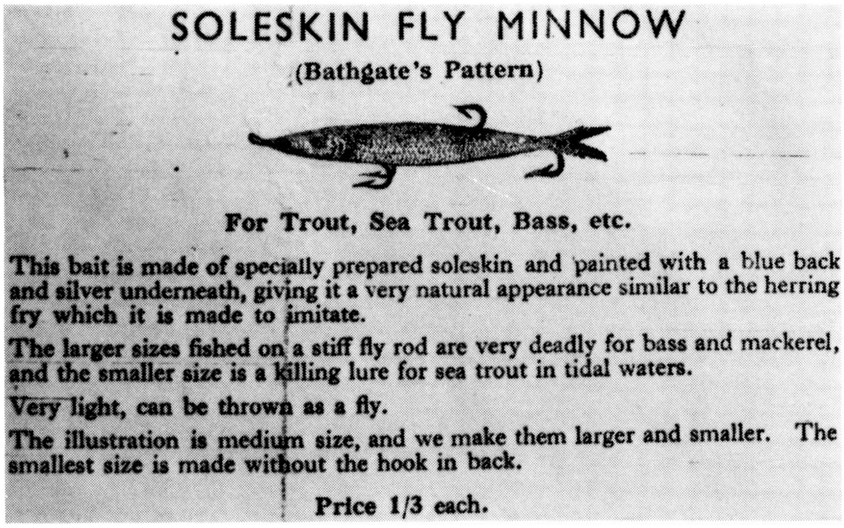

SOLESKIN FLY MINNOW

(Bathgate's Pattern)

For Trout, Sea Trout, Bass, etc.

This bait is made of specially prepared soleskin and painted with a blue back **and silver underneath, giving it a** very natural appearance similar to the herring **fry which it is made to imitate.**

The larger sizes fished on a stiff fly rod are very deadly for bass and mackerel, **and the smaller size is a** killing lure for sea trout in tidal waters.

Very light, can be thrown as a fly.

The illustration is medium size, and we make them larger and smaller. The smallest size is made without the hook in back.

Price 1/3 each.

Soleskin Fly Minnow 1905 – 1908

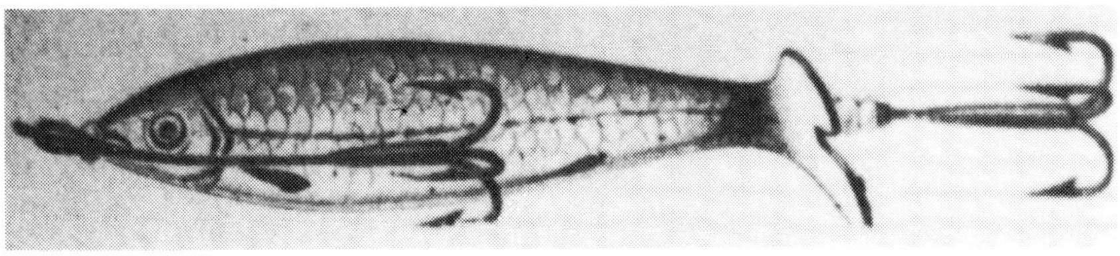

Perfect Spinning Bait 1908 – 1910.
Sizes 1½", 2", 2½", 3", 3½", 4", 4½"

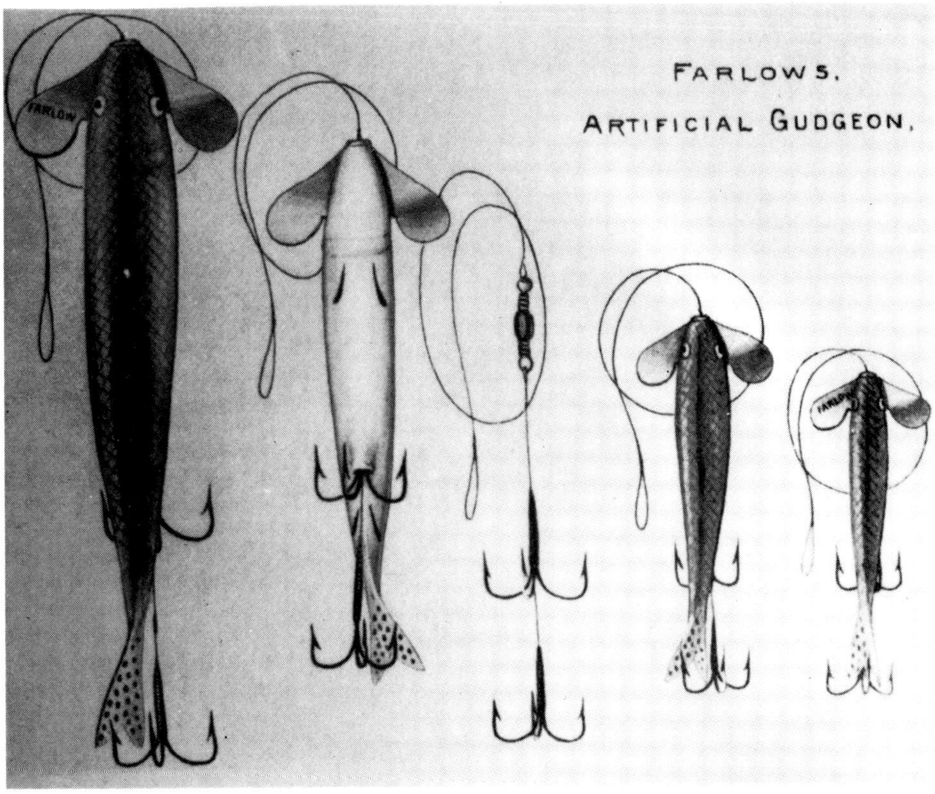

Artificial Gudgeon 1912 – 1915

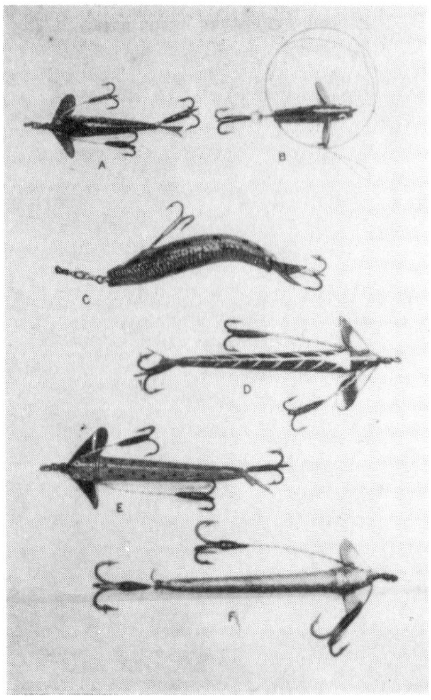

Trout Minnows A to F 1909 – 1940

A Extra Small Phantom
B The 'Enticer Minnow'
C Natural Artificial Minnow
D Whitebait Phantom
E Transparent Quill Minnow
F Silver Sand Eel

Tube Phantom 2″, 2½″, 3″, 3½″, 4″, 4½″ 1923 – 1940

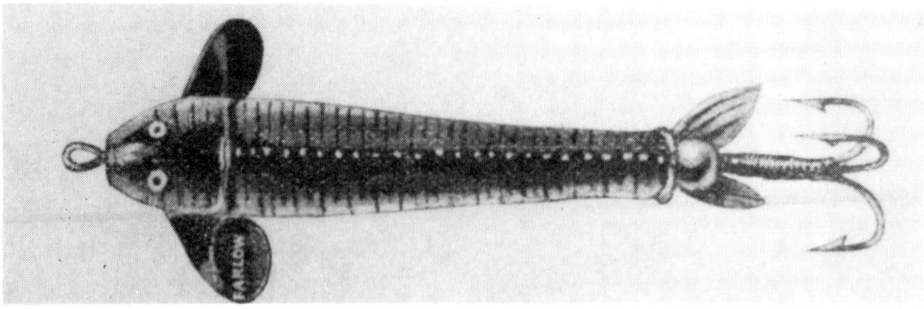

Wye Phantom 1¾″, 2″, 2½″, 3″, 3½″, 1923 – 1938

Tube Wagtail 2″, 2½″, 3″, 3½″, 4″, 4½″, 5″, 5½″ 1923 – 1940

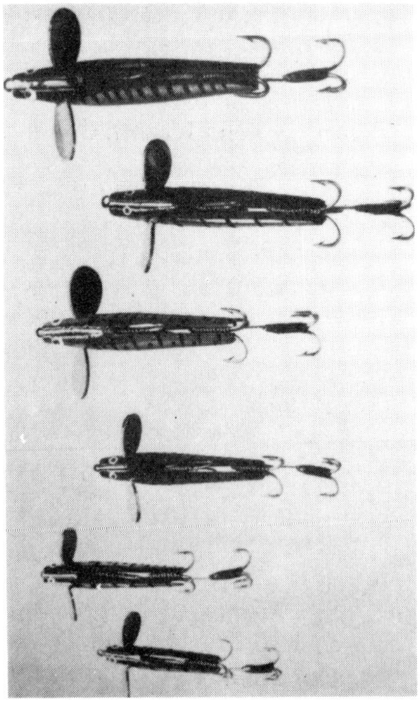

Excelsior Devon Bait c.1911 – 1912

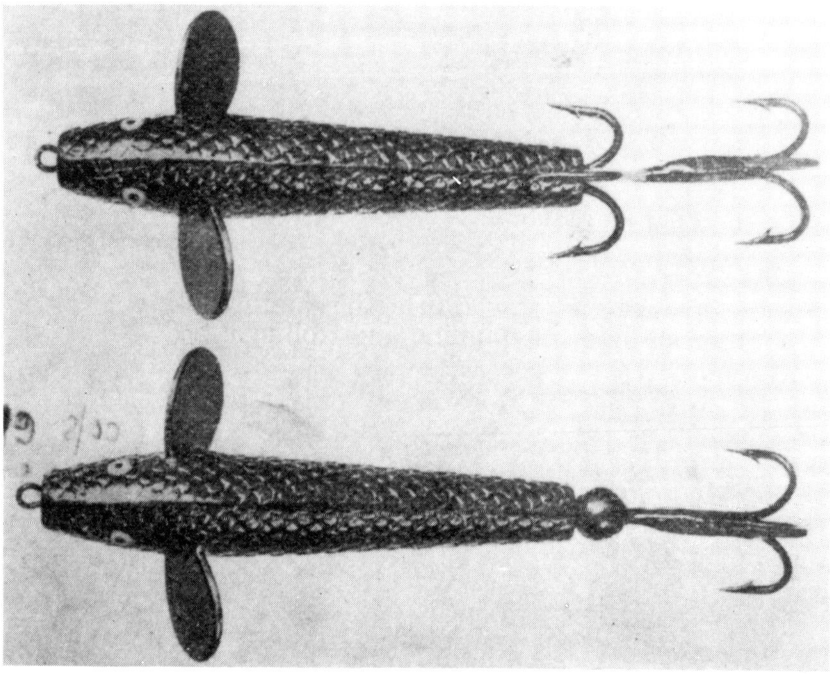

New Pattern Scaled Devon 1″, 1¼″, 1½″, 1¾″, 2″, 2¼″, 2½″, 3″ 1929 – 1940

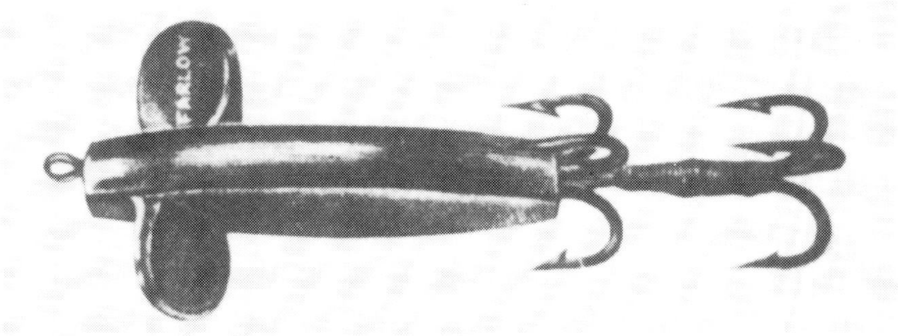

Reflet Minnow 1915 – 1960's.
Sizes 1½", 1¾", 2", 2¼", 2½", 3"

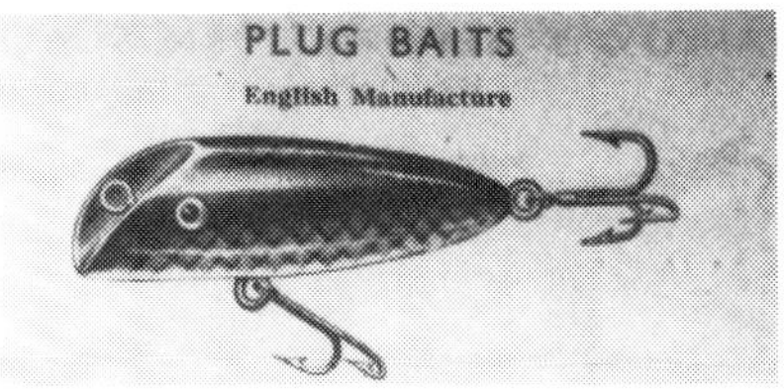

Plug Bait

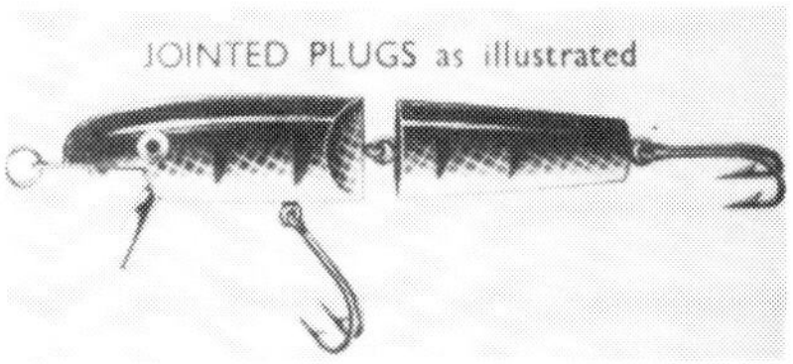

Jointed Plug Bait 1940

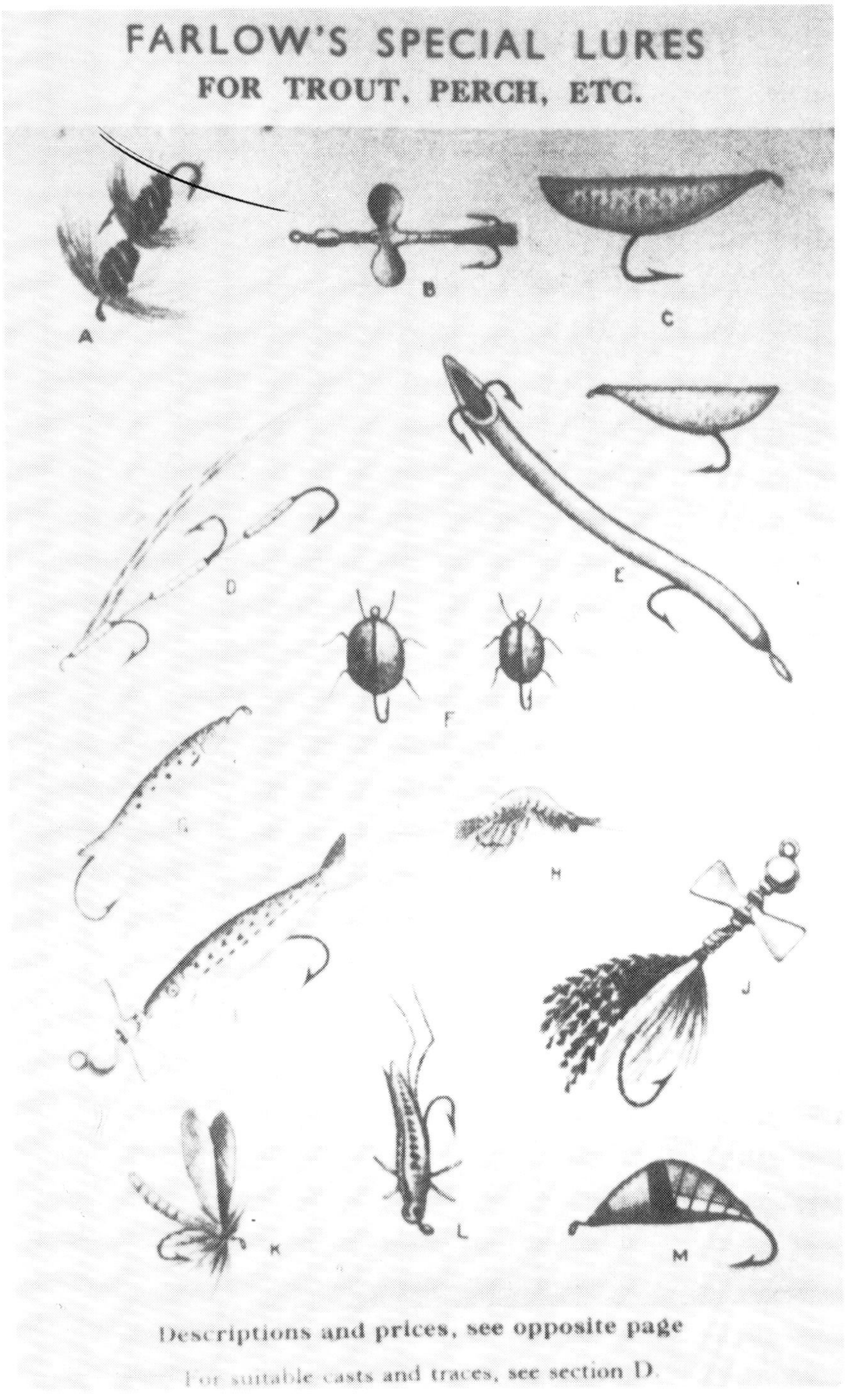

Special Lures 1930's

A Double hook worm fly. This is a double hook Peacock Palmer. 6/- per dozen.
B Magnet Spinner. Body and flanges silvered or gilt with red tails 1/- each.
C Wilson-Potter Soleskin fly. Body is bright silver and wings are tinted soleskin. In two sizes 6d each.
D 'Demon' or 'Terrier'. Bodies silvered. 6d each.
E Rubber Sand Worms. Green back with silver belly. 6d each.
F Floating Cochybondu. 1/- each.
G Transparent celluloid fly minnow. 1/6d each.
H Freshwater Shrimp. 1/- each.
I P.M. Fly Minnow. The flanges revolve. Spins in the slackest water. 1/6d each.
J P.M. Spinning Alexandra (Patent). The hook does not revolve. 1/6deach.
K Daddy Long Legs. 1/- each.
L Floating Green Grasshopper. 1/- each.
M Grasshopper grub. For grayling, leaded body covered with silk. Put two or three gentles on the point of the hook and work with a 'sink and draw' motion. 1/- each.

Foster Bros c1833 – 1960's

It is difficult to decide when the firm of Foster Bros. first started in the business of making fishing tackle. A catalogue in the 1890s had printed the words 'Established A.D. 1833' and yet in 1963 they decided to issue a booklet celebrating their bi-centenary.

This booklet says the firm of Foster Bros. was founded in 1763, but gives very little evidence. The only information offered to substantiate this claim was the statement – 'It is recorded that in 1763, J Barton had a business in Ashbourne for the sale of fishing tackle'.

The relationship of the Barton business to Foster's is not explained and the only other details of the early history in the booklet was the fact that in the fourteenth century a John of Ashbourne was buried in Ashbourne Parish Churchyard with the record that he was a fisherman. Hardly proof that the Foster's business as tackle makers had any connection with such an early date.

I would therefore prefer to accept 1833 as mentioned in the early catalogue as the date the firm was started and David Foster was the founder. In 1841 he invented a method of drawing gut through steel plates which produced extremely fine quality for clear waters, and he was a great exponent in the art of dry fly fishing. He was not a great innovator of tackle, which changed little until the next generation of Fosters arrived.

By 1880 the sons of the founder were running the business and their names were William Henry and David Foster. Their reign was to be a period of innovation, marked by several patents and flamboyant advertising for their products in contrast to the style of their father.

The height of their extravagant claims involved rods clad with steel wire. W H Foster patented an idea for binding the outside of the rod with steel wire in a criss-cross pattern in order to give extra strength and received patent No 1000 dated 19th January, 1892.

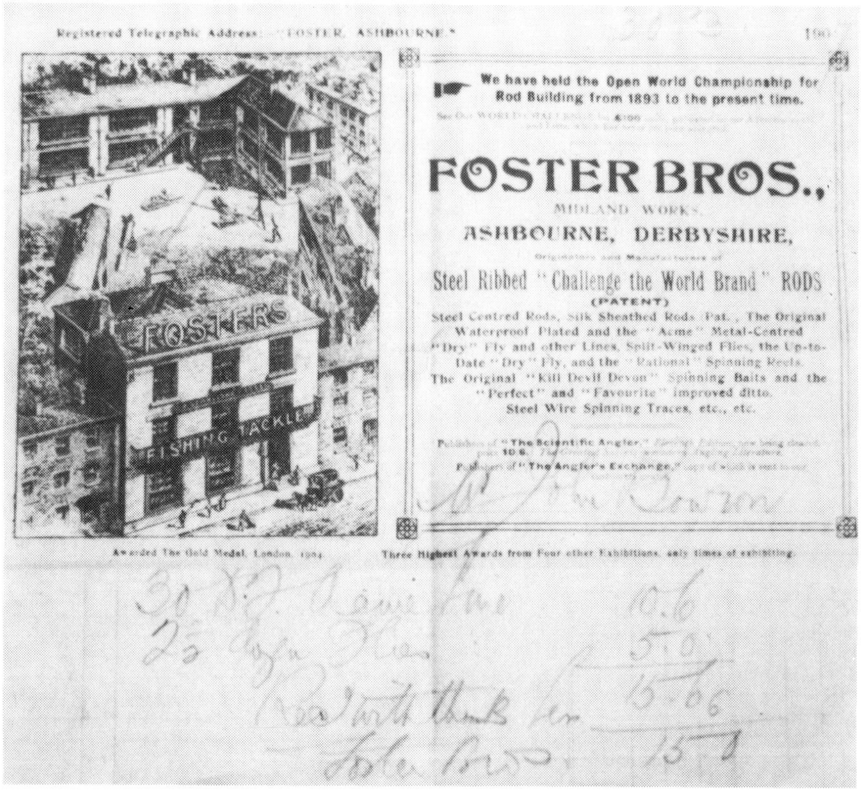

A Foster Bros bill from 1907

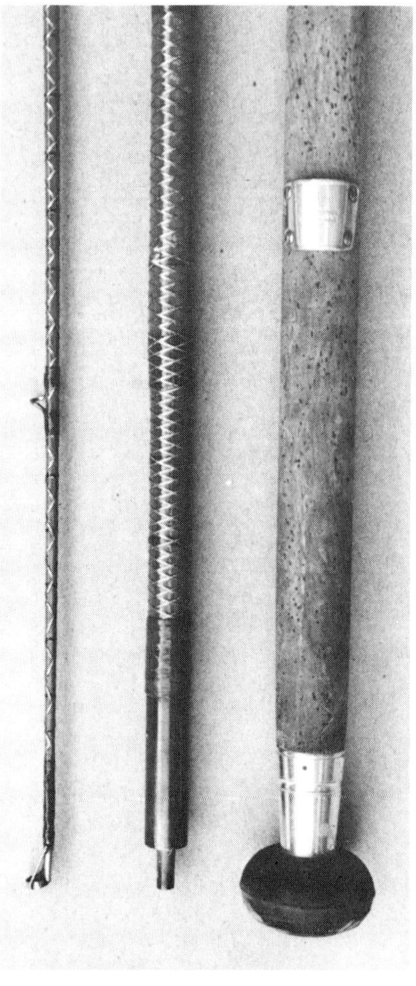

Foster's rod with wire cladding.

Foster's manufactured these rods and embarked on a sensational advertising campaign in which they 'challenged the world' to a contest. They were offering to back their steel ribbed patented rods against steel centered or jointed rods which they claimed would support more weights before breaking. There seems little logic in the design as any outer casing of this type would have no effect on breaking tolerance, nor would such a feature affect casting efficiency or guarantee excellence in a rod. Nevertheless, this gimmick gave their rods individuality and helped to sell Fosters' product, which was the object of the exercise.

It must have been quite successful as W H Foster was back at the Patents Office twelve years later with a similar idea for binding the outside of the rods, this time using silk, cotton, hemp or other textile material. The idea was nothing new as Hardy's had produced a rod twenty years earlier with a dark green binding but never continued with

An early Farlow brass winch with folding crank handle, diameter 4″

The New Zealand big-game sea reel

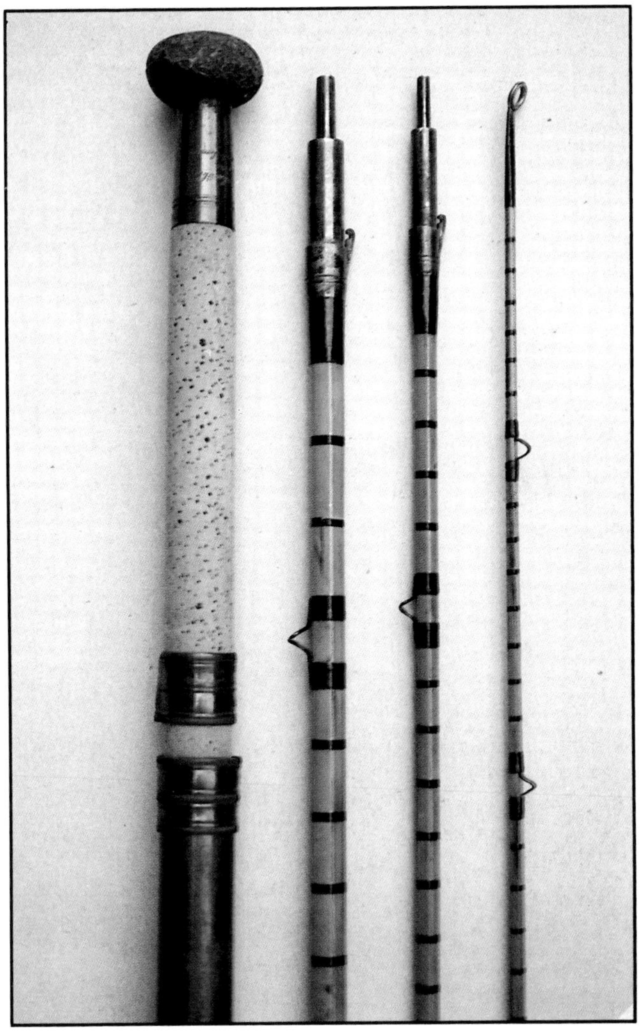

Big salmon rod in split cane with steel centre by C Farlow & Co, The Strand. It is a three piece rod with spare tip. Length 17ft, superb condition, date c. 1885 – 1895

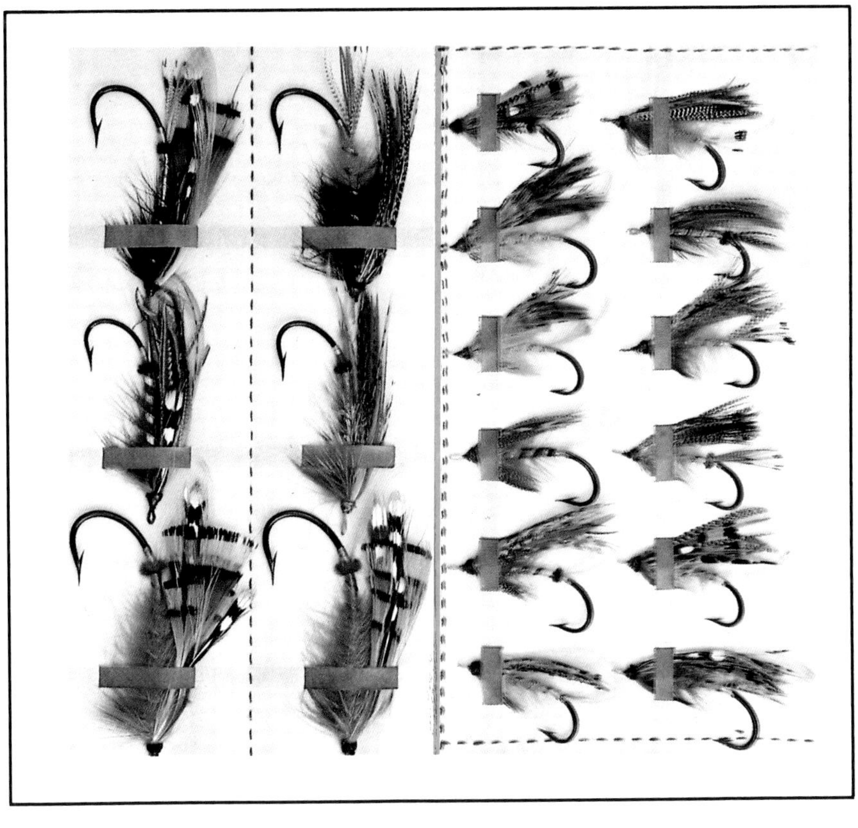

Ron Blackmore

Farlow salmon flies

Brown Trout by PD Malloch 1917

Below: Salmon Ferox by PD Malloch 1917

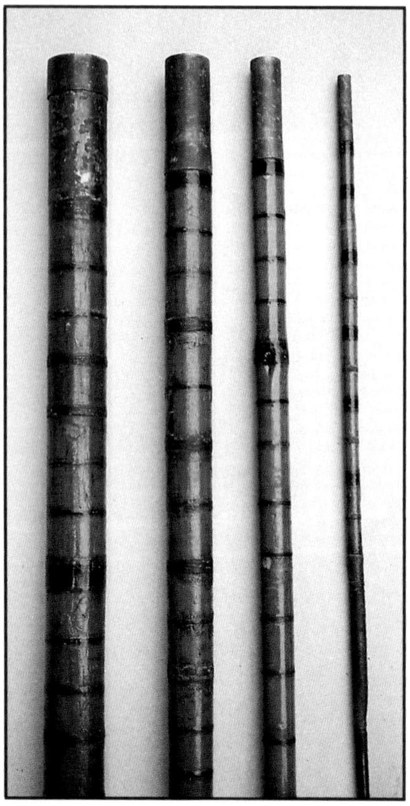

19th century Roach Pole. Length 17ft

Above left: A Slater Combination reel with an ebonite and brass star back plate and on/off check button, Slater drum release latch and nickel silver rim. Diameter 4½"

Left: A Nottingham reel in cherry wood with a Bickerdyke line guide

Above: The only known example of the first fixed spool casting reel in Britain by G R Holding. It is a wood Nottingham strap-back reel with painted drum, ebonite handle and a spring loaded swivel action

Left: Malloch all brass side caster of 2⅝″ diameter

Below: An Illingworth No. 1 alloy reel which could both cast and retrieve the line while the spool remained stationary

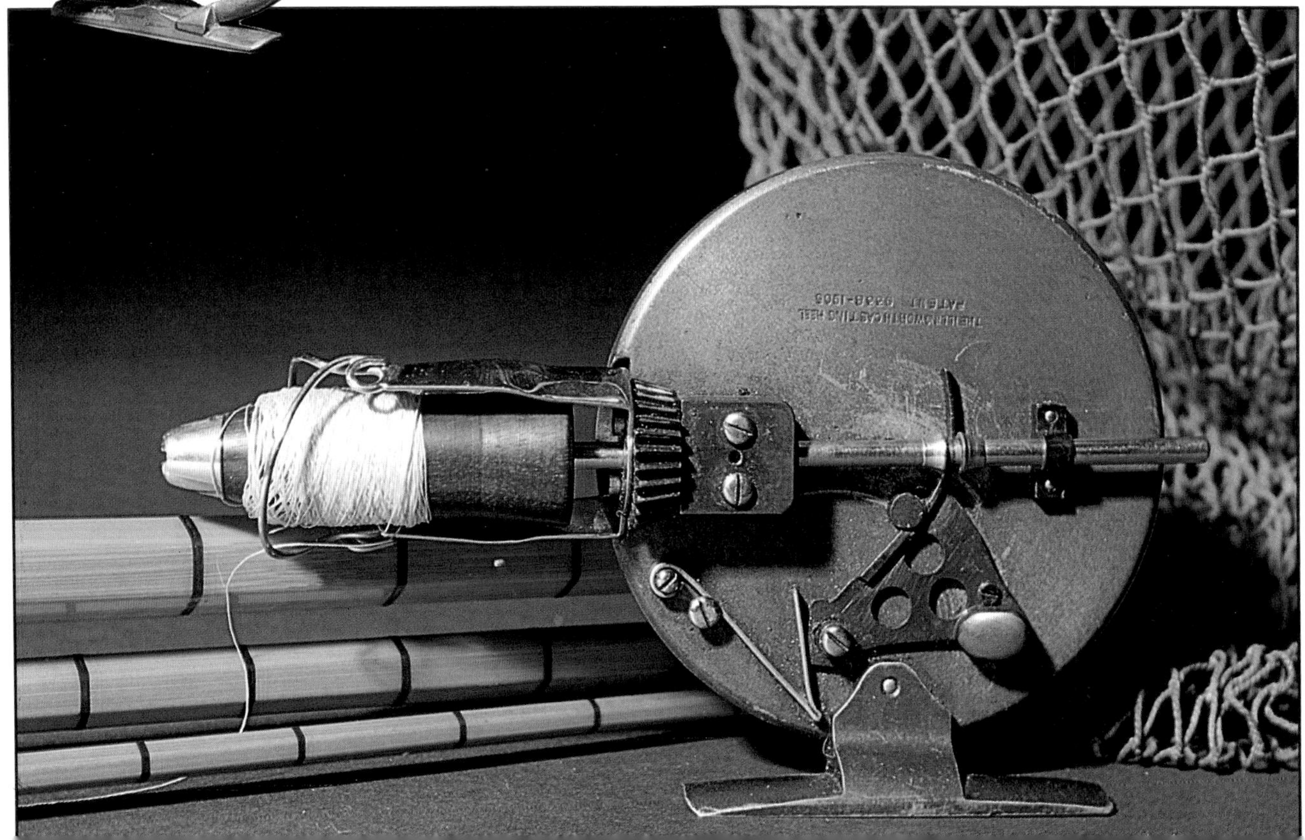

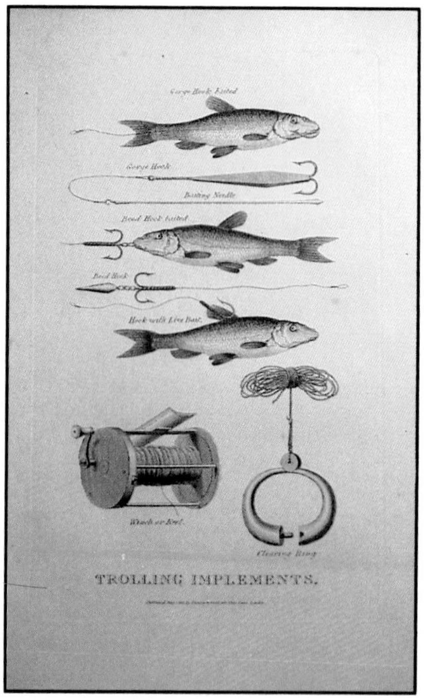

The earliest illustration of a multiplying winch which appeared in Rev WB Daniels Rural Sports *in 1801*

Right: Early coloured lures described as 'Minnows (artificial) or water-witch' from Rod and Line *by Hewett Wheatley 1849*

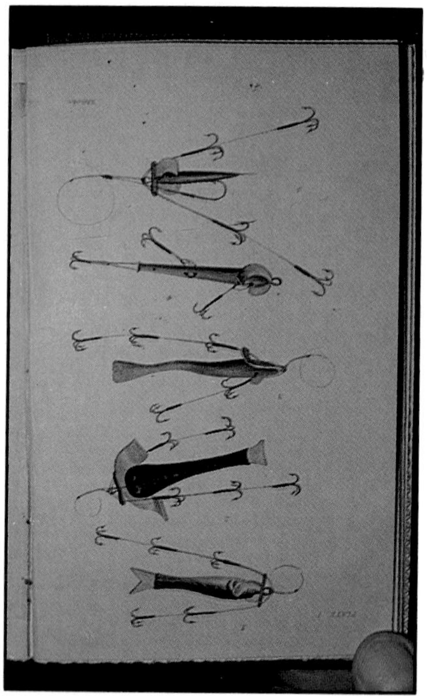

First coloured flies in English literature described as 'Natural Flies, Colored Red from Nature' in Fly Fishers Legacy *by George Scotcher c.1800*

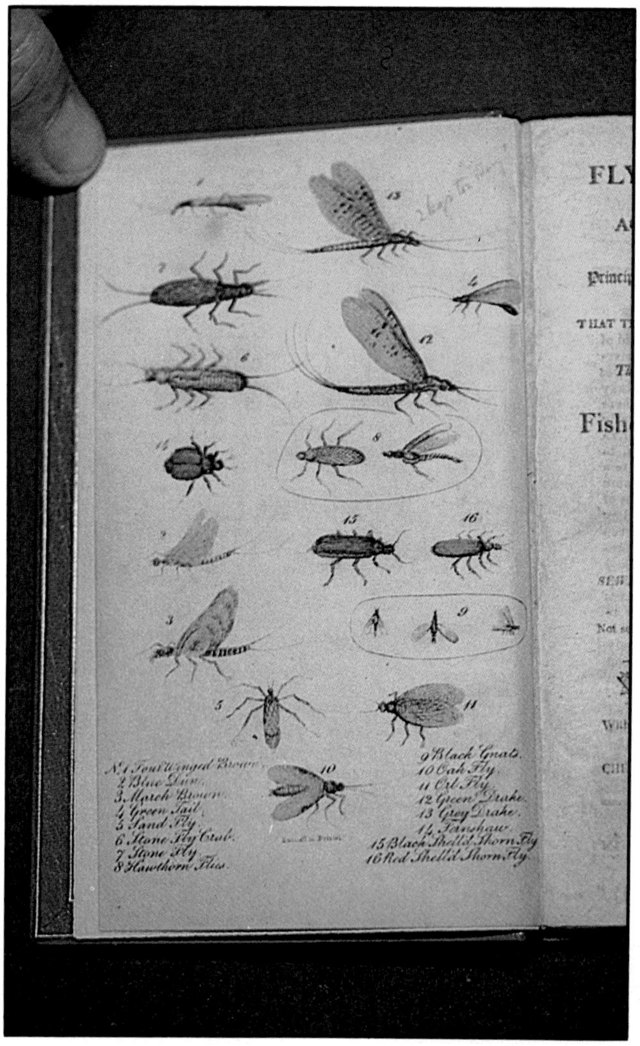

The first coloured salmon flies described as 'Specimens of Five Flies (artificial) which will be found very successful in raising salmon'. in The Fly Fishers Guide *by George C Bainbridge 1816*

Alloy Reel with ebonite handle, and on/off check button. Also a split-cane rod with steel ribbed cladding by Foster Bros. Diameter 4″

Alloy perfect style wide drum with line guard and ebonite handle. Diameter 3¾″

production. Foster received patent No 10721 dated May 10th, 1904 but must have realised that it was taking the idea of binding one step too far and never produced such rods in any quantity.

W H Foster patented several other ideas including – special type end rings (No 7459 – 1908), securing the steel centre in rods (No 27565 – 1911), brake for casting reels (No 5258 – 1913), colouring of lines (No 220814 – 1923).

In 1918 Wilfred Foster, the son of W H Foster, joined the firm and took over control in 1936 when his father retired. He kept the business together through the Second World War, enjoyed the boom years after the armistice and was going strong in 1965 when he issued what he claimed to be the Bi-centenary Booklet.

This old established firm is no longer with us today but should be remembered for its enterprise and drive even though their good quality tackle was sometimes not quite what the announcements claimed.

Alloy heavily perforated reel with ivorine handle. Diameter 3″

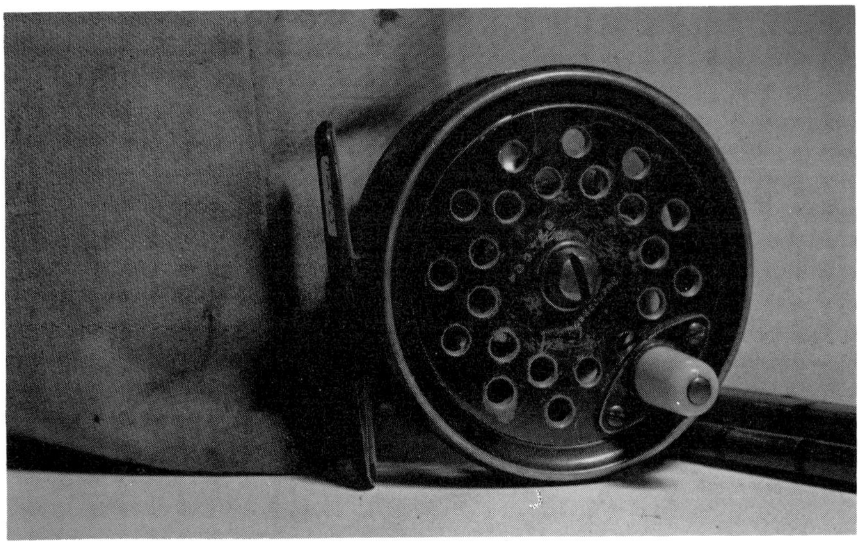

Alloy wide drum reel with tension screw, line guard and white composition handle. Diameter 4¼″

Haywood 1801 – 1839

In 1801 James Haywood was a brass-founder and manufacturer of brass lamps and chandeliers with premises at Morris's Court, High St, Birmingham. By 1803 he had moved to 71 Hill St and became a manufacturer of brass fishing reels. He made clamp foot winches in the early years, and later, ones with the modern type straight bar feet. He was one of the few early makers to stamp his name on winches, many of which must have been exported as they often turn up in America. In 1823 he was trading from No 102 Hill St and extended his activities to making brass ferrules and walking sticks. He died about 1828 and the business was carried on by his widow Mrs Mary Haywood. In 1833 she was listed as fishing reel maker at 101 Hill St and by 1839 she was selling reels and brass ferrules from a new address at Bath Row. On September 26th 1846 she died aged 83 years.

Illustrations are of the same reel but showing a Front and Rear Elevation

Hearder of Plymouth c.1820 – early 1900s

Jonathan Hearder was one of the oldest firms in the west of England to sell fishing tackle. He first appeared in the Plymouth Directory in 1814 as 'Umbrella Maker' at High Broad St and was still at the same address in 1823, but had extended his activities to gunsmith and fishing tackle maker. Mr A Courtney Williams in *Angling Diversions* suggested that he was the inventor of the 'Kill Devel' lure which is known to have been in use in the 1820s and probably earlier.

By 1830 he had moved to 28 Buckwell St and there was an additional registration in the directory of that year for a son, Jonathan Hearder (junior), described as schoolmaster at Buckwell St. In 1844 the firm was being run by a Jonathan Nash Hearder and by 1852 additional premises at 34 George St had become the main retail outlet. This arrangement lasted only a few years as in 1857 the address was 28 Buckwell St once more.

About 1873 the firm moved to 195 Union St and the title became Hearder & Son with the appearance of a new name – William Hearder D.Sc.FL.S., described as a 'Medical Galvanist'. They were still trading in fishing tackle and in 1895 placed the following text in the Plymouth directory.

> 'Hearder & Son, General Manufacturers, 195 Union St, Plymouth. The old established fishing tackle manufacturers of the West; inventors of the celebrated Spinning Sand Eels, and mounted lines for all parts of the world; Nets, Baits etc. Established 1770.'

The business was listed as a 'Sport's Warehouse' from 1900 to the beginning of the first World War in 1914, and it was probably at the end of this period that they ceased trading in fishing tackle. Hearder & Son continued to appear in the trade directories but without giving the nature of their business, and the title changed to Hearder Ltd about 1932. The final period in which they appeared in directories was 1938 to 1951 and their listed profession was that of chemist at 26 Westwell St, Plymouth.

Rare Hearder 3" diameter reel in brass and ebonite with nickel silver rims and horn handle

P D Malloch 1875 – 1981

Peter Malloch was born in 1853 in the little village of Almondbank, near Perth in Scotland. Of humble parentage, he did not have the advantage of higher education and spent his youthful days in the woods and fishing in the River Almond.

By the age of twelve he had a sound knowledge of all the birds and animals in the district, and by the age of fourteen he was able to mount birds, make a rod and tie flies.

In 1875 assisted by his brother James, he started a business in a small back room off High St, Perth as a taxidermist and fishing tackle supplier. From small beginnings he soon progressed and moved to a shop in High St. In 1903 a move was made to more spacious premises at 24, 26, 28, Scott St and Malloch was joined by his son Joseph, who remained in the business until 1933.

There was also one daughter and two other sons, one of which was in charge of an Estate Agency which the business incorporated. In 1918 at the end of World War I, the youngest son P J D Malloch joined the firm as secretary.

In 1884 Malloch was the second to patent a fixed spool casting reel in Britain and was the first to market it successfully. He produced a standard model with reversible drum and optional check, also a variant with the addition of a 'Gibbs' patented locking lever. Another model was introduced, known as the Malloch-Erskine which incorporated a set of geared cog wheels and modifications which allowed the angler to wind in the line using a clockwise turn of the handle. Another unusual reel sold by Malloch was the 'Sun and Planet' so named because of the relationship of a large cog wheel to a smaller one which controlled the amount of drag when playing a fish.

P D Malloch, the founder, was a notable fisherman and was the winner of the Loch Leven Championship in 1881, 1893, 1909 and also the National

Malloch Sidecaster with Gibbs Patent Lever

Ebonite and brass faced plate reel with ivorine handle. Diameter 4¾″

Angling Clubs competition in 1881, 1882, 1891, 1894, 1906 and 1912.

The famous artist and naturalist J G Millais described him as the best fisherman of his time and qualified this claim by saying he had fished with some of the best over a period of forty years.

Malloch's knowledge of the ecology of fish was in great demand in constructing new lochs, salmon pools and passes and improving the rivers of Scotland. He was the best authority on the life cycle of the salmon and trout being the first to study the importance of scale markings on salmon. He proved that every period of time, passed in river or sea, could be demonstrated by markings on the scales themselves. His intimate knowledge of the colour of scales made him one of the finest taxidermist of fish, and the dissection which this work involved gave him an insight into their diet. In 1910, Malloch's book – *The Life History and Habits of the Salmon, Sea-Trout and Other Fresh Water Fish* was published and accepted by many as the standard reference work on the subject.

Eleven years later in 1921 he died at the age of 68. The last member of the family, Miss Maggie Malloch remained in

Malloch Sun and Planet and internal mechanism. Diameter 4½″

control until 1964 when she retired at the age of 82. The business was sold and the new proprietors continued to operate until 1981 when an announcement was made in the *Perthshire Advertiser* on the 26th May, saying the business had been closed after 106 years of trading. The Managing Director blamed the current recession, plus the high rent and rates for an expensive city site.

The heaviest salmon (64lbs) ever caught in Britain was landed by Miss Ballantine in 1922 using a Malloch rod and reel (see page 144).

The 'Chippendale' reel by J E Miller marked only with patent No 22271 (1909)

J E Miller of Leeds 1898 – 1914

The first appearance of John Ernest Miller in the Leeds trade directories was in 1898 when he was recorded as trading as the 'Northern Anglers Depot' at 19 New Station St. The following year, 1899, the premises were listed for a Mr F M Walbran, who already had premises in Infirmary St, and had been selling fishing tackle from 1889 – 1897 at No 10 New Station St, a period when there was no mention of J E Miller. This is something of a mystery because in 1900 Miller was back in the trade list as the proprietor of 19 New Station St, and Walbran Ltd at 16 New Station St.

J E Miller continued to trade at the same No 19 address and on July 20th 1910, patent No 17250 was granted to J E Miller and H J Thomas for an improvement on a fixed spool multiplying reel. The Miller business produced Chippendale reels based on patent No 22271 of 1909 by S Payne and J T Chippendale and a multiplying model with the additional 17250 patent of 1910. The proprietor of the business was registered as J E Miller up to 1914 but for the final period of trading, 1915 – 1920, the name of Henry John Thomas appeared in the trade directories.

Multiplying Sidecaster with raised plate housing, straight crank, horn handle and Gibbs Patent Lever

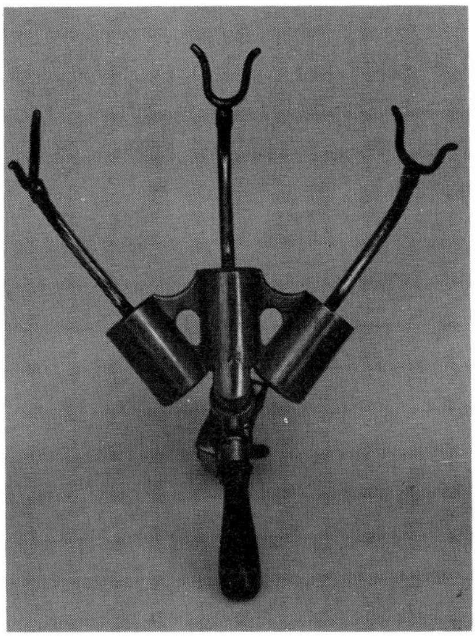

Malloch invented a multiple rod holder whereby rods could be fixed when trolling from the stern of a boat. He was granted patent No 1856 on January 26th 1895

The 'Chippendale Multiplier' which was a threadline multiplying casting reel with 2-1 ratio gear. Marked with Pat. 22271 (1909) and 17250 (1910). Spool in rosewood

Milwards Flycraft. An alloy reel with tension screw and line guard. Diameter 4″

H. Milward and Sons Ltd.

Henry Milward & Sons Ltd were manufacturers of needles, fish hooks and tackle with connections in needle making as early as the eighteenth century. They manufactured these products at Washford Mills, their premises at Redditch, up to the middle of the twentieth century. Their tackle had gained no less than thirty First Class awards at international exhibitions since the year 1853 including the Grand Prix awards at Brussels in 1910, at Turin in 1911 and two gold medals at Rio, Brazil in 1922.

Milward's shared the boom in needles and fish hooks and later under the control of Col C F Milward expanded into the sale of rods, reels and tackle. They made good quality rods and marketed other maker's reels as their own trade models, and sometimes adopted ideas which they considered had commercial potential.

One of the most unusual reels was the Milward Brownie designed by Simeon Brown of Carrie House, Thornton, Bradford and patented in 1922. It was a wooden reel designed to stand with its axis parallel to the rod similar to the Holden Mallock reels in order to cast with a fixed spool. Instead of the drum swivelling on the foot of the reel to adopt the required position, it achieved the same result by hinging outwards from the rod on a similar principle to the idea of Winans and Whistler of America. It is an interesting example to collectors of fixed-spool reels.

Milwards 'Brownie' which pivoted on a ball into a notched casting. This action allowed it to adopt a fixed spool casting position and then fold back to the rod to rewind normally. Diameter 3½″

J B Moscrop – Manchester

John B Moscrop was born in Bury, Lancashire in 1830 and attended Grammar School before becoming articled to a firm of Manchester architects. He very quickly left the profession and became a cotton spinner. Being scientifically minded, he invented the Moscrop steam and speed recorder which was so successful that it eventually found its way into every textile mill of the period.

He next invented and patented a machine for yarn testing by the single thread and this proved complementary to his first invention. Moscrop was a well-known and skilful angler and a prominent member of the Manchester Angling Society which was one of the oldest clubs in the country.

He took out reel patents No 2900 in 1888 and No 17501 in 1891 and invented a reel which the members of the society thought so good, that they adopted it as 'The Manchester Reel'. He was a lover of nature and sketched the lovely scenery of Ireland and Wales whenever his piscatorial activities took him there. Music was another interest and he was a clever pianist and great admirer of the old masters.

He lived at 'The Lodge', Platt Lane, Rusholme, Manchester, where he was registered in the trade directories of 1891 and 1892 as Moscrop, John, Engineer. From 1893 to 1903 he was registered as Moscrop J B Engineer, Patentee of Moscrop Recorder, 25 Market Place, Res. – The Lodge, Platt Lane, Rusholme.

Further research showed that the premises 25 Market Place was registered in 1895 as fishing tackle dealer trading by the name of Will Chambers & Co. Therefore it would seem reasonable to believe that John Moscrop had an interest in this business and it was an outlet for the Manchester Reel.

Moscrop died in 1903 at the age of seventy three and his famous reel continued to be popular for many years after his death. Allcock's acted as agent from 1893 – c.1929 and Farlows from 1898 – c.1915.

Moscrop's 'Manchester Reel'. Diameter 4″

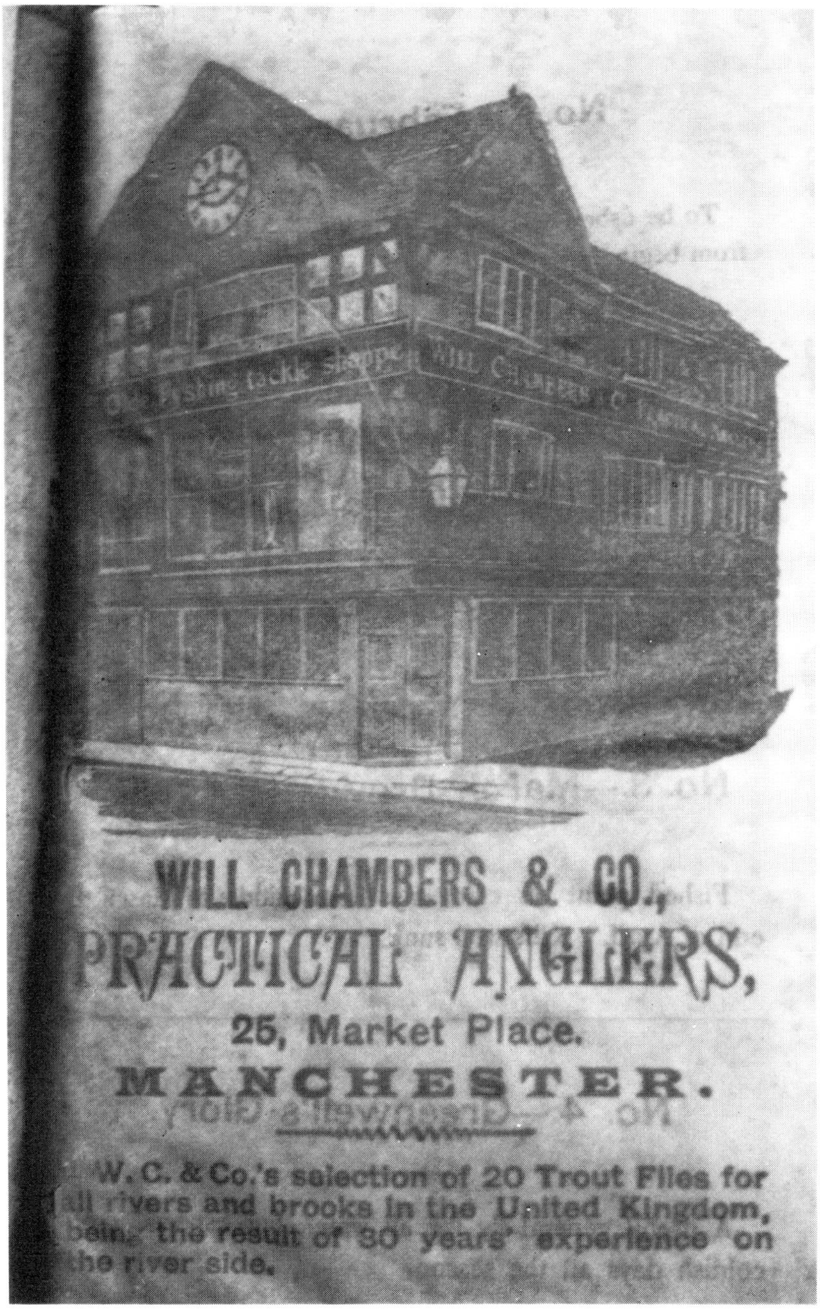

A picture of the shop in Manchester which appeared in a Chambers leather fly wallet

THE NOTTINGHAM WOOD WINCH

The Nottingham Centre Pin reel in cherry wood

The history of the Nottingham wood winch was outlined in an article by Henry Coxon which appeared in the *Fishing Gazette* on September 7th 1895, and the contents are the basis for my text of this model. Briefly what he said was that the earliest primitive patterns were made in Radford and Snieton, which were suburbs of Nottingham about the middle of the nineteenth Century.

The mechanic who first conceived the idea of a centre pin reel was a man called Joseph Turner of Pomfret St, Nottingham. He made several of this type of reel but soon after he began to market them, a Mr S Lowkes of Upper Parliament St, Nottingham introduced what he claimed was an improved version. However, it turned out to have certain defects, including a tendency for the line to become entangled in the aperture surrounding the spindle. This usually made it necessary to break off the line and on occasions to take off the entire line to reach the problem. Even with the early setbacks it proved to be very popular and was the best on the market at that time.

Another Nottingham maker was a man called Steers who produced large quantities of good quality 'centres' and just before his death was experimenting to produce a reel with two centres. A William Brailsford was another maker, who in the beginning, sold most of his production to Walter Wells of the Nottingham Worm Farm who retailed them to fishermen of the area.

One of the most famous of these anglers was a professional fisherman called George Holland or 'Nottingham George' and when he left the Trent for the Thames, he took with him the centre pin Brailsford reels. Eventually the secret got out and Brailsford started to supply other dealers.

Succeeding makers improved and perfected this type of reel including D Slater, Mr H Dale and Mr Eaton, a former employee of Slater. In about 1875, a Mr George Bates of the Nottingham Wellington Angling Society conceived the idea of a Silent Check Nottingham, and this form of centre pin was produced in 1895 by Mr E West, a fishing tackle dealer of 28 Sussex St, Nottingham in a wide variey of sizes.

The Nottingham wood reel was a very popular model and used in large numbers throughout the second half of the nineteenth century and well into the next.

It was made in a wide range of sizes with variations in design including a Sheffield pattern which had the inside of the wood drum hollowed out. A few early Nottinghams were even made with a collar or clamp foot attachment.

Some Nottinghams were made in this 'Sheffield Pattern'

David Slater

David Slater started off by making rods and his first was a six piece pocket roach rod in 1869. He worked in the coach making business and made three, four and five piece rods in his spare time. They were known as 'David's Rods' and the demand grew steadily until eventually he started up as a rod maker at 9 Portland St in Newark, Nottinghamshire.

In 1881 he extended his activities to making reels which were of the wood Nottingham variety and extended his range to what he called the 'Perfect Combination Centre Pin' which was usually made with ebonite back, wooden spool and annular line guard for which he was granted patent number 2551 on the 22nd of May 1883. By that date his premises had extended to Nos 8, 9 and 10 Portland St. A large number of Combination reels were also made with an ebonite brass star back, nickel silver rim and an ebonite drum.

David Slater was always keen on the tackle exhibitions and won his first Diploma Medal and a special money prize of £10 for 'excellence and cheapness' at Norwich in 1881. He went on to compete at the 1883 Fisheries Exhibition in London and secured four Diplomas and Medals and another special money prize. His Perfect Combination Centre Pin won the prestigious award of First Class Bronze Medal at the Cornwall Polytechnic Show.

The *Fishing Gazette* of the 22nd December 1883 reviewed Slater's New Patent Combination Winch described as having a new silent graduated check and made of the best well seasoned mahogany with light brass frame and side bars. It was priced at 15/- for a 4″, 12/6d for a 3½″, and 10/6d for a 2½″.

The same journal held a casting tournament in June 1886 and Slater beat nineteen other competitors to win the cup and 5 guineas with a cast of 177 feet 8 inches with a 2½ oz weight. He went on to gain other notable wins including a Diploma of Honour at Glasgow in 1888 and five Diplomas and Medals for reels at the Bolton Piscatorial Society in 1889.

He was the founder of the Newark Piscatorial Society and became famous for making fine quality reels and rods. He applied for a number of patents but there is no record because he never sealed and completed them.

One of these was probably the 'Slater Latch' which was a small latch near the centre of the reel plate which could release the drum for instant removal. Many other manufacturers took advantage and incorporated this idea on to their reels.

One patent which Slater and a Newark engineer called Arthur Thomas Allcock did complete was patent No 14803 and was granted in 1888 for a folding landing net.

The following history of this famous tackle maker and his business has had to be pieced together from articles and advertisements which appeared in the Fishing Gazette. He built a 'Fly Fishers Winch' in accordance to dimensions supplied by an amateur reel maker called T P Hawksley of the Fly Fishers Club. This model was initially produced in twelve sizes and later

A Combination reel with ebonite and brass star-back, Slater-latch, and nickel silver rim. 4½″ Diameter

The Zephyr narrow drum alloy and brass star-back reel with on/off button and Slater-latch. 4″ Diameter

with an enlarged winding drum in 2¾″ and 3½″ diameters, described as the 'S E J Fly Fishers Winch'.

In about 1892 Slater sold his celebrated business for a life of retirement and the firm traded as David Slater & Co. He probably retained some connection as the company expanded into a range of gunmetal reels for fresh water, light sea fishing, as well as mahseer and salmon. Advertisements appeared on the 16th December 1892 for the following tackle:

> *Rods*– Greenheart Salmon Rods 26/- to 42/-, Trout Rods 8′ to 12′ 21/- to 25/-, Greenheart Salmon & Like Rods 30/-, Thames Trout Rods 30/-, Newark Perfection Rods 10ft to 12ft, 21/- to 23/-, Sheffield Gem Roach Rod 10/6 to 15/- and the Nottingham New Style Rod 15/- to 17/6.
> *Reels*– Patent Combination Reels, Fly Fisher's Winch and Patent Combination Reels in Gunmetal for mahseer and salmon.
> *Patent Landing Nets* – 12/6 to 21/-.

In 1894 the business address became 60 Harcourt St, close to which was a second fishing tackle supplier called Charles Smith & Co trading in Lombard St.

On the 29th June 1895 a surprise advertisement appeared in the *Fishing Gazette* offering the David Slater & Co. business for sale at an asking price of £3000 due to ill health of the proprietor. This was followed by another on the 31st August announcing that David Slater had taken over his former business and was once again trading in his own name.

New reels were developed including the Zephyr which was a narrow drum model with wood front and aluminium back for bottom fishing and by 1898 the 'Jeffrey Jardine' handless reel, designed by Jas Jeffrey and Alfred Jardine with five large perforated flanges on the plate for control by the finger tips.

By 1912 Slater moved into the former Smith premises in Lombard St where he continued to trade until about 1920. The reels he produced were some of the best made in Britain and very beautiful ones to collect.

Below: The Scarborough reel plus passing dog

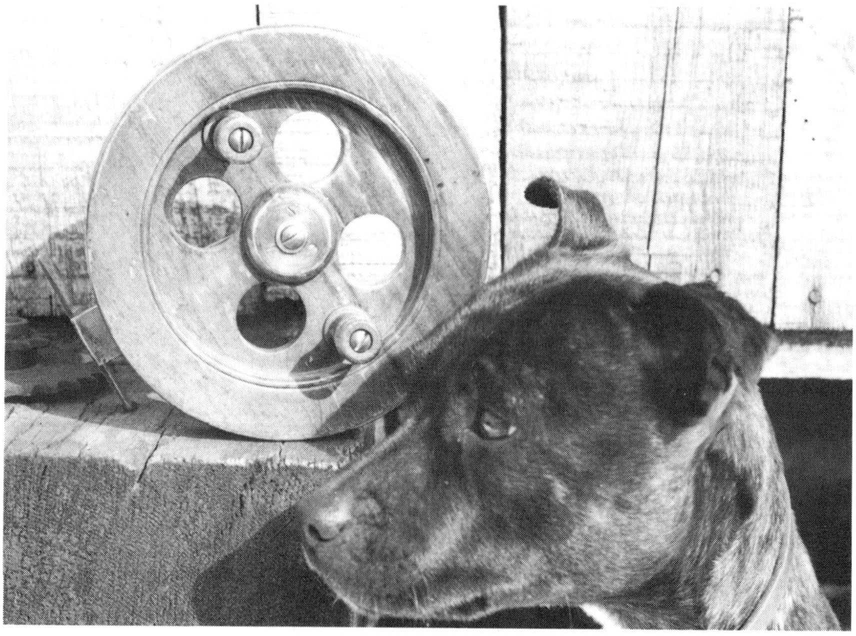

Scarborough Reel

The Scarborough was a dual handle wood reel with usually four large central perforations. It worked on a simple principle of a wood drum rotating on a metal bracket which was shaped to act as the foot. The drum was locked on by a wing nut which also acted as a friction brake.

Engraved Reels

Some brass reels were engraved with fishermen and fishing scenes and are very attractive and collectable.

A brass plate wind engraved with the scene of a fisherman in a boat

Small brass reel with the plate stamped out with the picture of a fisherman

EARLIEST FIXED SPOOL REELS AND PATENTS

Until the introduction of the fixed spool reel, anglers were restricted in the distance they could cast and the speed they could retrieve the line.

Their method had been to use long and powerful rods of between twelve and eighteen feet and to lay coils of line on the ground before casting. This did not always meet with success due to entanglement in plants and materials lying on the surface of the ground.

To overcome this problem, another way had been to lay the coils on a pan, attached to the waist of the angler, but this was obstructive and another additional restriction.

In the last quarter of the nineteenth century, there was an awareness of the advantage of being able to cast without involving the spool, and there was a race in Britain to perfect such a reel.

It is generally accepted that the idea of the fixed spool reel was a British invention and most people would credit either Malloch or Illingworth with being the inventor. In fact it was neither of these gentlemen who first devised a reel which could cast with a stationary drum.

The credit for the achievement lies between two patents, one by an Englishman, and the other by two Americans from Baltimore, and it would appear that the latter were the first to document the basic principle.

Drawing submitted to patent the reel of T Winans and T D Whistler

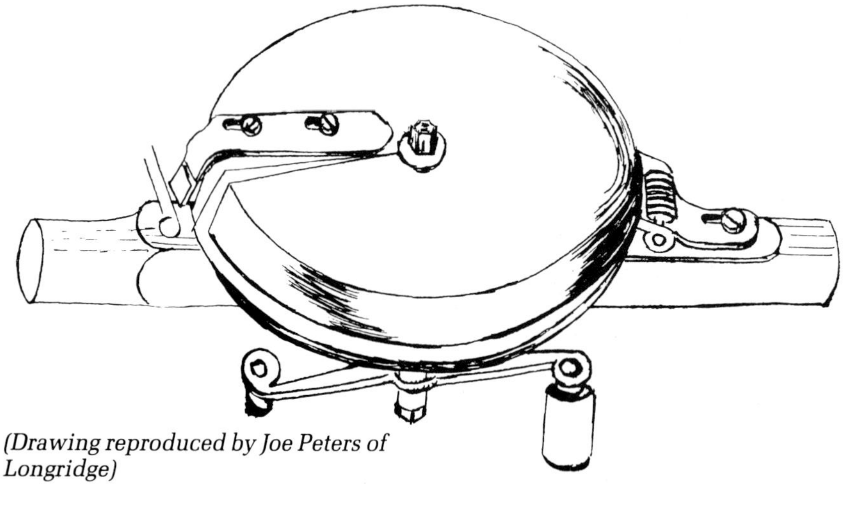

(Drawing reproduced by Joe Peters of Longridge)

PATENT NO. 161314

Fishing Reels
(Files February 27th 1875)

Thomas Winans and
Thomas D Whistler,
Baltimore,
Maryland,

'To all it may concern:

Be it known that we Thomas Winans and Thomas Delano Whistler, both of Baltimore, Maryland have invented certain new and useful improvements in fishing reels, of which the following is a specification. In these improvements in fishing reels it has been our principle object to prevent the line from over-running at the time of casting.

The liability of the line to overrun at this time is well known to fishermen. With the style of reel heretofore used, the over-running of the line, when making the cast, is very great if the reel is left free, and to prevent the over-running it is necessary to regulate the rotation of the reel by a friction brake of some kind. The operation, of course, requires the greatest amount of delicacy and experience, and even then there is great difficulty in preventing over-running. To accomplish the object we have in view, we combine with the reel a guide or line eye, placed by the side, and on the prolongation of the axis of the reel. The line passing over the side of the reel and through the eye, *can run freely from the reel without revolving the latter when the cast is made.*

The line eye is combined with, or forms part of, a cover or case which incloses the part of the reel that contains the line, and prevents, when the cast is made, the line being thrown out by centrifugal force. The arrangement above indicated is adapted for use in casting. After the cast is made it is desirable that the line should run from the reel in the ordinary way. To this end we provide an opening or slit, extending from the periphery of the cover into the eye, through which slit the line can, at pleasure, be passed into or removed from the eye. Other arrangements can however be employed for this purpose. The cover and eye can for instance, be stationary or fixed in a position at right angles with the pole, and the reel may be mounted on an axis or pivot, so located that the said reel can be swung out to enter the case or cover, in which case it will, like the cover, stand at right angles to the pole and will be in the required position for casting; or it may be swung back from the cover, so as to be parallel with the pole, in which case the eye will be nearly in line with the periphery of the reel, the parts thus being in the position required for their use after the cast has been made. Under this last indicated arrangement the eye rquires no lateral slit and the line will permanently pass through it.'

1875 Thomas Winans and Thomas D Whistler

The earliest patent which incorporates the method of casting with a fixed spool was granted to the two Americans, Thomas Winans and Thomas D Whistler. The main object of their idea was the improvement of a fishing reel by preventing over-running of the line, when casting.

The patent continues with two further pages of text giving detailed use of the reel with reference to the patent drawings.

Although the primary object of their design was the prevention of the line over-running, it is clear that they were able to cast with a stationary spool and incorporated a hinge feature which would allow the reel to move to a position with its axis parallel to the rod for an alternative method of fixed spool casting.

Front elevation

Back elevation

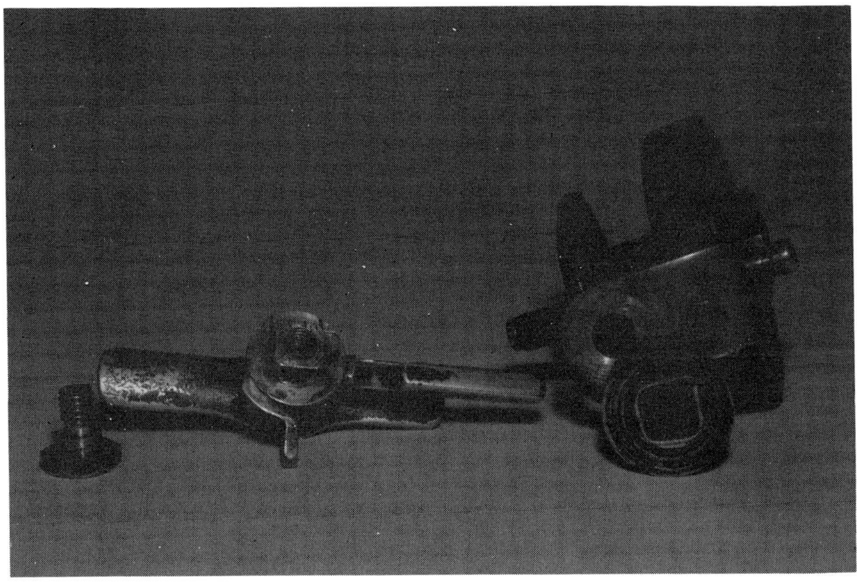

1878 George Richard Holding

The earliest British patent for a fixed spool casting reel was granted to G R Holding of Laurel Cottage, Beckenham, Kent. The patent was No 2121, applied for May 28th and granted November 28th 1878. It was described as 'a new pivot or swivel winch, the object being to enable a person to throw his or her line from the side of a winch or reel while the winch or reel remains stationary.'

The reel was basically a pivoting, strap-back Nottingham. In operation the reel was turned on its axis, one quarter of a revolution, which put the internal spring under tension and placed the face of the reel in the direction of casting. A trigger bar held the reel in the casting position and would then be released to allow the spool to spring back to the normal rewind position.

The Holding reel illustrated is at present the only known example. It is basically as the patent describes – a strap-back Nottingham with a brass trigger activating foot. When the reel was first discovered the section described as the 'holdfast' was coated with a grey compound and below it a black base coat. This was removed and it was possible to dismantle and examine the workings which were exactly as described in patent 2121 found marked on the holdfast casing. The small wood drum was coated with a black compound with a brass face plate and being only 2½″ diameter a single handle had been fitted. This reel takes a special place in the history of British tackle as it was the first to cast with a fixed spool and in the absence of any known example of the Winans and Whistler reel, it is possibly the earliest known documented reel of this type in either Britain or America.

The internal mechanism which causes the pivot action. Note the spring with a square centre which 'lodges on a square projection on the face of the holdfast' (foot) as described by patent 2121

A.D. 1878.—N° 2121.

Holding's New Pivot or Swivel Winch for Fishing Lines.

SPECIFICATION in pursuance of the conditions of the Letters Patent filed by the said George Richard Holding in the Great Seal Patent Office on the 28th November 1878.

GEORGE RICHARD HOLDING, of Laurel Cottage, Beckenham, in the County of Kent. "A NEW PIVOT OR SWIVEL WINCH FOR FISHING LINES."

The object of this Invention is to enable a person to throw his or her line from the side of the winch or reel while the winch or reel remains stationary, and also to enable a person to leave his or her rod and line while fishing without the chance of losing a fish which might have taken the bait during his or her absence.

The Invention consists of an improvement in winches or reels used in fishing.

I make the winch or reel after the pattern of what is known as the Nottingham winch or reel, that is to say, in wood, metal, or other suitable material, without cross bars. I then fix a strap of metal or other material on the back of the said winch or reel, and bring it at right angles, as in the ordinary way, immediately under the back of the winch or reel, extending about $^{2}/_{3}$rds of the width of the winch or reel proper, that is to say, the part of the winch or reel which is to rotate; on to the end of the said strap which comes under the rotating part of the winch or reel, I affix another piece of metal or other material, which I will call the scoop or holdfast, by a joint; the scoop or holdfast is made to fit the fishing rod, as in the ordinary way. I then put a screw pin or rivet of suitable substance, with a head or disc at one end, through the centre or other suitable part of the holdfast and the end of the before-mentioned strap which extends under the rotating part of the winch or reel. By this means I connect the strap and holdfast together, so that the whole of the winch or reel, that is, both the rotating part and back combined together with the strap, will turn upon the face of the holdfast. I then affix a spring of any suitable shape, made of steel wire or flat steel, on the before-mentioned strap, and bring it parallel with the strap under the rotating part of the winch or reel, and lodge it on a square projection on the face of the holdfast; or I place the said spring under the holdfast, and lodge it on the head of the before-mentioned screw or rivet. In this case I should make the head of the screw or rivet square, and omit the square projection on the face of the holdfast.

The object of the spring is to cause the whole of the winch or reel to turn on the holdfast in jumps of a quarter of a circle each time it is turned.

In some cases I omit the spring altogether, so that the winch or reel can be turned and left at any angle or part of a circle by means of a stiff joint.

I will now describe how my pivot or swivel winch is to be used:—If I am fishing for pike, jack, trout, or any other fish that requires running line, having got my bait and line ready for throwing in the water, I turn the pivot or swivel winch or reel a quarter of a circle; the face of the winch or reel will then be towards the top of the rod. I then throw the line by means of the rod, and the line comes quickly and without resistance over the side of the winch or reel, and the winch or reel remains stationary or nearly so. In throwing, no more line comes off the reel than is required, for the moment the bait falls the line stops running. When I wish to leave my rod and line I place the winch or reel in precisely the same position just described, and should a fish take the bait during my absence, the said fish can swim away and take what line it requires without feeling resistance until the whole of the line is off the winch or reel.

In all cases when winding up I turn the winch back to its former position, that is, with the face of the winch or reel towards the right or the left hand.

And in order that my said Invention may be more readily understood, I have annexed Drawings of the same, Figure 1 shewing the winch in the ordinary position, and Figure 2 shewing the winch in position for throwing the line or leaving during absence. The same letters of reference indicate similar parts in both Figs.

a represents the winch or reel; *b*, a strap of metal on the back of the winch or reel; *c* is the scoop or holdfast; and *d*, the joint which is made stiff.

1884 P D Malloch

P D Malloch is generally accepted as the inventor of the fixed spool casting reel but he was in fact several years too late. He could probably claim to be the first person to produce the type of reel on a successful commercial basis as the sidecasters he produced were very popular and sold in large numbers.

The Malloch reel was a much simpler device than the Holding and did not have a spring action to pivot back to the retrieve position from the casting position parallel to the rod. The fisherman simply turned the drum to the casting position manually and when required returned it by hand to the normal rewind position. A large guide eye remained stationary on a fixed arm through which the line passed in whatever position the reel was being used. The flange on the casting side of the drum had a convex surface which assisted the escape of line.

Patent AD 1884 3rd September No 11969. Peter Duncan Malloch of Perth, Scotland

Malloch Sidecaster

Left: Copy of patent No 2121 filed in 1878 by G R Holding

Right: Copy of patent No 9388 filed in 1905 by A H Illingworth

1905 Alfred Holding Illingworth

The first complete fixed spool reel which could both cast and retrieve line while the spool remained stationary was patented by Alfred Holden Illingworth of No 2 Highclere Villas, Ben Rhydding in Yorkshire.

He designed a reel with the unique action of a rotating flyer round a spindle and spool which moved backwards and forwards.

There were two versions of the Illingworth No 1 and the second is said to have an improved bell crank driven by a heart shaped variable speed grooved cam. I don't know what that means either. Mr Illingworth never made any money out of his inventions and assigned some production rights to the Light Casting Reel Co. Ltd. of 36 Sunnybridge Road, Bradford the manufacturers, and Mr F Barker of 26 Hinstock Road, Handsworth Wood, Birmingham.

Four more Illingworth models followed together with a whole series of other makers' 'threadline' reels. J E Miller of Leeds retailed the Chippendale, based on patent No 22271 dated 30th September, 1909 and followed it with a multiplying version as described in patent No 17250 of 20th July 1910, registered by J E Miller and H J Thomas. Illingworth's patent No 18723 dated August 1910 marked the introduction of his No 2 Model, which was a simple threadline reel sporting a rotating spool housing flyer and manual line pick up.

Morris Carswell of Glasgow had been experimenting with various reel improvements for some time and in 1912 he brought out a variation on the No 2 theme on patent 22701. His contribution to the Illingworth stable was an automatic line pick up device which meant the redesign of the reel's foot and stem to a 'T' shape as opposed to the crooked version originally designed.

In 1913 Illingworth rethought the features of the No 2 reel and on patent no 17157 he introduced the No 3 Model. The reciprocating spool feature was brought into use here and an optional handle extra

N° 9388 A.D. 1905

Date of Application, 4th May, 1905

Complete Specification Left, 3rd Nov., 1905—Accepted, 4th Jan., 1906

PROVISIONAL SPECIFICATION.

Improvements in and relating to "Bait Casting Reels" used in Angling.

I, ALFRED HOLDEN ILLINGWORTH, of 2, Highclere Villas, Ben Rhydding, in the County of York, Wool Merchant, do hereby declare the nature of this invention to be as follows:—

This invention relates to improvements in what are known as "bait casting reels," used in angling, and has for its object, the construction of a reel in such a manner that the axis of the spool or drum on which the line is wound always remains parallel to the rod to which the reel is attached, the said spool or drum remaining stationary either when "casting" or "recovering" the line in the operation of angling.

By the use of a reel constructed in accordance with my invention, better "casts" may be made owing to the decrease in friction hitherto experienced, and the line may be wound evenly on the spool or drum.

In carrying out my invention, the revolving disc of the reel is provided on or towards its outer edge with, by preference, bevel teeth, thus forming a toothed wheel, such toothed wheel engaging in turn a bevel toothed wheel which is revolubly mounted around a spindle of suitable length, such spindle being mounted and free to slide, but not to revolve, in suitable bearings attached to the plate which carries the before mentioned revolving disc. The said spindle is parallel to the rod, and one end of the same projects towards the point of the rod.

Attached to the bevel toothed wheel, is what is known to the textile trade as a "flyer" provided with one or more false eyes. On the revolving disc being operated by the angler, the bevel wheel and "flyer" will revolve around the spindle.

The spool or drum around which the line is wound is mounted on and towards the projecting end of the spindle in such a manner that the same may be retained securely thereon, and at the same time be removed therefrom when desired, but should a certain strain be placed on the line by reason of a fish being hooked, or the hook being held by weed or other matter, then the said spool or drum may revolve, the ease with which such revolution will take place being capable of regulation.

In order that the line may be evenly wound on the spool or drum, the line is passed through one of the false eyes of the "flyer", and the spindle is given a sliding motion, similar to what is known in textile industries as a "lifter motion." This motion may be imparted by the angler by means of a cam, lever, or the like. The said cam or the like may be operated by means of the revolving disc, or by the thumb or finger of the angler; in the latter case, the said cam or the like is engaged by a suitable spring which will always return same to its original position.

In operation, when "casting" or "recovering" the line, the spool or drum remains stationary. When "casting" the line slips off the end of the spool.

In "recovering" the line is passed through a false eye on the "flyer" and the "flyer" revolved as before described. The spindle, together with the spool. is moved backwards and forwards within the "flyer" by means of the "lift motion", thereby winding the line evenly over the spool or a portion of the same. When a fish is hooked or strain applied to the hooked end of the line, the spool is revolved and the strain may be adjusted, as before described, and the line let out as desired.

was the addition of a thimble hole in which to stick your finger to do the winding (a feature often used by Allcock's). The line pick up shoe was so designed that by backwinding, the line came free of it for casting.

Many minor changes took place on the No 3 including a fully enclosed body guard, and various versions of this model were produced.

In 1921 the No 3 Illingworth appeared under patent 187124. This reel featured an improved spool design, a new friction clutch arrangement and dummy backings to increase spool inner diameter. It often appears with the fully cased gear box.

In 1926 Arthur Allen of Glasgow brought out his Patent Spinnet reel under patent No 262706 which was a variation of Carswell's modified Illingworth of 1910 design. He had simply added a fine spring metal strip to press against the main drive toothed wheel to make a click and despite the fact that it was a dated model, it sold well.

Later that same year Walter Stanley was granted patent No 276861 for his now famous Allcock Stanley casting reel, which looked more like the Illingworth No 1 than any other reel. Once again, despite the fact it was a rehash of an old reel, it went on to sell thousands of units and was still available into the late 1950s.

The Illingworth No 4 was different in that the Patents were sealed by The Light Casting Reel Co Ltd and not the man himself. This heavier version of the reel was constructed of alloy and featured an extended rise and fall spool motion by a design change to the main shaft and winding gear. The gear casing was made in two parts and partially secured by a large brass knurled nut at the rear body. Patent No 361601 was registered in 1930.

A small time pirate venture was attempted by one P O'Reilly of

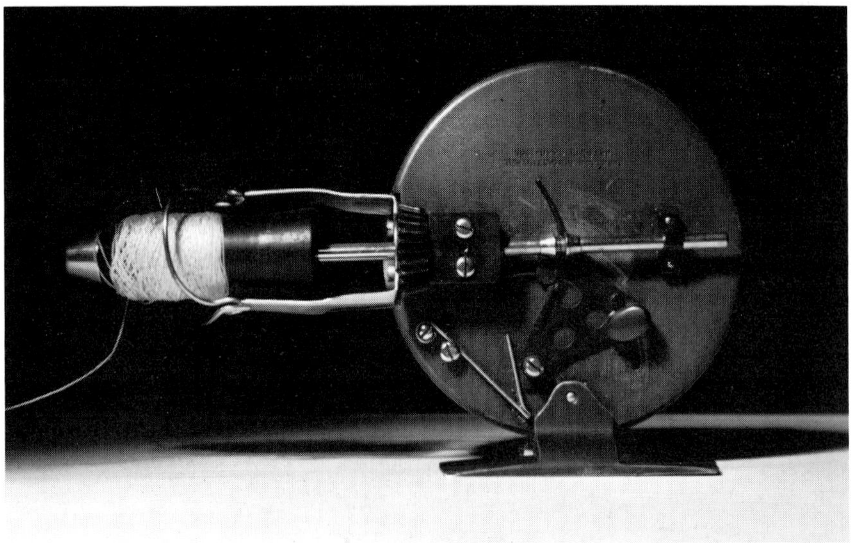

Illingworth No 1 First Version

Illingworth No 2 Second Versions

The later improved model of the Illingworth No 1 Second Version in which the loop wires have been shortened to small pickups

Ayrshire in 1931. His patent No 383423 relates to a Carswell/Allan reel with auto pickup engaged by an arrangement on the foot stem.

Allcocks followed the Illingworth theme in 1932 with their Duplex reel which had the novelty turn upside down feature which no one else used or copied. Threadlines as we know them were fading fast and the introduction of the Allcock Felton Cross Wind reel opened the flood gates to innovation and challenge to bring about the fixed spool reel of today.

The final Illingworth, the No 5, was basically the same as the No 4 except the main gear housing was encased in bakelite with anti-foul foot and stem characteristics.

Illingworth model numbers 2, 3, 4 & 5

Creels

Creels have been made from wood or whicker from earliest times with variations in shape as certain styles were fashionable. During the eighteenth century, and possibly earlier, leather creels were popular but eventually they were discontinued in favour of the cheaper and more serviceable whicker.

The earliest British patents for creels were taken out towards the end of the nineteenth century for designs which their inventors considered different and worth protecting for their potential financial gains.

The earliest man to apply for a British patent for a fishing creel was Harry Lewis Platt of 44 Shorrold Road, Fulham, London who was desribed as a 'Gun and Fishing Rod Maker'. He applied in 1889 for an idea to improve a fishing creel with a design which introduced a tray with fitted lid set into the top for the purpose of carrying lunch or refreshments. A patent No 14135 was issued but he failed to complete the necessary documentary procedure and the patent was abandoned. On December 21st 1891 he made a new application,

Some early creel patents included		
No 19949	Nov 17th 1891	Henry Angus Murton
No 3212	Feb 13th 1893	Phillip Green
No 14057	July 7th 1905	J. A. Mouls
Early Patents for fishing bags		
No 2661	July 30th 1874	E. T. Budden
No 4739	March 28th 1888	W. T. Hancock
No 8930	May 5th 1894	R. S. Bartleet

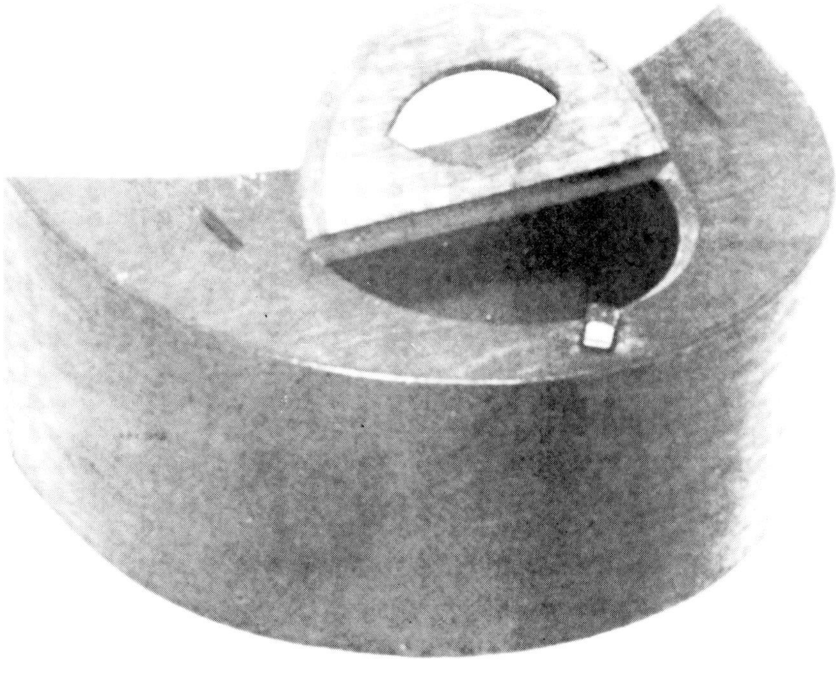

Oak creel constructed of thin sheets of oak with semi-circular hand lid.

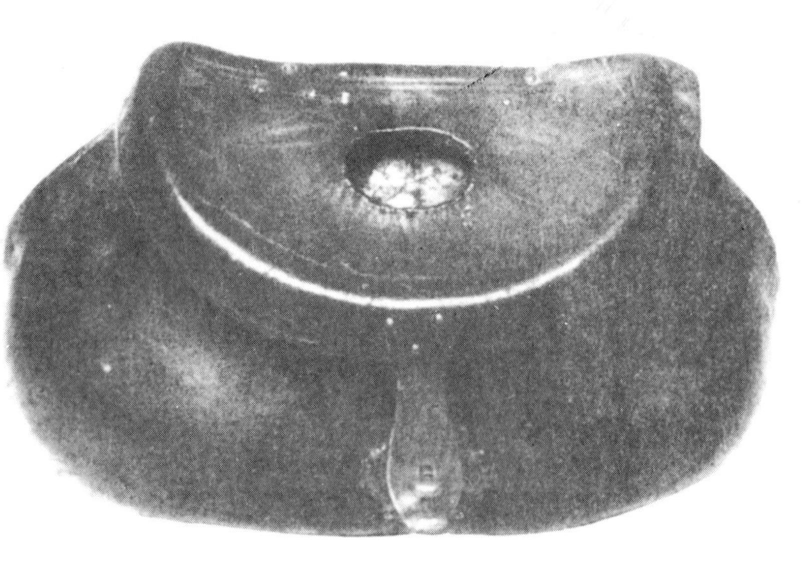

leaving complete specifications on September 12th 1892 and patent No 22305 was accepted on November 26th 1892.

On February 13th 1891 W Hardy and J J Hardy trading as Hardy Bros. made application and received patent No 2597 for a combined creel and tackle case. Although it was more like a tackle bag it had a basket section and a new bag on the front.

A pot-bellied leather creel by N Thompson with leather hinges, brass clasp and tooled lid

A rare Platts whicker creel with food tray and marked with Pat. No. 14135 which was the earliest for this piece of tackle but never completed. Date 1889

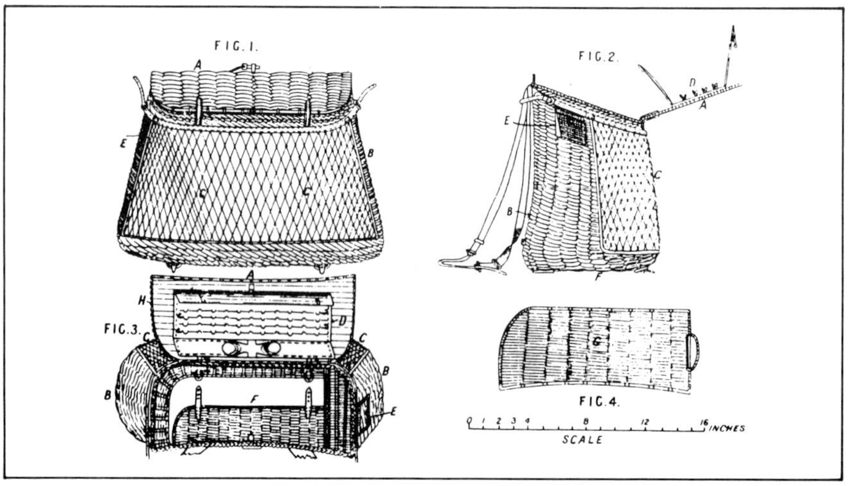

Combined creel and tackle bag by Hardy Bros patented Feb. 13th 1891

LIST OF SCOTTISH TACKLE MAKERS

ADAMS, Alex *Aberdeen* c.1870s
47 Woolman Hill

AIMER, James *Dundee* 1844 – 1850
1844 – 1845 4 Dallfield Walk
1846 – 1850 131 Murraygate

ALEXANDER, John *Edinburgh* c.1895
101 Dundee St.

ALLEN, Arthur *Glasgow* 1870 – 1978
144 Trongate and 12 London St.
By 1885 – 144 Trongate & 14 London St.
1895 – only 144 Trongate
1925 – 3 West Nile St.

ALLEN, David *Edinburgh* 1884 – 1891
1884 – 1888 112 Rose St.
1889 – 1891 108B Rose St.

ANDERSON, Roderick & Sons Ltd. *Edinburgh* 1880 – 1938
Princess St. (various premises)
1930 – 1938 49 & 51 Shandwick Place

ANDERSON, Thomas *Glasgow* 1880 – 1910
3 Batson St.
By 1900 30 Daisy St.
1910 – 1127 Pollokshaws Rd.

BAYLES, W *Glasgow* 1834 – 1835
3 New Wynd

BELL, David *Aberdeen* 1885 – 1891
36 George St.

BELL, George *Glasgow* 1855 – 1875
33 Queen St.

BLACKWOOD, H & Co. *Glasgow* 1875 – 1880
210 Buchanan St. & 67 Dundas St.

BLAIR, Alex *Glasgow* c.1885
28 Gordon St.
From 1890 8 West Nile St.
1895 31 Gordon St.
1900 69 Bothwell St.

Above: A Allan, Glasgow. Brass faced plate reel with nickle silver rims Diameter 3″

Rosewood & Brass with raised casing. Diameter 4½″. Marked – 'Anderson, Dunkeld'

BROWN, Hugh & Co. *Glasgow* 1885 – 1890
213 Argyle St.

BROWN, Peter *Perth* 1860 – 1872
41 George St.

BROWN, William *Aberdeen* 1835 – Current
Became W Brown & Co.
1835 – 1836 187 George St.
1836 – 1839 21 George St.
1839 – 1840 25 George St.
1840 – 1888 36 George St.
1888 – 1891 42 George St.
1891 – 1909 64 George St.
1910 – 1913 150 Union St.
1913 – Current 11 Belmont St.
Believed to have invented the 'Phantom' minnow.

Emslie, Dundee. Small brass plate reel with ebonite handle. Diameter 2½″

BRYSON, Charles *Perth* 1854 – 1882
Known Addresses
1854 64 South St.
1856 Barossa St.
1866 65 North Methven St.
1874 37 North Methven St.
1878 8 Athol St.
1881 – 1882 Watergate

BRYSON, Robert *Glasgow* 1895 – 1905
12 London St.
By 1905 38 Gallowaygate St.

BUCHANAN, James *Glasgow* 1855 – 1905
18 York St.
By 1870 St. En. Way
By 1875 62 Dale St.

CALDER, William *Aberdeen* 1901 – 1923
Guild St.

CALLAGHAN & Co. *Dundee* c.1925
10 Whitehall Crescent

CAMPBELL, Alexander *Inverness* c.1837
18 Church St.

CAMPBELL, Thomas *Glasgow* c.1860
29 Jamaica St.

CARFRAE, M'Duff *Edinburgh* 1840 – 1856
1840 64 Princess St.
1841 69 Princess St.
1842 – 1843 97 Princess St.
1844 – 1851 Mrs Carfrae
1848 – 1851 13 Frederick St.
1852 – 1856 Mrs Carfrae & Son
1852 96 Princess St.
1853 – 1856 3 Frederick St.

CARR, Alexander *Dundee* 1940 – 1950
1940 – 1945 35A Cowgate
1946 – 1950 12 South Lindsay St.

CARSWELL M & Co. *Glasgow* 1865 – 1925
80 Great Clyde St.
By 1870 90 Mitchell St.
By 1905 118 Howard St.

COBHAM, Charles (Rod Maker) *Perth* 1860 – 1865
1860 – 1861 11 Watergate
1862 – 1865 10 High St.

COCHRANE, William *Edinburgh* 1879 – 1903
1879 – 1885 4 Grove Place
1886 – 1887 169 Morrison St.
1888 – 1889 95 Rose St.
1890 – 1903 118 Rose St.

COWAN, Joseph A *Edinburgh* 1868 – 1898
1868 – 1870 18 Brunswick St.
1871 – 1877 146 Rose St.
1878 – 1881 33 Frederick St.
1882 – 1898 Rose St.

CROCKHART, D B *Perth* 1909 – 1970's
33 County Place

DAVIDSON, Alex *Aberdeen* 1885 – 1893
1885 – 1889 27 Carmelite St.
1890 – 1893 14 Carmelite St.

DAVIDSON & MANN *Aberdeen* 1880 – 1884
20 Carmelite St.

DEWAR, John F *Edinburgh* 1885 – 1905
1885 – 1904 48 Hanover St.
1905 88 Hanover St.

DICK D *Glasgow* c.1850
3 Saltmarket

DICK, William *Glasgow* c.1845
96 Jamaica St.

DICKSON, David *Perth* c.1899
15 South Methven St.

DICKSON, W & Co. *Edinburgh* 1876 – 1888
1876 – 1884 Gilmore Park.
1885 – 1888 15A Frederick St.

DICKSON, J & A *Edinburgh* 1892 – 1917
1892 – 1897 8 Braid Rd.
1898 – 1917 15 Comiston Rd. & 14 Braid Rd.

DICKSON, J & Son Ltd. *Dundee* c.1940
76 Ward Rd.

DOBBIE, John *Glasgow* 1875 – 1900
205 Argyle St.

DOUGALL *Glasgow* c.1834 – 1920
(Believed to have started in 1760)
Dougall J & J 1834 – c.1843
52 Argyle Arcade
Dougal James D c.1844 – 1894
c.1844 – 1849 52 Argyle Arcade
c.1850 – 1904 23 Gordon St
Dougall James D & Sons c.1895 – 1920
c.1905 – 1914 3 West Nile St
1915 – 1920 18A Renfield St

DOUGHERTY, James & Son *Glasgow* c.1865
6 Finniest St.

DOUGLAS, John & Co *Edinburgh* 1846 – 1851
Princess St.

DRYDEN, Adam *Edinburgh* 1862 – 1875
1862 3 Deanhaugh St.
1863 – 1873 24 Hanover St.
1874 – 1875 101 Rose St.

DUGUID, David *Aberdeen* 1854 – 1921
1854 – 1859 2 Flourmill Brae
1860 – 1904 3 Flourmill Brae
1905 – 1921 14 Carmalite St.
Became David Duguid & Son in the 1880's.

DUNCAN, William *Glasgow* c.1875
23 Queen St.

ELLIS, John *Edinburgh* 1830 – 1845
1830 – 1834 23 Leith St.
1835 – 1845 60 Princess St.

EMSLIE, Samuel *Dundee* 1900 – 1910
1900 – 1909 20 Barrack St.
1910 Emslie & Gellately at 80 Gellaley St.

EWEN, J.W. *Aberdeen* 1901 – 1916
20 Carmelite St.

FARQUARSON, A.H. *Edinburgh* c.1900
130 Georgie Rd.

FISHER, B A *Glasgow* c.1865
13 Hope St.

FORREST, John *Kelso* 1837 – 1967
Wood St.
Trading as Forrest & Sons as late as 1967 at 35 The Square

FRASER, William *Edinburgh*
1867 – 1870
1867 – 1869 117 High St.
1870 115 & 117 High St.

FULTON, A E *Edinburgh* 1905 – 1915
108 Rose St.

GARDEN, William *Aberdeen*
1869 – 1967
1869 – 1871 3 Belmont St.
1872 – 1937 122½ Union St.
1938 – 1967 216 Union St.
Became William Garden Ltd. in 1950's.

GIBSON, T & Son *Glasgow* 1880 – 1885
10 Renfield St.
1885 122 Nile St.

GILLESPIE, Lawson & Co. *Glasgow* 1870 – 1875
85 Buchanan St & 2 Gordon Lane.

GILMORE, James & Co. *Glasgow*
c.1865
158 Argyle St.

GLASS, J *Glasgow* 1834 – 1835
Thomson's Lane

GORDON, George *Aberdeen* 1854 – 1891
1854 – 1859 31 George St.
1860 – 1862 19 George St.

GORDON, J & G *Aberdeen* 1875 – 1900
1875 – 1878 12 St Nicholas St.
1879 – 1880 4 St Nicholas St.
1881 12½ Correction Wynd
1882 – 1898 73 Netherkirkgate
1899 – 1900 18 Carmelite St.

GORDON, James & Co *Glasgow*
c.1885
141 Renfield St.

GOW, John R & Sons *Dundee* 1880 – current
12 Union St.

GRAHAM, John & Co *Inverness*
1866 – current
27 Union St.
1980 – Current 71 Castle St.

GRANT, Alexander *Inverness*
c.1899
7 Baron Taylor's Lane

W'm Brown, Aberdeen. Curved crank handled brass reel inscribed '1877. Used for 30 years.' Diameter 4″

Scottish Trolling Reel. Diameter 5½″.

Forrest, dual ivorine handled alloy reel with rim tension screw

Gow & Son, Dundee All brass plate wind with horn handle. Diameter 4″

GRANT, James *Glasgow* c.1880
210 Maine St.

GRAY & Co. *Edinburgh* 1890 – 1910
1890 – 1904 27 Frederick St.
1905 – 1910 98 Lothian Rd.

GRAY, D & Co. *Inverness* 1897 – current
36 Union St.
By 1915 14 Union St.
By Mid 1960's 30 Union St.

GRIERSON, James *Glasgow* c.1845
21 Hutcheson St.

HAIGH, H *Edinburgh* c.1895
6 Shandwick Place

HAIGH, William *Glasgow* c.1880
21 Bothwell St.

HANNA, D & Co *Glasgow* 1770 – 1885
205 Thistle St.

HAY, T *Glasgow* 1885 – 1900
23 Nelson St.

HENDERSON, David *Aberdeen* 1845 – 1870
1845 – 1846 21 Loch St.
1847 – 1861 5 Castle Brae
1862 – 1870 39 Castle St.

HENDERSON, George
1870 – 1871
39 Castle St.

HENDERSON, J *Aberdeen* 1850 – 1874
1850 – 1859 89 Spring Gardens
1860 – 1872 1 Millbank Terrace
1872 – 1874 39 Castle St.
Became John Henderson & Son in 1871

HENDERSON, P & Sons *Dundee* 1880 – 1900
1880 – 1884 8 Tally St.
1885 – 1889 21 Barrack St.
1890 – 1894 20 Barrack St.
1895 – 1899 20 & 82 Barrack St.
1900 only 82 Barrack St.

HENDERSON, T G *Inverness* 1899 – 1906
39 High St.

HENRY, Alexander & Co. *Edinburgh* 1910 – 1920
(incorporated into Alex Martin about 1920)
22 Frederick St.

HILLIER, Fag & Co. *Glasgow* c.1900
2 Springfield Court

HISLOP, M *Glasgow* 1890 – 1900
21 & 32 Argyle Arcade

HOGG, Francis *Edinburgh* 1837 – 1887
1837 – 1844 11 Hanover St.
1845 – 1849 Fraser Hogg
1845 71 Princess St.
1846 – 1849 79 Princess St.
1850 – 1887 Mrs F Hogg, 79 Princess St.

HORTON, William *Glasgow* 1865 – 1910
29 Union St.
By 1880 11 Royal Exchange Square
1895 98 Buchanan St.

HUTCHIESON, Joseph *Glasgow* c.1885
70 & 72 Gordon St.

IMRIE, David *Glasgow* 1855 – 1870
7 Argyle St.
By 1865 12 Glassford St.

IMRIE, John *Perth* 1872
7 Watergate

INGRAM, Charles *Glasgow* 1895 – 1945
18b Renfield St.
By 1920 Additional premises at 4 Bothwell St.
1925 10 Waterloo St.

JACK, Alex & Co. *Glasgow* c.1875
9 Ardgowan St.

JONES, William *Edinburgh* c.1910
17 Haddington Place

KASSON, James *Dundee* c.1900
42 Castle St.

KENT, William *Glasgow* c.1900
519 Gallowgate

KIRKPATRICK, A & Co. *Glasgow* c.1885
24 Buchanan St.

LAING, John William *Aberdeen* 1880 – 1898
1880 – 1894 36 George St.
1895 – 1898 19 Stirling St.

LANDELL, William *Glasgow* 1895 – 1955
106 Trongate and 187 Broad St.
By 1920 106 & 108 Trongate

LANG, Samuel *Edinburgh* 1853 – 1874
1853 71 Princess St.
1854 59 Princess St.
1855 – 1863 5 Hanover St.
1864 – 1866 14 South St David St.
1867 – 1868 9 Brown St.
1870 – 1874 30 St. Andrew Square

LAWSON, James *Glasgow* 1875 – 1910
70 Argyle St.

LAWSON RANKIN & Co. *Glasgow* 1880 – 1915
85 Buchanan St.
1890 Lawson & Co.
By 1915 Lawson & Co. Ltd.

LAWSON, Robert *Edinburgh* 1880 – 1910
1880 – 1884 7 Hope St.
1885 – 1910 2 Hope St.
1905 – 1910 Mrs Lawson

LEES & WILSON *Edinburgh* 1880 – 1896
1880 – 1884 259 Leith Walk
1885 – 1896 4 Gayfield Place

LEES, James & Son *Perth* 1856 – 1895
George St.
1874 – 1895 Robert Lees

LEWIS, Stewart *Aberdeen* 1888 – 1890
St Peters Lane

LORIMER, John *Perth* c.1885
7 King St.

LUMLEY, F A *Edinburgh* c.1910
163–5, Leith St.

LYELL, John *Aberdeen* 1865 – 1879
128 Union St.
Traded as John Lyell & Co. from 1974

MACKAY, *Aberdeen* 1901 – 1910
50 Bridge St.

MACKENZIE, Alexander
Edinburgh 1806 – 1841
25 North Bridge

MACKIE, Alexander *Edinburgh*
1893 – 1920
8 & 9 Melbourne Place and 4 Victoria St.

MACLEAY, William Ashburton
Inverness 1873 – 1973
By 1899 W A Macleay & Son 65 Church St.
By 1925 43 Church St.

MACNAUGHTON, James
Edinburgh 1880 – 1900
26 Hanover St.

MACPHERSON BROS, *Inverness*
c.1899
36 Bridge St.

MACPHERSON, Duncan & Co.
Inverness c.1899
7 Drummond St.

MACPHERSON, John *Inverness*
1905 – 1977
24 Church St.
By 1925 6 Inglis St.

MALLOCH P D (1875 – 1981)

MARSHALL, Alex *Glasgow* 1890 – 1930
1890 – 1894 277 Argyle St.
1895 – 1899 277 & 213 Argyle St.
1900 – 1904 Also additional 176 London St.
1905 176 & 277 Argyle St.
1915 W. Marshall
By 1925 13 Union St.

MARTIN, Alexander *Glasgow*
1838 – current
79 Argyle St.
By 1845 18 Exchange Sq.
By 1850 20 Exchange Sq.
1905 20 Royal Exchange Sq. and 128 Union St, Aberdeen
1910 – 1920 incorporated with Alex Henry & Co. of 22 Frederick St, Edinburgh

MARTIN, Alex *Aberdeen* 1894 – 1967
1894 – 1936 128 Union St.
1937 – 1966 25 Bridge St.
Traded as Alex Martin Ltd. from 1950

MARTIN, Peter *Dundee* c.1880
77 Hill Town

Macleay, Inverness. Ivorine handled alloy, 'Hercules' type reel. Diameter 2¾″

Macleay, Inverness. Bronzed brass plate wind with ebonite handle. Diameter 4¼″

Scottish wooden Pirn with iron curved crank handle. Width 5″ Diameter 3½″ (with horse hair line)

M'DONALD, John *Edinburgh*
1898 – 1912
101 Dundee St.

M'GREGOR, Miss *Aberdeen* 1865 – 1872
1865 – 1867 59 Queen St.
1868 – 1869 80 Queen St.
1870 73 John St.
1870 – 1871 13 Lock St.
1871 – 1872 63 Union St.

M'GREGOR, Alexander *Perth* c.1909
44 George St.

M'GREGOR, David *Perth* 1889 – 1899
37 South St.

M'KINLAY, *Glasgow* c.1885
80 Renfield St.

M'KINLAY, John *Perth* 1868 – 1915
Became James M'Kinlay by 1880
By 1884 52 Athole St.
By 1885 – John M'Kinlay
1895 – 1915 8 County Place

M'KINLAY, William *Perth* 1852 – 1880
1852 7 Kinnoull St.
1859 17 Commercial St.
1860 6 Canal St.
1866 46 Athol St.
1868 34 St. John St.
1872 49 Commercial St.
1878 23 East Bridge St.

M'LAGEN, Peter *Perth* 1885 – 1915
274 High St.
1889 50 South Methven St.
1907 17 Princess St.
1915 21 Princess St.

M'LEOD, A & M *Glasgow* 1880 – 1890
1880 – 1884 361 Argyle St.
1885 – 1889 55 Norfolk St.
1890 349 Argyle St.

M'LEOD, D *Glasgow* 1834 – 1900
193 Argyle St.
From 1845 D M'Leod & Son.
1850 43 Clyde Place
1860 – 1880 46 Clyde Place
1885 58 & 62 Dale St.
1890 46 Clyde Place

M'LEOD, Peter *Glasgow* 1920 – 1970
345 Argyle St.
1930 – 1970 D M'Leod & Co.
118 Howard St.
By 1970 8 Springfield Court

McLEOD, William *Aberdeen* 1875 – 1880
8 Guild St.

M'NAUGHTON, John *Inverness*
1825 – 1837
1825 – 1836 Castle St.
1837 2 Beatons Close

McNAUGHTON, James *Perth*
1895 – 1899
44 George St.

M'PHERSON BROS *Glasgow* 1885 – 1945
134 Trongate
1890 134 Trongate & 156 Argyle St.
1895 78 & 156 Argyle St. & 115 Sauchiehall St.
1900 78 Argyle St.
1905 78 & 80 Argyle St.
1940 25 & 31 Queen St.

MILLAR, William *Dundee* 1890 – 1895
1890 – 1894 Drill Hall
1895 Charles L Millar at 40 Bell St.

MILNE, William *Aberdeen* 1870 – 1920's
1870 – 1874 60 North Broadford
1874 – 1881 25 North Broadford
1882 – 1884 32 Back Wynd
1885 – 1894 19 Stirling St.
1895 – 1898 8 Back Wynd
1899 – 1902 3 Trinity St.
1903 – 1909 29 Carmelite St.
1910 – 1922 39 Bridge St. & 22 College St.

MUIR, George E Y *Edinburgh*
1875 – 1890
1875 – 1884 1 West Crosscauseway
1885 – 1887 48 St. Patricks Sq.
1888 21 East Crosscauseway
1889 – 1890 Middle Arthur Place

MUNROE, Hugh *Edinburgh* 1833 – 1836
59 High St.

MURDOCK, James *Glasgow* 1880 – 1890
12 Kelburn Terrace
By 1885 46 Jamaica St.
1890 7 Croy Place

MURDOCK & SANDILANDS *Glasgow* c.1865
25 West Howard St.

NAPIER & CRAIG *Glasgow* 1885 – 1971
372 Scotland St.
By 1895 247 Paisley Rd.
1900 47 Park St.
1905 175 Park St.
1915 23 Wellington St.
1920 175 Park St.
1925 20 Sussex St.

NICOL, James *Aberdeen* 1892 – 1895
12 Correction Wynd

NISBET, A & Co. *Glasgow* c.1860
45 Union St.

ORMISTON, W & Co. *Glasgow* c.1885
120 Buchanan St.

PANTON, George *Glasgow* 1845 – current
Stockwell St.
By 1850 George Panton & Co.
1855 George Panton & Son.
By 1895 24 Miller St.
c.1900 George Panton & Son Ltd.
By 1945 44 Buchanan St.
1955 30 Buchanan St and 34 Argyle St.

PANTON, James & Co. *Glasgow*
1834 – 1860
59 Trongate
By 1840 114 Trongate
1850 85 Buchanan St.

PATERSON, James *Perth* c.1899
4 Abbot St.

PATON, Edward *Perth* 1860 – 1889
44 George St.
1872 – 1889 E. Paton & Son
also traded as Paton & Walsh

PHIN, William *Edinburgh* 1810 – 1894
1810 – 1820 92 High St.
1821 – 1831 34 North Bridge
Mrs W Phin 1832 – 1858
1832 – 1851 34 North Bridge
1852 – 1858 80 Princess St.
C A Phin 1859 – 1894
1859 – 1867 80 Princess St.
1868 – 1879 80B Princess St.
1880 – 1884 111 Princess St.
1885 – 1893 5 South St. David St.
1894 8 Dundas St.

PLAYFAIR, Charles *Aberdeen*
1820 – 1955
1820 – 1825 56 Union St.
1825 – 1845 94 Union St.
1845 – 1860 70 Union St.
1860 – 1882 138 Union St.
1775 Became Charles Playfair & Co.
1883 – 1924 142 Union St.
1925 – 1955 18 Union St.

POTTER, S & Co. *Edinburgh* 1895 – 1915
1895 – 1904 12 Elm Row
1905 – 1915 2 Gayfield Place

PROCTOR, John *Dundee* 1900 – 1905
82 Blackcroft

PURDEN, W *Glasgow* 1834 – 1835
153 Trongate.

RAWSON, William *Edinburgh*
1796 – 1846
William Rawson was one of the earliest tackle makers in Scotland having come from York to establish a business in Edinburgh.
1796 26 Leith St.
1797 – 1800 24 Leith St.
1801 – 1803 William Rawson & Sons 29 Leith St.
1804 – 1811 Rawsons (Rod Maker) 72 Leith St.
1812 – 1814 Rawson & Son (Rod Maker) 72 Leith St.
1814 – 1815 John Rawson (Rod Maker) 12 Princess St.
1816 – 1846 William Rawson (Rod Maker)
1816 – 1817 72 Leith St.
1818 – 1819 3 Calton St.
1820 43 Princess St.
1821 – 1822 91 High St.
1823 – 1826 97 High St.
1827 – 1846 153 High St.

ALSO LISTED
1820 – 1829 RAWSON, Joseph (Rod/maker)
1820 – 1822 12 Princess St.
1823 – 1827 13 Princess St. (Rod/hook/tackle)
1828 – 1829 38 Princess St.

RICHARD, James, B *Glasgow* 1880 – 1885
1880 – 1884 168 Argyle Arcade
1885 176 Argyle St.

RIGG, Thomas *Glasgow* 1838 – 1840
50 & 52 Hutcheson St.

Paton & Walsh of Perth. Scottish pattern – rosewood and brass with ebonite handle. Diameter 5″

J Wright, Edinburgh. Scottish type plate wind with ebonite handle. Diameter 3¾″

Scottish Trolling Reel. Diameter 5½″. Marked 'Harwood, Killin, Loch Tay'

RITCHIE, John *Aberdeen* 1882 – 1901
1882 – 1888 125 George St.
1889 – 1890 131 George St.
1891 197 George St.

ROBERTSON, John *Glasgow* 1865 – 1880
31 Argyle Arcade

ROBERTSON, John *Aberdeen* 1880 – 1893
128 Union St.

ROBERTSON, Thomas *Glasgow* 1865 – 1885
77 King St.

ROBERTSON, William *Glasgow* 1885 – current
Central Arcade 105 Hope St.
By 1890 5 Bothwell St.
1900 27 Wellington St.
c.1950 Became W'm Robertson & Co (Fishing Tackle) Ltd.

ROY, William *Aberdeen* 1865 – 1881
1865 – 1874 24 North Broadford
1875 – 1881 60 North Broadford

RUTHERFORD, D *Edinburgh* 1839 – 1841
45 Princess St.

RUTHERFORD, William *Edinburgh* 1836 – 1885
1842 – 1848 45 Princess St.
1849 – 1850 24 Princess St.
1851 – 1863 52 Princess St.
1864 – 1870 52 Princess St. Also 5 Hanover St.
1871 – 1885 Mrs William Rutherford
1871 – 1876 52 Princess St.
1877 – 1885 41A Princess St.

SANDERSON, Ludovick *Aberdeen* 1846 – 1881
118 King St.

SCOTLAND, G D *Glasgow* 1860 – 1865
29 Brunswick St.

SHANKS, *Edinburgh* 1842 – 1870
1842 – 1846 John Shanks & Co. 25 North Bridge
1847 – 1869 Thomas Shanks
1847 – 1859 25 North Bridge
1860 – 1869 5 Frederick St.
1870 Mrs Thomas Shanks, 5 Frederick St.

J S Sharpe of Aberden. 1920 – 1965

The founder of J S Sharpe of Aberdeen served his apprenticeship as a gunsmith with Davidson Gunmaker in Carmelite St Aberdeen. As a young man, he left to work in a north of England fishing tackle business, until this was interupted by the First World War. He saw service in Europe and the Middle East and after the war returned to Aberdeen. Although with very little capital, he set up in business in 1920 at 11 Belmont St, bringing in his two sons Jack & Alan. They struggled through the difficult times of the 1920's, making rods, collapsible landing nets and telescopic gaffs of unique designs.

Their sales extended to Canada, New Zealand, India, France and America and in the 1930's their name became known worldwide. In 1933 their rods were awarded the gold medal at the Milan Exhibition and they became the biggest rod maker in Scotland. The Second World War suspended manufacture of their tackle, but when it ended, the Sharpe family formed themselves into a private company. They introduced new machinery and produced a wide range of quality rods, the best of which were the 'Aberdeen' and the 'Scottie', and both sold in very large quantities. On December 18th 1957 the founder John S Sharpe died at the age of eighty six and his two sons carried on the family business.

In the year 1964/5 J S Sharpe Fishing Tackle Ltd joined C Farlow & Co. Ltd of 5b Pall Mall. Alan H Sharpe joined the board of Farlow's and three Farlow directors joined the board of the Aberdeen firm.

The following year the combined firm was sold to Mr A R Baxter and became a subsidiary of his Shawfield Street Securities Ltd. and continued as described for Farlow's of Pall Mall.

1920 – 1923 11 Belmont St.
1924 – 1926 37 Belmont St.
1927 – 1965 35 Belmont St.
1950 J S Sharpe (Fishing Tackle Ltd.)
1965 joined Farlow's & Co. Ltd.

SHERRIFF, Peter *Glasgow* 1855 – 1880
10 Renfield St.
By 1875 138 Sauchiehall St.
1880 J Sherriff, 200 Hope St.

SNOWIE, Hugh Lumsden *Inverness* 1860 – 1911
82 & 83 Church St.
By 1899 Hugh Snowie & Son 36 Church St.
By 1910 60 Academy St.

SOMERS, Jim *Aberdeen* 1950 – current
40 Thistle St.

SPICERS, P & Sons *Inverness* c.1915
60 Academy St.
(Succeeded H. Snowie & Son)

STEWART, Lewis *Aberdeen* 1890 – 1891
St Peters Lane

STIRLING & M'Lelland *Glasgow* 1895 – 1900
38 Queen St.

STRACHAN, James *Edinburgh* 1876 – 1885
1876 – 1884 64 Buccleuch St.
1885 2 Parkside St.

STRACHAN J Junior *Edinburgh* 1880 – 1881
16 Tobago St.

STRATON, James *Aberdeen* 1835 – 1851
1835 – 1847 5 St Katherine's Way
1848 – 1849 3 Kingsland Place
1850 – 1851 55 Netherkirkgate

SUTTER, John *Inverness* 1825 – 1860
Castle St.
By 1860 10 Church St.

TAIT, Archibald *Inverness* 1860 – 1866
19 Church St.

THOMPSON, Charles *Edinburgh* 1830 – 1837
44 Princess St.

THOMSON, J C & Co. *Glasgow* 1890 – 1895
12 St Enoch Sq.
By 1895 27 West Howard St.

THOMPSON, John T. *Edinburgh*
1889 – 1893
15 Frederick St.

TURNBULL, Robert *Edinburgh*
1905 – 1930
1905 – 1914 10 & 12 Hanover St.
1915 – 1930 5 South St. David St.

TURNBULL, William *Edinburgh*
1880 – 1930
1880 – 1890 68 Princess St.
1891 – 1893 60 Princess St.
1894 – 1941 Turnbull & Co.
1894 – 1928 60 Princess St.
1929 – 1941 37 George St.
The firm of Turnbull's carried on trading but ceased selling fishing tackle in c.1941.

WADDELL, Matt *Dundee* 1955 – 1960
12 South Lindsay St.

WALLACE & KERR (RODS) *Dundee* 1930 – 1935
76 Ward Rd.

WATSON, Donald *Inverness* 1899 – 1956
19 Inglis St.

WATSON, James *Aberdeen*
1922 – 1957 24 Guild St.
1927 – 1957 James Watson & Son

WELLS, B *Edinburgh* 1896 – 1899
11 Leith St.

WELLS, David *Edinburgh* 1873 – 1899
1873 – 1876 11 Leith St.
1877 – 1899 11 & 15 Leith St.

WILMOT, G Bernard *Edinburgh* c.1910
28 Nicolson St.

WILSON, *Edinburgh* 1820 – 1879
Wilson, R & G 1820 – 1832
1820 – 1822 14 Infirmary St.
1823 – 1832 23 Princess St.
Wilson, R 1833 – 1845
1833 – 1843 23 Princess St.
1843 – 1845 33 Princess St.
Wilson, A & G 1846 – 1879
1846 – 1860 34 Princess St.
1861 – 1879 19 Waterloo Place

WILSON, James *Glasgow* 1880 – 1905
62 Argyle St.

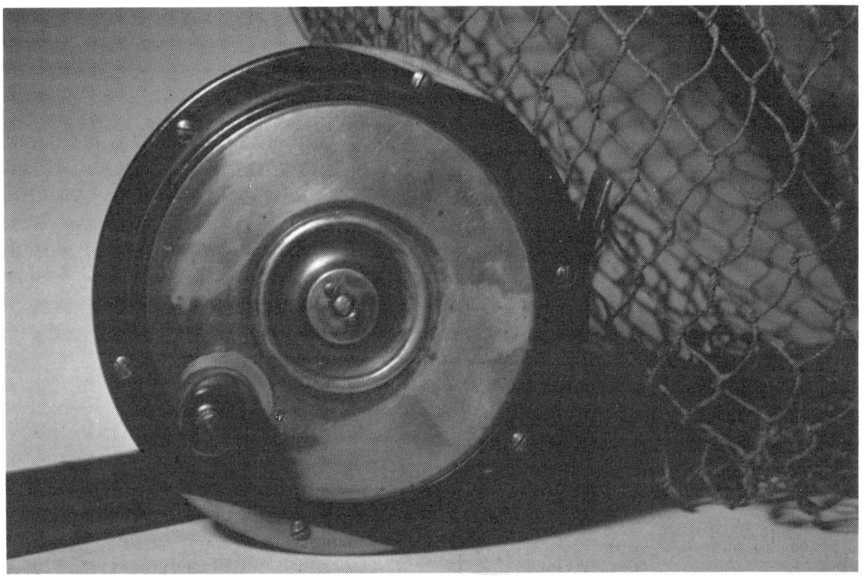

Robertson, Glasgow. Brass & rosewood. Diameter. 5″

P Sherriff, Glasgow. Rosewood and brass plate reel. Diameter 4″

A J S Sharpe's alloy reel 'The Scottie' Diameter 3½″

WILSON, J & C *Edinburgh* 1846 – 1863
1846 3 Abbeyhill
1847 – 1848 13 Abbeyhill
1849 – 1853 Parkside St.
1854 – 1858 Brand Place
1859 – 1863 Kings Place

WILSON, Robert *Aberdeen* 1863 – 1881
16 St Nicholas St.

WILSON, Edmund *Edinburgh* 1882 – 1893
Jeweller and fishing tackle maker.
1882 -- 1887 3A Frederick St.
1888 – 1891 154 Crosscauseway
1892 – 1893 60 Crosscauseway

WRIGHT, Robert *Edinburgh* 1871 – 1928
16 Princess St.
1888 – 1928 James Wright
1910 – 1930's John Taylor Wright (Junior) 24 West Preston St.

WRIGHT, Robert *Glasgow* c.1875
122 West Nile St.

YOUNG, William *Glasgow* 1875 – 1885
31 & 32 Argyle Arcade

Every Description of Sporting Ammunition in Stock

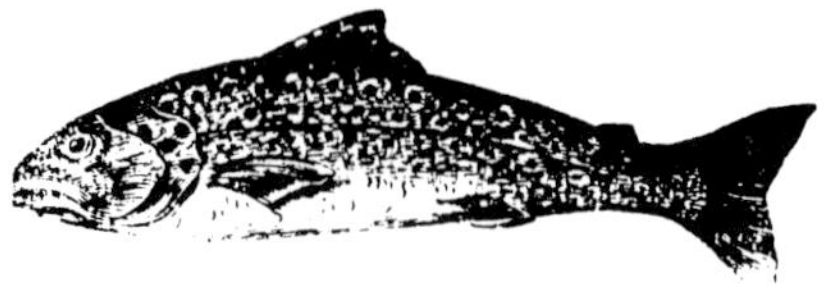

Salmon and Trout Rods, Reels, Lines, Baskets, Landing Nets, &c.
Fishing Rods and Reels Neatly Repaired.
Salmon and Trout Flies always on hand, or made to pattern
Fishes Stuffed and Preserved. Birds, Stags' Heads, &c.

D. WATSON & CO.,
PRACTICAL ANGLERS, GUN AND FISHING TACKLE MAKERS.
19 INGLIS STREET, INVERNESS
Telegrams—"Watson, Gunmaker, Inverness." Tel. No. 461.

D Watson, Inverness. All brass reel with straight crank anti-foul rim and ebonite handle. Diameter 4″

H Snowie (gunmaker) Inverness. Brass reel with serpentine crank and turned wooden handle. Diameter 4¼″

Above: M C Thorburn, Edinburgh, Ivorine handled brass reel with centre bar drum locking latch. Diameter 4″

Above Right: Turnbull, Edinburgh. Brass plate reel with nickel silver rims and ebonite handle. Diameter 4″

Right: Wells, Edinburgh. Curved crank handled brass reel with ebonite handle. Diameter 4″

Above: A & G Wilson, Edinburgh. Curved crank handled brass reel. Marked 'Maker to HRH Prince Albert'. Diameter 2⅝″

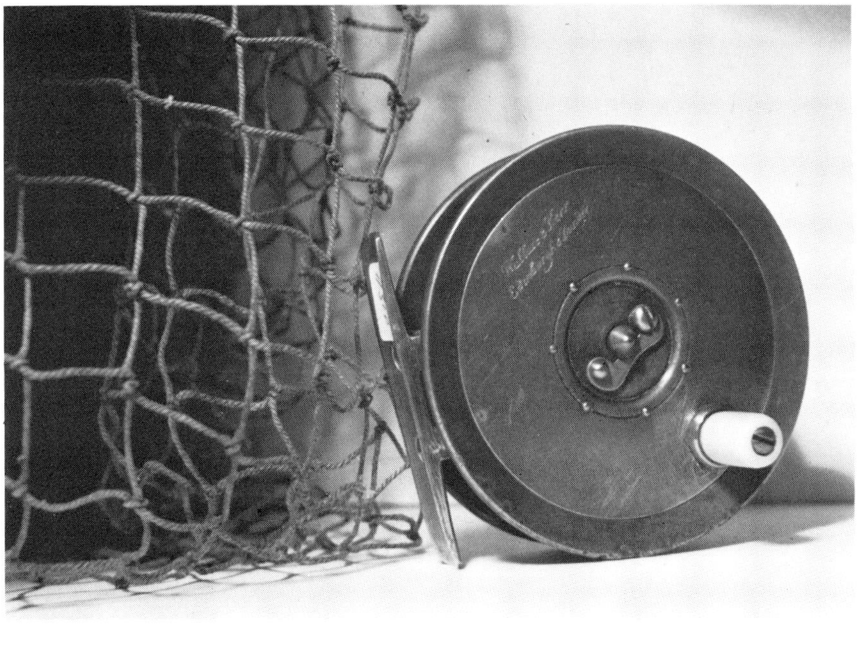

Right: Wallace & Kerr, Edinburgh and Dundee. Ivorine handle and drum locking latch. Diameter 3″

HOOK MAKERS

The Kirby family of hook makers dominated the market up to the middle of the 18th century with Denton of Yetland in Yorkshire, their main competitor. The last Kirby advertisement I have been able to find was in 1768 from premises at St Anne's Lane, Aldergate, London in which Mr Ustonson is named as their sole agent.

By that time however, hook makers were in business in various parts of the country, and London which had been the centre and home of the industry began to decline.

Kendal in Cumbria was a town associated with hook making. Hutchinson had started in 1745 as a sideline to needle manufacturing and quickly extended his activities to making creels and other forms of tackle. He was still in business a century later which was confirmed by William Shipley and E Fitzgibbon in *Fly Fishing* in 1838. Another hook maker was Adlington, while a James Garnett was listed in 1868 as maker of flies at No 5 Yard, 56 Highgate, Kendal.

Limerick in Ireland became famous for production of hooks and the best known were made by the O'Shaughnessy family who were established in 1795. On the 9th of March 1848 Robert O'Shaughnessy placed the following advertisement in the Limerick Chronicle:

> 'Fishing Tackle: Facts are stubborn things: O'Shaughnessy has the honour of informing the Piscatorial World, that he is now the only person in existance, manufacturing the real O'Shaughnessy Hooks and Flies; any other person professing to sell Hooks or Flies as O'Shaughnessy is imposing on the public. There is but ONE ESTABLISHMENT for getting the real genuine article, in which has attained so much celebrity, and that is solely at O'Shaughnessy's'.

Copying and misrepresentation must have been part of the hook industry as O'Shaughnessy's announcement suggests that he met with the same problems that John Kirby experienced over a century earlier.

Hook making in the beginning required very little skill. A simple device called a hook bender was all that was required and even children could use it successfully. Production was run on the basis of a cottage industry but eventually demand outpaced the supply. Mechanisation and centralisation had to be introduced with a larger and better controlled labour force. Redditch was the place chosen and makers sprang up to cope with the growing market. Firms like Allcocks, Milwards, Bartleet, Boulton, Davies, Moore, Sealey, Smith, Hemming, James and Woodfields sent hooks to all corners of the globe. Redditch became the hook centre of the world supplying both fishing fleets and sportsmen.

The theory of how it all started is that the monks of Bordesley Abbey were skilled artisans in metal which they had learned from their links with Toledo in Spain. Henry VIII dissolved the brotherhood and the monks were hidden and looked after by local people. There was a transfer of the skill of making needles which the monks possessed and the recipients were the people of the local villages. Eventually hook making developed as a sideline to the needle trade and one of the earliest makers was Charles Tolley at Sambourne near Redditch. There were a number of makers of which there are no records except John Andrews of Tardebigg village who patented a process for tempering hooks.

By the middle of the 19th century the Redditch firms were the market leaders in the fish hook industry and won all the premier awards at the prestigious Great Exhibition of 1851:

PRIZE MEDAL:
Bartleet & Son (Redditch) – Fish Hooks and Needles
PRIZE MEDAL:
Boulton W & Son (Reddith) – Fish Hooks and Needles
PRIZE MEDAL:
Hemming H (Redditch) – Fish Hooks
PRIZE MEDAL:
Horsefall H (Birmingham) – Pins and Wire for Fish Hooks
PRIZE MEDAL:
James J (Redditch) – Fish Hooks and Needles

The Exhibition catalogue gave the following description of the manufacture:

> 'Fishing hooks are formed by simple tools: a bundle of wire is cut into lengths and straightened; the barb is formed by a simple blow with a chisel; the opposite end is flattened – the barbed end pointed; they are then case-hardened, the surface being partly acted on and rendered extremely hard by means of immersion in hot animal charcoal; they are subsequently brightened by friction and tempered; in some cases they are japanned, in others tinned, but this refers only to the larger sizes – WCA'.

It is difficult to establish when the eyed hook was first used in Britain as what few records have been quoted are relatively late. Mr H S Hall and Mr Blankart perfected and brought eyed hooks to prominence in 1879 but in a letter to the Fishing Gazette said they had purchased them two years earlier. The vendor had been a Mr Aldham who wrote the *Quaint Treatise* in 1876, but although he mentioned eyed hooks he said they had been produced for the book but did not know the maker.

It is recorded that Allcock of Redditch made some for J S Holroyd of London in 1867 and it has been suggested that they were the makers of the ones for Aldham's book. Eyed hooks were mentioned eighteen years earlier in 1849 by Hewett Wheatley in *Practical Hints and Dainty Devices of the Sure Taking of Trout, Grayling etc* in which he says they have been used for a long time.

There is a needle and hook museum at Redditch.

In 1823 Redditch and district had about 800 houses and a population of over four thousand. It was a principle place of needle and fish hook manufacture, listing the following persons trading—

Fish Hooks
Allcock
Bartleet, W'm & Sons
Boulton, W'm & Sons
Clarke, Joseph
Cook, T & E
Cooper, Jno
Harrison, Jas
Hemming, W'm
Holyhoake, T & J
James, Jos
James, R
Milward, Henry & Sons
Mills, Matthew
Prescot, J & Son
Reading, Joseph
Smallwood, W'm
Tandy, Thomas

Tackle and Floats
Cox, C E
Hollington, W'm
Harrison, James
Turner, Thomas
Wyers & Son
Yoxall & Co

Fly Makers
Harrison, James
James, Joseph
Wells, Susan
Yoxall & Co

Needle Makers
Allcock Polycarp
Bartleet, W'm & Co
Boulton, W'm & Co
Chambers, Aron
Chilingworth & Cooper
Field, W'm & Co
Field, Thomas
Gould, W'm
Hemming, R & Son
Holyhoake, T & J
Lloyd, E & Co
Milward, Henry & Sons
Mills, Matthew
Reading, Jos
Smallwood, W'm
Swann, Chas & Co
William, Jos
William, Thomas

The earliest evidence I have found of an eyed hook was in a journal called *The Working Man: A Weekly Record of Social and Industrial Progress* dated Saturday April 7th 1866. It contains an article on fish hooks with details of their manufacture based on a visit to the factory of Messrs Henry Lewis & Son of Redditch. In the process of 'shanking' it says '. . . Some are tapered at the end with a file, while others are simply curled round or bowed to provide a fastening for the line.' This would be the early form and had probably been in use far longer than is generally believed.

The following text is taken from *Secrets of Angling* by John Denny 1652

Cutting the wire into lengths suitable for the hook about to be made is the first operation, and is performed in two ways. The small and medium sizes are cut from the bundle or coil in quantities, between the blades of a pair of large upright shears, in the same manner as needle wires (see page 130); but large sea-hooks, made from thick wire, are cut singly, each length being placed separately upon a chisel fixed in a block or bench, and struck with a hammer. What are called "dubbed" hooks, are "rubbed" after being cut—that is, placed in a couple of iron rings, then made red-hot, and rubbed backwards and forwards with an iron bar until the friction has made every wire straight. Hooks, in general, are not rubbed, but are at once taken to be "bearded," or barbed, which is thus performed: The bearder, sitting at a work-bench in a good light (see engraving), takes up three or four wires with his left hand, between the finger and thumb, and places the ends upon a piece of iron, somewhat like a very small anvil, fixed in the bench before him. In his right hand he holds the long handle of a knife of peculiar shape, the blade of which, having the edge turned from him, is placed flat upon the wires, the knife-point at the same time being passed under a bent piece of iron firmly fixed, which enables him to obtain sufficient leverage to cut the soft wires and raise the barb, or "beard," this being done by *pushing* the handle forward, whilst the point remains fixed, as described. It becomes a laborious operation in the case of very large sizes, requiring, not merely a forward motion of the arm, but a strong push with the body against the handle.

They are next taken by the filer, who makes the points. (See illustration.) Each barbed wire is taken up separately, fixed in small pliers held by the left hand, then placed upon the end of a slip of box-wood, and filed to the degree of sharpness required. This is a matter of great nicety and delicacy. Common hooks are pointed with one file, but the finer sorts require two or three, flat and half-round. Large sea-hooks have the ends flattened, and the burr cut off on each side with a sharp chisel into a roughly-shaped point, previous to being filed. The points of "dubbed" hooks are not filed, but ground upon a revolving stone, and this process is called "dubbing."

When the points are made, the "benders" proceed to operate upon them. The woman seen in our illustration holds in her left hand a piece of wood, at the upper end of which is inserted a curve, or "bend" of steel, projecting slightly. Taking a wire in her right hand, she catches the beard upon one end of the steel curve, and pulls the wire round into the proper "hook" shape. For the larger sizes, the "bends" are fixed, not held in the hand.

Nothing now is necessary to perfect the formation but "shanking," which is done in various ways. Hooks are flattened at the shank end by a workman, who holds the curved part in his left hand, rests the end upon the edge of a steel anvil, and strikes it one sharp blow with a hammer. Some are tapered at the end with a file, whilst others are simply curled round, or "bowed," to provide a fastening for the line.

With steel hooks, hardening is the next process; but iron ones require converting, or "pieing," before they will harden. The pie-hole is a recess with a large, open chimney, and in this recess is placed an iron pot, filled with alternate layers of hooks and bone-dust. At a little distance from the pot, bricks are built up all round, and the space filled with coal, which, when lighted, creates an intense heat, and to its action the hooks are exposed for about ten or twelve hours, allowed afterwards to cool, and are then fit for hardening. To effect this, they are exposed to a great heat upon pans in a fire-hole, and, whilst red-hot, poured into a cauldron of oil. Small hooks are afterwards tempered in a kind of frying-pan, partly filled with drift-sand, and placed over a fire. The larger ones are tempered in a closed oven, at a low heat.

When these operations are completed, they are taken to the scouring-mill, of which we have given an illustration. It is occupied by a number of revolving barrels, driven by steam-power, and containing water and Soft soap into which the

two latter are performed in the ordinary way, and the blueing is done by exposing them to a certain degree of heat in drift-sand over a fire, in the same way as small hooks are tempered. Counting, papering, labelling, and packing, complete the series, and the goods are then ready for the market.

Readers of the foregoing description can hardly fail to notice the extreme simplicity of most, or all, of the processes; and it seems strange that in such an age as ours there should be little improvement in the mode of production, as compared with the fireside practice of amateurs 200 years ago. In the "Secrets of Angling," before referred to, the author describes the making of hooks (as practised by himself) in the following terms:—"Soften your needles in an hot fire in a chafer. The instruments—First, an hold-fast. Secondly, an hammer to flat the place for the beard. Thirdly, a file to make the beard, and sharpen the point. Fourthly, a bender, viz., a pin bended, put in the end of a stick, an handfull long. When they are made, lap them in the end of a wier, and heat them againe, and temper them in oyle or butter."

The heaviest salmon caught in Britain was landed by a Miss Ballantine on the River Tay, Perthshire, Scotland, in 1922.
The salmon weighed 64lbs and was caught using a Malloch rod and reel.
The picture below shows Miss Ballantine with her prize trophy.

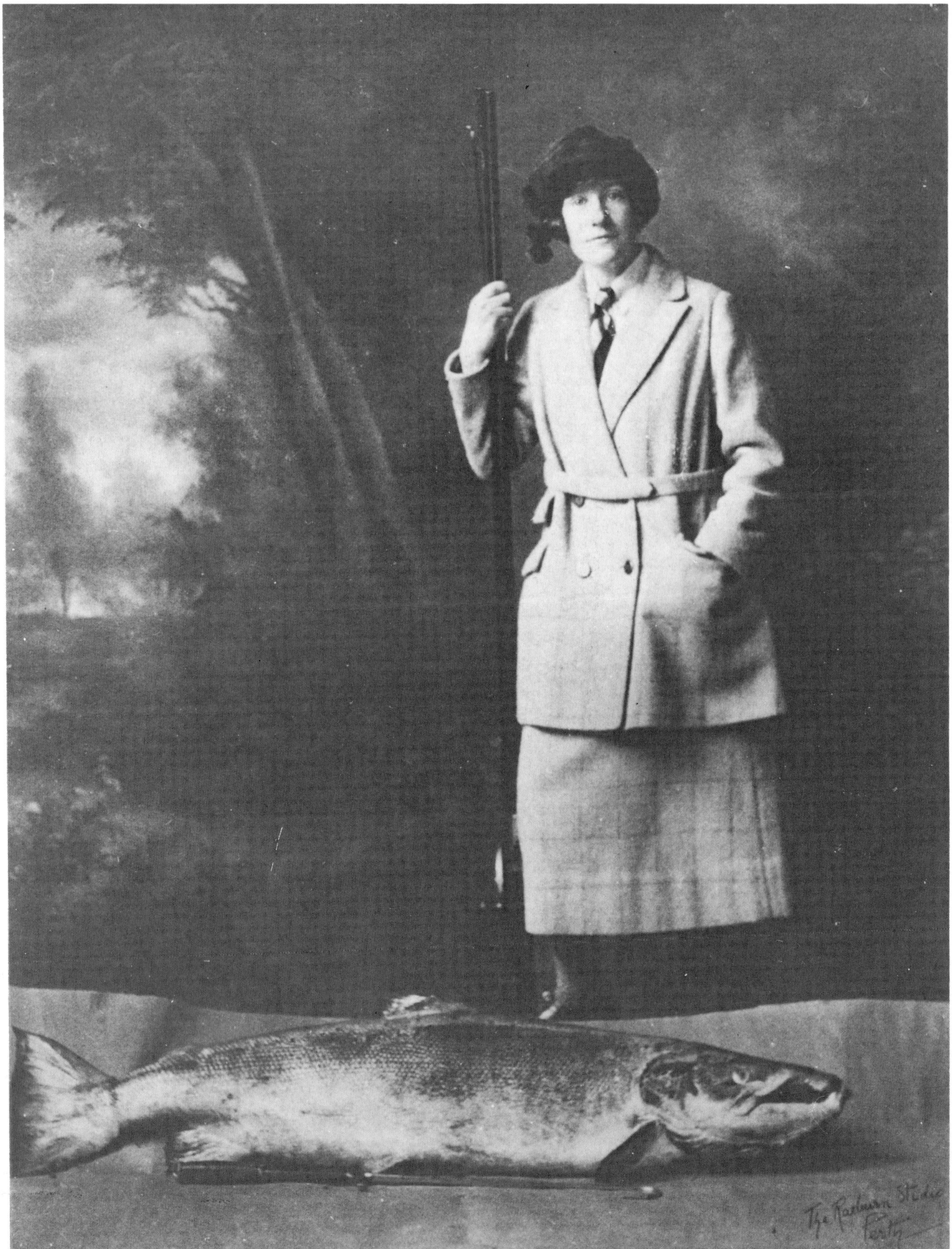

Transitional Perfect 2½″ diameter

One of the most valuable reels in the world – the ORIGINAL PERFECT in the 2¼″ diameter size. It is the ultimate Hardy Bros collector's reel with only two known examples at the present time

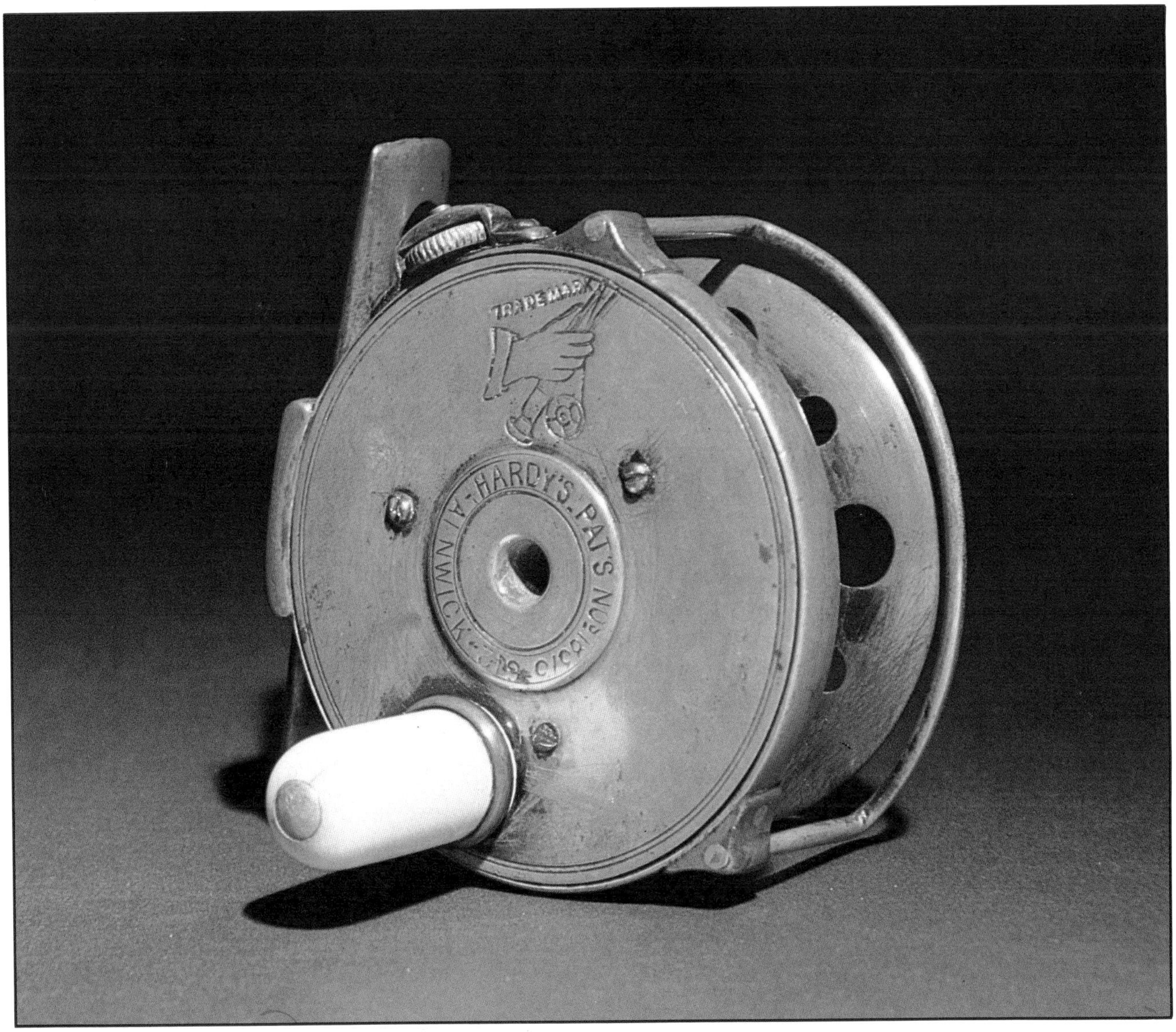

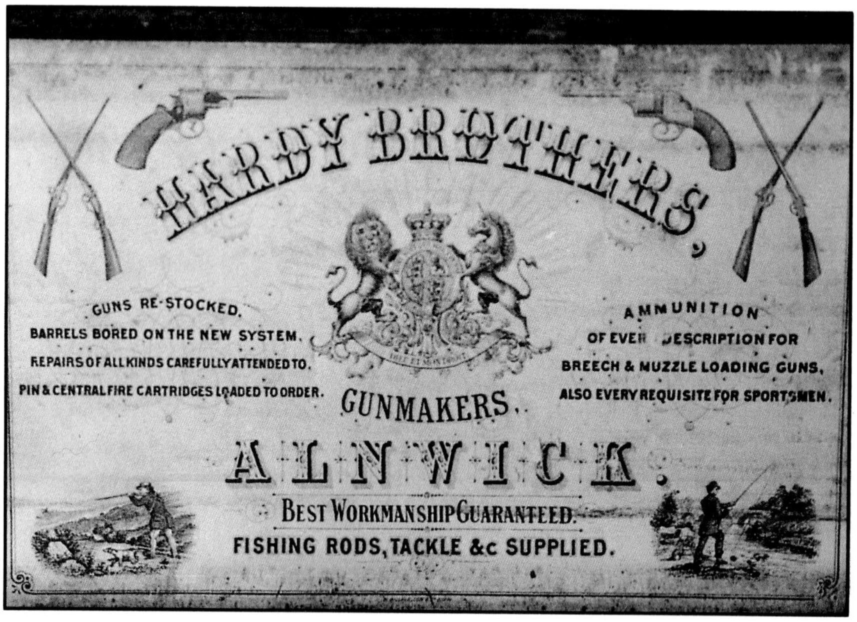

Paper trade label which Hardy Bros glued into the earliest leather rod cases

Below left: Wood handled split cane rod. It is a three piece with two spare tops (one shorter). Lengths 17ft and 15ft. The number is 6059 (no letter) c.1880s

Below: Wood handled split cane rod (wrapped), three piece and two extra spare tops (one shorter). The number is 5423 (no letter) c.1880s. Lengths 13ft and 11ft

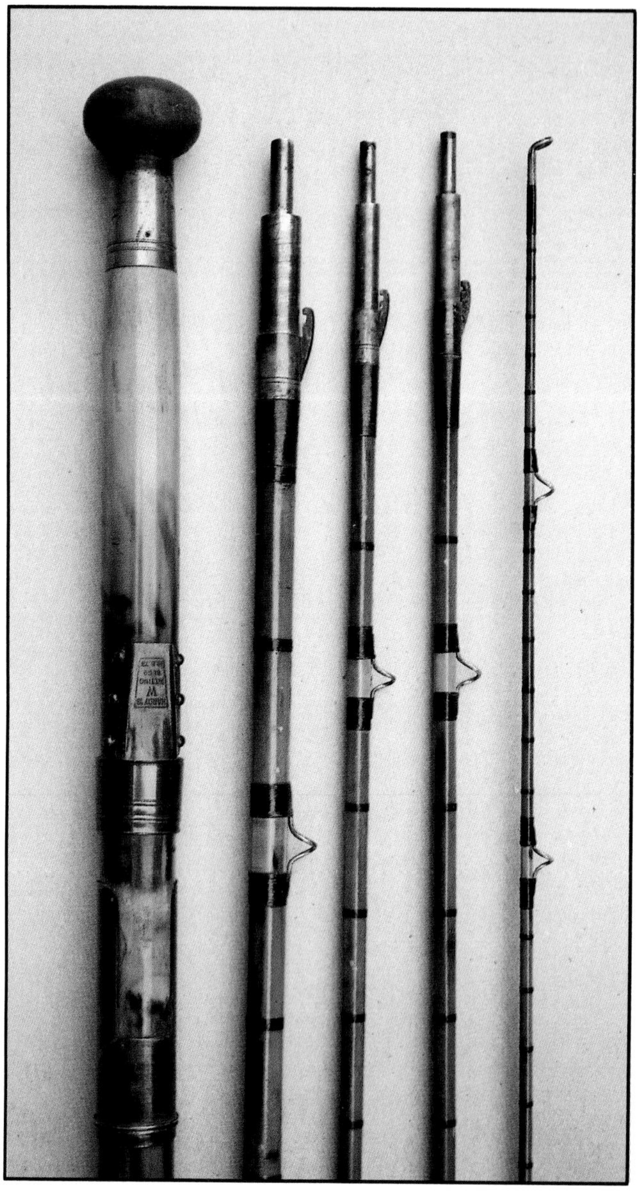

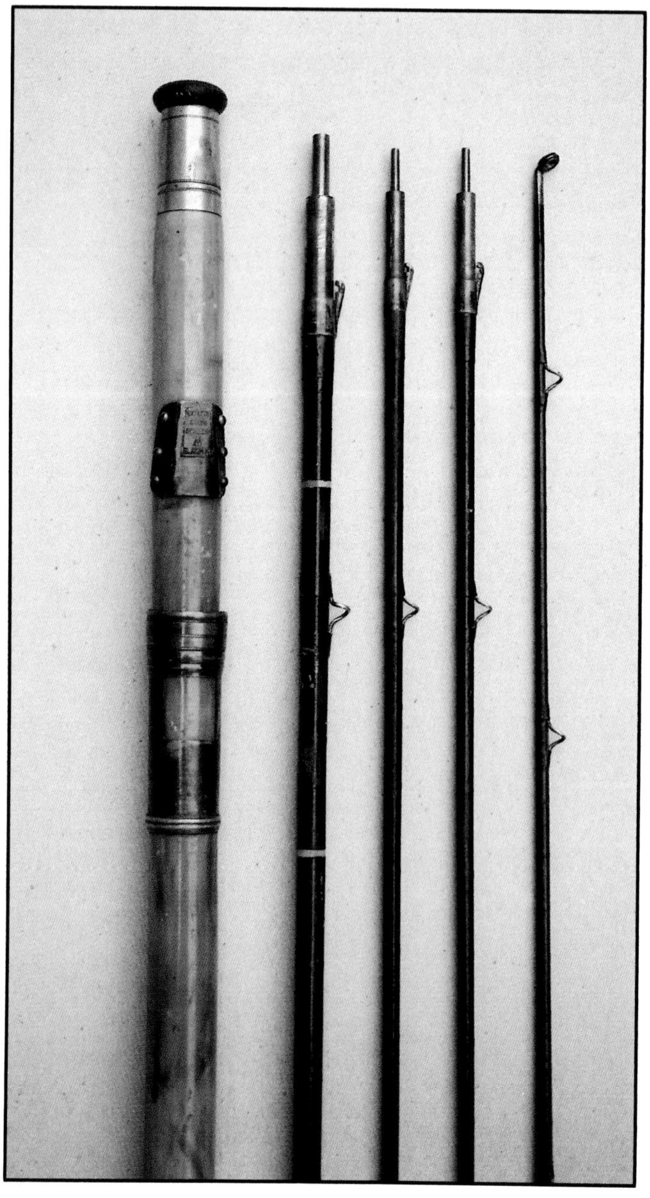

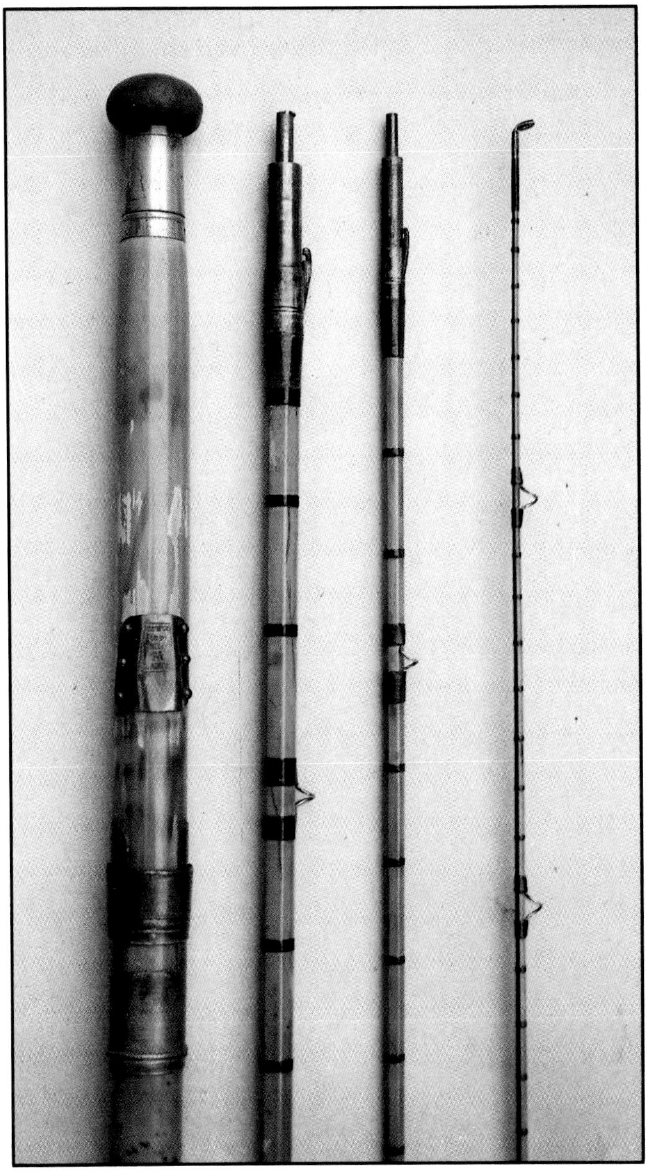

Wood handled split cane rod of three pieces with spare top. Length 15ft. The number is 9769 (no letter) c.1880s

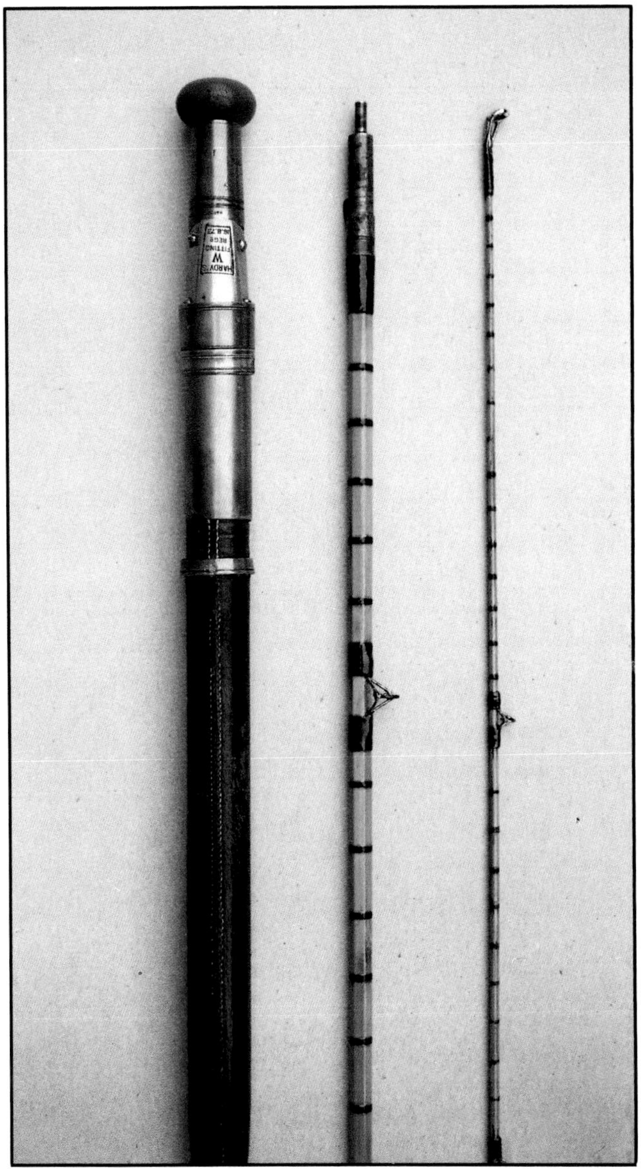

Leather handled 3 piece split cane rod 'The Combination.' Length 10ft 6". Number 15573 c.1891

Wye split cane rod, 3 piece with spare top. Length 13ft 6in. The number is H1880 (1955) condition unused

1896 Perfect. Sizes 2½", 2⅝", 2¾", 3¼", 3½", 4", 4¼", 4¾"

1896 Perfect Unperforated. The finest example ever seen of an all brass 1896 Perfect with all the original bronzing. Diameter 3"

Hercules. Sizes 2½", 2⅝", 2¾", 3", 3¼", 3½", 3¾", 4", 4¼", 4½", 4¾", 5"

Brass Faced Wide Drum Perfects. Sizes 2½", 2⅝", 2¾", 3", 3¼", 3½", 3¾", 4", 4¼", 4½", 4¾", 5"

HARDY BROS

The name of Hardy Bros has always been synonymous with quality. So much so, that Rolls-Royce Motor Company used their Pall Mall shop as a background for their company catalogues. Hardy reels and tackle are collected in many countries of the world and the history of their reels, rods and lures has been eagerly awaited for many years.

William Hardy, the founder of Hardy Bros

Hardy Bros. was started in 1872 by William Hardy, son of the late J J Hardy, in Paikes Street, Alnwick, and was joined one year later by his brother John James. Having served their time as engineers, they later learned the craft of gun-making which gave them the skills for their initial business as gunsmiths, whitesmiths and cutlery makers and quickly extended their activities to making fishing tackle. They built a good country business, supplying the sportsmen and gentry of Norththumberland with sporting goods, but soon concentrated their efforts on rod making which offered the greatest potential and profit. It was the time when split bamboo rods were coming into favour and they turned from the traditional wooden rods to making ones of split bamboo cane of superb quality, the more expensive of which had steel centres. The Hardy catalogue of 1885 included various sizes of the following rod models – *Gold Medal – Gem – Ladies Rod – H Cholmondeley-Pennell – Marston – Portmanteau – Tourist Portmanteau – Composite – Hotspur – Guinea* and *Hollow Butt Rods.* Other products included fly tackle, hooks and four varieties of plug lure – *Angel* or *Devon Minnow – Quill Minnow – Famed Phantom – Excelsior Spinner.* Reels offered were limited to *Birmingham Half-Ebonite, Birmingham Plate Reel, a Birmingham* in German silver, and the *Bronzed Crank.*

The 1886 catalogue included the same four models with the addition of a 3½″ and 4″ Malloch Sidecaster together with one described as a 'Plain Reel'. The latter was offered in very small sizes – 1¼″, 1½″, 1⅝″, 1¾″, 2″, 2¼″, 2½″, 2⅝″, 2¾″ and 3″ priced from 1/3d to 9/–. This cheap range was probably manufactured outside the company and unmarked. Both these additional models disappeared from the 1888 catalogue and the only new reel was a cheap strap-back Nottingham in one size of 4″ at 10/6d. The premises at Paikes St had been abondoned for a larger workshop in Fenkle St, but this in turn proved cramped and inadequate. By 1890 they were in production in an entirely new factory at Bondgate and were supplying distinguished anglers in Britain, Europe and America. The success and volume business up to that time had been mainly in rods while sales of reels were relatively small and confined to the Birmingham and Nottingham style, similar to the ones being sold by their longer established British competitors.

It would appear from the early Hardy catalogues up to 1890, that there was very little interest in the reel side of the business, but this was not true.

The Hardy catalogues can be very misleading, because reels were often developed and put into production before they appeared in print and when illustrations did appear, they were sometimes prototype drawings which were out of date before the catalogue was even printed. That was the case of the Perfect, acknowledged to be the finest of all Hardy products. The catalogue of 1890 announced only three traditional reels, but the Perfect was already being made and sold, although its official year of introduction in the company literature was not until 1891.

By January of that year six patents had been lodged by Hardy Bros. The first was for a reel fitting and the Lockfast Joint in 1881; the second for an idea to lengthen and

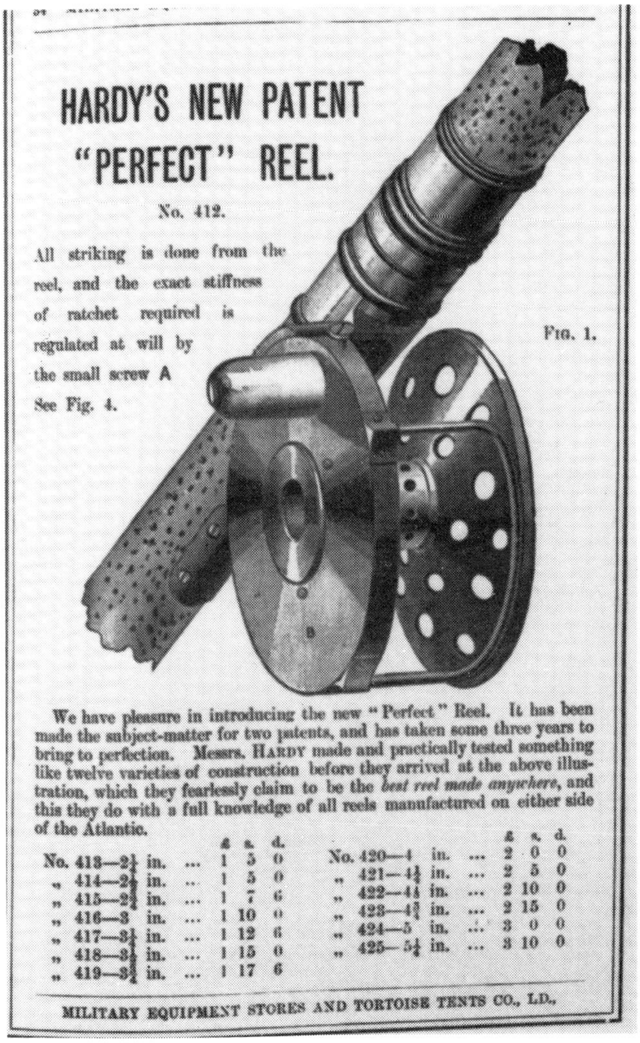

HARDY'S NEW PATENT "PERFECT" REEL.

No. 412.

All striking is done from the reel, and the exact stiffness of ratchet required is regulated at will by the small screw A See Fig. 4.

FIG. 1.

We have pleasure in introducing the new "Perfect" Reel. It has been made the subject-matter for two patents, and has taken some three years to bring to perfection. Messrs. HARDY made and practically tested something like twelve varieties of construction before they arrived at the above illustration, which they fearlessly claim to be the *best reel made anywhere*, and this they do with a full knowledge of all reels manufactured on either side of the Atlantic.

	£	s.	d.		£	s.	d.
No. 413—2¼ in. ...	1	5	0	No. 420—4 in. ...	2	0	0
" 414—2½ in. ...	1	5	0	" 421—4¼ in. ...	2	5	0
" 415—2¾ in. ...	1	7	6	" 422—4½ in. ...	2	10	0
" 416—3 in. ...	1	10	0	" 423—4¾ in. ...	2	15	0
" 417—3¼ in. ...	1	12	6	" 424—5 in. ...	3	0	0
" 418—3½ in. ...	1	15	0	" 425—5¼ in. ...	3	10	0
" 419—3¾ in. ...	1	17	6				

MILITARY EQUIPMENT STORES AND TORTOISE TENTS CO., LD.

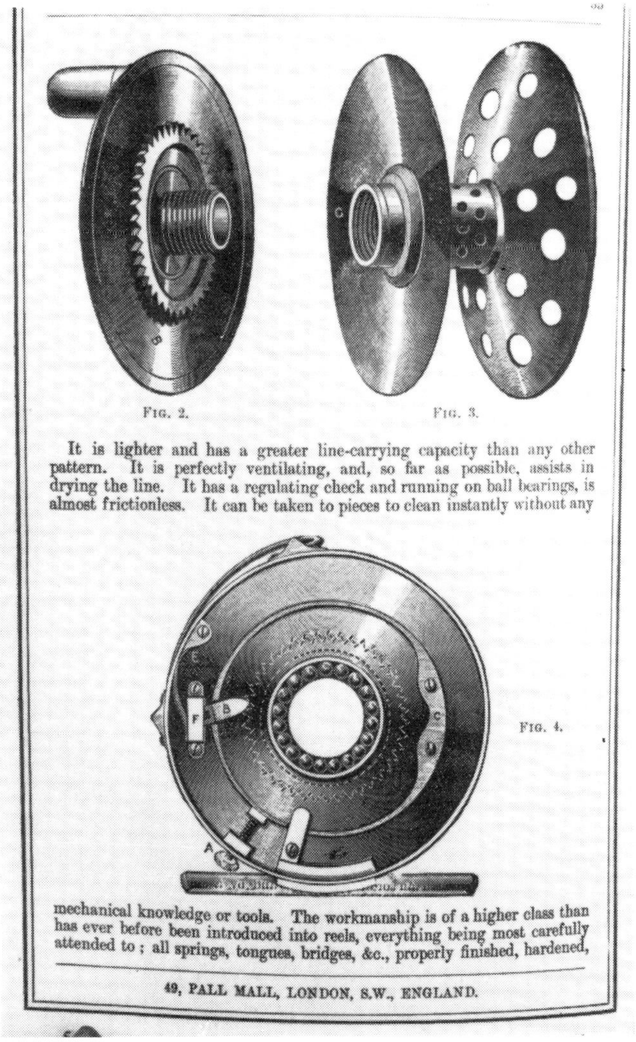

FIG. 2. FIG. 3.

It is lighter and has a greater line-carrying capacity than any other pattern. It is perfectly ventilating, and, so far as possible, assists in drying the line. It has a regulating check and running on ball bearings, is almost frictionless. It can be taken to pieces to clean instantly without any

FIG. 4.

mechanical knowledge or tools. The workmanship is of a higher class than has ever before been introduced into reels, everything being most carefully attended to; all springs, tongues, bridges, &c., properly finished, hardened,

49, PALL MALL, LONDON, S.W., ENGLAND.

Illustration of drawings of Original Perfect and check mechanism which appeared for the first time in the 1891 catalogue

shorten rods in 1887; the third for a spinning live bait and gorge in 1888; and a fourth for placing adjustable weights in a hollow butt to balance the handle. The next two patents for the first time concerned reels and were registered by a new name Forster Hardy, who was a third brother to join the firm. He had taken charge of the reel department and invented a far reaching, revolutionary reel, using ball bearings on which the drum would run. Patent No 18373 dated December 17th 1888 described the workings and Patent No 612 dated January 13th 1891 was the second, consolidating the idea of incorporating ball bearings.

This revolutionary idea was the basis of the Perfect, and its delayed announcement, until it appeared in the 1891 catalogue, was probably due to waiting for the second of the patents to be registered.

Hardy Bros were premature in having printing blocks made to illustrate the new model, as the drawings which appeared in the 1891 catalogue were different from the Perfect which was actually put into production. Possibly one or two prototypes were made to the illustrated design, but I have no knowledge of any being found except claims which cannot be substantiated. Therefore, I consider the original production Perfect as having a bridge over the rim tension regulator screw and the check mechanism usually described as the '1896 Check', which I will re-name the 'Early Check'. Evidence of this has been kindly supplied by Mr J L Hardy, in the form of a photograph of an Original Perfect which was sold in 1890, a year before it first appeared in the catalogue, and it clearly has the features described. The reel was sold privately to an American collector for £5000 in the early 1980s.

The emphasis of Hardy Bros was on quality and producing the best, which in turn attracted the top people, many of whom exerted great influence on sales. Customers included Prince Albert Victor, Mr C Pennell, Major Turle, Mr G Selwin Marriott, Mr H S Hall, Mr W Senior *(The Field)*, Mr R D Marston *(Fishing Gazette)*, Mr G M Kelson and Mr F M Halford.

Hardy Bros had cleverly involved many of these influential people in rod design and used their names to make the rods very fashionable. The 1891 catalogue offered the following rod models in a variety of sizes – *Gold Medal – Special – Perfection – N B Perfection – Ideal – Gem – Ladies Rod – H.S. Hall – Quadruple – Norwegian – Albert Victor – H. Cholmondeley-Pennell – Major Turle – Hotspur – Redspinner – Marston – Composite – Badminton – Yorkshire Club – Dee – Kelson – Hi-Regan – Portmanteau – Tourist Portmanteau – General – Thames Punt – Hollingworth Cyclist* – and spinning, trolling and dapping rods. The plug lures offered were *Silk Phantom – Excelsior Spinner – Soleskin Phantom – New Pearl Phantom – Spiral Minnow* and *Angel* or *Devon Minnow.*

This Original Perfect was sold in 1890 and clearly shows a bridge over the rim tension regulator screw and what is usually described as the '1896 Check' which I have re-named the 'Early Check'

RODS BY HARDY BROS.

Hardy rods were marked with numbers only pre-1900 and with a letter and a number from just after the turn of the century. The most attractive and collectable are the early split cane ones with wood handles and brass fittings.

Year	**Numbers**
1890	(March) 13452
1892	17197–19000
1893	19001–21660
1894	21661–27498
1895	27499–31705
1896	31706–34956
1897	34957–40187
1898	40188–43929
1899	43930–49019
1900	49020–55066
1901	55067–59440
1902	59441–95552
1903	95553–101390
1904	101391–101679
	A1028–A5631
1905	A5632–A12935
1906	A12936–A19313
1907	A19314–A27256
1908	A27257–A35341
1909	A35342–A44905
1910	A44906–A55752
1911	A55753–A66152
1912	A66153–A76109
1913	A76110–A86335
1914	A86336–A94721
1915	A94722–A100041
1916	A100042–A100158
	B1021–B7889
1917	B7890–B12146
1918	B12147–B16425
1919	B16426–B23556
	C11–C186
1920	C187–C10405
1921	C10406–C16732
1922	C16733–C25725
	D171–D2041
1923	D2042–D3399
1924	D3400–D5930
1925	D5931–D7375
	E1045–E2030
1926	E2031–E5882
1927	E5883–E9435
1928	E9436–E13508
1929	E13509–E17685
1930	E17686–E20904
1931	E20905–E22530
1932	E22531–E25275
1933	E25276–E28278
1934	E28279–E31422
1935	E31423–E35277

Year	Numbers
1936	E35278–E39798
1937	E39799–E45174
1938	E45175–E49492
1939	E49493–E52331
1940	E52332–E53644
1941	E53645–E55130
1942	E55131–E56090
1943	E56091–E56399
1944	E56400–E56855
1945	E56856–E57900
1946	E56901–E60708
1947	E60709–E63386
1948	E63387–E67200
1949	E67201–E70990
1950	E70991–E75100
1951	E75101–E81000
1952	E81001–E86200
1953	E86201–E91000
1954	E91001–E96202
1955	E96203–E98999
	H101–H4600
1956	H4601–H10121
1957	H10122–H14127
1958	H14128–H20678
1959	H20679–H27533
1960	H27534–H35183
1961	H35184–H48465
1962	H48466–H52737
1963	H52738–H58199
1964	H58200–H62932
1965	H62933–H69100
1966	H69101–A
1967	S
1968	J
1969	B
1970	K
1971	Z
1972	O
1973	C
1974	Y
1975	L
1976	D
1977	X
1978	M
1979	Q
1980	H
1981	V
1982	E
1983	W
1984	G
1985	T
1986	IA
1987	IS

Two early Hardy Bros split bamboo rods with wooden handles and brass fittings. One three piece with spare tips, lengths 17ft and 15ft (No 6059). The other, three piece with spare tip, length 15ft No 9769 (No letters)

RODS BY HARDY BROS.

MODEL	MATERIAL	PIECES	ORIGINAL LENGTHS	YEAR
Gold Medal	Split Bamboo	3	10′–20′	1885–1967
Perfection	Split Bamboo	2	9′–11′	1885–1871
Gem	Split Bamboo	3	8½′, 9′	1885–1903
H S Hall	Split Bamboo	3	10½′	1885–1921
H Cholmondeley-Pennell	Split Bamboo	3	14′	1885–1925
Marston	Split Bamboo	2	—	1885–1897
Portmanteau	Split Bamboo	4	9′, 9½′, 10′, 10½′, 11′	1885–1924
Tourist Portmanteau	Split Bamboo	6	14′	1885–1895
Composite	Greenheart/Split Bamboo	3	10′–20′	1885–1894
Third Quality Wood Rods	Wood	3	10′–20′	1885–1917
Celebrated 'Guinea' Fly Rods	Hickory/Greenheart	3	10′–12′	1885–1921
Plain Quality Spin and Trolling	Greenheart/Split Bamboo	3	11′–14′	1885–1905
Second Quality Spin and Trolling	Greenheart/Split Bamboo	3	11′–16′	1885–1905
Best Quality Spin and Trolling	Greenheart	3	11′–16′	1885–1905
Hotspur	Greenheart	2	9′, 9½′, 10′	1885–1956
N B Perfection	Split Bamboo	2+handle	—	1885–1900
Ideal	Split Bamboo	1	9′–11′	1885–1939
Perfection Two Handed	Split Bamboo	2	13′, 14′	1885–1921
Albert Victor	Split Bamboo	3	10½′	1886–1921
Major Turle's Pattern	Split Bamboo	3	11′	1886–1906
Redspinner	Split Bamboo	Telescopic	9½′, 10½′	1886–1887
Quadruple	Split Bamboo	8	11′, 11½′, 12½′, 13′	1886–1910
Perfection Spinning	Split Bamboo	2	10½′	1886–1921
Badminton	Split Bamboo	3	12½′, 14′	1886–1908
Anglo-Indian Mahseer	Split Bamboo	3	16′, 18′	1886 only
Kelson Salmon	Split Bamboo	3	18′	1886–1923
Celebrated 'Alnwick' Greenheart	Greenheart	3	9′–20′	1886–1952
Second Quality Wood Rods	Wood	3	10′-20′	1886–1892
Yorkshire Club Dee Spinning	Greenheart/Split Bamboo	3	15½′	1891–1897
Hi Regan Salmon	Split Bamboo	3	16′	1891–1952
Norwegian	Split Bamboo	3	10′–14′	1891–1895
Hollingworth	Greenheart/Split Bamboo	3	11′ (2 Tops 9′6″)	1891–1939
Thames Punt	Greenheart/Split Bamboo	3	10½′	1891–1911
Cyclist's Rod	Greenheart/Split Bamboo	3	10½′	1891–1924
Dapping Rod	Greenheart/Split Bamboo	3	17′, 17½′	1891–1957
Gold Medal with Steel Centre	Split Bamboo	3	10′–20′	1892–1957
Driver Perfection	Split Bamboo	2	10′, 10½′	1894–1897
Hi Regan Perfection	Split Bamboo	2		1894–1897
Houghton Dry Fly	Split Bamboo	3	11′	1894–1957
Princess	Split Bamboo	3	9′, 9½′, 10′	1894–1924
H Cholmondeley–Pennell's Trout	Split Bamboo	3	10′7″	1894–1939
New Zealand Rods	Split Bamboo	3	11′–16′	1894–1913
Compressed Cane Built up to 12′	Split Bamboo			1894–1903
Breadalbane	Split Bamboo	3	14′–16′	1894–1909
Prawning Rod	Bamboo/Split Bamboo	3	14′	1894–1897
Ladies Salmon Rod	Split Bamboo	3	14′, 15′, 15½′	1894–1901
Special Salmon Rod	Split Bamboo	3	16½′–17′	1894–1939
Shannon Salmon Rod	Split Bamboo	3	19½′	1894–1897
Perfection Composite	Greenheart/Split Bamboo	2	9′–12′	1894–1919
C S Composite	Greenheart/Split Bamboo	3	9′–20′	1894–1919
Second Quality Hotspur	Greenheart/Split Bamboo	2	10′, 12′	1894–1908
Second Quality Alnwick Greenheart	Greenheart	3	10′–20′	1894–1917
Shannon Castle Connell Balance	Greenheart			1894–1901
Special Spin/Trolling/Worming				
Prawning – Plain Quality	Greenheart/Bamboo			1894–1939
– Second Quality	Greenheart/Bamboo	3	11′–14′	1894–1920
– Best Quality	Greenheart/Bamboo	3	11′–14′	1894–1923

MODEL	MATERIAL	PIECES	ORIGINAL LENGTHS	YEAR
Special Chub and Barbel	Greenheart/Bamboo	3	12′	1894–1925
Guinea Roach, Perch, Bream,	Greenheart/Bamboo	3	10′–12′	1894–1912
XL Roach, Perch	Greenheart/Bamboo	2	10′–12′	1894–1909
Short Sea Rods for Boat	Bamboo	2 & 3	8′–14′	1894–1924
BSAS Combined Whiffing Deep Sea	Bamboo/Greenheart	3	11′	1894–1939
John Bickerdyke General Sea	Bamboo/Greenheart	3	11′–15′	1894–1924
Sea Fly Rod	Greenheart	3	16′	1894–1911
Hardy Composite	Greenheart/Split Bamboo	3	10′–20′	1895–1911
Halford Priceless	Split Bamboo	3	10′3″ (Top Pentagonal)	1897–1913
Champion Salmon Fly	Split Bamboo	3	17′9″	1897–1924
Murdock Spinning/Prawning	Split Bamboo	2 & 3	11½′	1897–1956
Thames Trout-Wheeley	Split Bamboo	3	11′	1897–1902
Special Worming	Hickory/Lancewood/Split Bamboo	3	16′	1897–1925
Farne Sea Rod	Greenheart	3	8′	1897–1939
Hussey Sea Rod	Bamboo/Greenheart	3	8½′	1899–1911
Extra Heavy Sea Rod	Bamboo/Greenheart			1899–1901
Pope Dry Fly	Split Bamboo	2	10′	1899–1970
Harden Dry Fly	Split Bamboo	3	10′3″, 11′	1899–1903
Booth Derbyshire Dry Fly	Split Bamboo	3	10′	1899–1914
Special Spinning for Tasmanian Great Lake	Split Bamboo	3	10½′–14′	1899–1909
Tarpon Sea Bass and Tuna	Split Bamboo	1+ Handle	7′2″	1899–1903
Special Worming	Split Bamboo	3	12′3″, 14′	1899–1934
R B Marston	Split Bamboo	3	10′9″	1899–1902
Reffitt Wet Fly	Split Bamboo	2	11′	1900–1914
Featherweight Perfection	Split Bamboo	2	8½′	1900–1957
Nonagonal	Split Bamboo	3	18′	1900–1908
Spey Twitching	Split Bamboo	3	17′3″	1900–1908
Boy's Rod	Bamboo/Greenheart	2	9′–12′	1900–1928
Sir Edward Grey Perfection	Split Bamboo	2	10½′	1902–1921
Octagonal Trout	Split Bamboo	3	11′	1902–1934
Halford Salmon	Split Bamboo	3	16½′	1902–1909
Royal Salmon	Split Bamboo	3	16′0″	1902–1910
Victoria Salmon	Split Bamboo	3	14′–17′	1902–1939
Scarboro Sea Rod	Greenheart	2	10½′	1902–1913
Crown Houghton	Split Bamboo	3	9′9″, 10′, 10′4″, 10′7″	1903–1969
Baden-Powell	Split Bamboo	3	11′	1903 only
Octagonal Perfection	Split Bamboo	2	9½′, 10′, 10½′, 10′9″	1903–1926
New Hardy-Marston	Split Bamboo	3	10′4″	1903–1927
Gem Featherweight	Split Bamboo	3	8½′–10½′	1903–1939
Wee Murdock Spinning	Split Bamboo	3	10′, 10½″, 11′	1903–1939
Tournament	Split Bamboo	3	10′, 10½′, 11′	1903–1948
Fairy	Split Bamboo	3	8½′, 9′, 9½′	1903–1956
Paradox Mahseer	Split Bamboo	3	14′	1905–1934
Victor Casting Rod	Split Bamboo	2	8½′	1905–1909
The Raymond	Bamboo/Greenheart	3	10½′	1905–1917
Ludovic Cameron All Round	Greenheart	3	14′	1905–1908
Murdock	Greenheart	3	10½′–12½′	1905–1934
Coquet Sea Rod	Split Bamboo	2	8′, 8½′	1905–1957
Whitby Sea Rod	Bamboo	1		1905–1912
The St. Leonard Sea Rod	Hickory/Greenheart	2	7½′–9′	1905–1957
Fort Myers Tarpon	Split Bamboo	1+Handle	7′2″	1905–1913
Captiva Tarpon	Greenheart or Hickory	1+Handle	7′2″	1905–1913
Halford Dry Fly	Split Bamboo	3	9½′	1905–1915
Eddystone Sea Rod	Split Bamboo	2	9′9″	1906–1914
Beresford	Split Bamboo	1	6′	1906–1913
Extra Light Salmon	Split Bamboo	3	14′–17′	1907–1934
Shaw Special Perfect Dry Fly	Split Bamboo	3	9′9″	1907–1912

MODEL	MATERIAL	PIECES	ORIGINAL LENGTHS	YEAR
Dorchester	Split Bamboo	3	9′9″	1908–1911
River Eden Spinning	Split Bamboo	2	11½′, 12′	1908–1920
Salmo-Esox Spinning	Split Bamboo	3	10′9″	1908–1925
Fairchild	Split Bamboo	3	8′, 9′, 9½′	1908–1957
Connemara Salmon	Split Bamboo	3	16′	1909–1934
Loch Lomond	Greenheart	3	14′	1909–1924
Knockabout Special Dry Fly	Split Bamboo	2	9½′	1910–1971
Norwegian Salmon	Split Bamboo	3	17′	1910–1952
Victor and Overhead Casting Rods (1910)	Split Bamboo			1910–1956
Half-Guinea Pike Rod	Bamboo/Greenheart	2	10′–12′	1910–1915
Surf and Beach	Split Bamboo		7′	1910–1911
Casting Club de France	Split Bamboo	2	7′, 8′	1911–1961
Itchen	Split Bamboo	3	9½′, 10′	1912–1967
Allinone Combined Fly and Spinning	Split Bamboo	3	5½′-10′	1912–1952
Norsk Murdoch	Split Bamboo	3	11½′	1912–1939
Natal Surf or Beach	Split Bamboo	2 & 3	10½′, 12′	1912–1948
Halford (1912 model)	Split Bamboo	3	9½′	1912–1948
Kennet Dry Fly	Split Bamboo	3	9′9″	1912–1923
Poole Combination	Split Bamboo	3	8′9″	1913 only
England's Ideal Roach	Bamboo/Greenheart	3	11′	1913–1925
Perfect F W K Wallis Nottingham	Bamboo/Split Bamboo	3	10′, 11′, 11½′	1913–1931
Wye	Split Bamboo	2 & 3	10½′, 11′, 12′, 12½′, 13′	1914–1978
Decantelle Spinning	Split Bamboo	2	10½′, No. 1, 2, 3, 4	1914–1952
Perfection Roach	Split Bamboo	2	10′, 10½′, 11′	1914–1966
Featherweight Roach	Split Bamboo	3	10′, 10½′, 11′	1914–1933
Channel Bass	Bamboo/Greenheart	3	12′	1914–1923
Salt Water Rods, No. 1, 2, 3, 4	Split Bamboo			1914–1957
Deluxe	Split Bamboo	3	9′, 9½′	1915–1957
Rising	Hickory	2	11½′	1915–1939
Henning	Split Bamboo	2	8′	1915–1929
Special Salmon Fly	Split Bamboo	3	14½′	1917–1931
Special Pike	Bamboo/Greenheart	2	10′–12′	1919–1951
Hardy-Marston (1920 model)	Split Bamboo	3	9′8″	1920–1930
Corbett Spinning	Split Bamboo	2	9′3″	1920–1957
Princess Mary Salmon Fly	Split Bamboo	3	14½′	1921–1939
Viscount Grey	Split Bamboo	2	10½′	1923–1956
J J Hardy No. 1 Dry Fly	Split Bamboo	3	9′, 9½′	1923–1948
J J Hardy No. 2 Wet Fly	Split Bamboo	3	9′9″	1923–1948
New Zealand Tournament	Split Bamboo	3	11′	1923–1934
Princess Mary Trout	Split Bamboo	3	9½′	1923–1924
Aydon Fly Rods	Greenheart/Hickory	3	9′-11′	1923–1939
Captiva	Greenheart	1	6′10″	1923–1924
Salt Water No. 5	Split Bamboo			1923–1962
Salmon Deluxe	Split Bamboo	3	9½′, 10′	1923–1952
J J H Spinning No. 1	Split Bamboo	2	10′	1924–1957
J J H Spinning No. 2	Split Bamboo	2	10½′	1924–1930
Composite Fly	Greenheart/Split Bamboo	2 piece	9′, 9½′, 10′, 10½′	1924–1952
Match Roach	Split Bamboo	2	10½′, 11′	1924–1953
White Wickham Fairchild	Split Bamboo	3	8′	1925–1927
Marvel	Split Bamboo	3	7½′	1925–1970
Hebridean Fly	Split Bamboo	3	13′9″	1925–1956
A H E Wood, No. 1, 2, 3	Split Bamboo	3	12′	1926–1952
H Cholmondeley-Pennell Combination	Split Bamboo	3	14′	1926–1934
General	Bamboo/Split Bamboo	3	13′	1926–1955
Upstream Worming	Split Bamboo	3	12′	1927–1953
L R H Dry Fly	Split Bamboo	3	9′4″	1928–1971
Prince Leopold	Split Bamboo	3	9′9″	1928–1939
Hardy-Marston Double Handed	Split Bamboo	3	10′4″	1928–1939

MODEL	MATERIAL	PIECES	ORIGINAL LENGTHS	YEAR
Hardy-Marston Blagdon	Split Bamboo	3	10′9″	1928–1939
White Wickham	Split Bamboo	3	8′	1928–1939
St Joe	Split Bamboo	2	5′, 5½′, 6′	1928–1952
St Croix	Split Bamboo	2	5′, 5½′, 6′	1928–1952
Spliced Greenheart Fly Rod	Greenheart	3	14′, 15′, 16′	1928–1934
No. 6 Salt Water	Split Bamboo			1928–1948
Loch Leven	Split Bamboo	3	11½′, 12½′	1929–1939
A E M Sussex Brook	Split Bamboo	2	8′	1929–1939
Junior	Greenheart	2 & 3	8½′, 9′, 9½′, 10′, 10½′	1929–1956
Featherweight Roach	Split Bamboo	3	11′	1929–1939
Davy	Split Bamboo	3	8′9″	1930–1939
Locksplice Spinning	Greenheart	2	9′9″	1930–1934
Valencia	Split Bamboo	1 + handle	8½′	1930–1948
Teviot	Split Bamboo	3	9′, 9½′, 10′, 10½′	1931–1939
Deluxe Double Built	Split Bamboo	3	8′, 8½′, 9′, 9½′, 10′	1931–1939
J J H Spinning	Split Bamboo	3	10′, 10½′	1931–1939
Ideal Spinning	Split Bamboo	1		1931–1933
No. 1 Dual Purpose	Split Bamboo	6	11′–13′4″	1933–1939
No. 2 Dual Purpose	Split Bamboo	4	8′, 10′	1933–1939
Keith Rollo	Split Bamboo	3	9′, 9½′	1932–1957
J J H Triumph	Split Bamboo	2 & 3	8′9″	1933–1971
			(Reintroduced in 1980	*for 1 year)*
Hardy-Wanless	Split Bamboo	2	7′–10′	1933–1970
Hardy-Wanless	Split Bamboo	2	10′	1933–1952
Hardy-Wanless	Split Bamboo	3	10′	1933–1952
Hardy-Wanless	Split Bamboo	2	10′ Upstream Worming	1933–1956
Hardy-Wanless	Split Bamboo	3	10′ Upstream Worming	1933–1952
Hollow Built	Split Bamboo	3	11′, 12′, 13′	1932–1939
Hardy-White-Wickham Salt Water	Split Bamboo	2	5′1″	1933–1948
RCB	Split Bamboo	2	10′	1934–1948
Rogue River	Split Bamboo	3	9½′, 10′	1934–1962
Kenya	Split Bamboo	3	8′	1934–1957
Casting Club de France	Split Bamboo	3	8′, 9′	1934 only
J J H Special Salmon	Split Bamboo	3	14′, 14½′	1934–1952
Hardy-Zane Grey Extra Heavy	Split Bamboo/Hickory	2	5′1″	1934–1957
FWK Wallis All Round	Bamboo/Split Bamboo	3	11′, Nos. 1,2,3	1934–1955
FWK Wallis Avon	Bamboo/Split Bamboo	3	11′, Nos. 1, 2, 3	1934–1953
Lightweight Match	Bamboo/Split Bamboo	3	11′, 12′, 13′	1934–1953
Ideal Roach	Bamboo/Split Bamboo	2 & 3	11′–14′	1934–1955
Special Pike Spinning	Bamboo/Greenheart	2	10½′, 11′, 12′	1934–1939
Perfection Roach	Split Bamboo	2	11′	1934–1955
Masterpiece Pike	Split Bamboo	3	10′	1934–1952
Popular Pike	Greenheart/Split Bamboo	3	10′	1934–1952
Everyman Pike	Greenheart	3	10′	1934–1952
Recruit Pike	Bamboo/Greenheart	2	10′	1934–1952
Edward Louche	Greenheart	2	8′, 9′	1934–1939
Multex No. 1	Split Bamboo	2	10′	1935–1939
Multex No. 2	Split Bamboo	2	10′	1935–1939
Koh-i-noor	Split Bamboo	2	8′9″	1935–1972
Surestrike	Bamboo/Greenheart	3	10½′, 11′	1936–1953
Punt	Bamboo/Greenheart	2	8′	1936–1939
Tourney	Split Bamboo	2	8′, 8½′, 9′	1937–1957
Super Decantelle	Split Bamboo	2	10½′	1937–1957
L R H Spinning No. 1 and No. 2	Split Bamboo	2	9½′	1937–1978
Wye Spinning	Split Bamboo	2	9′, 10′	1937–1939
Farcast No. 1 and No. 2	Split Bamboo	2	5½′	1937–1957
Vibration Spliced	Greenheart	3	14′, 15′, 16′	1937–1939
Upstream Select Worming and Grayling	Bamboo/Split Bamboo	3	12′	1937–1953
Hickory Salt Water	Hickory			1937–1939

MODEL	MATERIAL	PIECES	ORIGINAL LENGTHS	YEAR
L R H Double Handed Greased Line	Split Bamboo	3	13′	1938–1963
Connoisseur Double Built	Split Bamboo	3	11′, 12′	1938–1952
Hardy-Jock Scott	Split Bamboo	2	5½′	1938–1956
Favourite Spinning	Greenheart	2	7′	1938–1952
Live Baiting Pike	Split Bamboo	3	10′	1938–1952
Coquet Salmon	Split Bamboo	3	13′1½″	1937–1957
Match Fishers	Bamboo/Split Bamboo	2	10½′, 11′	1939–1953
Truecast	Bamboo/Split Bamboo	3	10′, 11′	1939 only
Outfit	Bamboo/Split Bamboo	5	11′, 13½′	1939 only
Connoisseur	Bamboo/Split Bamboo	3	12′	1939 only
LRH Dry-Wet	Split Bamboo	3	9′3″	1948–1957
LRH Wet	Split Bamboo	3	9′3″	1948–1950
LRH Salmon	Split Bamboo	3	14′	1948–1967
LRH Spinning No.3	Split Bamboo	2	9½′	1948–1952
West Country Fly	Split Bamboo	3	9′4″	1951–1956
West Country Greased Line	Split Bamboo	3	11′3″	1951–1956
Wanless Light Line Fly No.1	Split Bamboo	3	9½′	1951–1952
Wanless Light Line Fly No.2	Split Bamboo	3	12½′	1951–1952
Wanless Light Line Fly No.3	Split Bamboo	3	11′–14′	1951–1952
Marksman Spinning	Split Bamboo	2	8′3″	1951–1963
West Country Spinning	Split Bamboo	2	7′	1951–1957
NAAF Fly and Spinning	Split Bamboo	4	6′10″ – 8′10″	1951–1956
No. 1 Coronation	Split Bamboo	3	9′	1954–1956
No. 2 Coronation	Split Bamboo	3	9′	1954–1957
No. 3 Coronation	Split Bamboo	3	12′	1954–1956
No. 4 Coronation Spinning	Split Bamboo	2	7′	1954–1956
Palaglass Fly	Glass Fibre	2 & 3	7′9″–12′	1954–1957
Palaglass Salmon Spinning	Glass Fibre	3	9½′	1954–1957
Palaglass Threadline	Glass Fibre	2	7′	1954–1957
HE Accuracy	Split Bamboo	2	8′	1954–1956
Javelin Pike Spinning	Split Bamboo	2	8½′	1954–1955
Carp	Split Bamboo	2	10′	1954–1955
Expert	Bamboo/Split Bamboo	3	12′, 13′	1955–1962
Nocturnal	Split Bamboo	2	10′	1957–1962
L R H Spey Casting	Split Bamboo	3	13′9″	1957–1963
Spintrole	Split Bamboo	2	10½′	1957–1959
Traveller	Split Bamboo	5	6′10″, 8′10″	1957–1963
Nusea	Split Bamboo	2	9′ 3″	1957–1964
Pira Yura	Split Bamboo	2	11½′	1957–1962
Wanless Sea Rod	Split Bamboo	2	7′	1957 only
Surf Casting (Natal)	Split Bamboo	2 & 3	10′–12′	1957 only
Taupo	Split Bamboo	3	10′	1957–1964
County Spinning	Split Bamboo	2	8½′	1960–1967
Hollolite Trout Fly	Split Bamboo	3	8′, 8½′, 9′, 10′	1960–1967
Hollolite Salmon Fly	Split Bamboo	3	12½′	1960–1966
Hollokona Salmon Deluxe	Split Bamboo	3	8½′, 9′, 9½′	1961–1966
Glaskona Trout Fly	Glass Fibre	2	8′, 8′9″	1961–1966
Glaskona Spinning	Glass Fibre	2	6′10″	1961–1966
Phantom	Split Bamboo	2	6′10″, 8′, 9′	1962–1972
Glasavon	Glass Fibre	3	10′9″	1962–1964
Glaskona Expert	Glass Fibre	3	12′, 13′	1962 only
Glaskona Pier	Glass Fibre	2	8′	1962–1966
Glaskona Beach	Glass Fibre	2	11′	1962–1964
Glaskona Light Sea Spinning	Glass Fibre	2	4′4″	1962–1964
Gold Crest	Split Bamboo	3	8′, 8½′, 9′, 9′ No. 2	1963–1965
Fire Crest	Split Bamboo	2	8′, 8½′, 9′, 9′ No. 2	1963–1965
Dipper	Split Bamboo	2	9½′	1963–1965
Ibis	Split Bamboo	3	12′	1963–1965
Shearwater	Split Bamboo	3	14′	1963–1965
Pintail	Split Bamboo	2	7′	1963–1965

MODEL	MATERIAL	PIECES	ORIGINAL LENGTHS	YEAR
Egret	Split Bamboo	2	8½′	1963–1965
Teal	Split Bamboo	3	10′	1964–1965
Mallard	Split Bamboo	2	10′	1964–1965
(*Bird Range of Neocane changed name to Glen Range in 1966*)				
Corsair Boat	Solid Glass			1964 only
(*Glen denotes Neocane – Ben denotes Neoglass*)				
Glen Farrar	Split Bamboo	3	8′, 8½′, 9′ No.1, 9′ No.2	1966–1967
Glen Beg	Split Bamboo	2	8′, 8½′, 9′ No.1, 9′ No.2	1966–1967
Ben Hope	Glass Fibre	2	8′, 8′9″	1966–1967
Glen Etive	Split Bamboo	3	10′	1966–1967
Glen Cassley	Split Bamboo	2	10′	1966–1967
Glen Loy	Split Bamboo	2	9½′	1966–1967
Ben Screel	Glass Fibre	3	9′9″	1966 only
Glen Locky	Split Bamboo	3	12′	1966–1967
Ben Nevis	Glass Fibre	3	12½′	1966 only
Glen Cova	Split Bamboo	3	14′	1966–1967
Glen Rinzie Spinning	Split Bamboo	2	7′	1966–1967
Ben Lomand Spinning	Glass Fibre	2	7′	1966 only
Ben Cairn	Glass Fibre	2	8½′	1966–1967
Ben More	Glass Fibre	2	8½′, 9½′	1966 only
Matchquest	Glass Fibre	3	12′, 13′	1966–1970
Matchquest	Glass Fibre	4	14′	1966–1970
Conquest	Glass Fibre	3	11′, 12′, 13′	1966–1969
Matchman	Glass Fibre	3	12′, 13′	1966–1969
Fenquest	Glass Fibre	2	9½′	1966–1969
Avon Quest	Glass Fibre	2	10′	1966–1969
Carpquest	Glass Fibre	2	10′	1966–1969
Sidewinder Nos. 1,2,3,4	Glass Fibre	2	7′	1966–1969
Longbow	Glass Fibre	2	11′, 11′9″, 12′3″	1966–1969
Reservoir Fly	Split Bamboo	2	9½′	1967–1969
Invincible	Glass Fibre	2	8′–14′3″	1967 only
Invincible Spinning	Glass Fibre	2	7′, 8½′, 9½′	1967 only
Jet	Glass Fibre	2	8′, 8½′, 9′	1967–1975
WF Hardy	Split Bamboo	3	7½′, 8′, 8½′, 9′	1969–1971
			Re-introduced for one year in 1980	
Continental Special	Split Bamboo	2	6′8″, 7′, 7½′, 8′4″	1969–1972
Riccardi	Glass Fibre	2	7′	1969–1972
Smuggler	Glass Fibre	4	8′	1969–1980
Jet Salmon	Glass Fibre	3	12½′, 14′3″, 15′5″	1969–1975
Richard Walker Reservoir	Glass Fibre	2	9½′	1969–1970
Esk	Glass Fibre	2	10′	1969–1980
No. 1 Fibalite Spinning	Glass Fibre	2	6′, 7′	1969–1970
No. 2 Fibalite Spinning	Glass Fibre	2	8½′	1969–1970
No. 3 Fibalite Spinning	Glass Fibre	2	9½′	1969–1970
Norsk Spinning	Glass Fibre	2	10′	1969 only
Float Quest	Glass Fibre	3	12½′, 13′	1969 only
Endrick Pike	Glass Fibre	2	10′	1969 only
Richard Walker Avon	Split Bamboo	2	10′	1969 only
Richard Walker Carp	Split Bamboo	2	10′	1969 only
Coastmaster	Glass Fibre	2	9′	1969–1980
Riccardi	Split Bamboo	2	7′	1969–1971
Richard Walker Avon	Glass Fibre	2	10′	1970 only
Richard Walker Carp	Glass Fibre	2	10′	1970 only
Hardy Swing Tip	Glass Fibre	2	8′9″, 9½′	1970–1983
Tourney Surfcasting	Glass Fibre	2	11′9″, 12′3″	1970–1984
Saltwater Boat	Glass Fibre	2	7′	1970–1980
Richard Walker Superlite	Glass Fibre	2	9′3″	1971 only
Mooching Rod	Glass Fibre	2	10′	1971–1980
Matchmaker	Glass Fibre	3	12′, 13′	1971–1981
Jet Spinning	Glass Fibre	2	6′1½″, 7′, 8′, 8½′, 9½′, 10′	1972–1973

MODEL	MATERIAL	PIECES	ORIGINAL LENGTHS	YEAR
Saltwater Deluxe Boat	Glass Fibre	2	7′	1972–1977
Midge Fly	Glass Fibre	2	6′3″	1973–1978
Palakona	Split Bamboo	2	6′, 6′8″, 7′2″, 7′, 8′, 8½′, 8′9″	1973–1978
Invincible	Glass Fibre	2	10½′	1973–1980
Fred Taylor Trotter	Glass Fibre	2	11′3″	1973 only
Victor Surfcaster	Glass Fibre	2	12′	1974–1981
Fibalite Spinning	Glass Fibre	2	6′1½″, 7′, 8′, 8½′, 9½′, 10′	1974 only
Richard Walker Little Lake	Glass Fibre	2	9′	1975–1978
Tourney Mk II	Glass Fibre	2	11′, 11′9″, 12′3″	1975–1977
B C Ten Ten	Glass Fibre	2	10′10″	1975–1980
Hardy Graphite	Carbon Fibre	2	7½′, 8′, 8½′, 9′	1976–1983
Fibalite	Glass Fibre	2	7′, 7½′, 8′, 8½′, 8′9″, 9′, 9′3″	1976–1978
Fibalite Salmon	Glass Fibre	3	12½′, 14′	1976–1984
Swim Feeder	Glass Fibre	2	8′9″, 9½′	1976–1981
Fred Buller Drifter	Glass Fibre	2	10′9″	1977–1980
Richard Walker Farnborough	Carbon Fibre	2	9′	1978 only
Graphite Carp	Carbon Fibre	2	10′	1978–1983
Fred Buller Pike	Glass Fibre	2	11′	1978–1981
Fred Taylor Touch Ledger	Glass Fibre	2	9′	1978–1980
Graphite Saltwater Deluxe Boat	Carbon Fibre	2	7′	1978–1980
Tourney Mk III	Glass Fibre	2	12′, 12′3″	1978–1980
Graphite Surfcaster	Carbon Fibre	2	12′, 3-5oz, 5-8oz	1978–1980
Fibalite Perfection	Glass Fibre	2 & 3	7′, 8′, 8½′, 8′9″, 9′, 9½′, 10′, 10′3″, 10½′	1980–1983
Graphite Salmon	Carbon Fibre	3	11′, 12′, 12½′, 13′9″, 15′4″, 16′, 18′, 20′	1980–1983
Graphite Spinning	Carbon Fibre	2	8½′, 10′, 11′	1980–1983
Graphite Swing Tip	Carbon Fibre	2	9½′	1980–1983
Light Match	Glass Fibre	3	12′, 13′	1980–1980
Graphite Match	Carbon Fibre	3	12′, 13′, 14′, 15′	1980–1983
Graphite Smuggler	Carbon Fibre	6	7′	1981 only
Fred Buller Drifter	Carbon Fibre	3	11′	1981 only
Victor Boat	Glass Fibre	2	30lb, 50lb	1981–1982
Atlantic Canada Big Game	Glass Fibre	2		1981–1983
Boron Reservoir	Boron	2		1981–1983
Graphite Smuggler	Carbon Fibre	7	8′2½″	1983 only
Graphite Smuggler	Carbon Fibre	8	9′5″	1983 only
No. 2 Graphite Match	Carbon Fibre	3	12′, 13′, 14′	1983 only
Graphite Favourite	Carbon Fibre	2	7½′, 8′, 8½′, 9′, 9′3″, 9½′	1983 only
Graphite Favourite Salmon	Carbon Fibre	3	12½′, 14′, 16′	1983 only
Graphite Favourite Spinning	Carbon Fibre	2	7′, 8½′, 10′	1983 only
Graphite Favourite Carp	Carbon Fibre	2	11′	1983 only
Boron Fly	Boron	2	7½′, 8′, 8½′, 9′, 10′	1983 only
Deluxe Trout	Carbon Fibre	2	7½′, 10½′	1984 only
Deluxe Salmon	Carbon Fibre	3	13′9″, 15′4″	1984 only
Deluxe Smuggler	Carbon Fibre	6, 7 & 8	7′, 8½′, 9′	1984 only
Favorite Match	Carbon Fibre	3	12′, 13′, 14′, 15′	1984 only
Deluxe Smuggler Spinning	Carbon Fibre	6 & 7	7′, 8½′	1984 only
Fibalite	Glass Fibre	2	8′, 8½′, 9′	1984 only

Hardy Works

It was not quality alone which led to the rapid growth and fame of Hardy Bros. They were fortunate to be located at the centre and head of the British Empire when it dominated large areas of the world. It was a time when Britain exerted great political and social influence and the people in the front line were the landed gentry and the more affluent, many of whom sported Hardy rods and reels. They mixed with the upper classes around the world, with the result that their home grown sports and pastimes spread abroad, and Hardy's were one of the leading beneficiaries of the popularity of fishing in these countries.

Orders poured in from all over the world and gave the brothers confidence to produce a wide variety of tackle. With the new enthusiasm injected by Forster, they produced both narrow and wide drum reels. Their rods, which had earlier been the main product of the business, were sold in increasing numbers with a bigger range of models and sizes.

The early Perfects were made of brass but a new alloy was introduced called Alumin from which the Perfect Narrow Drum was made and first announced in the catalogue of 1897. This was followed by similar contracted models, one of which had a brass-faced handle plate (1899 – 1901) and then more all-alloy versions. There was also a brass-faced wide drum range of Perfects which succeeded the early brass models and in turn was phased out when the all-alloy reels became established. Some bear numbers or letters inside the casing which indicate the initials of the maker who worked on the reel and represents the pride which existed before the age of mass production.

The Hardy brass and brass-faced reels were usually given a permanent coating to stop tarnishing and is referred to as 'bronzing'. No-one seems to know exactly what it was, but it gave a black-lead appearance. A few brass-faced reels were given a 'silver-bronzing' which made them even more attractive. These

REEL MAKERS' NAMES

Initials	Names	Reels
RB	Robert Borthwick	Fly
TP	Thomas Pattinson	Fly
WS	Wilf Sinton	Fly
RR	Robert Richardson	Fly
TH	Thomas Hall	Fly-Hardex
TA	Thomas Appleby	Silex
EB	Ernie Broadford	Jock Scott, Altex
AP	Addie Pringle	Hardex
RM	Robert M'Lean	Longstone
JBW	Joe Wallace	Silex
AHW	Arthur Wall	Silex
GT	Gordon Talbot	Altex, Silex
JAJ	Joe Johnson	Jock Scott, Altex, Fly Mult.
PW	Percy Walsh	Silex
WO	William Ord	Hardex
JD	James Dodds	Silex
TW	Thomas Wilkinson	Longstone
NMH	Norman Heatherington	Sea Reels
JS	James Smith	Fly
TAG	Thomas Armstrong	Fly
MS	Marshall Scott	Jock Scott, Altex, Elarex, Exalta
JL	Jack Luke	Altex, Elarex, Exalta
RH	Raymond Humble	Altex, Elarex
JRJ	Jack Johnson	Altex, Exalta, Elarex
TM	Terence Moore	Hardex
EW	Eric Willcox	Hardex, Sea Reels
MH	Main Hudson	Hardex, Altex, Fly
MR	Maurice Richardson	Hardex
IR	Isobel Richardson	Hardex
DW	Dennis Ward	Silex
JSD	James Davison	Sea Reels
JLH	James Hardy	Perfect, Altex

are rare and their individuality makes them very collectable. The material and characteristics of the apendages of reels changed over the years, and one can get a quick approximation of the age from these points. Again it is difficult to be exact due to Hardy's continuing to use illustrations long after the model and materials had been changed, and their practice of producing unusual reels from their normal range. Ivory was used for reel handles of the Birmingham Half-Ebonite and Hercules in the 1880s and up to the time when it was used on the Original and Transitional Perfects as late as c.1893. After that date it was replaced by a man-made substitute called ivorine, which looked almost identical but did not crack, as was the tendency of the natural material.

Horn was used on models such as the early Birmingham Plate reel but does not give an accurate dating because it was used on a number of models well into the 1900s. The way to tell the difference between the natural and man-made products is by the sense of touch, the ivory and horn being colder. A surer way, but not to be recommended, is to place a lighted match to the material. The man-made products will melt and burn. The foot or saddle of some reels changed about 1922, from having a smooth top to one with rows of grooves which allowed the seating ring to screw more securely on to the foot.

The 'Rod-in-Hand' trade-mark was stamped on the plate of some models and is an indication of an early reel, as it was discontinued after about 1903. Evidence to suggest this comes from the fact that none of the alloy Perfect Wide Drum range, introduced with the new check mechanism in 1905, have the mark, but it appears on many of the alloy Wide Drum (Early Model) reels made c.1899 to 1905 which also have the Early Check mechanism. Some Brass Faced Perfects made to the 1905 design do have the trade-mark but these are the exception and are possibly the last reels on which it appeared. The Bouglé was introduced in 1903 and occasionally an early one turns up with one on, while the Perfect Early Silent Check (1908 – 1910) reels of which I have knowledge have no trade-mark. A shaded form of 'Rod-in-Hand' trade-mark occasionally appears and is generally believed to be the earliest version.

Hardy Bros can claim to be one of the few firms whose products became so synonymous with quality, that Rolls Royce used the Hardy Bros Pall Mall shop as a background for their catalogues.

I have attempted to piece together a fairly accurate history of their products. In describing the features of reels I sometimes use the words 'production model'. By this I mean the official model being sold, which usually appeared in company catalogues as opposed to the 'odd' reels which were produced as prototypes, market-trials, special orders or for whatever reason.

Some collectors will pay high prices for oddities but although I find them interesting and desirable, they have not the same appeal as a rare production model from the maker's range which would have been offered to the fishermen of a particular period. I have tried to produce a full and complete record of Hardy reels and resisted the temptation to keep the data general and non-specific. Collectors and historians want to know exactly in which years an item was made and not 'early' or 'late' century. Therefore I have attempted to give a full account of every reel model, together with the sizes and dates of production, accepting, as I trust the reader will, that such an ambitious undertaking will inevitably attract some anomalies.

It should be noted that there was a period of eight years from 1940 when no catalogues were issued and this gap, up to the Export Catalogue of 1948, makes it impossible to follow the progress of a reel which was being sold in 1939, unless its production life carried on up to 1948. Therefore when the last date of a reel is shown as c.1939, it should be understood that it could have finished that year or at any time in the following eight years. The year 1939 was the start of the second world war, which brought production of most recreational products to a halt and it is highly probable that production of most reels being sold at that time did indeed cease, or was suspended for a number of years.

Top: A bordered oval logo, a straight line logo with the words – 'Hardy's Pat Perfect Reel,' and a Rod-in-Hand trade-mark

Middle: An unbordered oval logo

Bottom: A bordered oval logo

Birmingham Half-Ebonite

Birmingham Plate Reel

Hercules

Birmingham Half-Ebonite
c.1880 – 1896

Sizes 2¼″, 2½″, 2¾″, 3″, 3¼″*, 3½″, 3¾″*, 4″, 4¼″*, 4½″, 4¾″*, 5″*
** From – c.1890.*

A bronzed Birmingham type reel with ebonite back plate, nickel silver rims, ivorine handle (ivory c.1880s) and referred to in Hardy catalogues as the 'Composite Reel' in the last two years of production. The handle plate was stamped with a bordered oval logo and some also had a Rod-in-Hand trade-mark.

Birmingham Plate Reel
c.1880 – 1921

Sizes 2¼″, 2½″, 2¾″, 3″, 3¼″, 3½″, 3¾″*, 4″, 4¼″*, 4½″, 4¾″*, 5″*
*Sizes marked * from c.1890 – from 1911 only the four smallest sizes.*

An all metal Birmingham type reel with horn or ebonite handle, described as 'Bronzed Gunmetal Reel' and made from the finest hammer hardened gunmetal. It continued in production until 1920. The handle plate was stamped with a bordered oval logo and some also had a Rod-in-Hand trade-mark.
There was a cheaper version described as suitable for boys in sizes 2¼″ and 2½″ priced 5/– and 5/6d from 1911 to 1921.

Birmingham Special New Pattern
1885 – 1886

In 1885 and 1886 a luxury quality Birmingham in German silver and described as 'Special New Pattern' was offered in sizes 2¼″, 2½″, 4″, 4½″, priced 23/– to 50/–.

Hercules c.1880 – 1904

Sizes 2½″, 2⅝″ (from 1894), 2¾″, 3″, 3¼″, 3½″, 3¾″*, 4″, 4¼″*, 4½″, 4¾″*, 5″**
*Sizes marked * from 1891*

This reel was described in its early years as the 'Special Pattern and Hardmetal' and was designed for lightness over the traditional brass reels. It was made from what the company finally called their 'Hercules Metal' which had a warm bronze attractive colour. The handle plate was stamped with either a bordered or unbordered oval logo and some also had a Rod-in-Hand trade-mark. It had an ivorine handle (ivory c.1880s).

Bronzed Crank c.1880 – 1909

Bronzed Crank, sizes 2″, 2¼″, 2½″, 2¾″, 3″, 3¼″, 3½″*, 3¾″*, 4″*, 4¼″*, 4½″ (from 1889) Sizes marked * from 1894*

The Bronzed Crank was a simple crank-handled, fixed check reel with ebonite knob, which appeared in the early catalogues with the Birmingham reels and continued in production up to 1909. There was either a bordered oval logo on the handle plate or the company name stamped on the crank arm.

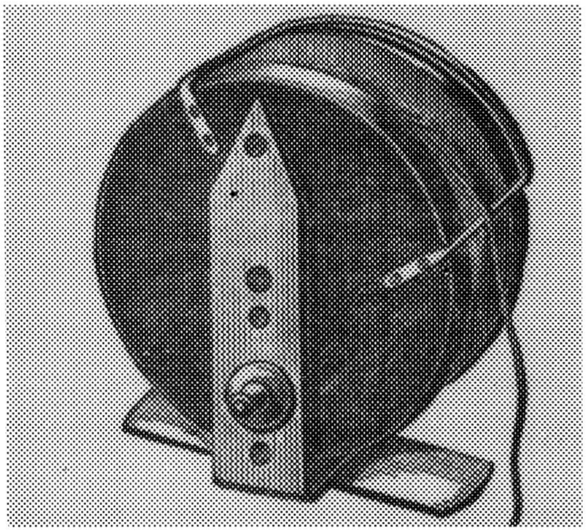

Hardy Nottingham 1888 – 1921

Strap-back Nottingham 1888 –1893 In two sizes 3½″, and 4″.

A 4″ diameter wooden Nottingham was marketed in 1888 in the form of a plain wooden reel with line guide and brass strap-back support, on which was a simple on/off check at the base. It was later made in two sizes, 3½″, and 4″ diameters up to 1893, but the following year changed to the better known Starback Nottingham with a brass foot, Bickerdyke line-guard, on/off check and horn handles. It went absent from the catalogues from 1905 to 1913 when the Nottingham Silex was being shown but was probably still being produced. It re-appeared in the catalogue of 1914 described as the Plain Nottingham and remained in production up to 1921.

Starback Nottingham 1894 – 1921 Sizes 3″, 3½″, 4″, 4½″, 5″

Nottingham Silex 1899 – 1911

Left: 1899 – 1910 Nottingham with Silex Action
Sizes 3½", 4", 4½", 5", 6"

The Nottingham was available with Silex action from 1899 to 1911

Below left: 1911 Nottingham Silex No 2 Action
Sizes 3½", 4½", 5"

Below: Internal workings of the 1911 Nottingham Silex No 2 Action

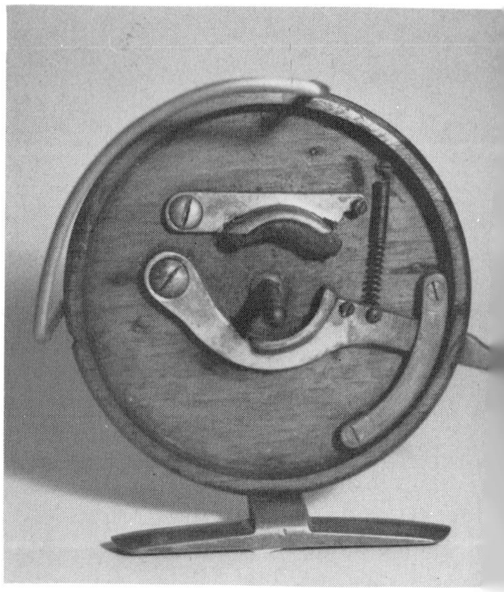

Combined Fly and Spinning reel 1894 – 1898

Sizes 2¾", 3", 3½", 4", 4½", 5"

This centre-pin spinning reel was a short lived alloy model. Features included a smooth brass foot, dual ivorine handles, adjustable bearing and check button on the back plate and carried an oval logo and Rod-in-Hand trade-mark. It was not usually marked with the name of the model.

Nottingham Lever Action Reel 1912 – 1922

Sizes 3½", 4", 4½", 5", 6"

This model had a ratchet check on a moveable arm which overcame the possibility of the ratchet locking. It had a rim lever which would throw the check in or out of gear and a centre adjustable tension nut fitted.

It was in production from 1912 to 1922, starting off as the 'New Nottingham' (1912 – 1913) and became the 'Improved Nottingham' (1914 – 1922).

Silex No. 2 Patent Surf Reel 1912 – 1913

Sizes 4½", 5" and 6". (priced 50/–, 55/–, and 60/–)

It was a heavy duty sea reel made of the best seasoned walnut with bulbous horn handles, a 'Duralumin' spindle plate and brass lined back plate. It had the No 2 patent lever action, with dual pressure levers acting on the hub, and was designed for those who cast heavy weights long distances, either through surf, from a pier or for heavy boat work.

External Pillared Crank c.1880s

Very little is known about this reel as it did not appear in the company catalogues. It was a brass crank-handled model with external pillars, smooth brass foot, horn handle and anti-foul rim and made in a range of sizes, probably outside the company. Great care should be taken when purchasing this reel as I believe some are still being made outside the company. It is the easiest of all Hardy models to copy.

The Early Check mechanism of the Original Perfect production model

Original Perfect 1890 – 1891/2

Sizes 2¼", 2½", 2¾", 3", 3¼", 3½", 3¾", 4", 4¼", 4½", 5", 5¼" (price 25/– to 70/–)

The Original Perfect was based on a new concept of ball bearings as described in the Hardy Bros patents No 18373 (1888) and 612 (January 1891), which were inscribed in a circular central channel on the face of the handle plate. The ball bearings were made of brass but in the small sizes of 2¼" and 2½", tiny steel ones were used and they are not replacements as everyone believes. The final design of the reel, which had evolved from a number of experimental varieties, had been perfected and was in production as early as 1890. Almost all the earliest Perfects have a Rod-in-Hand trade-mark stamped on the handle plate.

The first model was illustrated in the catalogues of 1891 and 1892 and had an unfamiliar un-bridged rim tension regulator screw and a strange check mechanism which appeared in successive years up to the 1895 edition, although by that year two new model Perfects had evolved. Sales of the Original Perfect ceased in 1891 or 1892. The characteristics of the production model were a rim tension regulator screw with guard, large and small plate perforations, ventilated drum core, Bickerdyke line-guard, a hole at the centre of the plate leading through the drum core, smooth brass perforated foot and an ivory handle. There was also an unventilated version of this model produced which was never illustrated in the company literature.

The Hardy Perfect had enthusiastic reviews from its very inception and it has appeared in many models and sizes for almost a century. The Original Perfect is the most sought-after of all Hardy reels, and represents the beginning of the longest running and finest quality fly reel in the world.

Unventilated Original Perfect with iron wire Bickerdyke line guard. Diameter 3½"

Transitional Perfect 1892/3

Sizes 2¼", 2½", 2⅝." 2¾", 3", 3¼", 3½", 3¾", 4", 4¼", 4½", 4¾", 5", 5¼"

The Transitional Perfect was made of brass and usually had nickel silver pillars or both rim and pillars, ivory handle, and a similar check mechanism to the earlier Perfect. It represented the half-way stage of development between the two early brass models of the 1890's. Features retained from the Original Perfect were rim tension regulator screw with bridge, a hole in the centre of the plate leading through the drum core, a perforated smooth brass foot and the same inscription pattern on the handled plate which included a Rod-in-Hand trade-mark. In profile it resembled its better known successor the 1896 Perfect, as it had no line-guard and the drum core had lost most of its ventilations.

Transitional Perfect variants were sold, including one which had no perforations and no ball bearings, while another was made with the handle plate design of the 1896 Perfect. The odd reel was made which had a similar handle plate design to the Original Perfect but had introduced a left-hand threaded brass drum locking screw at the centre of the backplate (c.1893). There has even been one which turned up with the locking screw on the handle plate. These have to be considered as experimental oddities.

The Transitional Perfect was never sold as such in the company literature although a picture of one did appear in a leaflet marked 'Supplement to "C" catalogue' and also appeared in the catalogues of 1894 and 1895. However, the reel was shown lying on its side and was in fact being used to sell its successor – the 1896 Perfect. Hardy Bros had simply added additional text describing a left-hand threaded drum locking screw.

1896 Perfect c.1894 – 1897

This reel has always been referred to as the 1896 Pattern Perfect and although it was being sold earlier than that date, there seems little point in changing its name now. Two pieces of evidence suggest that it was in production as early as 1894. On April 24th 1985, Sotheby's held an auction which included lot No 235 described as a cased 1896 Pattern all brass Perfect and engraved on the reel 'ASMS July 1894', and on the blue lined case, a gift inscription 'ASMS July 1895'. In the absence of a better explanation, it would seem that one of these items had been wrongly dated, giving an element of doubt to the date on the reel. However, the catalogue of 1894 gives much more conclusive proof in the form of a Transitional Perfect reel laid on its side, but accompanied by text which described a left-hand threaded locking screw for dismantling. Although the odd examples of a Transitional Perfect have turned up with a drum locking screw, it is highly probable that it was the 1896 Perfect being sold from the advertisement in the catalogue of that year.

A problem to be considered is the question of whether a 2¼″ size was made for this model. The Transitional was offered in this size but when its picture was used to sell the 1896 Perfect in the catalogues of 1894 and 1895, the 2¼″ continued to appear. The question is whether the company dropped the size when the new

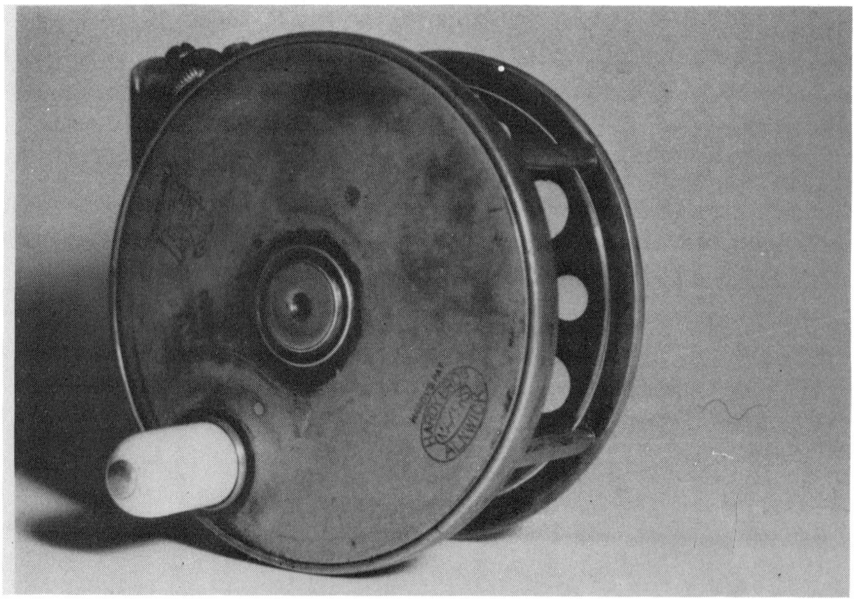

Sizes 2¼″?, 2½″, 2⅝″, 2¾″, 3″, 3¼″, 3½″, 3¾″, 4″, 4¼″, 4½″, 4¾″, 5″, 5¼″

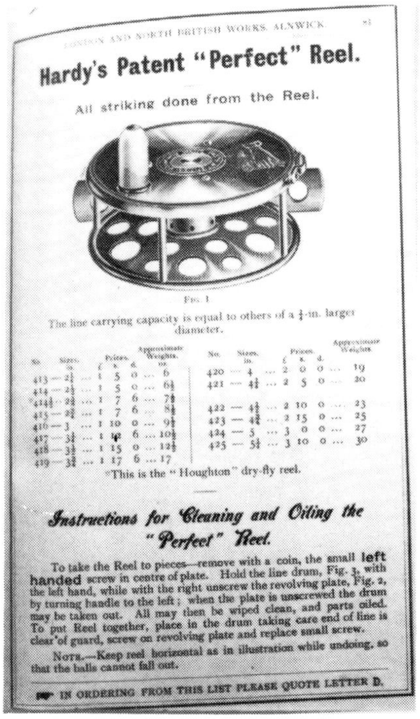

LONDON AND NORTH BRITISH WORKS, ALNWICK.

Hardy's Patent "Perfect" Reel.

All striking done from the Reel.

FIG. 1.

The line carrying capacity is equal to others of a ¼-in. larger diameter.

No.	Sizes. in.	Prices. £ s. d.	Approximate Weights. oz.	No.	Sizes. in.	Prices. £ s. d.	Approximate Weights.
413	2¼	1 5 0	6	420	4	2 0 0	19
414	2½	1 5 0	6½	421	4¼	2 5 0	20
*414½	2⅝	1 7 6	7½	422	4½	2 10 0	23
415	2¾	1 7 6	8½	423	4¾	2 15 0	25
416	3	1 10 0	9½	424	5	3 0 0	27
417	3¼	1 12 6	10½	425	5¼	3 10 0	30
418	3½	1 15 0	12½				
419	3¾	1 17 6	17				

*This is the "Houghton" dry-fly reel.

Instructions for Cleaning and Oiling the "Perfect" Reel.

To take the Reel to pieces—remove with a coin, the small **left handed** screw in centre of plate. Hold the line drum, Fig. 3, with the left hand, while with the right unscrew the revolving plate, Fig. 2, by turning handle to the left; when the plate is unscrewed the drum may be taken out. All may then be wiped clean, and parts oiled. To put Reel together, place in the drum taking care end of line is clear of guard, screw on revolving plate and replace small screw.

NOTE.—Keep reel horizontal as in illustration while undoing, so that the balls cannot fall out.

IN ORDERING FROM THIS LIST PLEASE QUOTE LETTER D.

Rare unperforated all brass 1896 Perfect retaining almost all the original 'bronzing'. Diameter 3″

An illustration of a Transitional Perfect being used to sell the 1896 Perfect in the 1894 catalogue

Illustration showing the major difference between the 1896 Perfect with a centre screw and the Transitional Perfect with a hole through the drum core which was also a feature of the Original Perfect

reel was introduced and never bothered to cross out the obsolete size, or if indeed the 1896 Perfect was made in the 2¼" diameter.

In the catalogue of 1897 the first new, true picture of the model appeared, but there was no mention of the 2¼" size and I have no knowledge of the existence of such a reel at present. However, as it was included in the sales literature in the first two years of its production, I have no alternative but to include the size.

The 1896 Perfect was usually of all brass construction, but a few had nickel silver pillars or both rim and pillars, and one or two have turned up with an alloy frame and brass drum. It retained the Early Check mechanism, rim tension regulator screw with bridge, smooth brass foot and the large and small plate perforations of the earlier models, but like the Transitional had no line-guard. New features included an ivorine handle (possibly the odd early one in ivory), left-hand threaded drum locking screw at the centre of the plate, which meant that it could not be dismantled without first removing the screw with a tool. The markings on the handle plate had changed with the removal of the central channel containing the patent numbers and maker's name. Instead it had a plain face with usually a straight line logo, bordered oval logo and on most reels a Rod-in-Hand trade-mark.

A picture of the reel continued to be shown in catalogues up to 1908, but it is clear from the fact that so few are about today, that it had finished long before that date. An 1896 Unventilated Perfect variant is known to have been made but it is extremely rare and only the odd reel must have been produced. The 1896 Perfect production model was replaced about 1898 by the Perfect Brass Faced Wide Drum which had a similar handle plate design and the same check mechanism up to 1904.

The continued illustration of the early reel was another example of the company using out of date pictures to sell new models.

Perfect Brass Faced Wide Drum 1898 – 1908

The Perfect Brass Faced Wide Drum succeeded the 1896 Perfect and although it was a longer running model it was never illustrated with its own picture in the catalogues. This has always been something of a mystery and it was only when the production years were analysed for the specification of reels that the full explanation was found. The 1896 Perfect was only fitted with the Early Check mechanism and is a relatively rare reel, and therefore it is obvious that its later appearances in catalogues up to 1908 were included to sell the next model which was the Perfect Brass Faced Wide Drum.

Hardy Bros must have considered the picture of the reel sufficiently similar, having the same inscription design with only a new plate perforation pattern changing the large and small perforations to two rows of holes ⅛" and ¹⁄₁₆" diameters, in a circular pattern on the new model.

As there is no mention of a Perfect Brass Faced reel in any of the catalogues, it seemed that it would not be possible to identify when the new model was introduced. However, when the weights, which accompanied the reels in the illustrations, were analysed, evidence was found which showed when the transfer occurred. Surprisingly, it was in the data accompanying the out of date picture of the 1896 Perfect in the catalogue of 1899, an illustration familiar to most serious collectors. The weights in the text had been crossed out and written alterations made to introduce new lighter weights, all of which were incorporated into the text of the catalogue of 1901. I checked these weights against the ones in my collection of Perfect Brass Faced Wide Drum reels and found they corresponded fairly accurately with what the catalogues described as 'approximate weights'. The weights of my reels were – 2½" - 6oz, 2⅝" – 6oz, 2¾" – 7oz, 3" – 8oz, 3¼" – 10oz, 3½" – 11½oz,

Sizes 2½" 2⅝", 2¾", 3", 3¼", 3½", 3¾", 4", 4¼", 4½", 4¾", 5", 5¼", 6".

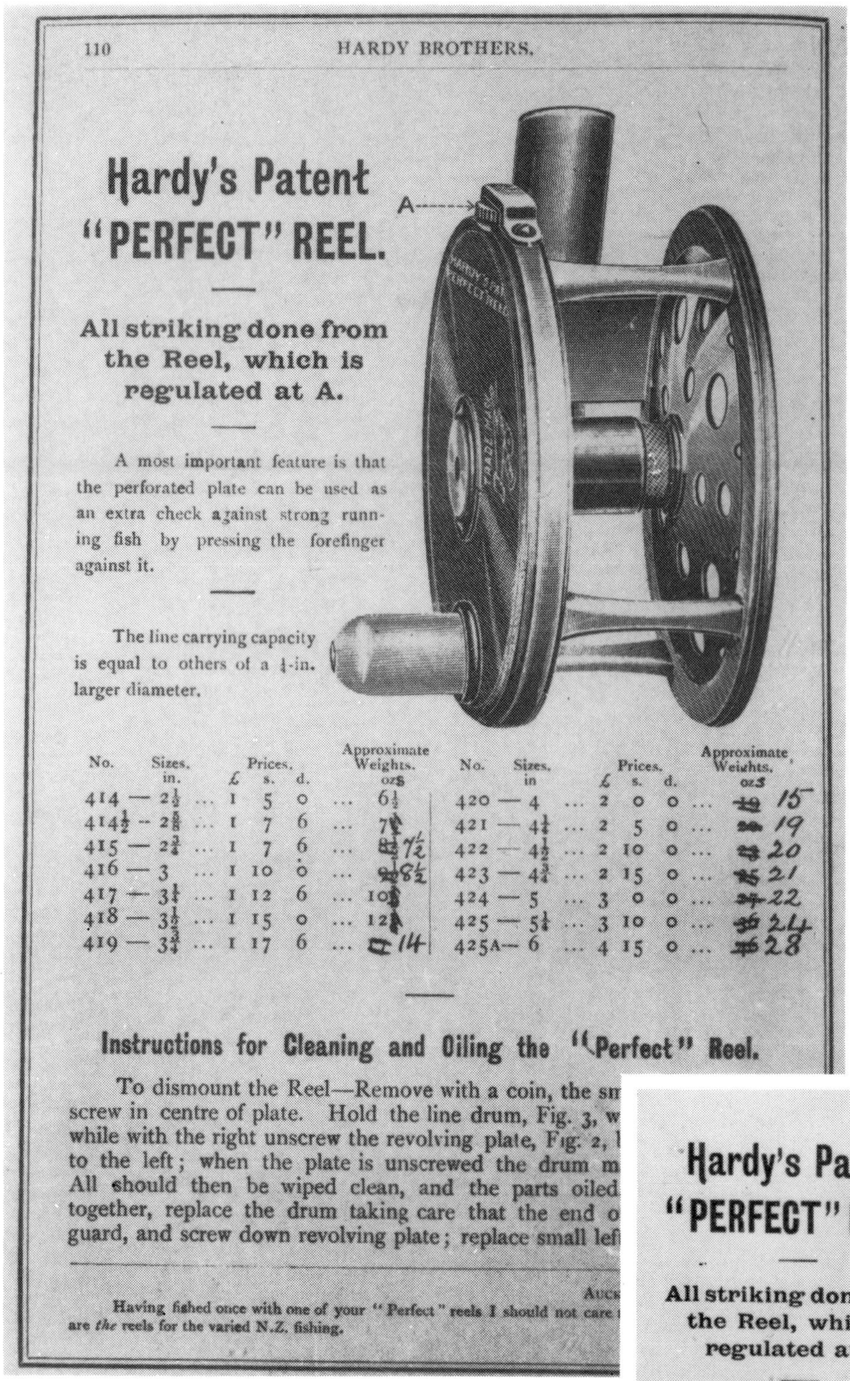
110 HARDY BROTHERS.

Hardy's Patent "PERFECT" REEL.

All striking done from the Reel, which is regulated at A.

A most important feature is that the perforated plate can be used as an extra check against strong running fish by pressing the forefinger against it.

The line carrying capacity is equal to others of a ¼-in. larger diameter.

No.	Sizes. in.	Prices. £	s.	d.	Approximate Weights. ozs	No.	Sizes. in	Prices. £	s.	d.	Approximate Weights. ozs
414	2½	1	5	0	6½	420	4	2	0	0	[illegible] 15
414½	2⅝	1	7	6	7½	421	4¼	2	5	0	[illegible] 19
415	2¾	1	7	6	[illegible] 7½	422	4½	2	10	0	[illegible] 20
416	3	1	10	0	[illegible] 8½	423	4¾	2	15	0	[illegible] 21
417	3¼	1	12	6	10[illegible]	424	5	3	0	0	[illegible] 22
418	3½	1	15	0	12[illegible]	425	5¼	3	10	0	[illegible] 24
419	3¾	1	17	6	[illegible] 14	425A	6	4	15	0	[illegible] 28

Instructions for Cleaning and Oiling the "Perfect" Reel.

To dismount the Reel—Remove with a coin, the sm screw in centre of plate. Hold the line drum, Fig. 3, w while with the right unscrew the revolving plate, Fig. 2, to the left; when the plate is unscrewed the drum m All should then be wiped clean, and the parts oiled together, replace the drum taking care that the end o guard, and screw down revolving plate; replace small lef

Auck

Having fished once with one of your "Perfect" reels I should not care are *the* reels for the varied N.Z. fishing.

Catalogue of 1899 showing alterations

3¾" – 12½ oz, 4" – 16½oz, 4¼" - 19oz, 4½" – 22oz, 5" – 25oz. All the small sizes were under the new lighter weights, three of the larger sized reels were over but none reached the heavier weights given in the catalogues before 1899.

Therefore it is clear that it was the Brass Faced Perfect which was being sold from the illustration which appeared from 1899 to 1908. Considering the fact that models were often on the market in advance of their appearance in company catalogues, it would seem reasonable to record the beginning of sales as 1898. Features included ivorine handle, rim tension regulator screw with bridge, straight line logo, most with Rod-in-Hand trade-mark, a bordered or unbordered oval logo, smooth brass foot and a drum locking screw. It used the Early Check for a number of years but adopted the new check when it was introduced in 1905.

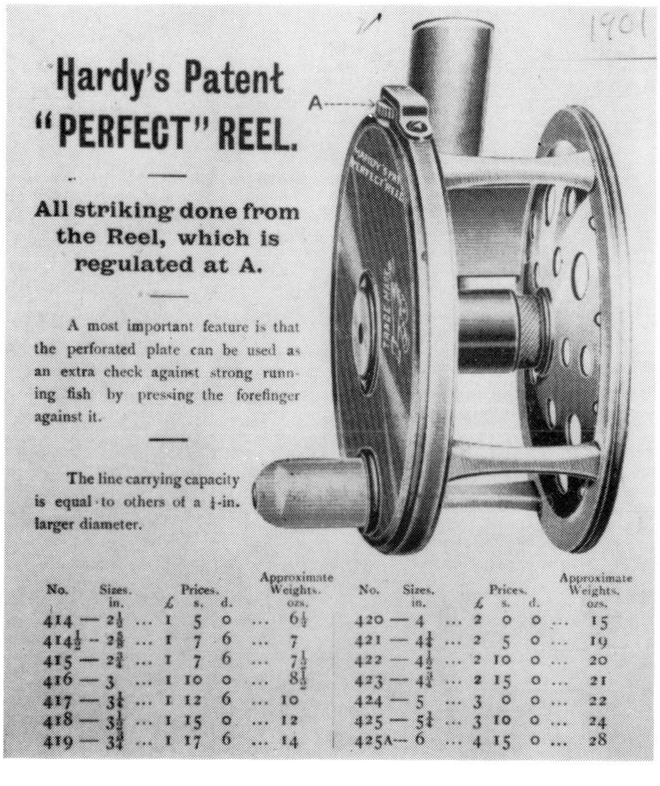
1901

Hardy's Patent "PERFECT" REEL.

All striking done from the Reel, which is regulated at A.

A most important feature is that the perforated plate can be used as an extra check against strong running fish by pressing the forefinger against it.

The line carrying capacity is equal to others of a ¼-in. larger diameter.

No.	Sizes. in.	Prices. £	s.	d.	Approximate Weights. ozs.	No.	Sizes. in.	Prices. £	s.	d.	Approximate Weights. ozs.
414	2½	1	5	0	6½	420	4	2	0	0	15
414½	2⅝	1	7	6	7	421	4¼	2	5	0	19
415	2¾	1	7	6	7½	422	4½	2	10	0	20
416	3	1	10	0	8½	423	4¾	2	15	0	21
417	3¼	1	12	6	10	424	5	3	0	0	22
418	3½	1	15	0	12	425	5¼	3	10	0	24
419	3¾	1	17	6	14	425A	6	4	15	0	28

Catalogue of 1901 with the earlier alterations incorporated into text

The perforated plate pattern of two rows of tiny holes

The Early Check

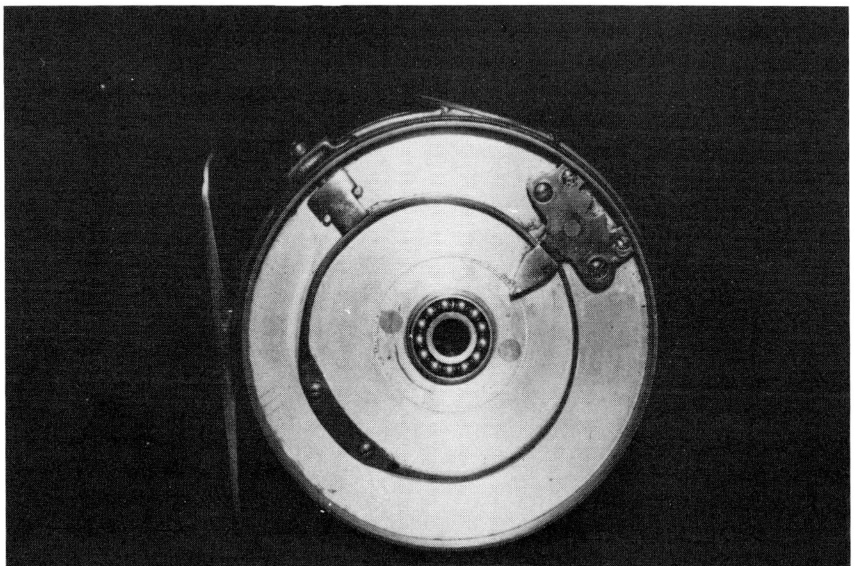

The 1905 Check

Perfect Wide Drum c.1899–1905. Sizes $2\frac{1}{2}$", $2\frac{5}{8}$", $2\frac{3}{4}$", 3", $3\frac{1}{4}$", $3\frac{1}{2}$", $3\frac{3}{4}$", 4", $4\frac{1}{4}$", $4\frac{1}{2}$", $4\frac{3}{4}$", 5"

Perfect Wide Drum (Early Model) c.1899 – 1905

Although the catalogues would have us believe that the alloy Perfect Wide Drum started in 1905, examination of reels provides evidence of an earlier beginning. A few rare ones turn up whose handle plate has an oval unbordered logo, a straight line logo and some with an additional Rod-in-Hand trade-mark. Most have the Early Check mechanism but later ones the 1905 Check. Features included a rim tension regulator screw with bridge, drum locking screw, ivorine handle, smooth brass foot (occasionally alloy) and plate perforations of two rows of tiny holes, $\frac{1}{8}$" and $\frac{1}{16}$" diameter in a circular pattern. Examples of this model are very collectable but difficult to find. An unventilated version was made in the $2\frac{5}{8}$" size.

Perfect Wide Drum 1905–1921. Sizes $2\frac{1}{2}$", $2\frac{5}{8}$", $2\frac{3}{4}$", 3", $3\frac{1}{4}$", $3\frac{1}{2}$", $3\frac{3}{4}$", 4", $4\frac{1}{4}$", $4\frac{1}{2}$", $4\frac{3}{4}$", 5", $5\frac{1}{4}$", 6"

Perfect Wide Drum 1905 – 1921

The catalogue of 1905 announced a new alloy model and a new check mechanism. It had a different inscription design on the handle plate with only a small central channel usually containing the words 'Hardy's Patent, Alnwick' and on the larger sizes 'Hardy Bros Ltd, Alnwick – Patent "Perfect" Reel.' The perforated plate had the same pattern as the earlier model and an optional line-guard was available on the $3\frac{1}{2}$" and above sizes. A number of check mechanisms were used during the life of this model (excluding the Early Check), and the main ones are illustrated on the opposite page. Other features included a rim tension regulator screw with bridge (from c.1917 without bridge), drum locking screw, ivorine handle and smooth brass foot. There was a Eunuch version with no ball bearings, but unlike the contracted Eunuch Perfect still retained the left-hand drum locking screw.

Perfect Wide Drum without a bridge over the rim tension regulator screw (1917–1921)

Early Check

1905-11 Check.

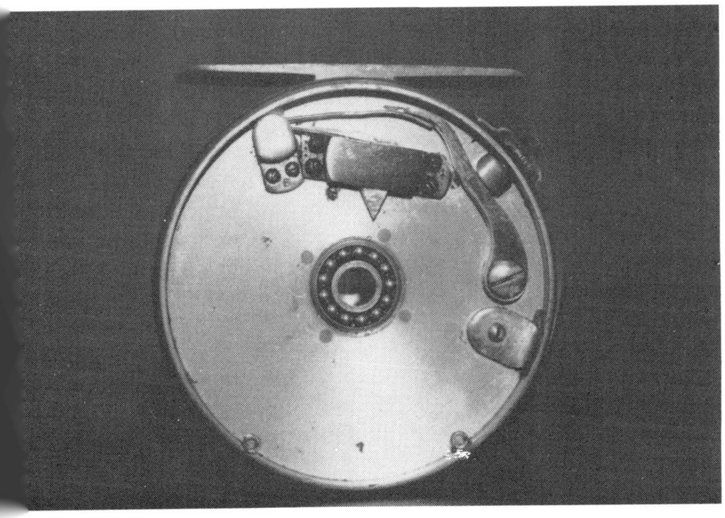

1912 Check described as 'New Patent Compensating Check'

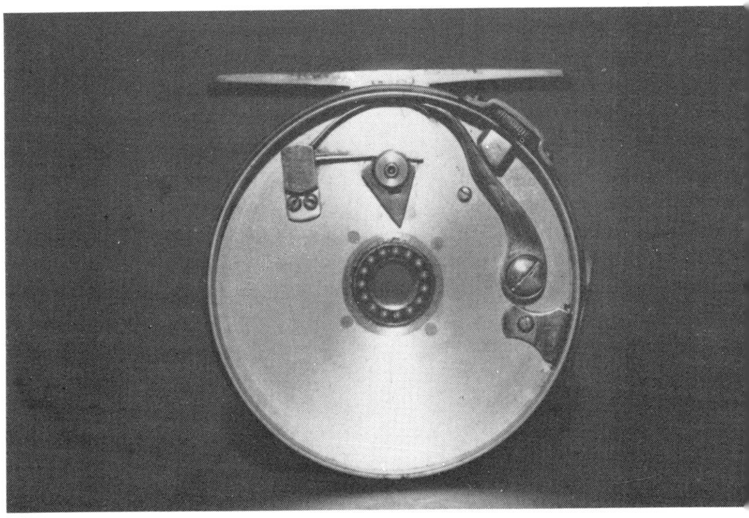

1912 Check

The Eunuch design with no ball bearings c.1917

1917 Check

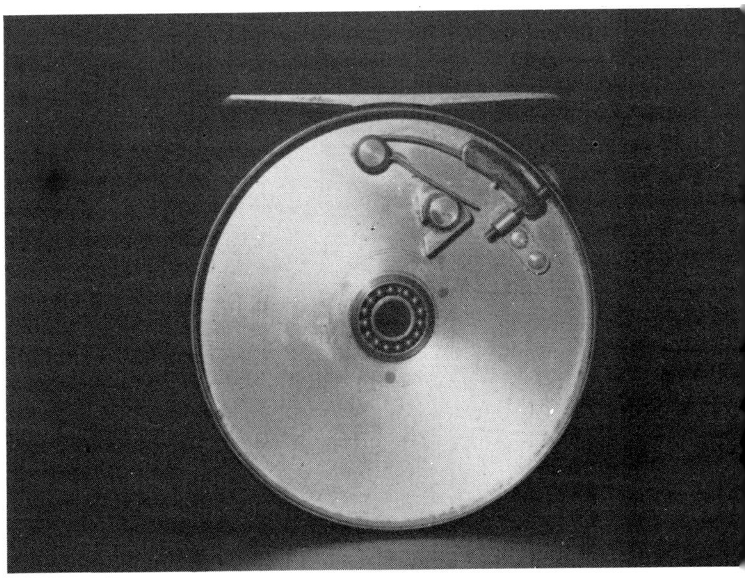

Perfect Mark II Wide Drum 1922 – c.1945

Sizes 3", 3¼", 3½", 3¾", 4", 4¼". 4½" (The larger sizes 4¾", 5", 5¼", 6" were made to order from 1922 – 1924).

In the early years of standardization between 1917 and 1921 when the catalogues showed a single check mechanism with various duplication marks, the illustrations were all confined to the contracted model. At the present time I have no knowledge of any wide drum standardized reel with the early Mark I/II/III Duplicated marks and characteristics. Therefore the Perfect Mark II Wide Drum has to be regarded as the one with the new features introduced in 1922. These included an ebonite handle, grooved brass foot, rim tension regulator screw without bridge, new handle plate inscription design and usually the check mechanism with the spare spring and tonge. It retained the left-hand threaded drum locking screw with the exception of the small sizes 3" and 3¼", which had replaced it with a stud like the new contracted model. Some Wide Drum Perfects with the Duplicated Mark II handle plate inscription introduced in 1922 were made with a single check mechanism in the period of transition. I have found the rare sizes of 3" and 3¼" and also a Special Perfect Mark II with single check mechanisms.

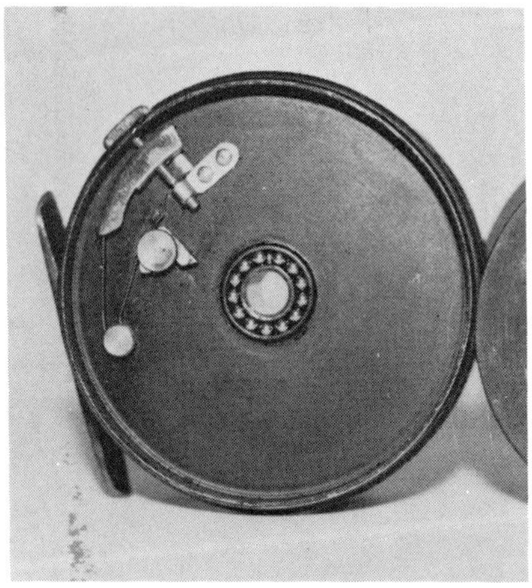

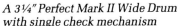

A 3¼" Perfect Mark II Wide Drum with single check mechanism

Perfect Post War Wide Drum c.1946 – 1966

Sizes 3" (dropped in 1948), 3¼", 3½", 3¾", 4", 4¼", 4½". From 1957 only three sizes 3¾", 4", 4½" (dropped in 1960)

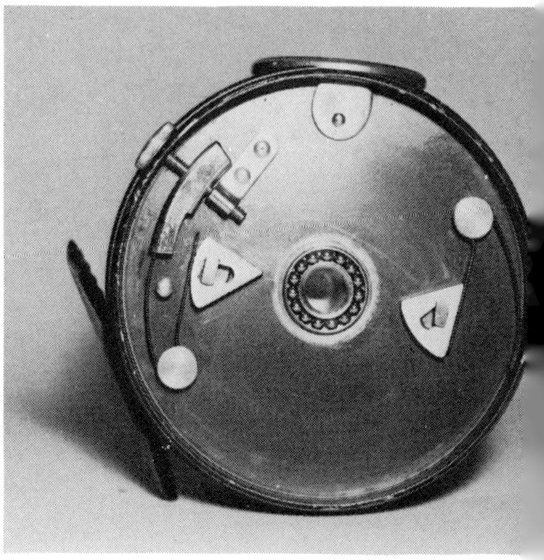

Special Perfect 1903 – 1922

The Special Perfect was first introduced in the catalogue of 1903. It was a Perfect variant designed for lightness and capable of carrying sufficient amount of line for dry fly or general fishing. Features included a rim tension regulator screw with guard (from c.1917 without guard), ivorine handle, left-hand threaded drum locking screw, smooth brass foot and the Perfect check mechanisms as they developed.

Special Perfect 1903 – 1922. Size 3¼″

Special Perfect Mark II. Size 3¼″

Special Perfect Mark II 1923 – 1939

In 1923 a Mark II model evolved with the new features introduced on the Perfect Mark II and remained in production until 1939.

Bouglé Mark II 1923 – 1939

In 1923 the Bouglé Mark II evolved with the usual Mark II features, and continued in production up to the Second World War.

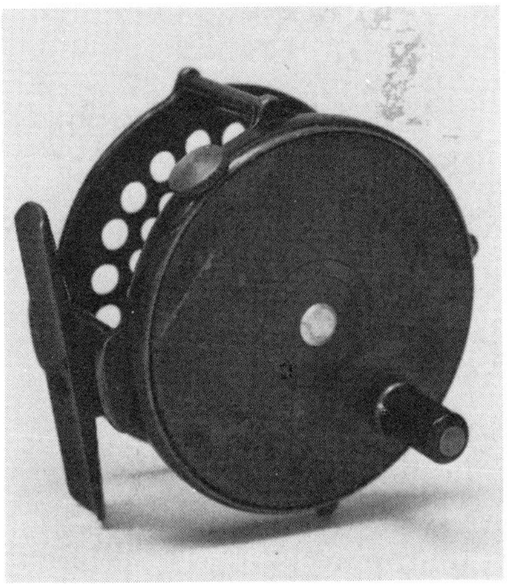

Bouglé Mark II. Sizes 3″, 3¼″

Bouglé 1903 – 1922

This reel was a Perfect variant described as a new design by M Bouglé for a light reel with great line capacity. It was made of Alumin alloy with a heavily perforated plate, brass or alloy smooth foot, rim tension regulator screw with guard (from c.1917 without guard), ivorine handle, external pillars, left-hand threaded locking screw and the usual check mechanisms as they developed.

Sizes 3″, 3¼″ (from 1905). The diameter includes the external pillars

Evolution of the Contracted Perfect

A contracted alloy Perfect was introduced in the catalogue of 1897 with the claim that the new large barrel would retrieve the line quickly and almost serve the same purpose as a multiplier. It was made of alumin with a rim tension regulator screw and bridge, ivorine handle, left-hand threaded drum locking screw, smooth brass foot and the Early Check mechanism.

The illustration of the first one showed a contracted reel with large and small perforations in the drum plate which is unfamiliar to known examples of this model. Two reels have been found which have large and small perforations. One had an extra inner circle of tiny holes of two alternating sizes and perforated pillars. The other had the early perforation pattern but no rim tension regulator screw. Both these examples are experimental oddities and different from the first one illustrated. However, in June 1989, I received a telephone call from a collector in Yorkshire to say he had acquired an early contracted Perfect with large perforations and a Rod-in-Hand trade-mark. I expected it to be another rare prototype but was very excited to find it was the real thing. It exactly matched the one illustrated in the catalogue of 1897. The reel which collectors had only seen on a picture drawing had at last become a reality.

I would class the discovery of this reel as one of the most important finds, with the exception of the 2¼″ Original Perfect it must be the most collectable of all Hardy reels. The model was introduced at the time the large and small perforation pattern was being changed to two rows of tiny holes ⅛″ and 1/16″ diameters, in a circular pattern. One or two reels must have been sold before the Perfect Narrow Drum (Early Model) went into production. All the reels had the plate design of a centre circle, a straight line logo, Rod-in-Hand trade-mark and usually an oval logo.

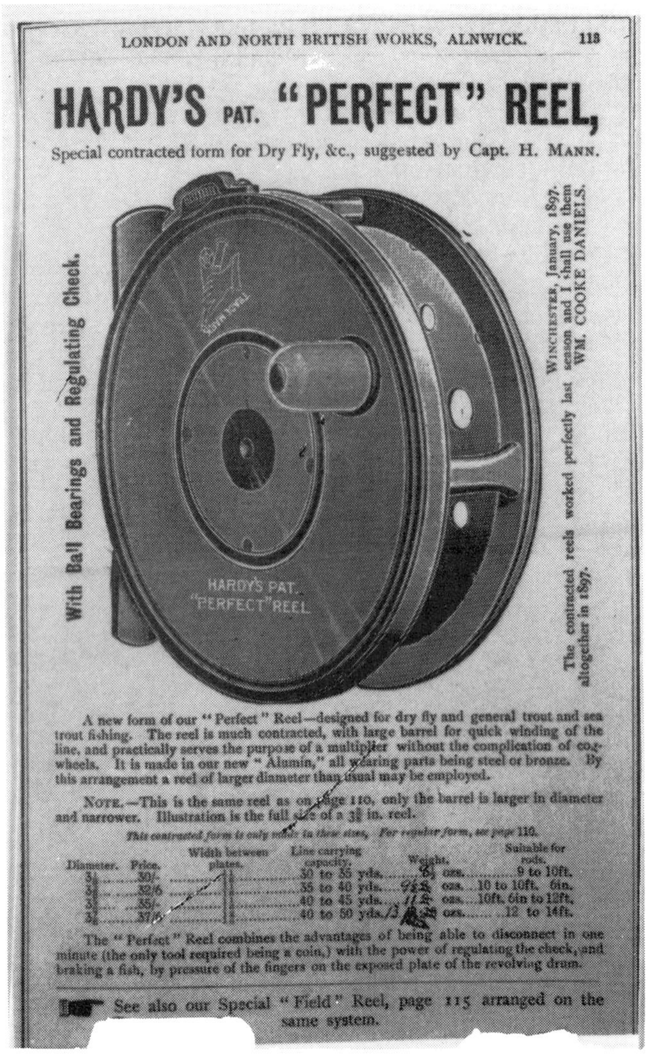
LONDON AND NORTH BRITISH WORKS, ALNWICK. 113

HARDY'S PAT. "PERFECT" REEL,

Special contracted form for Dry Fly, &c., suggested by Capt. H. MANN.

With Ball Bearings and Regulating Check.

The contracted reels worked perfectly last season and I shall use them altogether in 1897.
WINCHESTER, January, 1897. WM. COOKE DANIELS.

A new form of our "Perfect" Reel—designed for dry fly and general trout and sea trout fishing. The reel is much contracted, with large barrel for quick winding of the line, and practically serves the purpose of a multiplier without the complication of cog-wheels. It is made in our new "Alumin," all wearing parts being steel or bronze. By this arrangement a reel of larger diameter than usual may be employed.

NOTE.—This is the same reel as on page 110, only the barrel is larger in diameter and narrower. Illustration is the full size of a 3⅜ in. reel.

This contracted form is only made in these sizes. For regular form, see page 110.

Diameter.	Price.	Width between plates.	Line carrying capacity.	Weight.	Suitable for rods.
3⅛	30/-	[illegible]	30 to 35 yds.	[illegible] ozs.	9 to 10ft.
3⅜	32/6	[illegible]	35 to 40 yds.	[illegible] ozs.	10 to 10ft. 6in.
3⅝	35/-	[illegible]	40 to 45 yds.	[illegible] ozs.	10ft. 6in to 12ft.
3⅞	37/6	[illegible]	40 to 50 yds.	[illegible] ozs.	12 to 14ft.

The "Perfect" Reel combines the advantages of being able to disconnect in one minute (the only tool required being a coin,) with the power of regulating the check, and braking a fish, by pressure of the fingers on the exposed plate of the revolving drum.

See also our Special "Field" Reel, page 115 arranged on the same system.

Written alterations to the weights in the catalogue of 1899

It is generally believed that the alloy contracted Perfect ran continuously from its inception and the Brass Faced version was an early additional range. It would seem from research that this was not the case and the data suggesting a different progression came from the weights of the reels which appeared in the catalogues. In 1896/97 when the model was first introduced the weights listed were: 3⅛″ – 6½oz, 3⅜″ – 8oz, 3⅝″ – 9oz and 3⅞″ – 10oz.

No catalogue was printed in 1898 but when the 1899 edition came out, it contained dramatic increases to the weights of the contracted Perfect, and appeared in the form of hand-written alterations to the text. Having already examined similar alterations in the same catalogue, which marked the advent of the Brass Faced Wide Drum Perfect, it would seem that the original all alloy contracted Perfects had changed to a heavier model which could only be the Brass Faced Narrow Drum Perfect. The fact that the company had gone to the trouble of changing the weights would suggest that the earlier model had been discontinued.

The new weights were: 3⅛″ – 8½oz, 3⅜″ – 9½oz, 3⅝″ – 11oz, and 3⅞″ – 13 oz.

These weights were incorporated into the text of the catalogue of1902, with the exception of the 3⅜″ size which had the printed 9½oz crossed out and a reduced weight of 6¼oz written in. This suggests that a much lighter alloy reel had been re-introduced in that size and in 1903 all the weights of the contracted Perfect reels had been reduced even lower than the figures given for the original alloy model of 1896/97. The new set of weights were: 3$\frac{1}{8}$″ – 5$\frac{3}{4}$oz, 3$\frac{3}{8}$″ – 7$\frac{1}{4}$oz, 3$\frac{5}{8}$″ – 8oz and 3$\frac{7}{8}$″ – 8$\frac{3}{4}$oz. I checked these weights against the only other contracted Perfect model, which was the later alloy range with the central channel inscription design and found the weights of the ones I examined matched almost perfectly.

Therefore the story that the catalogue weights seems to tell, is that the original alloy models were short lived, being succeeded by the Brass Faced which in turn was replaced about 1902 by the more familiar all alloy reel.

Perfect Narrow Drum (First Model) 1896 – 1897

The beginning of the contracted Perfect range and the first illustrated record of this model

Left: Back Plate with large and small perforations.
Right: Handle Plate. The only known example of this model at the present time. Size 3$\frac{1}{8}$″, 3$\frac{3}{8}$″, 3$\frac{5}{8}$″, 3$\frac{7}{8}$″

Perfect Narrow Drum (Early Model) 1897 – 1898
This was the early production Narrow Drum Perfect design which the company settled on and marketed. Features included a rim tension regulator screw with bridge, smooth brass foot, ivorine handle and plate designed with a centre circle, straight-line logo and Rod-in-Hand trade-mark, and occasionally an unbordered oval logo. The drum was perforated with two rows of tiny holes of $\frac{1}{8}$″ and $\frac{1}{16}$″ diameters in a circular pattern and locked by means of a left-hand threaded screw. It had the Early Check mechanism.

Sizes 3$\frac{1}{8}$″, 3$\frac{3}{8}$″, 3$\frac{5}{8}$″, 3$\frac{7}{8}$″

Rear elevation

Perfect Brass Faced Narrow Drum. Sizes 3⅛", 3⅜", 3⅝", 3⅞"

Perfect Brass Faced Narrow Drum 1899 – 1901

This alloy contracted Perfect was basically the same as the earlier model and had a similar handle plate inscription design of a straight line logo, Rod-in-Hand trade-mark and usually a bordered oval logo. The difference was in having a bronzed, brass handle plate, otherwise it had all the usual features of a rim tension regulator screw with bridge, ivorine handle, smooth brass foot, Early Check mechanism and two rows of tiny perforations in a circular pattern on the drum which was locked by a left-hand threaded screw. The rarity of this model would suggest that only a few were sold which was probably the reason it was quickly dropped in favour of a much lighter all alloy reel.

Perfect Narrow Drum. Sizes 2¾" (1911/1912), 2⅞" (from 1911), 3⅛", 3⅜", 3⅝", 3⅞"

The 2¾" Perfect Narrow Drum made only in 1911/1912

Perfect Narrow Drum 1902 – c.1921

The contracted Brass Faced Perfect was dropped in c.1902 and replaced by a similar model which had an alloy handle plate on which was a plainer design of only a central channel which contained the words – 'Hardy's Alnwick Patent'. Features included a rim tension regulator screw with bridge (from c.1917 without bridge), ivorine handle, smooth brass foot and drum locking screw. This model used various check mechanisms and internal arrangements as they were developed including the Early Check, 1905 Check, 1912 Check, 1917 Check and also appeared in an unusual form called the Eunuch Perfect. This was designed without ball bearings and the knurled left-hand drum locking screw had been replaced by a small brass stud which was the tip of the handle plate shaft, making it possible to dismantle the reel without the use of a tool.
There has always been a mystery about the production of a contracted 2¾" Perfect since the size was discovered listed for the

1896 Perfect diameter 2½″

Above: Perfect Brass Faced Wide Drum diameter 3¼″

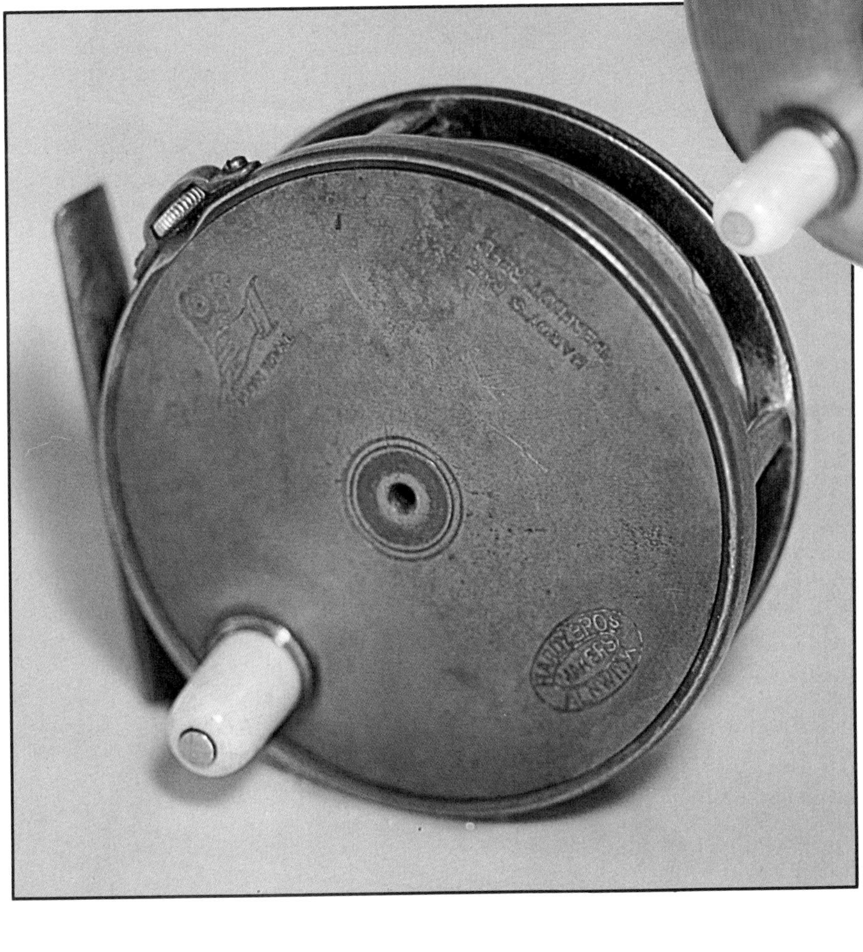

Perfect Brass Faced Narrow Drum diameter 3⅜″

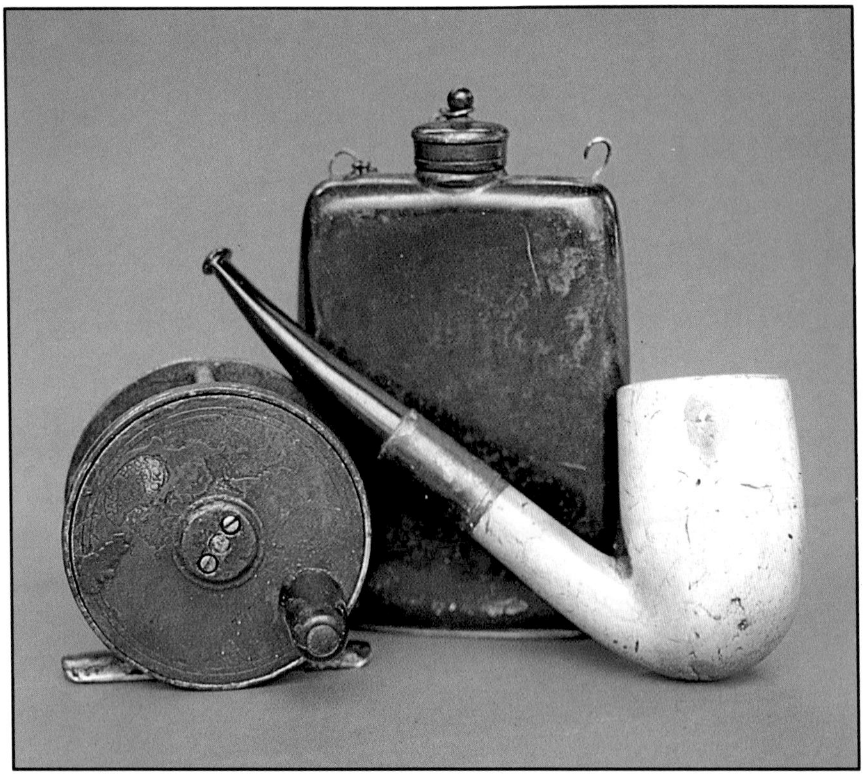

Lord Carmichael's Birmingham Plate Reel diameter 2½″ also his hip flask and pipe

The SS Medina which was sunk in 1917 by a German 'U' boat

P&O Line

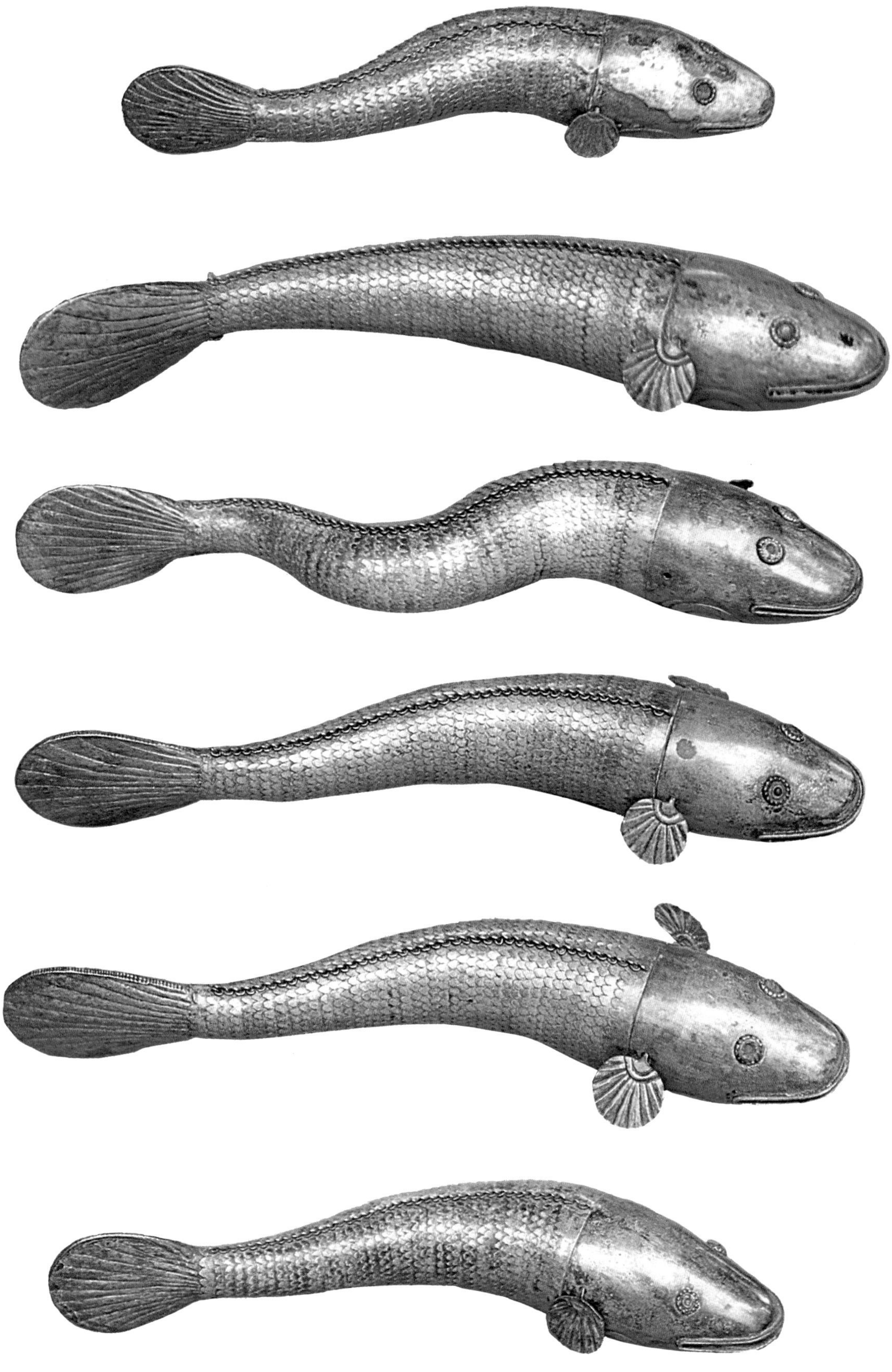

The six Medina fish recovered from the wreck of the SS Medina along with other artefacts belonging to Lord Carmichael

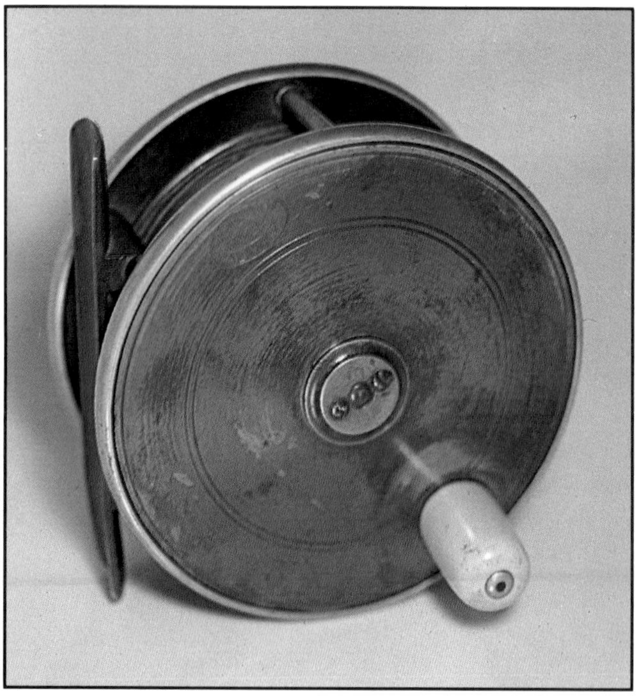

Birmingham Half-Ebonite diameter 4″

Bronzed Crank diameter 2½″

Birmingham Plate Reel diameter 2¼″

Hercules diameter 2½″

Perfect Narrow Drum in the catalogues of 1911 and 1912. In the 1913 edition the 2¾″ size was crossed out by hand and the generally held belief, in the absence of knowledge of any such reel, has always been that it was a printing error. However, I have discovered the existence of two examples, both of which are exactly 2¾″ diameter. One has the 1905 – 1911 Check and the other the 1912 Check which would appear to support the intentional production of the size by Hardy Bros in the two years it was advertised. The reason for making the size in addition to the introduction of the 2⅞″, was probably to fill the gap left behind when the smaller sizes of Perfect Wide Drum below 3″, were dropped in 1911.

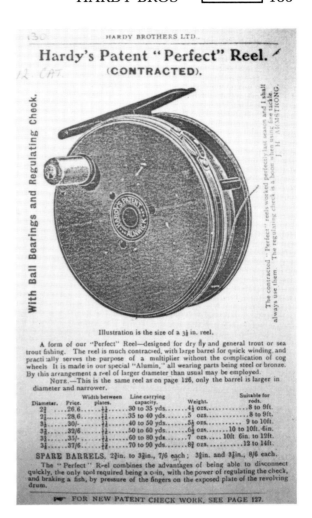

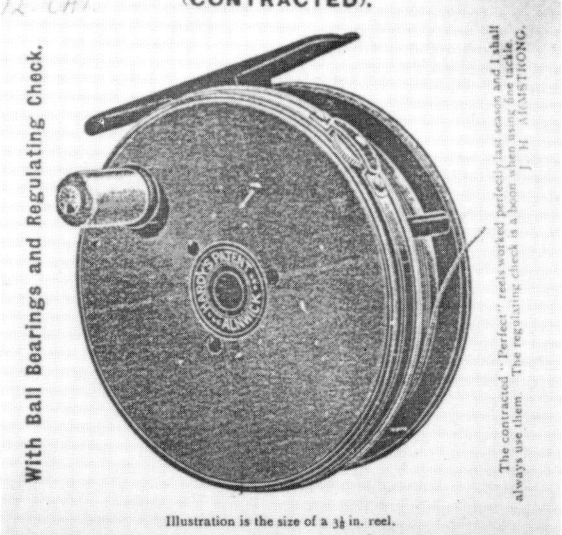

130 HARDY BROTHERS LTD.

Hardy's Patent "Perfect" Reel.

(CONTRACTED).

12 CAT.

With Ball Bearings and Regulating Check.

The contracted "Perfect" reels worked perfectly last season and I shall always use them. The regulating check is a boon when using fine tackle. J. H. ARMSTRONG.

Illustration is the size of a 3⅛ in. reel.

A form of our "Perfect" Reel—designed for dry fly and general trout or sea trout fishing. The reel is much contracted, with large barrel for quick winding, and practically serves the purpose of a multiplier without the complication of cog wheels. It is made in our special "Alumin," all wearing parts being steel or bronze. By this arrangement a reel of larger diameter than usual may be employed.

NOTE.—This is the same reel as on page 126, only the barrel is larger in diameter and narrower.

Diameter.	Price.	Width between plates.	Line carrying capacity.	Weight.	Suitable for rods.
2¾	26/6	[illegible]	30 to 35 yds.	4½ ozs.	8 to 9ft.
2⅞	28/6	[illegible]	35 to 40 yds.	5 ozs.	8 to 9ft.
3⅛	30/-	[illegible]	40 to 50 yds.	5½ ozs.	9 to 10ft.
3⅜	32/6	[illegible]	50 to 60 yds.	6½ ozs.	10 to 10ft. 6in.
3⅝	35/-	[illegible]	60 to 80 yds.	7 ozs.	10ft 6in. to 12ft.
3⅞	37/6	[illegible]	70 to 90 yds.	8¾ ozs.	12 to 14ft.

SPARE BARRELS. 2¾in. to 3⅜in., 7/6 each; 3⅝in. and 3⅞in., 8/6 each.

The "Perfect" Reel combines the advantages of being able to disconnect quickly, the only tool required being a coin, with the power of regulating the check, and braking a fish, by pressure of the fingers on the exposed plate of the revolving drum.

FOR NEW PATENT CHECK WORK, SEE PAGE 127.

Catalogue of 1912

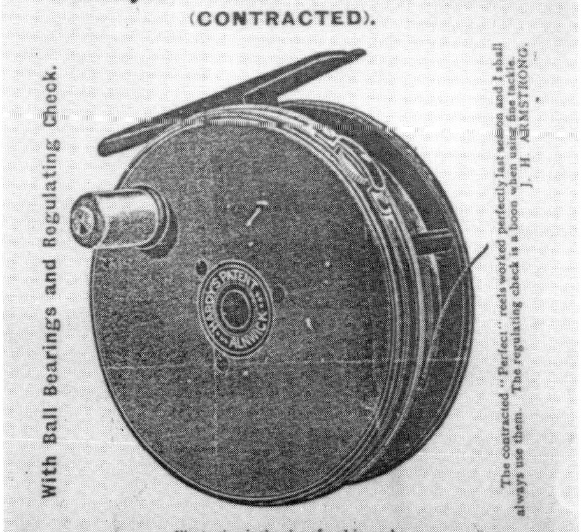

131 HARDY BROTHERS LTD.

Hardy's Patent "Perfect" Reel.

(CONTRACTED).

With Ball Bearings and Regulating Check.

The contracted "Perfect" reels worked perfectly last season and I shall always use them. The regulating check is a boon when using fine tackle. J. H. ARMSTRONG.

Illustration is the size of a 3⅛ in. reel.

A form of our "Perfect" Reel—designed for dry fly and general trout or sea trout fishing. The reel is much contracted, with large barrel for quick winding, and practically serves the purpose of a multiplier without the complication of cog wheels. It is made in our special "Alumin," all wearing parts being steel or bronze. By this arrangement a reel of larger diameter than usual may be employed.

NOTE.—This is the same reel as on page 128, only the barrel is larger in diameter and narrower.

Diameter.	Price.	Width between plates.	Line carrying capacity.	Weight.	Suitable for rods.
~~[illegible]~~	~~26/6~~	~~[illegible]~~	~~[illegible]~~	~~[illegible]~~	~~8 to 9ft.~~
2⅞	28/6	[illegible]	35 to 40 yds.	5 ozs.	8 to 9ft.
3⅛	30/-	[illegible]	40 to 50 yds.	6 ozs.	9 to 10ft.
3⅜	32/6	[illegible]	50 to 60 yds.	7 ozs.	10 to 10ft. 6in.
3⅝	35/-	[illegible]	60 to 80 yds.	7¾ ozs.	10ft 6in. to 12ft.
3⅞	37/6	[illegible]	70 to 90 yds.	9¼ ozs.	12 to 14ft.

SPARE BARRELS. 2⅞in. to 3⅜in., 7/6 each; 3⅝in. and 3⅞in., 8/6 each.

The "Perfect" Reel combines the advantages of being able to disconnect quickly, the only tool required being a coin, with the power of regulating the check, and braking a fish, by pressure of the fingers on the exposed plate of the revolving drum.

FOR NEW PATENT CHECK WORK, SEE PAGE 129.

7/-

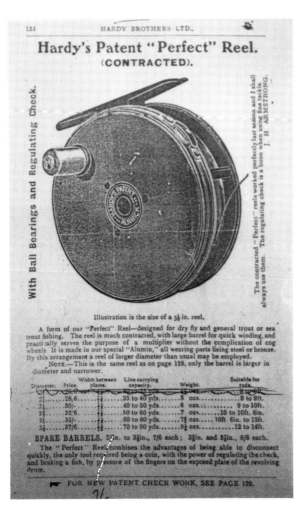

Catalogue of 1913

Standardization and Duplication Marks

Hardy Bros learned the advantages of interchangeability of parts during the First World War and made efforts to standardize the parts of their popular models. It would appear to have taken a few years to become fully organised, during which time there was some confusion as to how the standardized reels should be marked. The new rationalisation would appear to have been introduced gradually and probably a limited number of reels were given trial markings. The birth of the Mark II model has always been something of a mystery and the generally held belief is that Mark II was inscribed on reels to denote a double check mechanism.

I have always been of the opinion that the mark was first devised to indicate interchangeability of parts between models, because it first appeared in the catalogues before the Dual Check was introduced and a number of reels marked Duplicated Mark II have only the single check mechanism inside. To find the truth, it is essential to carefully examine the catalogues and the reels of the years when standardization was being introduced.

The idea was first announced in the catalogue of 1917 with an illustration of a contracted Perfect check mechanism with a single spring and tonge and described as Mark III. The same Single Check was shown in the 1919 and 1920 editions but the sign had been changed to Mark I, and strandardization up to that period was confined to the Uniqua and Perfect models. In 1921 the same single spring and tonge check mechanism was again illustrated but the mark had changed to what was to prove its permanent name of Mark II, and the St. George had been included in the scheme. To add to the confusion the catalogue of 1923 announced a double check mechanism, which for the first time had a spare spring and

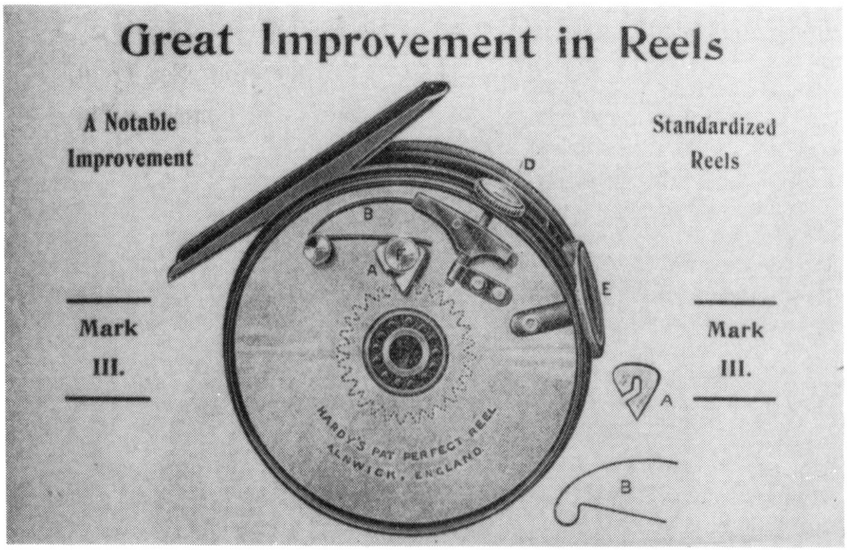

1917 catalogue

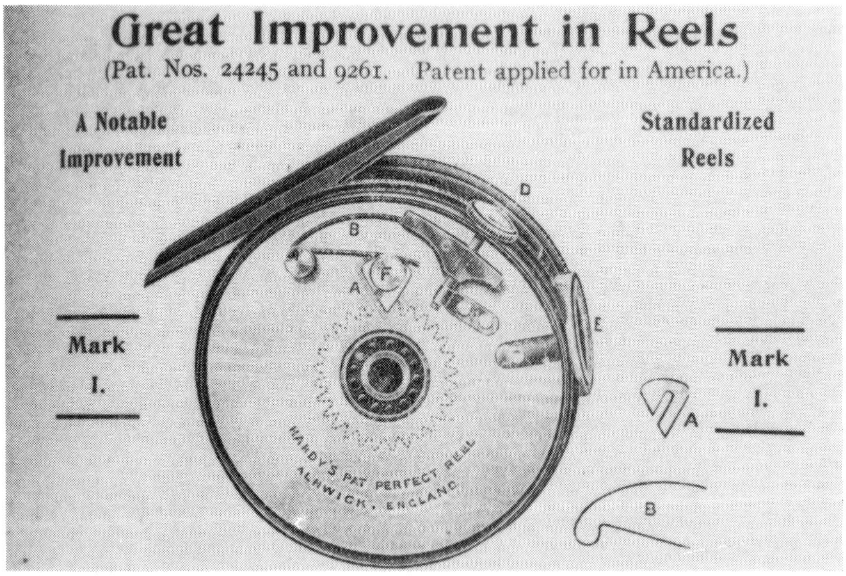

1919 and 1920 catalogues

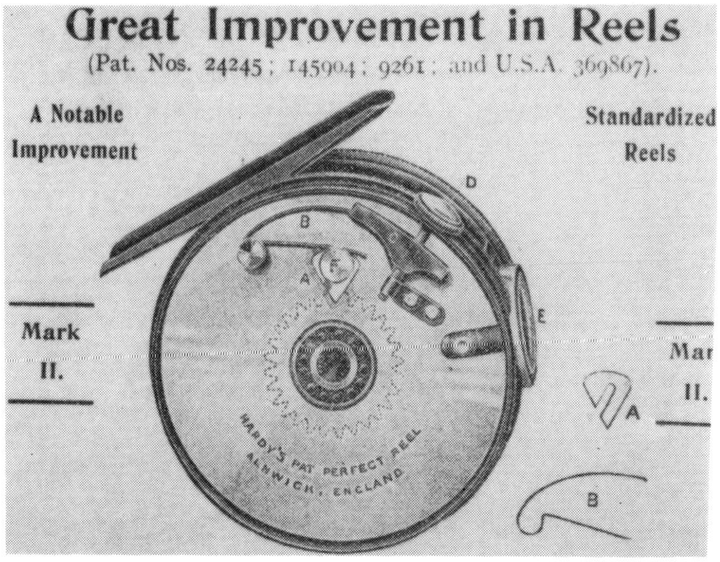

1921 catalogue

tonge, and the Special Perfect and Bouglé were added to the list; while in 1924 the St. John was also included. This is the total relevant information which can be obtained from the catalogues but it is of little use without knowledge of what was actually happening to the reels themselves at that period.

Standardization Marks on Reels 1917 to 1921

There has been a lack of knowledge of the reels described in the catalogues of 1917 to 1921 which are obviously very rare. After an extensive search I eventually found a reel which gave me reason to believe that some were produced with the marks described in the years when standardization was being introduced. It was a contracted Uniqua 3⅜″ with ivorine handle, smooth aluminium foot but with an unusual plate inscription – 'Mark 1', underlined and below the word 'Duplicated' – (Mark I/Duplicated). This reel appeared to be an example of the one described as Mark I in the catalogues of 1919 and 1920. Subsequently, I found a second example and this time it was a contracted Perfect 3⅝″ with similar features of ivorine handle, smooth aluminium foot and the same unusual plate inscription design – 'Mark II' underlined, and below, the word – 'Duplicated' (Mark II/Duplicated). These models had dispensed with the bridge or guard over the rim tension regulator screw.

Soon after finding the two reels with the early duplication marks, I heard of two similar ones, a Uniqua Mark I and another Perfect Mark II. Both had similar features including the unusual inscription design, ivorine handles and smooth aluminium feet. The dealer who sold the reels informed me that he had also handled a Perfect Mark I Duplicated which had similar characteristics. Therefore Hardy Bros must have been introducing standardization and marking some reels exactly as described in the catalogues and probably experimenting with materials.

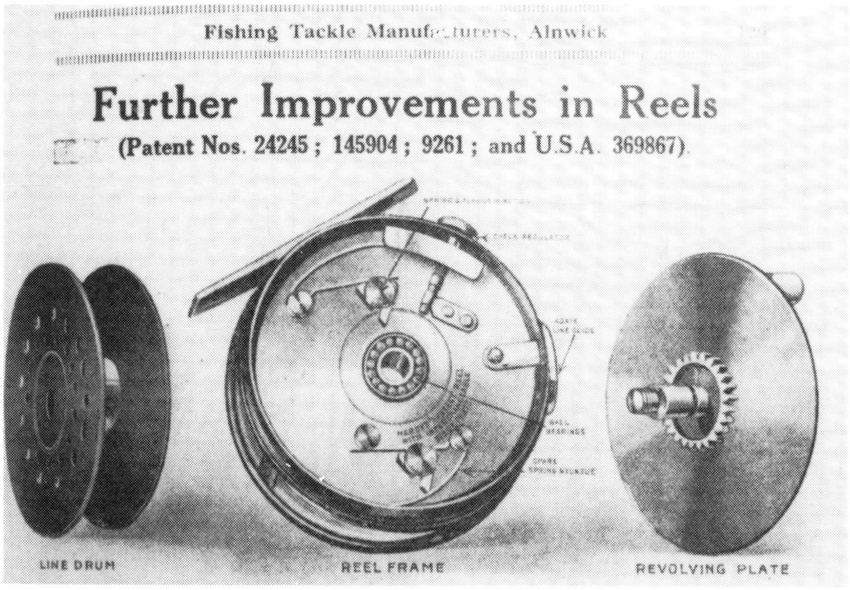

1923 catalogue

It could be argued that all the duplication marks used between 1917 and 1921 were experimental and should be disregarded, but the fact that some reels were stamped with the various marks means that no history of the model can be complete without including them. The Mark III and Mark 1 Duplicated data shows clearly that the company introduced the mark to denote interchangeability of parts and the fact that they finally settled on Mark II was possibly influenced by the development of the double check mechanism. Although the new check did not appear in the catalogues until 1923 it was probably being developed in 1920 and 1921 and marketed in 1922.

Some people believe that the Mark III which appeared in the catalogue of 1917 was a misprint and should have read Mark I. At the present time I have no knowledge of a Perfect or Uniqua reel with the early Mark III/Duplicated inscription which would support the idea of a misprint. However, I will reserve judgement in case it turns out to be similar to the 2¾″ contracted Perfect of 1911/1912, which everyone also thought was a misprint, but eventually two have been found.

The early duplication mark

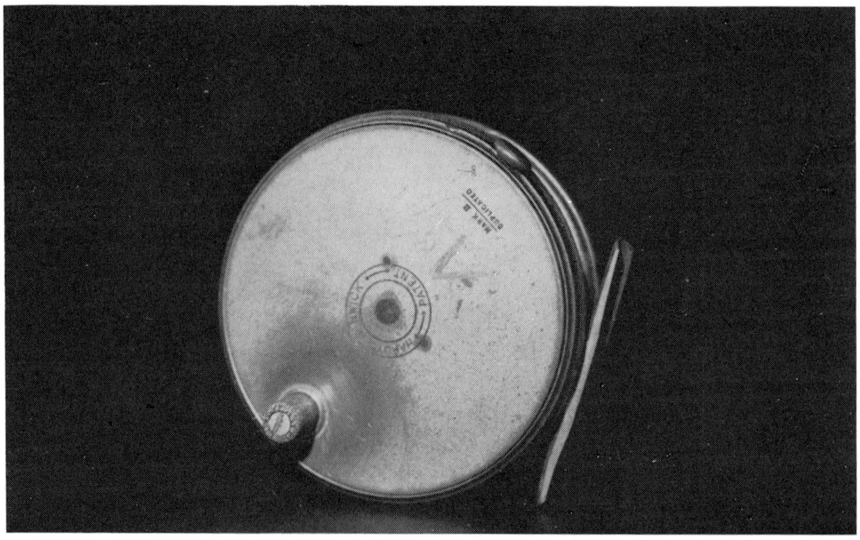

Perfect Mark II (1921) Narrow Drum.
Sizes 2⅞", 3¼", 3⅜", 3⅝", 3⅞"

The single check mechanism.

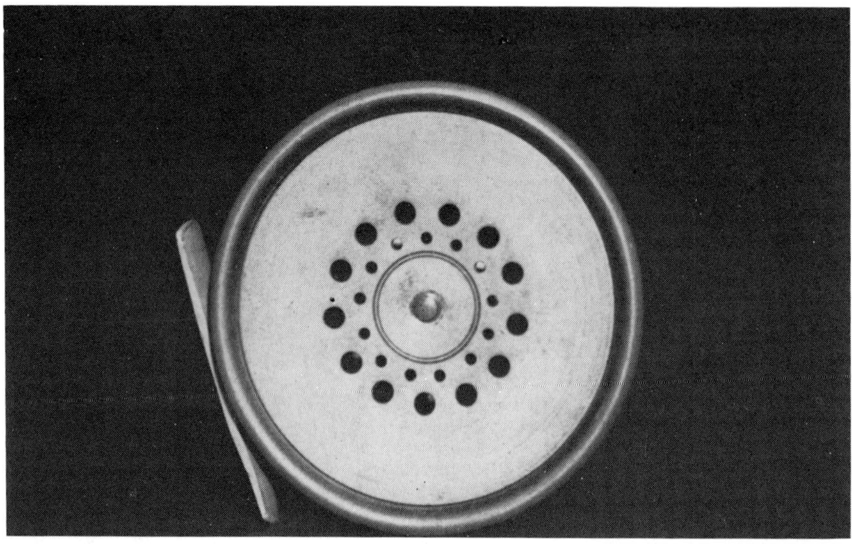

A rear view showing the centre stud

Perfect Mark I Narrow Drum 1919 – 1920

Sizes 2⅞", 3⅛", 3⅜", 3⅝", 3⅞"

Reels stamped with the early duplication mark had the same features as described for the Perfect Mark II (1921) Narrow Drum.

Perfect Mark II (1921) Narrow Drum 1921

The earliest Perfect Mark II which was introduced in 1921 had a rim tension regulator screw without bridge, an ivorine or composition handle, single check mechanism, smooth alloy foot (occasionally brass) and an inscription design – 'Mark II', underlined, and below the word – 'Duplicated'. (Mark II/Duplicated).

Earliest Mark II/Duplicated inscription

The new feature of the Perfect Narrow Drum Mark I and Mark II Duplicated was the introduction of a stud which replaced the left-hand threaded locking screw. This feature had only previously been used on the Eunuch version of the contracted model Perfect but would be incorporated on to the next generation of contracted Mark II Perfects and some of the smallest sizes of the Perfect Mark II Wide Drum model.

Perfect Mark II Narrow Drum 1922 – 1945

The fact that few Single Check contracted Perfects with the unusual early inscription 'Mark II/Duplicated' have been found, would suggest that it appeared in its early form for only the one year and had been replaced in 1922 by the redesigned Mark II.

The new reel had a rim tension regulator screw without bridge, ebonite handle, brass foot with grooves along the top, and a complete new inscription design on the handle plate. This included the retention of the central channel but the enclosed wording quickly changed to 'The "Perfect" Fly Reel'. On the plate was a lot of information in small $\frac{1}{16}''$ setting, between the channel and the rim, giving the name of the company and the reel size on one side, and on the opposite, patent numbers, below which was 'Duplicated Mark II'. It had the stud, replacing the drum locking screw, first seen on the Eunuch Perfect Narrow Drum and incorporated on to the Perfect standardized models between 1917 and 1921.

Sizes $2\frac{7}{8}''$, $3\frac{1}{8}''$, $3\frac{3}{8}''$, $3\frac{5}{8}''$, $3\frac{7}{8}''$

New double check mechanism

The five sizes of the Perfect Mark II Narrow Drum

New Features introduced in 1922

A central stud which replaced the drum locking screw

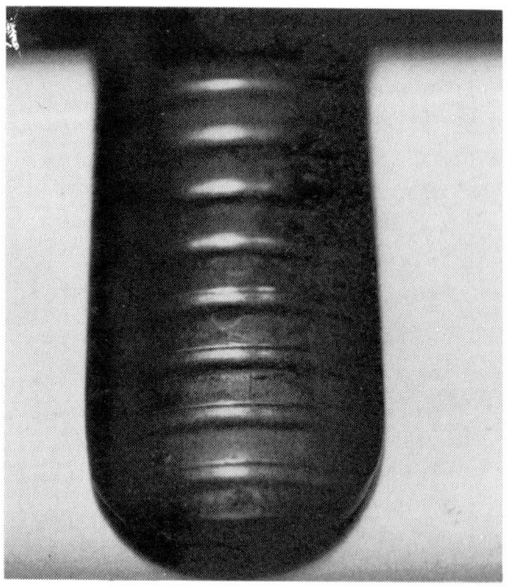

Grooved brass foot

Ebonite handle

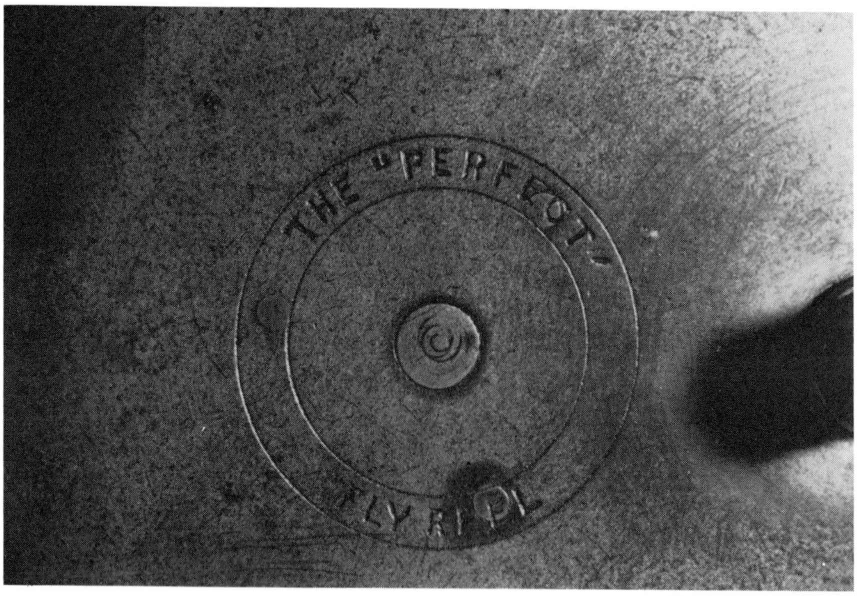

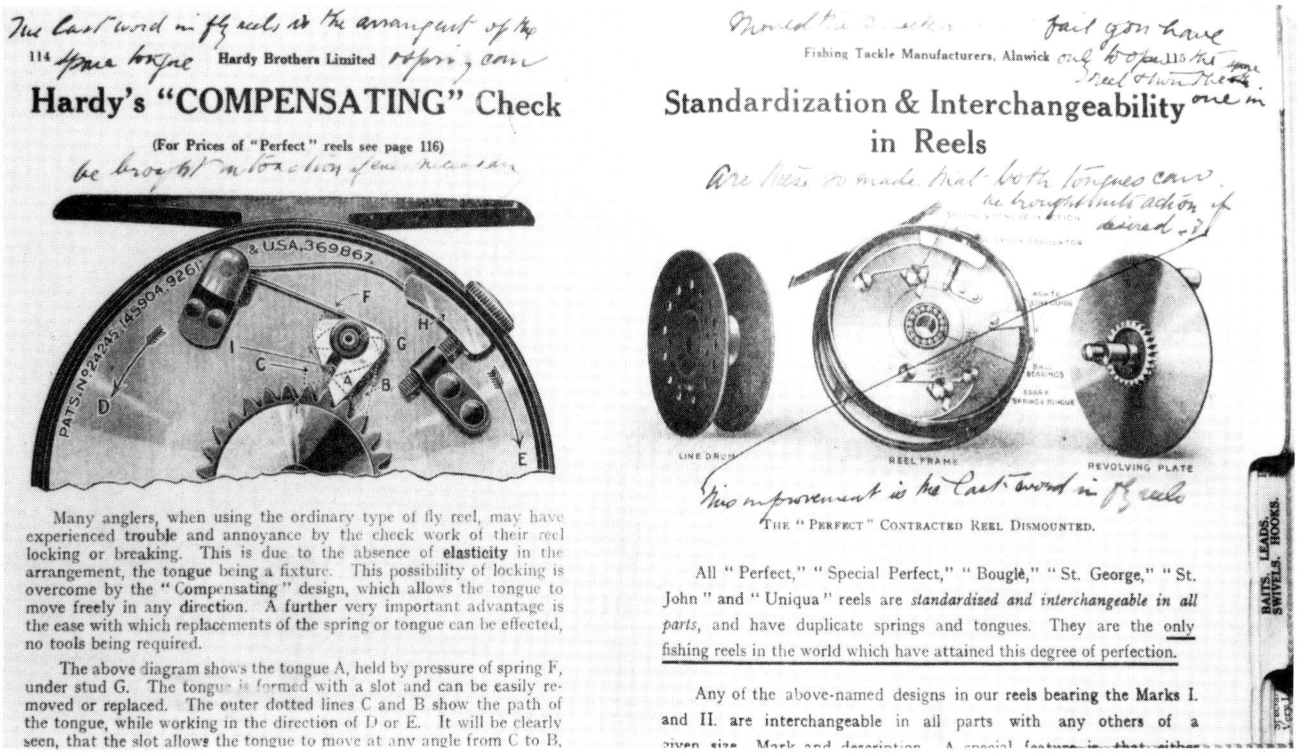
114 Hardy Brothers Limited

Hardy's "COMPENSATING" Check

(For Prices of "Perfect" reels see page 116)

Many anglers, when using the ordinary type of fly reel, may have experienced **trouble** and annoyance by the check work of their reel locking or breaking. This is due to the absence of **elasticity** in the arrangement, the tongue being a fixture. This possibility of locking is overcome by the "Compensating" design, which allows the tongue to move freely in any direction. A further very important advantage is the ease with which replacements of the spring or tongue can be effected, no tools being required.

The above diagram shows the tongue A, held by pressure of spring F, under stud G. The tongue is formed with a slot and can be easily removed or replaced. The outer dotted lines C and B show the path of the tongue, while working in the direction of D or E. It will be clearly seen, that the slot allows the tongue to move at any angle from C to B,

Fishing Tackle Manufacturers, Alnwick 115

Standardization & Interchangeability in Reels

THE "PERFECT" CONTRACTED REEL DISMOUNTED.

All "Perfect," "Special Perfect," "Bouglé," "St. George," "St. John" and "Uniqua" reels are *standardized and interchangeable in all parts*, and have duplicate springs and tongues. They are the only fishing reels in the world which have attained this degree of perfection.

Any of the above-named designs in our **reels bearing the Marks I. and II.** are interchangeable in all parts with any others of a

Check mechanism illustrated in the catalogue of 1927 with hand-written notes describing the new arrangement of the springs and tonges

The new Mark II was fitted with what is called the double check mechanism (Dual Check), which was first illustrated in the catalogue of 1923. This carried a spare spring and tonge which could easily be removed to replace the original if required. Eventually they had the simple but clever idea of positioning the spare tonge in such a way that it could be brought into action by simply turning to a working position. The catalogue of 1929 showed the first illustration of the new arrangement, but I found evidence that the company had the idea at least two years earlier. The catalogue of 1927 in the board-room of Hardy Bros contains hand-written notes on the illustration of the Perfect check mechanism and says 'the last word in fly reels is the arrangement of the spare tonge and spring can be brought into action if necessary.'

The contracted Perfect Mark II continued in the same form up to about the time of WW II and by the late 1940s the Mark II inscription had been dropped and a Perfect with a plainer handle plate design was being sold.

The Improved Dual Check illustrated in the catalogue of 1929

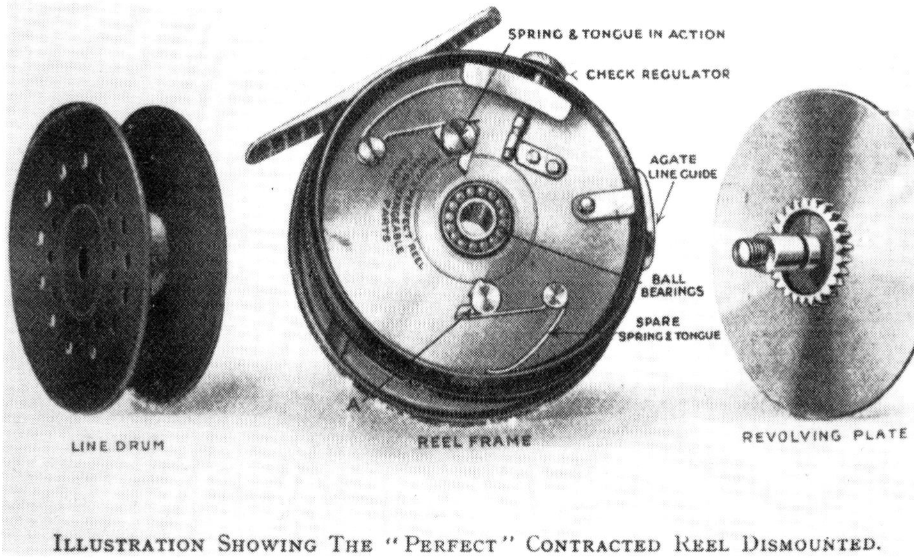

ILLUSTRATION SHOWING THE "PERFECT" CONTRACTED REEL DISMOUNTED.

Perfect Post War Narrow Drum c.1946 – 1966 and 1978 to current

In 1978 the contracted Perfect was re-introduced in modern form in sizes – 3⅛″, 3⅜″ and 3⅝″.

Sizes 2⅞″ (dropped in 1956), 3⅛″, 3⅜″, 3⅝″, 3⅞″

The double check mechanism of the Perfect Post War Narrow Drum

Perfect Taupo 1958 – 1964

This was an additional 3⅞″ contracted post war Perfect with a slightly wider drum

Size 3⅝″

Perfect Early Silent Check 1908 – 1910

The reel was introduced in 1908 as a variation of the normal Perfect range, for anglers who disliked the noise of the check when playing a fish. The mechanism had eliminated the toothed cog but otherwise worked like the other production model. It was made in one size of 3⅝″, retailing at 40/–, with an extra 7/6d for an agate guide ring. Externally it looked liked any other other 3⅝″ contracted Perfect except that the width between the pillars was ¾″ instead of the usual 1¹⁄₁₆″. This early model had a distinctive heavily perforated inside casing behind the handle plate and is a rare reel, with only three years in production.

130 HARDY BROTHERS LTD.

HARDY'S

Patent "Silent Check" Fly Reel.

Suitable for Dry Fly or any kind of Trout Fishing.

Silent Check, with Regulator and Ball Bearings. Holds 50 to 60 yards of line.

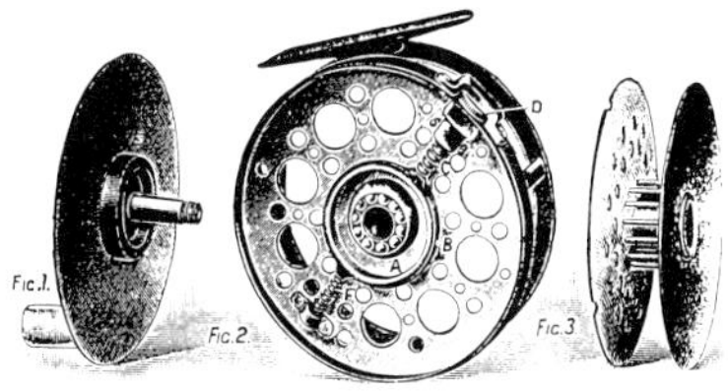

This is a new design of a silent check reel. As may be seen from Fig. 2, the clutch B is actuated by spring C at F and bears on hub E (see Fig. 1) which fits into space A on Fig. 2, the pressure being regulated by milled nut D on the rim, which may be increased by turning screw to the left or decreased by turning to the right, as may be desired. The arrangement is practically the same as in our Patent "Perfect" reel. This is the only Silent Check reel which has a smooth easy action and may be regulated to any required stiffness.

The reel is fitted with ball bearings and may be taken apart in the same manner as that described on page 122. The diameter is 3⅝ in., width between plates ¾ in. It carries 40 yds. of heavy double tapered trout line with 20 yds. of backing, while the weight is only 6½ ozs. It is an ideal reel for those who dislike the noise of a check, and while mainly intended for trout fishing, may, from its large line carrying capacity, be used for loch, sea trout and even grilse. Price 40/-, if fitted with agate guide ring as on page 129, 7/6 extra.

Perfect Silent Check 1931 – 1936

This model was simply a standard Perfect Mark II with a modified check mechanism, having an arm which braked on a hub on the revolving plate to eliminate the noisy ratchet check action.

Sizes – Wide Drum 3¾″, 4″, 4¼″, 4½″
Narrow Drum 3⅛″, 3⅜″, 3⅝″, 3⅞″

Field Narrow Drum c.1879 – 1902

The Field contracted model was made of Alumin, with fixed check, smooth brass foot, ivorine handle. The company logo and usually a 'Rod-in-Hand' trademark were stamped on the back plate.

Field Brass Faced c.1899

Some brass-faced versions of the Field model were made but not mentioned in the company catalogues.

Field Narrow Drum c.1897 – 1902. Sizes 3 1/8", 3 3/8", 3 5/8", 3 7/8", (width between plates 12/16")

Field Wide Drum 1897 – 1907

The Field Wide Drum was made of Alumin, with fixed check, smooth brass foot, ivorine handle. The company logo and usually a 'Rod-in-Hand' trademark were stamped on the back plate.

Sizes 2 5/8", 2 7/8", 3 1/8", 3 3/8", 3 5/8", 3 7/8", 4 1/8", 4 3/8", 4 5/8", 4 7/8", 5 1/8"
Width between pillars 13/16", 14/16", 1 1/16", 1 2/16", 1 3/16", 1 4/16", 1 6/16", 1 8/16", 1 9/16", 1 10/16", 1 10/16"

Ocean Reel (First Model)
1894 – 1902

The beginning of the Ocean range of sea reels was a plain dual handled model with a centre knurled edged drum locking nut which when tightened acted as a brake.
It was resurrected in similar form as the Coquet (1911–1922).

Dr S Harrison

The Ocean (First Model)
Sizes 4 1/2" to 7"

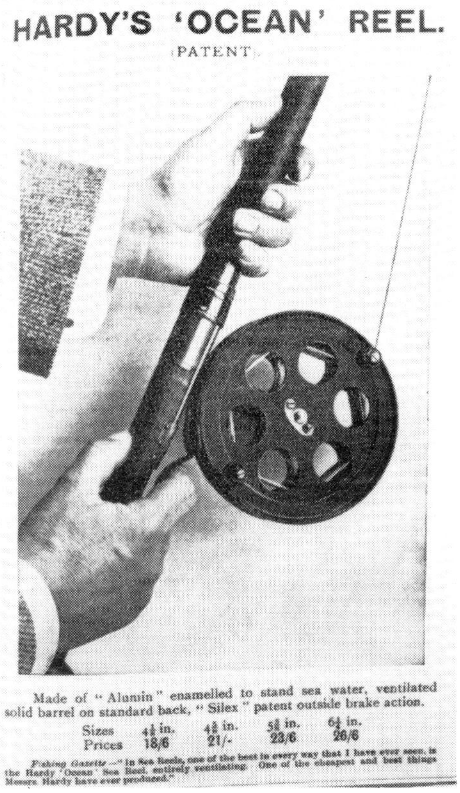
HARDY'S 'OCEAN' REEL.
(PATENT).
Made of "Alumin" enamelled to stand sea water, ventilated solid barrel on standard back, "Silex" patent outside brake action.
Sizes 4⅛ in. 4⅝ in. 5⅝ in. 6¼ in.
Prices 18/6 21/- 23/6 26/6
Fishing Gazette.—"In Sea Reels, one of the best in every way that I have ever seen, is the Hardy 'Ocean' Sea Reel, entirely ventilating. One of the cheapest and best things Messrs. Hardy have ever produced."

The Ocean (Second Model) illustrated in 1903 Sizes 4⅛″, 4⅝″, 5⅝″, 6¼″

Ocean Reel (Second Model) 1903 – 1904

This was a heavily perforated reel made of Alumin with a ventilated solid barrel and a Silex brake action. It was a cheaper version of the Farne (Second Model) with no line-guard.

Patent Ocean Reel. Size 4⅝″

Patent Ocean Reel 1905 – 1910

It was a large sea reel and had a strong metal back strap fixed to a large smooth foot. The drum was made of Ebona with two horn handles and secured by a centre knurled edged tension nut. Fixed to the foot was a heavy duty Bickerdyke line-guard and lever operated external brake with pad.

The Improved "Ocean" Reel
1911 MODEL. (EBONA.)
With "Silex" action and "Bickerdyke" Line Guard.
A newly designe
sea reel with Pa
"Silex" lever ac
ion, see Fig. 2.
pressing the lever
towards the rod,
drum becomes fr
either in casting
or letting down le
etc., in boat fishi
The moment
lever is released.

Improved Ocean Reel 1911

This model was similar to its predecessor, made in Ebona but without the external brake. It was fitted with the patent Silex lever action.

Size 5⅛″

WEYBRIDGE, January, 1897.
I am immensely pleased with the new reel. I can throw just as far as with the ordinary loose barrel Nottingham reel, but the curse of fast reels is practically done away with by the new check arrangement. During the whole afternoon I only had one slight over-run, and that entirely my own fault, through trying too much—endeavouring to reach an impossible distance. I consider the reel invaluable, especially to beginners. I find the throw can be regulated with ease; the adjustable check put on with the finger for a moment and then released, the bait falling steadily into the water, and the final pace slackening properly. I was quite surprised to find I could do so well with it on the first trial. The silent check is excellent, no jar or scraping.
CHAS. H. WHEELEY.

Above: Silex (First Model) which at present has not been found

Below: Silex with single rim lever control

Silex 1896 – 1911

In the catalogue of 1897 the Silex was first illustrated with the dual handled drum side full of large ventilations which is unfamiliar to the present known early examples of this model. Therefore, until the Silex (First Model) is found, I must accept the Silex shown in the 1899 catalogue as the earliest production model. This had two ivorine handles connected by a cross-bar on an unperforated drum, near the centre of which was a drum release button. It was an alloy reel with smooth brass foot, rim cut-out and a single rim lever. In 1902 this early model evolved to a more sophisticated version with three rim controls, one being an automatic presser brake lever, another an adjustable auxiliary check and the third was a regulator screw. The Silex was also made without the cross-bar which joined the two handles and a picture of one being used in casting appeared in the catalogue of 1905. An unusual feature of the early Silex was the cageing round the drum core.
Silex sizes 3″ (dropped in 1901), 3¼″ (from 1902), 3½″, 3¾″ (from 1899), 4″, 4¼″ (from 1902), 4½″, 4½″EW (from 1908)

Check mechanism for three rim control model

Silex with three rim controls

Silex No 2 1911 – 1922

The Silex No 2 was an alloy spinning reel with a smooth brass foot and a number of new or modified features. There was a new check/brake mechanism with ivorine rim lever, dual ivorine handled drum side with a row of perforations and a ventilated drum core. The first version of this model was illustrated in 1911 with a bridge over the rim regulator screw, a central knurled locking nut and had no rim cut out. In 1911 the earlier Silex made its final appearance, but after its demise the Silex No 2 later re-introduced two of its features. The un-bridged rim regulator screw was used and the rim cut out was made available on the larger sizes of 3½" upwards. The new version also had a new plate inscription design and by 1914 the central knurled drum locking screw had been replaced by a three drum screw release latch and a bar latch on the smallest 2⅞" size. The three smallest sizes of this model were available with a rectangular rim lever for single handed casting.

The Silex No 2 spinning reel introduced in 1911. Sizes 2⅞" (from 1913), 3¼", 3½", 3¾", 3¾"EW (from 1920), 4", 4¼", 4½", 4½"EW

Silex No 2 with rectangular rim lever

Silex No 2 check mechanism

Silex No 2 later version with new plate design

3 screw drum release latch

Silex No 2 in the small size 2⅞" with guard over regulator screw and bar latch

Silex No 2 Silent Wind-In c.1920 – 1922

This was a standard Silex No. 2 which could run silently in one direction only and was developed towards the end of the production period. This was done by changing the toothed wheel against which the pawl worked to produce a click sound, from fixed, to one which could run freely in one direction only.

By 1921, many of the larger sizes had been sold with the new feature and in the catalogue of that year it was offered as an additional range described as Silex No 2 Silent Wind-in, although still marked as before and externally indistinguishable from a standard Silex No 2. The idea lasted only a couple of years as in 1923 the Silex No. 2 reels were replaced by the Silex Major which incorporated 'Silent Wind in' on the larger sizes.

Silex Minor 1923

This model was a cheaper version of the Silex Major and had no regulator, a silent variable brake instead of a ratchet check and was fitted with jewelled bearings and latch fastener. Very little is known about the model except from the text of the catalogue of 1923 in which it made its only appearance. A rare and collectable reel.

Silex Minor. Sizes 3", 3¼", 3¾", 4"

Little Silex Tournament 1905 – 1911

This was a 3¼" Silex, intended for competitive bait casting and used with the Victor rod. At the Crystal Palace Tournament in 1904, Mr J J Hardy easily beat all comers in the special light bait casting contest both for accuracy and distance. Mr L R Hardy won the professional light bait casting event with the reel and Victor rod at the Eleventh International Casting Tournament in London in 1908.

Silex Major 1923 – 1952

This model was introduced in 1923 and features included no rim cut out, grooved brass foot, ebonite handles, although ivorine was retained for the rim operating lever and there was a drum release button similar to the one of the earliest Silex model. The plate carried the new inscription of the 'Silex Major' which was accompanied by patent numbers, the size and company name. The early Silex Major had a circular turning button regulator on the plate which had replaced the rim screw of the earlier model. In 1928 this was changed to a white dial indicator on the plate and a regulator screw on the rim once more.

Sizes 3" (1924 – c.1939), 3¼" (dropped 1950), 3½", 3¾", 3¾" EW, 4", 4¼", 4½", 4½" EW

Above; The early Silex Major with turning brake regulator on the plate

Left; The Silex Major of 1928 with indicator dial and screw regulator on rim

JJ Hardy Silex 1924 – 1928

This model was described as merely a Silex Major with two additional movements. One was a secondary rim lever which had two positions, giving either free, or partially free running. The second was a portion of exposed drum rim which allowed extra control by thumb or fingers when playing a fish. The 3¼″ size had ordinary ratchet check while the other sizes had Silent Wind-in action.

J J Hardy Silex. Sizes 3¼″, 3½″, 3¾″

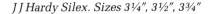

Silex Multiplier 1924 – 1939

This reel was an alloy multiplier with gearing of approximately 2¼ to 1 and made in two sizes, 2¾″ for trout and 3½″ for salmon. It had a grooved brass foot, ebonite handle, ivorine thumb bar, adjustable check on rim with white indicator dial on the reverse side.

Silex Multiplier. Sizes 2¾″, 3½″ (1925 – 1935)

Super Silex 1928 – 1953

The Super Silex was described by the company as 'embodying all the features of the Silex Major and to add a simple action to enable the reel to be used when casting without touching any part of it'. Features of the reel included the usual grooved brass foot, regulator screw on rim with white dial indicator, ivorine rim check lever with on/off set positions and drum release button latch.

Super Silex. Sizes 3″ (dropped c.1939), 3¼″, 3½″, 3¾″, 3¾″EW, 4″, 4¼″, 4½″, 4½″EW

Super Silex Multiplier
1930 – c.1939

This model was similar to the Super Silex reel but with an additional multiplying gear which was disengaged when casting. Features were a grooved brass foot, ebonite handle, ivorine rim lever which engaged or threw out the gears, and a regulator screw on the rim with white indicator dial on the front. The range was discontinued in c.1939.

Right: Super Silex Multiplier. Sizes 3¼", 3½", (also listed in EW but unknown at present)

Silex Rex 1935 – 1937

The Silex Rex was a short-lived quadruple multiplying bait casting or spinning reel, with level-wind distributor.
The number of reels sold was 1935 – 53, 1936 – 28 and 1937 – 13.

Left: Silex Rex. Size 2⅛"

Silex Jewel 1954 – 1959

Features of the reel were grooved brass foot, black handles on perforated drum, white rim lever on/off check and regulator with white dial and two screw latch drum release. It had a bright and enamelled finished.

Below: Silex Jewel. Sizes 3¾", 4", 4½"

Silex Superba 1960 – 1971

This reel succeeded the Silex Jewel having a similar bright and enamelled finish. Features were a grooved alloy foot, black handles on perforated drum, white indicator dial with adjustment lever on the face, black rim presser brake lever and a two screw latch drum release.

Below: Silex Superba. Size 4"

Farne Reels

The Farne sea reel range began in 1897 with a 6″ unperforated dual handled model which changed in 1903 to a heavily perforated reel made of enamelled alumin, and fitted with a Silex Check mechanism and Bickerdyke line-guard. In 1905 it changed to an unperforated version in one size of 5⅛″ and was made of Ebona. A new model was announced in 1911 and called the 'New Farne', which was still made of Ebona but had adopted the No 2 Silex action. There were in fact three versions of this reel available and described as Nos 1, 2 and 3. In 1914 a new alloy model called the 'Improved Farne' was marketed in four sizes and continued in production until 1939.

Farne (First Model) 1897 – 1902
Size 6″

Farne (Second Model) 1903 – 1904
Sizes 4⅜″, 5″, 5¾″, 6⅝″

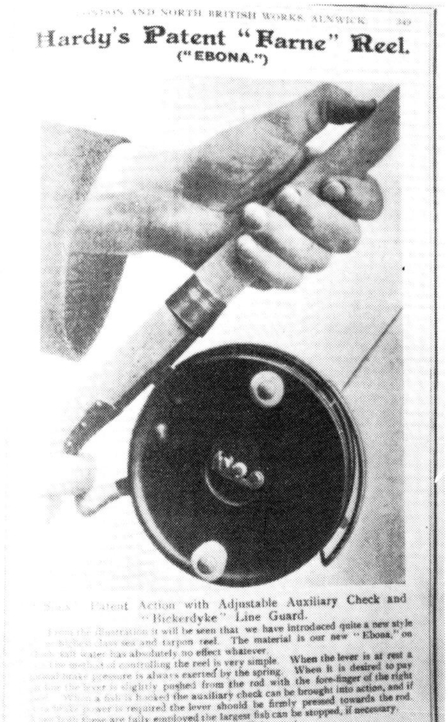

Farne Patent Ebona 1905 – 1910
Size 5⅛″

New Farne 1911 – 1913
Externally the same as the previous model but fitted with the No 2 Silex action
Size 5⅛″

Improved Farne 1914 – 1939
Sizes 4½″, 5″, 6″, 7″

Uniqua Narrow Drum
1903 – c.1921

The Uniqua Narrow Drum was a light alloy contracted reel with a fixed check, smooth brass foot, ivorine handle and horseshoe drum release latch.

Sizes 2⅝", 2⅞", 3⅛", 3⅜", 3⅝"

Uniqua Mark I Narrow Drum
1919 – 1920

A light alloy contracted reel with single check mechanism, smooth alloy foot (occasionally smooth brass) and the early duplication mark.

Sizes 2⅝", 2⅞", 3⅛", 3⅜", 3⅝"

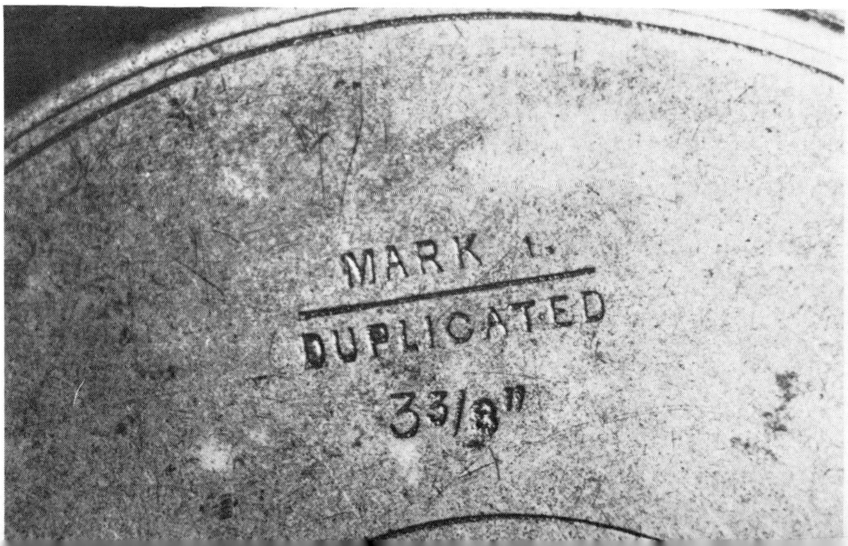

The early duplication mark

Uniqua Mark II (1921) Narrow Drum **1921**

The earliest Uniqua Mark II Duplicated was made in 1921. It was a lightweight alloy contracted reel with a single check mechanism, ivorine handle, smooth alloy foot (occasionally smooth brass) and the early duplication mark design. This model was the beginning of the Mark II range.

Sizes 2$\frac{5}{8}$", 2$\frac{7}{8}$", 3$\frac{1}{8}$", 3$\frac{3}{8}$", 3$\frac{5}{8}$"

Early Mark II/Duplicated inscription

Single check mechanism

Uniqua Mark II (1921) Narrow Drum, with alloy drum, ivorine handle and horseshoe latch

Uniqua Mark II Narrow Drum 1922 – 1959

The early Mark II (1921) model was quickly replaced by the more familiar version with the new features. These included an ebonite handle, grooved brass foot, double check mechanism, optional rim regulator screw and a new plate inscription design giving the maker, size, model, patents and Duplicated Mark II in $\frac{1}{16}$" setting.

Sizes 2$\frac{5}{8}$", 2$\frac{7}{8}$", 3$\frac{1}{8}$", 3$\frac{3}{8}$", 3$\frac{5}{8}$"

Uniqua Wide Drum 1909 – 1921

This wide drum range was introduced for salmon fishing and was a light, strong, fixed check alloy reel with smooth brass foot, ivorine handle and two screw oval oil latch.

Sizes 3½", 3¾", 4", 4¼", 4½"

Uniqua Mark II Wide Drum 1922 – 1959

In the absence of any evidence of a wide drum reel, with the early Mark I/II/III/Duplicated inscription together with a single check and early characteristics, the Uniqua Mark II Wide Drum has to be recorded as the one with the new features. These usually included an ebonite handle, grooved brass foot, horseshoe or bar latch, optional rim regulator screw, double check mechanism and the new Mark II handle plate inscription design. The 'Uniqua' name was revived on a model for a period between 1981 and 1983.

Sizes 3½", 3¾", 4", 4¼", 4½" (the two larger sizes were dropped in 1949/50)

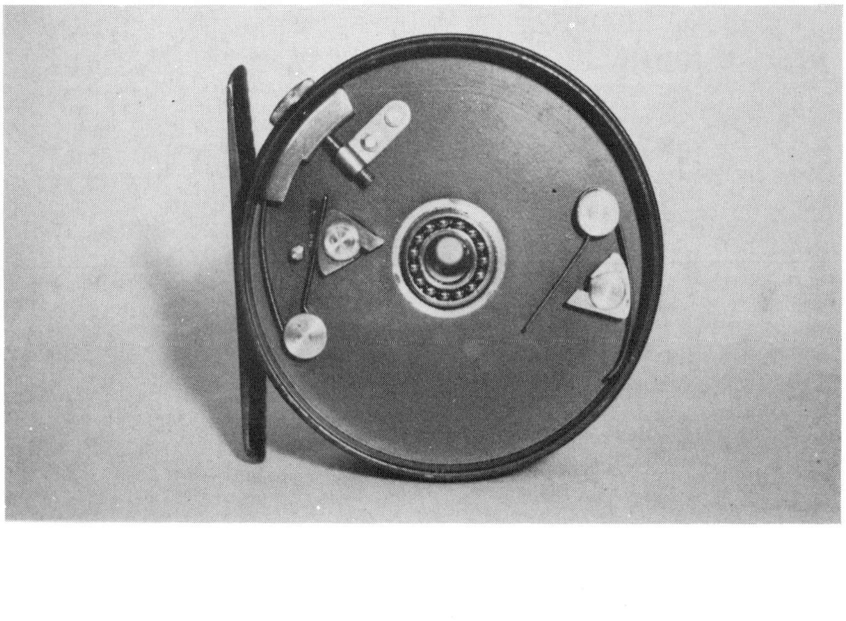

New double check mechanism

Longstone Ebona 1905 – 1920

The earliest Longstone was introduced in 1905 in one size of 5⅛″ diameter and was a plain double horn handled sea reel made of Ebona. It had a wide rim on the drum, Bickerdyke line-guard, and a milled tension nut to obtain the required brake power.

Size 5⅛″

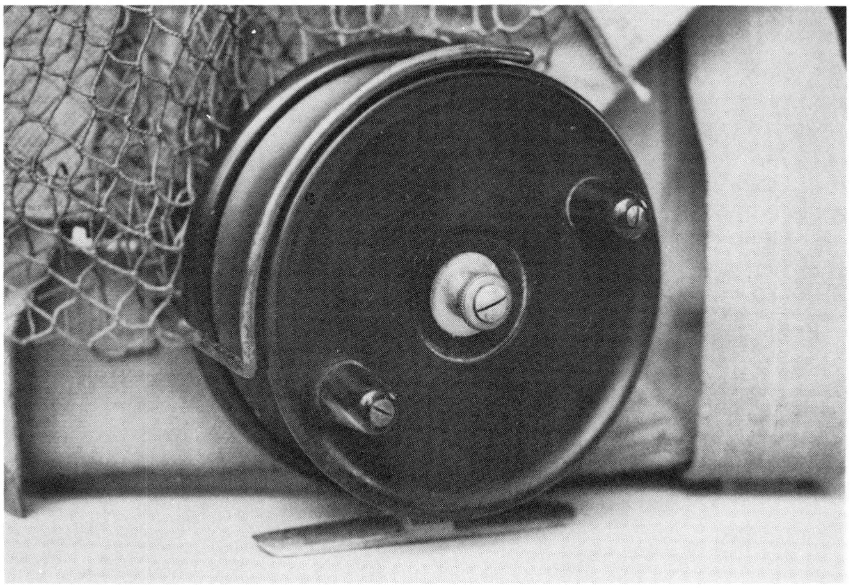

Longstone Walnut 1921 – 1922
Sizes 4″, 4½″, 5″, 6″

Longstone Alloy with a Single Row of Perforations 1923 – 1927

The Longstone made of anti-corrosive alloy was introduced in 1923 and was basically similar to the earlier model. It had dual black handles, Bickerdyke line-guard and central tension regulator nut, on the front of which was a drum locking screw. The new additional feature was a rim lever which operated on/off check mechanism.

Sizes 3½, 4″, 4½″, 5″, 6″

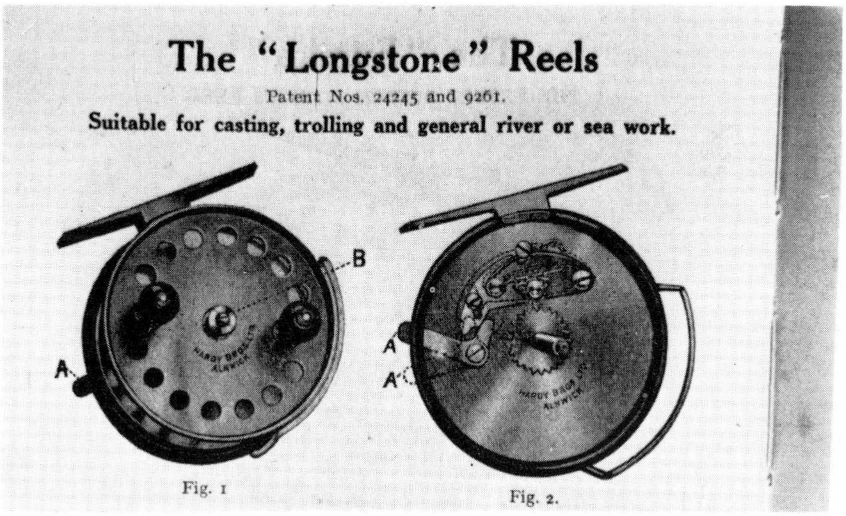
The "Longstone" Reels
Patent Nos. 24245 and 9261.
Suitable for casting, trolling and general river or sea work.
B
A
A
A
Fig. 1
Fig. 2.

Longstone Alloy with Two Rows of Perforations 1925-1936

The catalogue of 1925 offered an additional alloy version which had two rows of perforations and the usual Longstone features. It continued to be offered in this form up to 1936.

Sizes 3½″ (from 1928), 4″ (from 1928), 4½″, 5″, 6″

Longstone Alloy Unperforated 1937 – 1959

This model was similar to earlier alloy Longstone sea reels but was unperforated, and continued in production until 1959. A modern form of Longstone was re-introduced in 1969 in a 4½″ size and is currently in production.

Sizes 1937 – 1956 3½″, 4″, 4½″, 5″ (dropped in 1954), 6″ (dropped in 1954). 1957 – 1959 only a 4″ size

"LONGSTONE" Reels for Dorado

Reels originally designed for Dorado Fishing and suitable for Casting and Spinning in fresh or salt water in any part of the World where a strong, sound, reel with plenty of line capacity is required; also make excellent fly reels.

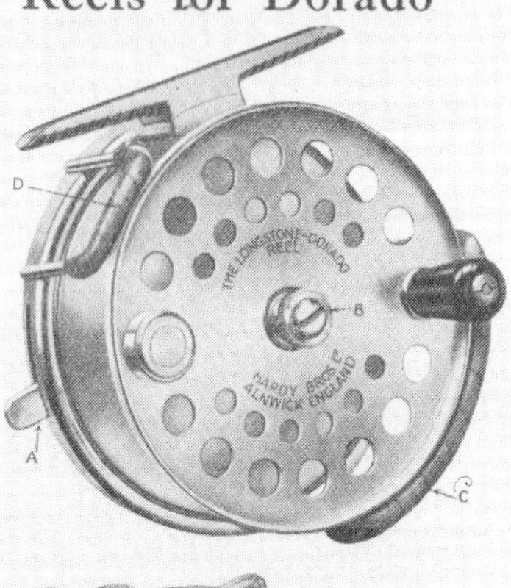

Mr. Mallet's Pattern.

Fitted with a raw hide thong wound round the line guard for pressing against the drum to form the auxiliary brake against a fish.

Size - - 4½″
Price - - 60/-

Solid leather case (velvet lined) **26/-**

General Harrison's Pattern.

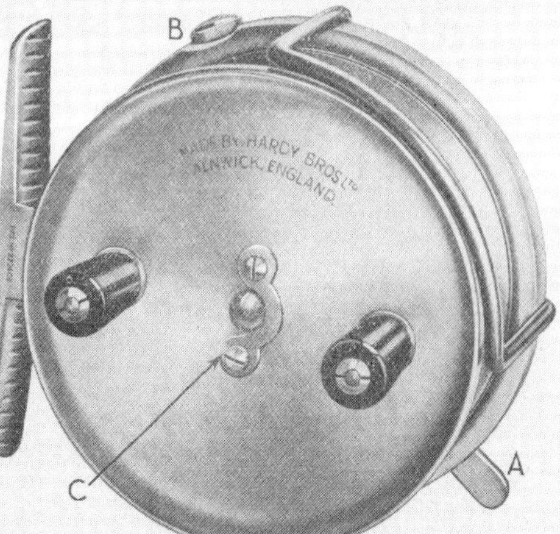

Designed to a specification given us by Brig. General Harrison. Made from a light non-corrosive metal, composed of a back plate to which is firmly fixed the carbon steel spindle of generous size for wear and strength, on which the drum, bushed with best phosphor-bronze, revolves. The large comfortable handles are of sound construction, the pin and spindle, base and screw are all turned from one solid piece of metal, and screw nuts assist to secure them to the front drum plate.

The ratchet check action is of an improved type, conveniently operated by lever "A" projecting through the rim of the back plate. The casting brake and regulator are of the same design as those fitted to our "Super Silex" Reels, see page 152 for instructions to adjust. The brake face which bears on the hub is of oil-soaked blocked felt giving a very sensitive touch, and the brake regulator operated by milled nut "B" permits of the finest adjustment.

In conjunction with this regulator is our patent No. 288101 brake indicator and dial same as used on our "Super Silex," page152, which records the amount of brake pressure controlling the reel. To dismount the drum for cleaning and oiling, screw the regulator nut till the indicator registers FREE, then unscrew "C" two turns, slip back the latch when the drum can be removed from the spindle.

The line spool is provided with a generous sized well rounded and polished flange for braking a fish with ball of finger or thumb. It can also be used to control the Reel when casting.

Made in 3 sizes only - -	4½″	5″	6″
Price - - - - - -	80/-	85/-	92/6

Solid leather case (velvet lined), 37/6

Thumb and Finger Stall.—Hand crochetted of best macramé twine, to protect finger and thumb when playing a fish. Thumb or finger, 1/6 each.

Longstone Dorado 1928 – 1939

An additional model to the Longstone range was introduced in 1928 and described as being designed for Dorado fishing. It was suitable for casting or spinning in fresh or salt water in any part of the world, and could also be used for fly fishing. Two forms were available, a Mr Mallet pattern in a 4½″ size and a General Harrison pattern in 4½″, 5″ and 6″.

A General Harrison pattern. An extremely rare reel and the only example I have ever seen.

Megstone Ebona 1905 – 1922

The Megstone was introduced in 1905 and was a plain sea reel made of Ebona. Features included a central milled nut which controlled the brake pressure, a circular line-guard with arm attachment to the foot and two horn handles on an unventilated drum.

Size 4⅝″

Megstone Walnut 1923 – 1927

In 1923 the Megstone was offered with the same features as the earlier model but made of well-seasoned walnut. It continued in this form until it was phased out in 1927, when just three 4½″ size reels were sold.

Sizes 4½″, 5″

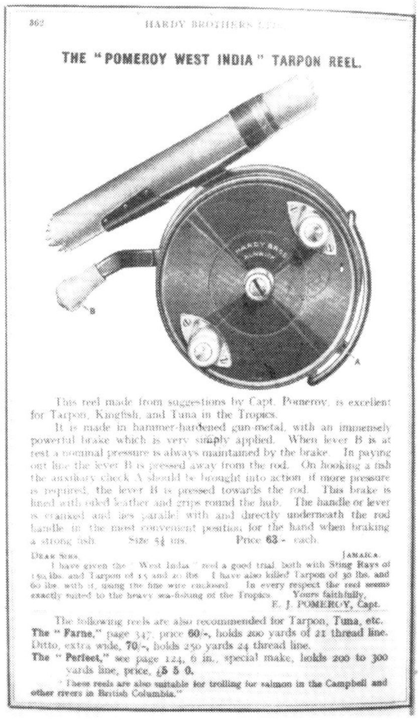

362 HARDY BROTHERS LTD.

THE "POMEROY WEST INDIA" TARPON REEL.

This reel made from suggestions by Capt. Pomeroy, is excellent for Tarpon, Kingfish, and Tuna in the Tropics.

It is made in hammer-hardened gun-metal, with an immensely powerful brake which is very simply applied. When lever B is at rest a nominal pressure is always maintained by the brake. In paying out line the lever B is pressed away from the rod. On hooking a fish the auxiliary check A should be brought into action, if more pressure is required, the lever B is pressed towards the rod. This brake is lined with oiled leather and grips round the hub. The handle or lever is cranked and lies parallel with and directly underneath the rod handle in the most convenient position for the hand when braking a strong fish. Size 5⅛ ins. Price **63/-** each.

Dear Sirs, Jamaica.

I have given the "West India" reel a good trial, both with Sting Rays of 150 lbs. and Tarpon of 55 and 20 lbs. I have also killed Tarpon of 30 lbs. and 60 lbs. with it, using the fine wire enclosed. In every respect the reel seems exactly suited to the heavy sea-fishing of the Tropics. Yours faithfully,

E. J. POMEROY, Capt.

The following reels are also recommended for Tarpon, Tuna, etc.

The "Farne," page 347, price **60/-**, holds 200 yards of 21 thread line.

Ditto, extra wide, **70/-**, holds 250 yards 24 thread line.

The "Perfect," see page 124, 6 in., special make, holds 200 to 300 yards line, price, £5 5 0.

"These reels are also suitable for trolling for salmon in the Campbell and other rivers in British Columbia."

Size 5⅛″

The Pomeroy West Indian 1909 – 1912

The reel was made in hammer-hardened gun metal with an immensely powerful lever brake and designed for tarpon, kingfish and tuna in the tropics. It made its first appearance in 1909 in one size of 5⅛″ priced at 63/– and was short lived making its last appearance in 1912.

Coquet 1911 – 1922

The Coquet was introduced in 1911 and was a plain strong sea reel made from walnut with gunmetal back and spindle and fitted with an adjustable tension nut. It continued in production up to 1922.

The "Coquet" Sea Reel.

Model 1911 (WALNUT).

Size 5″ and 6″

Saint George 1911 – 1983

The Saint George was a contracted trout fly reel similar to the Perfect Narrow Drum and introduced in one size of $3\frac{3}{4}''$, with agate line-guard and rim regulator screw with bridge (without bridge from c.1917). The early version had a left-hand threaded knurled drum locking nut which changed to a three screw latch in 1913, and this in turn was succeeded by a two screw latch in the 1940's. The features of the reel followed the same path as the Perfect and Uniqua models except that it was not given the Duplicated Mark II inscription which would have created a new model, although the mark was used on the Saint George at a later period. The early version up to and including 1921 had an ivorine handle, single check mechanism and surprisingly many with a smooth alloy foot.

Although some examples have a smooth brass foot, a study of the early Saint George reels showed a high percentage fitted with smooth aluminium feet, and far more than could reasonably be attributed to replacements. There is no evidence of the early 'Mark II/Duplicated' standardization mark of 1921 on this model at the present time. In 1922 it adopted an ebonite handle, double check mechanism and usually a grooved brass foot.

Saint George reel c.1917–1921

Single check mechanism.

Sizes – $3\frac{3}{4}''$ (1911 – 1980s), $3\frac{3}{8}''$ (1913 – 1968), $3''$ (1920 – 1968)

The Saint George introduced the double check mechanism in 1922 and the improved version (illustrated) from c.1927

Two forms of 3" Saint George showing a three and a two screw latch.

Saint George Wide Drum 1920 – 1924

This was a short lived salmon model with dual handles (or single), three screw latch, steel line-guard, regulator screw and silent winding in action. It is a rare and collectable reel.

Size 4½" (priced 110/–)

Saint George Silent Check 1920 – 1926

A Silent Check variation was offered in the early 1920's with a regulating brake fitted.

Sizes 3″, 3⅜″, 3¾″

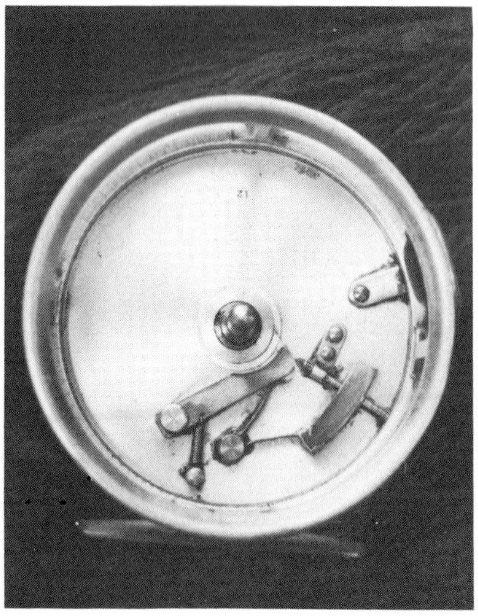

Saint George Junior 1928 – 1964

This small alloy reel had all the features of the larger Saint George reels but was specially designed to correctly balance with the various patterns of lightweight fly rods.

Size 2 9⁄16″

Saint George Multiplier 1927 – 1939

This reel was designed for quick recovery of line having an approximate 2 to 1 gear ratio. The 3¾″ was intended for dry fly fishing for salmon using a light, single-handed rod.

Saint George Tournament Fly Reel 1938

A Tournament Fly Reel of lightweight alloy construction with a fully ventilated drum, the backplate reduced to a simple cross-piece with black handle and fixed check. It is believed that only three of these reels, which never appeared in the catalogues, were sold in 1938. The illustrated reel has a section of rim missing.

Sizes-1927 3⅜″, from 1928 – 3⅜″ and 3¾″ (Both sizes also offered in a deeper drum version)

Right; Saint George Tournament Fly Reel. Size 3¼″

Eureka (Early Model) 1913 – 1921

The Eureka was a much contracted reel with only 13⁄16″ between the plates and designed to facilitate quick recovery of line. It had a brass foot, ventilated lightweight drum, dual ivorine handles, on/off check rim lever and bar release latch. The feature which distinguished this model from the later one was a section of rim cut-out.

Size 3½″

Eureka 1922 – 1955

In 1922 the Eureka got rid of the cut-out rim section in favour of a full rim and the handles changed to ebonite. It appeared in the catalogues up to 1953 and recorded by Hardy Bros as finishing in 1955.

Sizes 3½″, 4″ (from 1934)

USA Fly Reel 1922 – 1923

This was a short-lived model made in Alumin and fitted with what the company called their patent 'Radio' action which featured a silent automatic variable brake. It is a reel which can be easily overlooked as it is not stamped USA but marked 'Uniqua Mark II,' but with a silent action.

Sizes 2⅝″, 2⅞″, 3⅛″, 3⅜″, 4″, 4¼″

Rhodesian Reel 1921

Sea Silex with Two Rim Controls 1914 – 1924

The Sea Silex was an all-round sea reel made of non-corrosive alloy which could withstand the action of sea water. In the beginning, the reel was inscribed 'Silex No. 2' and after about a year adopted its permanent name of Sea Silex. Features were perforated drum and two rim lever controls.

Sizes 4½" (dropped in 1915), 5", 6", 7"

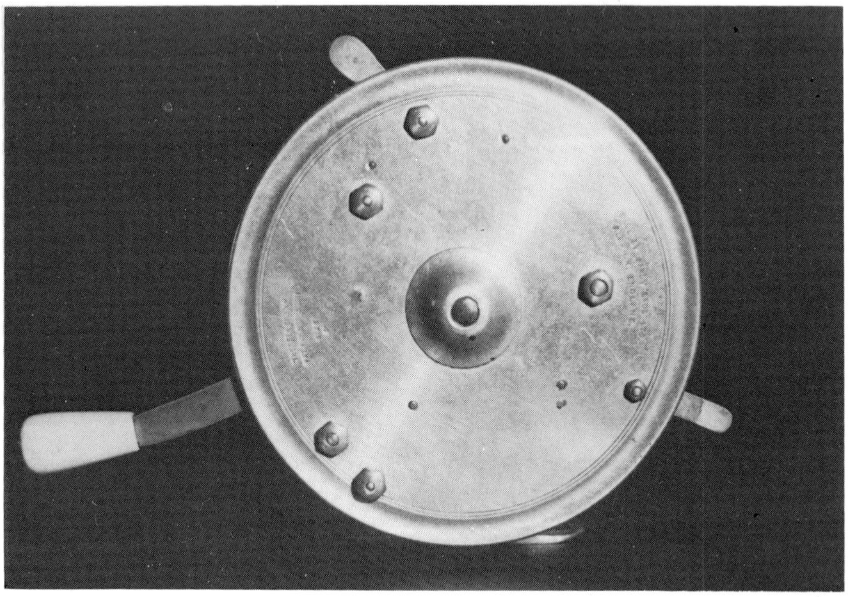

Sea Silex with Three Rim Controls 1925 – 1929

In 1925 the Sea Silex was illustrated with three lever rim controls which included a hand lever pressure brake, a compression drag and a on/off ratchet check lever.

Sizes 5", 6", 7"

Sea Silex with Four Rim Controls 1930 – 1959

In 1930 a new model was introduced, which in addition to the three rim lever controls, also had a milled nut on the rim which adjusted the brake pressure and registered between Heavy and Free on a white indicator dial.

Sizes 5", 6", 7"

The Natal 1923–1948

The Natal was introduced in 1923 and designed to meet the requirements of sea anglers in South Africa. It was constructed of alloy, unventilated, dual handled and with a pressure brake regulating nut.

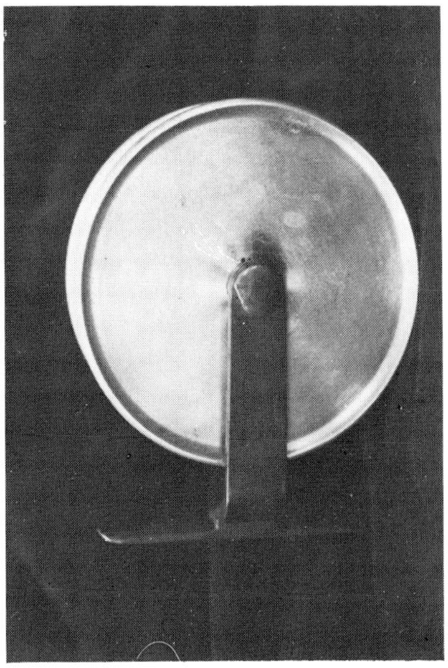

Above: Rear elevation of the Filey. Size 4½″

The Filey 1925 – 1939

The Filey was actually the 4½″ size of the Natal which in 1924 was offered at 50/–. When it was dropped it re-appeared in 1925 as a new model called the Filey and priced at 30/– and continued in production up to the Second World War.

Triumph (1936 Model) 1936 – 1951

A Triumph model was re-introduced in 1936 and new features included a traditional type line guard, on/off check control on the back, dual black handles, central locking screw and was a light alloy free running reel.

Above: Triumph, 1936–1951. Sizes 3¼″ and 4″ in a wide drum (1$\frac{1}{16}$″ between plates). Also a 3¼″ narrow drum (½″ between plates) was produced c.1939

Triumph (1923 Model) 1923 – 1928

The Triumph model made its first appearance in 1923 and continued to be produced up to 1928. It was a light, dual black handled reel made of alumin and on the back was a circular turning button pressure regulator which was marked Free, Light, Medium and Strong Pressure. Later ones had a rim screw regulator and both versions had an on/off rim lever check control and the traditional button release latch.

Sizes 3″ (from 1924), 3¼″ (from 1924), 3½″, 3¾″, 4″, 4½″ (from 1924)

Below: The two versions of the Triumph (1923 Model)

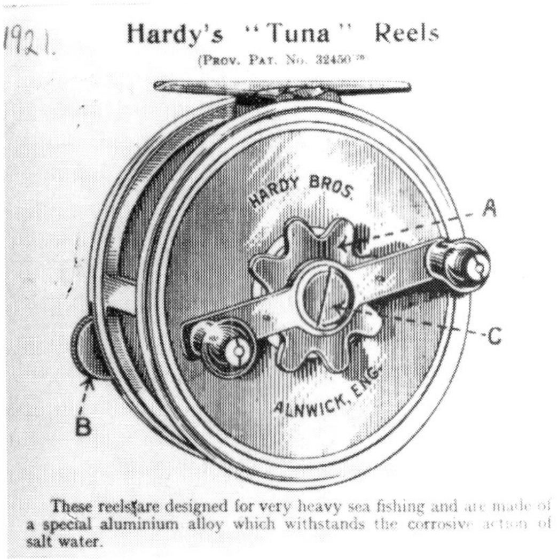

Tuna Sea Reel. Sizes 5″, 6″, 7″

Tuna Sea Reel 1921 – 1922

In 1921 a large heavy alloy sea reel was offered in three sizes and called the 'Tuna'. Features included a star drag pressure brake washer, dual handles on a handle-bar, and a disc shaped on/off control. It did not appear as the Tuna in the catalogue of 1923, as it had adopted a new name of Fortuna.

Fortuna with Capstan Star and Plate Lever c.1929 – 1933

In the catalogues of 1929 to 1934 a Fortuna reel was illustrated which had no rim lever but had a lever control on the back of the reel. In 1934 the text accompanying the illustration did not contain any mention of this lever which suggests that it had been dispensed with. This reel was usually shown in the larger sizes but in the odd year such as 1931, when the Fortuna Fly Reel did not have its own illustration, the sizes 4¼″ and 5″ were included in the list of this model.

Fortuna with Capstan Star and Rim Lever c.1923 – 1928

The Fortuna was first announced in the catalogue of 1924 although it was probably being sold in 1923. It was similar to the Tuna except a rim lever control had replaced the disc-shaped one. In the first year it was offered in a range of sizes from 3½″ to 7″ although the smaller sizes may have been included to sell the Fortuna Fly Reel which was not illustrated until the following year. It continued to be shown in this form up to 1928 and mainly in the larger sizes.

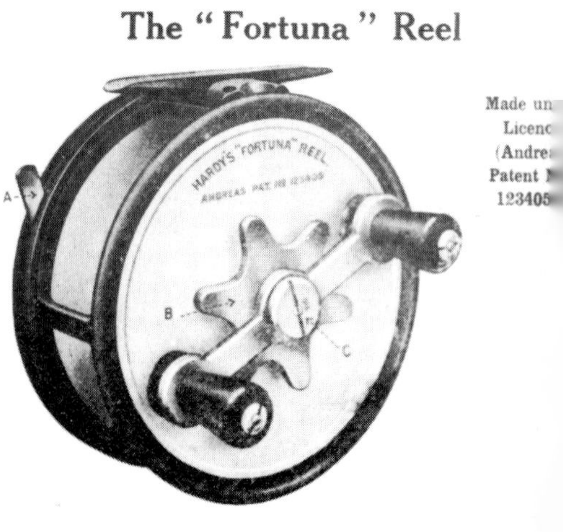

Sizes 3½″, 4¼″, 5″, 6″, 7″, 8″, 9″

Fortuna with Capstan Star and Plate Lever
Sizes 6″, 7″, 8″, 9″

Fortuna with Capstan Wheel c.1934 – 1956

The Fortuna Sea Reel was not illustrated in the home catalogues between 1935 and 1938, but hand written ledger records at Hardy Bros show all the sizes were being sold. In 1939 it was illustrated with a captain's wheel pressure brake washer which had replaced the star shaped one. This change probably occurred earlier, as the 1929 catalogue showed a Fortuna with Auxiliary Brake model with the captain's wheel washer.

Sizes 6″, 7″, 8″, 9″, 9″EW (from 1934)

Fortuna with Auxiliary Brake
c.1929–1956

Fortuna with Auxiliary Brake. Shown fitted with the Van Brunt adjustable brace

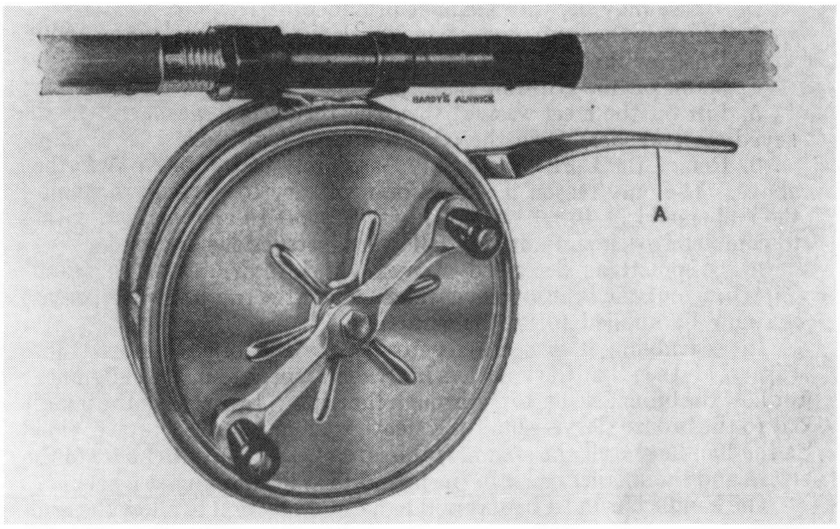

Fortuna with Auxiliary Hand Brake
c.1934 – 1939

Fortuna Perforated Fly Reel
1924 – 1934

The Fortuna Perforated Fly Reel was illustrated in the catalogues 1925 – 1934 but was probably being marketed in 1924. It was a smaller version of the Fortuna sea reel with dual black handles on a handle-bar, a circular pressure brake washer and a single row of perforations on the side of the drum.

Above: Fortuna Perforated Fly Reel. Sizes 3½″ (dropped in 1932), 4¼″, 5″

Fortuna Junior Fly Reel
1935 – 1939

The Fortuna Junior was sold in the late 1930s and was an un-ventilated version of the Fortuna Perforated Fly Reel.

Below: Fortuna Junior Fly Reel. Sizes 4¼″, 5″

Saint John 1923 – current

Saint John Reel. Size 3⅞″

The illustration shows the two forms of drum. The No. 1 is built up and the No. 2 is deeper and carries more line

The Saint John reel was originally made for John James Hardy for trout fishing with a light rod, and had a quick recovery contracted line drum which was made of alumin. Its features included a grooved brass foot, ebonite handle, rim regulator screw, three screw latch, double check mechanism and was made with two sizes of drum core which carried variable quantities of line. There was a No. 1 reel with a built up drum which carried 35 yards of tapered line and designed for use with light rods and sold until about 1939. The No. 2 was intended for dry fly fishing for salmon with single-handed rods and carried 35 yards of double tapered line and 80 yards No.2 silk backing.

Below: Silex Major with Auxiliary Brake

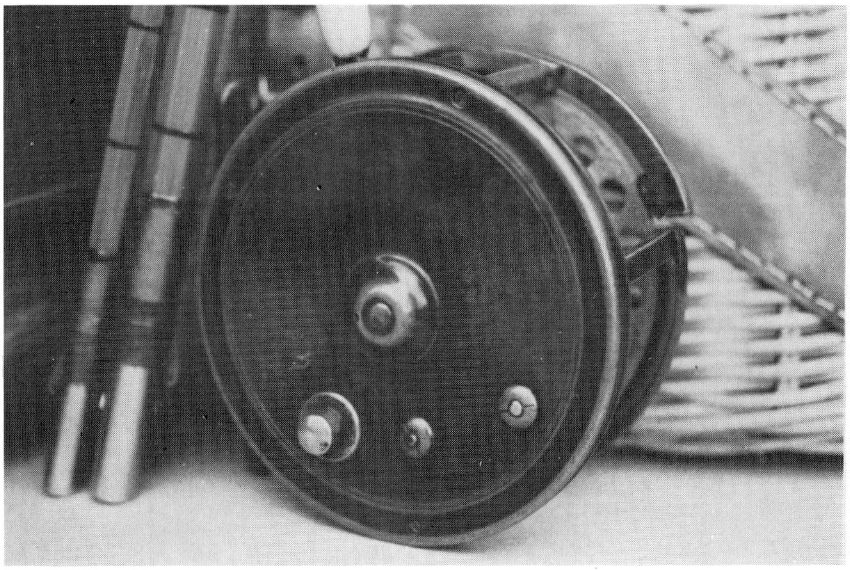

Auxiliary Brake c.1924 – 1929

The Auxiliary Brake appeared in the 1924 catalogue as an optional extra on the Silex Major on sizes 3½″ upwards at a cost of 10/6d and on existing reels 15/–. In 1925 the extra feature was extended to the same sizes of Perfect Mark II and Uniqua Mark II wide drum reels, and in the following year it was confined to sizes 3½″ to 4½″. It was not solely fitted to these models, as I have knowledge of it appearing on a Silex No. 2 which ceased in 1922 and the St. George Salmon (1920 – 1924). I have treated sea reels with this feature as something separate.

A rare Silex No. 2 with Auxiliary Brake

The legendary story is that James Heddon, who was a citizen of Dowagiac, Michigan, one day tossed a piece of wood he had been whittling, into the water of Dowagiac Creek. He saw a large bass strike at it and this led to the Heddon lure and tackle empire which became the largest producer of artificial baits of their time. Prior to forming the Heddon Tackle Co, James Heddon carved a few frogs for himself and friends and only 8 authentic frogs are known to exist.

Clyde A Harbin

Heddon Catalogue

Dowagiac Creek

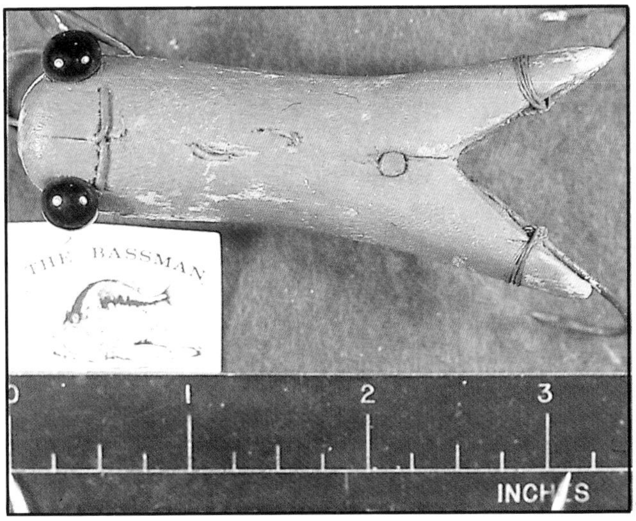

Clyde A Harbin

Hand carved frog made by James Heddon c.1898

The Kentucky History Museum

No 1 Trout Reel in brass with crank handle, marked 'JF & BF Meek/Frankfort/KY./No1' (c.1839-52)

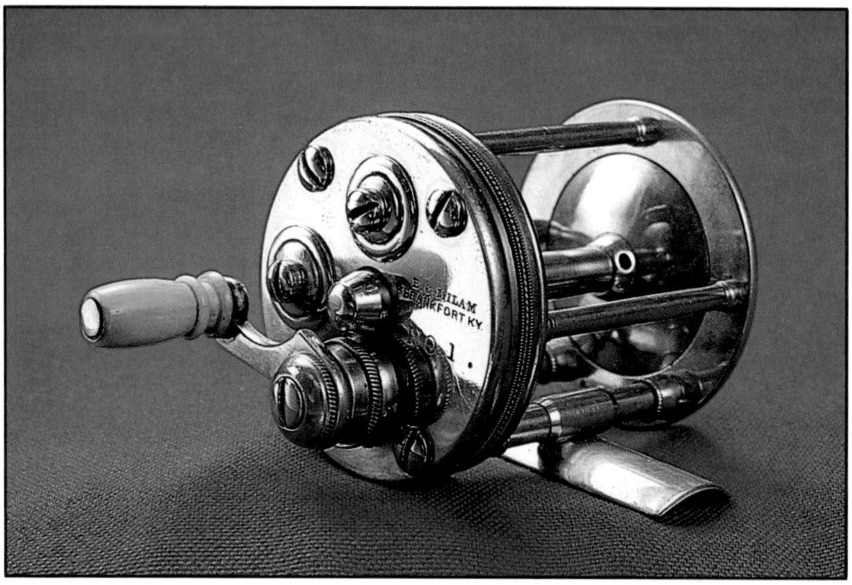

The Kentucky History Museum

No 1 Trout Reel in German silver with crank handle, marked 'BC Milam/Frankfort/Ky. No.1' (c.1881-96)

The Kentucky History Museum

No 2 Bass and tournament casting reel in German silver, marked 'The Frankfort Kentucky Reel/No2/BC Milam/Frankfort/KY' (c.1896-1900)

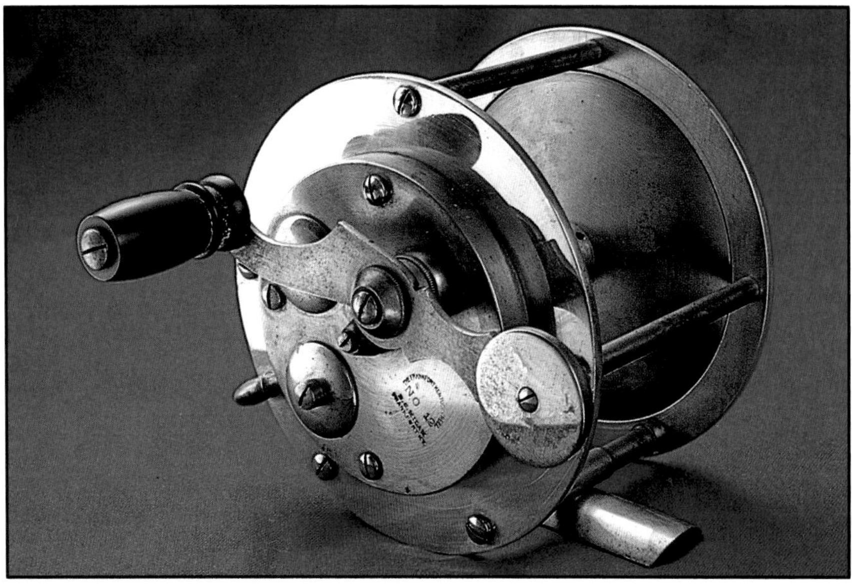

The Kentucky History Museum

No 12 Tarpon reel in German silver, marked 'The Frankfort Kentucky Reel/No12/BC Milam/Frankfort/KY' (c.1896-1900)

The Kentucky History Museum

No 3 General utility reel in brass with balance crank handle (end plate stamp: 9426). Marked 'The Frankfort Kentucky Reel/No3/BC Milam & Son/Frankfort/Ky' (c.1900-1928)

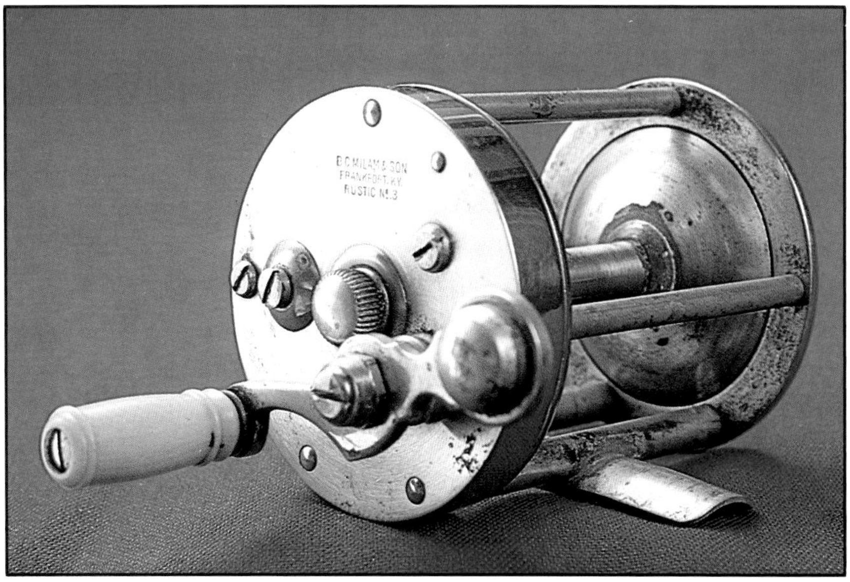

The Kentucky History Museum

'BC Milam & Son/ Frankfort/Ky/Rustic No3' in German silver (c.1900-1928)

Gary L Miller

Group of typical Northern Michigan fish decoys from the 1930s and 1940s sizes 5″ to about 10″ long

Bass, Perch and Brook Trout decoys (top to bottom). All by Oscar W Peterson of Cadillac, Michigan. Circa 1930 sizes 6″ to 9″

Above: Uniqua Mark II with Auxiliary Brake

Perfect Wide Drum Mark II with Auxiliary Brake

Sunbeam and Sunbeam Mark II 1924 – 1956

This trout fly reel was introduced in 1924, made of alumin and fitted with a line guide. It had a compensating and single check mechanism and later became the Sunbeam Mark II which was stamped on the reel. The name was revived for a final period from 1978 to 1983.

Sizes 2¾", 3", 3¼"

Alma 1925 – 1936

This was a big game multiplying reel made in strong light metal and described as a two geared free spool reel having gear ratios of one to one and two and a half to one. It was expensive costing £25, with the option of a leather case for an extra £3 when it was first introduced in the 5¼" size in 1925. The old sales ledger at Hardy Bros shows that its final year was 1936 when only one 5¾" size was sold.

Left: Alma. Sizes from 1926 3½", 4¼" (1935 only), 4¾", 5¼" (1925–1929), 5¾", 7"

Hardy Zane Grey c.1928 – 1957

Sizes 3½", 4³⁄₁₆", 5", 5½", 6". Also special orders for 7" and 8½"

This reel was designed to meet the requirements of the famous angler and author Mr Zane Grey with his stipulation that it must be the best big game fishing reel in the world. It was priced at £30 and made from Monel which the company claimed to be the strongest non-ferrous metal known. The multiplying gear was 'single helical, the teeth of the involute type, and running silently.' The reel was offered in a range of sizes in home and export catalogues up to 1957. A Zane Grey reel of modern form was re-introduced in 1983.

Davy 1930 – 1939

The Davy was a contracted quick winding light reel made from Alumin. Its features were dual handles on perforated drum, bar latch, regulator rim screw and grooved brass foot. (187 reels sold).

Size 3½"

South African Surf Casting Reel 1930 – 1948

This reel was designed specially to meet the requirements of anglers who fished from the coast of South Africa or cast heavy weights long distances from the shore. The drum and back were made from non-corrosive Duralumin with a strong gunmetal foot secured to the back plate. The reel was fitted with an optional ratchet check and adjustable brake for use when casting. It was dual handled and had a centre locking screw in front of the adjustable tension nut for dismantling. Hardy Bros sold one 6″ reel in 1930 and continued to sell this model in small quantities up to 1948.

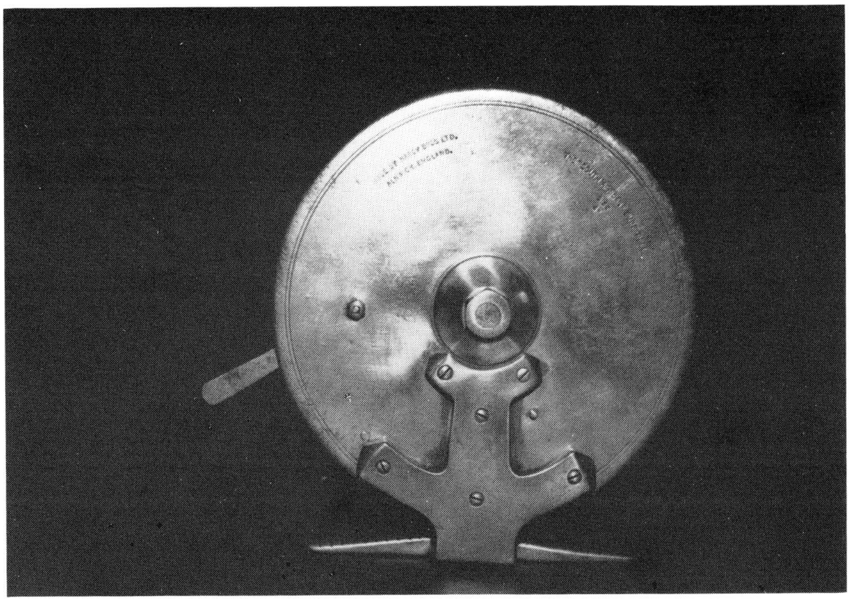

Sizes 6″, 7½″ (from 1934), 9″

Cascapedia 1932 – 1939

This was a high class multiplying fly reel for salmon fishing with a 1¾ to 1 gear ratio. It had an optional check stud on the plate, a check brake pressure lever with indicator and a revolving pillar.

The Cascapedia is a very desirable reel for any collector but similar to many of the quality American models.

Below; Cascapedia. Sizes 1932 – 1936 3⅛″, 3⅜″, 3⅝″, 1937 1938 3⅝″, 3¾″

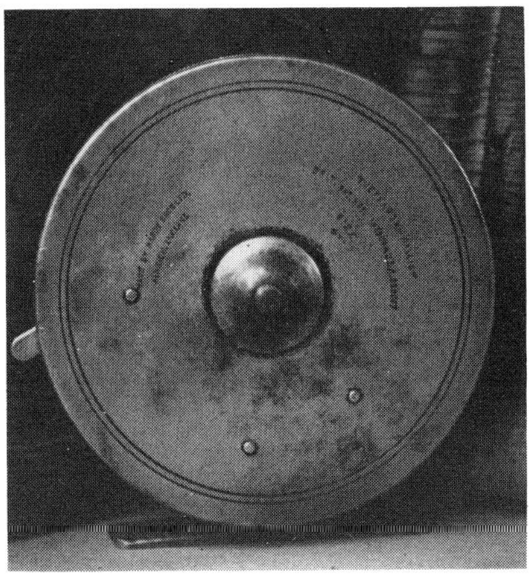

Hardy Wallis c.1931 – 1939

The Hardy Wallis was a light but strong alloy reel made for bottom fishing. Features included dual handles on an un-ventilated drum, grooved brass foot, on/off rim lever check control and drum release button. It was perfectly balanced and ran on a ground tool steel spindle in a phospor-bronze bush and had jewelled bearings.

Left; Hardy Wallis. Size 3½″, 4″ and a special 4½″

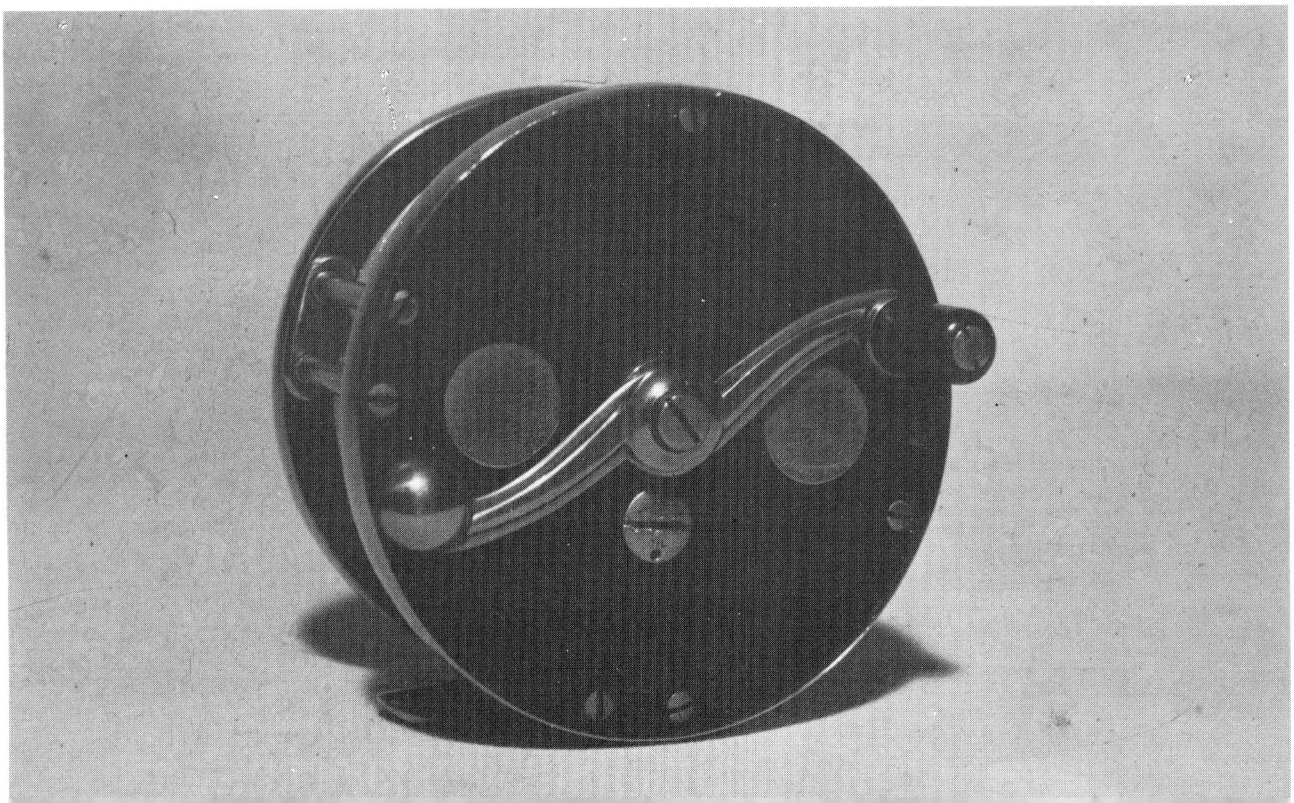

G Thornton

Tournament Reel 1931 – 1939

Hand-written ledger records at Hardy Bros show that the Tournament Reel was sold between 1931 and 1939. It was designed for competitive casting with baits up to and including ½oz. In casting the very light drum was entirely free from the winding handle, and in addition was balanced on fine adjustable pivot bearings, which offered the minimum of inertia to be overcome at commencement of casting. During the flight of the bait when the reel was paying off line, the drum was automatically controlled by governors which prevented over-running, but did not retard the flight of the bait.

Hardy-Decantelle 1931 – 1950

Sales of this reel started in 1931 and it was announced in the catalogue of the following year. The information given was that the French spinning reel known as the Decantelle had been purchased by Messrs. A P Decantelle and Hardy Bros Ltd., and the sole manufacture and selling rights were to be controlled by Hardy Bros. The reel was called the Hardy-Decantelle. It was in fact a simple form of Silex, made of aluminium alloy with dual ebonite handles and ebonite rim lever control, rim regulator screw and brass foot.

Above: Hardy-Decantelle. Sizes 3½", 4"

Match Fishers Reel 1936 – 1939

This was a fixed spool casting reel, which swivelled to turn the reel with its axis parallel to the rod to face the direction of casting, after which it could be turned back to the normal re-wind position. This model was not illustrated in the catalogues. Sales of the reel began in 1936 when just 4 were sold, followed by 130 in 1937 and 80 in 1938. It finished in 1939 for which year no sales records are available. This model has been overlooked by collectors.

The Barton 1934 – 1939

This reel was designed at the suggestion of Dr Barton the president of the Fly Fishers' Club, and produced as the ideal reel for dry fly fishermen. Features included an off-set grooved brass foot, large reverse tapered black handle, adjustable rim screw check, and quarter frame metal line-guide. Hand-written ledger records at Hardy Bros. show it was sold from 1934 to 1939.

Size 3¼" (weight 7¾ oz price 63/–) The Hardy Bros catalogues gave the size as 3" but this must have been a printing error as the only known examples have been 3¼"

Christies (Glasgow)

Altex Reels 1932 – 1966

The Altex was a stationary drum reel, having the axes of the reel parallel to the rod, allowing the line to slip off and cast with a fixed drum. An automatic pickup was fixed to a flyer which revolved round the drum to wind in the line.

It was introduced in 1932 in No. 1 and No. 2 models, each of which was available in two variations, one being automatic pickup and the other by finger. In 1935 an additional No. 3 model designed to use heavier line had been added to the range. The Altex production years were as follows – Altex No. 1, 1932 – 1965. Altex No. 2, 1932 – 1966. Altex No. 3, 1935 – 1963.

There was also a Sea Altex (1937–1959) with an aluminium drum and anodised outer parts.

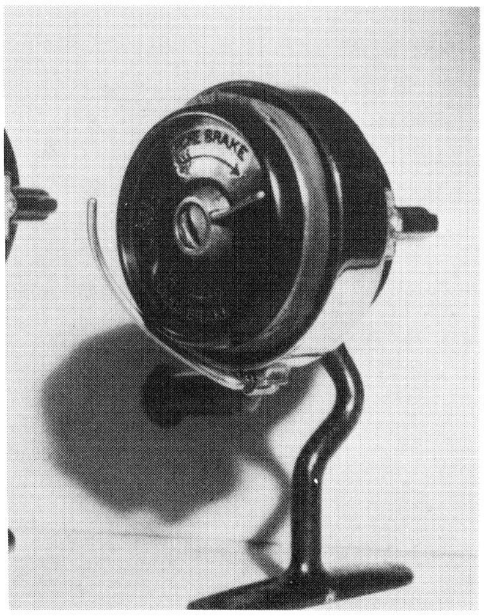

Hardex Reels 1937 – 1959

This model was introduced in 1937 and was basically similar to the Altex fixed spool reel but more moderately priced.

Two versions were offered, a No. 1 for trout, sea trout, grayling and small fish and No. 2 with a larger spool capacity for larger species. The models improved over the years as new features came along and finished in 1959.

Left; The Hardex reel

Above; Hardy White-Wickham. Size 8″

Lightweight 1936 – 1964

This was a light, 3¼oz. contracted reel for quick winding which was easily taken apart for cleaning.

Below; Lightweight. Size 3³⁄₁₆″

Hardy White - Wickham 1934 – 1939

This reel was made to comply with the ideas and requirements of the famous big game sea angler Mr H White-Wickham. It was made from the strongest non-ferrous metal, with a large diameter partly contracted drum to give quick line recovery. The handles remained stationary when the line was being taken off the reel and brake pressure could be quickly applied to any tension by means of the central star pressure brake washer.

Special Tournament Casting Reel c.1938

The Tournament Casting Reel was hand built purely for distance casting. It was made of light alloy with adjustable automatic reflex wire brake and adjustable tension.

Drum diameter was 2⅝″, drum width 1″, depth to core ⁹⁄₁₆″. This reel was not illustrated in the catalogue.

I have seen an example of this model without the Hardy Bros name and stamped 'B te SGDG FRANCE'.

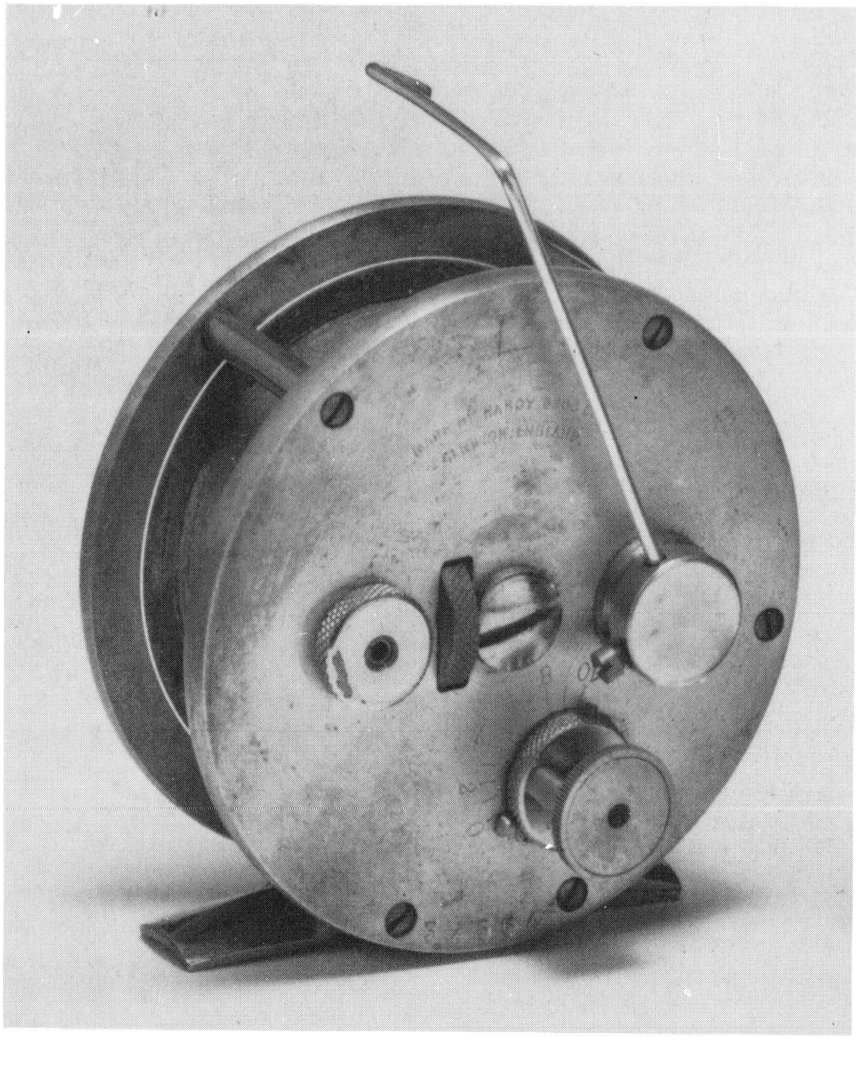

Fin De Lange 1937 – 1939

New Brunswick 1938 – 1939

Hardy Jock Scott 1938 – 1952

The HJS was a small multiplying reel with a gear ratio of four to one, and could disengage the gears on casting by moving a tiny lever on the edge of the rim, and re-engage automatically immediately the reel handle was turned. It was made from Duralumin alloy, weighed only 5¾oz and was given a black anodised finish and chrome plated fittings. An exclusive feature of this reel was the line drier supplied, with which it was possible to carry two lines. Upon reaching the water the angler was able to choose the line most suitable to the prevailing conditions. Similarly, should a change of line be needed during the day, it was only a matter of a few minutes to wind the line in use on to the drier, where it would remain drying, and to wind the spare line on to the reel. The HJS reel, together with cork abhor and oil bottle, was initially retailed at £13.18.6d plus £1.1.9d purchase tax and the line dryer was £1.9.0d plus 6/5d purchase tax.

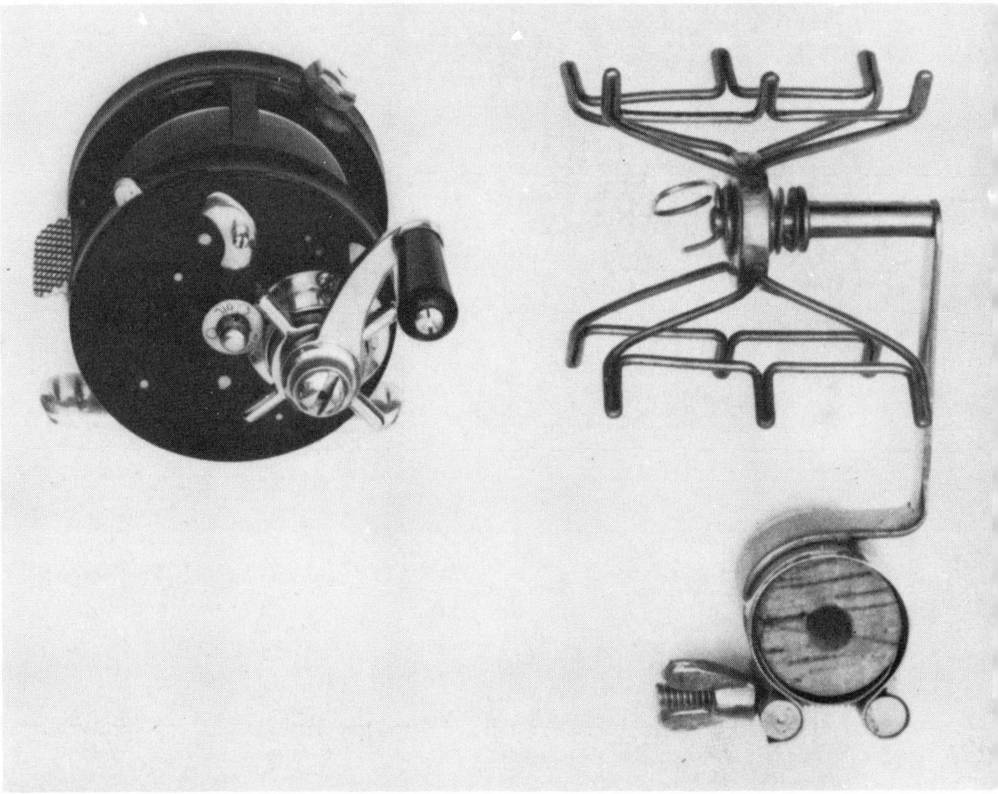

Hardy Jock Scott Tournament c.1952

A multiplying reel in Duralumin specially designed for tournament casting.

Above; Hardy Jock Scott Tournament reel

Elarex c.1939 – 1964

The Elarex was a 4 to 1 gear ratio multiplying reel made from aluminium alloy with dual handles, thumb rest and automatic level-wind line distributor. Hardy Bros. record the production years as 1939 – 1964.

Fly Reel Narrow Drum
c.1940s – c.1950s

This plain alloy contracted fixed check reel did not appear in any catalogues and its years of production can only be a matter of speculation. Features included a black handle, smooth brass foot which is unusual, brass central drum retaining screw and a double check mechanism.

It appears to be a reel which was designed to use up parts left in stock from an earlier period.

Size 3⅜″

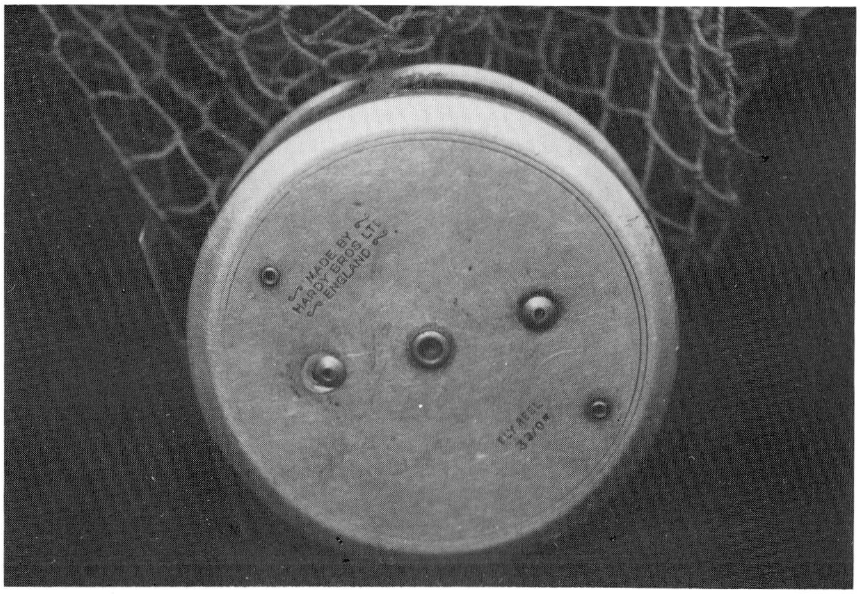

Fly Reel Wide Drum
Post-War

This is an alloy wide drum reel with perforated handle plate, grooved brass foot and Dual Check mechanism. The rarity of this model would suggest that it was only made for a short period and never appeared in any catalogue. Although produced relatively late it is a valuable collectors reel. I have only seen three examples and all were 3¾″ diameter.

Size 3¾″

Goodwin 1940 – 1959

The Goodwin sea reel was made in two versions. No. 1 was the plain reel controlled by hand when casting, and ratchet check and hand when playing a fish. No. 2 was similar but fitted with a spring adjustable screw controlled brake for casting and holding a fish, similar to that fitted for many years to the Longstone. It was operated by turning the control nut in the centre of the drum. The No. 1 was dropped after 1953 and the No. 2 remained in production until 1959.

The Goodwin No. 2. Size 4″

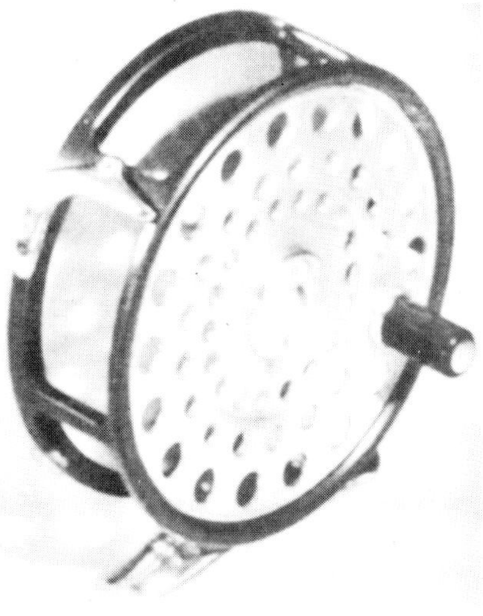

Above: LRH Lightweight. Size 3 3/16"

LRH Lightweight 1948 – current

The LRH Lightweight Fly Reel had compensating check and a line guide of hard stainless steel metal which prevented the line wearing grooves in the frame.

LRH Lightweight Multiplier 1974 – 1980

Monogram Reel	c.1950
Princess	1953 – 1959 and 1962 – current
Princess Multiplier	1974 – 1980
Taupo Perfect	1958 – 1964
Zenith	1958 – 1980
Zenith Multiplier	1974 – 1980
Featherweight	1958 – current
Silex	1972 – current
Featherweight Multiplier	1973 – 1977
Husky	1964 – 1969 and 1978 – 1980
Fly reel 3 3/16" (contracted). Also supplied with Silent Wind-In	1967
Viscount 130, 140, 150	1969 – 1978
Viscount	1981 – 1983
Viscount Silent	1982 – 1983
LRH Lightweight Multiplier	1974 1980
Marquis No.4 – 10	1969 – current
Marquis Salmon No.1 & No.2	1970 – current
Marquis Multiplier	1971 – current
Marquis Salmon No.3	1981 – current

Princess 1953 – 1959, 1962 – current

Featherweight 1958 – current

Husky 1964 – 1969 and 1978 – 1980

Zenith 1958 – 1980

Marquis 1969 – current

Viscount 1969 – 1978, 1981 – 1983

Conquest. Size 4⅛" 1955 – 1966

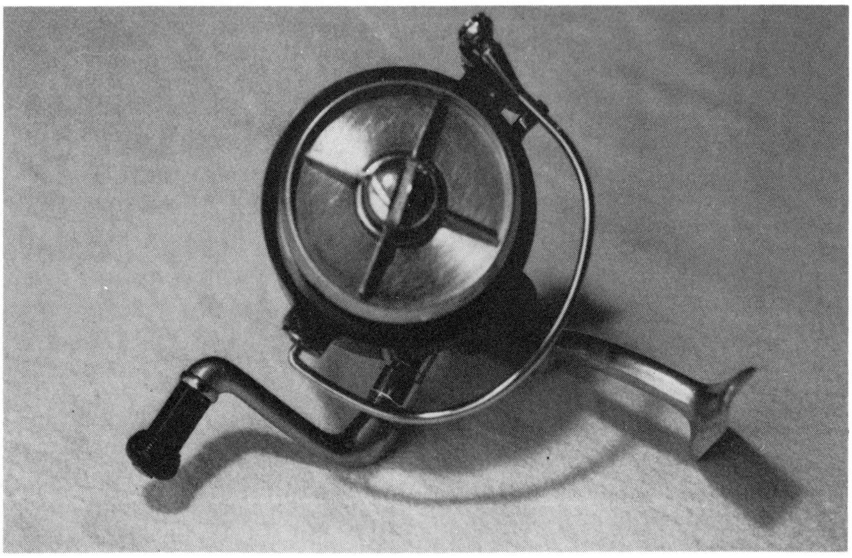

Exalta 1958 – 1965

Marquis Salmon No.1,2,3 Silent	1982 – 1985
Marquis 2/3	1985 – current
Marquis Silent Check	1985 – current
Sunbeam 5/6 6/7, 7/8, 8/9, 9/10	1978 – 83
Prince 5/6, 7/8	1983 – current
Golden Prince 5/6, 7/8	1984 – current
Ocean Prince Two	1984 – current
Golden Prince 9/10, 11/12	1985 – current
Ocean Prince One	1985 – current
Conquest	1955 – 1966
Exalta	1958 – 1965
Hydra	1958 – 1967
Flyweight	1961 – current
Saint Andrew	1962 – 1969
Gem	1962 – 1969
Eddystone	1964 – 1966
Saint Aiden	1964 – current

Flyweight 1961 – current. Size 2½"

Hydra 1958 – 1967. Sizes 3⅛", 3½", 3¾", 4⅜"

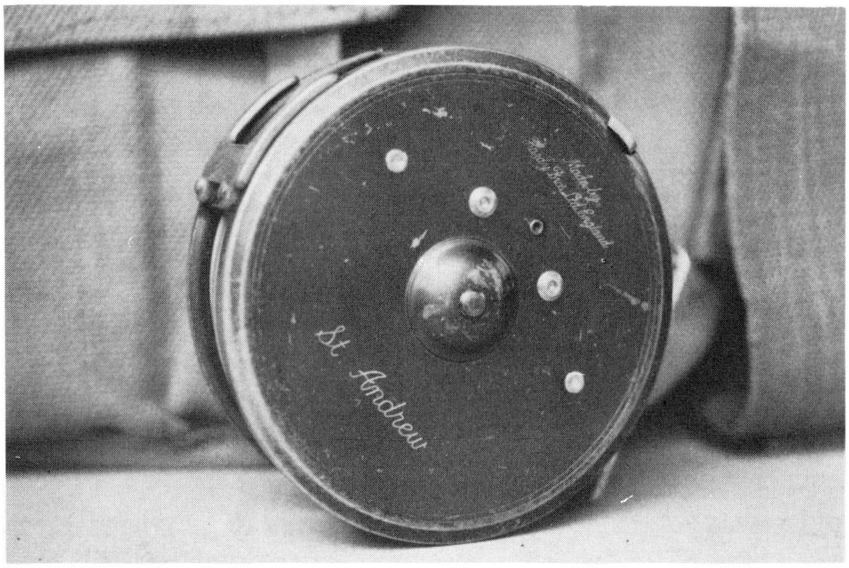

Saint Andrew 1962 – 1969. Size 4⅛″

Saint Aiden 1964 – current. Size 3¾″

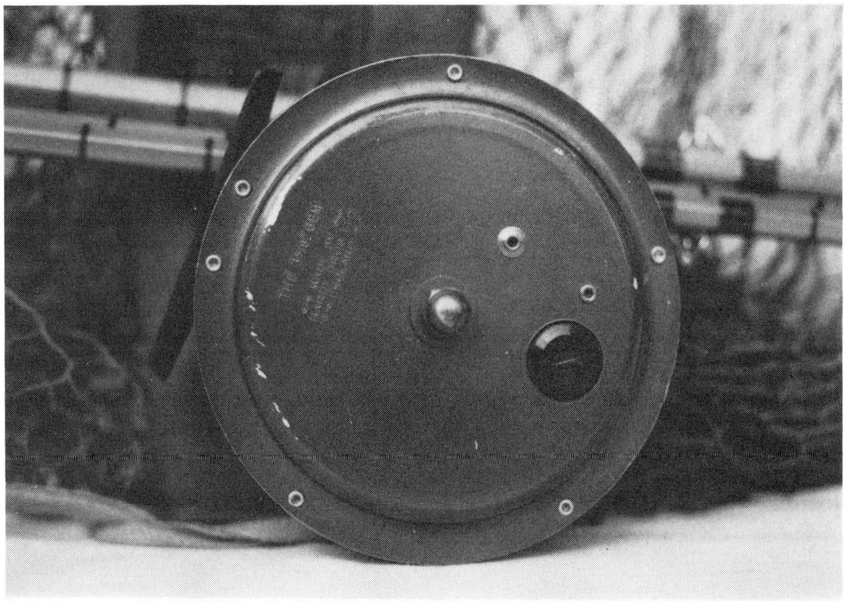

Gem 1962 – 1969. Sizes 3¼″, 3⅝″

Eddystone 1964 – 1966. Size 6″

THE MEDINA REEL

Lady and Lord Carmichael, 11th Baronet and 1st Baron Carmichael of Skirling. GCSI, GCIE, KCMG 1859 – 1926

No item of fishing tackle in any collection in the world can match the provenance and incredible story of the 'Medina Reel'. It was probably made before 1900 and although only a relatively cheap 2½" diameter Hardy Bros Birmingham Plate Reel, (c.1880's-1921), it was destined to have a very special owner and witness dramatic historical events.

It became the property of Sir (later Lord) Thomas David Gibson Carmichael and was used by him in all parts of the British Empire when he held office as – Governor of Victoria 1908 – 1911, Governor of Madras 1911 – 1912, and Governor of Bengal 1912 – 1917.

Carmichael was a remarkable art collector, having gone to Italy in 1885 as a young man with George Curzon (future Viceroy of India). From then on he collected works of art voraciously with the enthusiasm that characterised many late nineteenth-century connoisseurs. Parts of his collection are scattered round the world in museums and galleries.

He enjoyed shooting and fishing and was a keen entomologist whose enthusiasm was rewarded in India, when a new species of daddy-long-legs was named 'Tipula Carmichaeli' after him.

One of the highlights of his tours abroad was the visit of King-Emperor George V and Queen Mary to India in 1911, when they attended the Delhi Durbar, which was a huge gathering at which the Indian Princes paid homage.

The royal couple had sailed to India on the Medina, P&O's most up-do-date steamship, built at Greenock in 1911 for the mail run to Australia. She had been specially fitted out as a royal yacht in red, white and blue instead of her usual black and buff livery.

At the Dunbar, George V announced that the capital would be moved from Calcutta (in Bengal NE India) to Delhi, which was more central. Carmichael was made Governor of the re-organised Province of Bengal, the first since Warren Hastings in 1771, and raised to the peerage as Baron Carmichael. His Indian service brought him three orders of chivalry – Knight Commander of the Order of St. Michael and St. George, Knight Grand Commander of the Order of the Indian Empire and Knight Grand Commander of the Star of India.

In the spring of 1917 the Carmichaels prepared to leave India as the new Governor arrived to take up his duties. It was the time of World War 1 and Lady Carmichael thought the exchange absurdly dangerous when English ships were constantly being attacked by German gunboats, but both she and her husband looked forward to going home.

Their ship was the Medina which had come from Australia carrying a valuable cargo of tin and meat, much needed in the blocade of Britain. The Carmichaels loaded eighty chests of possessions and travelled with them as far as Port Said where they transferred to HMS Sheffield, while the Medina continued with

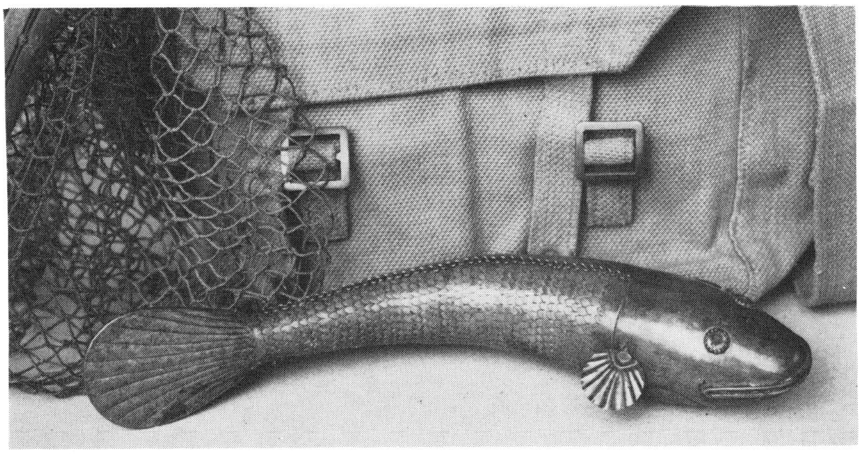

Above; One of the six Medina articulated brass fish

Lord Carmichael's reel, hip flask, pipe and watch case recovered from the wreck of the SS Medina

their baggage. The steamship reached Portsmouth safely and had started out for Tilbury when she was torpedoed off Start Point, Devon in the late afternoon of April 28th 1917. Five members of the crew were killed by the explosion while the rest took to the lifeboats as the Medina sank, taking with it the possessions of Lord Carmichael.

British morale was very low during that period of the war because of German successes on the Western Front and in the U-boat war. The government suppressed press reports of the sinking of the Medina and the *Times* merely reported that Lord Carmichael had returned without mentioning the calamity which had befallen his possessions. Medina's cargo of tin was salvaged in 1932 but it was not until 1984 that Consortium Recovery Ltd tried to locate Lord Carmichael's possessions. Their attempt failed and was finally abandoned because of severe weather conditions.

In late 1986 the project was resurrected with the Consortium using the very latest equipment from the vessel 'Holger Dane' owned by Henning Faddersbøll. Pairs of divers worked eight hour shifts for twenty four hours a day from a diving bell lowered 220ft to the wreck. Although protected from the intense cold by specially heated suits, the divers faced the hazard of unstable decks and compartments filled with mud. Several times they cut through the steel only to find rotting butter and meat. It was decided to abandon the project until on a final descent, one of the divers, Simon Barnes, came on a box marked GCIE (Knight Grand Commander of the Indian Empire), proof that they had at last found Lord Carmichael's belongings.

The mud was sucked away to unearth the contents of the cases, turning the water into swirling inky blackness in which the divers had to work by feel. Baskets of discoveries were hauled to the surface and included a large Oriental art collection, Indian brassware, Japanese porcelain, Chinese carving, netsuke, ancient Egyptian beads striped in gold, and an Assyrian cuneiform seal. Among the more personal effects were readable letters to Lord Kitchener and Lord Rosebery, masonic jewellery, amethyst and diamond cufflinks, his KCMG order and Lord Carmichael's personal brass fishing reel – the 2½" Hardy Birmingham Plate Reel. It had travelled an incredible journey across the world with Lord Carmichael, to the bottom of the sea with the SS Medina and after seventy years on the seabed it came back from the deep.

Fortunately the reel had been made almost entirely of brass and although the moving parts had fused, it was fully intact.

A young engineer and collector named Christopher Wilson was commissioned to bring the reel back to working order, which he did most successfully while retaining all the original main parts.

Other items of Lord Carmichael's property recovered from the SS Medina included a brass hip flask, empty watch case, pipe and six articulated brass fish, which had aquired a wonderful patina and were in remarkably good condition.

This history of the Medina reel will remain unique, while the Medina fish and other artefacts must be the ultimate in piscatorial memorabilia.

Hardy Bros Lures and Circa Dates of Sales

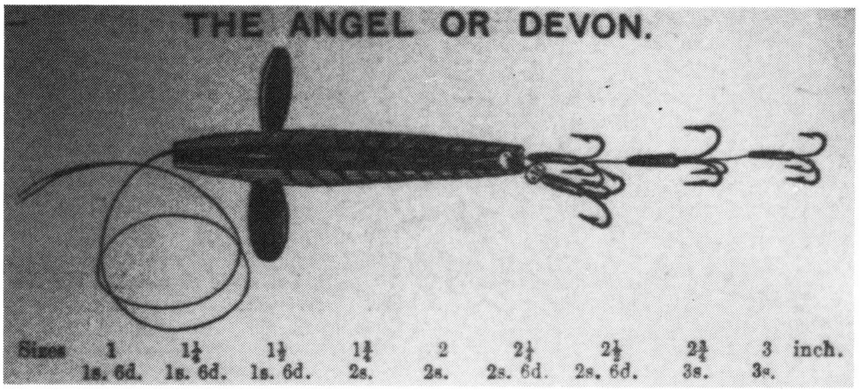

Angel or Devon. Early – 1893

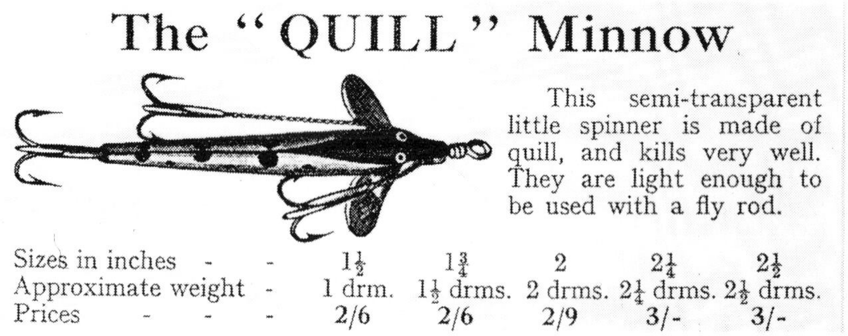
The "QUILL" Minnow
This semi-transparent little spinner is made of quill, and kills very well. They are light enough to be used with a fly rod.
Sizes in inches - - 1½ 1¾ 2 2¼ 2½
Approximate weight - 1 drm. 1½ drms. 2 drms. 2¼ drms. 2½ drms.
Prices - - - - 2/6 2/6 2/9 3/- 3/-

Quill Minnow. Early – 1965

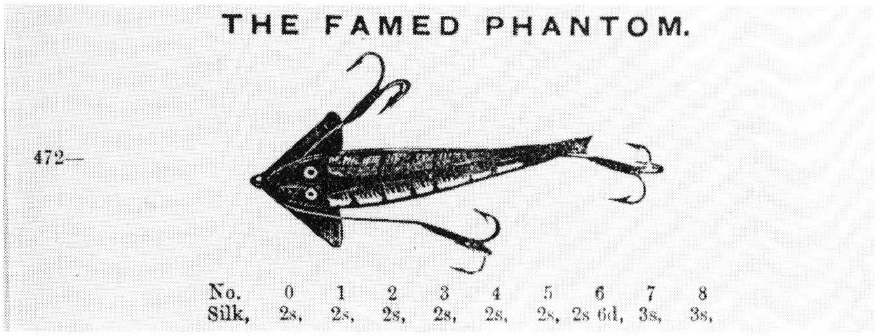
THE FAMED PHANTOM.
472—
No. 0 1 2 3 4 5 6 7 8
Silk, 2s, 2s, 2s, 2s, 2s, 2s, 2s 6d, 3s, 3s,

Famed Phantom 1885

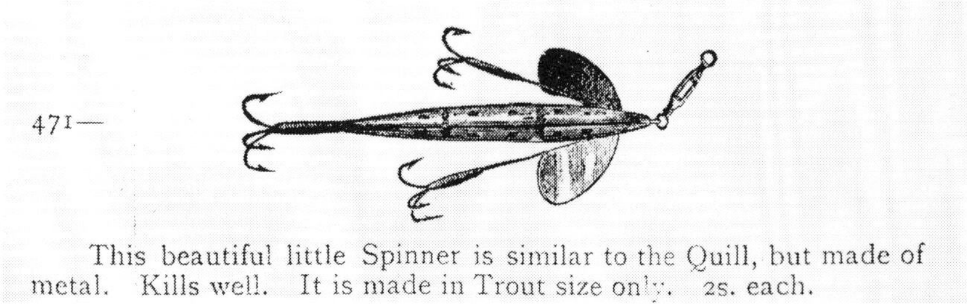
471—
This beautiful little Spinner is similar to the Quill, but made of metal. Kills well. It is made in Trout size only. 2s. each.

Excelsior Spinner. Early – 1896

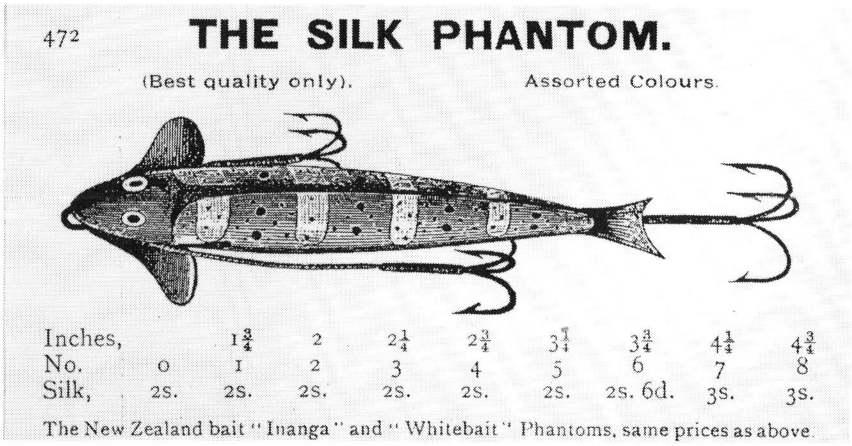
472
THE SILK PHANTOM.
(Best quality only).
Assorted Colours.
Inches, 1¾ 2 2¼ 2¾ 3¼ 3¾ 4¼ 4¾
No. 0 1 2 3 4 5 6 7 8
Silk, 2s. 2s. 2s. 2s. 2s. 2s. 2s. 6d. 3s. 3s.
The New Zealand bait "Inanga" and "Whitebait" Phantoms, same prices as above.

Silk Phantom 1888 – 1896

SOLESKIN PHANTOMS.

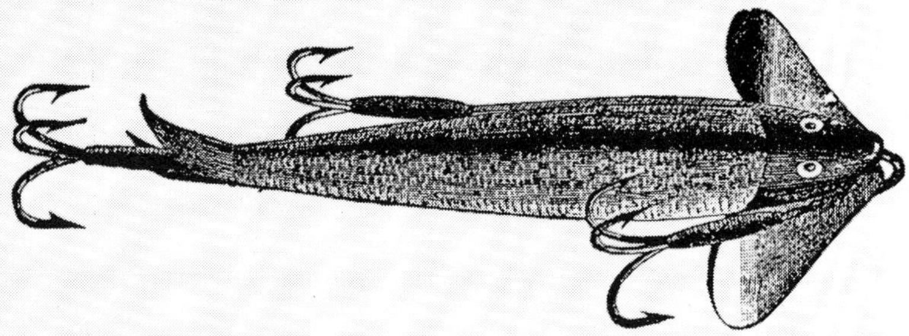

473—$1\frac{3}{4}$ and $2\frac{1}{4}$ inch	... ...	2s. od. each.
474—$2\frac{1}{2}$ and 3 inch	... ...	2s. 6d. ,,
475—$3\frac{1}{2}$ inch	... ...	3s. od. ,,
476—4 inch	... ...	3s. 6d. ,,
477—$4\frac{1}{2}$ inch	... ...	4s. od. ,,

Soleskin Phantom 1888 – 1901

$479\frac{1}{2}$— NEW "SPEAN" BAIT.

Trout Size, 2s. each. Salmon Size, 2s. 6d. each.
A very bright Metal Bait.

New Spean Bait 1888 – 1890

$477\frac{1}{2}$— THE NEW PEARL PHANTOM.

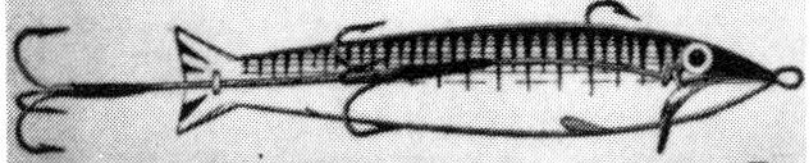

SIZES—	1 in.,	$1\frac{1}{4}$ in.,	$1\frac{1}{2}$ in.,	$1\frac{3}{4}$ in.,	$2\frac{1}{4}$ in.,	$2\frac{3}{4}$ in.,	3 in.,	$3\frac{1}{2}$ in.
PRICES—	2/6,	2/6,	2/6,	2/6,	3/-,	3/6,	4/-,	4/6.

One of the most brilliant and life-like baits ever produced, and very killing.

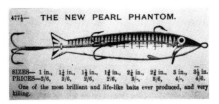

New Pearl Phantom 1890 – 1893

$479\frac{3}{4}$ THE SPIRAL MINNOW.

Best Quality—Stamped. (Geen's Patent.)

Sizes—	$1\frac{1}{2}$	$1\frac{3}{4}$	2	$2\frac{1}{4}$	$2\frac{1}{2}$	3	$3\frac{1}{2}$
	1/9	1/9	2/3	2/3	2/9	3/-	3/6

Spiral Minnow 1890 – 1896

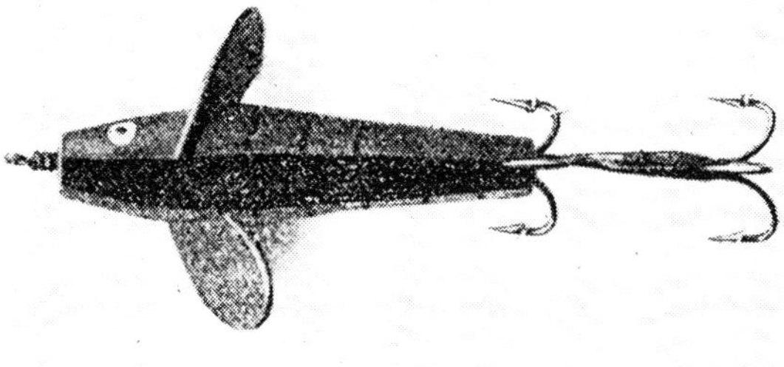

Excellent baits for all kinds of spinning. The advantage of a light minnow is that it does not sink so quickly as a heavy one, and remaining longer in midwater, can be spun more slowly. The fins being extra large help to keep the minnow up; the result is, it can be worked for a longer time over the lie of the fish.

Colours—Silver, Blue and Silver, and Brown and Silver.

Sizes	$1\frac{1}{4}$	$1\frac{1}{2}$	$1\frac{3}{4}$	2	$2\frac{1}{2}$ in.
Approx. weight	2	$3\frac{1}{2}$	5	$5\frac{1}{2}$	10 drms.
Prices	2/3	2/6	2/9	3/-	3/3 each.

Fitted with Hardy "Oval" wire treble hooks for Mahseer, etc., 9d. each extra.

Right: Pennell Minnow 1894 – 1908
Became Aluminium Pennell
1909 – 1936

Phantom Minnow 1894
Became McPatent Phantom
1895 – 1901
Became Rubber Phantom 1902 – 1909
Became Hardy Phantom 1910 – 1940

The "M.C. PATENT PHANTOM MINNOW"

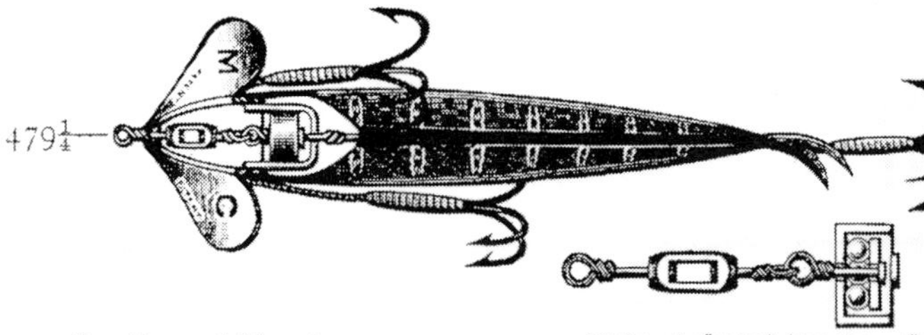

Section of Head. Patent Combination Swivel.

spins beautifully without any Swivel Trace. The Patent Combination Swivel is on the **Ball Bearings** principle, so that there is almost no friction.

These baits are made of transparent Soleskin with silvered leads inside. They are very lifelike, and kill well anywhere. We have supplied them largely to New Zealand, as they are a good imitation of the natural baits found there, and kill well.

Inches	$1\frac{3}{4}$	2	$2\frac{1}{4}$	$2\frac{3}{4}$	$3\frac{1}{4}$	$3\frac{3}{4}$	$4\frac{1}{4}$	$4\frac{3}{4}$
Prices	3/3	3/3	3/6	3/6	3/6	3/9	4/-	4/6

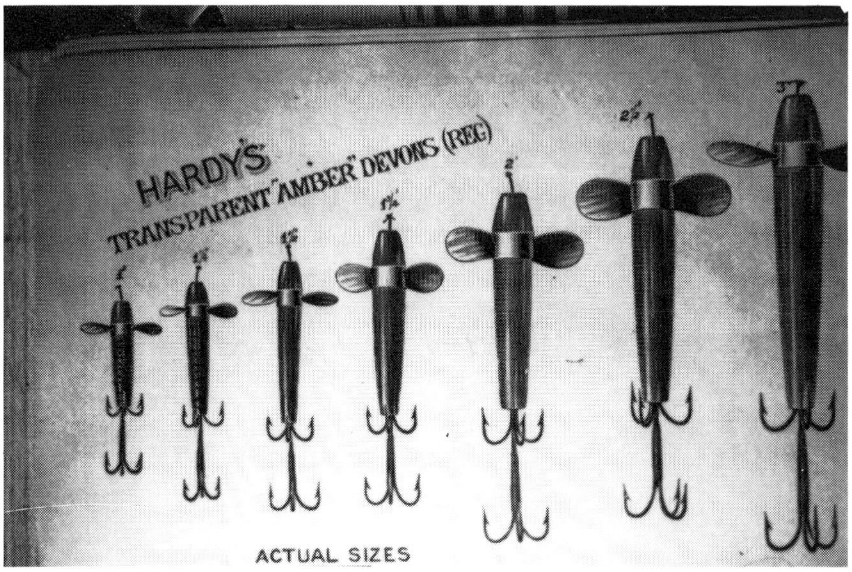

Transparent Amber Devon
1897 – 1910
Sizes 1″, 1¼″, 1½″, 1¾″, 2″, 2½″, 3″

Improved Quill Devon 1897 – 1924

Also manufactured was the Moori-Inanga or New Zealand Minnow 1899 – 1909. No illustration is available

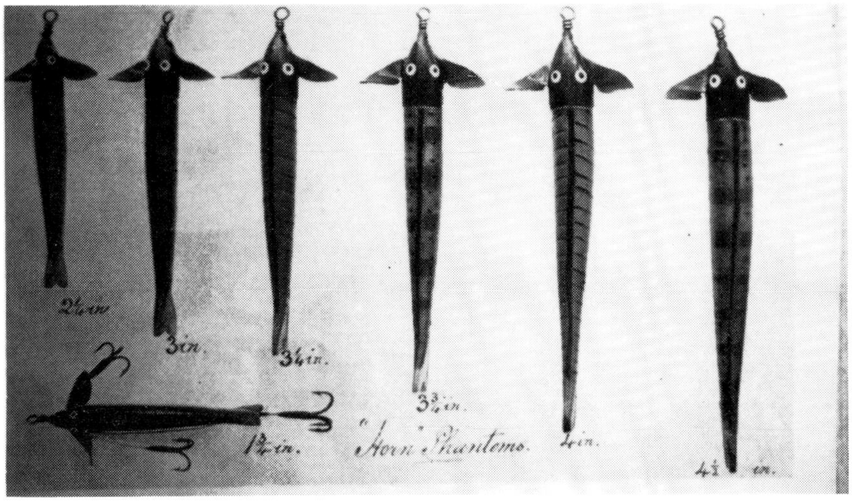

Horn Phantom 1899 – 1909

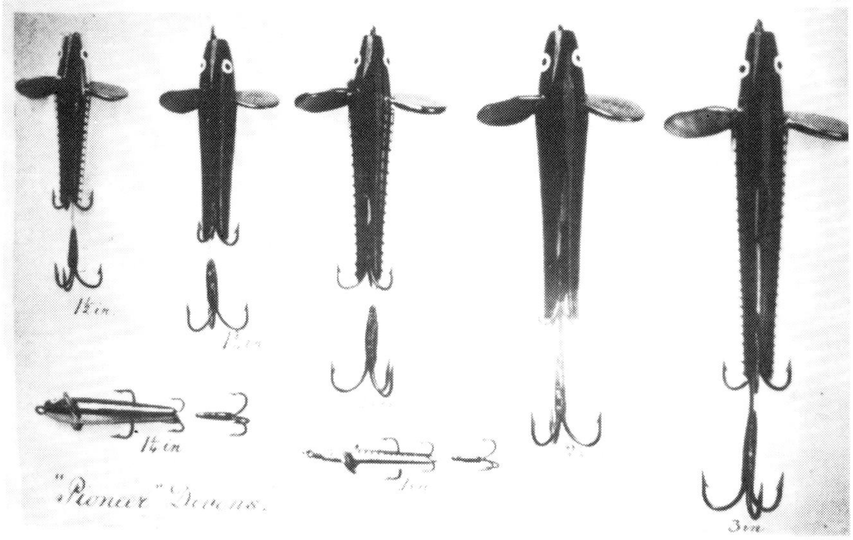

Above: Pioneer Devon 1899 – 1940

Above: Special Phantom 1902 – 1940s

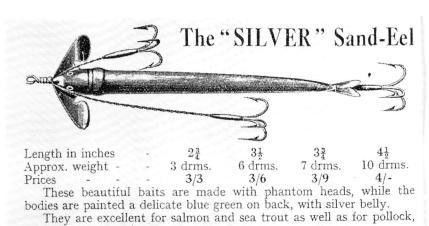

The "SILVER" Sand-Eel

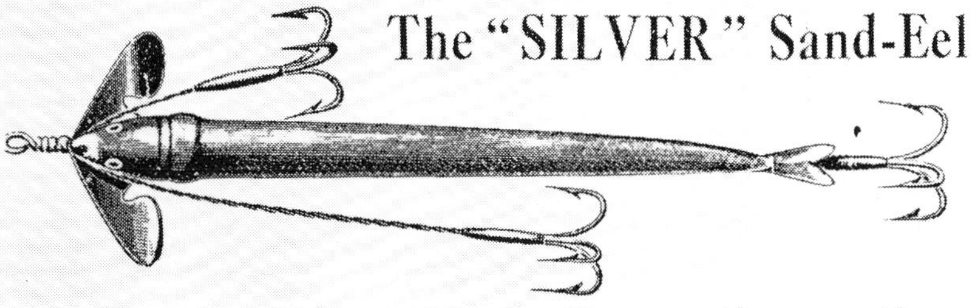

Length in inches -	2¾	3½	3¾	4½
Approx. weight - -	3 drms.	6 drms.	7 drms.	10 drms.
Prices - - - -	3/3	3/6	3/9	4/-

These beautiful baits are made with phantom heads, while the bodies are painted a delicate blue green on back, with silver belly.

They are excellent for salmon and sea trout as well as for pollock, bass, etc., in estuaries.

Above: Silver Sand Eel 1902 – 1954

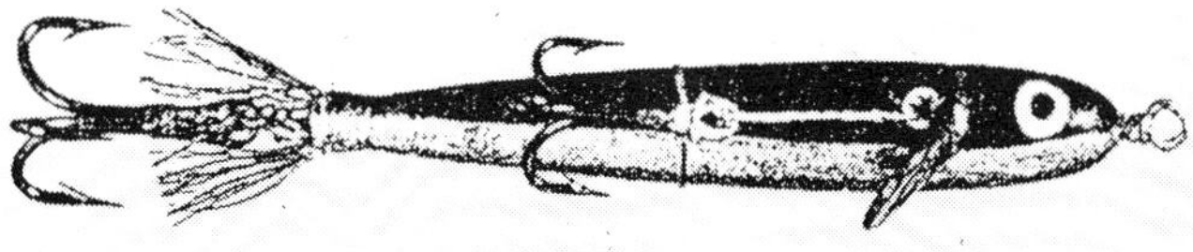

Ideal Phantom 1902 – 1940's

Ideal Phantom 2¾" Gudgeon

Swallow Tail Bait, Blue & Silver, 2½"

'Swallow' Tail Bait 1903 – 1953

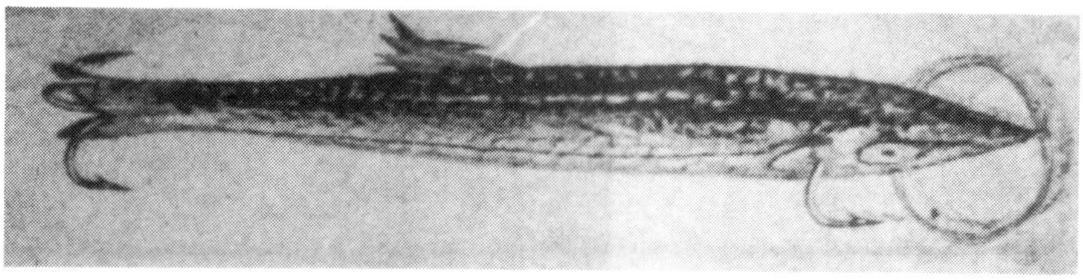

Vuoska or 'Whiskie Bobbie Bait'
1905 – 1907 Sizes 4¼", 3½", 3"

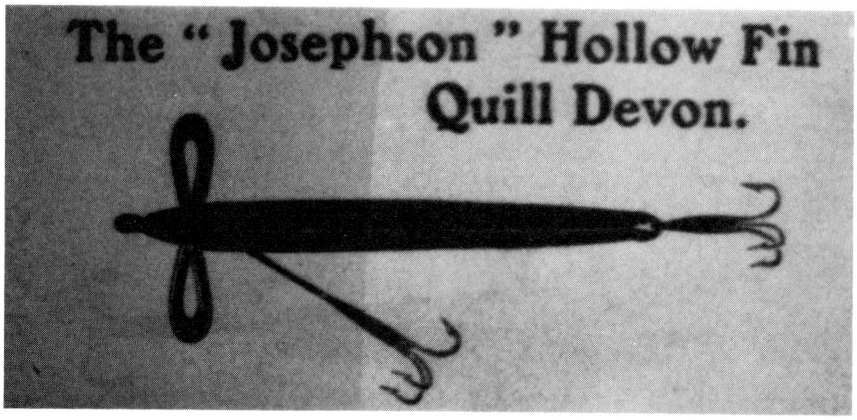
The " Josephson " Hollow Fin
Quill Devon.

'Josephsons' Hollow Fin Quill Devon
1906 – 1911

The " Halswell " Devon.
This Devon is specially recommended for use in New Zealand, and it is made after the design sent to us by one of our New Zealand clients. Made in either the style of our " Pennell " or " Pioneer " Devons.
Colour dull grey. Size 1¾ in. 1/6 each.

The 'Halswell' Devon

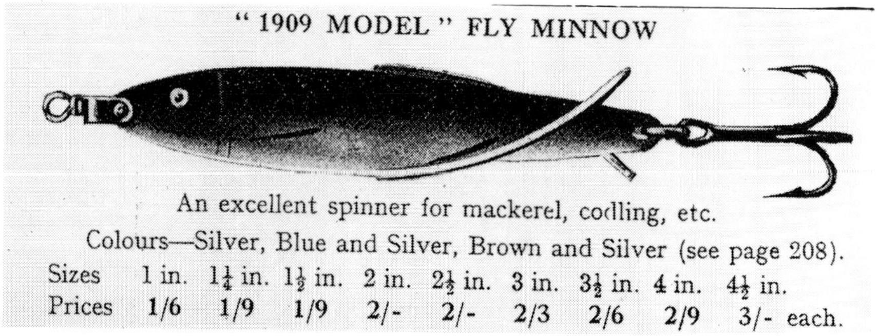
" 1909 MODEL " FLY MINNOW
An excellent spinner for mackerel, codling, etc.
Colours—Silver, Blue and Silver, Brown and Silver (see page 208).
Sizes 1 in. 1¼ in. 1½ in. 2 in. 2½ in. 3 in. 3½ in. 4 in. 4½ in.
Prices 1/6 1/9 1/9 2/- 2/- 2/3 2/6 2/9 3/- each.

'1909' Model Fly Minnow
1909 – 1926 (Became Model Fly Minnow 1927 – 1960's)

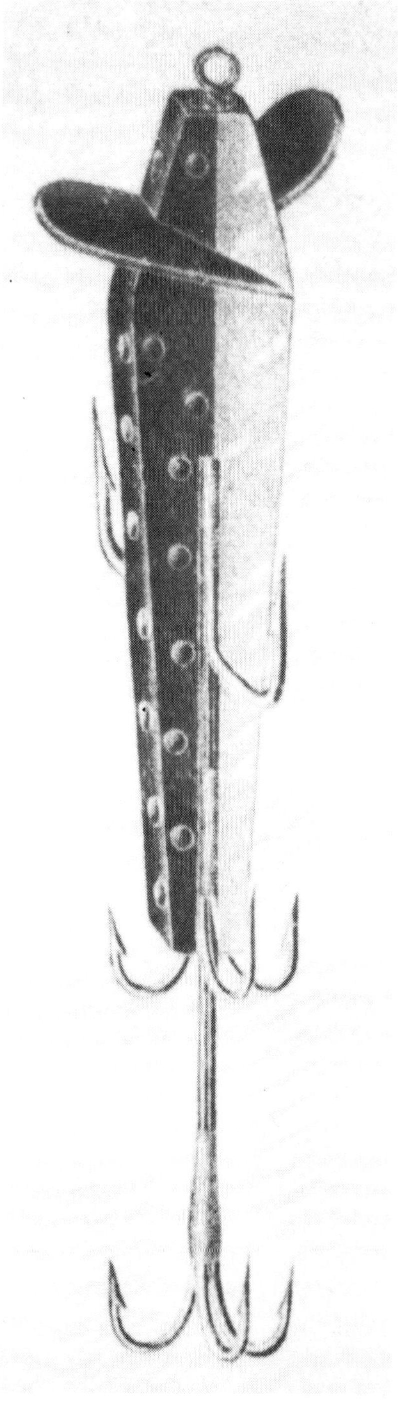

Forward Rectangular Devon
1906 – 1909

"ANTI-KINK" BAITS—*Contd.*

The "HARDY" Devon

Pat. Nos. 220000 and 155523.

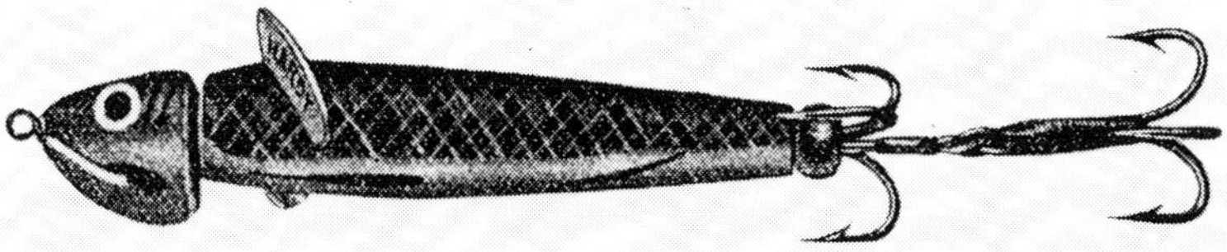

In colour, see Plate 18. Opp. page 206.

The heads of these Devons are fixed to a hollow spindle upon which the body revolves, and through which the hook flight is passed. The body only revolves—the head, spindle and hooks remaining stationary.

The body is made of metal and scaled, which gives it a realistic effect, while the colouring seats deeply, and is not easily rubbed off.

Colours: Silver, Gold, Blue and Silver, Brown and Gold, Gudgeon.

Sizes - - - - - - -	$2\frac{1}{2}$	3	$3\frac{1}{2}$	in.
Approximate weight - - -	$\frac{7}{8}$	1	$1\frac{1}{2}$	ozs.
Prices - - - - - -	4/6	4/9	5/-	each.

Hardy Devon 1914 – 1940s

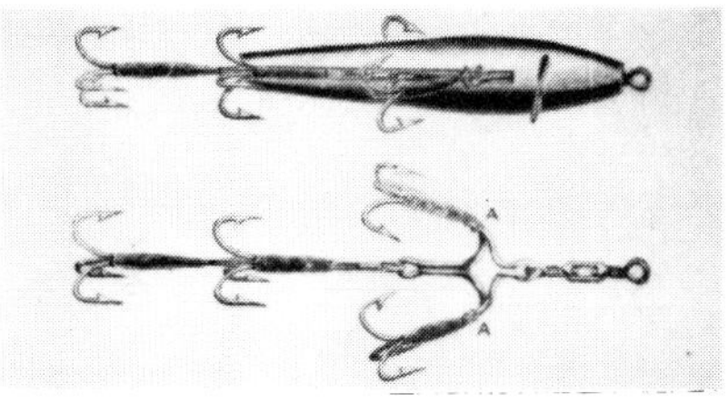

Devon Oval 'Murdock' 1909 – 1912
Sizes 2", 2½"

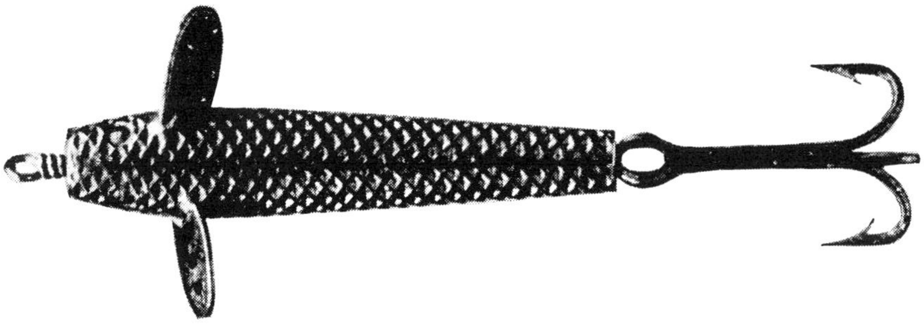

Improved Pennell Devon 1914 – 1925
Became Pennell Devon 1926 – 1962
Sizes 1", 1¼", 1½", 1¾", 2", 2¼", 2½", 3", 3½"

The "HUTTON-WYE" Phantom

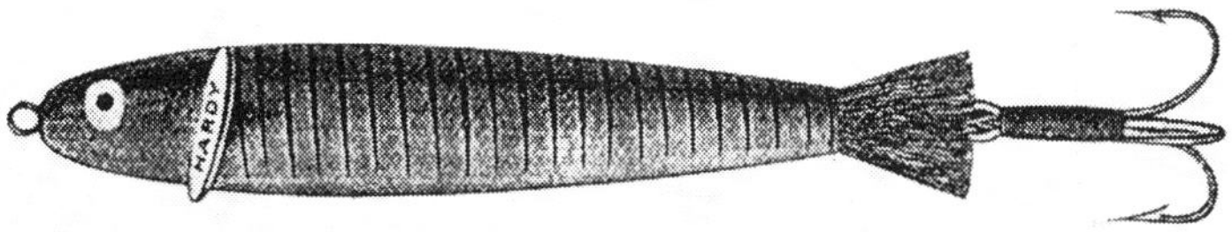

In colour, see Plate 18 opposite.

This bait is made as a Devon, the body being free to slide up the trace when a fish is hooked. It is therefore less liable to be destroyed, and cannot be used as a lever by the fish to rid itself of the hook. The flight is one treble hook, mounted on strong six-ply single gut and swivel.

The head, with fins, is in one piece of metal, under our Patent No. 155523. The tail is formed of strands of coloured gut, and is most realistic.

Mr. Hutton writes :—" The head is good and must be much stronger, being in one piece of metal. The bodies are excellent. The tails are very nice."

Colours: Brown and Gold, Silver and Blue, and Gudgeon.

Sizes - - - - -	3	$3\frac{1}{4}$	$3\frac{1}{2}$	$3\frac{3}{4}$	in.
Approximate weight -	6	7	8	9	drms.
Prices - - - - -	3/6	3/6	4/-	4/-	

'Hutton-Wye' Phantom 1921 – 1940s

The "BULLY" and "WHITEBAIT"

In colour, see plate 17.
Opp. page 206.

These baits are used in the lakes in New Zealand, etc., for large trout. The method of using is to cast out with a stout fly rod and work the bait by long slow strokes. As the attachment ring is on the underside of the head and immediately in front of the vane, the bait has a most natural and attractive action, resembling that of a small fish.

Illustrations are exact sizes. Painted to represent the Bully and Whitebait as found in the New Zealand lakes. Price 3/- each.

Bully and Whitebait 1924 – 1936

This bait is made of copper with leaded head. The tail can be set to give a quick or slow spin as desired. The leaded head, while assisting casting, also keeps the bait in correct position when fishing.

Right: Beadnell Spinner 1924 – 1936

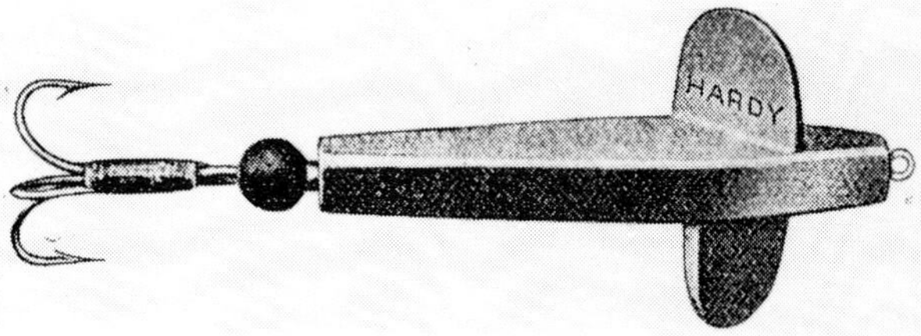

Left: Reflex Devon 1924 – 1955

The "HARDY SWIMMER" Bait

Pat. No 155523

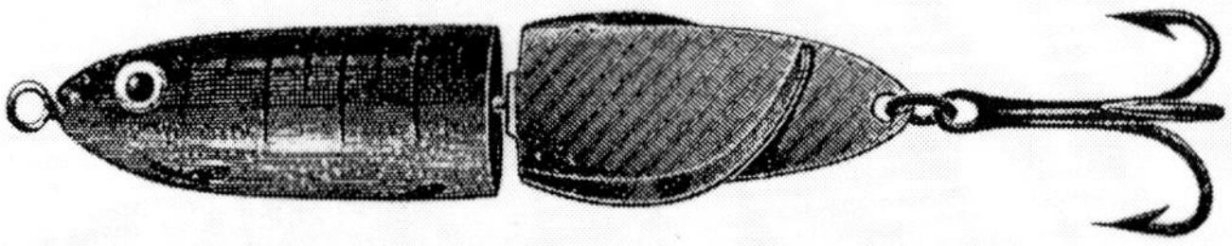

In colour, see Plate 18. Opp. page 206.

This form of bait is most attractive and realistic. The front portion being stationary acts as an "Anti-Kinker," whilst it also adds to the realistic appearance of the bait. As only the lower part of the bait moves, the whole has a very natural and fish-like action.

The present forms of Devon, Phantom, etc., although killing very well, do not give such a realistic imitation of the actual movement of a swimming fish, in such a way as the Hardy Swimmer, which has proved very deadly when ordinary baits have failed.

Colours: Blue and Silver, Brown and Gold, Gudgeon colour.

Sizes - - -	1¾	2	2¼	2½	in.
Approximate weight -	6	8	12	13	drms.
Prices - - - - -	3/-	3/3	3/6	3/9	each.

CALGARY, ALBERTA, CANADA, 14/5/28.

The "Hardy" 2 in. Swimmer Bait, Blue Silver is the best artificial bait I ever used, unfortunately lost the one you sent me last Summer.

G. A. HAWKES.

Right: Swimmer Bait 1924 – 1959

The "SYLPH" Minnow

A MOST REALISTIC ARTIFICIAL BAIT.

Patent Nos. 223078 and 221545.

Regd. No. 713182.

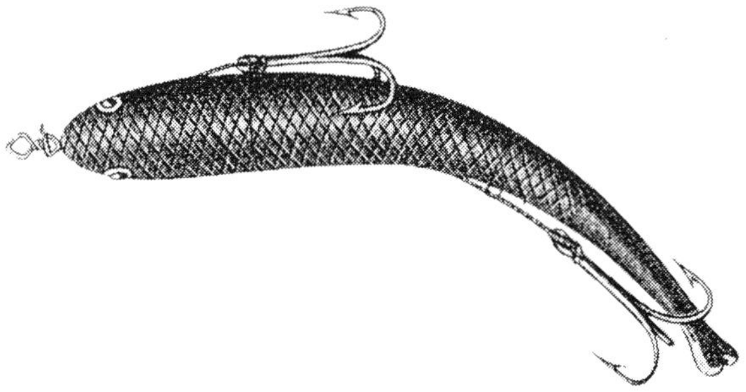

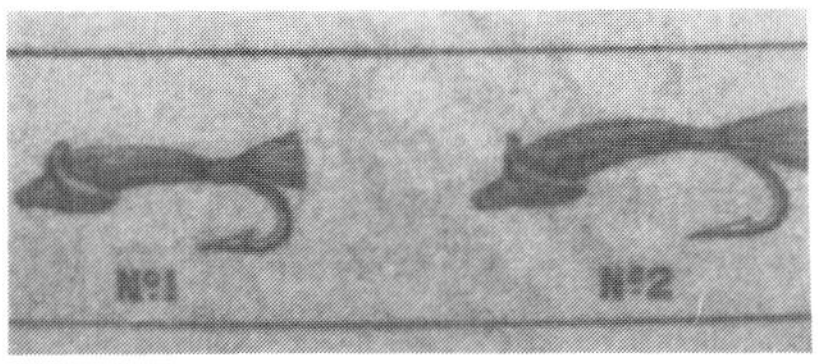

New Fly Minnow 1927 – 1933

Sylph Minnow 1925 – 1940s
Sizes 1½", 1¾", 2", 2½", 3", 3½"

The "GOLDEN" Sprat

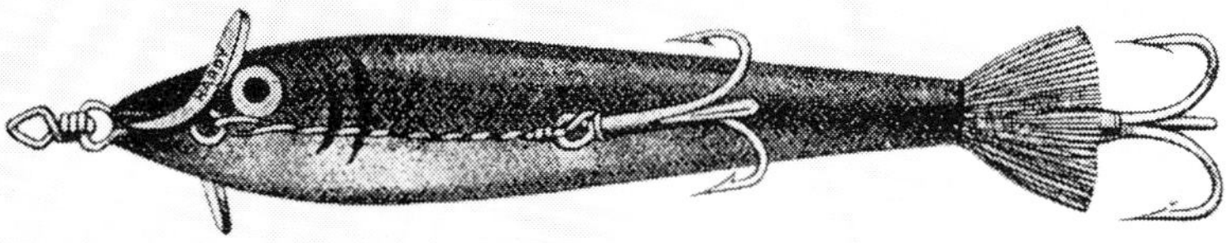

In colour, see Plate 18. Opp. page 206.

The golden coloured natural sprat is much to the fore as a salmon bait in the early part of the season, so we have introduced an accurate representation called the Golden Sprat, which has a Patent "Hardy" swivel at its head.

We also stock this sprat in its natural colouring, viz., Silver.

Sizes - - - - -	2	2½	3	3½	4 in.
Approximate weight -	2½	4½	7	10	15 drms.
Prices - - - - -	2/9	3/-	3/6	3/9	4/- each.

Golden Sprat 1925 – 1962

THE "WETHERAL" BAIT

Regd. No. 726391.

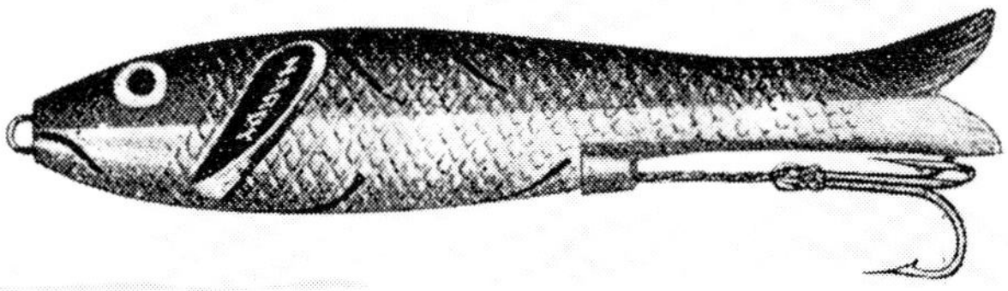

Wetheral Bait 1927 – 1940s

Darting and Diving Baits

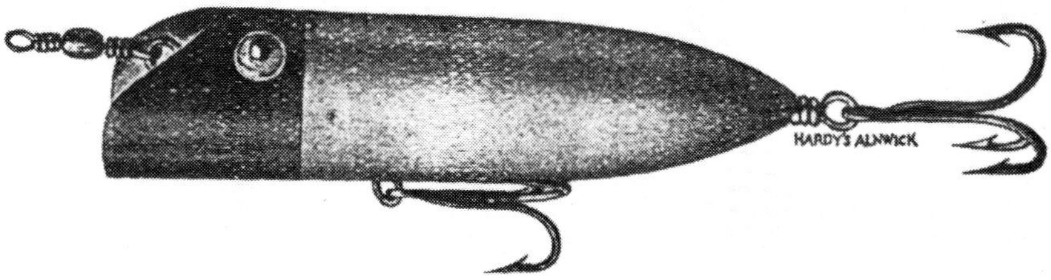

Darting and Diving Bait 1929 – 1940s

Genuine Mother-of-Pearl Devons

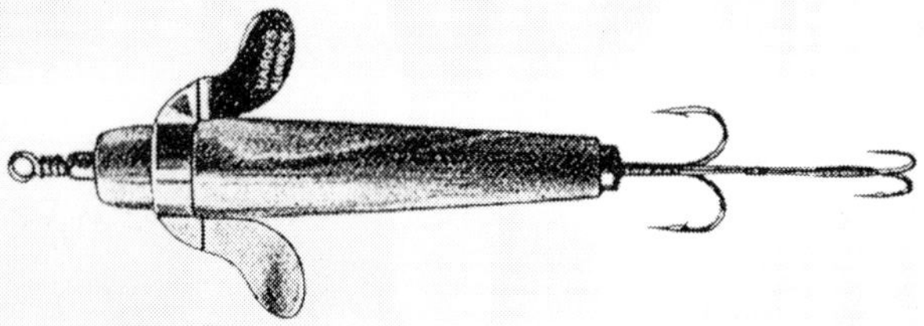

A very attractive bait with all the beautiful shades of colour contained in real mother-of-pearl. Also in Pink Shades.

Very life-like in appearance; really something out of the ordinary, and a bait no angler, who spins, should be without. Good for either clear or coloured water.

Sizes	1	1¼	1½	1¾	2	2¼	2½	3 in.
Prices	3/3	3/6	4/-	4/6	5/-	6/6	8/6	10/6 each.

Mother of Pearl Devon 1929 – 1936

The L.R.H. "Semi-buoyant" Devons

A new series of Devons made specially to fish shallow rivers. The bodies being made of wood over a thin metal tube prevent the bait from sinking rapidly and consequently catching on the bottom.

Colours—Blue and Pearl White, Gold and Silver, Pearl White and Red. Mounted with single round bend treble and red bead, or if desired two trebles.

Size.	Approx. Weight.	Price each.	Size.	Approx. Weight.	Price each.
1½ in.	2 drs.	2/6	2¼ ins.	4 drs.	3/3
1¾ in.	2¼ drs.	2/9	2½ ins.	6 drs.	3/6
2 in.	3½ drs.	3/-			

These weights are nearly half of that of the "Pennell" Devons.

LRH Semi-Buoyant Devon 1933 – 1940s

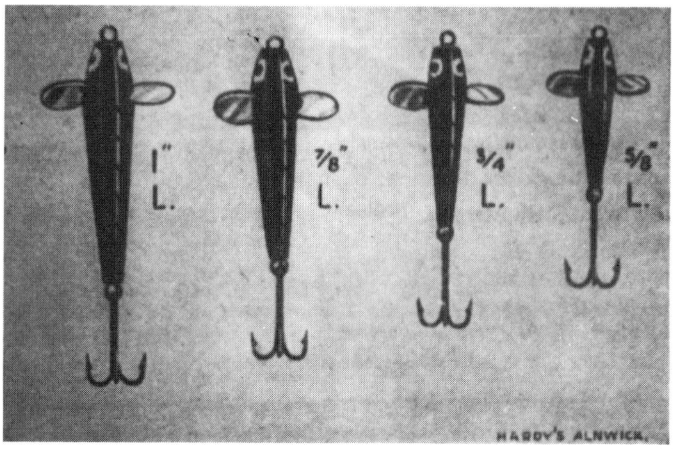

Threadline Pennell Devon 1933 – 1963

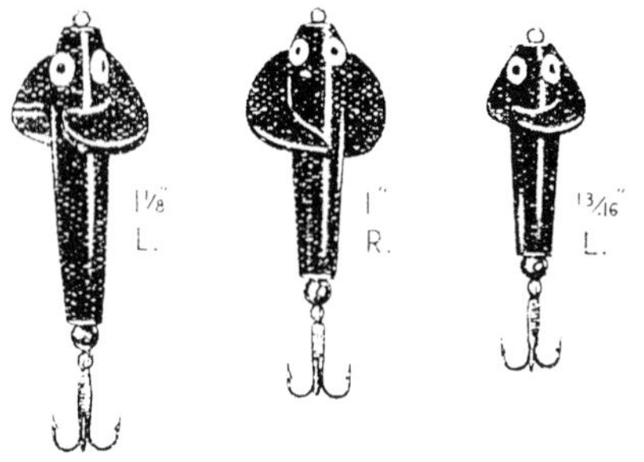

Heavyweight Devons 1937 – 1963

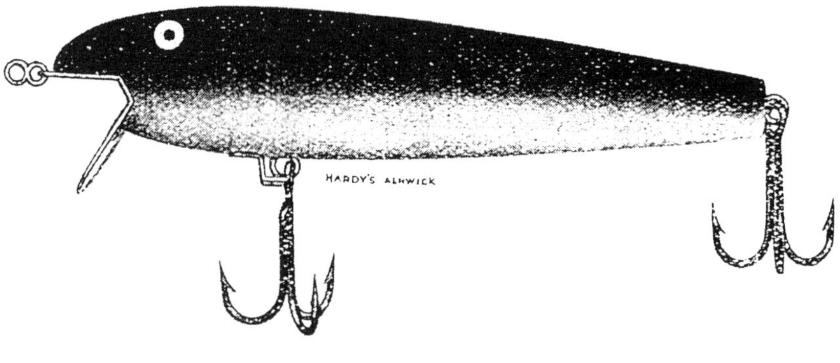

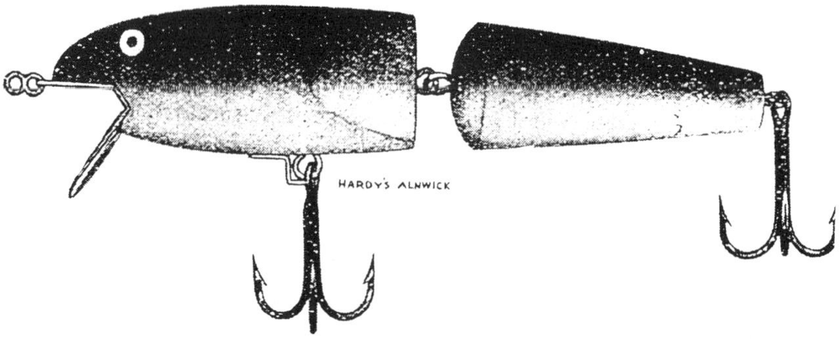

Wigglers Bait 1937 – 1940s (Two models)

Sprat Devon 1937 – 1965
Sizes 1½", 1¾", 2", 2¼", 2½", 3", 3½"

The 'Yellow Bellies'

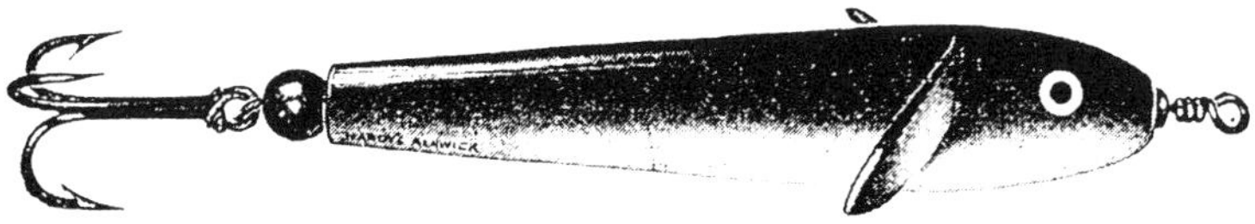

This now famous bait—introduced by us a few years ago, has proved to be outstandingly successful as a salmon and sea-trout lure in all rivers. In fact it can be said there is not a fishery where it has been tried and not found very successful.

It is designed to swim on a level keel, it is semi-buoyant, flirting in the varying undercurrents of the stream, greatly adding to its attractions. The blend of colours proved, after considerable experiment, to be extremely attractive to fish. To fish it properly it should be allowed to drift round with the stream, raising the rod point gradually, occasionally dropping it slightly, to give even more life and movement to the bait. Do not use any lead on the trace except in very strong streamy water.

Stocked in one colour only—the true, original yellow belly shades. Always carry a few in the tackle box. They are also made to order in brown and gold, and blue and silver.

SIZES:	1¾	2	2¼	2¾	3¼ ins.
WEIGHTS: (approx.)	3	4	4	7	8 drms.

These weights are nearly half that of the 'Pennell' Devons.

Yellow Bellies 1951 – 1963

'West Country' Devon

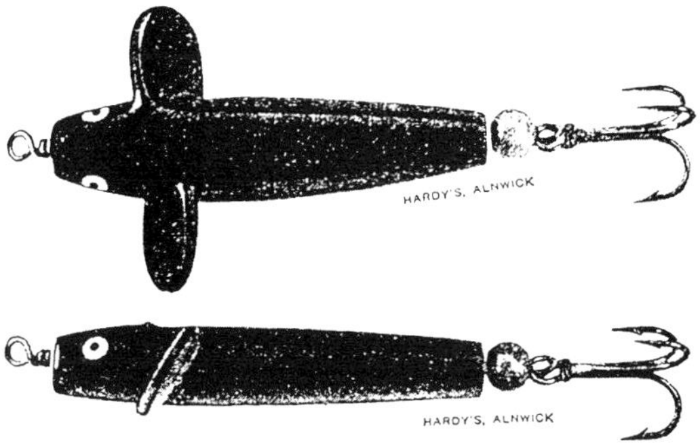

Above: West Country Devon
1951 – 1963
Sizes 1½", 2", 2⅜"

Roses' Reversible Spin Devon

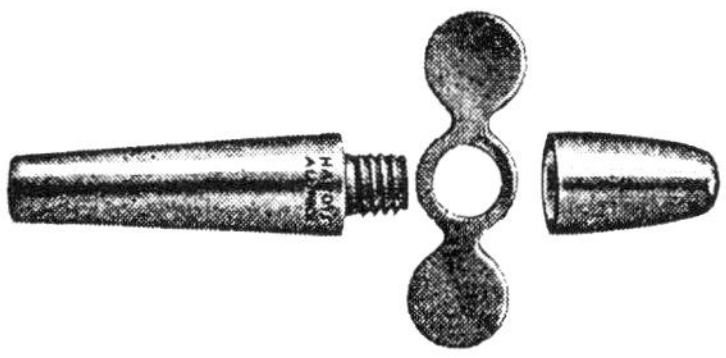

Fig. 1 *Devon showing 3 component parts*

A very simple and new idea of how to change the direction of the spin of a devon to prevent the line becoming twisted and snarled.

The fins are made of ductile metals and easily twisted to produce a spin in either direction for which use a key is provided.

The devon is made in three parts: head, fins and body.

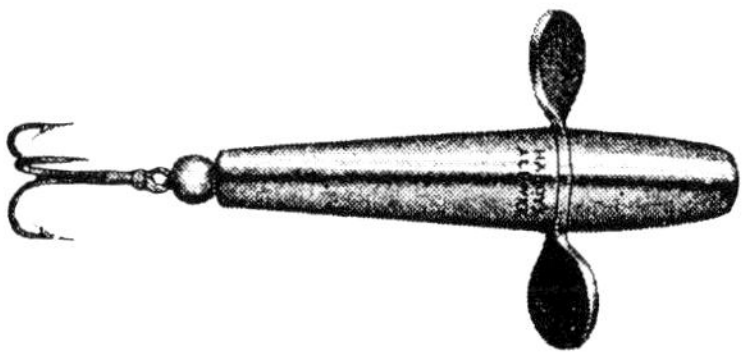

Fig. 2 *Devon Assembled*

Roses Reversible Spin Devon
1954 – 1959
Sizes 1¼", 1½", 2"

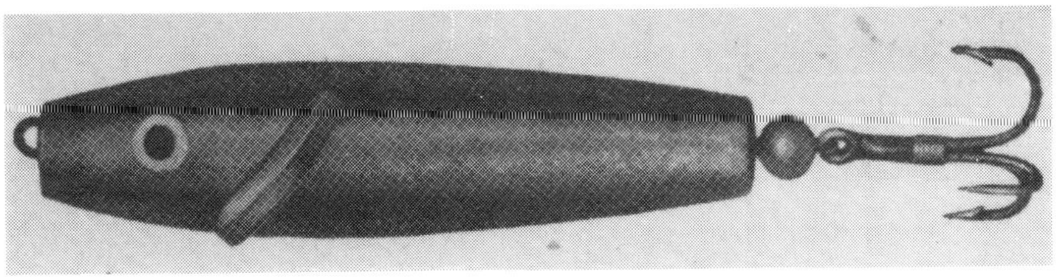

Driftex 1957 – 1965

LEATHER EEL TAIL

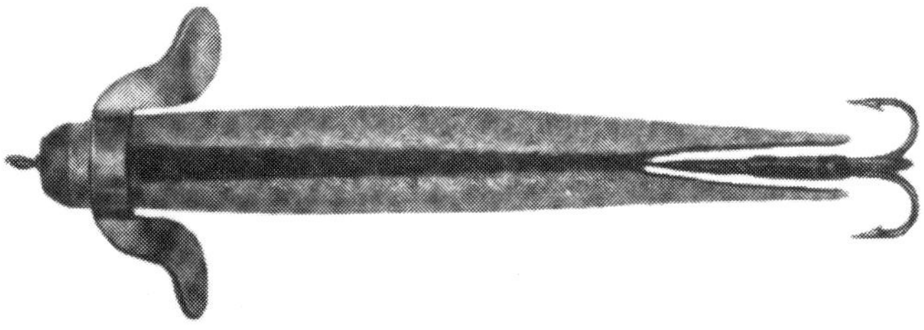

This bait is used with considerable success both on the Irish rivers and on the Spey.
It has a weighted head and the body is made of two strips of leathers joined together for approximately two-thirds of their length.
This bait is made in one size only, namely 3 in.

Leather Eel Tail 1957 – 1962

Selection of Hardy Bros Fishing Tackle

Hardy Bros 'Perfect' Creel

The "EDEN" Trout and Sea Trout Bag

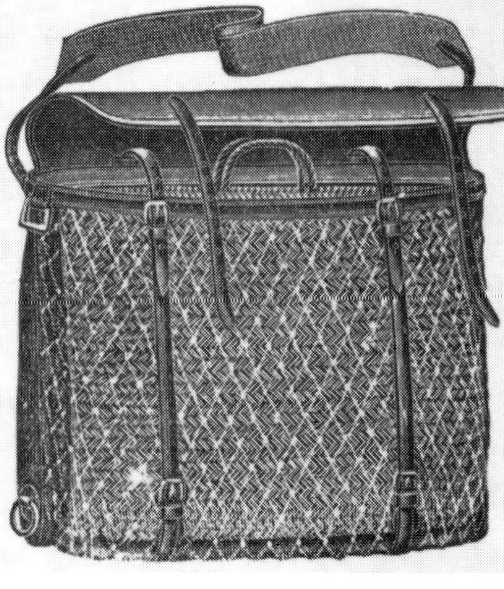

Made of stout waterproof mole colour sateen with two compartments. The outer one or net is for the fish, and is fitted with a bass bag, supported on a stiff fibre bottom, so that fish do not get squashed. By replacing the bass the bag does not become foul.

The inner compartment is intended for lunch, tackle, etc.

Size 16 in. × 12 in.

Price 27/6 each.

For suitable Bass Bags, see page 377.

FISHING TACKLE MANUFACTURERS, ALNWICK 323

The "CARRY ALL" Creel

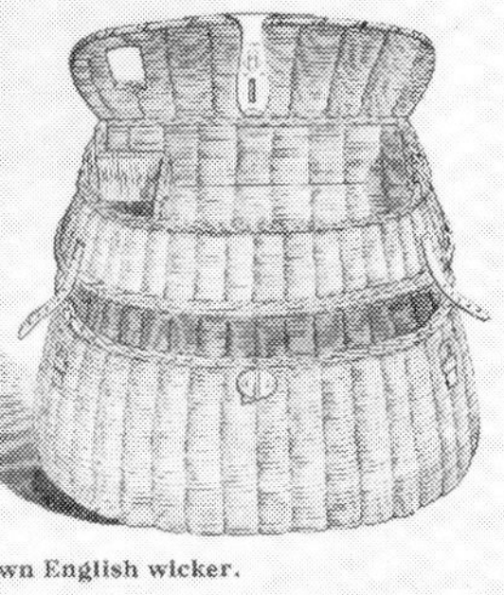

In this basket the lunch, etc., compartment is above and quite clear of the fish.

The straps are arranged so that the basket may be worn over the shoulder in the ordinary manner, or with strap over both shoulders as a knapsack—a welcome relief when 10 lbs. of fish are to be carried any distance.

Made of best brown English wicker.

No. 1.—10 in. × 14 in., for 10 lbs. of fish, **32/6.**
No. 2.—11 in. × 15 in., for 15 lbs. of fish, **34/6.**
No. 3.—12 in. × 16 in., for 20 lbs. of fish, **36/6.**

The "CURRAGH" Creel

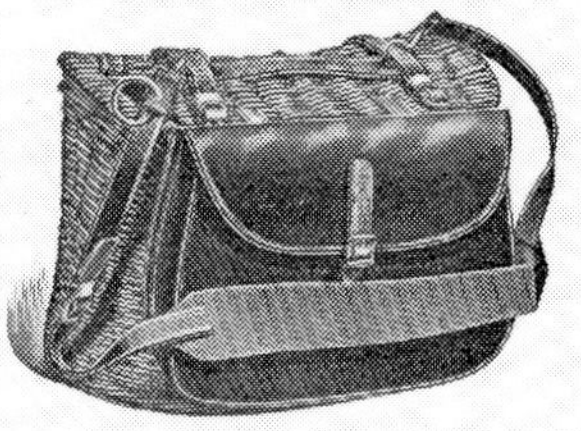

A combined fish basket and lunch or tackle bag. The bag is detachable, and the shoulder strap can be attached to it, so that either may be used separately.

The basket is made of best brown English wicker and fitted with a waterproof lining.

The straps are designed so that a waterproof coat may be carried. This arrangement should commend itself to those who consider an ordinary basket too bulky and heavy, and a bag no protection for fish.

Length 15 in., depth $8\frac{1}{2}$ in. Size across top 3 in., across bottom 4 in. Price, complete, 41/6. Price, without lunch bag, 32/6.

FOR THE "ANGLER'S PIPE," SEE PAGE 384.

324 HARDY BROTHERS LIMITED

The "HOUGHTON" Creel

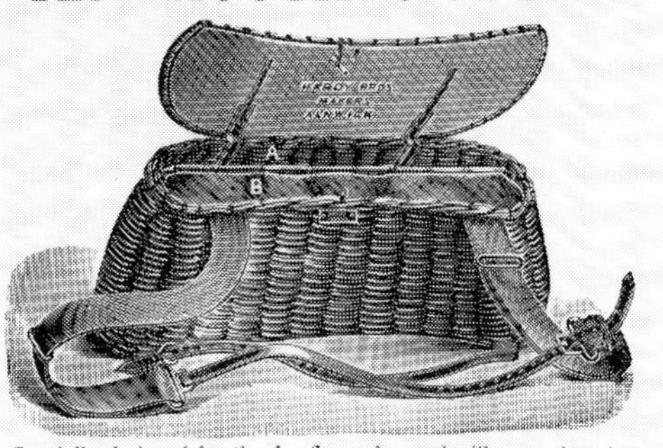

Specially designed for the dry fly angler, and will carry three brace of "Test" fish. Strongly made of brown English willows. Size 19 in. long by 6 in. deep and 7 in. high.

Fitted with shoulder strap and straps to carry coat on the lid. The lid is lined inside with waterproof material, and opens away from the angler. Price **28/6.**

Is fitted with removable inner lining (**B**) for fish and separate compartment (**A**) for lunch and tackle as in illustration. Price **33/6.**

The "ENGLISH WICKER" Creel

A light basket made of best brown English willows, with ordinary web shoulder strap, and straps for light waterproof coat.

No. 1, to carry 9 lbs.	No. 2, to carry 12 lbs.	No. 3, to carry 20 lbs.
19/6	**21/6**	**23/6.**

FOR THE "ANGLERS' PIPE," SEE PAGE 384.

FISHING TACKLE MANUFACTURERS, ALNWICK 327

The "BASKET" Bag

This combination of basket and bag is made of stout waterproof mole colour sateen, with two inside compartments, and pocket on outside. The outer compartment, intended for fish, is fitted with a removable waterproof lining. The inner one is divided into two divisions for lunch, tackle book, etc. (see dotted lines). Fish rest on the stiff flat bottom **A**, and do not get squashed. The expanding gusset ends, when in use, form a spout-shaped mouth (as shown by dotted lines **B**), and so permit fish being easily slipped in. When it is desired to carry large fish, both gussets may be pulled out. It folds like an ordinary bag for packing, is very light, has a handle for carrying as well as a special shoulder and body strap, and a square eye for carrying a net at **C**. An excellent bag for all-round trout or sea trout fishing, particularly when one occasionally kills a salmon.

Size 15 in. × 10 in. Weight 2 lbs. 4 ozs.

Price **52/6** each.

"ROYDE" NET, SEE PAGE 311.

323 HARDY BROTHERS LIMITED

The "CARRY ALL" Trout and Sea Trout Bag

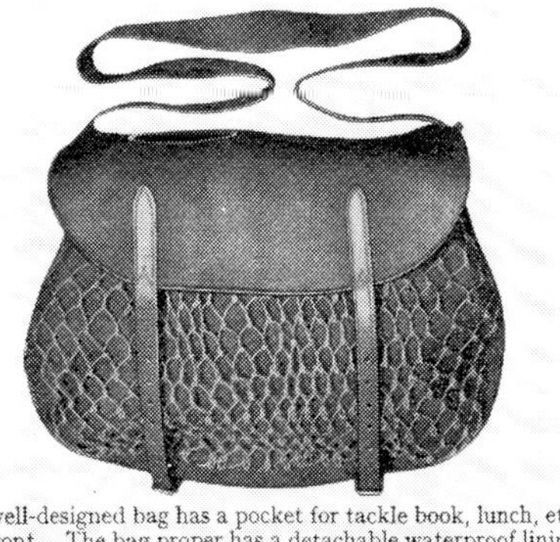

This well-designed bag has a pocket for tackle book, lunch, etc., and a net in front. The bag proper has a detachable waterproof lining, into which fish are passed through the hole in lid.

Made of very fine drab cashmerette, with web girdle sewn to the gusset of bag. The two long straps can be used to carry a coat or waders.

Sizes:	15 × 11 in.	16 × 12 in.	17 × 12 in.	19 × 14 in.
Price:	No. 1, **28/6.**	No. 2, **33/6.**	No. 3, **38/6.**	No. 4, **43/6.**

The "SLIP IN" Trout Bag

No. 1.—10 × 15 in. **14/6**
No. 2.—11 × 16 in. **16/6**
No. 3.—13 × 17 in. **18/6**

A bag of simple but useful design. The spout-shaped mouth is shown open as in use, which permits fish to be easily slipped in; when not in use this mouth is folded into bag. The bag is waterproof, and has a lunch or tackle compartment in front.

FOR THE "UNIQUA" FLY REEL, SEE PAGE 139.

The "TWEED" Salmon Bag

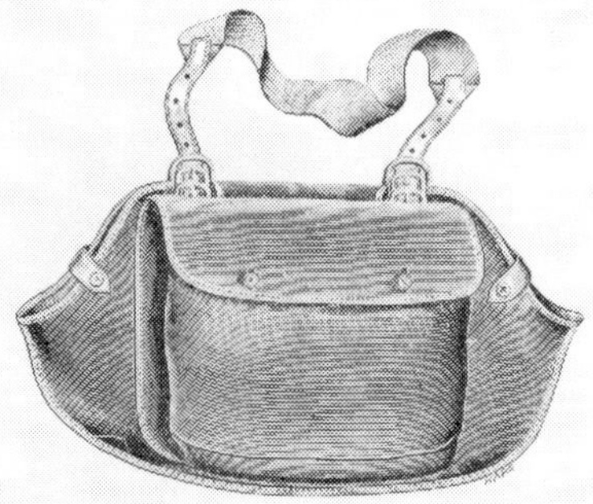

Made in Brown Cotton Duck, with the inside white waterproof enamelled, which can be washed. It is fitted with a detachable bag in front, for carrying fishing requisites, etc. The bag is fitted with straps and buckles in place of the buttons as shown.

Sizes in inches	20 × 12	22 × 13	24 × 14	30 × 18
	32/-	35/6	40/-	44/-

The "TAY" Salmon Bag

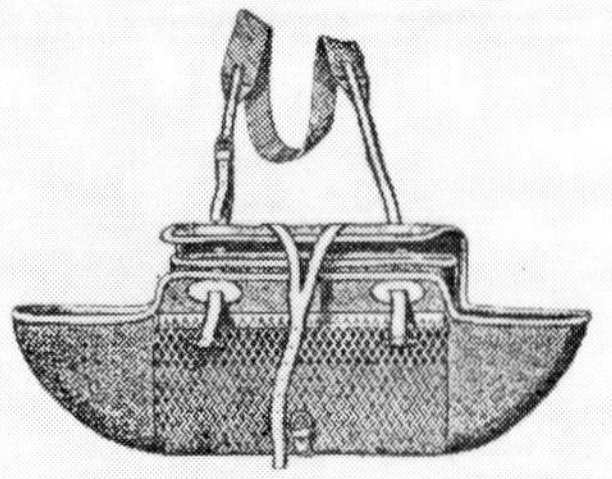

Made of the best Brown Duck, white waterproof enamelled inside, and with net on outside, and an inside compartment for tackle, etc. The expanding gussets when not in use can be folded into the bag.

Sizes in inches	32 × 10½	36 × 12	40 × 14	44 × 15
	33/-	36/6	41/-	45/-

FOR THE "PERFECT" SALMON FLY REEL, SEE PAGE 132.

The "COQUET" Trout Bag

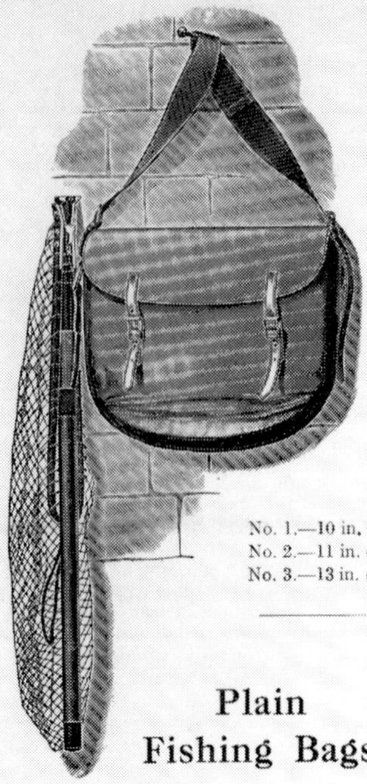

Made of stout waterproof material, with two full-sized compartments; the inner one, intended for fish, is waterproof lined inside, the outer being intended for tackle, lunch, etc.

The special features are:

(1) The shoulder strap has provision made to carry a waterproof coat in the military fashion when desired.

(2) The waterproof cover or lid of bag can be detached and used as a seat. It is a plain but very practical arrangement.

(3) Ring at side to carry net.

No. 1.—10 in. deep by 12 in. long, **23/6.**
No. 2.—11 in. deep by 14 in. long, **28/6.**
No. 3.—13 in. deep by 16 in. long, **34/6.**

Plain Fishing Bags

A very good bag for boys, or for carrying as an extra bag with lunch, etc. Made of canvas, waterproof lined and fitted with adjustable web shoulder strap. No. 1, **8/-**; **No. 2, 8/6.**

FOR THE "JUNIOR" RODS, SEE PAGE 293.

The "ALLINONE" Fly Fisher's Case

CONTAINS:

FLY BOX—CAST CASE—CAST DAMPER AND SPORTSMAN'S BALANCE

The case is divided into compartments, **B** to hold an Aluminium Fly Box; **A**, a Chamois Leather and Parchment three-pocket Cast Case, and **C**, a Cast Damper with felt pads. On the Cover is a pocket to hold a Sportsman's Balance.

No. 1. For Salmon, with the "USK" box (see page 97), Cast Case, Damper Pouch and No. 687 Sportsman's Balance to weigh 30 lbs. × ½ lb., **37/6** each.

No. 2. For Sea Trout and Trout, with No. 6 box (page 98), Cast Case, Damper Pouch, and No. 684½ Balance to weigh 4 lb. × 1 oz., **32/6 each.**

FOR RODS, SEE PAGE 222.

The "UNIQUE" Salmon Fly Cabinet

A very handsome and convenient Mahogany Cabinet, 10½ in. high by 9¾ in. wide by 6¾ in. deep, fitted with ten Salmon Fly Trays with clips to hold 270 flies. The trays have washable tablets, on which may be written the names of the flies. The space at bottom has a perforated lid to hold albo carbon, to keep away moths. The cabinet is made with a lid, to lock in front of trays. Sunk brass handle and name plate. Price **£6 15s. 6d.**

If fitted with one or more of the Trays with clips for Sea Trout Flies. Price **8/6** to **10/6** per tray extra.

Solid Leather Case, with Handle Straps and Lock complete. To contain cabinet. Made to order only. Price £4 17s. 6d.

Any particular tray can be taken out without disturbing the others, a vast improvement over the old-fashioned box, with trays dropping in one over the other, in which the particular fly wanted was often in the bottom tray, necessitating the removal of all the others to get to it.

FOR SALMON FLIES, SEE PAGE 69.

The "J. T. E." General Angler's Box

With Tackles Ready for Use, etc.

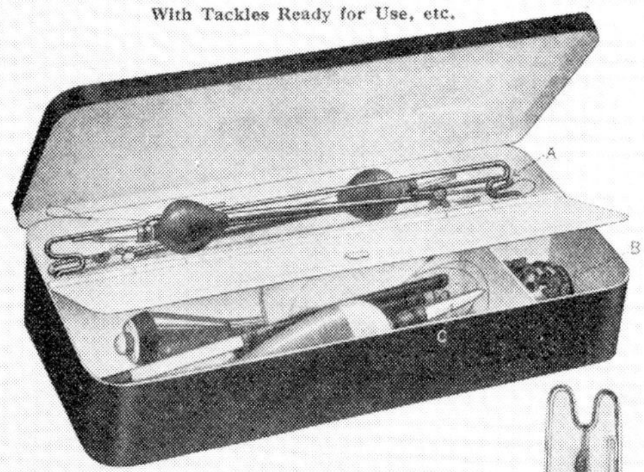

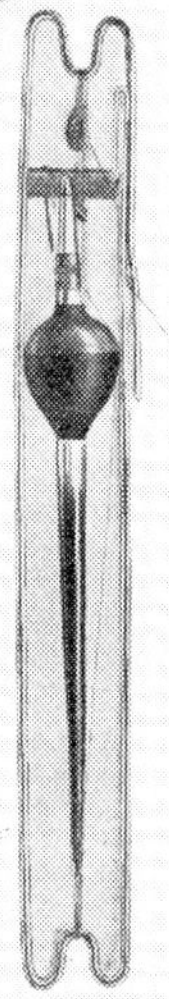

The "J. T. E." Carrier mounted. Regd. No. 717226.

This bottom fisher's outfit has been developed by Mr. J. T. Emery. As listed it is a general equipment, but may be had in any variation to suit individual requirements.

The " J. T. E. " Carrier for mounted tackles is neat and simple, the hook being held in a pad is protected.

The box is made of Japanned Tin, size $6\frac{1}{2} \times 3\frac{3}{4} \times 1\frac{1}{2}$ in. with division **A** to hold 6 mounted tackles, **B** for split shot and float caps, and **C** (which has a movable partition), for floats, gut bottoms, hooks to gut, etc.

The outfit supplied with the box is four float and two ledger tackles on " J.T.E. " carriers, 6 gut bottoms, 2 doz. hooks to gut, coil of lead wire, box of split shot, 1 doz. No. 5 " Simplex " leads, 6 float caps and two ledger bars.

The mounted tackles, which are leaded ready for use, are—

No. **1.**—1 yd. bottom, No. 9 " Sidebarb " hook, pat. J. float.

No. **2.**—1 yd. bottom, No. 9 " Sidebarb," 4 in. pat. A float.

No. **3.**—1 yd. bottom, pat. K hook, $3\frac{1}{2}$ in. pat. C. float.

No. **4.**—2 yd. bottom, No. 8 hook " Pennell " tackle, 3 in. pat. D float.

No. **5.**—Heavy Ledger, 18 in. bottom, No. 8 " Pennell " tackle, Ledger bar with $\frac{1}{2}$ in. bullet.

No. **6.**—Light Ledger, 18 in. bottom, No. 2 " Pennell " tackle, Ledger bar, with five $\frac{1}{8}$ in. bullets.

Price complete, **21/-**.

Prices separately, Box, **6/-**, " J. T. E." Carriers, $6\frac{1}{2}$ in. for float tackles ; $3\frac{1}{2}$ in. for ledgers, **3d.** each ; Ledger bars $2\frac{3}{4}$ in. with leads, **2d.** each.

See pages, Floats, 178 " Simplex " leads, 200 ; Pierced bullets, 201 ; Hooks to gut, 175 and 176.

FOR THE "GENERAL" ROD, SEE PAGE 298.

Hardy's "SECURITY" Fly Holder

Pat. No. 18086.

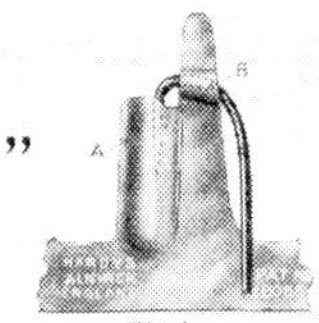

Fig 1.

Pat. No. 18086.

An improved holder for carrying flies in a box. The advantages are, the flies are securely held in correct position (compare Fig. 2 and Fig. 3), while the point and barb of the hook are perfectly protected. In fixing a fly, the point of the hook must enter the shield at **A**, before it is pulled into the clip at **B**, Fig. 1.

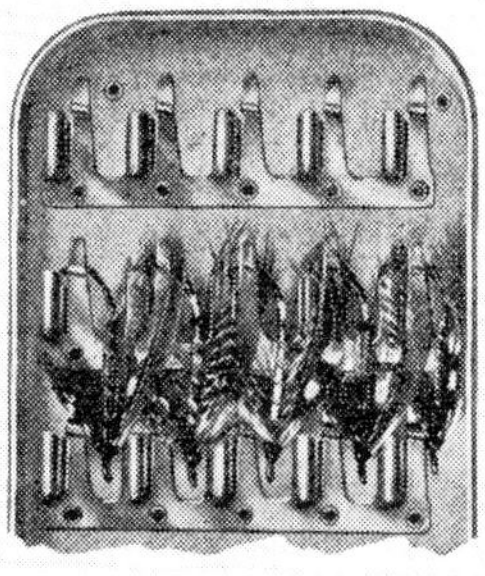

Fig. 2.—The " Security," showing all flies in correct position with points and barbs protected.

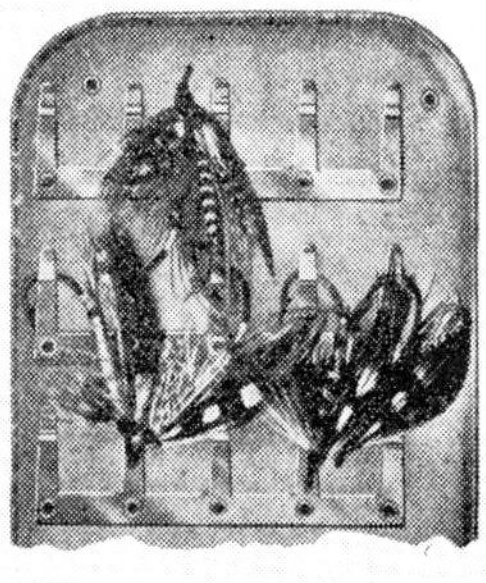

Fig. 3.—The old way, showing how the flies may be disarranged and point and barb broken.

Aluminium Salmon Fly Boxes fitted with pat. "Security" Clips

The " CREE."—8 in. by 4 in. by $1\frac{1}{2}$ in., to hold 50 single or double flies, sizes Nos. 7 to 2/0 hooks, and 32 single flies, sizes 2/0 to 6/0, **31/-.**

The " NAVER."—7 in. by $3\frac{3}{8}$ in. by $\frac{3}{4}$ in., to hold 30 single or double flies, sizes 7 to 2/0, and 12 single flies, sizes 2/0 to 6/0, **14/-.**

The " USK."—6 in. by $3\frac{3}{8}$ in. by 1 in., to hold 40 single or double flies, sizes 7 to 2/0, **10/-.**

The "DART."—$4\frac{3}{4}$ in. by $3\frac{3}{8}$ in. by $\frac{5}{8}$ in., to hold 30 single flies, sizes 7 to 2/0, or 30 double flies, 7 to 4, **8/6.**

FOR THE " LOW WATER " SERIES SALMON FLIES, SEE PAGE 71.

The "HALFORD" Dry Fly Boxes

MADE OF JAPANNED TIN

No. 1.

MAY FLY BOX.

Size, $7\frac{1}{4} \times 3\frac{1}{2}$ in. $\times \frac{7}{8}$ in.

Price 22/6

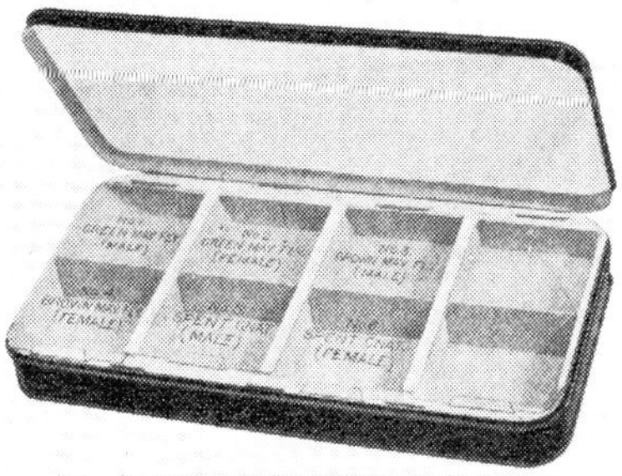

No. 2.

SMALL FLY BOX.

Size, $5\frac{3}{4}$ in. $\times 4$ in. $\times 1\frac{3}{16}$ in.

Price 35/-

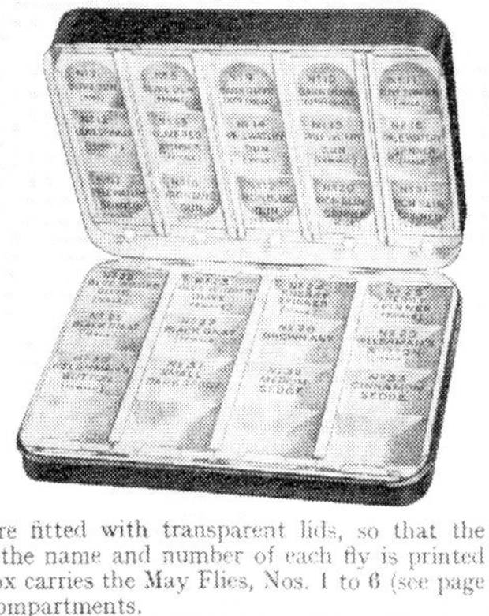

The compartments are fitted with transparent lids, so that the flies may be seen, while the name and number of each fly is printed on the lid. The No. 1 box carries the May Flies, Nos. 1 to 6 (see page 65), and has two spare compartments.

The No. 2 Box holds the flies Nos. 7 to 33 (see page 60), and has four spare compartments.

The idea of the boxes is educational as well as general handiness ; everyone does not know his " Halford " by heart, nor can he remember the various flies. By using these boxes, however, he soon becomes acquainted with the flies and their spinners by the constant reference.

Supplied with unprinted lids at same prices.

FOR THE " DRIFLYDRESSER," SEE PAGE 80,

The "J. W. DUNNE" Dry Fly Boxes

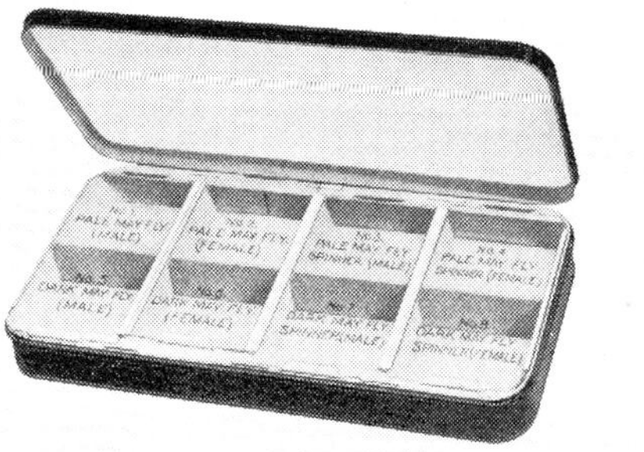

No. 1.

We will make any of our Fly Boxes in silver or gold for presentation

No. 2.

Made of Japanned Tin and arranged to carry the " J. W. Dunne " dry flies, see page 62. Fitted with transparent lids, so that the flies may be seen and on which the number and name of each fly is printed.

No. 1. The May Fly Box, size $7\frac{1}{4} \times 3\frac{1}{2} \times \frac{7}{8}$ in. carries the May Flies. Price **22/6** each.

No. 2. The Small Box, size $5\frac{3}{4} \times 4 \times 1\frac{3}{16}$ in. holds the remainder of the series. Price **35/-** each.

FOR SUITABLE GUT CASTS, SEE PAGE 105.

194 HARDY BROTHERS LIMITED

The "COMPACTUM" Case

For carrying Artificial Baits, Natural Bait Tackles, Traces, Leads, Spare Hooks, etc.

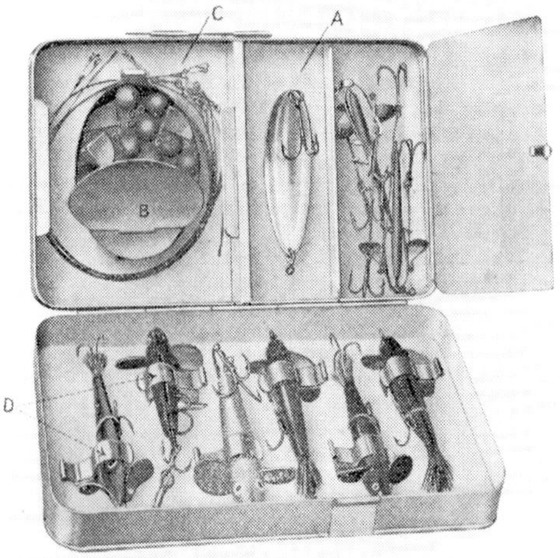

Made in Japanned Tin, and designed to carry all that is required for spinning. The method of holding the baits is novel, and permits of easy selection, while it prevents the baits being entangled and damaged.

Each size will hold 6 phantoms, devons or minnows, securely held in a spring clip, see **D.** The division **A,** which has a movable partition, holds spoons, natural bait tackles, devon mounts, etc., while **C** is for traces and **B** for leads, swivels, spare hooks, etc.

No. 1.—Size $7\frac{1}{4}$ ins. by $4\frac{1}{2}$ ins. by $2\frac{1}{16}$ ins. Price **21/-** each.
No. 2.—Size 6 ins. by $3\frac{3}{4}$ ins. by $1\frac{1}{4}$ ins. Price 17/6 each.

FOR LEADS, SEE PAGE 198, Etc.

FISHING TACKLE MANUFACTURERS, ALNWICK 195

Hardy's New "Multum-in-Parvo" SPINNERS BOX

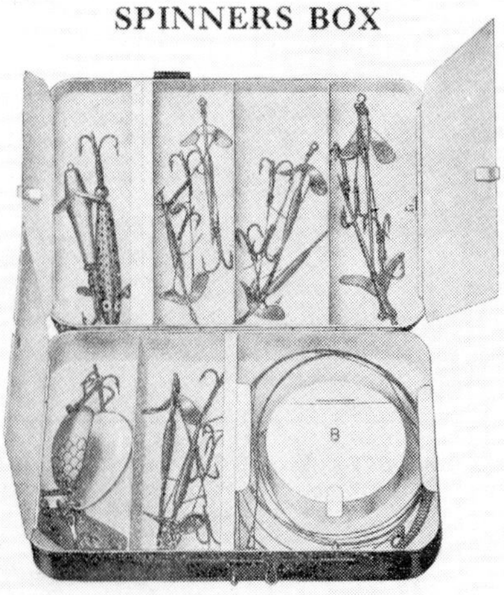

Made in Japanned tin. As the partitions are movable, the compartments may be arranged to hold a large assortment of artificial baits, natural bait tackles and traces. The circular box **B** holds leads, spare hooks, swivels, etc.

The lid cover is fitted with guides in which the movable partitions are carried when not in use.

The three right-hand spaces in the lid may be converted into two large horizontal compartments, and the two compartments in the bottom of box made into one large space.

A practical and useful box :

No. 1.—Size $7\frac{1}{4}$ ins. × $4\frac{1}{2}$ ins. × $2\frac{1}{16}$ ins. Price **22/6** each.
No. 2.—Size 6 ins. × $3\frac{3}{4}$ ins. × $1\frac{13}{16}$ ins. Price **19/6** each.

FOR "PUNJAB" TRACES, SEE PAGE 113.

FISHING TACKLE MANUFACTURERS, ALNWICK 93

The "TEST (MONTAGU)" Fly Box

WITH CAST DAMPER
(Registered No. 654474)

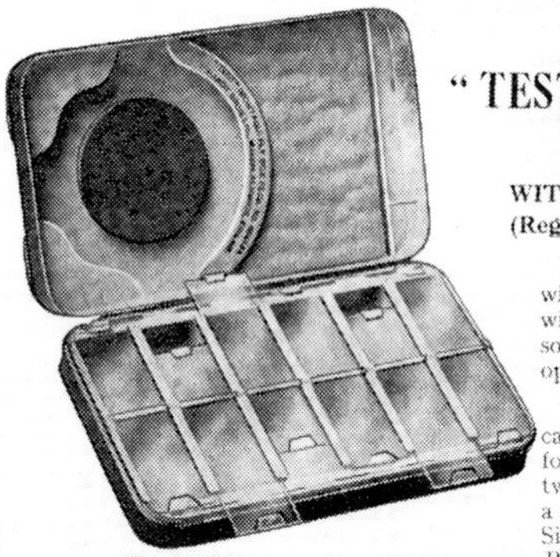

Fig. 1.—Shows the Interior

Made of Japanned Tin with twelve compartments with transparent lids, made so that one space only is open at a time.

The lid has a space for casts, a felt and a cork pad for flies, and space for tweezers. On the outside is a damping pouch, see Fig. 2. Size $5\frac{1}{4}$ in. × $3\frac{1}{4}$ in. × $1\frac{1}{4}$ in. Price **32/6** each. Tweezers, **2/6** per pair.

The *Field* writes :—"This seems to us a really excellent box, on which its sponsors are to be congratulated. We know from sad experience how trouble comes from the accumulation of separate items required in fishing. The more such items can be combined (within reason) the better."

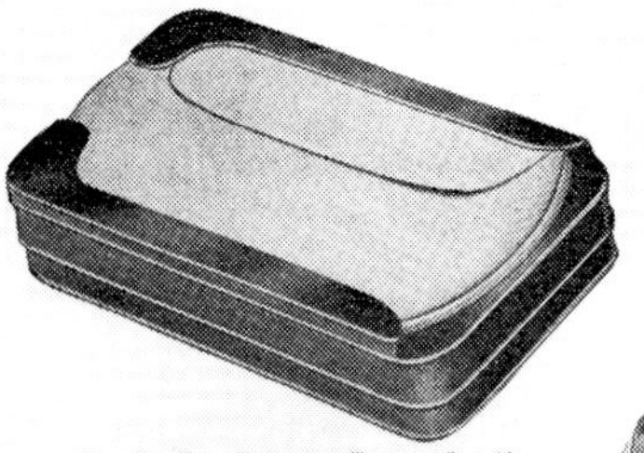

Fig. 2.—The Damping Pouch, Outside.

The "ALLSEEN" Eyed Fly Box

Japanned Tin, with 12 compartments with **transparent** sliding lids.

Size—5 in. × $3\frac{1}{4}$ in. × $\frac{7}{8}$ in.

Price **14/6** each.

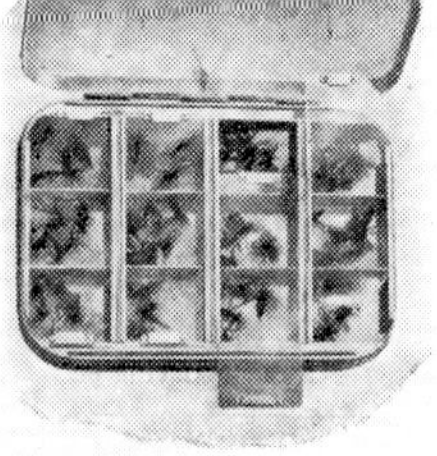

94 HARDY BROTHERS LIMITED

The "GLENNOE" Mounted Cast Case

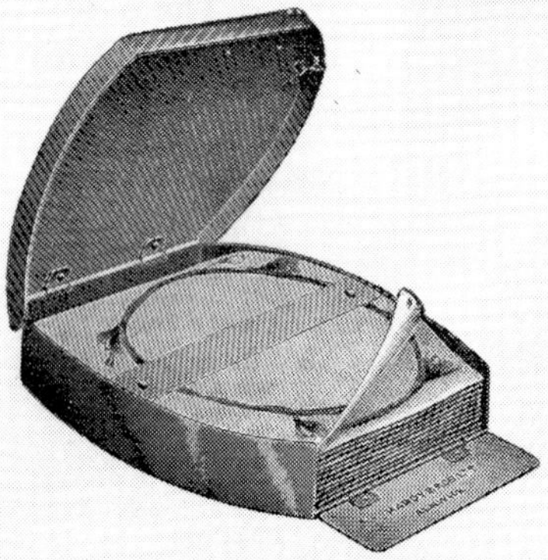

Made of Japanned Tin and fitted with twelve leaves to hold mounted casts. Each cast is held by a keeper, and is separate from its neighbour. By this arrangement the casts and flies cannot possibly entangle.

The box is of convenient shape to fit into a coat pocket. Size, $4\frac{1}{2}$ in. × $4\frac{1}{2}$ in. Price **8/6** each.

Aluminium Eyed Fly Box

WITH TRANSPARENT SPRING LIDS

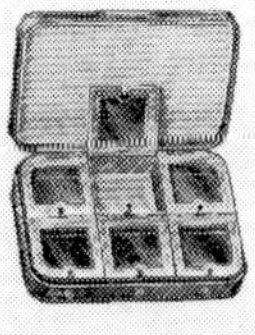

$3\frac{1}{2}$" Box with six compartments and washable contents tablet in lid. Price - - - **7/-** each.
$4\frac{3}{4}$" Box with twelve compartments and felt drying pad in lid. Price - - - **8/6** ,,
6" Box with sixteen compartments and felt drying pad in lid. Price - - - **11/6** ,,

FOR DRY FLIES, GENERAL PATTERNS, SEE PAGE 64.

The "CARRY ALL" Case

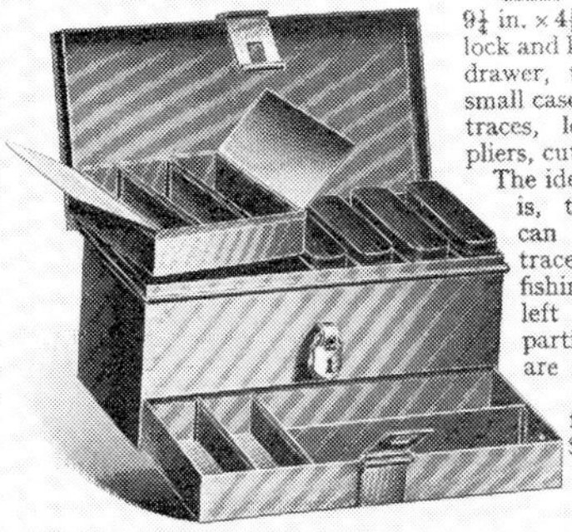

Made of Japanned Tin, size 9¼ in. × 4⅝ in. × 4¾ in., with padlock and key. Fitted with large drawer, three trays and four small cases, to hold 3 doz. baits, traces, leads, hooks, swivels, pliers, cutters, etc.

The idea of this arrangement is, that the small cases can be filled with baits, traces, etc., for the day's fishing, and the stock box left at home. The partitions in the trays are movable. Price **50/-**

Pliers and Cutters for wire work, etc. Size 3½ ins. Price **1/9**

Box to Carry Mounted Natural Baits

A plain aluminium box with hinged lid in two sizes. Each box is supplied with two felt pads which are damped in cold water to keep the baits fresh. It is very convenient to mount up a selection of baits before leaving home especially in cold weather and have them ready at the water side.

Size 8″ × 4½″ × 2″ - **12/6** Size 6″ × 4″ × 1½″ - **10/6**

Also in Japanned Tin, 6½″ × 3¾″ × 1″, price, 7/6 each.

The "HOUGHTON" Eyed Fly and Cast Box

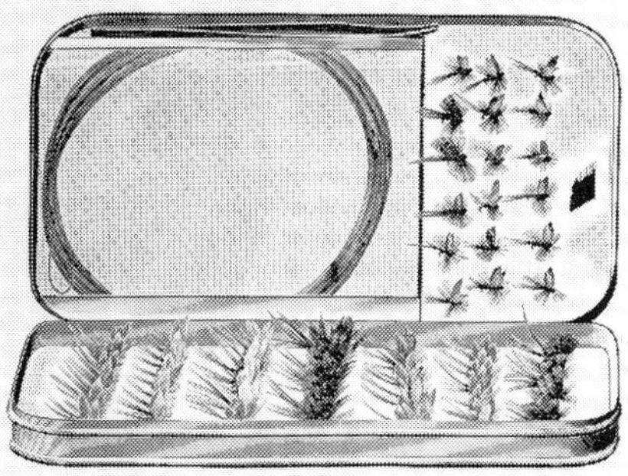

Made of **Japanned Tin**, with felt lining. Will hold 20 doz. eyed flies and one doz. gut casts. Size, 7 × 3⅝ × ⅞ ins. Price **14/-**.

With corrugated cork bars, instead of felt lining, **16/6**. "Pennell" Fly Tweezers and Cutters, **2/6** extra.

The "GIRODON PRALON" Fly Boxes

MADE OF JAPANNED TIN

"**Improved G.P.**" with washable tablet. The name of the fly is written against the number for reference. **A**—Division to hold tweezers

No. 1. 6 × 3½ × ⅞ in. with 15 compartments, **23/6**.

No. 2. 4 × 3 × ¾ in. with 9 compartments, **19/-**.

PLAIN PATTERN without tablet and with plain lids. **No. 1.** Size as above Price **18/6**.

No. 2. Size as above. Price **13/-**. "Pennell" Fly Tweezers and Cutters, **2/6** extra.

Hardy's "RELEASE" Leads

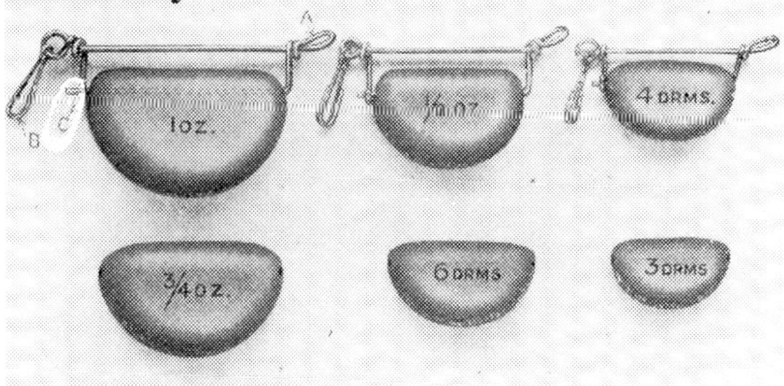

An Antikink lead, which can be released from the mount when caught between the rocks, etc., and so free the trace and the tackle; the lead only being lost. A steady pull of about 4 lbs. on the reel line, which is attached to the eye A, will disengage the catch C from the end of the carrier bar, and so free the trace. At B is fitted a link spring for easy attachment to the swivel or loop of the trace. Each carrier is supplied with two leads of different weights as illustrated. After releasing the carrier, it is advisable to bend outwards the bar carrying the lead before fixing a new lead in place so as to ensure a good hold at C. Price, No. 1 with leads 1 oz. and ¾ oz., **1/-** each; No. 2 leads ½ oz. and 6 drms., **1/-** each; No. 3 leads 4 and 3 drms., **10d.** each.

Spare leads, 1 oz., ¾ oz., ½ oz., 6 drms. Price, **4/-** per doz. 4 drms., 3 drms., **3/-** per doz.

Lead Carrier for use in Rocky Rivers

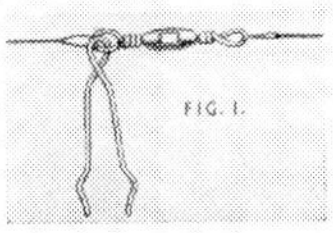

FIG. 1.

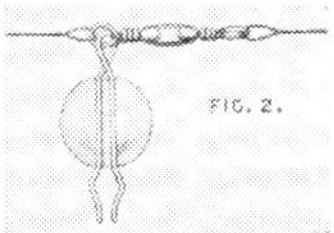

FIG. 2.

Regd. No. 710935.

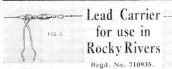

A Spring Clip Carrier for use when spinning, trolling or prawning in rocky rivers. The carrier is attached to the trace by springing it into the eye of a swivel as in Fig. 1. In Fig. 2, a pierced bullet is shown fixed on the carrier, the arms being passed through the hole in the lead.

If when using the carrier the lead gets fast, all one has to do is to give a steady pull and the carrier is pulled out of the lead. This saves breakage of trace, etc.: the only loss being the lead.

To carry pierced bullets	No. 1. ¼ oz.	No. 2. ⅜ oz.	No. 3. ½ oz.	No. 4. ¾ oz.
Price per dozen carriers	**1/4**	**1/4**	**1/6**	**1/6**

FOR "PUNJAB" WIRE, SEE PAGE 112

Rod Rest for Trolling or Sea Fishing

The socket and spindle with pinching screw permits the direction of the rod to be altered, while the arms are so arranged that the angle of the rod can be adjusted as desired. Price, **15/6** each.

The 'Ford' Fish Carrier

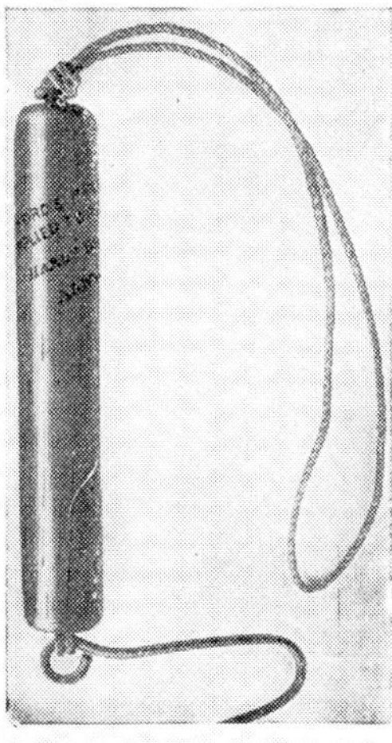

The "Ford" Carrier in use.

The cord loop is put over the base of the tail and the wood handle passed through, when it grips the part firmly. The fish is then bent until the metal hook can be pushed under the gill cover. Length, 6½ ins. Price, **2/-** each.

FOR THE "TWEED" SALMON BAG, SEE PAGE 326

The "ONVIEW" Fly Book and Mounted Cast Case

Pigskin Cover, with divisions for scissors, etc., and two cover pockets. Fitted with twelve transparent pockets for mounted casts; six unmounted cast pockets marked fine, medium, and strong; two felt leaves. The 5 in. book has twenty-four fly pockets and the 6 in. thirty-six fly pockets.

Size 5 in.—Price **14/6** each. 6 in.—Price **15/6** each.

Circular Cast Boxes and Dampers

1. **JAPANNED TIN,** 4¼ in. by ¾ in.; the left side protected by flanges holds the casts. The right has a waterproof leaf and felt pad, which may be damped and the casts placed between to soften.

Price **6/6** each.

2. **ALUMINIUM,** size 4⅛ × ⅝ in. deep, **3/-** each.

Felt pads—Extra.

Cast Damper and Carrier

Damper Side. Illustration shows the "Damper" Side with a cast lying in one of the felt leaves.

Carrier Side. Illustration shows the "Carrier" side with casts. 7 parchment pockets for carrying spares.

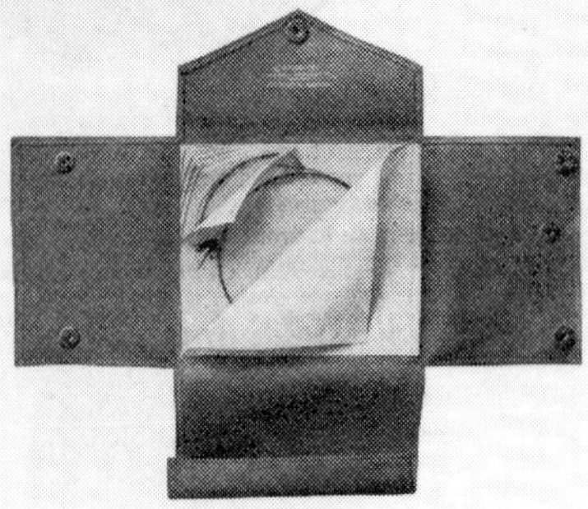

A very compact Cast Carrier and Damper 5″ × 5″. One side is arranged to carry spare casts—mounted and unmounted—in the other side are two felt leaves which are dampened to soften casts intended to be used during the day's fishing. Made of sound waterproof material with rigid back to protect the casts.

Price **5/-** each.

FOR ALUMINIUM SALMON FLY BOXES, SEE PAGE 97.

The "HARDY" Cast Damper

(Regd.)

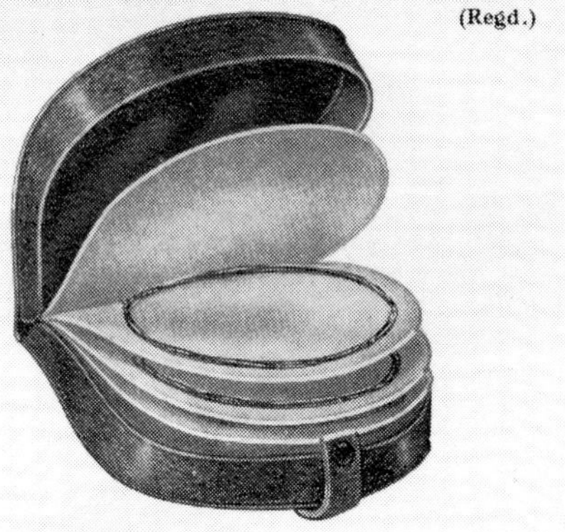

This is a practical and serviceable form of Cast damper which has been used by members of our firm for some years.

The case is made of hide, lined with rubber. The "leaves" or divisions are of felt and are secured by an elastic band and are readily removed to dampen or dry.

Five Casts, salmon or trout, can be carried separately.

Size 4 in. × 4 in. Price, **7/6.**

The "TWEED" Salmon Fisher's Cast Case

Made of Crocodile Calf Leather, in very superior style, with four non-deleterious Chamois Leather Pockets, having parchment flaps, each marked with strength of gut.

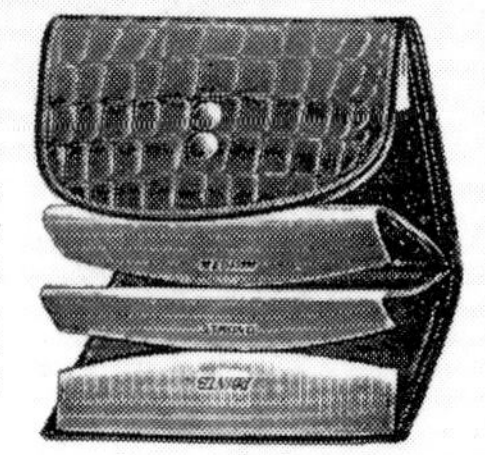

A very compact and excellent case, capable of holding a considerable number of casts, traces, etc. One size only, 6½ inches.

Price **19/-** each.

IN ORDERING FROM THIS LIST, PLEASE QUOTE LETTER L 1.

The "GLEN" Fly and Cast Case

Transparent Pockets for Mounted Casts.

Double leather cover with patent fasteners. Fitted with 12 divisions for flies; 4 transparent pockets for casts and two cover pockets. A handy form of pocket book.

Price **8/6** each. Size 4 × 5½ in.

CAST AND FLY POUCH. Leather cover with parchment leaves. To carry mounted or unmounted casts, flies, hooks, etc. Price **2/9** each.

DOUBLE ZINC BAIT KETTLES, 9 in., **11/10**; 10 in., **13/-**; 11 in., **15/6.**

The "HOUGHTON" Trout Fisher's Cast Case

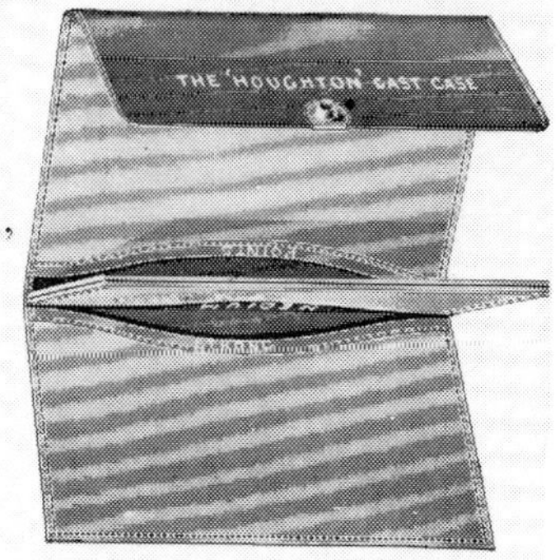

• The four pockets are made of unbleached chamois skin and are marked—strong, medium, fine and points. Selection is rendered easy. We need hardly remind anglers that chamois is the very best of all materials to protect gut in any climate. The cover is solid leather.

Size 6 in. by 4½ in. **11/6** each.

Dry Fly Requisites

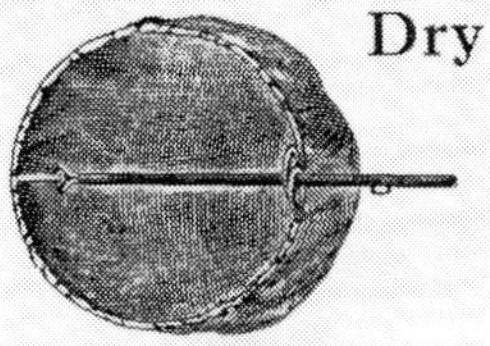

FLY CATCHER

A useful little net, 3½ in. dia. Can be quickly attached to the rod top to pick a natural fly from the water for inspection.

Price **1/3** each.

A perfect preparation for reel lines. It is non-adhesive, clean to handle, keeps the line pliant and in good order. For dry fly work it floats the line perfectly. It may be used to proof the fly, by gently rubbing on wings and hackle.

Waterproof dressed spinning lines keep in good condition when rubbed over with "Cerolene."

Undressed lines may be proofed by steeping in melted "Cerolene." In addition, it is excellent for cleaning reels, etc. Price **1/-** per tin.

KNEE PAD

Made of grained cowhide, with pad and two straps for buckling on. A great protection when kneeling on wet grass, gravel, or loose sand.

Price **9/6** each.

THE "CURATE." (Regd. 557672.)

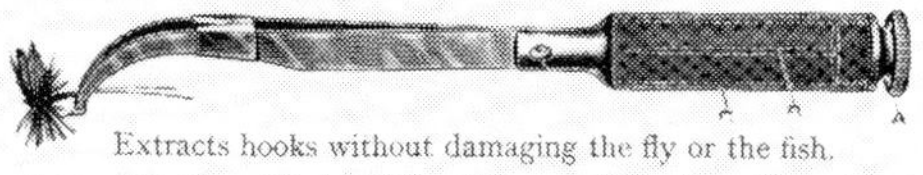

Extracts hooks without damaging the fly or the fish.

A combination of the following useful anglers' tools.—Small Priest; Tweezers, or a disgorger; Gut Cutter **E**; Reservoir **C**, to hold oil for reels; Stiletto **B**, to apply oil or clean the eye of a hook. The handle may be used as a match striker. Price **6/6** each.

FOR SPINNING LINES, SEE PAGE 124.

The "DRIANOIL" Dry Fly Drier and Oiler

The case is fitted on one side with Amadou to dry a damp fly and on the other with a pad of felt to hold odourless paraffin or "Cerolene," on which the fly is pressed to prepare it before using.

Price **5/6** each.

EXACT SIZE.

"**Amadou,**" an excellent absorbent to use for drying water-logged flies.

Price **1/-** per piece.

Waistcoat Pocket Fly Oil Bottle

A convenient form for the waistcoat pocket. The interior is fitted with a long sleeve, which prevents the oil flowing back when filled to line mark.

PRICE **4/6** each.

POCKET LINE GREASER

For rubbing down dry fly or spinning lines with "Cerolene." Price **1/3** each.

A dry fly preparation which is perfectly clean and harmless to feathers or wax. It has no stickiness like the usual dry fly oils, and is an absolutely perfect preparation for floating flies. As it does not discolour the fly, the full effect of all the delicate colourings is retained. Price **1/-** per bottle.

Note.—This preparation cannot be sent abroad by post.

"SUNSHINE" OIL, FOR "DUNNE" DRY FLIES, SEE PAGE 62. PRICE 1/- PER BOTTLE.

The "DRIFLYDRESER" Pat. No. 19101/25.

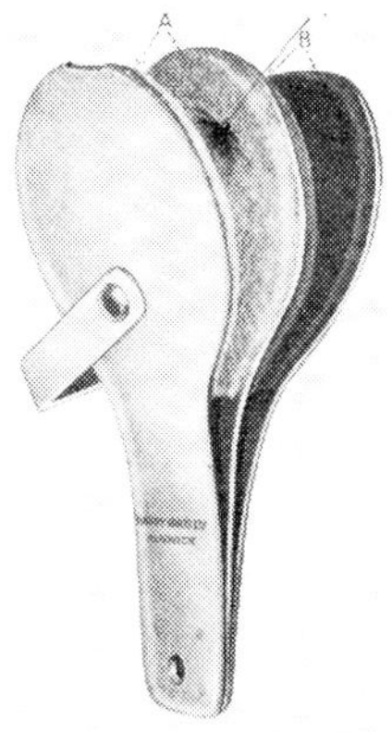

This novel arrangement is, without doubt, the handiest and most convenient form of dry fly dresser. It hangs from the coat, and consequently is always at hand when required, while it relieves the necessity for carrying bottles, etc.

It is shown in use. The leaves **AA** are fitted with pads of Amadou to dry a fly, and **BB** with prepared felt to proof it. All that is required is to place the fly between **AA** or **BB** as may be desired and press the leaves together with the finger and thumb. Price **4/6** each.

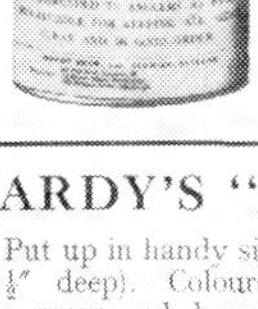

"RUSTPRUF"

A preparation for applying to steel articles to prevent them being attacked by rust.

… per bo…

HARDY'S "CELLULOSE VARNISH"

Put up in handy sized tins (2¼" dia. × 1½" deep). Colours—black, white, blue, green, red, brown, yellow, silver, gold and clear. Handy for all sorts of jobs—Can be used for varnishing to protect reels, rods, painting spoons, baits, etc.—See all traces of grease and dirt are removed before applying the varnish. Dries in a few minutes.

Price per tin **1/6** each.

Brushes to apply varnish to baits, reels, rods, etc., etc. Price **9d.** each.

TWEEZERS, GUT CUTTER AND DISGORGER

A useful article for cutting off gut ends, or extracting flies from the box or fish. The handle end is formed as a disgorger and turn screw. Illustration is actual size. Price **3/6** each.

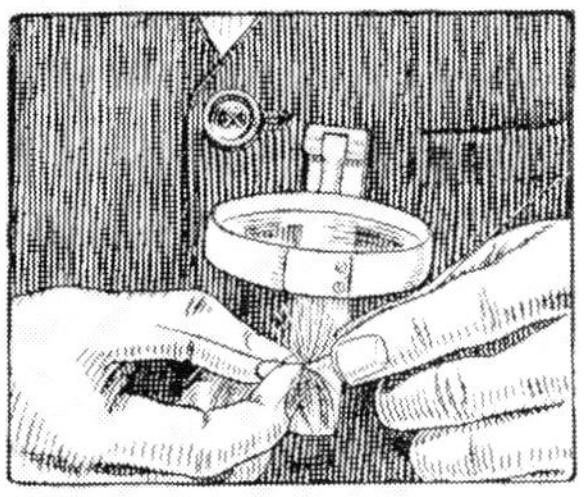

The "WARDLE" MAGNIFIER

Regd. No. 704251.

We are indebted to Major Wardle for this excellent idea. The magnifier is carried by a safety pin fastening to the coat and is always handy for immediate use. When not in use it closes up against the body quite out of the way.

Price **13/-** each.

ANTI-MIDGE

A healthy, clean compound of essential oils, pleasant in odour, and without the slightest deleterious effect on the skin. Some form of midge preventative is a necessity for anglers, and this compound does all that is required. The bottle which is fitted with a sprinkler stopper is of a convenient form to fit the waistcoat pocket.

Price **1/3** each.

FOR TERMS OF BUSINESS, SEE PAGE 5.

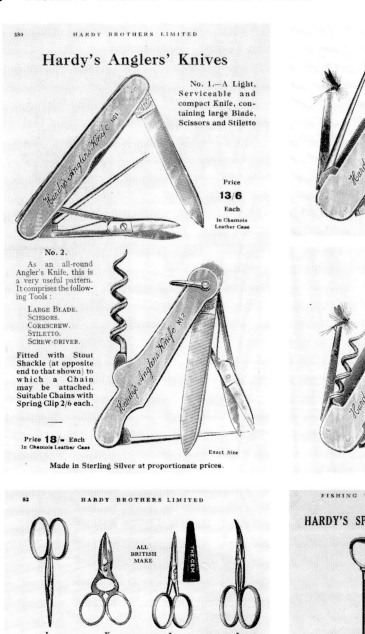

Hardy's Anglers' Knives

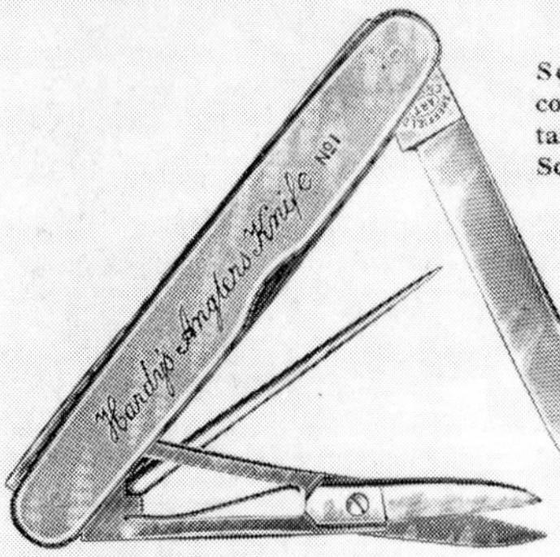

No. 1.—A Light, Serviceable and compact Knife, containing large Blade, Scissors and Stiletto

Price **13/6** Each
In Chamois Leather Case

No. 2.

As an all-round Angler's Knife, this is a very useful pattern. It comprises the following Tools:

LARGE BLADE.
SCISSORS.
CORKSCREW.
STILETTO.
SCREW-DRIVER.

Fitted with Stout Shackle (at opposite end to that shown) to which a Chain may be attached. Suitable Chains with Spring Clip 2/6 each.

Price **18/-** Each
In Chamois Leather Case

Exact Size

Made in Sterling Silver at proportionate prices.

Price **24/-** Each
In Chamois Leather Case

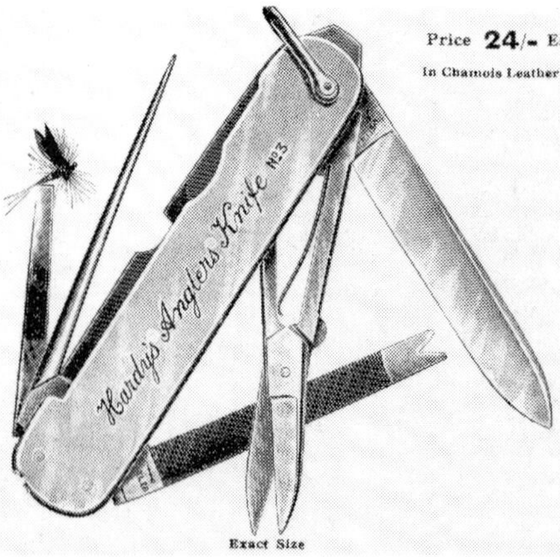

Exact Size

Price 27/6 each
In Chamois Leather Case

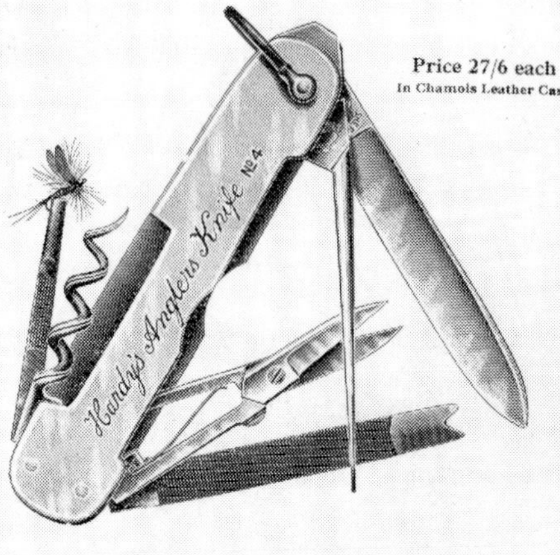

Exact Size

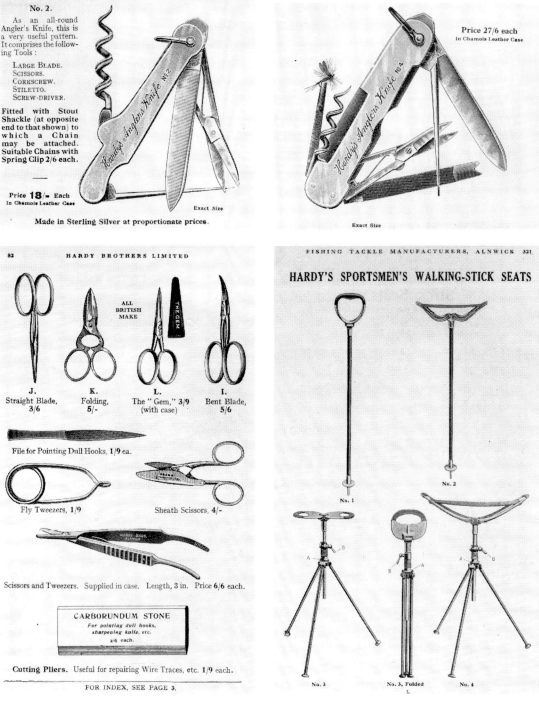

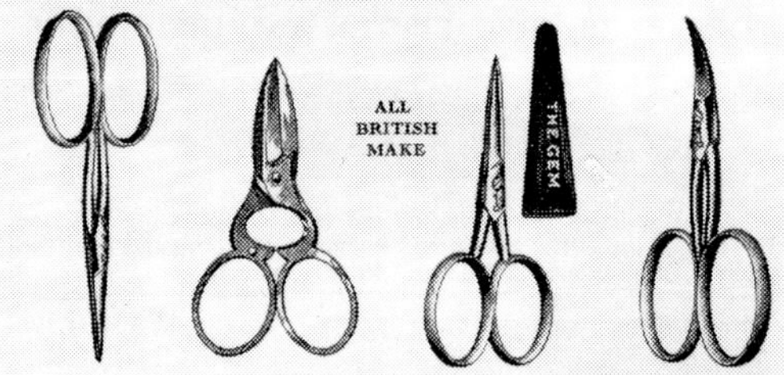

J.	K.	L.	I.
Straight Blade, **3/6**	Folding, **5/-**	The "Gem," **3/9** (with case)	Bent Blade, **5/6**

File for Pointing Dull Hooks, **1/9** ea.

Fly Tweezers, **1/9**

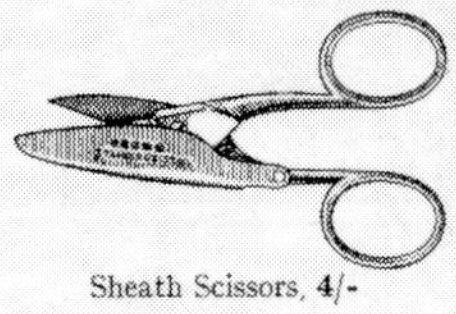

Sheath Scissors, **4/-**

Scissors and Tweezers. Supplied in case. Length, 3 in. Price **6/6** each.

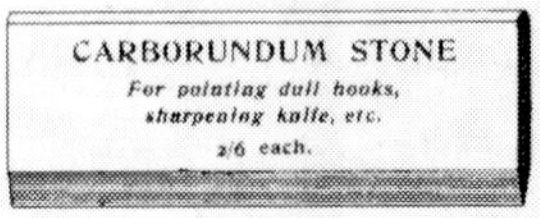

CARBORUNDUM STONE
For pointing dull hooks, sharpening knife, etc.
2/6 each.

Cutting Pliers. Useful for repairing Wire Traces, etc. **1/9** each.

FOR INDEX, SEE PAGE 3.

HARDY'S SPORTSMEN'S WALKING-STICK SEATS

No. 1

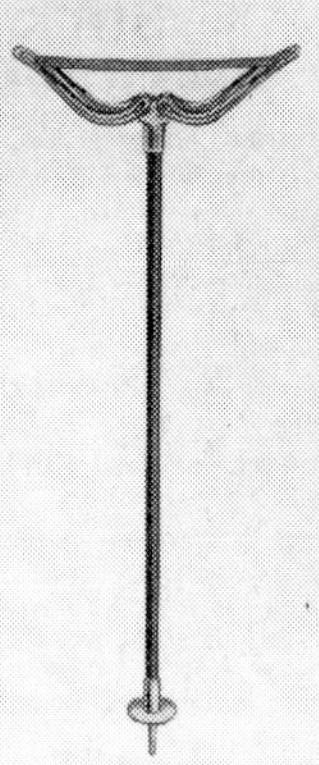

No. 2

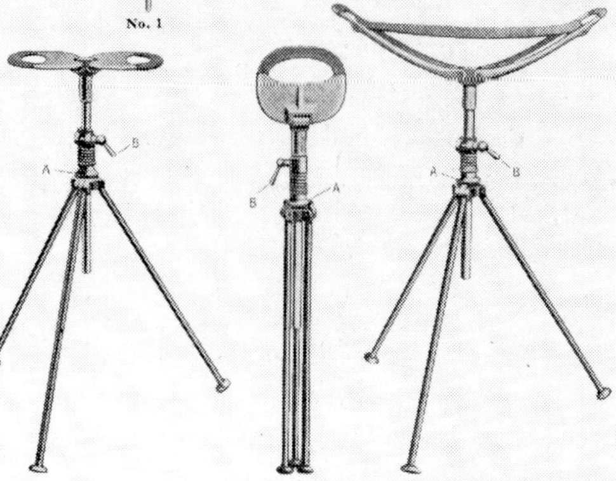

No. 3 No. 3, Folded No. 4

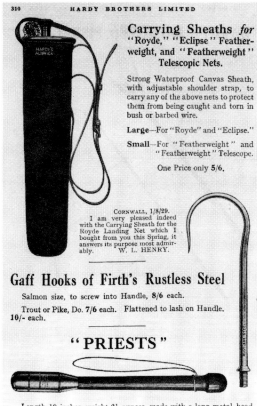

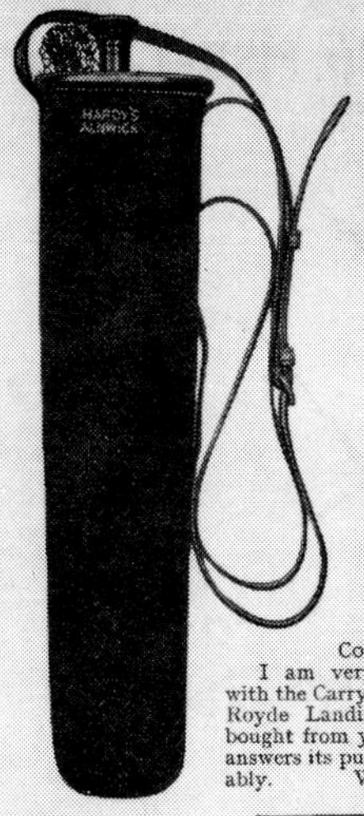

Carrying Sheaths *for* "Royde," "Eclipse" Featherweight, and "Featherweight" Telescopic Nets.

Strong Waterproof Canvas Sheath, with adjustable shoulder strap, to carry any of the above nets to protect them from being caught and torn in bush or barbed wire.

Large—For "Royde" and "Eclipse."

Small—For "Featherweight" and "Featherweight" Telescope.

One Price only **5/6.**

CORNWALL, 1/8/29.
I am very pleased indeed with the Carrying Sheath for the Royde Landing Net which I bought from you this Spring, it answers its purpose most admirably. W. L. HENRY.

Gaff Hooks of Firth's Rustless Steel

Salmon size, to screw into Handle, **8/6** each.

Trout or Pike, Do. **7/6** each. Flattened to lash on Handle. **10/-** each.

"PRIESTS"

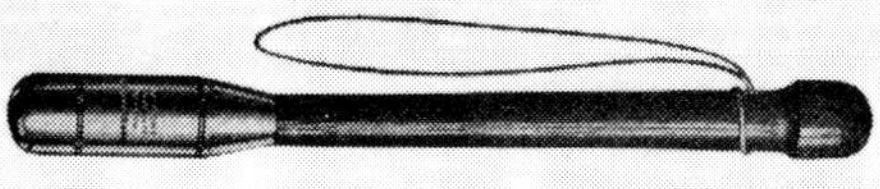

Length 10 inches, weight 6½ ounces, made with a long metal head heavy enough to dispatch a salmon or pike. Price, **5/-** each.

For trout, weight 2¼ ounces, length 9 inches. Price **3/6** each.

FOR THE "CURATE," SEE PAGE 78.

The "FEATHERWEIGHT" Landing Nets

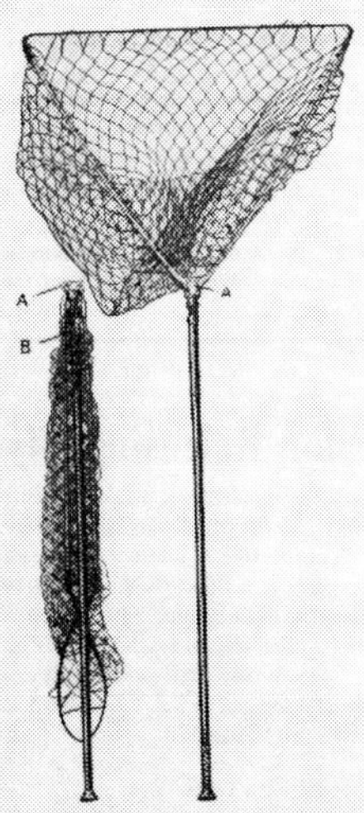

FIG. 1.—NON-TELESCOPIC.
Length Folded - 27 ins.
Open - - - 39½ ins.
Weight - - - 9 ozs.

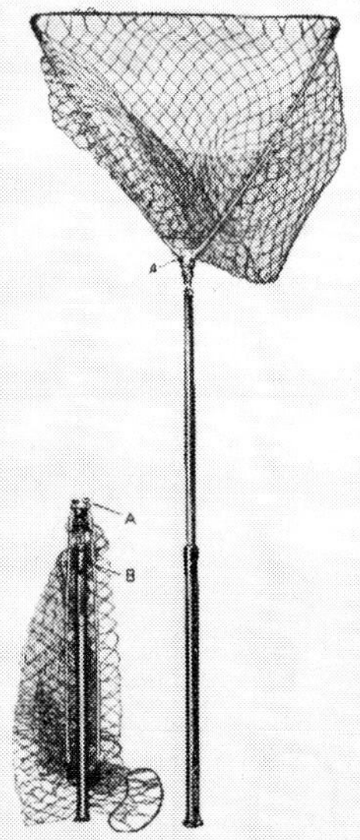

FIG. 2.—TELESCOPIC.
Length Closed, 18 ins. overall.
Extended and Open - 44 ins.
Weight, - - - 14 ozs.

A light folding net made to meet the requirements of those who favour a "light" kit. The action is similar to the "Improved Royde," page 311. It is a strong light little net of convenient type. The net is solid plaited hook-proof silk. The length of arms is 15 ins. Price, non-telescopic, Fig. 1, **35/6.** With telescopic handle, Fig. 2, measuring when closed, 18 inches over all, Price **47/6.** Carrying Sling, **2/6 extra.**

FOR "FEATHERWEIGHT" RODS, SEE PAGE 267.

The "COQUET" Landing Net

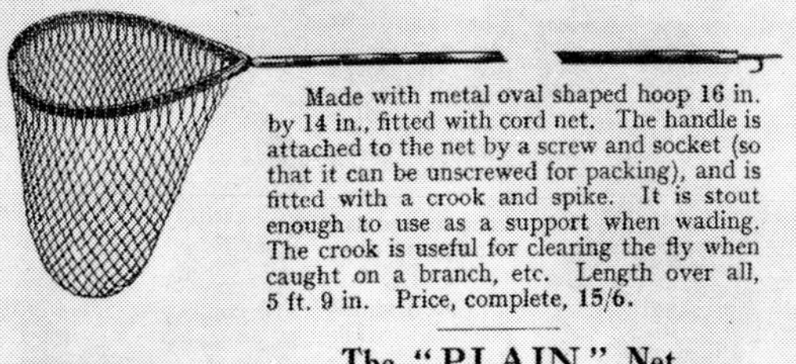

Made with metal oval shaped hoop 16 in. by 14 in., fitted with cord net. The handle is attached to the net by a screw and socket (so that it can be unscrewed for packing), and is fitted with a crook and spike. It is stout enough to use as a support when wading. The crook is useful for clearing the fly when caught on a branch, etc. Length over all, 5 ft. 9 in. Price, complete, **15/6.**

The "PLAIN" Net

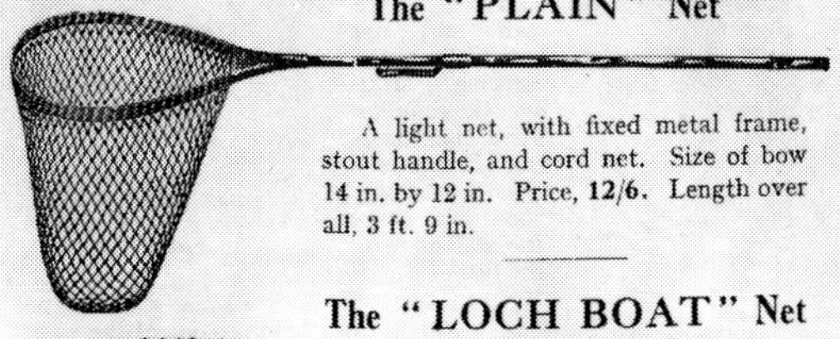

A light net, with fixed metal frame, stout handle, and cord net. Size of bow 14 in. by 12 in. Price, **12/6.** Length over all, 3 ft. 9 in.

The "LOCH BOAT" Net

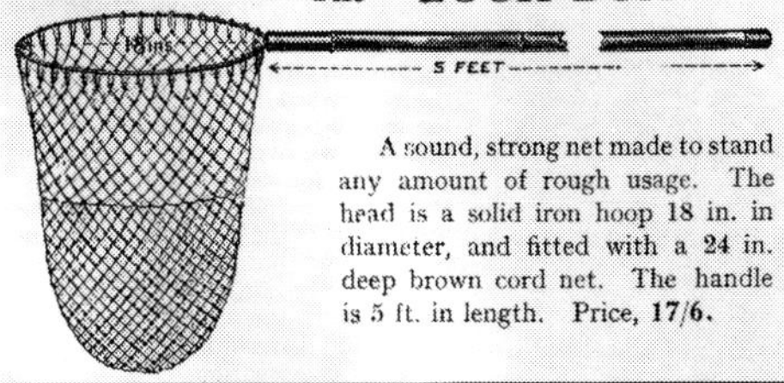

A sound, strong net made to stand any amount of rough usage. The head is a solid iron hoop 18 in. in diameter, and fitted with a 24 in. deep brown cord net. The handle is 5 ft. in length. Price, **17/6.**

The "WETHERED" Net Carrier

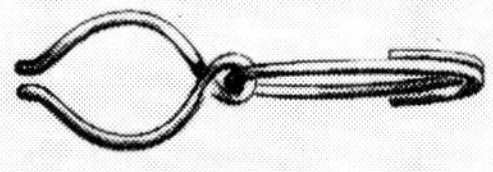

A handy little clip which may be placed on the creel strap, and will carry net or gaff by pushing the handle through the clip. To remove, the handle is simply forced out. Price, **1/-** each.

FOR REELS, SEE PAGE 129.

The "Duplex" Landing Net

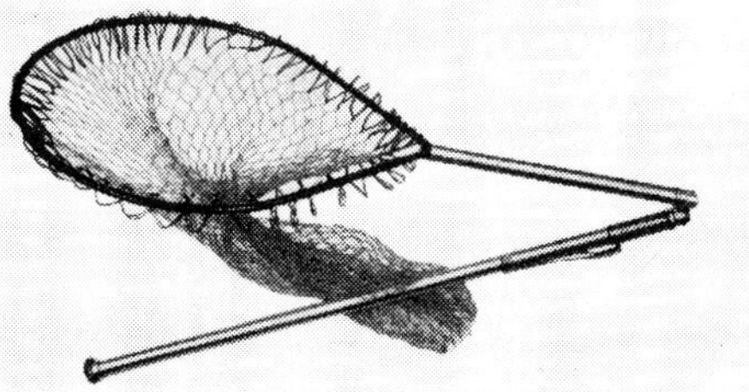

A strong light net with an improved Knuckle joint—the handle is of Duralumin tubing—the head is rigid, pear-shaped, and measures 14″ × 12″—it is provided with a Carrying Clip and plain cord net. Extra for silk net, **4/-**

Extended 4 ft., Folded 2 ft.; weight 1 lb. 4 ozs.; Price, **30/-** each.

The "SIMPLEX" Landing Net

WITH PATENT SELF-LOCKING HEAD

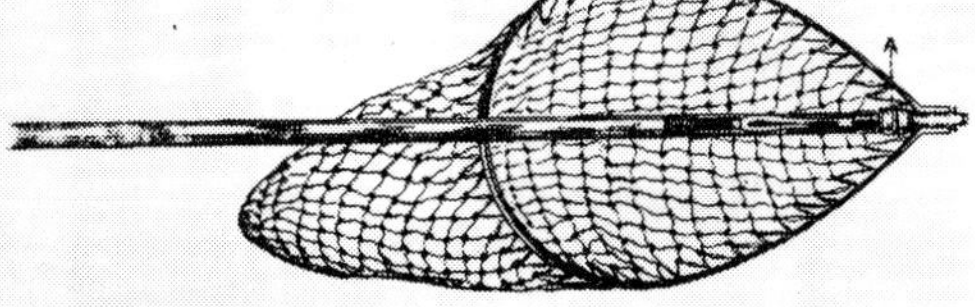

A light, handy, and convenient folding net. To bring into play, simply throw head over, when it locks and is ready for use. To fold, draw back the locking ring A, when head will fall into position as illustrated.

The hoop, being made of a non-corrosive aluminium alloy, is very light and impervious to the action of water.

Price, **24/-.** With solid plait silk net, **4/-** extra. Carrying sling, **2/6** extra. Length open 44 ins. Closed 30½ ins.

FOR WADERS, SEE PAGE 330.

The "ROYDE" Folding Landing Nets

FIG. 1.—Extended in use. Length overall 47 ins.
FIG. 2.—Folded as carried. Length overall 32 ins. This illustration also shows the Walking Stick design with handle B.
WEIGHT 18½ ozs.

Fig. 1.
Fig. 2.

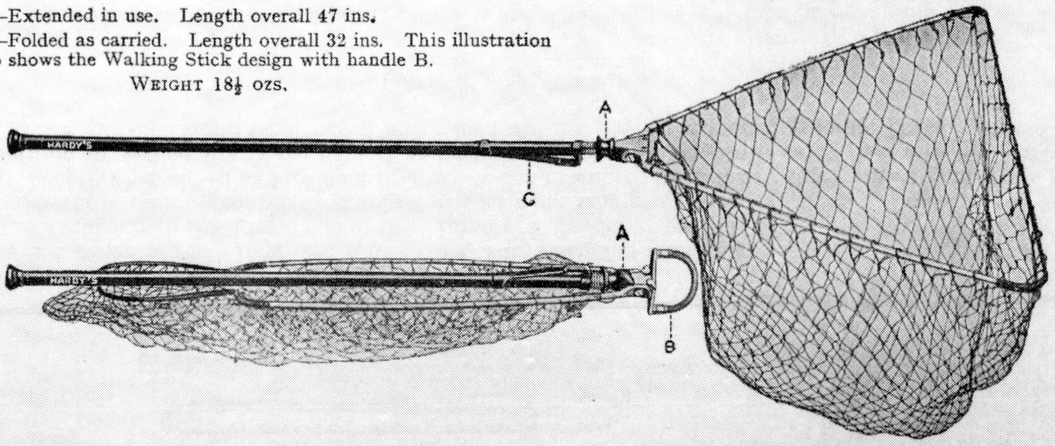

The "**Improved Royde.**" The arms and shaft are made of special non-corrosive light-weight metal.

The head folds up so that the net hangs quite out of the way on the creel strap or clip. It can be quickly brought into action with one hand; as by simply throwing the head over it opens, the locking bolt **A** securely fastening it. The reverse action closes the net, as when held vertically, and the locking bolt pulled back, the weight of the head causes it to fall over when the net closes. **C** is the carrying clip.

With 16½ inch arms and waterproof plaited silk net, **45/-.** With handle **B** as a walking-stick, the shaft being of Hickory, Fig. 2, **10/6** extra.

"**Grilse Size,**" with 24 inch arms and cable laid net, suitable for large fish, **63/-.** Overall and Open, 53 ins. Closed, 33 ins. Weight, 35 ozs.

The "**Plain Royde,**" 16½ inch arms, wood handle and cord net. This pattern is not fitted with the locking bolt **A.** Price, **28/6**; waterproof Silk Net, **4/-** extra. Carrying Sling to any pattern, **2/6** extra.

FOR THE "SUPER SILEX" REEL, SEE PAGE 152.

The "ECLIPSE" Folding Landing Net

WITH TELESCOPIC HANDLE AND SELF-LOCKING HEAD

Extended as in use - 60 ins.
Closed and Folded - 27 ins.

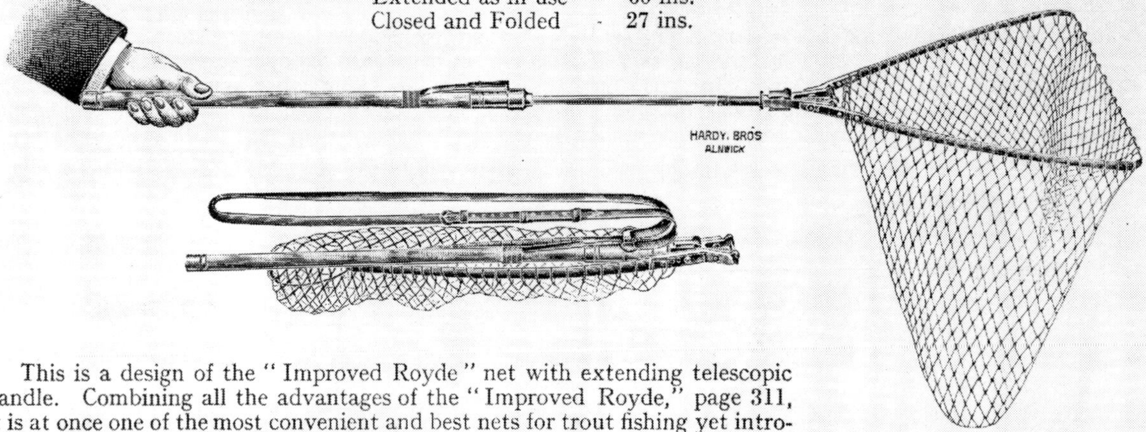

This is a design of the "Improved Royde" net with extending telescopic handle. Combining all the advantages of the "Improved Royde," page 311, it is at once one of the most convenient and best nets for trout fishing yet introduced. Length when closed and folded 2 ft. 3 in. When extended about 5 ft. Price, with 16½ in. arms, **60/-.** **The Salmon or Grilse** size is the lightest and handiest design for those who carry their own net. Made to order. Price, **80/-.** Length when closed and folded 29½ ins. When extended as in use 71 ins. Arms 22 ins. Weight 50 ozs.

Carrying Sling **2/6** extra.

CHIEF CONSTABLE'S OFFICE, TAUNTON, 28/5/29.

I bought my Landing Net from you in 1907 so it does not owe me much! It has landed a 9¾ lb. salmon.

(Lt.-Col.) H. C. METCALFE.

FOR THE "HEBRIDEAN" FLY ROD, SEE PAGE 271.

FOR SALMON FLIES, SEE PAGE 69.

The "BEART" Collapsing Salmon Nets

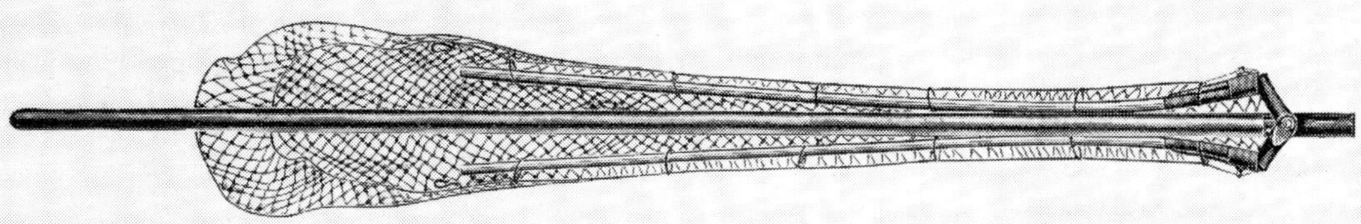

CLOSED

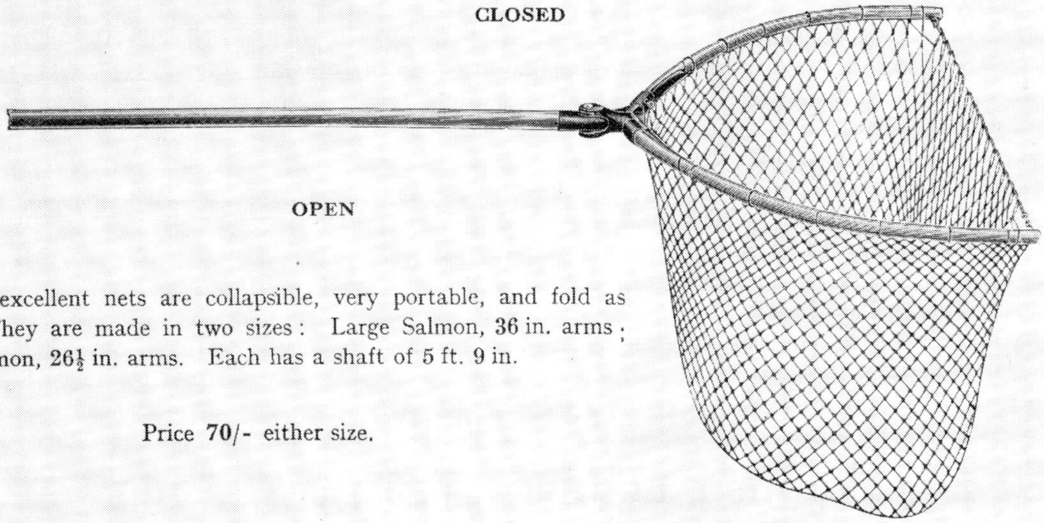

OPEN

These excellent nets are collapsible, very portable, and fold as shown. They are made in two sizes: Large Salmon, 36 in. arms; Small Salmon, 26½ in. arms. Each has a shaft of 5 ft. 9 in.

Price **70/-** either size.

The "TWEED" Salmon Landing Net

WITH DETACHABLE HEAD

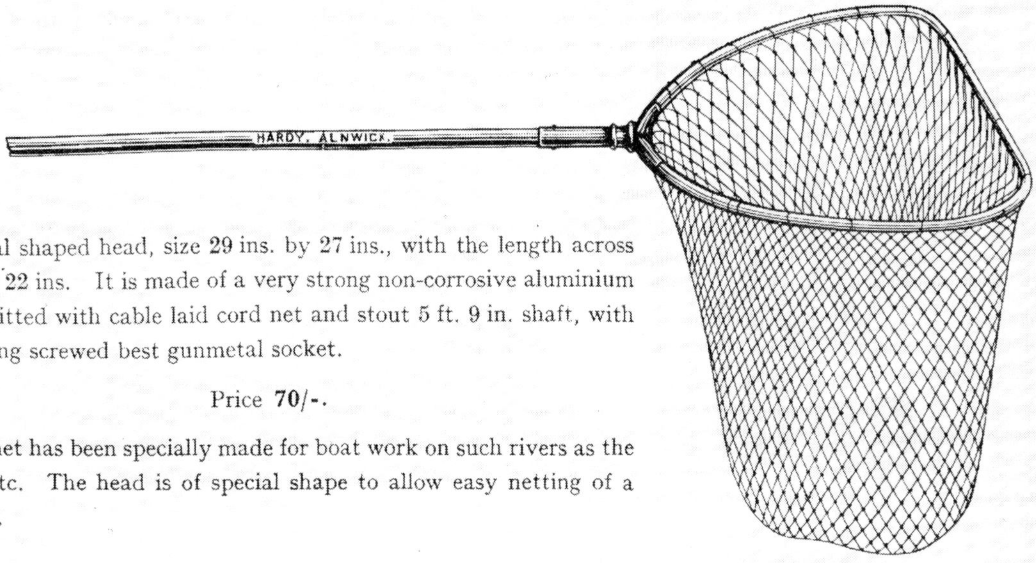

Special shaped head, size 29 ins. by 27 ins., with the length across front end 22 ins. It is made of a very strong non-corrosive aluminium alloy. Fitted with cable laid cord net and stout 5 ft. 9 in. shaft, with very strong screwed best gunmetal socket.

Price **70/-**.

This net has been specially made for boat work on such rivers as the Tweed, etc. The head is of special shape to allow easy netting of a large fish.

The "TYNE" Wading Staff and Gaff

THE ORIGINAL WAS DESIGNED IN 1880

With Hardy's Point Protector. Patent No. 181906.

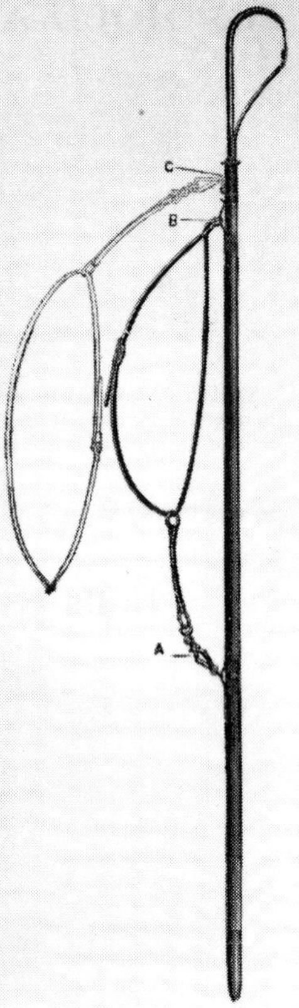

A most useful article, being indispensable when wading, and where the angler wishes to reach the bank quickly after hooking a fish, then it serves as a third leg. It may be carried in the hand as a staff, when fastened by the leather strap over the shoulder (as shown by dotted lines). After wading into position, allow the gaff to hang by the strap, the leaded end keeping it in position. When the cast is finished it can be taken in the hand and used in making the next step, and so on. The staff is also usefui to gauge the depth in coloured water.

The strap may be adjusted, so that the gaff can also be carried over the shoulder, as shown in illustration A to B, when it is quite out of the way.

In either position it can easily be detached with one hand by pressing the scissor clip at A or C.

Very strongly made, **Firth's stainless steel,** fitted with Patent steel point protector. The shaft can also be used as a landing net handle. Length over all, 4 ft. 9 in.

Price, **37/6.**

FOR THE "TWEED" SALMON LANDING NET, SEE PAGE 320.

The "ORCHY" Wading Staff and Gaff

IMPROVED DESIGN. Reg. No. 710349.

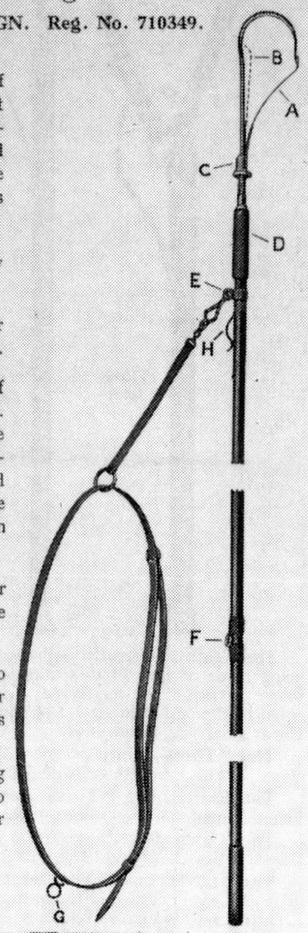

The "Orchy" Wading Staff and Gaff combines all our latest improvements. Our original pattern, called the "Tyne" and shown on page 306, has been made by us for nearly 50 years; and is a great favourite.

The improvements in this new design are:

1. A perfected form of our patent point protector A.
2. A simple and handy method of releasing the protector. On pulling down the sleeve C, the protector A is released from the point and springs to position B quite out of the way when gaffing.
3. A comfortable india rubber hand grasp is fixed on the shaft at D.

The strap may be adjusted so that the gaff may be carried over the shoulder or for wading as illustrated.

When required for carrying over the shoulder slip ring G into clip at H, and scissors clip over ring F.

Length over all, 4 ft. 9 in.

Price, **47/6.**

FOR THE "HI REGAN" SALMON FLY ROD, SEE PAGE 277.

Hardy's "TELESCOPIC" Gaffs

With Spring Point Protector.

Patent No. 181906.

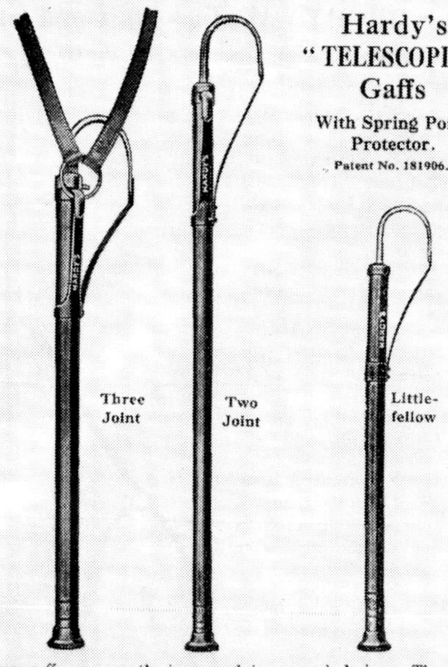

These gaffs are greatly improved in general design. The hooks being made of best **Firth's stainless steel,** the handles and telescopic portions of non-corrosive aluminium alloy, with a tensile strength equal to the best mild steel. The two and three joint patterns have Hardy's Carrying arrangement.

The "Three Joint," weight 16½ oz. Price, **36/6** each. Length closed, 17½ ins. Length extended, 42 ins. Carrying Sling, **2/6** extra.

The Extra Long "Three Joint," weight 21 oz. Price, **41/6.** Length closed, 23 ins. Length extended, 58 ins.

The "Two Joint," weight 13 ozs. Price, **28/6** each. Length closed, 20 ins. Length extended, 36 ins. Carrying Sling, **2/6** extra.

The "Littlefellow" Two Joint Telescopic. A very light handy little gaff, easily carried in the bag or creel. Length extended, 24 ins. Length closed, 14½ ins. Weight, 8 ozs. Price, **18/6.**

FOR THE "VICTOR" SPINNING RODS, SEE PAGE 288.

HARDY'S IMPROVED FISH-TAILER

Pat. applied for

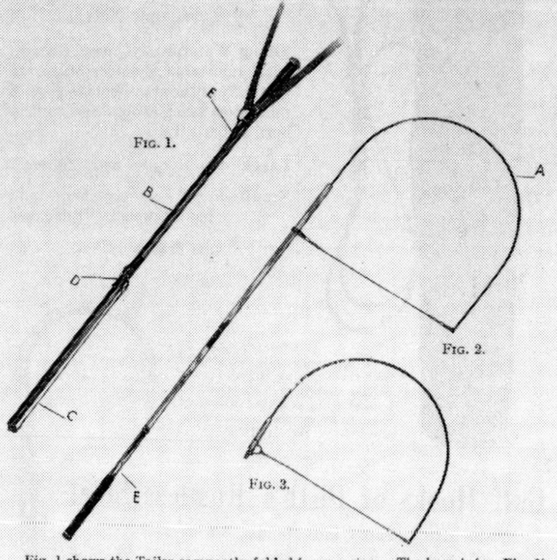

Fig. 1 shows the Tailer compactly folded for carrying. The bow A (see Fig. 2) is telescoped into shaft B (Fig. 1). The noose C lies close against the shaft and is held in a simple and quickly released fastener D. The carrying clip E is our well-known pattern used on our nets and gaffs. When a fish is hooked and the Tailer is required the carrying clip is easily released from the sling with one hand, the fastener D opened and the bow and noose set as shown in Fig. 2. When the fish is sufficiently played out the bow is slipped over the tail, the Tailer brought forward up the body, a sharp stroke away from the fish releases the bow and the fish is securely noosed when it may be lifted out of the water. The lift should be in a straight line with the shaft of the Tailer. An efficient, strong and easily handled part of an angler's equipment.

Fig. 3.—A Tailer head without the telescopic shaft and carrying clip.

Price of telescopic pattern, Figs. 1 and 2, **37/6.** Weight **15 ozs.**

Price of head only, Fig. 3, **22/6.** Weight 8 ozs.

HALTWHISTLE, 2/8/30.

Thank you for yours of July 31st and my Tailer which arrived to-day. I am delighted with it, you have done all that I suggested and I don't think it could be improved upon. You have got the loop quite rigid which I consider a very important point.

R. K. ARMSTRONG.

Hardy's "Drop" Knife

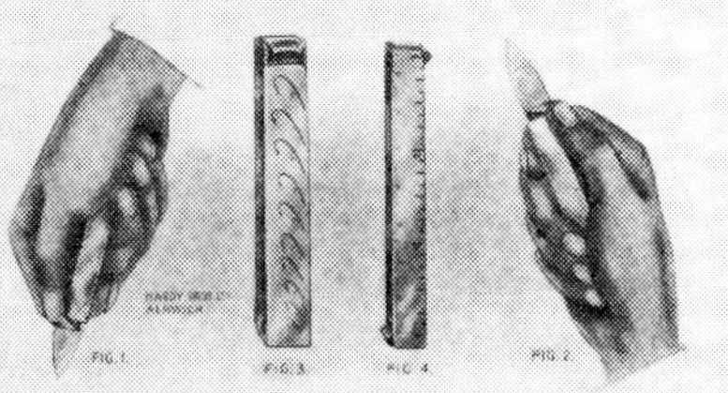

A handy and practical form of pocket knife. A tool you will always find a use for. The blade can be **opened** and **securely locked** and closed with one hand.

Knife No. 1 contains at one end a stout knife blade and at the other end a screw-driver, one side of which is cut as a nail file. The screw-driver can be locked at its full length or at half length.

Knife No. 2 contains a stout knife blade and Fig. 1 shows the knife being held with the catch lifted by the thumb allowing the blade to drop and lock.

Fig. 2 shows how the knife is held to close the blade—pull the catch over with the thumb when the blade will drop into the haft and is securely held.

Figs. 3 and **4** show two of the faces of the knife haft. The measure in Fig. 4 is in inches and centimetres. Fig. 3 is a scale of fly hooks.

Overall length 3 ins. Prices—No. 1, **6/6**; No. 2, **5/-** each.

Hardy's Pocket Tool Outfit

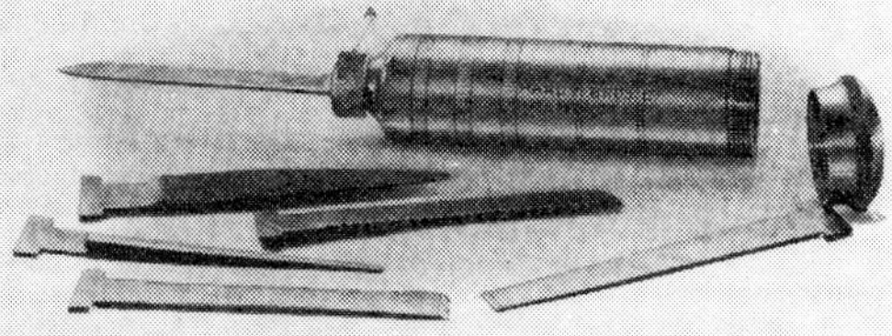

A substantially made, practical, compact tool outfit which can be comfortably carried in the pocket—Length 3¾"; weight 2½ ozs. The handle contains six tools of best Sheffield steel comprising a strong knife blade—a screw-driver—a chisel—a saw—a tapered reamer, and a half round file. When it is desired to fix a tool into the handle—unscrew nut A, insert the tool into the slot and screw on nut A.

A tool with many uses which can frequently relieve a difficult situation. No trouble to carry, but a boon when required. It's a tool, not a toy.

Price **10/6**

Fly Makers' Vices

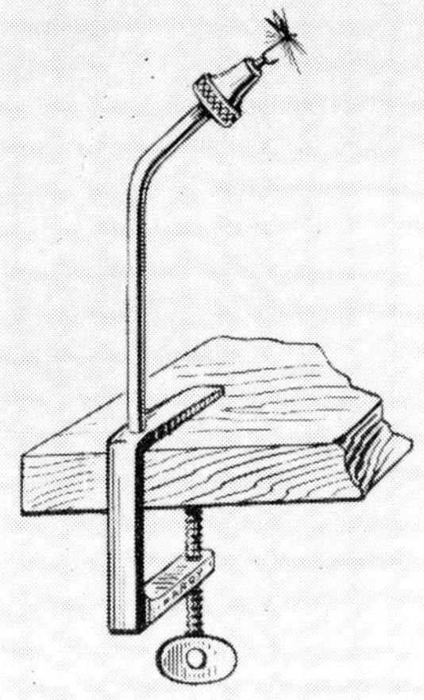

The "Hardy-Coulin"

Suitable for Small Flies.

In designing this vice we have been kindly assisted by Mons. E. Coulin, an ardent amateur fly dresser.

The vice and locking ring being perfectly plain there is no liability of the tying silk, etc., becoming entangled with parts of the vice whilst working. The work is held at an angle which permits both hands to operate with ease. Fitted with adjustable table clamp.

Price **9/-** each.

The "AMATEUR"

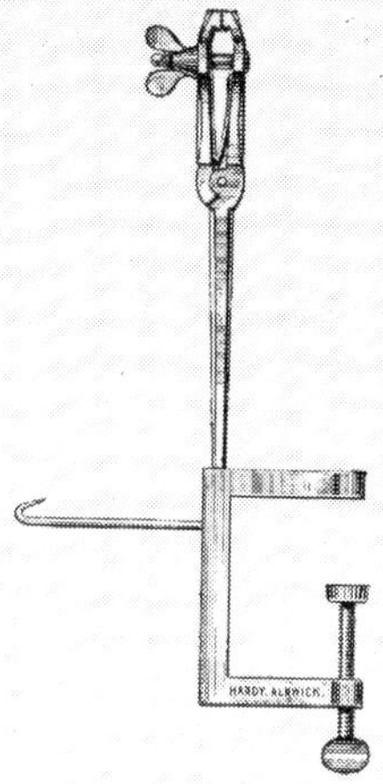

Made with strong adjustable vice, operated by fly nut, and adjustable table clamp.

The hooked arm is made to screw in and a rubber washer is provided with a slot to hold the silk.

Price **10/6** each.

READING, 1929.

I have a "Hardy-Coulin" Fly-tyers' Vice, with which you supplied me last year. I would like to take this opportunity of expressing my admiration of this vice. It is reliability and simplicity combined.

PATRICK H. EVANS.

Artificial Baits for Big Game Fish, Etc.

THE "WILSON" SPOON, made of white colour metal and fitted with "Hardy" Swivels.

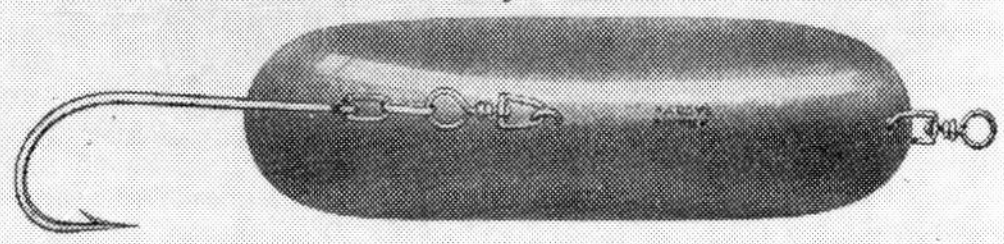

Sizes in inches	4	4½	5	6
Prices, each	**4/3**	**4/6**	4/9	5/-

THE "STEWART" SPOON, made of white colour metal and fitted with "Hardy" swivels.

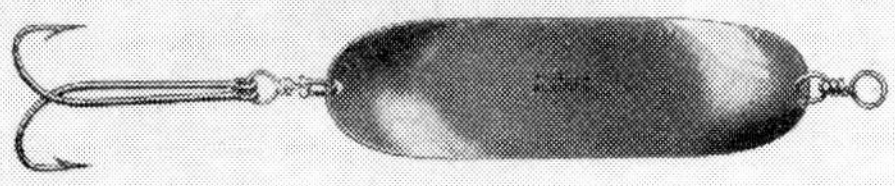

Sizes in inches	3	3½	4	4½	5	6
Prices, each	3/3	3/9	4/3	4/6	4/9	5/-

THE "INDIAN" SPOON

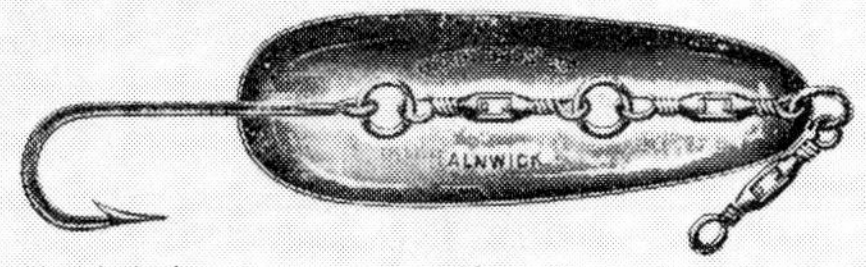

Sizes in inches	2½	4	5
Prices, each	3/-	4/3	4/9

HERRING OR SPRAT BAIT

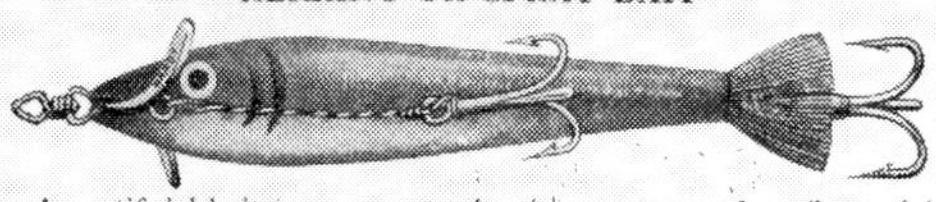

An artificial bait to represent a herring, sprat or other silvery fish. Excellent for big game sea fish or large pike. Painted any colour to order.

Sizes in inches	6	8	10
Prices, each	15/-	18/6	21/-

Larger sizes made specially to order.

FOR ARTIFICIAL SPINNING BAITS, SEE PAGE 202.

The "FARNE" Spinner

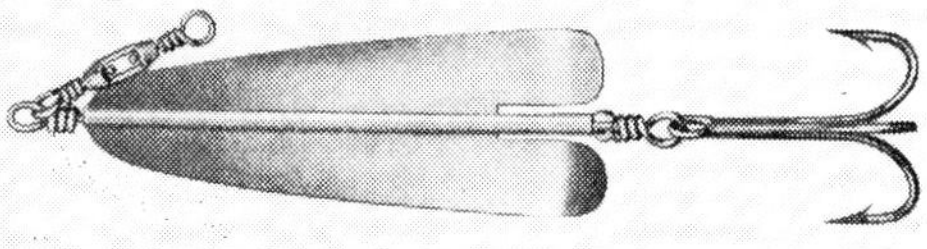

A deadly bait. Colour Silver. Sizes 2½ in. × ⅜ in. **1/-** each.

The "OTTER" Bait

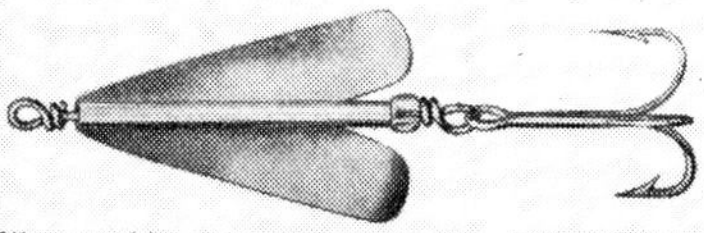

Colour Silver. 1¼ in., **6d.**; 1½ in., **7d.**; 2 in., **10d.**; 2¼ in., **1/2** each.

Improved "SILVER OTTER"

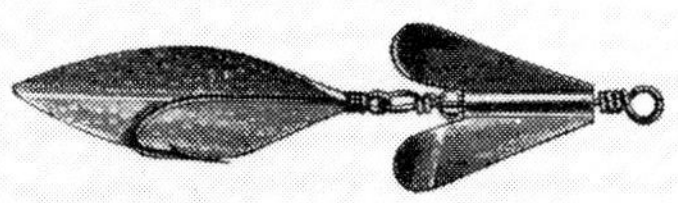

EXACT SIZE.

A combination of the "Otter" Bait and "Soleskin" Fly. Specially suitable for Mackerel, Bass, Pollock, etc. Price **9d.** each.

India-Rubber Tube Bait

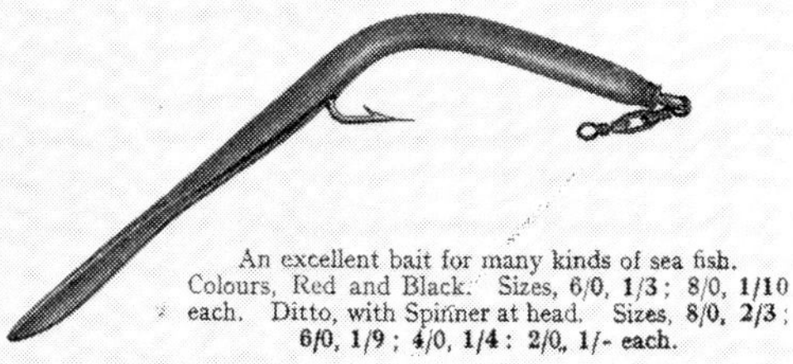

An excellent bait for many kinds of sea fish. Colours, Red and Black. Sizes, 6/0, **1/3**; 8/0, **1/10** each. Ditto, with Spinner at head. Sizes, 8/0, **2/3**; 6/0, **1/9**; 4/0, **1/4**: 2/0, **1/-** each.

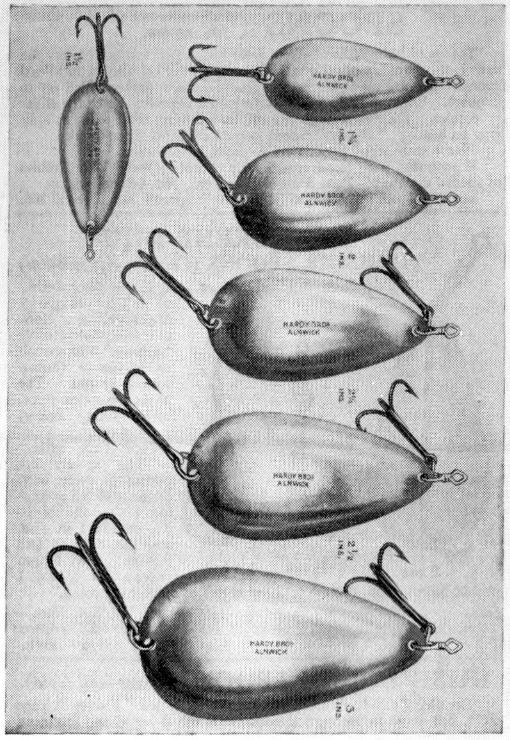

EXTRA HEAVY "SPECIAL" SPOONS

Genuine Sheffield Plate. Colour: Copper outside, Silver inside.

Sizes - - - - - -	$1\frac{1}{2}$	$1\frac{3}{4}$	2	$2\frac{1}{4}$	$2\frac{1}{2}$	$2\frac{3}{4}$	3	in.
Approximate weight - - -	4	5	8	11	13	16	20	drms.
Prices - - - - - -	1/6	1/9	1/9	2/-	2/-	2/3	2/6	each.

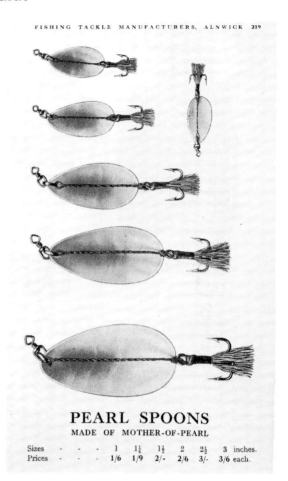

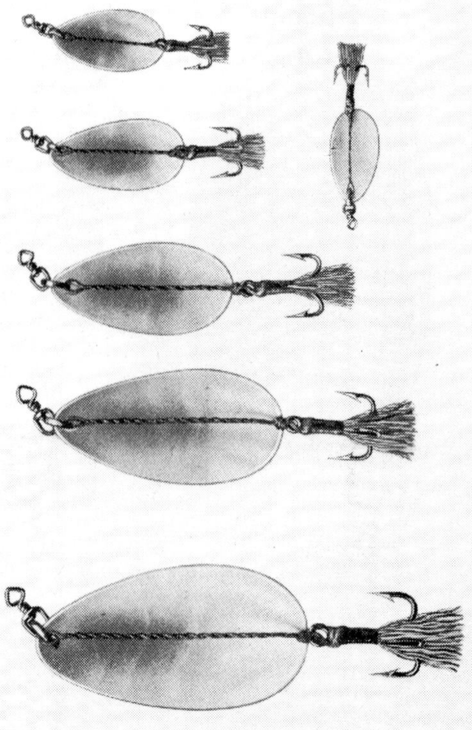

PEARL SPOONS

MADE OF MOTHER-OF-PEARL

Sizes - - -	1	$1\frac{1}{4}$	$1\frac{1}{2}$	2	$2\frac{1}{2}$	3	inches.
Prices - - -	1/6	1/9	2/-	2/6	3/-	3/6	each.

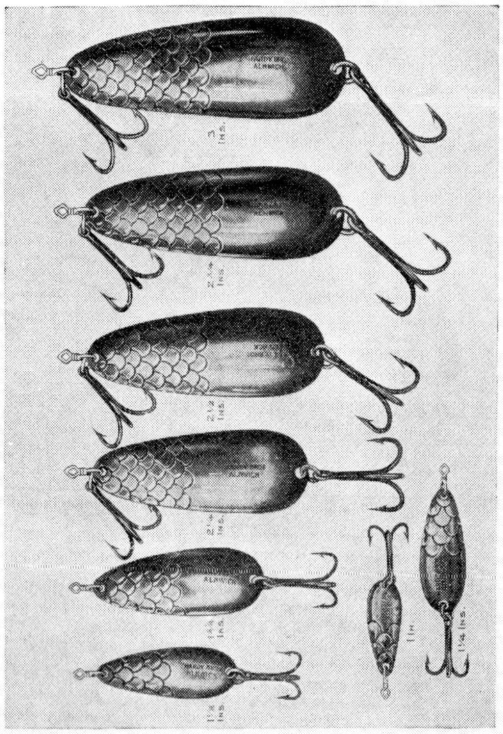

EXTRA HEAVY "KIDNEY" SPOONS

Half-scaled Genuine Sheffield Plate.
Colour: Copper outside, Silver inside.

Sizes - - - - -	1	$1\frac{1}{4}$	$1\frac{1}{2}$	$1\frac{3}{4}$	$2\frac{1}{4}$	$2\frac{1}{2}$	$2\frac{3}{4}$	3	ins.
Approximate weight -	$2\frac{1}{2}$	3	4	5	8	10	11	12	drms.
Prices - - - - -	1/-	1/-	1/3	1/6	1/9	1/9	2/-	2/3	each.

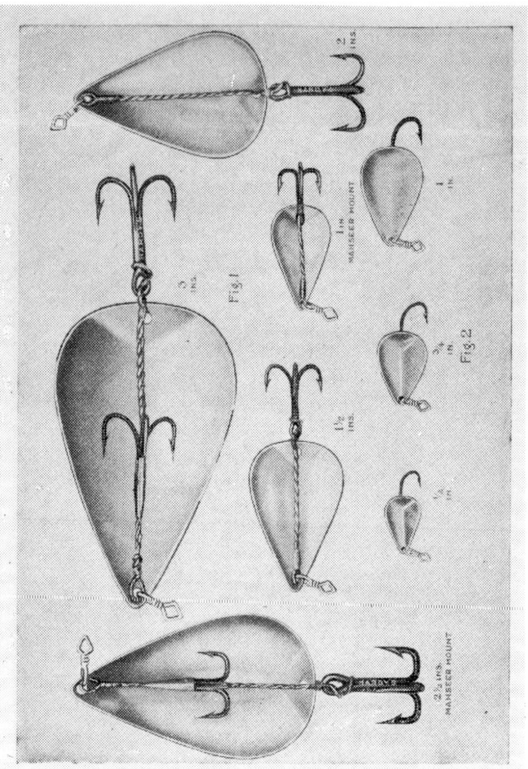

"HOG BACKED" SPOONS. Colour: Gold outside, Silver inside.

Sizes - - - - -	1	$1\frac{1}{2}$	2	$2\frac{1}{2}$	3	ins.
Approximate weight - -	2	4	8	12	20	drms.
Price - - - - -	1/3	1/6	1/9	2/3	2/9	each.

FLY SPOONS. Colour: Silver.

Sizes - - - - - -	$\frac{3}{8}$	$\frac{1}{2}$	$\frac{3}{4}$	1	in.
Price - - - - - - - -	7d.	8d.	9d.	9d.	each.

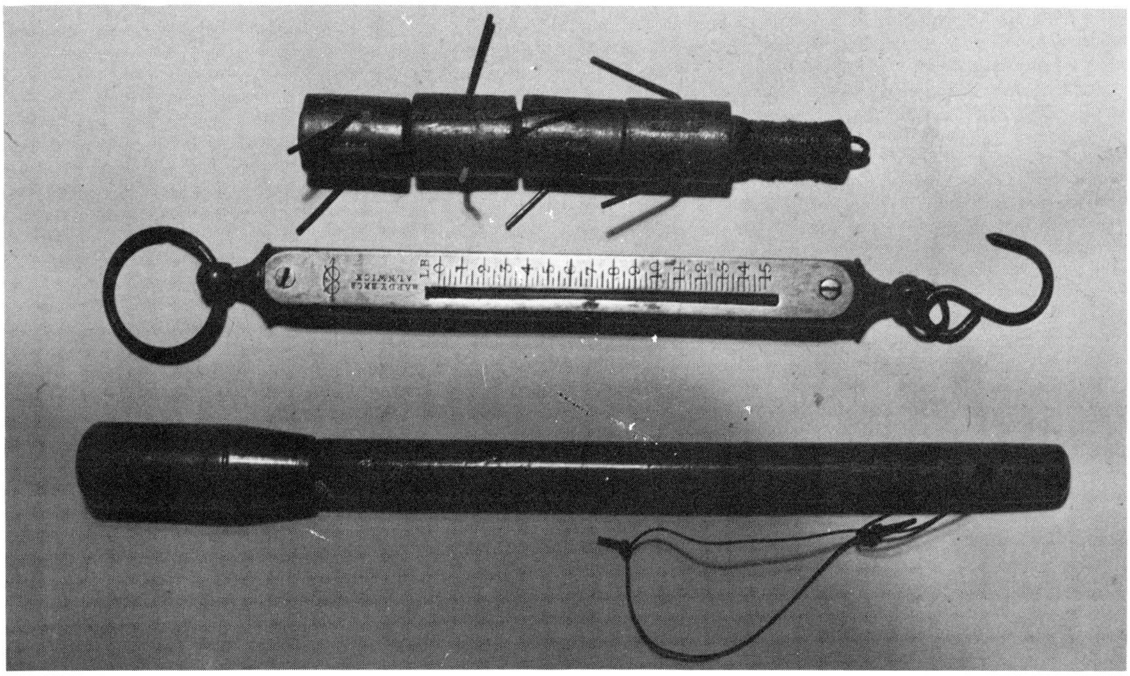

Hardy wood and brass gaff
Hardy spring balance
Hardy sea lead, made of rubber cord, lead casting and brass spikes

Spring balance, Hardy tool kit, matchbox dismantler, Wardle magnifyer, oilbottle, pipe cleaner oiling pen, Patent non spill line greaser, oil bottle, split shot box, weed cutter tackle retriever, spring balance, pocket gaff gut gage, scissors with protective guard 3 spanners (for winch fittings), curate, disgorgers (two)

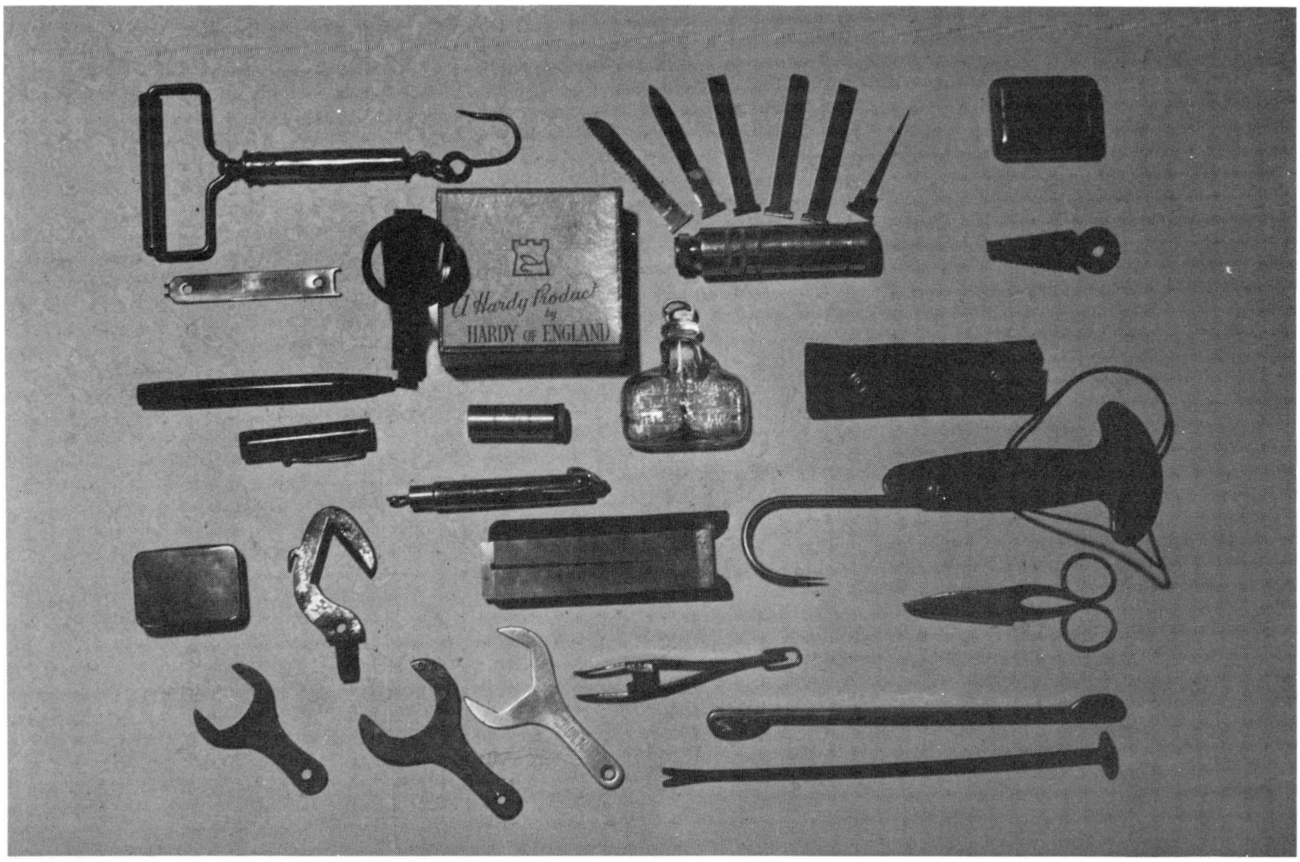

Selection of Hardy Bros Line Driers and Line Winders

The "Compact" Line Drier

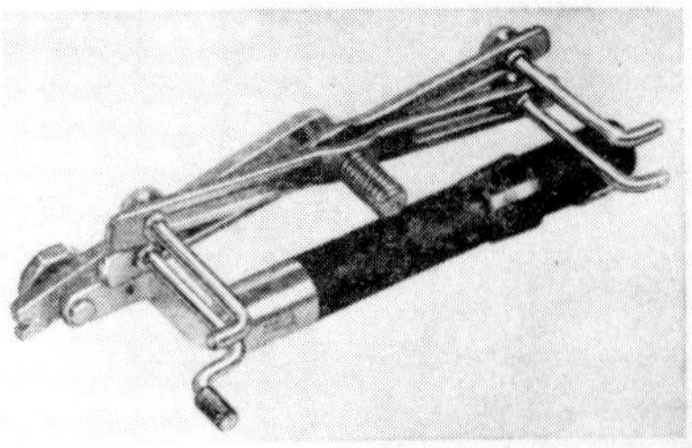

Fig. 1.—The Line Drier with Handle folded for packing

A light, compact and quickly assembled line drier with no loose parts t… and assemble.

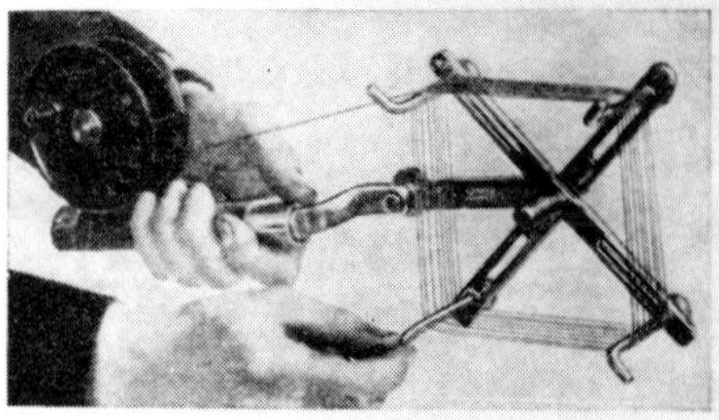

Fig. 2.—The Line Drier with Handle in use

Measurement across arms, 6 in.

THE "PRACTICAL" LINE DR…

126 HARDY BROTHERS LTD.,

Improved Line Drier

In Use

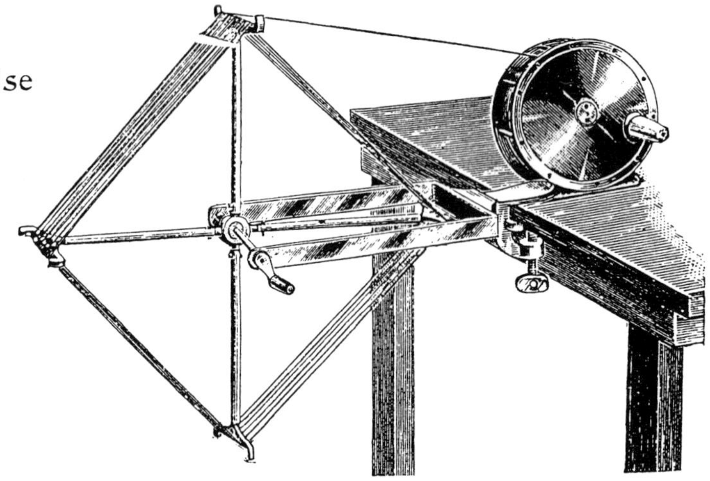

374L.—Can be screwed to a table and the line unwound from the reel in a few minutes. The drum is 11 inches in diameter. It takes to pieces and packs into small space. A splendid and practical winder.

Price, in box, complete, 15/6.

The "Ward" Line Drier

COLLAPSIBLE.

Made to the idea given to us by Dr. Ozier Ward.

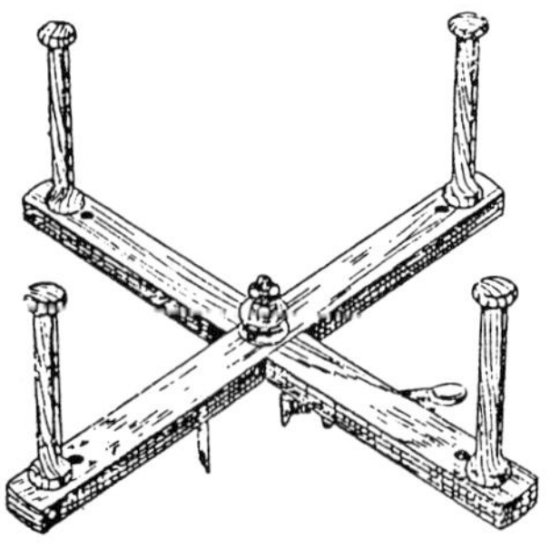

This is a strongly made and handy line drier, which can be fixed to a table by means of the usual screw clamp. The arms are of hickory mounted with detachable wood pegs, upon which the line is wound. A milled nut with cushion spring is fitted on spindle end, and allows the tension to be regulated when winding line on to reel.

Packed in neat box, size 12 in. × 4 in. × $1\frac{3}{8}$ in.

Price 6/6 each.

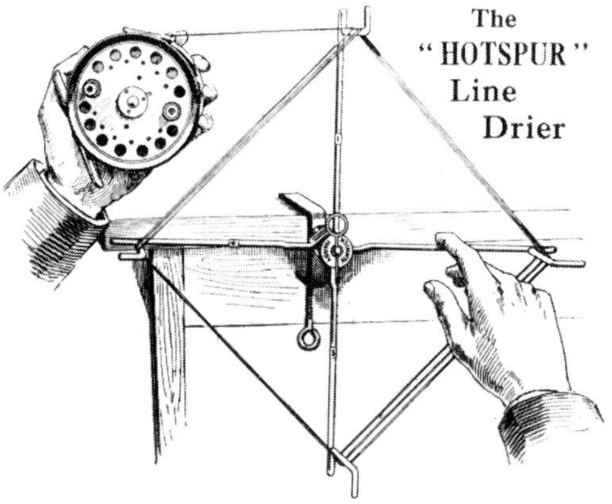

The "HOTSPUR" Line Drier

The 1911 Model Line Winder

COLLAPSIBLE.

THE "FACILE" LINE DRIER.

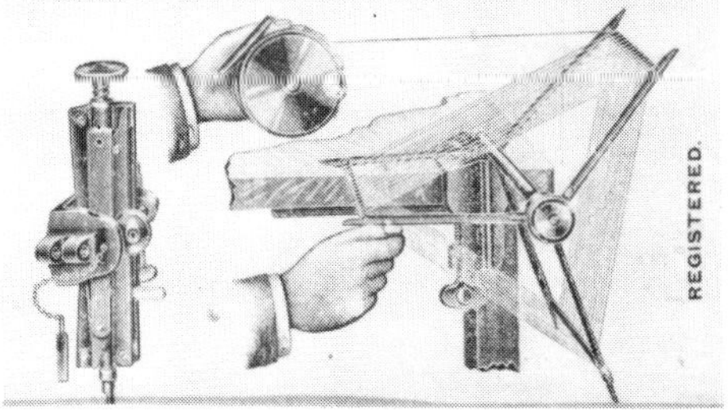

The "Bethune" Line Winder.

(HARDY'S PATENT)

THE invention of C. C. Bethune, Esq., and is one of the best and most compact yet invented. The illustration shows it in use. The reel is put on the handle, exactly as on a rod butt, the fittings being the same. The winder works between two spiral springs, and can be oscillated in winding, thus the line is not all wound in one place, but is evenly distributed.

In winding line off the reel, the small thumb screw should be eased. When as much line as desired has been wound off, this screw is then tightened, and keeps all taut. When the line is being wound back on to the reel again, the thumb screw should be eased a little to allow winder to travel steadily.

When line is wound off reel on to winder, both the reel and winder may be hung up until they are again wanted.

They are made in two sizes, Trout and Salmon, and packed in neat cedar wood boxes, with slide lids.

To Pack.—Simply unscrew arms and handle.

Sizes—Trout—$6 \times 4 \times 2\frac{1}{2}$.		Salmon—$6\frac{3}{4} \times 5\frac{1}{4} \times 3$.
Prices—	TROUT, 8/6.	SALMON, 10/6.
Suitable for 2 to $3\frac{1}{4}$ in. Reels.		Suitable for $3\frac{1}{2}$ to 5 in. Reels.

☛ FOR LANDING NETS, SEE PAGES 285 TO 296.

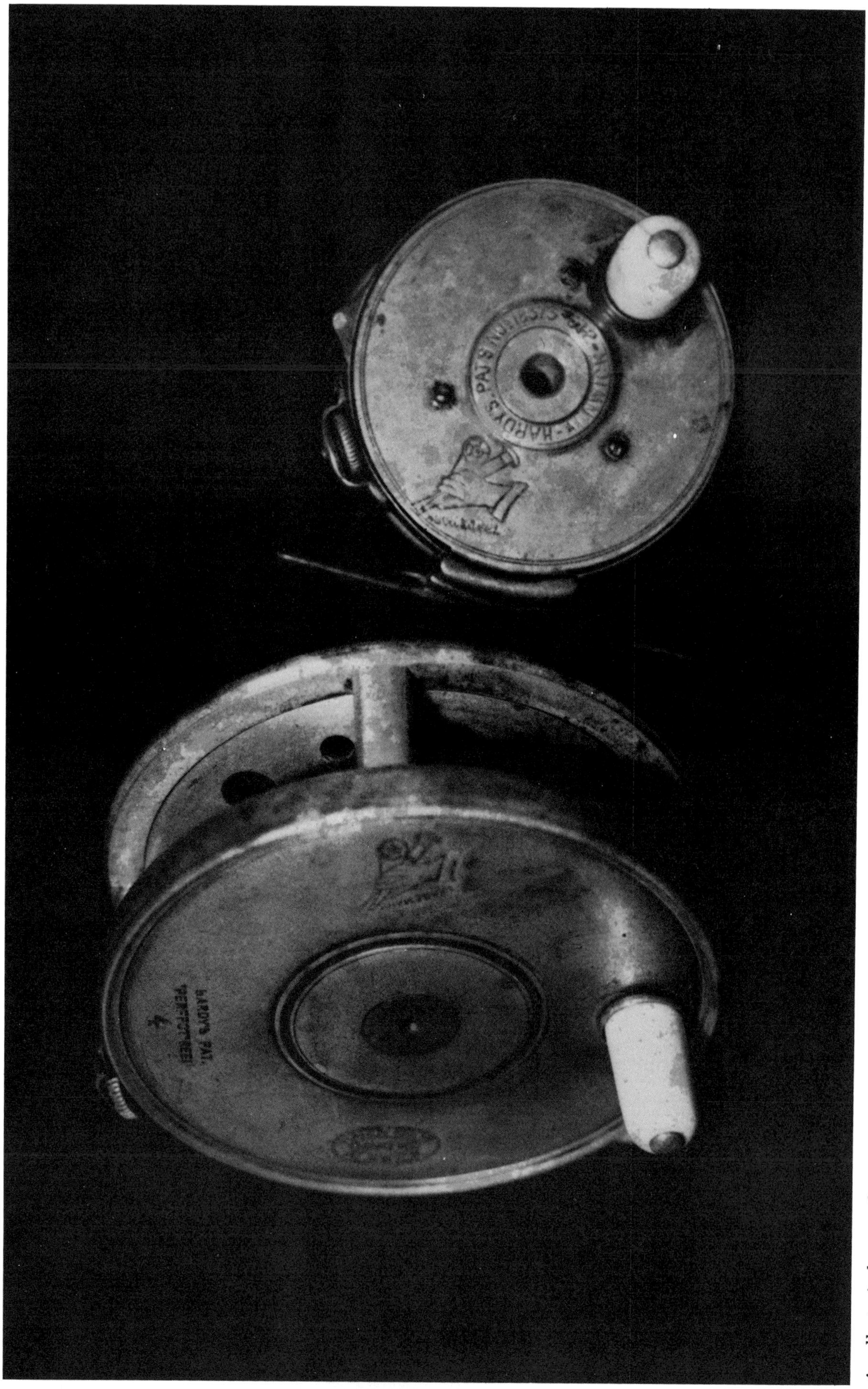

A collector's dream—the two most important Hardy Bros reels. The 2¼" Original Perfect and the only known example at the present time of the Perfect Narrow Drum (First Model) Size 3⅝"

AMERICA

The finest multiplying reels have always been made in America, since a watchmaker by the name of Snyder introduced precision engineering and marked the beginning of the legendary Kentucky Reels.

The first known American fishing book was Joseph Seccombe's *Business and Diversion, inoffensive to* GOD, *and necessary for the Comfort and Support of human society. A DISCOURSE utter'd in Part* AT *Ammauskeeg-Falls,* IN THE *Fishing Season. 1739.*

Evolution in America

The date of man's first arrival in America is at present not known but is assumed to be between 25,000 and 35,000 years ago, although some authorities suggest 50,000. He is generally believed to have gained access by following migratory animals over a land or ice bridge, which once joined Asia to North America, at what is now the Bering Straight. Early man spread throughout the Americas and established various cultures. In the north he became the Palaeo-Indian, and eventually the American Indian, who was flourishing when the country was first discovered by the Europeans in the fifteenth century.

There are people in America who refuse to accept the simple truth that their country remained completely cut off from the peoples of other continents after the land bridge disappeared. Visits from outside would have necessitated hazardous voyages across oceans of which very little was known, with no guarantee that the return passage would be possible. However, there have been numerous claims of landings and colonisation by Vikings, Egyptians, Chinese, Greeks and Romans, which if true, would have meant the introduction and use of the fishing rod, reel and other items of tackle many centuries in advance of Britain and the accepted history of America.

It is therefore important to examine these ideas, the validity of which should be based on collective archaeological finds and not on supposition, probabilities or capabilities, nor on the discovery of isolated artefacts without supporting evidence. Whenever a race of people inhabit an area they invariably leave behind all kinds of evidence of their existence. The ground on which they lived usually contains materials of their dwellings, utensils, weapons, bones of animals and fish included in their diet and remains of the people themselves. It is a cross section of these finds that is required to prove the existence of a people, otherwise any claims can only be treated as myths and legends.

Many books have been written to try to prove these ideas, while museums have been built and even a football team named after a civilisation which is supposed to have colonised the United States.

The most respectable of the claimants are the Vikings who appear to have a large amount of supporting evidence. Had they colonised parts of America they would have had little influence on the development of fishing tackle because their methods were basic. However, their case is worth examining in order to get an overall picture of colonisation and their success would give a fair indication of the chances of others.

Some citizens of Alexandria in the state of Minnesota, where a large number of Scandinavian immigrants settled during the nineteenth century, have built the Runestone Museum, outside which stands a 28 feet high statue of a Viking. The founders believe that Vikings landed and settled in part of the state of Maine which they called 'Vinland', and the museum contains a map showing the area of the settlement.

This corresponds with the Vikings' own literature in the form of Icelandic sagas which relate a voyage in the eleventh century to a land called 'Vinland'. It is generally accepted that the Vikings sailed west from their Scandinavian homeland to colonise Iceland and to establish settlements in Greenland, while trading with Europe in deep-sea trading ships.

However, there is little support for the idea that they reached the coast of North America and it seems strange that Alexandria claims association as it is a thousand miles or more away from the Atlantic coast. The alleged evidence stands inside the museum in the form of a fourteenth century Viking stone called the Kensington Runestone, named after the locality near Alexandria where it was found on the land of a farmer of Scandinavian descent. The carving on the stone tells of a party of eight Swedes and twenty two Norwegians going on a voyage of exploration from Vinland; also of a fishing expedition in which ten of the party were killed.

The stone has been the subject of fierce controversy since it was first put forward as tangible proof of Vikings in North America and the experts have expressed doubt as to its age and authenticity. It contains a mixture of Scandinavian words from several centuries and the words and language could not have been inscribed in the period claimed for the stone.

The second piece of evidence was the Vinland Map which was an old parchment of skin on which was drawn an island called Vinland, together with a section bearing a Latin inscription telling the story of two men having discovered and explored the new land. Although the map appeared authentic, examination of the writing found that the ink could not have been pre-twentieth century. Another claim for possible Viking presence in America can be found at a small sea port south of Boston, on the ocean coast of Rhode Island. It is a mysterious building at Newport, the famous home of the America's Cup, and known as the Newport Tower.

In the early nineteenth century a Danish archaeologist visited and decided it was built by the Vikings in the twelfth century. Some people have described it as a circular church, which if true, would have made it the earliest in America. Eventually the truth was discovered. A will was found, which had been prepared by Benedict Arnold, a one-time Governor of Rhode Island, and it contained reference to 'My stone mill at Newport' which proved it to be a colonial building.

None of the supposed Viking artefacts were accompanied by the associated finds one would have expected, and do not prove that the Vikings were ever in America. Archaeological evidence would suggest that the Vinland of the sagas was in fact the northern tip

Haida halibut hook attached to line made from twisted spruce root. Found on Queen Charlotte Island 1884

of Canada – Newfoundland, where Scandinavian homes and iron workings have been found.

Many books claim that regular return crossings from the old world have been taking place for the last fifteen hundred years. Some describe Phoenician, Celtic, Libyan and Iberian visitations, but there are no collective artefacts to prove these ideas. Large quantities of stones with markings have been put forward, together with scratchings on rock faces, but professional archaeologists say these can be anything: Indian drawings, geological markings or simply modern plough scratches and not old world scripts.

Another school of thought believe that the Egyptians sailed to America. Considering the fact that they were using the rod around 2000 BC, this would have changed the history of American fishing tackle. It is known that the Egyptians built and used wooden boats on the Nile, and an explorer, Thor Heyerdahl, built a giant boat of papyrus reeds in an attempt to

A map of the Americas in a 1592 Ortelius Theatrum Orbis Terrarum

prove that the Egyptians were capable of reaching America.

He sailed from Morocco to within six hundred miles of the American coast before his craft became unseaworthy, forcing him to discontinue the voyage. He showed the passage was possible but failed to prove whether the Egyptians ever made the crossing. Heyerdahl and his supporters point to the Mexican pyramids as evidence of Egyptian influence, but these were built two thousand years after the Egyptians had abandoned pyramid building. Also, they are not the same type, as unlike the Egyptian ones, they have temples on top of them. These buildings of high platform construction were probably an independent design. There have never been any Egyptian artefacts found in America, and stories of their presence can only be treated as legends.

Other books tell of Roman and Greek voyages to America and the evidence put forward by this school is as follows.

A few coins of the Roman Emperor Hadrian (117 – 138 AD) were excavated by workers when digging foundations on a building site. They were found several feet below the surface in what appeared to be undisturbed soil.

Old-world pottery lamps have been found in America. An early Greek example made before 480 BC turned up at the Boston Antiques Fair, and another was reported to have been found by an archaeologist in Connecticut. A third discovery was made in a cave along the Coosa River, which flows through north western Georgia and eastern Alabama. This time it was another Greek lamp dating back to 250 BC and found with it were many other pieces, all of which showed no sign of use. They appeared to be a sack full of trade goods.

Archaeologists consider these isolated finds as modern losses and stray items which have come across the Atlantic since the time of Columbus.

China is the other great civilisation believed to have made regular trips to America, which if true, would have greatly influenced both materials and tackle for fishing. There was a book in China written between AD 502 and 557 called *The History of the Liang Dynasty*, which tells of a Buddhist monk who voyaged over the ocean to a magical land where people dressed in a different way.

Some writers have suggested that this country was America and were very excited some years ago, when what appeared proof of the theory was discovered. Some Chinese junk anchors were found off the coast of California at Palos Verdes Peninsula, which is now part of Los Angeles.

There was no doubt that these stone anchors were similar to the ones used in junks in China for centuries. A more cautious group of archaeologists examined the material from which the anchors were made. They found that their composition was Monterey shale which is a widely distributed rock along the coast of California.

This created a mystery as to why Chinese junks should have anchors made in California. Further investigation showed that it was not a visiting boat, but a resident one, as there were hundreds of Chinese fishermen living on this coast in the nineteenth century and working from junks built in California. In the early part of the twentieth century they were driven out of business by competition and all

Haida halibut hook

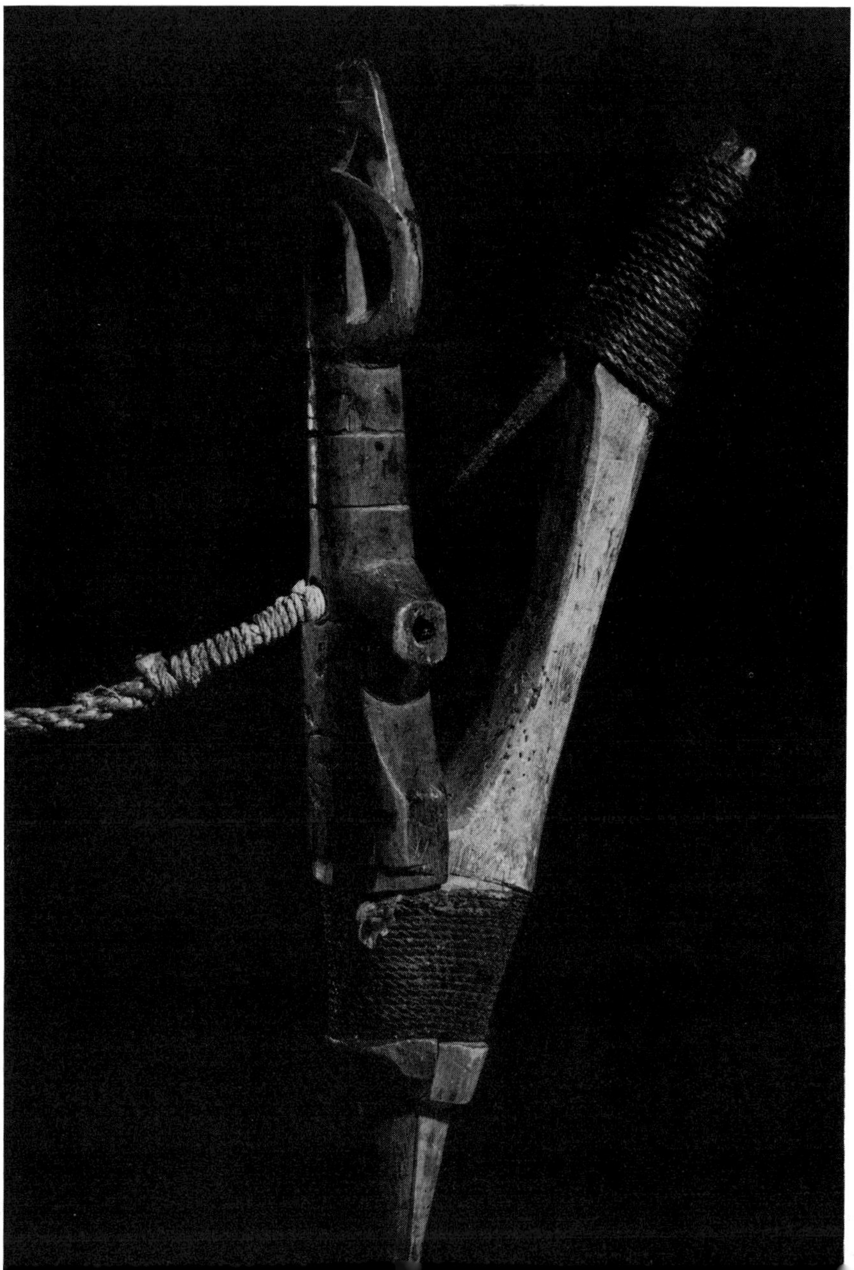

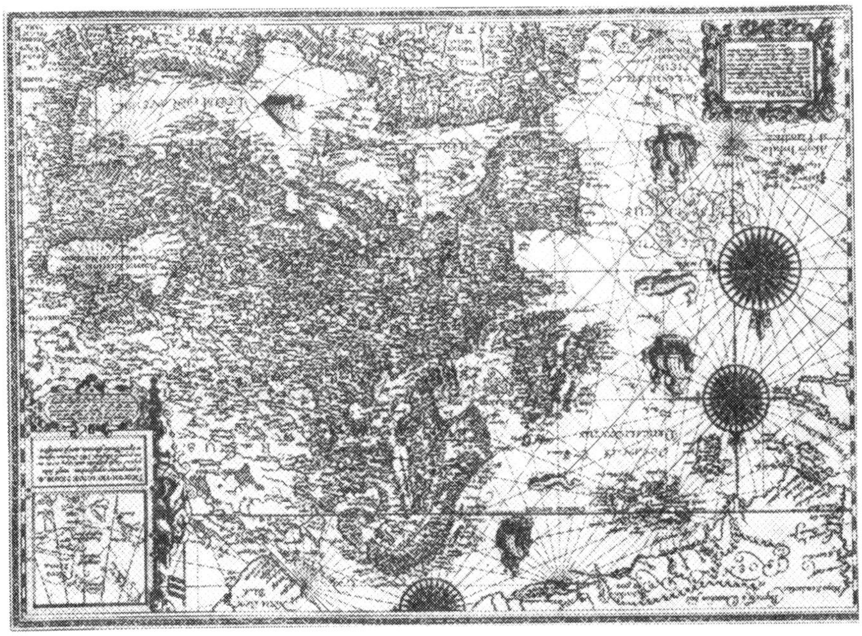

Baptista van Deutecom's map of Europe c.1599

the boats disappeared.

None of the claims for early colonisation of America can meet the requirements of professional archaeologists and there is no firm evidence to suggest there was any but the Indian culture up to the sixteenth century AD. There must have been the odd landing on the coast of America where a craft was blown by trade winds, but there is nothing to suggest that civilisations of the old world made regular crossings and colonised in numbers that would have influenced the development of the country, or introduced the fishing rod and reel to America at an early period.

The earliest implements and methods of catching fish in America evolved and were practised by the Indian. Like his Palaeolithic ancestor, he was an expert hunter-fisher and although the tackle he used throughout his history may appear crude by modern standards, there is no doubting his efficiency.

He used a wide range of designs and materials for fish hooks, depending on availablility and wariness of the fish. Probably the gorge and the plain hook made from wood or bone were the earliest. The shell-heaps of Santa Barbara have produced gorges while the Ohio Mounds have unhearthed unbarbed hooks of bone, according to Frederick Webb Hodge's *Hand-book of American Indians* (Bureau of American Ethnology Bulletin No 30 Part 1 1905, Smithsonian Institution, Washington DC.) and this publication gave details of various type of Indian hooks and lines. These included hooks made from wood, bone, shell, stone, copper and natural hooks from cactus spines, and hook shapes found in the bones of animals and birds. The best known are the large halibut compound hooks from the nineteenth and early twentieth century. Some tribes made a 'V' shaped hook by lashing together two sections of wood, with a bone point lashed to the end of one side and facing inwards. Others made a 'U' shaped hook by bending a section of wood and lashed a point to the end of one side facing inwards at an angle of 45°. I am grateful to the British Columbia Provincial Museum, Victoria BC, Canada and the Museum of Archaeology and Anthropology of Cambridge, England for supplying photographs of these types of hooks, and information on the methods of their construction. The Indians made the bend in the 'U' formed hook by placing a straight shaped piece of wood, which had been soaked with water, into a hot crude oven in the ground. A steady supply of water was thrown in and turned to steam. Eventually the wood became pliable and was then removed and pegged to the required shape on a board and soaked with fat.

Phillips Fine Art Auctioneers

Indian fish arrows

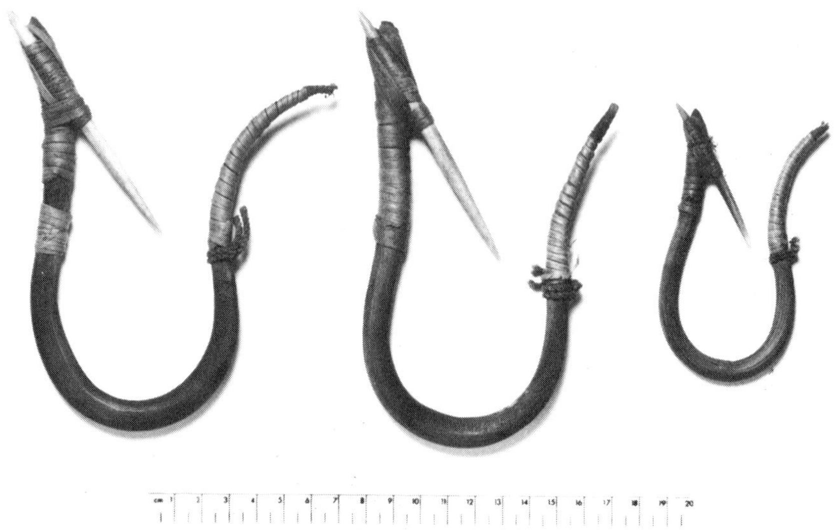

'U' shaped halibut hooks

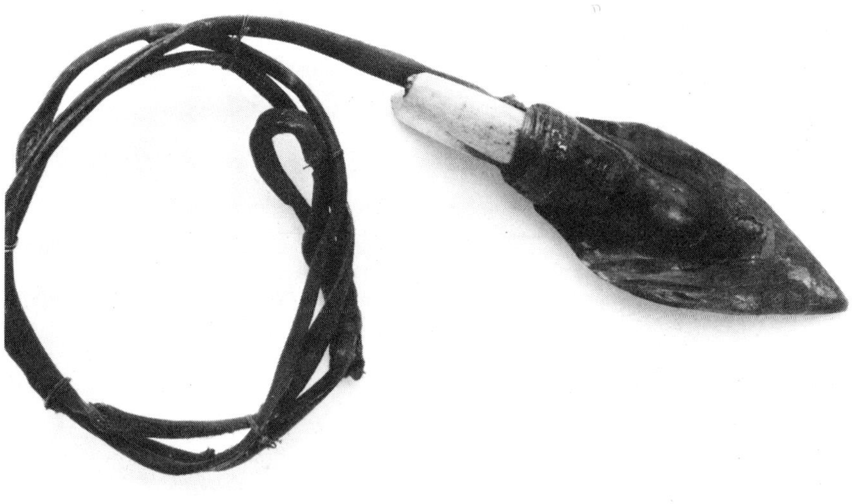

Harpoon head which became detached from the shaft on penetration and was retrieved by means of the line

Some wooden hooks made by the Indians had the ability to sink. This was achieved by selecting the wood which forms the knot, where a branch grows from the trunk, at which point it is very dense and heavy.

Indians had the knowledge and ability to make fishing lines and nets from natural materials, including twisted bark, roots, nettle and kelp, and these were used in a wide variety of ways.

Spears and harpoons were used to kill fish and the difference in the two depended on the method of use and the design of the head. The spear had a pointed head fixed to a shaft which remained in the hands of the fisher while retrieving the fish. The harpoon had either a fixed head, or one detachable from the shaft when the fish was penetrated, but both forms were retrieved by means of a line.

The spear was better suited for the capture of smaller fish which had not the power to break the shaft, while the harpoon was used against the bigger, more powerful ones. The bow and arrow has always been considered the Indian's hunting weapon, but it was equally as effective in the killing of fish. It was necessary to judge the pace of a fish swimming and at the same time make allowance for light refraction. Once the skill had been acquired the fish arrow became as deadly as the harpoon gun. The capture of large numbers of fish was achieved by the use of river traps and weirs constructed from stone, wood, and nets in the same way as practised by early man.

The book *Indian Fishing: Early Methods on the North West Coast,* by Hilary Stewart (Published by Douglas & McIntire of Vancouver) gives a full and illustrated account and is the most informative work on the subject. Stewart describes how large nets made from the stinging nettle (*Urtica Lyallii*) were used, together with stone sinkers across large sections of a river. This was often a communal activity organised on a regular basis where the fish were both caught and dried. There were two methods of preservation, one

The Haskell Minnow

'Philbrook & Payne, Makers – Pat. Apld For' Marked Trout Reel. Made before the granting of the 1877 Philbrook patent and its subsequent assignment to the H L Leonard Rod Co., who marketed the 'Leonard Reel' for a century. Only one other of these orange and black side plate reels is known to exist in collections and one other is reported to have been found. This 2⅜" diameter click reel of German silver and orange with black hard rubber is in sparkling near mint condition

SALESMAN'S WALLETS BY S ALLCOCK & CO.

Folding wallet of six compartments displaying trout flies

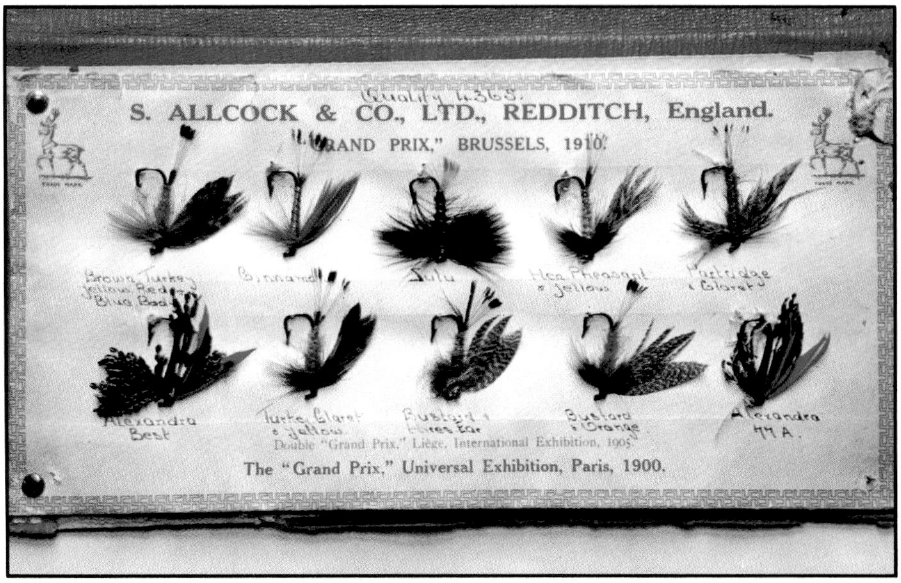

Folding wallet of four compartments displaying forty wet flies

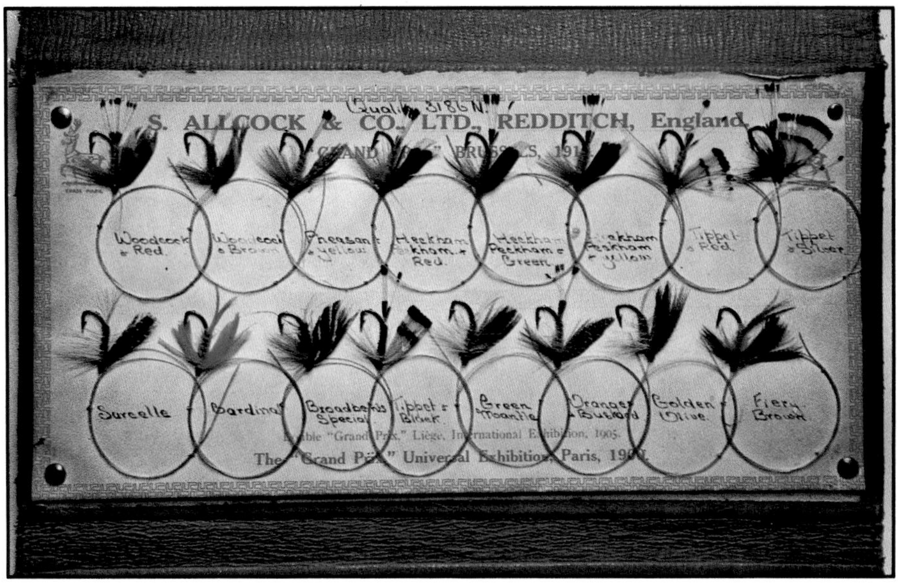

Folding wallet of four compartments displaying 62 wet flies

The worn condition of the wallets bears witness to the countless displays in fishing tackle shops throughout Britain in the first half of the twentieth century. They are of supreme importance to the history of fishing tackle

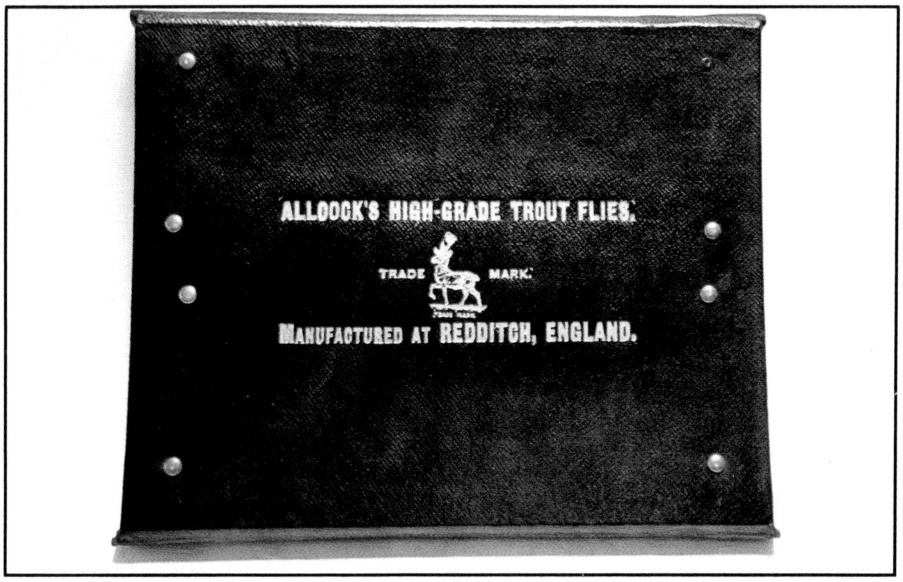

Salesman's case 9½" x 7½" containing forty two trout flies displayed in four compartments

Folding display card containing five salmon flies with spinning heads

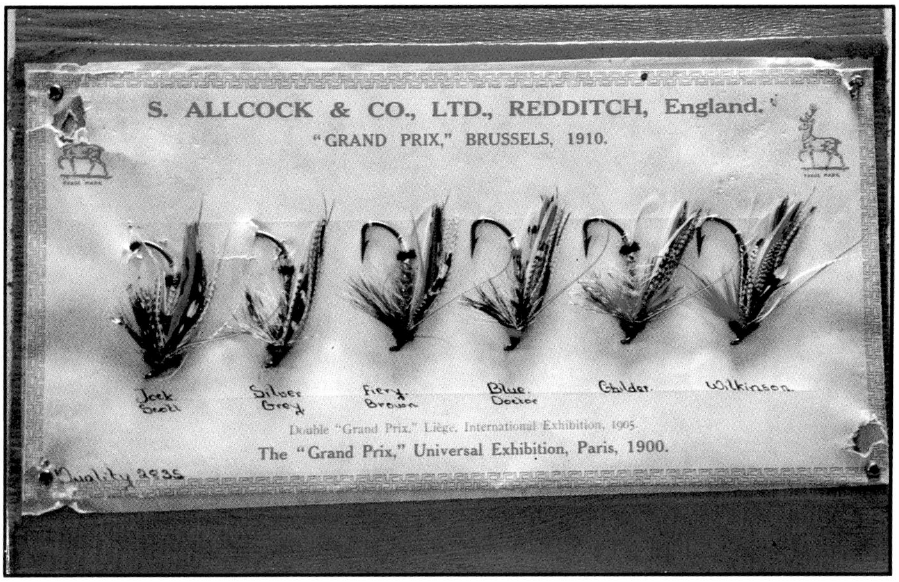

Folding wallet of eight compartments displaying 61 steel-eyed salmon flies

Julius Vom Hofe, Maker, N Y marked trout reel, with back sliding click button (2¼″ diameter)

The Kent Double Spinner Artificial Minnow manufactured exclusively by F A Pardee & Co, Kent, Ohio. Size 3⅞″ long

Early E D W Vom Hofe N Y and Pat Jan 23 83 marked reel in German silver and hard rubber with back sliding click button. Diameter 2⅜″

A Bonafide Aluminium Minnow lure based on the 1907 patent of Hiram H Passage who assigned half to George E Van Decar of the Bonafide Manufacturing Company. Size 3¼″ long

Left: William Mills & Son N Y marked (Leonard) multiplying reel in German silver and hard rubber with back sliding click button. Diameter 2¾″

using drying racks which could utilise the sun and wind and the other the use of heat and smoke in specially constructed Smoke Houses.

The Indian has always shown a great reverence for natural resources as his ancestors would have done. He believed in many forms of spirits and often carved their forms on hooks and other fishing implements. The fact that migratory fish and wildfowl returned in great numbers, while in other years there were very few, gave him the belief that some great supernatural force in the form of spirits were exercising an influence. The Indian's ceremonies were to give thanks for the natural resources, which he respected and treated as something far more important and spiritual than merely as food.

A Fox Chief from M'Kenney's History of the Indian Tribes of North America 1837 – 88

Phillips Fine Art Auctioneers

THE NEW AMERICA

Drawing by Fraser Jay

Replica of the Mayflower, the ship which carried the early Pilgrims to America in 1620

The first English fishing tackle would have reached America in the sixteenth century, arriving with the first British settlers. There were probably various types of rods, ranging from a simple one-piece bottom rod to ones with a number of pieces as described by Dame Juliana, together with hooks, horse-hair line and possibly artificial baits of the period.

The first of these settlements was the ill-fated first colony at Roanoke Island. A party of 108 men sailed from England on April 9th 1585 with instructions from Sir Walter Raleigh to settle in what at the time was called Virginia. It was a big area of North America, stretching from what today is Pennsylvania to South Carolina. They would have been well aware that their initial survival would depend upon the limited provisions from the ship and the animals, fish and fruit of the new territory. Therefore a number of the men would most certainly have included fishing tackle among their implements and weapons when they planned their requirements.

The voyage across the Atlantic was completed and they landed on Roanoke Island but experienced great difficulties. After a year they returned to England on the ships of Sir Francis Drake. A second party of colonists arrived and they in turn returned to England, leaving only 15 adventurers in America.

In 1587 Raleigh sent a party of 117 settlers under the leadership of John White, with instructions to settle on the shores of Chesapeake Bay. The ship's crew refused to sail further than Roanoke Island, so everyone had to disembark on July 22nd 1587. Not one of the earlier party was found alive. On August 18th, only twenty eight days after the colonists landed, a baby girl was born. It was John White's grandchild and christened Virginia Dave, being the first English child to be born on the American continent.

White sailed home to England for badly needed supplies, but due to the Spanish War did not get back to America until 1590. When he landed on the site of the first British colony, he found that everyone had disappeared leaving behind only 'Croaton' carved on a tree. Historians believe that Indians called Lumbee, in the area of north Carolina, were originally the Croaton tribe and were involved in the disappearance.

The first permanent British settlement in America was established in 1607 when one hundred settlers reached Chesapeake Bay and founded Jamestown. It had been planned and financed by a group of London merchants and blessed by the Church of England, who wished to spread Protestant Christianity to the New World.

In 1620 a small band of religious separatists formed the second colony at Plymouth, New England. They had left England to escape religious persecution and, after an unhappy period in the Netherlands, sailed to America. These were followed by new settlers to Massachusetts Bay, New Hampshire, Maine and all the new colonies flourished and grew.

British fishing tackle would have accompanied many of the earliest settlers to the new colonies, but their attempts at

First American patent for a lure in 1852 – Buel's Trolling Spoon

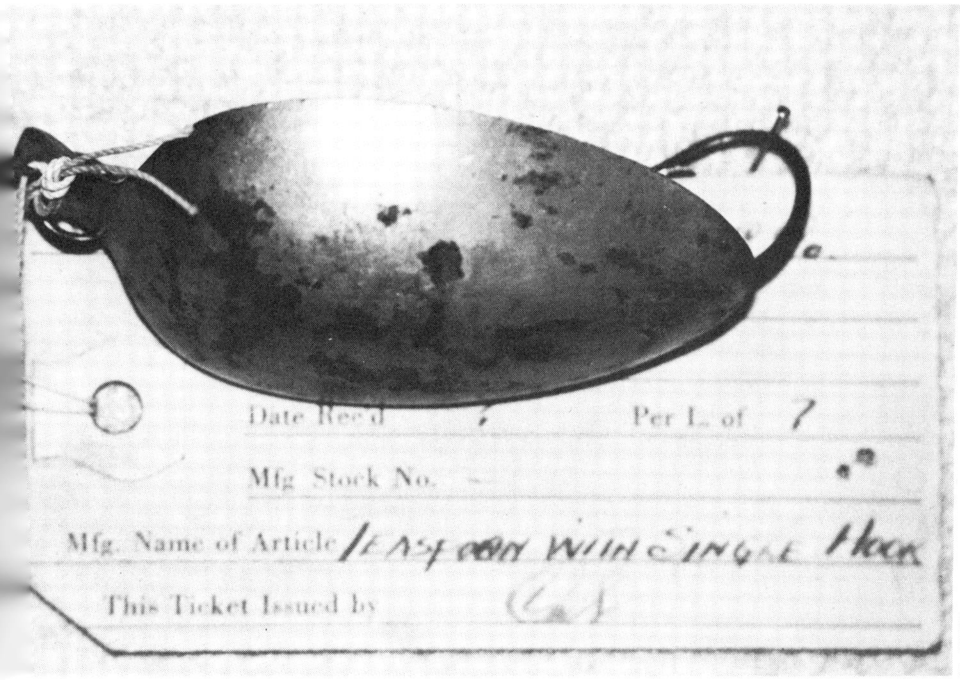

Karl White

Buel's hand-made spoon believed to be the earliest spoon made in America

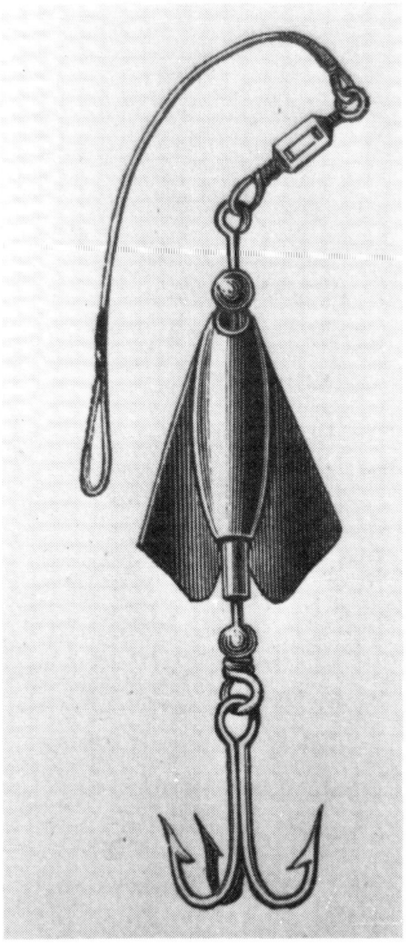

'Devil Killer' lure sold by Ustonson to King George IV in 1828

fishing would have proved ineffective in comparison to the skill of the Indian. The difference was due to the fact that fishing and tackle evolved in Britain mainly as a sport or pastime, whereas the Indian possessed a far superior knowledge of local fish ecology and used simple but deadly implements on which generations of his people had depended for food.

The new settlers never adopted the superior basic fishing methods of the indigenous semi hunter-fisher. The agricultural economy of the new colonies permitted the continuation of fishing mainly as a pastime, in the same way as practised in Britain, and it was from the old country that the new settlers continued to take supplies of tackle until the demand grew large enough to sustain makers of their own.

By 1750, the population which started with 100 British settlers in 1607, had reached one and a third million, with immigrants from Germany, France, Holland and Ireland. Almost everyone worked in rural activities and the first towns, roads, schools and churches were built. Small industries had been established for essential goods and other commodities were brought in from the countries of Europe using local agents. Fishing rods and reels continued to be purchased mainly from Britain until towards the end of the eighteenth century, although some would have been made by local craftsmen.

It was the beginning of the nineteenth century before makers really considered fishing tackle as a viable commercial enterprise, and turned their minds to producing goods which could outsell the imports from Britain. Up to that time the London tackle makers found America a very lucrative market for their brass winches, rods and accessories which included hooks, lines and a wide range of artificial baits. Eventually by the 1840s, American manufacturers had become established and their products replaced all the imported tackle with the exception of artificial baits. Evidence to support this comes from a publication called the *American Angler's Guide*, printed in 1846 and sold at the Angler's Depot, 122 Fulton St, New York by John J Brown, who was probably the author. It gave details of the goods sold and an insight into the state of the American tackle trade, which by the 1840s was turning out everything the fisherman required. It said:

> 'American reels have almost entirely superseeded the foreign; in fact, with the exception of artificial baits, all articles of tackle made in this country, are equal if not superior to those of England, and if the angler can procure the American, he should patriotically avoid anything else.''

The hobby of collecting lures, which are mainly in the form of simple metal baits or what are termed 'plugs', is very popular in America, and has now reached such proportions that a National Fishing Lure Collector's Club (NFLCC) is active with members across America and as far away as Canada, Britain and Japan.

The generally accepted history is that although Indians and early man practised the use of simple lures, the modern versions were not introduced until the

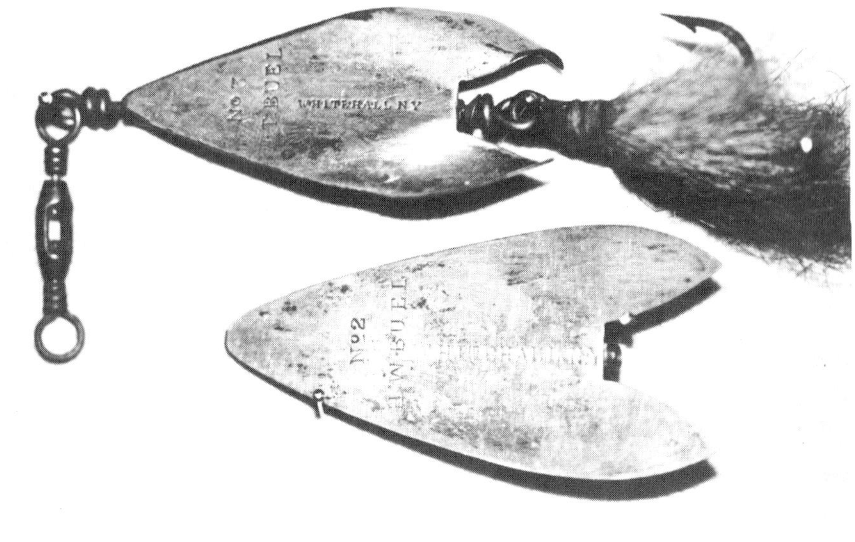

Buel's Trolling Spoons No 2 and No 3. Based on the patent of 1852

nineteenth century. It is believed that a few crude forms called Devons, Angels and Phantoms came into America and it was from these simple beginnings that they evolved. The first was the spoon bait of Julio T Buel in about 1830, which he discovered when he accidentally dropped a spoon into Lake Bomoseen and saw a fish strike at it. A similar colourful story is told of James Heddon, who in c.1898 threw a piece of wood into Dowagiac Creek and saw it taken by a bass, which set him on the road to building a plug empire. They are wonderful stories and may be true, but the history of commercial lure making has a much earlier beginning.

American patents have usually

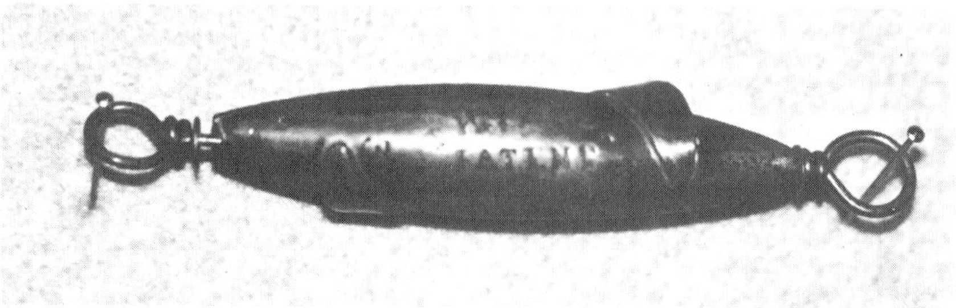

Charles DeSaxe of New York was granted a patent on June 12th, 1855 for an 'Improved Serpentine Spinner'. It was assigned to the Thomas H Bate Company

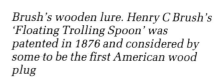

Brush's wooden lure. Henry C Brush's 'Floating Trolling Spoon' was patented in 1876 and considered by some to be the first American wood plug

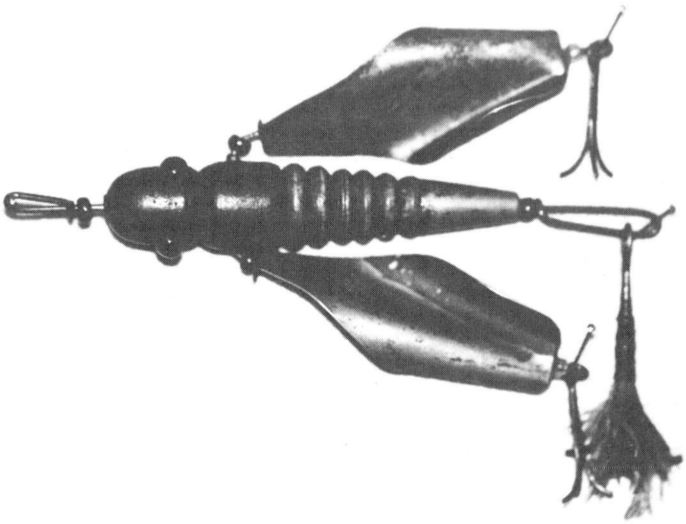

Flying Helgramite.

been the basis for piecing together that country's history of fishing tackle but there is a problem with using these documents. The records did not start until 1790 and the earliest surviving patent for fishing is dated 1838. The weakness of using these patents is the fact that one cannot be sure whether the idea is not the product of another generation's ingenuity.

The earliest American lure patent was taken out by Julio T Buel for a trolling spoon in 1852, and this had a remarkable resemblance to Kill Devils which Ustonson is known to have sold to King George IV in 1828. I believe these to be the same metal bait described as Devil Killer and

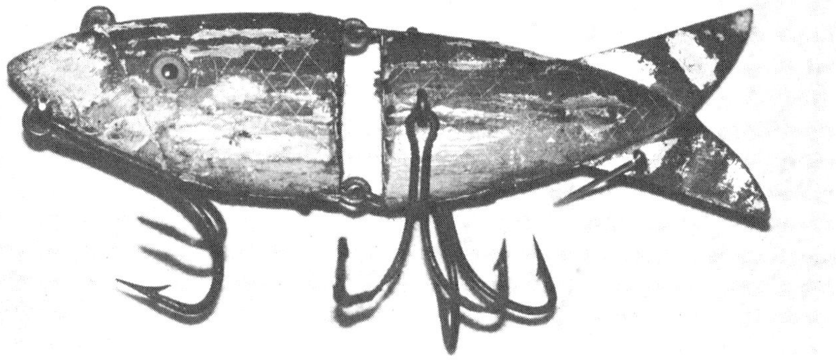

Karl White

K & K Animated Minnow. Believed by some to be the first jointed bait to be made in America

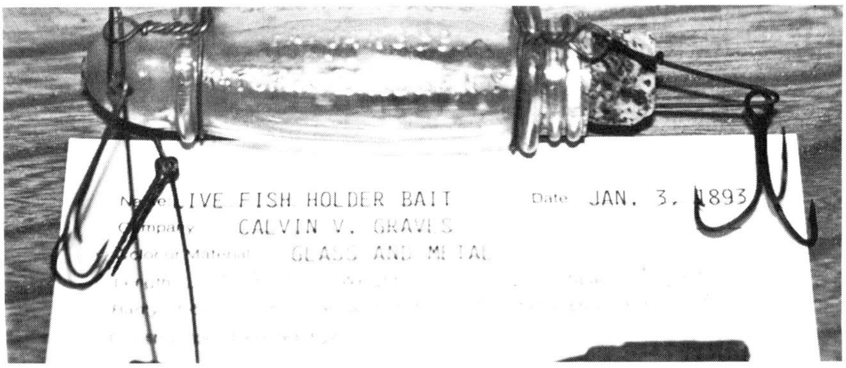

Karl White

The Welsh and Graves Minnow Tube was patented January 3rd, 1893. It was an embossed clear brown glass tube with a hole drilled to circulate water and contained a live minnow. It was the first glass plug

Harry Comstock's Flying Helgramite was patented in 1883 with a wood body early American wood plug

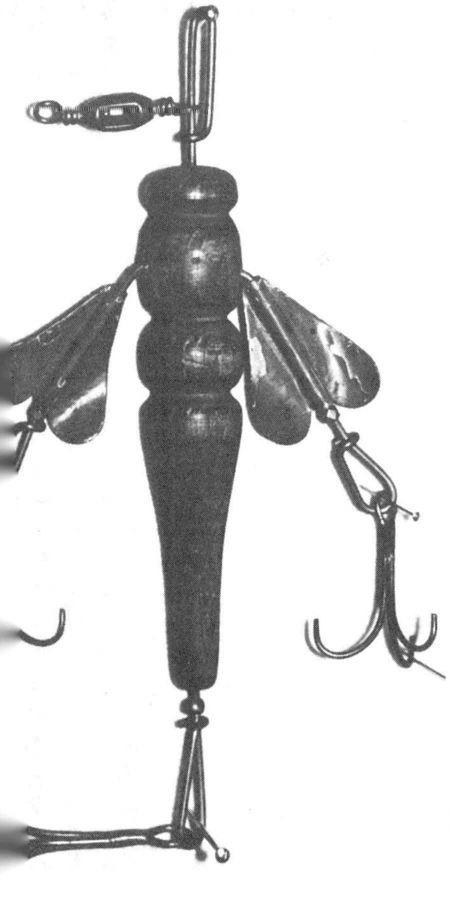

Karl White

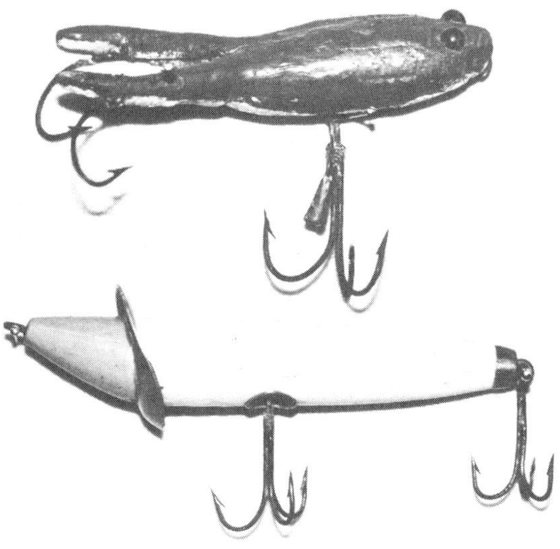

Karl White

Heddon hand carved frog (c1898) and the Slope Nose Expert based on Heddon's patent granted April 1st, 1902

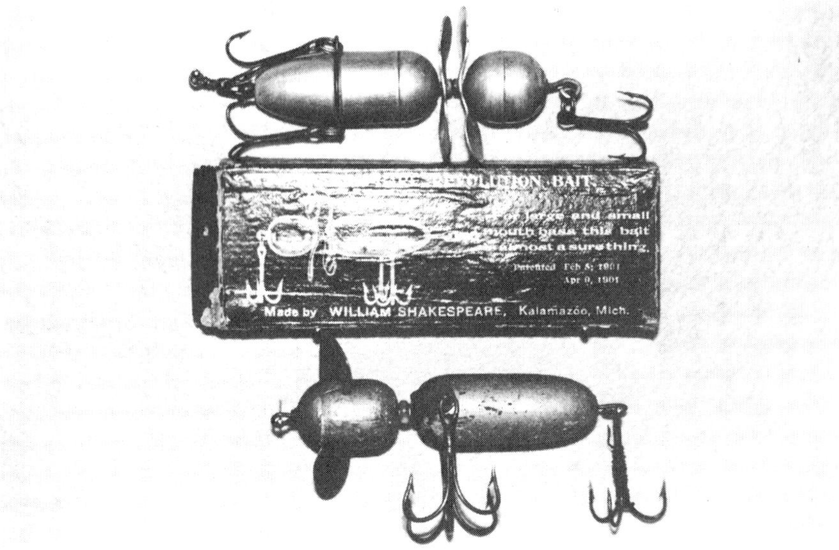

Karl White

Shakespeare wood Revolution, patented in 1901. Also an aluminium Revolution

E & B D Barne's plug c.1906

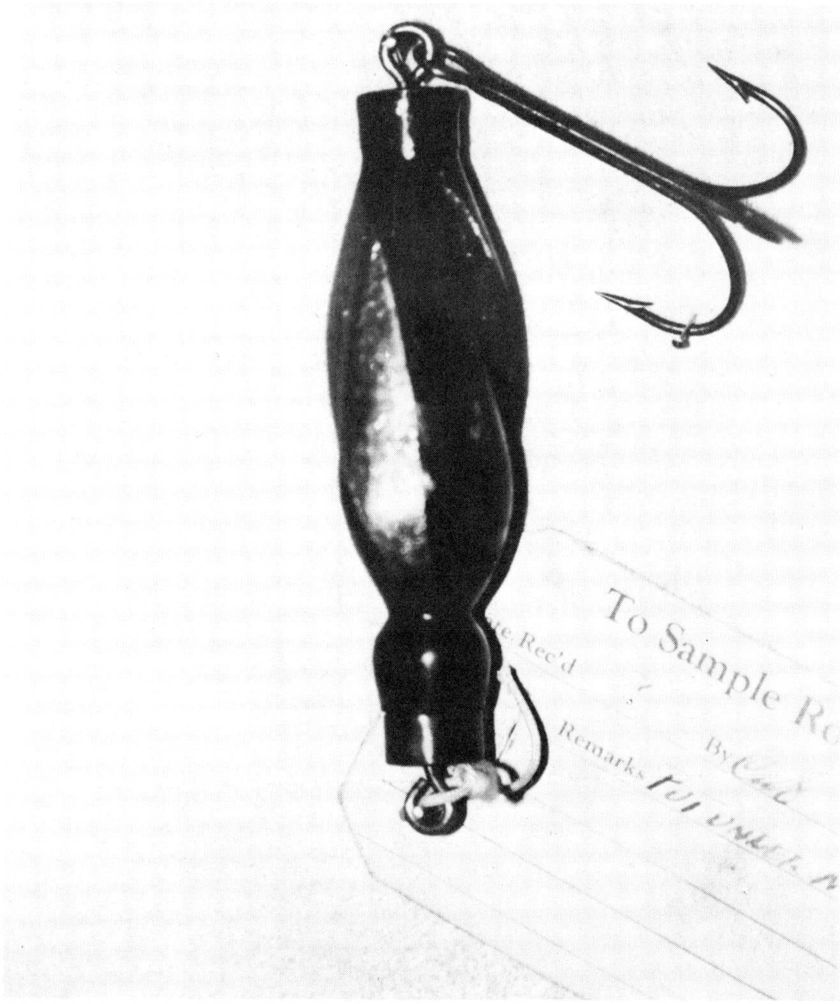

Karl White

illustrated in *Fishing Tackle* by J H Keene in 1886. This author confirmed that the lure had been in use for at least fifty years.

It is now clear from research into early angling books and the information on newly discovered bills and trade cards, that a wide variety of lures were being sold throughout the eighteenth century, and possibly earlier in Britain. These included painted metal imitation fish and numerous plugs, such as artificial mice, frogs and many varieties of fish. They would be individually hand made of cloth, silk and other materials and of a beautiful life-like quality. All these baits were being sold to America in the early period and were so good that sales continued into the early part of the nineteenth century.

Eventually American makers started in the tackle business and extended their activities to producing lures. Fashions changed and new cheaper forms of artificial baits captured the market. American flair and ingenuity resulted in a steady flow of new ideas, designs and materials, many of which were patented, to take full advantage of a profitable and ever expanding market.

Excellent American specialist publications have been produced for lure collectors. Many of these contain large numbers of illustrations to assist in the identification of the thousands of American plugs, a large number of which are listed in the Price Guide section of this book. It has only been possible to include a few illustrations of the earliest examples. All have been kindly supplied by Mr Karl White, and are a small sample of the ones on display at his National Fishing Tackle Museum at Luther, Oklahoma which houses one of the largest collections of tackle in the country.

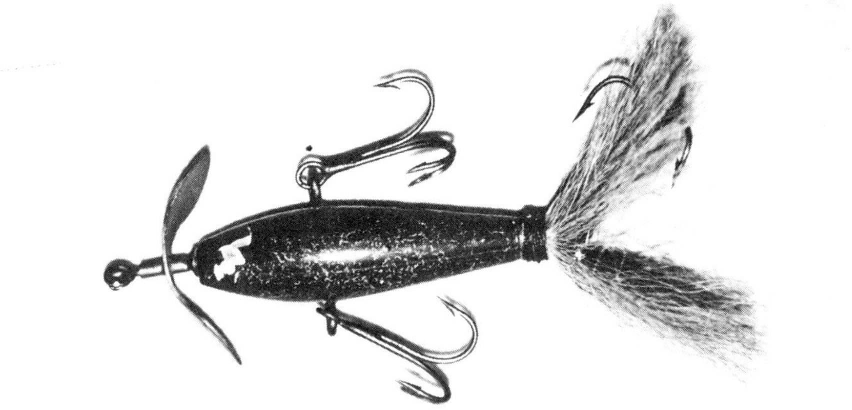

Worden's Combination Minnow. An early plug by South Bend Bait Co

Karl White

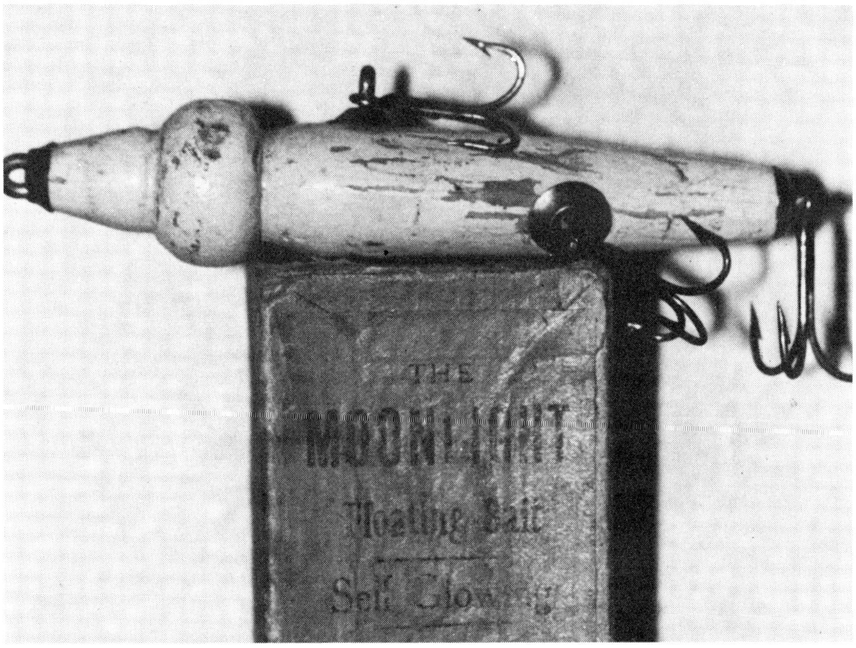

Moonlight Floating Bait. One of the earliest Moonlight plugs

Karl White

Henzel Booster Bait which was made of muslin type material and contained food. Henzel's patent of 1907 recommended that the food should be 'flour, rice, potato, egg or any other food stuff'

Karl White

Izaac Walton was the first to record the construction and use of an artificial minnow in Britain

Charles Cotton claimed that Walton was 'the best Angler with a Minnow in Britain' but did not approve of its use and said – 'for though we do it with a counterfeit fly, me thinks it should hardly be expected that a man should deceive a fish with a counterfeit fish.'

MEEK & MILAM | B. C. MILAM | B. C. MILAM & SON

"HARK TO THE MUSIC OF THE REEL!
WE LISTEN WITH DEVOTION:
THERE'S SOMETHING IN THAT CIRCLING WHEEL
THAT STIRS THE HEART'S EMOTIONS!"

SOME ACCOUNT OF THE NATURE, CAPABILITIES AND MANIFOLD VIRTUES OF

THE MILAM
"FRANKFORT, KENTUCKY"
FISHING REEL

MANUFACTURED BY

B. C. MILAM & SON
FRANKFORT, KENTUCKY, U. S. A.
ESTABLISHED 1839

KENTUCKY REELS

The finest multiplying reels have always been made in America and one may forgive Dr James A Henshall, author of *Book of the Black Bass*, for erroneously crediting the early American maker Snyder with being the inventor. Henshall was one of the few people to have first-hand experience of the earliest Snyder multiplier, which was the beginning of the legendary Kentucky reels. The multiplying reel was invented and in common use in England in the eighteenth century and two sorts were being used. One had the crank in the centre of the box, while the more common form positioned it between the centre and the edge of the rim. Some could wind up to three and four times with one turn and in 1808, Williamson's *The Complete Angler's Vade Mecum* described and gave drawings of a nine fold compound multiplying reel.

The earliest record of a brass multiplying winch was on a trade card issued in the late 1760s by Onesimus Ustonson of London, who placed a similar advertisement in a book *The Art of Angling* in 1770. An Ustonson multiplier was reported to have been found in a store about sixty miles from the Kentucky river, which was inscribed 'Ustonson, Maker to his Majesty, Temple Bar, London' and the foot support stamped with his trade mark 'U'. It is probable that Snyder based his design on such a reel, the first of which was made about 1820. Henshall said that Snyder made his first reel in 1810 while living in Paris, Bourbon County, Kentucky. However, he may have been less than accurate, because there is no record of such an early reel nor a resident by the name of Snyder in Bourbon County which pre-dates 1820. What we can be sure of is that Snyder, a watchmaker, introduced precision engineering and made the first smooth running reel which could cast a longer distance and retrieve the line more quickly. He was the first important maker of the quality Kentucky reels and was the inspiration for other watchmakers to diversify their activities to making fishing reels.

In 1830, a Mr Theodore Noel and his brother were watchmakers at Frankfort, Kentucky and made a brass fishing reel. Benjamin C Milam was apprentice to Theodore's brother until they went out of business.

In 1835 Johnathan Fleming Meek moved from Danville to Frankfort, carrying on in business as a watchmaker and jeweller. He had a younger brother Benjamin Fleming Meek, born in 1817, who he employed as an apprentice. It is believed that their interest in reels developed from repairing those of local fishermen and progressed to designing their own superior model. By 1837 they were so busy that they took on a sixteen year old apprentice called Benjamin Cave Milam, who was born July 1st, 1821. This enabled Johnathan to concentrate on watchmaking and jewellery and his brother Benjamin to make reels. The younger brother became a partner in 1839 and the reels produced were marked 'J F and B F Meek'.

The apprentice Milam proved most capable and made reels up to June 1846, when he left to serve one year as Captain of a Kentucky

FAMOUS KENTUCKY REEL MAKERS

Benjamin F Meek (1817–1901)

Benjamin C Milam (1821–1904)

John W Milam (1859–1928)

George W Gayle (1834–1896)

Clarence Gayle

Volunteer Company in the Mexican War. He returned in 1847 and became a partner in the Meek business in 1848, when the firm changed its name to J F Meek and Co. The reels continued to be marked 'J F and B F Meek, Frankfort Ky,' but in 1852 the business failed.

Johnathan F Meek moved to Louisville, where he worked until his death in the trade of watchmaker for W'm Kendrick. On January 1st 1853, B F Meek and B C Milam formed a new firm named Meek and Milam.

They used premises at 222 Main Street, with Meek attending to the jewellery and watchmaking on one floor and Milam resumed reel making on the one above. The reels were stamped 'Meek and Milam, Frankfort Ky,' but in 1855 the partnership was dissolved.

They continued to work independently from the same premises, Meek as a watchmaker and Milam in the reel trade. The reels continued to be stamped 'Meek and Milam' up to 1880, although Meek had no interest for the last 25 years of this period. The stamp was changed in 1881 to 'B C Milam Frankfort, Ky.'

In 1887, John the son of B C Milam, started in his father's workshop, having worked two years previously during the summers, and assisted in the sale of reels which had become internationally known for fine quality. They were smooth running with low friction steel to brass gears of a 4 to 1 ratio and described in a catalogue – 'The friction of the parts is so slight that a smart strike of the handle causes it to take about 50 revolutions.'

In 1890 John was fully skilled and appointed as a partner in the business. Although the name of the firm was changed to B C Milam & Son, the stamp on the reel remained the same 'B C Milam, Frankfor, Ky' with the words 'The Frankfort Kentucky Reel'.

In 1900 a new stamp was introduced with the words 'B C Milam & Son' and continued for the next twenty eight years. On January 29th, 1904 Benjamin Cave

Richard W Oliver

Extremely rare c.1845 'J F & B F Meek, Frankfort, KY' marked brass reel with horn handle and sliding click button. The logo marking used 1839 – 1852. Size 2⅛" diameter and 2" wide spool.

Frank Stewart

Above: 'Meek & Milam No 3 Frankfort KY.' Brass with click, head cap screws unnumbered, c.1875, (Buffalo horn grip)

'Meek & Milam No 2 Frankfort KY.' German silver with click, 3 number head cap screws, c.1853 (counter balance handle may be replacement for crank). German silver is another name for nickel silver

Frank Stewart

Milam died, leaving the son John to run the firm until his own death in March 1928.

There are additional Milam markings to confuse the already difficult saga, namely a maker's stamp with the words 'B C Milam & Son, Frankfort, Ky Rustic No,' and sold in the ten year period prior to Milam Junior's death. It is believed that this reel was not made in Frankfort by John, who like his father had worked initially single-handed throughout many years in business. Instead it was a reel he had designed to compete with the competitors such as Meek, and made elsewhere by a manufacturer of cheaper mass produced reels. These 'rustics' were offered in a variety of sizes for about $7.50 each.

Some Milam reels were made after the death of John Milam from the remainder of the parts from his workshop. Clarence Gayle was the surrogate manufacturer and a further story says that when Gayle died in 1948, some remaining Milam parts were sold off to a gunsmith called W G Farmer of Lexington, Kentucky.

It is believed that he made one or two reels which were purchased on his death by an antique shop. These in turn were purchased by a discerning citizen of the area, who donated them to the Kentucky History Museum in Frankfort.

After the partnership broke up in 1855, B F Meek continued to trade in watchmaking and jewellery at 222 Main St, below his former partner. In 1882 he moved to a new home at 839 Seventh St, Louisville and re-located his business there. By that time two sons, Pitman and Sylvester, had joined the firm and Meek had extended his activities to making reels once more.

At first the reels were marked 'B F Meek' but quickly changed to 'B F Meek & Sons'. The quality of the reels which they made were of the highest order in both materials and design. All were hand made and production rarely exceeded seven reels per month.

In 1898 Pitman Meek died and his father, who by that time was

Frank Stewart

'BC Milam No 3 Frankfort KY.' German silver with click and drag. c.1883

Frank Stewart

'BC Milam & Son No 3 Frankfort KY, The Frankfort Kentucky Reel.' Brass with German silver trim, click and drag, c.1904

Below: 'BF Meek & Sons No 3 Louisville KY.' German silver with click

Frank Stewart

Frank Stewart

'J L Sage No 3 Frankfort KY.' Brass with click and drag, Buffalo horn grip, c.1880s

Frank Stewart

'G W Gayle & Son, Frankfort KY.' German silver, Kentucky style. (No 3 size unmarked). c.1900–1940

Below: 'G W Gayle & Son, Frankfort KY.' German silver and new style. c.1900–1940

Frank Stewart

eighty-one years of age, decided to sell the business. It was purchased by J H Sutcliffe who formed a corporation with two other men called Ron Carter and James O'Conner of Louisville, Kentucky. Benjamin Fleming Meek returned to Frankfort where he lived until his death. The new partnership continued to trade as B F Meek & Sons, but immediately started to advertise 'the original Frankfort Kentucky Reel', which the Milam family had spent many years making famous.

Legal proceedings were started by B C Milam & Son, while Sutcliffe and Co started the Blue Grass Reel Works Co. In 1901 Judge Shackleford Miller ruled in favour of Milam and Son and stopped Sutcliffe and partners using any of the words 'Frankfort Kentucky' and awarded damages based on the profit made by the sale of the falsely described reels.

In 1916 Sutcliffe and partners sold the business to Horton Manufacturing Company of Bristol, Connecticut, who continued to manufacture Meek reels up to 1945 but stamped them "Horton M'F'G Co, Bristol, Connecticut." Also "Meek No." or "Bluegrass No."

Some reels bearing the Meek name were made by the American Company. Sylvanus Meek, a son of BF Meek stayed on with the business when it was sold to JH Sutcliffe & Co and eventually he ended up at the American Company who used his famous name.

In 1881, J L Sage started making reels at Frankfort. He had served his time as a gunsmith and operated a gun repair shop. During the spare time he had available between jobs, he made fishing reels which he stamped 'J L Sage'. His total output was about one hundred and he later moved to Lexington, Kentucky where he died about 1897.

George W Gayle was another old-time watchmaker who began making hand-made reels in Kentucky in 1883. He was born in 1832 and died in 1896 leaving a son Clarence who had been associated with him in the business. The reels they made were stamped 'W Gayle and Son.'

Clarence Gayle continued to run the family business and produced quality hand made reels, similar in beauty and dependability to the 'Meek' until about 1920 when he changed over to lesser quality single action fly reels. It is believed that Clarence obtained a stock of Milam reel parts when John Milam died and assembled some Milam reels. Some of these parts were still in stock when Clarence Gayle died in 1948 and, as already recorded, these were sold off and eventually ended up in the Kentucky Historical Museum in Frankfort.

I thank Frank Stewart, Steve Vernon, Ron Gast and the Kentucky Historical Museum for assistance with the history of Kentucky reels and the photographs kindly supplied.

Steve K Vernon

'BF Meek & Sons No 25 Blue Grass.' German silver with Carter's patent No 764348 quick-takedown design, but built with pillars and head plates. Not Carter's one piece drum frame

EARLIEST AMERICAN REEL PATENTS

In 1790 the US Patent Bill was introduced aimed at providing inventors with an exclusive monopoly for their ideas for a period of 14 years (it became 17 years in 1861). The cost was only a few dollars, and providing the patent was approved, the patentee could theoretically enjoy protection against commercialisation by anyone else. After a few years the work and responsibility for vetting patents by the authority was scrapped in favour of a simpler, quicker, but less effective registration system. In 1836 a fire destroyed the Patent Office and all records, believed to contain about 10,000 patents. It is doubtful whether there would have been many concerned with fishing as only one was registered in the following twenty years. After the fire, all patents were numbered and a better system of checking their validity was introduced.

There are hundreds of American patents relating to fishing tackle, but it has only been possible to include the earliest and most important which pioneered certain features on which successive generations of reels were based.

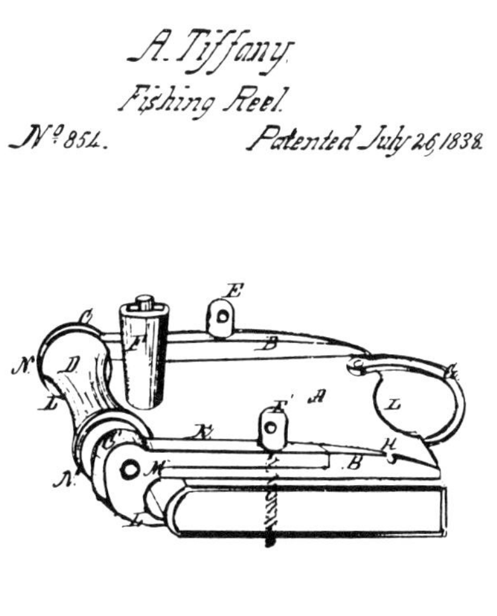

Tiffany patent

I have to thank the Science Reference Library in London where copies of American patents are housed, for their assistance in my research and supplying the patent documents and drawings included in this book. The ones detailed are familiar to collectors and historians of American tackle. I have been unable to find any new evidence of earlier patents than those well documented by earlier authorities. Steven K Vernon's book *Antique Fishing Reels,* (Stagpole Publications) gives details and drawings of all the important patents for reels of the USA.

The earliest surviving patent for a fishing device was No 854 granted to Arunah Tiffany of Gibson, Pa, on July 26th 1838. The invention was described as a fishing reel although it had little resemblance to one. It was a form of roller contraption which was meant to be attached to the rail of a boat for the manual hauling in of a line or net.

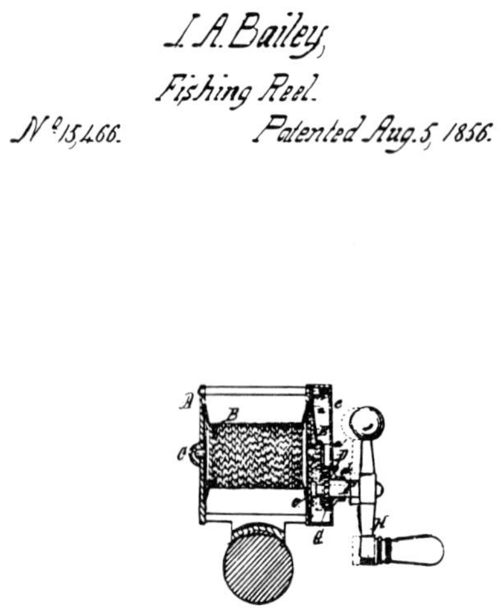

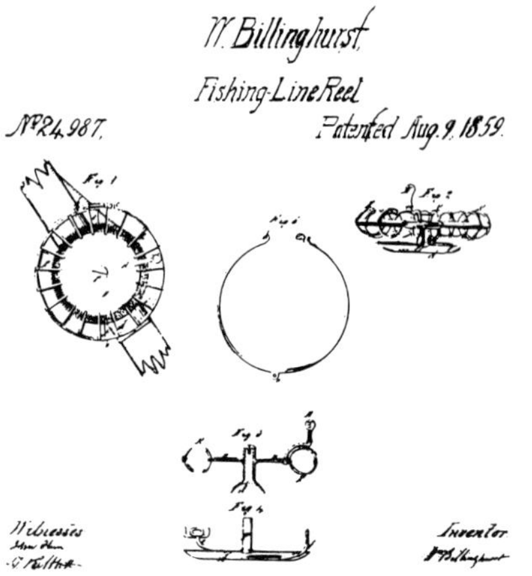

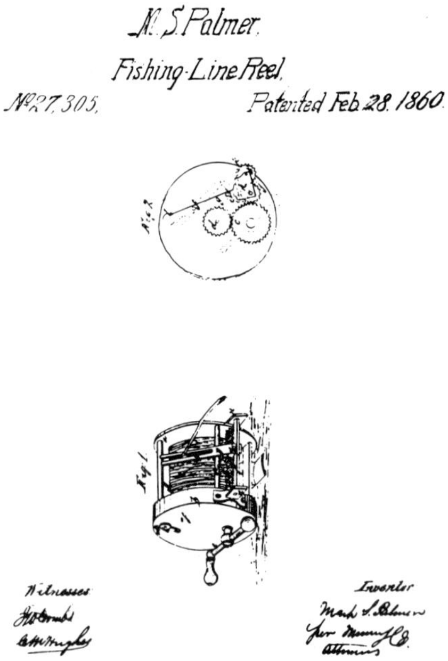

JOHN A BAILEY OF JERSEY CITY, NEW JERSEY. Patent No 15466 – August 5th 1856.

This was the first patent which could throw a reel in and out of gear using a type of clutch and is the earliest surviving patent for a true fishing reel. Bailey's design concerned a ball handled reel with a crankshaft, which could be worked laterally in a socket or collar attached to the end of the end plate of the reel frame. It could be thrown out of gear by moving the crank outwards and a flat spring maintained the free spool position. The gear was re-engaged by pressing the crankshaft inwards. He assigned the patent to John Warrin, a New York maker.

W BILLINGHURST OF ROCHESTER, NEW YORK. Patent No 24987 – August 9th 1859.

This was the first patent specifically for a reel frame and the skeletal design was claimed to offer a number of improvements. The principle idea was better line drying described in the patent as 'so constructing the reel that when the line is wound up, it shall form a ring instead of a cylinder, thus providing efficiently for its drying without unwinding the line.' Other advantages claimed were reduction in weight and cost and a quicker rewind of 'nearly ten times the amount taken up by one turn of the common reel-handle'. Billinghurst also said, 'the general form is much more convenient for carriage in the pocket, as the whole thing, line and all, forms a flat disc of no very great dimensions and which lies snug and close to the person.'

Many variations of the level-wind were patented including:

Charles L Noe	135283	Jan.	28th	1873
Simon W Wardell Jr	220776	Oct.	21st	1879
George L Crandel	336092	Feb	16th	1866
Andrew B Hendryx	351598	Oct	26th	1886
William D F Jarvis	368922	Aug	23rd	1887
Joseph P Costigan	396469	Jan	22nd	1889
Christian E Moller and Charles Raettig	401049	April	9th	1889
Samuel L Bean	467849	Jan	26th	1892
Curtis N Wilcox	477196	June	14th	1892
Thomas Greason	477754	June	28th	1892
Nelson H McGregor	520607	May	29th	1894
	522079	June	26th	1894

MARK S PALMER OF NEW BEDFORD, MASSACHUSETTS. Patent No 27305 – February 28th 1860.

This was the first patent for a level-wind mechanism and the design was remarkably similar to the ones used today. It was described in the patent as follows: 'This invention consists in the employment or use of a travelling or reciprocating line guide attached to the reel and operating automatically and in such a way as to cause the line, as it is wound up, to be adjusted evenly on the shaft of the reel'.

Several level-wind patents were registered including two from a man called Nelson H McGregor. His first patent was No 520607 (May 1894) and a second No 522079 (June 1894) for a gear train to drive the reel wind more efficiently. The makers, Wheeler & McGregor, marketed the Milwaukee reel which was probably the first with a level-wind device to be a commercial success.

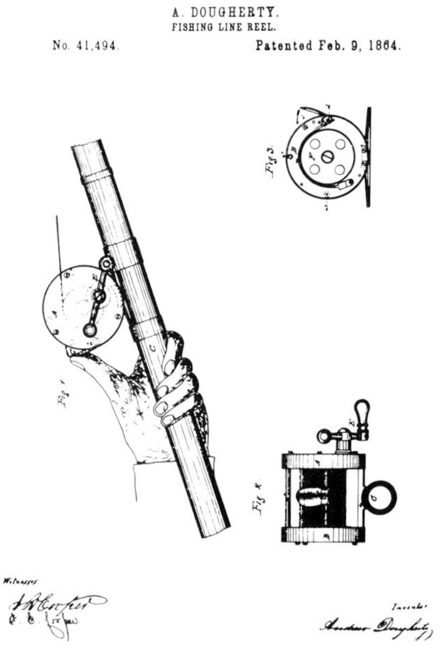

A DOUGHERTY OF BROOKLYN, NEW YORK. Patent No 41494 – February 9th 1864.

This was the earliest patent for a braking device. The text of the patent stated that some devices for controlling the speed at which fishing line could be taken off had been used at that time, 'but from defects in the construction or plan, such reels have not been used to an extent, and anglers of the present day prefer to control the unwinding of the line by the pressure of the thumb'.

The Dougherty invention was a thumb brake in the form of a plate mounted on a revolving pillar on the opposite side of the spool to the crank handle.

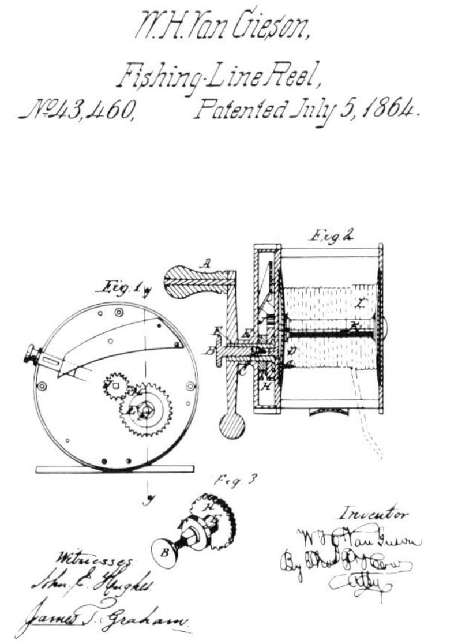

W H VAN GIESON OF NEW YORK. Patent No 43460 – July 5th 1864.

This was the first patent to slow the rotation of the spool by utilising an adjustable friction wheel usually described as a 'drag'. Van Gieson was the first to document this type of mechanism and assigned his patent to Thomas H Bate and William Mills. His idea was to 'clamp the cog wheel that worked the shaft, about which the line was wound between the wheels which revolved with the crank and thus revolved the cog wheel and shaft by friction.' It worked 'by turning thumb screw B, the coiled spring C forces the pin D along the slot in the crankshaft F and this forces the friction wheel E against one side of the cogwheel H'.

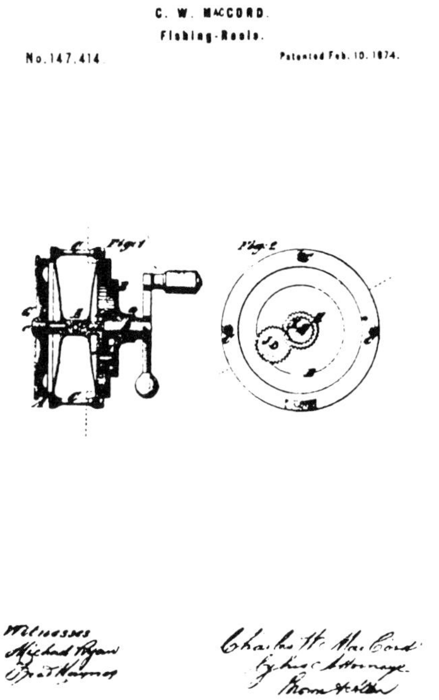

CHARLES W MacCORD OF WEEHAWKEN, NEW JERSEY. Patent No 147414 – February 10th 1874.

This was the earliest patent for the idea of easily dismantling a reel. MacCord did this by designing an annular rear back plate A with the inner circumference slightly larger than the spool and threaded for the reception of a cap or cover. The spool could be removed simply by unscrewing off the plate cap. He also suggested that the cap could be hinged.

FRANCIS A LOOMIS of ONONDAGA, NEW YORK. Patent No 235157 – December 7th 1880.

This was the first patent for the automatic rewind of a reel. It was a simple device with a helical spring. When the line was cast it tightened the spring and when a brake was released, the spring would rewind with the assistance of gearing. It was the fore-runner of automatic reels and was manufactured by Loomis, Plumb & Co, Syracuse, New York.

The first Automatic Fly Reel by Loomis, Plumb & Co

EARLIEST AMERICAN BOOK ON ANGLING

The first known American fishing book is Joseph Seccombe's *Business and Diversion, inoffensive to God, and necessary for the Comfort and Support of human Society* which takes the form of *'A Discourse utter'd in Part at Ammauskeeg-Falls in the Fishing-Season 1739'.* It was published in Boston in 1743 in 21 pages but contained no information about the tackle of the period. Swann Galleries in New York sold a copy on October 23rd 1986, for $14,000.

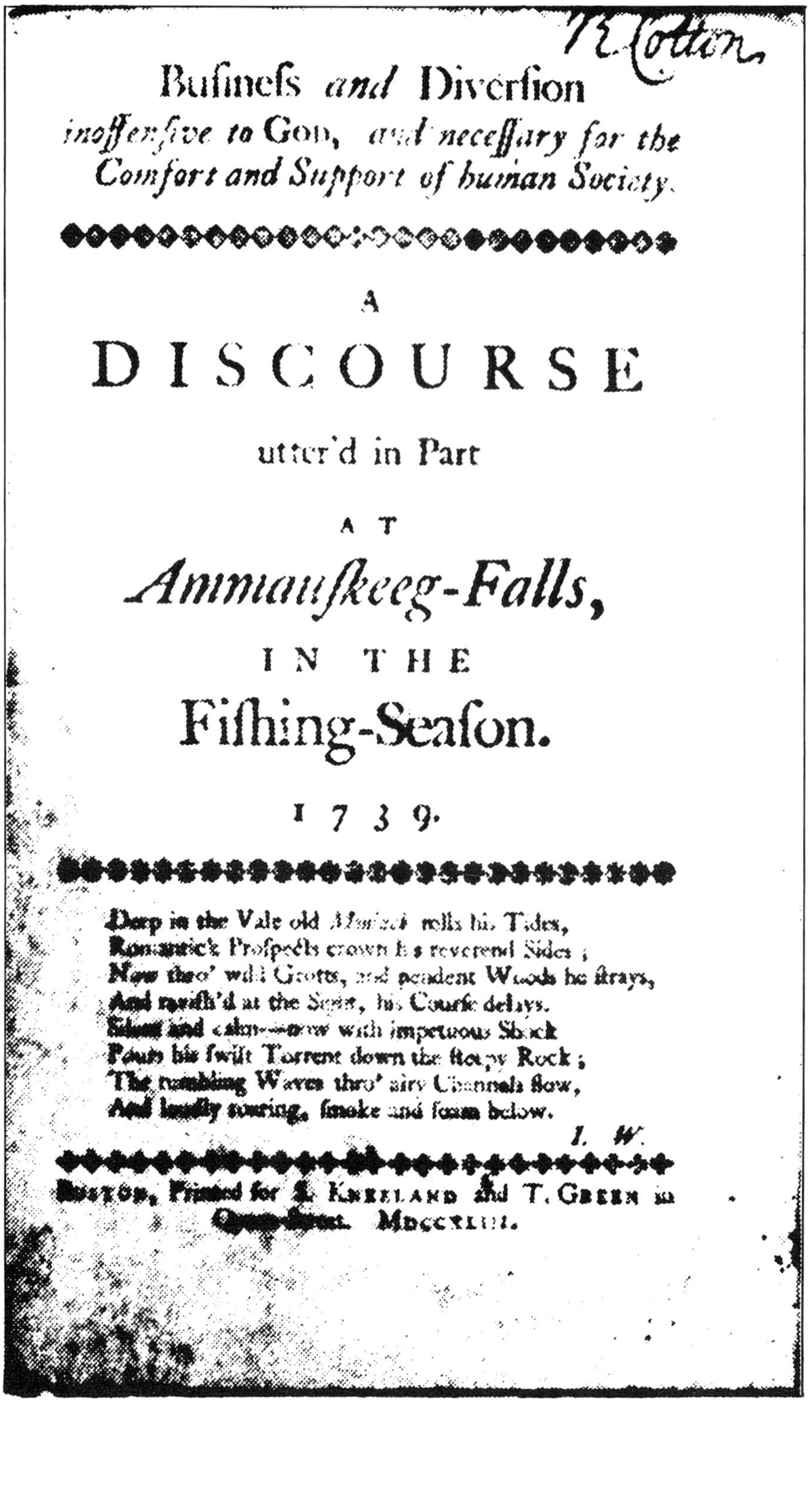

R. Cotton

Buſineſs *and* Diverſion

inoffenſive to GOD, *and neceſſary for the Comfort and Support of human Society.*

A

DISCOURSE

utter'd in Part

AT

Ammauſkeeg-Falls,

IN THE

Fiſhing-Seaſon.

1739.

Deep in the Vale old *Merimack* rolls his Tides,
Romantick Proſpects crown his reverend Sides;
Now thro' wild Grotts, and pendent Woods he ſtrays,
And raviſh'd at the Sight, his Courſe delays.
Silent and calm——now with impetuous Shock
Pours his ſwift Torrent down the ſteepy Rock;
The tumbling Waves thro' airy Channels flow,
And loudly roaring, ſmoke and foam below.

I. W.

BOSTON, Printed for S. KNEELAND and T. GREEN in Queen-Street. MDCCXLIII.

AMERICAN REELS

ABBEY & IMBRIE

Abbey & Imbrie started in the business of selling fishing tackle in 1820 in New York, and an early address was 48 Maiden Lane, New York. They were also located at 18 Vesey St, and by 1923 were trading from 97 Chambers St in the same city.

They were large traders in all kinds of fishing tackle throughout the nineteenth century.

Some of the quality makers including Leonard, Julius Vom Hofe and many others sold tackle through Abbey and Imbrie.

Steve K Vernon

A Julius Vom Hofe casting reel made for Abbey & Imbrie. Nickel plated on brass and equipped with the 1889 pivot on the rear and the 1882 pivot on the front

AMERICAN COMPANY OF ROCKFORD, ILLINOIS

The American Company of Rockford, Illinois made fishing reels to customer's specifications and ran a range of quick-takedown reels in aluminium and nickel silver in the 1900s.

Design of their reels was based on patent No 693459 dated February 18th 1902 which was granted to William S Sutton of Belvidere, Illinois.

They also made an American Meek No 22. This was produced as a result of Sylvanus Meek, son of B F Meek, who stayed on with the Meek business when it was sold to J H Sutcliffe & Co, and later worked for Gayle, finally ending up with the American Company. Probably he was employed for the use of the Meek name which was used on reels.

Another inventor who influenced American Company reels was Harry H Richardson, of Beaver Falls, Pennsylvania, who was granted patent 817987 on April 17th 1906 for an endless-groove level-wind also patent 824438 on June 26th 1906 for the first micrometer drag. Both these patents he assigned to the American Company and the level-wind was incorporated into their reels, and was an optional extra on their Meek model.

Tarpon reel marked only 'Abbey & Imbrie' and 'Pat'd Jan.14th '02' which was the date Francis J Rabbeth patented his famous drag handle known as the 'Rabbeth' which was the forerunner of the star drag

BATES COMPANY

The Bates Company was established in 1822 when two brothers, Thomas and James Bates, who were fish hook and needle makers in Redditch, England, sent over a representative to open an agency in America. When the business became established in the late 1820s, Thomas came over and took control, and the reels at that period were stamped 'T J Bates'. The brother James had a son called Thomas and a daughter Elizabeth, and in 1843 the son Thomas joined his uncle and the firm took the new title of T & T H Bate. The daughter Elizabeth had married a man called William Mills and in 1853 he also became a partner and the firm then traded and stamped their reels 'T & H Bate & Co NY', until 1873 when the last Bate died. William Mills had a son called Thomas Bate Mills who also worked in the business and in 1873 the name of the firm became William Mills & Son. (See page 299 for William Mills & Son).

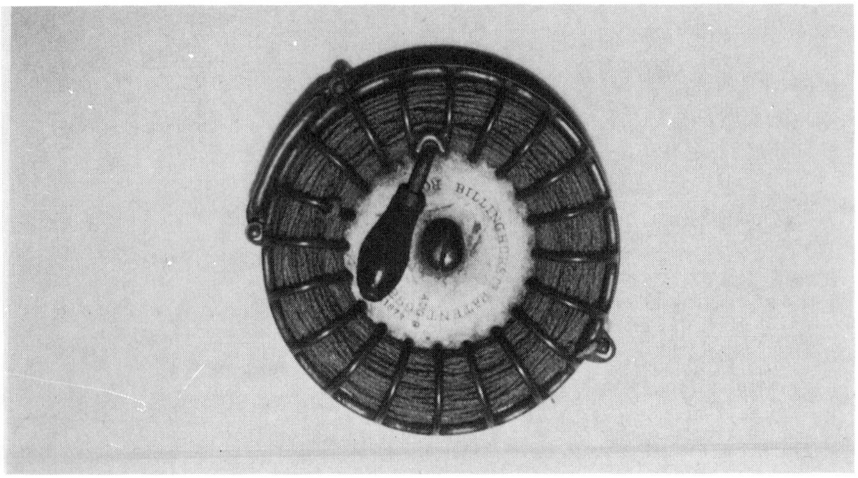

The Billinghurst constructed from nickel plated brass wire

BILLINGHURST

William Billinghurst traded in Rochester in the state of New York and was the first person to patent a reel frame in the United States. His patent No 24987 on August 9th 1859 was a design which would permit the line to dry without removing it from the spool, while at the same time decreasing the overall weight. It was made of nickel plated brass and sported a wooden handle knob which could be folded down for carrying. The reel was the ancestor of the late fly reels and was similar to the larger 'Follett' model and is very scarce and collectable.

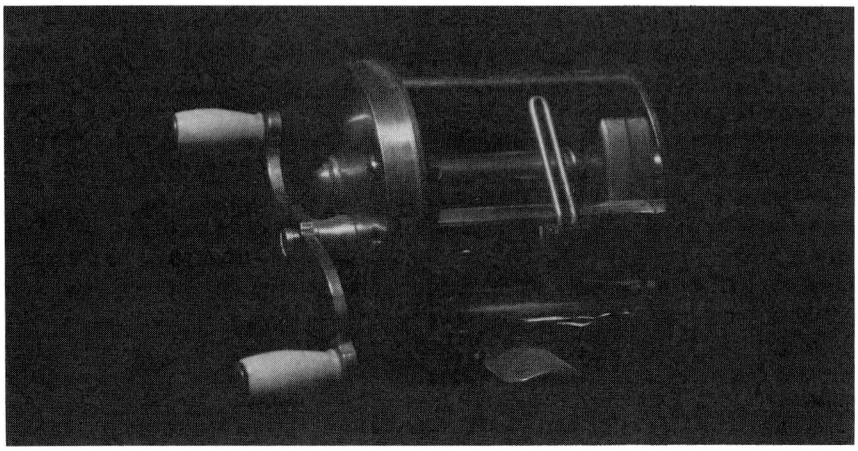

Bronson multiplying reel with level-wind

BRONSON & CO

Bronson & Co have made interesting and inexpensive multipliers with level-wind from the early 1900s and the following include some of their models:- *Altoona, Blue Heron, Fleetwing, Flyer, Lashless, Meadowlark, Mercury, Silver Princess, Sure Kast, Union Jack, Veteren.* Bronson reels are good quality, interesting, very attractive and offer an opportunity to collectors in the lower price range.

Steve K Vernon

Carlton 4X casting reel. German silver with hard rubber spacing rings. It includes patent features, extendable crank, drag and rim click button. The crank knob is loosened to allow the crank to slide for variable torque

CARLTON MANUFACTURING COMPANY

Carlton Manufacturing Company were located at Rochester, New York. On October 27th 1903, Harvey B Carlton received patent No 742587 for a nine to one multiplying reel which the company produced in nickel silver with a balance handle. This gear ratio was not new, as in 1808 Williamson's *The Complete Angler's Vade Mecum* gave drawings of both conventional multiplying gears and his improved four gear train which produced nine spool rotations. In 1905 Carlton received a second patent No 790676 for a free-spool clutch, drag and click, each operated with a rim positioned sliding button. Both patents were assigned to Carlton Manufacturing Company.

CHAMBERLAIN CARTRIDGE & TARGET COMPANY

The Chamberlain Cartridge & Target Company made the Hunter Reel about 1904, which had a spool of hard rubber and was made of German silver, with aluminium alloy inserts in the head and tail plates. It had a thumb bar on the back pillar which allowed disengagement of the gearing from the spool and it was equipped with a quick-takedown release.

The events and the development up to the agreement between Robert L Hunter, the inventor and Chamberlain Cartridge & Target Co were as follows: Robert L Hunter received patents on July 31st 1899, May 19th 1903 (No 728717) and January 19th 1904 (No 750054) and assigned the rights to American Signal and Power Co. It is doubtful whether this company ever made any Hunter reels and it seems that Hunter got the patent rights returned and re-assigned them to Chamberlain Cartridge & Target Co who manufactured a number of reels, bearing the patent date of May 1903. Hunter was granted another patent which was No 842551 on January 29th 1907 but it is possible that production of Hunter reels had ceased by that date.

Ron Gast

The Hunter Reel

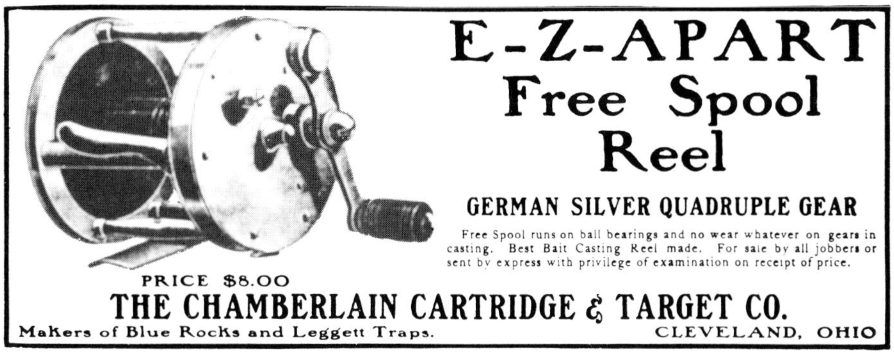

THOMAS H CHUBB

Thomas H Chubb started making fishing tackle at Post Mills, Vermont in 1869 and introduced the Henshall Van Antwerp Four Multiplying Black Bass Reel in 1885, with an adjustable drag and adjustable click. It was made for use with the standard Henshall Black Bass Rod.

Within a short period of time, changes were made to the drag mechanism of the reel because the drag-lever was on the wrong side for playing a fish.

The second Henshall Van Antwerp reel appeared in 1888 with the drag-lever moved to the tail plate side which allowed easier variation in the drag, but

Ron Gast

First model Henshall-Van Antwerp Reel

Steve K Vernon

Conroy Maker. Brass, balance ball handle reel with an adjustable brake. The pitting is due to exposure to salt water

Steve K Vernon

A J C Conroy & Co German silver reel with 'S' handle, bone knob, swivelling oil caps. This was the typical New York style reel of the mid-19th century for salt water fishing

Below: A 'Coxe No 60' German silver casting reel clamped together by a shaft running through the spool arbor

Steve K Vernon

the lever was still in an awkward position when casting.

In 1891 Montague City Rod Company purchased the Chubb business and a third model of the reel was introduced within a short time. This model bore Chubb's design patent No 13921 (1883) and patent No 370684 (1887) although it is not clear whether the design described in the patents was used.

JOHN CONROY

John Conroy was one of the earliest makers who started in business about 1830 at premises in New York and developed and competed with the Kentucky makers.

His reels were hand made and he also produced a range of other tackle, including rods of various woods with guides and ferruled tips, and a wide variety of flies. Conroy reels were made of brass or nickel silver and many were inscribed with the retailer's name rather than the maker. They were finely made and are scarce and highly collectable.

Conroy eventually went into partnership about 1880, with two men called Bissett and Malleson and continued to make high quality tackle from premises at Fulton St, New York.

At the beginning of the 1880s, the company lost one of its partners, Malleson, who started up in business on his own account, and the name of the firm was changed to Conroy & Bissett.

J A COXE

J A Coxe made some of the finest fresh and salt-water reels including big-game fishing models from California. In later years the J A Coxe Reel Company operated from Bronson, Michigan and produced a variety of level-wind multipliers in nickel silver over brass.

The J A Coxe big game reels included the No 950 Foulfish and Marlin Trolling Reel and the No 1215 Lightsurf Reel.

FOUR BROS

Four Bros made a variety of multipliers including the Sumco which incorporated patents from 1923, 1926 and 1927.

Other models included Pontiac which had a two to one gear ratio and was made of brass, Capitol of nickel silver and hard rubber, Mohawk with raised pillars, Regal which was a Kentucky type non-backlash reel with thumb click and drag, and the Eclipse Surf Casting Reel.

HAWKS & OGILVY

Hawks & Ogilvy was another maker based in New York and made quality multiplying reels in the 1800s. These reels are scarce and very collectable.

HEDDON

James Heddon is better known for his plug business which traded at Dowagiac, Michigan from c.1898. His earliest work was a few hand carved frogs and he was granted his first patent on April 1st 1902 for a plug which is known to collectors as the Slopenose. The company also made reels and other fishing tackle.

A few of the reels marketed included – Heddon No 45, No 3, range, No 4–18 with level-wind No 31 Waltoniam, No 4 Chief Dowagiac, No 3AB Indian Chief and Automatic Fly reels No 37 and No 87.

The Eclipse Surf Casting Reel

Four Bros – Sumco multiplier

D A Smith

Hawks & Ogilvy reel in German silver

Steve K Vernon

Heddon 3-25 in German silver with level-wind, on/off sliding click button

Hendryx multiplier in hard rubber and nickel silver

The 'Utica' automatic reel marked – 'Pat FEB 28 1888' and 'JUNE 16/91' also 'Ye Auto Reel'. Made by Horrocks & Ibbotson when they took over Yawman & Erbe

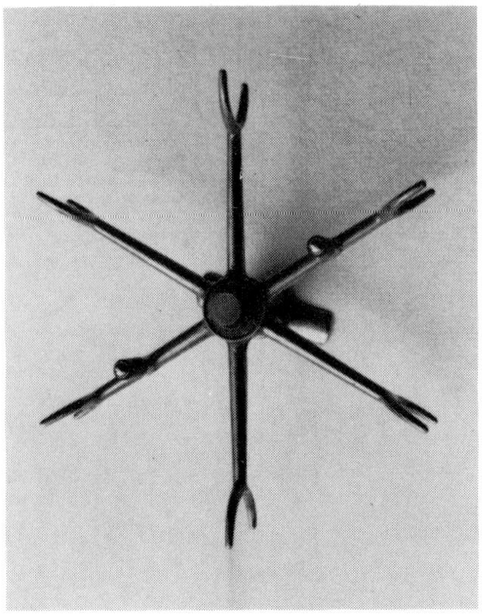

Frank Stewart

'Henry A Kiest, Knox Ind' marked cast aluminium Indiana style reel. It was also called 'Reel Foot Lake Side' in later years

HENDRYX

Hendryx started in business in the 1870s in New Haven, Connecticut trading as Andrew B Hendryx Company. He took out several patents before 1900 and sold a wide variety of reels.

Some were of standard design, some with raised pillars and ranged from small economy reels to large salt-water models.

HORROCKS & IBBOTSON COMPANY

Horrocks & Ibbotson Company were tackle makers from the early 1800s at Utica, New York. They made a variety of reels including the following level-wind bait casting models – *Captain, Captain's Best, Commodore, New Admiral, Caster* and *Top Flight.* They eventually took over Yawman and Erbe, who were manufacturers of automatic combination reels, and continued with their production.

HENRY A KIEST

Henry A Kiest of Knox, Indiana made a large frame reel of 7¼″ diameter which allowed the line to dry more quickly. It was sold with an aluminium can for storage.

H H KIFFE COMPANY

H H Kiffe Company of 523 Broadway, New York started in 1875 and made a number of multiplying reels in nickel over brass and hard rubber and nickel silver. They were good quality and are collectable reels.

KOSMIC

Kosmic reels and rods were made for only about five years from c.1890. The business was owned by US Net & Twine Co which was stamped on their products. Their reels usually had external pillars and were constructed from German silver and hard rubber. Models included fly reels and multipliers with balance handles. Both rods and reels are scarce and command high prices at auction. It should be noted that there was later a trade reel called the Kosmic Reel which has only a nominal value.

H H Kiffe trolling reel of hard rubber and nickel plated brass. Probably made by Julius Vom Hofe, two of whose patent dates are stamped on the reel c.1890

Original Kosmic multiplying reels

Rare original Kosmic trout fly reel. Marked on the front – 'The Kosmic Reel'. German silver parts with raised pillars, plates containing hard rubber. Diameter 2″

Late reel which used the title 'Kosmic Reel'

A very collectable Leonard raised pillar multiplier

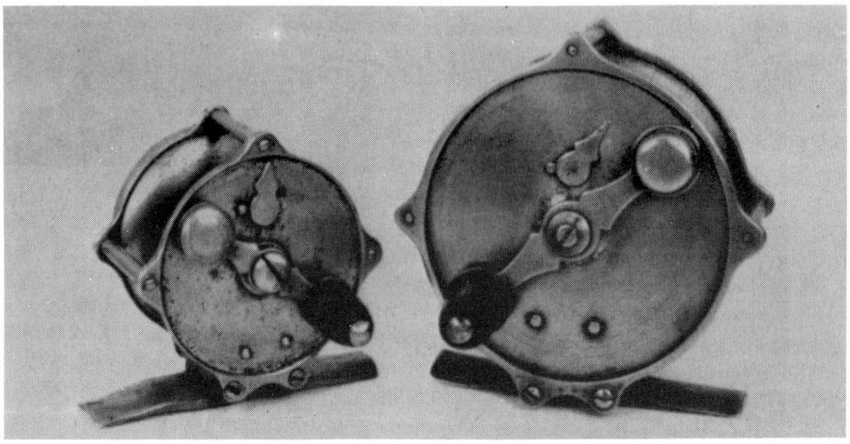

Above: Rare multiplying Malleson reels each with centre mounted handle, gear system located in a raised gear housing and with a novel 'arrow head' click indicator. Nickel plated on brass

Below: Aluminium automatic reel marked 'Martin Auto Fish Reel Co, Mohawk NY No 2' and 'Pat applied for'. This was probably made about 1920/22 and referred to the October 9th 1923 patent

Frank Stewart

HIRAM LEWIS LEONARD

Hiram Lewis Leonard was a gunsmith and fishing tackle maker who started at Bangor, Maine in about 1870. He was a craftsman and made quality rods and reels. From the 1870s he made a raised pillar reel in nickel silver and hard rubber in different sizes.

He made quality split cane rods and marketed much of his tackle through a sole agent, who he often jointly named on the equipment 'H L Leonard Maker. W'm Mills & Son New York'.

Reels are very collectable and command good prices.

FREDERICK MALLESON

Frederick Malleson was a partner in the firm of Conroy, Bissett & Malleson at Fulton St. New York in 1881. By 1883 Malleson had left and gone into business on his own account. On September 4th of that year he was granted patent No 284217. He produced high quality multipliers with raised pillars.

MARTIN AUTOMATIC FISHING REEL CO INC

Martin Automatic Fishing Reel Company Inc were early pioneers of the automatic fly reel, trading from 1885 in New York at addresses 1500 Martin St. and 600 Main St. They took out patents in the 1890s and 1923 and produced many models.

A F MEISSELBACH & BROS

August F Meisselbach, together with his brother William and nephew William Jnr, were fishing tackle makers in the 1880s trading as A F Meisselbach & Bros at Newark, New Jersey. A F was granted his first two patents (No 336657 and No 352926) in 1886 and continued to patent new ideas with his brother. They worked on designs with Pliny Catucci who assigned a number of his patents to the Meisselbach business. The patent of Louis M Sanders No 1228606 dated June 5th 1917 was also assigned to the Meisselbachs. Over the years they produced many reels with the take-apart feature and incorporated level-wind and free-spool into reels at quite an early stage. Some of their models included: *Good Luck, Expert, Flyer, Okeh, Featherlight, Neptune, Surf Models, Tripart* and *Takapart.* Sometime in the 1920s the firm split up and A F moved to Elyria, Ohio where he traded as A F Meisselbach M'f'g Co of Elyria, Ohio. The brother remained in Newark and continued to trade as Meisselbach – Catucci M'F'G' Co, 51–55 Stanton St, Newark, N J.

WILLIAM MILLS AND SON

William Mills and Son was the new name of the Bates Company adopted in 1873 when the last of the Bates died. The Mills who had been partners took full control and eventually the next generation of children came into the family business. William Mills senior died in 1883 and his son Thomas Bate became the owner and survived to the age of ninety, dying in 1941. Three of his six children came into the firm whose names were Eddie, Chester and Arthur. Arthur had a son also called Arthur, who, together with his uncle Eddie, bought out the others members of the family. Arthur (junior) became sole owner when his relative died and when he retired the business was taken over by two of his three sons.

William Mills & Son became agent for Hiram L Leonard split cane rods and soon bought an interest in H L Leonard Rod & Co, marking both names on rods. The big profit side of the Mills business was selling tackle wholesale to hardware and general stores in rural communities and cities from their New York premises at 21 Park Place.

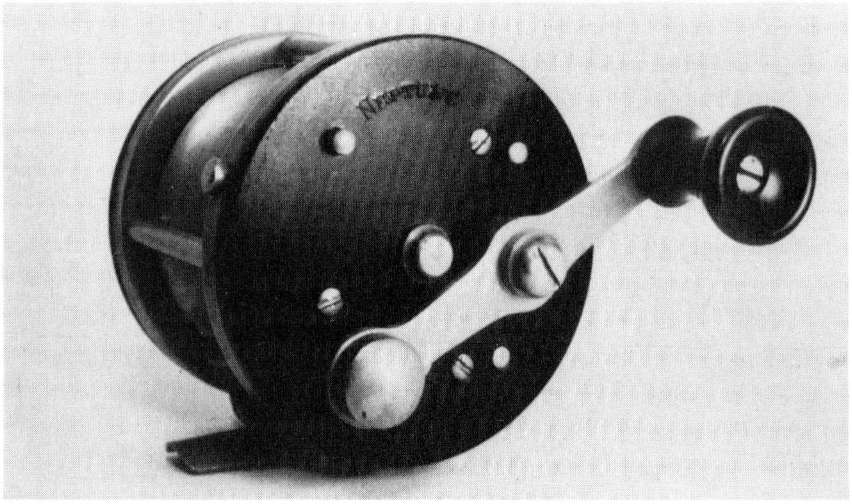

Steve K Vernon

Meisselbach Neptune with German silver frame, hard rubber plates, free spool clutch and a sliding button operated drag

Steve K Vernon

Meisselbach 'Tripart' No 580. Built with the patented one-piece frame and quick-takedown device and was a very efficient reel

Steve K Vernon

W'm Mills & Son multiplier with raised pillars, plated brass frame and hard rubber cover. The rim button pops out to operate a spring brake and the knurled button operates a click. The frame consists of a piece of folded brass supported by pillars (Kopf's 1885 patent)

Steve K Vernon

'W'm Mills & Son'. It is a saltwater reel with German silver frame and hard rubber side plates and knob. The rim lever operates a drag patented in 1906

Steve K Vernon

Ocean City Surf Casting Reel of German silver and hard rubber, with a free spool clutch (lever). A Rabbeth drag handle (1902) has been substituted for the original crank

Orvis Fly Reel

Steve K Vernon

Pflueger 'Supreme,' earliest design, Case's level-wind with Douglass clutch. The level-wind pivots down for casting. When retrieving, it is automatically lifted into the line guide by one of the pivoting dogs on the front of the level-wind case

OCEAN CITY REEL COMPANY

Ocean City Reel Company were located in Philadelphia, Pennsylvania and purchased the Edward Vom Hofe reel making business in 1940. They sold a variety of reels in the 1940s including the fresh water Ocean City, Smoothcast, a heavy duty Imperial Reel, Smoothflite and the No 81 St. Charles. In the 1950s they adopted new model numbers and made a full range of salt-water surf casters including the Inductor free spool reel. In addition they sold the Farcaster, Hampton, Topsail and a non level-wind free spool salt water reel named the Fantum and others.

CHARLES F ORVIS

Charles F Orvis started in business in Manchester, Vermont, about the beginning of the 1870s and invented the glass minnow trap. On May 12th 1874 he was granted patent No 150883 for a fly reel which had heavily perforated side plates. It was a crank handled very narrow drum reel and even had the flanges and shaft of the spool perforated to eliminate dampness.

The Orvis family had literary ability, with the founder, Charles F Orvis, co-authoring with Cheney, to produce *Fishing With The Fly* in 1883. Mary Orvis Marbury, a daughter, had been introduced into the firm as a fly-tyer and in 1892 had a book published entitled *Favourite Flies and Their Histories.*

Orvis offered a wide variety of flies and a range of salmon and trout rods.

PFLUEGER

Pflueger, The Enterprise Manufacturing Co, Akron Fishing Tackle Works, Akron, Ohio, started in business in the 1860s. The Pfluegers patented many new ideas and were involved in others and it is only possible to mention a few of the earlier ones. Ernest F Pflueger was granted patent No 560925 on May 26th 1896 and Joseph E Pfleuger No 720063 on February 10th 1903 for a reel with the first laminated side plate in which the rubber and metal were fixed during vulcanisation, making riveting unnecessary. This method of plate was used on the Golden West model.

Joseph E Pflueger also received patent No 866060 on September 17th 1907 for a thumb pad which could be carried and pivoted on the back reel pillar, and in the same year had earlier combined his inventive talents with T J Llewellyn and were jointly granted patent No 841796 for a reel whose spool had a shaped shaft which stepped down in diameter to form shoulders.

Charles T Pflueger took out many patents, one of which was patent 1730331 on October 1st 1929, granted jointly with Frank B Koehler for a rotatable cap to cover oil parts which was incorporated on to the T M Williams design patented in 1909 which eventually resulted in the Pflueger-Williams handle drag. The Pflueger reels of the twentieth century are good quality, attractive and made in a large number of models. They offer the opportunity to put together a good collection of reels without spending a lot of money. Models include: *Akron, Alpine, Autopla, Avalon, Buckeye, Capitol, Captain, Eclipse, Everlaster, Farcaster, Freespeed, Gem, Golden West, Hawkeye, Interocean, Martin, Medalist, Nobby, Norka, Ohio, Okerite, Pakron, Pal, Pelican, Pontiac, Redifor, Rocket, Saltrout, Seaview, Skeliton Fly Reel, Skilkast, Summit, Superex, Supreme, Taxie, Temco, Templar, Triumph, Worth, Pflueger-Williams, Shwartz Trolling* and others.

ROCHESTER REEL CO

The reel models of Rochester Reel Co, 90 Chambers St, New York included: New Gem, Ideal models, Triumph and the Rochester Fly reel. The patents of Andrew Wollensak of Rochester were assigned to Wollensak Optical Co and used in Rochester reels. On September 6th 1910 he was granted two patents, one was No 969234 for an anti-backlash device and click on a

Pflueger 'Golden West' marked with patent number 1450738, 1559496 and 1608287

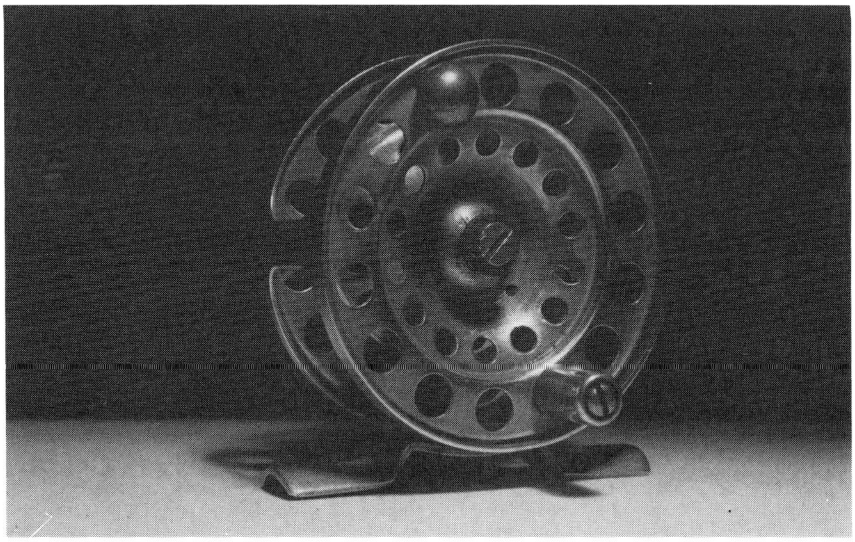

Above: Rochester 'No 1 Ideal Fly' and marked 'Rochester Reel Co, 90 Chambers St NY.'

Below: W'm Shakespeare JR 'Service'. A small casting reel of German silver with a patented brake (1903) and quick-takedown design using knurled screwable pillars (patent 1906)

Steve K Vernon

Steve K Vernon

Steve K Vernon

Above: M A Shipley. A nickel plated brass raised pillar reel. Almost every American reel maker included reels of this type in its production line

Below: 'South Bend Bait Company' Model 1131-A. One of their earlier anti-backlash casting reels of German silver, c.1915

Frank Stewart

quick-takedown type reel and the other No 969235 for a heavily perforated flanged spool and radial lever operated brake. Both were used in the design of the Rochester model.

SHAKESPEARE CO

Shakespeare Co started in business in the 1890s in Kalamazoo, Michigan. Some of their reel models included: *Alamo, Beetzsel, Criterion, 1905 De-luxe, Delux Wondereel, Deuce, Freespool, Glaskyd, Ideal, Jupiter, Kalamazoo, Marhoff, OK Automatic, Precision, President, Quad, Russell, Service Take Apart, Silent True Art Automatic, Sportcast, Standard Professional, Superior, Thrifty, Tournament, True Axis, True Blue, Triumph, Uncle Sam, Universal, Wonderful* and many more.

MALCOLM A SHIPLEY

Malcolm A Shipley made reels rods and fishing tackle in the latter part of the 1800s from premises in Market St, Philadelphia. He was granted patent No 699825 on May 13th 1902 for an add-on drag handle which was marketed as the 'Gem'. By the early 1900s he was trading from Chestnut St, Philadelphia. He made quality standard multiplying reels with and without raised pillars in brass and also nickel plated brass and hard rubber. The reels are scarce and collectable.

A B SHIPLEY & SON

A B Shipley & Son were in business at Commerce St, Philadelphia, Pennsylvania, and produced quality rods and all manner of accessories including fittings, hooks, lines, flies and artificial baits. They also made multiplying reels of brass, also brass and hard rubber, and are very collectable.

SOUTH BEND

South Bend made many functional, anti-backlash reels with level-wind from the early 1900s at very competitive prices. They made a No 1200 model with level-wind, a No 1131 anti-backlash in nickel silver with jewelled bearings, also a very cheap model with level-wind for $9 called the Oreno Anti-Backlash reel. There were a large number of model numbers marketed including a 3 piece take-down reel No 400 and a Perfectoreno model range. South Bend also sold automatic fly reels with the No 1100 Oreno single action which was $7 in 1928 plus more expensive models No 1120 and No 1140 Orenomatic reels.

WILLIAM H TALBOT

William H Talbot started making fishing reels in about 1892 in Nevada, Missouri and later moved to Kansas City, Missouri. Models included the Comet, Jupiter, Mars and the Tournament reel. A Talbot Star was made to the specifications of patent No 666398 granted to W H Talbot on the 22nd January 1901. Talbot reels are highly collectable.

UNION HARDWARE CO

Union Hardware Co traded from about the middle of the nineteenth century at Torrington, Connecticut. One of their best known models was a single action fly and bait casting take-apart reel called the Samson.

A feature was a hinged head plate, patented (No 832291) on October 2nd 1906 by Thomas W Bryant of Torrington and originally suggested by MacCord's patent No 147414 in 1874. The company also made multipliers in nickel silver over brass with both internal and external pillars and balance handles.

Frank Stewart

'William H Talbot Reel Co, Nevada MO.' A German silver Comet reel, c.1910

Frank Stewart

Above: 'Talbot Reel M'fg Co KC MO USA', German silver check reel, c.1916

The Samson reel

Below: 'Union Hardware Co Torrington Conn.' The head plate is hinged at the bottom and swings outwards to service the gears

Edward Vom Hofe small ebonite and German silver reel with 'S' handle, 2⅜" diameter. Marked 'Pat Jan 23.83.' On/off click button

Richard W Oliver

Scarce Edward Vom Hofe Special Star. Size 2/0 c.1907

EDWARD VOM HOFE 1867–1940

Edward C Vom Hofe was the brother of Julius Vom Hofe and started making rods and reels in 1867 at 92 Fulton St, New York. He was granted his first reel patent No 219328 on September 2nd 1879 for a tension device, and on January 23rd 1883 patent No 271166 for an improved design incorporating an arrow shaped pawl held between two curved springs and operated by a sliding button on the rear. Patents were often stamped on the oil caps of Edward Vom Hofe reels, one being patent No 563964, dated July 14th 1896 for an automatic drag; also patent No 700424, dated May 20th 1902 for a star-drag. Like his brother he made some of the finest reels, and any bearing his name is guaranteed to create interest. Some models such as Perfection, Peerless, Restigouche, Col Thompson command high prices and are much sought after by American collectors.

JULIUS VOM HOFE

Julius Vom Hofe was the son of Frederick and the elder brother of Edward Vom Hofe. He started in business in 1857 in South Fifth St, Brooklyn, and made a wide variety of fine quality reels which are very collectable. He took out many reel patents and played an important part in the development of American reel design and was possibly the inventor of spiral gears.

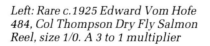

Left: Rare c.1925 Edward Vom Hofe 484, Col Thompson Dry Fly Salmon Reel, size 1/0. A 3 to 1 multiplier

Richard W Oliver

Right: An early Julius Vom Hofe bait casting reel with sculptured plate rims and back plate. Size # 3½. Diameter 2¼". Rear cap with 1885 and 1889 patent dates

A rare jewel in the form of a tiny 2⅛″ diameter reel with rear sliding click button, marked with only 'Julius Vom Hofe Maker NY.' Condition – mint

A Julius Vom Hofe raised pillar bait casting reel with a nickel plated cross frame and hard rubber side plates. Patented in 1886

Left: Early Edward Vom Hofe Perfection Model 360 Trout Fly Reel with 1883 patent date, sliding click button and adjustable drag under the handle, 1/0 size. Diameter 3⅛″

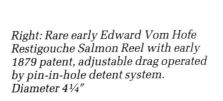

Right: Rare early Edward Vom Hofe Restigouche Salmon Reel with early 1879 patent, adjustable drag operated by pin-in-hole detent system. Diameter 4¼″

Frank Stewart

Above: Wheeler & McGregor, Milwaukee, Wisconsin. Nickel plated on brass and based on the patents of 1894

Richard W Oliver

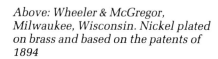

Left: Otto Zwarg Salmon Reel, Model 300. A 4/0 size reel with Vom Hofe adjustable drag with red dot indicators on the back and a 'Z' logo on the bearing cap cover

Richard W Oliver

Below: Otto Zwarg 9/0 size, 'Maximo' custom built big game reel of German silver and hard rubber

WHEELER & McGREGOR COMPANY

Wheeler & McGregor Company started in business in Milwaukee, Wisconsin towards the end of the nineteenth century.

On May 29th 1894 Nelson H McGregor was granted patent No 520607 for a level-wind and a month later on June 26th he received patent No 522079 for an improved version incorporating an original gear train. The new feature was used on a reel called the Milwaukee which the catalogue of 1895 offered in nickel silver over brass, in a No 3 size and a No 4 wide drum version. The company was one of the earliest to market a reel with the level-wind feature successfully.

YAWMAN & ERBE MANUFACTURING CO

Yawman & Erbe Manufacturing Co, Rochester, NY made automatic fly reels based on the patents of Philip H Yauman which were – No 378565 (February 28th 1888), No 454319 (June 16th 1891), 629842 (August 1st 1899).

The company was taken over by Horrocks & Ibbotson who continued to produce automatic models including the Utica automatic.

OTTO ZWARG

Otto Zwarg was another maker of Brooklyn, New York, who made quality reels.

OTHER AMERICAN MAKERS AND DEALERS

New York: A Clerk & Co; J B Crook & Co; H B Hartill; Peck & Snyder; Henry C Squires; Willsher & Damerel.
Boston: Bradford and Anthony succeeded by Dame, Stoddard & Kendal, 374 Washington St.
Chicago: Wilkinson Co (Est 1872), 83 Randolf St.
Philadelphia: John Krider, Walnut St, (Fishing Tackle outfitters).

THE EARLIEST AMERICAN ROD MAKER

The early rods in America up to 1800 had been imported mainly from Britain and one or two other European countries and were made from a variety and sometimes combination of woods. These included hickory, bamboo, greenheart, lancewood, crab, ash, yew and many others and usually tapered from the centre of the handle out to the tip.

Split cane was being used in Britain for tip sections as early as the turn of the nineteenth century and like the early winches would have quickly found its way across to the USA.

American makers eventually started up and began to produce split cane rods of the finest quality. It is only possible to give a brief mention of the earliest American maker to use split bamboo on rods and I thank the State Museum of Pennsylvania and the Pennsylvania Historical and Museum Commission for the history and illustrations of the work of the American pioneer rod maker.

SAMUEL PHILLIPPE

Samuel Phillippe was the earliest American rod maker to use three-strip glued up bamboo end pieces on his rods, and pioneered a four-strip construction for the same purpose between 1845 and 1855. He had a son, Solon, who built rods with a six-strip end piece, while working as his apprentice in 1859.

It is generally believed that the first American to build a rod completely of split cane was A E Green and the earliest fellow countryman to make a six-strip rod was Charles F Murphy.

Information about the rod

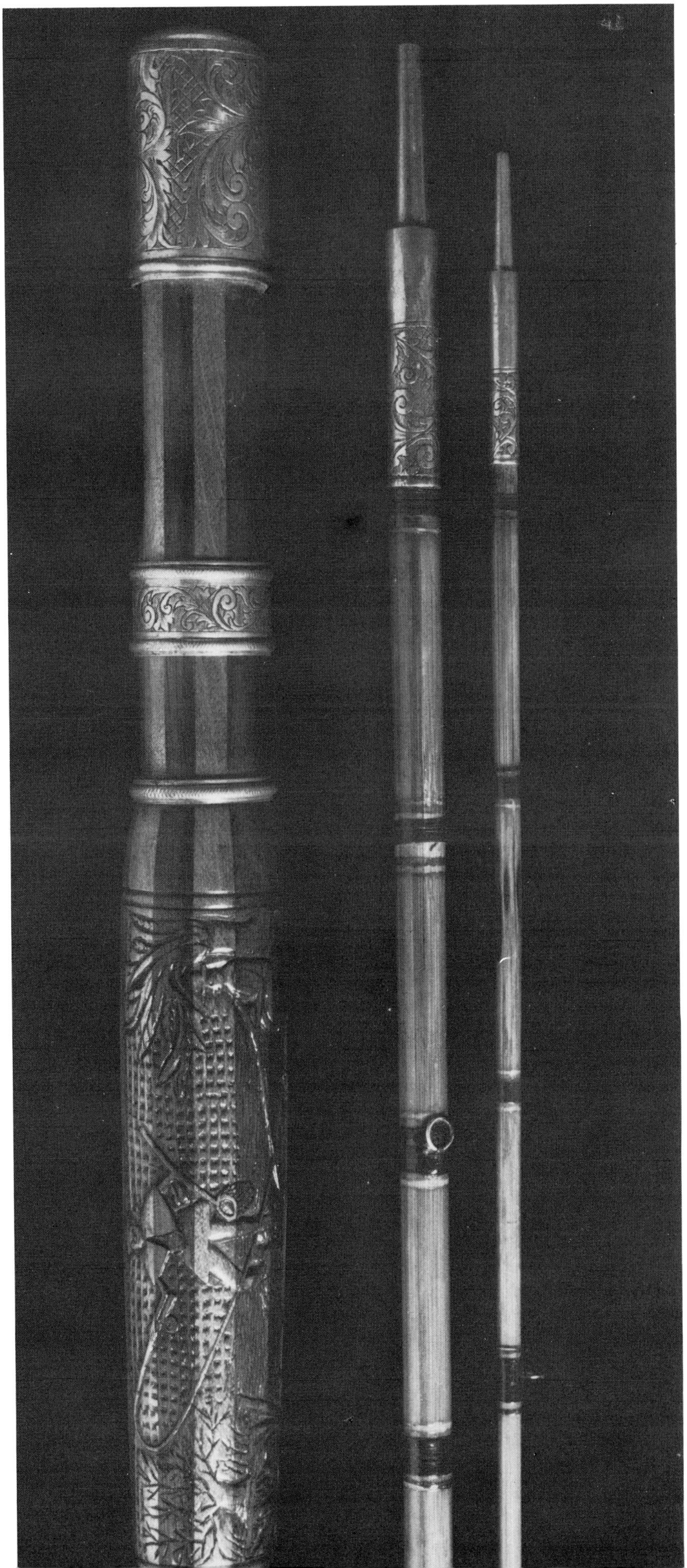

Phillippe Fly Rod of split bamboo with engraved silver fittings and carved hand piece. Inscribed 'S C Phillippe, Maker, Easton'. The rod was donated by the Harrisburgh Fly Fishing Club to the State Museum of Pennsylvania Historical and Museum Commission who have kindly given permission for the illustrations

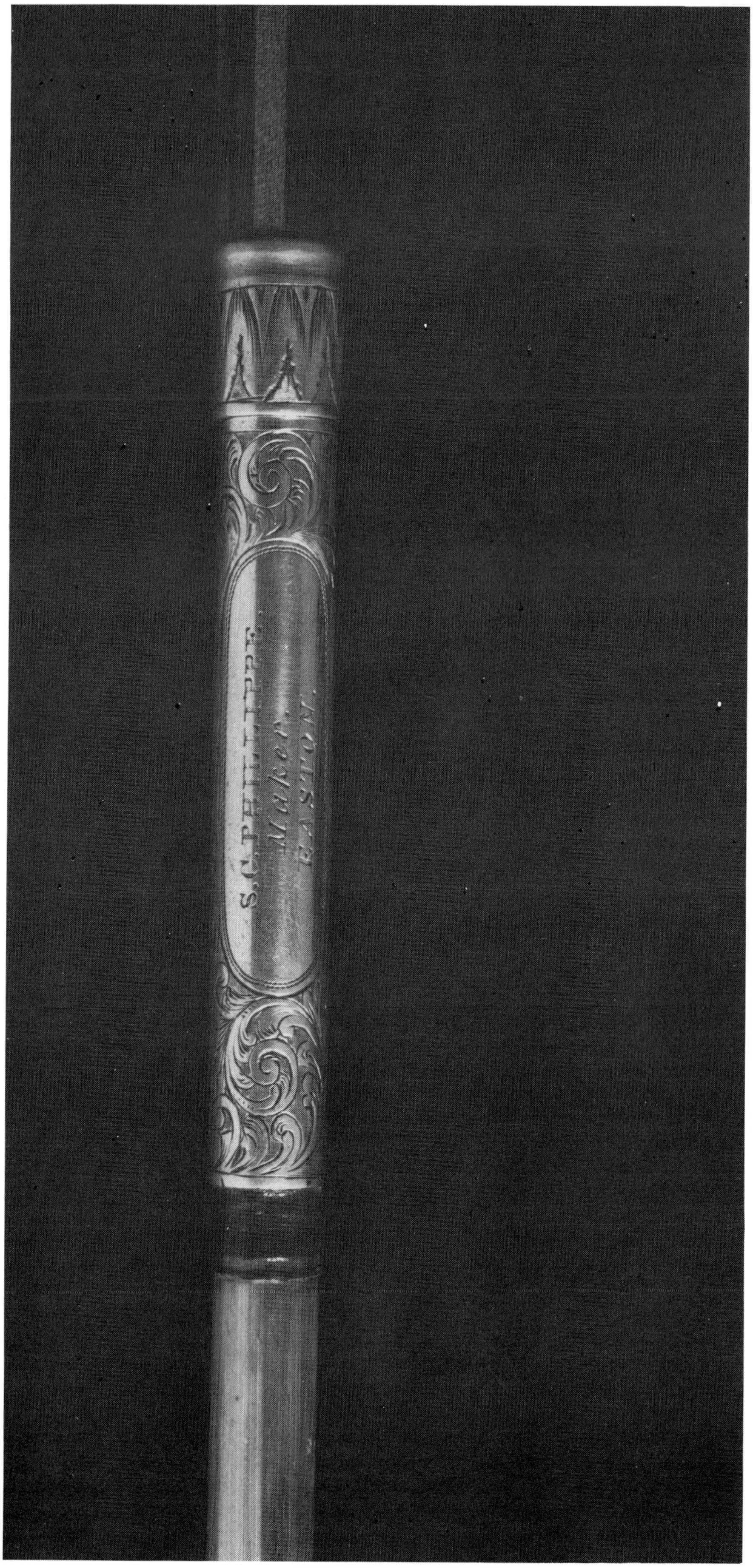

making of Phillippe was given by James A Henshall in *Book of The Black Bass* with the following

'Samuel Phillippe was born August 9th 1801 in Reading, Pa, and died in Easton, Pa, on May 25th 1877. He went to Easton when about sixteen years old, where he learned the trade of gunsmith with Mr Peter Young. He was a skilled workman in wood or metal, and made violins and fishing rods in addition to his regular work as a gunsmith. He received a silver medal for one of his violins from the Franklin Institute Fair at Philadelphia. He made the first Kinsey fishing hooks from patterns furnished by Phineus Kinsey of Easton, Pa. He was a good trout fisher and fished at times in company with Thad Norris of Philadelphia, and Judge Jas Madison Porter, Colonel T P Sitgreaves, W Green, Phineus Kinsey, John and Abraham Dehart, Sherriff Heckman and others of Easton'.

The Phillippes were followed by a succession of fine quality American makers whose work commands high prices at the Richard W Oliver auctions and include – Charles Murphy, Hiram Lewis Leonard, E F Payne, Thomas and Edwards, F E Thomas, Charles F Orvis, Harold Steel Gillum, Edmund Everett Garrison, H W Hawes & Co and many others.

Details and prices of American rods sold in the last six years are given in the Price Guide section.

Phillippe Rod

FISH DECOYS

The ice-spearing fish decoy has been used for centuries by Indians, Eskimos and probably by our palaeolithic ancestors. They have been made from a variety of materials including wood, bone, horn, ivory, in all manner of shapes and sizes, with one purpose, to attract fish within range of a spear. Although decoys are usually shaped in the form of a fish, they can be something as simple as a tiny leaf shape, which when drawn through the water would stimulate the curiosity of a predatory fish and cause it to follow to within range of the waiting fisherman.

By carving the decoy fish with special features such as a curved tail or unusual body shape, it was possible to give the decoy peculiar movements in the water which would simulate the actions of an injured fish. The line was usually secured to a single eye on the decoy, but on some there were a number of eyes placed along the dorsal fin, so that by varying the tie position, the performance in the water could be altered. Its use would have become a skilled art and necessitate an understanding of the ways and feeding of fish. Many of the fish decoys were exact copies of their live counterpart and the range extended to all forms of life including mice, frogs, muskrats, turtles and products of the imagination of the carver. Sizes varied from ¾″ to over three feet in length depending on which fish it was to be used against. These were often pike, sturgeon or whatever predatory fish were present. Unfortunately, most of the carvers who created the imitation fish remained unknown and produced both fish and duck decoys. Some of the early creations are now recognised as a form of American folk art and can command high prices.

Most of the ones around today have usually been made between 1900 and 1950 and it was during that period that the factory models were produced, which, although generally not as good as the individual makers, tend to bring quite high prices. They include

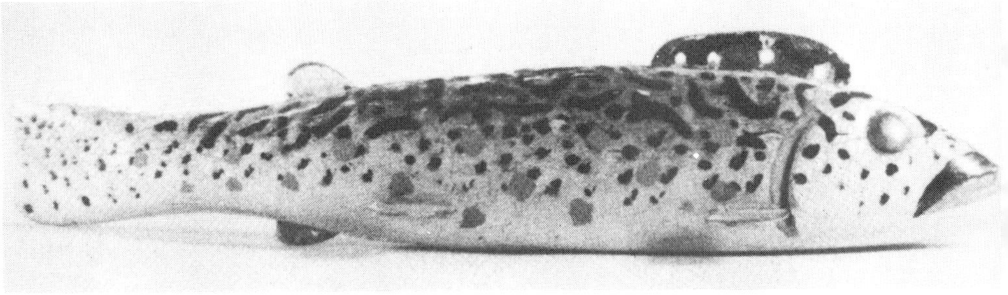

Oscar Peterson carved spear fishing trout decoy. Length is 7″ with tack eyes and one piece wood

Tom Schroeder fish spearing decoy. This dace or chub is 5″ long and has a curved tail

One of the most extreme examples of escalating prices for any collectable recently occurred in the field of duck decoys. On April 16th 1986 a decoy by Elmer A Crowell of East Harwich, Massachusetts was sold for $64,000. In May 1986 a decoy Black Drake by Joe Lincoln (illustrated) was sold by William Doyle Galleries for an astonishing $205,000. Since then the record for a decoy has gone above $300,000

Pflueger, Heddon, South Bend, Moonlight, Paw Paw, Bear Creek Bait Company, Creek Chub, Randall and Sletten.

The decoy fish range included finely carved trout, pike, bass, suckers, minnows, sturgeon and many others. They featured individually shaped tails, incised gills, carved scales and fins which were made from a variety of materials.

Of the individual carvers, one of the best known is Oscar W 'Pelee' Peterson of Grayling, Michigan, who lived from 1887 to 1951. He was a man of all trades who carved everything from people and boats to animals, ducks and fish. His fish decoys had his particular style, being usually one piece, curved, long, smooth and sleek. Other features were often incised gills, metal gills, flat underside, and usually two inlet weights in the base. He carved in a wide range of sizes from three inches to over a foot, although most of his work was in the mid-range. The variety of fish included trout of all kinds, various suckers, perch, smelt, tadpoles, frog, turbot, bass and many forms of no known species.

Peterson had an individual style in the painting of his creations. Although he was tied to producing the natural colours of the fish, he tended to paint a touch of bright red on the gill, mouth and the tail end. He used all manner of eyes including glass, tack, and painted, all with contrasting coloured eyebrows. He worked as an individual and carved in pine and white cedar with simple tools including chisels, drawshave, knife and sandpaper. He produced his own paint and used only one colour at a time on a number of decoys, which meant that he took weeks to complete a decoy but produced a number at a time and each one different. He also made plugs and took out a patent in 1927 for one with a special shaped underside which caused a wobbling motion when drawn through the water, but was never as well-known for his plugs as he was for his decoys.

The sport of spearing through ice is still legal and practised in Michigan and other Great Lake states, and the methods have probably changed little from the ways of the Eskimo or early man in the ice age. In January and February the shanties or 'coops' are hauled out on to the ice and placed over holes cut in the frozen lake. Snow is banked up against the base of the shanty to block out light and the ice is shovelled clean in a wide band round the shanty to allow a little winter light to illuminate the water below. Crushed egg shells, white pebbles or other light coloured material are thrown into the water to line the bottom in order to reflect the light and give a clearer underwater view.

A fire is lit in the little stove and the spear rope is made fast to a bolt in the ceiling with the spear head submerged and the shaft resting on the edge of the ice. In this position it is not necessary to break water with the spear, which would frighten the fish. The decoy is then introduced with the fisherman's other hand and it swims clockwise or antic-clockwise depending on the curve of its body and tail. Some decoys have fins and tail which can be bent to vary the performance, while the position of attachment of the line can alter the movement through the water.

Top: Pair of fish decoys. Larger one from Wisconsin (maker unknown). Other by Leonard Selinsky of Clare, Michigan.
Below: Group of five small fish by D C Revit, Bay City, Michigan, c.1928-38

There are certain regulations which govern what can be used and the minimum size which can be killed. In Michigan a fisherman is permitted two lines with hooks in the water at a given time, one of which can be the decoy. The minimum size of fish which can be killed varies from state to state and lake to lake. Some spearmen use a sizing decoy which gives an instant comparison with a target so that he can be sure it is a permitted size before killing. The variety of decoys and the techniques are endless and a spear fisherman can be extremely skilled, I thank William Doyle Galleries of New York for the black and white illustrations and Gary L Miller, a specialist authority and collector of decoys, for information and colour photographs of the subject.

Fish decoys, together with duck decoys, are uniquely American and due to the current fashion for folk art, they have become a sporting collectable.

Group of five fish decoys makers unknown. Probably from the Michigan area

The most unusual and primitive form of decoy fishing has been practised for centuries and still continues with the older generation of the men of a small village called Kontu in Papua New Guinea. They don't actually use an imitation fish, but prefer to kill the real thing and use the dead fish as a decoy, instead of using it as a lure on a hook and line. They believe that sharks are possessed by spirits of their ancestors and traditional practices must be followed when catching one, with certain taboos strictly adhered to.

The fisherman is careful not to step over the droppings of pigs or flying-foxes, nor does he sleep with his wife before putting out to sea, alone in a narrow canoe with outriggers.

First of all he paddles into the shallow waters and spears small fish which he will use as decoys. He then heads for the open sea and follows a ritual passed down to him by his forefathers. On his way out to sea he spears the reef several times and drops a number of small stones to awaken the spirits and identify himself to them. Once he has reached open water he calls the shark by means of smacking his paddle and shaking a wooden rattle on the surface. This simulates a fish in distress and attracts the shark to his small canoe. He then takes a spear, on the end of which is impaled a dead decoy fish, and tempts the big fish close to the canoe. His method is to manipulate the fish decoy with one hand, while he holds ready a rope formed in a slip-noose to which is attached a large propeller shaped wooden floater about four feet long. As the shark swims alongside on the surface he slips the noose over the head and immediately throws the harpoon into the fish. He drags the fish out of the water and against the side of the boat where he rains blows on the head with a heavy wooden club. Only when the fish has been subdued does he pull it into the canoe.

The sharks he selects are usually about 12 feet long which are both manageable and a size which will fit into his canoe. He believes he has called and captured the spirit of the shark and in order to preserve his magical powers he must keep the heart, liver and fin for himself and his family although he may divide up the rest of the fish for the people of his village.

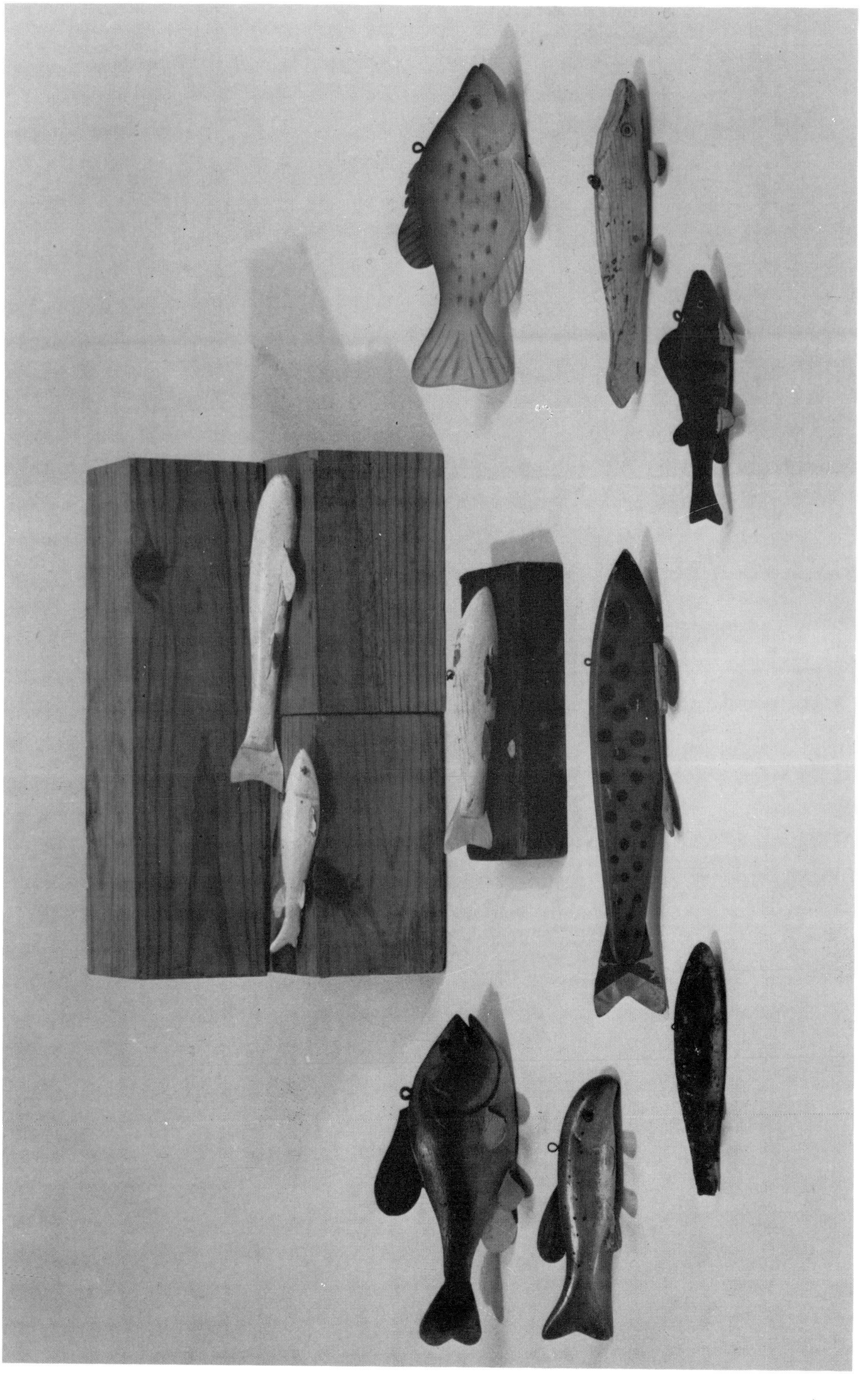

Group of ten fish decoys

PRICE GUIDE

The Price Guide Section of this book is possibly unique in the field of collecting, because it provides an almost complete record for all time, of everything sold when fishing tackle came of age and established itself as part of the antique trade.

The figures given are the actual prices paid, and includes a 10% buyer's premium. The data has been taken from all the specialist sales in Britain and America over a period of six years.

In the first two years there was an abundance of the finest British collector's reels for sale, when the entire collection of David Petty was disposed of through the specialist sales of Sotheby's. Eventually everything was sold at what now seems extremely low prices, with many of the best examples going to collectors overseas.

In America, Richard Oliver Galleries have greatly promoted the collecting of fishing tackle by organising first class specialist sales with quality illustrated catalogues in both black and white and colour. They hold two specialist sales, per year and organise full media coverage, particularly when items make record prices, such as a Haskell Lure ($22,000), Philbrook & Payne reel ($20,900), H S Gillum rod ($19,250) and a fish decoy ($6,325).

The data in the Price Guide gives the record of prices and the number of times a model has been sold, which may reflect its rarity. There will be a fluctuation in prices of the same item of tackle, caused by either variation in condition, or the market forces of supply and demand. As a guide it is probably better to take the average of prices given.

I would like to sound a warning to any new collector who may be tempted to copy the mistake of some antique traders, who clean the age colour from the brass on reels and other items of tackle. Turning a grubby old reel into a gleaming piece of brass may ensure a quick sale in the bottom price range, but would be wrong and damaging to quality antique examples. The correct procedure is to clean and polish without affecting the patina, as one would an antique piece of furniture.

A collector who intends to purchase from auctions, should whenever possible attend the viewing and always take along a measure and a lens. Catalogues produced by some auction houses in Britain usually contain mistakes in sizes, models and descriptions and it is good policy to automatically check out any items on which bids are to be made. There is no substitute for experience which usually has to be aquired the expensive way, and it is only by regular handling that the knowledge is acquired.

Reels need careful examination to check for replaced parts, hair-line cracks to rims, pillars and plates or anything which would suggest that the example is not honest or genuine. Similar care should be taken with rods, lures and any other items of tackle.

Collectors of British and American fishing tackle can now be counted in many thousands and the interest has spread to over twenty five countries. The Price Guide gives a permanent record of the *'beginning'* of a field of collecting which will become increasingly international.

HARDY REELS

Prices shown in italics denote amounts realised at auction during the last two years

ALMA
12/0 size – $750 (R A Bourne Auction)

AUXILIARY BRAKE SILEX MAJOR
3¾″ – £88, £77
4″ – £154
4½″ – £143

AUXILIARY BRAKE UNIQUA
– *£250*

AUXILIARY BRAKE SILEX No 2
– *£400*

PERFECT AUXILIARY BRAKE
– *£500, £400.*

ALTEX No 1
– £121 (marked PATENT APPLIED FOR), £30, $22

ALTEX No 2
– £44, £30, $33, £44, *£71* (three), *£71* (two), *£49, £55, £71, £77, £44*

ALTEX No 3
– £27, *£42, £49*

THE BARTON
3¼″ – £902, £660, £990, *£1265, £1100, £1815, £880*

BIRMINGHAM HALF-EBONITE
4¼″ – £132, *£150*
4½″ – £93, *£170*
5″ – £350

BIRMINGHAM PLATE
2¼″ – £187, £121, £104, *£150, £144*
2½″ – £66, £71, $121, £93 (damaged), *£150, £154, £209*
3¼″ – £121
3½″ – £60, *£90, £220*
4″ – £49, $77, £99, *£130*
4½″ – £44, *£110*

BRONZED CRANK
3¾″ – £319, *£638* (3″), *£600*

CASCAPEDIA
3⅝″ – £2100 (private)
3¾″ – Size 4/0 *£3300*
3⅜″ – £5720

COMBINED FLY AND SPINNING
– £935, *£900*

CONQUEST
4⅛″ – £41, £22, *£78, £49.*

COQUET
Est. from £400

DAVY
– £850, *£1200*

DECANTELLE
– *£33, £33*

EDDYSTONE
6″ – £24, £22, £55

ELAREX
– £49, £44, £38, £33, $82, £61, *£71, £33, £88, £44, £30*

EUREKA (Early model)
– *£250*

EUREKA
3½″ – £132, £110, £80, £77, £71, *£66, £160, £176*
4″ – £88, £77, £22, *£44, £55, £61, £130, £190, £200*

EXALTA
– £44, £27

EXTERNAL PILLARED CRANK
2¼″ – £858, *£500*
2⅞″ – £610
3¾″ – £770

FARNE REELS

FARNE (First Model)
Est. from £400
FARNE (Second Model)
Est. from £300

FARNE EBONA
Est. from £300

NEW FARNE
5⅛″ – £484

IMPROVED FARNE
6″ – £121

FEATHERWEIGHT
– £35, £44, £49, *£61, £60*

FIELD NARROW DRUM
3⅛″ – £220
Other sizes
– £308, £143, *£270, £350*

FIELD WIDE DRUM
2⅝″ – £374
4⅛″ – £143, £280

FIELD BRASS FACED
3⅞″ – £638

FILEY
4½″ – £55

FLY REEL
3⅜″ – £71, £150

FLYWEIGHT
2½″ – £55, *£49, £66*

FORTUNA
6″ – $220, £143, *£132, £240*
7″ – £176, £110, £104, *£178*
8″ – *£341*

FORTUNA PERFORATED FLY REEL
3½″ – £935, £352

FORTUNA with Capstan Star and Plate Lever
Est. from £500

FORTUNA JUNIOR FLY REEL
– £500, *£280, £290*

GEM
3¼″ – £38, $42

GOLDEN PRINCE FLY REELS
– Limited edition set of three in case *$577*

GOODWIN
4″ – £104, *£60, £95, £47, £140*

HARDEX No 1
– £44, £19

HARDEX No 2
– *£27*

HARDY DECANTELLE
4″ – *£77, £65, £55*

HARDY JOCK SCOTT
– £242, £187, £165, £154, *£270 £377*

HARDY JOCK SCOTT TOURNAMENT
Est. from £500

HARDY NOTTINGHAM
– £143, £132, *£270, £264*

HARDY NOTTINGHAM LEVER ACTION
4″ – £220
4½″ – £132, *£200*

HARDY NOTTINGHAM SILEX
– £120, £160, *£200, £209*

HARDY WALLIS
3½″ – £121
4″ – £154, £110, £77, *£150*

HARDY WHITE – WICKHAM
Est. from £400

HARDY ZANE GREY
3½″ – £770
4 $^3/_{16}$″ – £726
6″ – £682

HERCULES
2½" – £253, *$800*, $467, *$1320*
2⅝" – *£500* (rare size)
3" – £88, £88, £160
3½" – £71, *£120*
4" – £99, £44, *£180, £104*
4¼" – £121, £143, £209, *£187*
£220
4½" – £49, *£170*

HUSKY
– £60

HYDRA
3½" – £30, *£35*

LIGHTWEIGHT
3³⁄₁₆" – £45, *£44*

LONGSTONE EBONA
5⅛" – £231

LONGSTONE WALNUT
Est. from £300

LONGSTONE ALLOY REELS
3½" – £61
4" – £41, *£61, £60*
4½" – £55, £38, *£66, £66*
5" – £66, £49
6" – £49, £49, *£38, £80*

LONGSTONE DORADO
– £500

LRH LIGHTWEIGHT
3³⁄₁₆" – £44, £35, *£77* (two), *£60*

MARQUIS
3¼" – £44
3½" – (two) £71
3¾" – £24, £55, *£44* (two), *£44*
3⅞" – Salmon No 1 £55
4⅛" – Salmon No 2 £60, £71,
£88, £55
3⁷⁄₁₆" – Marquis No 7 £38
3⅝" – Marquis 8/9 £55, £60

MATCH FISHERS REEL
– £220, *£198, £290*

MEGSTONE EBONA
Est. from £300

MEGSTONE WALNUT
Est. from £300

NATAL
Est. from £300

OCEAN REELS

OCEAN (First Model)
Est. from £400

OCEAN (Second Model)
Est. from £300

PATENT OCEAN
Est. from £300

IMPROVED OCEAN
Est. from £200

PERFECT MODELS

ORIGINAL PERFECT
2¼" – £4400
2½" – £3740, £3630, £2970
Phillips (Exeter)
2¾" – £1980
3" – £4840
3½" – £2750
4" – £1320

TRANSITIONAL PERFECT
2½" – £3300
2⅝" – £3300
2¾" – £2227
2¾" – with the face plate of the succeeding 1896 model Perfect – £1265
4" – An unusual variant with brass drum retaining screw which was incorporated on to the succeeding model, the 1896 Perfect, *£2035*

1896 PERFECT
2½" – £1870, £590(polished, replaced foot), *£1200*
2⅝" – £1155, £990, £770,
– £682
2¾" – *£990*
3" – £1490 (unventilated)
– £682
3½" – £572, £440
4" – £590, *£770*
4½" – £825
4¼" – *£1680*
4¾" – £902, £748
5" – £1210
(All prices in 1989 from £1000)

PERFECT BRASS FACED WIDE DRUM
2½" – £726, £682, *£1000*
2⅝" – £660, £495, £330, £264,
£800, £330
2¾" – £297 (damaged), *£1078*
3" – £682
3¼" – £840, £770
3½" – £209, £198, *£300*
3¾" – £110, £104, *£341, $400*
4" – £165, £143, £132, £121,
£110, £104, £187, *£363,*
£198, £616
4¼" – £132, £110, £99, £88,
£165, *$600, $450, £209*
4½" – £176, £154, £104, *£214,*
£93, £88, £220, *£330,*
£400, £220
4¾" – £1000 (private)
5" – £1000 (private), £800

A non-production Original Perfect which had been the property of William Hardy. Sold for £4840

Transitional Perfect

Original Perfect

PERFECT WIDE DRUM (EARLY MODEL)
2½″ – *£685*
3½″ – £220, *£300, £400*
4″ – *£440*

PERFECT WIDE DRUM
2½″ – £600 (private), £374 (replaced foot)
2⅝″ – £308, £220, *£154*
2¾″ – £308
3″ – £220 (unmarked), £104, *£400, £352* (worn condition)
3¼″ – £400, *£300*
3½″ – £120, £110, *£140, £165, £110*
3¾″ – £143, £121, £93, £77, *£176, £209*
4″ – £121, £88, £82, £60, £275, *£132, £165, £198* (in case)
4¼″ – £82, £77, £55, $275, £121, *£200, £418* (superb reel in case), similar £418, £93
4½″ – £104, £82, £77, £55, *£170, £396* (superb reel in case)
4¾″ – *£650*

PERFECT EUNUCH MODEL
4″ – (no ball race) £132

PERFECT MARK II WIDE DRUM (Also includes POST WAR model)
3″ – £500
3¼″ – £440
3½″ – £99, £93, £88, £82, $132, *£176, £187*
3¾″ – £110, £88, £82, £71, £66, £55, $132, £165, *£154, £132, £209, £110, £176, £165, £187*
4″ – £154, £132, £121, £110, £99, £88, $132, £154, £155, *£198, £132, £165, £374* (bright finish), *£264*
4¼″ – £110, £99, £176, £66 (drum screw replaced), *£165*
4½″ – £60, £143 (with case), *£165*

From left to right: 1896 Perfect, Field (top), Transitional Perfect, 1896 Perfect

PERFECT NARROW DRUM (EARLY MODEL)
3⅛″ – *£350*
3⅜″ – *£400, £230*
3⅞″ – *£590*

PERFECT BRASS FACED NARROW DRUM
3⅛″ – £638, £460 (Phillips Chester)
– £396, £720 (with original bronzing)

PERFECT NARROW DRUM
2⅞″ – £286, £253, *$1,150*
3⅛″ – £242, £176, £132, £44 (replaced foot), £165, £60, *£264, $375, £132,* $412, *£89*
3⅜″ – £126, £110, £55, $110, *£99, $190,* $220, *£110*
3⅝″ – £104, £93, £71, *£70, £209, £220, £170*
3⅞″ – £176, £165, £115, £143, *£198, £205*

PERFECT EUNUCH
3⅛″ – £100

PERFECT MARK I NARROW DRUM
Est. from £300

PERFECT MARK II (1921 MODEL) NARROW DRUM
Est. from £400

PERFECT MARK II NARROW DRUM (also includes POST WAR model)
2⅞″ – £220, £176, £143, £121, £110, £104, $198, £187, £132, £176, *£132, £221, £176, £99, £137*
3⅛″ – £154, £115, £99, £88, £77, £66, £60, £49, £121, £55, *£82, £77, £71, £104, $71, $83, $93, £86, £71, £77, £154* (in case), *£104, £82*
3⅜″ – £99, £93, £77, £60, £55, £49, £46, £82, £66, *£61, £126, £44, £94, £82*
3⅝″ – £77, £49, £46, £41, £198 (left handed), £121, £66, *£93*
3⅞″ – £143, £121, £110, £77, £49, £99, *£82, £121*

PERFECT VARIANT
with large and small perforations
– £638

Hardy reels from left to right – Brass Faced Perfect Wide Drum 2½″ diameter, Brass Faced Perfect Narrow Drum 3⅛″ diameter, 1896 Perfect 5″ diameter, 1896 Perfect 2⅝″ diameter, Original Perfect 2½″ diameter

BOUGLÉ
3″ – £490, $990, £660 (toe broken), *£1320*
3¼″ – £638, *£1100, £935* (spring missing)

BOUGLÉ MARK II
3″ – £528, $770
3¼″ – £858, £688, $1100, $880

SPECIAL PERFECT
3¼″ – £528, £420, £330, *£685*

SPECIAL PERFECT MARK II
3¼″ – £308, £264, *£400*

PERFECT EARLY SILENT CHECK
Est. from £800

PERFECT SILENT CHECK
4″ – £418
3⅛″ – £150, *£440*

PERFECT TAUPO
– *£400, £500*

POMEROY WEST INDIAN
Est. from £300

PRINCESS
– £30, £22, £44, *£55*

RHODESIAN REEL
Est. from £300

SAINT AIDEN
3¾″ – £40, *£99, £44, £22, £49*

SAINT ANDREW
4⅛″ – £77, £44, *£52, £60*

SAINT GEORGE
3″ – £231, £176 (3 screw), *£165, £132, £330, $302, $962* (mint), *$550,* £148, £143 (2 screw), *£88, £93, $225, £143, £99*
3⅜″ – £121 (3 screw), £115 (3 screw), £82, £38, £88, *£60, £49, £55, £55, £77, £49, £88, £49, £70*
3¾″ – £44, £38, £34, £30, £38, £165, *£49, £44, £71, £38, £35, £60, £47, £88, £50, £77, £154*

SAINT GEORGE JUNIOR
2 9/16″ – £242, £209, £687, $357, $302, £165 (section of rim missing) *$525, $632, $660, $715*

SAINT GEORGE MULTIPLIER
3⅜″ – £176, £77 (agate ring cracked), *£280*

SAINT GEORGE SILENT CHECK
Est. from £300

Silex Multiplier 2¾″ diameter (top left), Silex Superba (top right), Sea Silex 6″ (bottom left), Silex Major with Auxiliary Brake 4″ diameter (bottom right)

SAINT GEORGE TOURNAMENT FLY REEL
– £550

SAINT GEORGE WIDE DRUM
4½″ – £1,000 (private), *£900*

SAINT JOHN No 2
3⅞″ – £49, *£41, $170, £60, £60, £55, $385* (in original box), *£49*

SAINT JOHN No 1
(with built up drum)
3⅞″ – £90

SEA SILEX
5″ – £165, £110, £66, $176
6″ – £520 (Early Mark – 'Silex No 2')
7″ – £220, £143

SILEX
3¼″ – £60
3½″ – £77
3¾″ – £60, *£121* (in leather case), *£143*
4″ – £66, *£93, £88, £132, £77*
4¼″ – £60, £33, *£99*
4½″ – £77, £66, £71, £93, *£66*

SILEX No 2
2¾″ – £165
3¼″ – £55, £49, *£71*
3½″ – £33, *£110*
3¾″ – £34, £33, £27, £27, £24, *£55*
4″ – £55, £30, £49, £20, *£44, £33, £82, £71, £77*
4¼″ – £88, £60, *£38*
4½″ – £44, *£44*

SILEX SILENT WIND-IN
3¾″ – £110

SILEX MAJOR
3″ – £242, £121, £121, *£132*
3¼″ – £88, £49, £38, £77, *£71, £82*
3½″ – £55, £41, £33, £27, £55, *£42, £77*
3¾″ – £55, £49, £44, £38, £30, $99, £55, *£93*
3¾″ EW – £77, £66, *£220* (superb reel in case)
4″ – £60, £44, £35, £33, £22, £38, £22, £38, *£55, £82, £99, £165* (in leather case), *£71, £60*
4¼″ – £77, £38, £30, £33, *£49, £286* (superb reel in case), *£60*
4½″ – £38, £34, *£59, £187 (left hand wind in case)*
4½″ EW – £77

SILEX MINOR
Est. from £500

LITTLE SILEX TOURNAMENT
Est. from £700

SILEX MULTIPLIER
2¾″ – £264, £231, £165, *£240*

SUPER SILEX
3" – £176
3¼" – £121, £104, *£77, £126*
3½" – £165, £132, £82, £93, *£130*
3¾" – £120, *£330* (mint in case), £110, *£110, £121*
4" – £176, £176, £151, £121, *£82,* £104, £82, £121, £154, *£99, £99, £150, £110, £110*
4¼" – £88, *£93*
4½" EW – £187, *£121*

SUPER SILEX MULTIPLIER
3½" – £209, £300, *£350, £325*
3¼" – £286, £320

SILEX REX
Est. from £1500

J J HARDY SILEX
3½" – £242, *£400*

SILEX JEWEL
3¾" – £132, £93, £110, *£121*
4" – £187, *£154, £140*

SILEX SUPERBA
4" – £143, £99, £88, £82, *£71*

SILEX No 2 PATENT SURF REEL
4½" – £200

SOUTH AFRICAN SURF CASTING REEL
Est. from £400

SPECIAL TOURNAMENT CASTING REEL
– £510

SUNBEAM
2¾" – £38
3¼" – £60, £30, £19
4" – (with case) £88

SUNBEAM MARK II
2¾" – £38, £30, *£71, £49*
3" – £38, £49

TOURNAMENT REEL
Est. from £1000

TRIUMPH (1923 MODEL)
– £375

TRIUMPH (1936 MODEL)
3¼" – £110, *£82*
4" – £220

TUNA
7" – £143

UNIQUA NARROW DRUM
3⅛" – £44, *£132, £44*
3⅜" – £66, *£60*

UNIQUA WIDE DRUM
4" – £55
4¼" – £71
3¾" – £33, £27, £24, £38
3½" – £33
3¾" – £88, *£61*

UNIQUA MARK I (1919/20 MODEL) NARROW DRUM
Est. from £300

UNIQUA MARK II (1921 MODEL) NARROW DRUM
Est. from £300

UNIQUA MARK II NARROW DRUM
2⅝" – £104, £99, *£88*
2⅞" – £93, £55
3⅛" – £30, £22, $242, *£71, £55, £49*
3⅜" – £16, *£44*
3⅝" – £11, £55, *£44, £35*

UNIQUA MARK II WIDE DRUM
4" – £33, *£198, £71*
4¼" – £66, *£176* (superb reel in case), *£55, £104*

U.S.A.
Est. from £500

VISCOUNT
– £55, *£27, £71*

WALLIS
– £220

ZENITH
– £99, £77, £77, *£39, £60, £44*

Hardy reels from left to right – Eureka 3½" diameter, Hardy Wallis 4" diameter, Conquest 4⅜" diameter, Silex Multiplier 2¾" diameter

HARDY RODS

All rods listed are split-cane unless otherwise stated

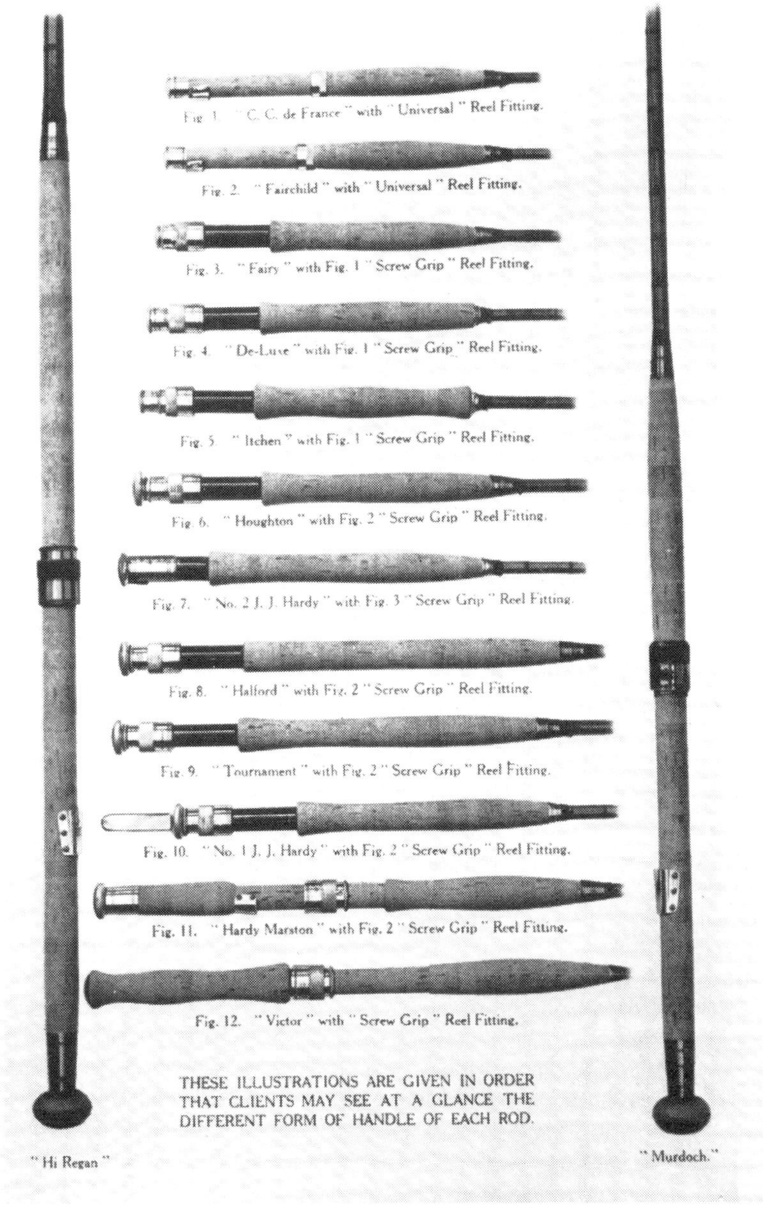

ALNWICK GREENHEART
15ft – £22

AHE WOOD No 2
3 piece + spare tip
12ft – E 55770 £93, £88 E 56982

AHE WOOD No 3
3 piece + spare tip
12ft – H6394 £88, E68666 £55, H51551A £49, E70383 £49, H51551A £71, £55

AYDON
3 piece + spare tip, greenheart
8ft – two rods G/4375 and G14376 £198

CARP
2 piece
9ft 11″ – No H11243 £38

C C DE FRANCE
2 piece
9ft – H13925 £66, E35346 £60, E23393 £41, 33939 £49, E48097 £115, E38698 £110, £104, E46822 £115, 35346 £71
8ft 6″ – Sold with Princess Reel £143, rod only $187
8ft – No 33617 in leather tube £176, E54410 £66, E47699 £60, H58404 £220
7′ 9″ – H8005 £132, E33718 £44, E41465 £99
7′ – E69782 £132, £198, $495, $605
6′ 10″ – 2 piece + spare tip $467
6′ 6″ – E51259 £242

COQUETTE
3 piece + spare tip
13′ – H7835 (+ gaff) £99, H7121 £71
8′ – 38843 £71

CORBETT No 1
9′ 3″ – 2 piece No 28767, £16

THE COUNTY
8′ 7″ – 2 piece H35174 £33

CROWN HOUGHTON
3 piece + spare tip
10′ – No H3794 (plus aluminium tube) £49

DAPPING
14′ – 3 piece + spare tip £44, £60

DE-LUXE
3 piece + spare tip
10′ – B22883 £77
9′ 6″ – E86518 £70, £60 No 57576
9′ 4″ – E11238 £44

9′ – H23039 £88, No 58469 £77, H32862 £33, H3833 £66, £68, H41551C £60
8′ 10″ – E95874 £82
8′ 6″ – E73949 £71, G 73949 £60, E51406 £61
8′ – 3 piece £49

5½ oz DE-LUXE
3 piece + spare tip
9′ – E95874 £104, H37469 £88, E95874 £60

EXTRA HEAVY ZANE GREY
6′ 10″ – No 43777 £132

FAIRY
10′ – 3 piece + spare tip $55
9′ 7″ – 3 piece No E58344 $49
7′ – 2 piece 'H W Favorite 10 lb,' G31247 £38

FAIRCHILD FLY ROD
7½′ or 8′ – 3 piece + two tips of different lengths. Moderate set but otherwise excellent $341

FEATHERWEIGHT PERFECTION
2 piece
9′ 3″ – E89622 £61, £104

GLEN LOY
9′ 6″ – E6982 £49

GOLD MEDAL
3 piece + spare tip
14′ – £49
13′ – £22, £104
10′ – H3346 £71, £44, £71, H16687 £44
9′ 10″ – E49866 £88, No H15688 £71
9′ 5″ – H57010 £66, £71
9′ – E57741 £38, C46120 £33, £93
8′ 1″ – No 246936 £93

HALFORD KNOCKABOUT
2 piece
9′ 6″ – H66021 £77, H24588 £55, 61993 £77
9′ 6″ – 3 piece + spare tip, 'The Halford 1905 Model' £99

HARDY ZANE GREY
6′ 10″ – Big game rod marked 'Hardy Zane Grey, Steel Centre, Test Curve 56 lb'. Old over varnish, good condition $1650

H E ACCURACY
2 piece
8′ – No 3202 £44

HEBRIDEAN
3 piece + spare tip
13′ 10″ – No 196216 £24

H E WOOD No 2
12′ – 3 piece + spare tip No E76333 £82

H J S ROD
2 piece + spare tip
5′ 6″ – E46512 £110

HOLLOLITE
3 piece + spare tip
12′ 6″ – H22397 (unused) £143, £157, £105, H29171 £99, H36281 £93, H31814 £82, H26781 £72, H31847 £176, £88 H36266
10′ – 3 piece + spare tip $176
9′ – 3 piece + spare tip $247, £176 H60865
8′ 6″ – H35394 £154

HOUGHTON FLY ROD
3 piece + spare tip
10′ – c.1984 £60, E31874 £77, £93
9′ 6″ – E58259 £38
9′ 6″ – B10989 (with rod tube) £121, £88 E5523

HOUGHTON MARSTON
2 piece + spare tip
10′ 6″ – No 93914 £38

IDEAL
9′ 6″ – 1 piece E36240 £110
9′ – E298320 1 piece + case £104
8′ 6″ or 8′ – Two 1 piece rods with cases £99

ITCHEN
3 piece + spare tip
9′ 6″ – £77, £93, £61, H39237C £82, £132

J J HARDY
3 piece + spare tip
10′ – E23019 £66
10′ – 2 piece, No E31678 £30
9′ 3″ – 3 piece E55983 £27

J J H TRIUMPH
3 piece + spare tip
8′ 9″ – E43684 £71, E97575 £38
8′ 6″ – No. 673 £24
8′ 3″ – 2 piece E66997 £88

KEITH ROLO
9′ – 3 piece + spare tip £136

KOH-I-NOOR
2 piece H20212 £60
8′ 9″ – £99, £77 H12385, £44 H19089
7′ 10″ – E80913 £33

LIGHTWEIGHT-THAMES STYLE
Whole cane 3 piece + spare centre section
13′ 3″ or 11′ 3″ – G14789 £33

LOCH-LEVEN
3 piece + spare tip
11′ 6″ – No 41336E £86

L R H DRY FLY
3 piece + spare tip
8′ 9″ – H4009 (sold with L R H reel) £88, £99

L R H No 1
2 piece
9′ 6″ – H4727 £44, H11459 £41, E59200 £38, H15256 £55, H8100 £49

L R H No 2
2 piece
9′ 6″ – H10442 £49, £27, £99, No HC42744 £55, NOH 26952 £61, £77, 65597 £99

L R H No 3
2 piece
9′ 6″ – E 88103 £71, H26814 £88

L R H GREASED LINE
3 piece
13′ – E62435 £71

L R H SALMON FLY
14′ – 3 piece + spare tip £142

MARKSMAN
8′ 3″ – 2 piece H1484 £49, £60

MARSTON 1920
3 piece + spare tip
9′ 8″ – C13612 £38
10′ 4″ – B14332 £60

MARVEL
7′ 6″ – 3 piece + spare tip, 2¾ oz. Mint $797

MULTEX No 2
2 piece
9′ 9″ – E35484 £27

MURDOCK
3 piece + spare tip (steel centre)
11′ 6″ – No E 32907 £24
10′ 3″ – £49

N B PERFECTION Combination Rod
– 13 piece including 5 tops and 2 two piece pigskin and brass handles No 14061. An early rod £286

NEOCANE
3 piece
14′ – NE2418 £13

PALAKONA
3 piece + spare tip
13′ – A84576 £27
12′ 3″ – No 101448 £55
10′ – A34015 £27
11′ 1″ – No 99596 £90
9′ 9″ – 2 piece No 1515C £27
8′ 9″ – 2 piece A68898 £22, £71
8′ – 2 piece £143

PENNELL
14′ 6″ – 3 piece + spare tip, £92

PERFECT
2 piece
8′ 6″ – £61

PERFECTION
2 piece
10′ 3″ – A98088 £60, No 100256 £22
10′ – H68029 £60, E5287 £27, H7944 £93
9′ 10″ – £38
9′ 6″ – E5660 £27, H59932 £30, E30865 £20, E34345 £121, H433930 £71, E28609 £44, £38
9′ – H53600 A. AFTM 5 £82, H53600 A £44, H 64496 £44, E26309 £35, H1585 £77, E71231 £33, £66, £71, E13337 £77, £99
8′ 6″ – 2 piece £82
8′ – H21724 £82, H9514 £60, E54333 £38

PHANTOM
2 piece
9′ – H52772 £82, H60212 £66, H64905 £60, £66
8′ 6″ – £110, £71
8′ – H57703 £110
6′ 10″ – New condition $247
6′ – £110, £232

POPE
2 piece
10′ – No 58324 £60, H283 £60, £44, No C13369 £49, H58299 £77, H38292 £33, £44, £88, 13197C £86
9′ – £60

PRINCESS
3 piece
9′4″ – A16800 (presentation rod) £99

ROACH PERFECTION
2 piece
10′ 2″ – No 4896E £30

ROGUE RIVER
10′ – + spare tip, H7891, £71
9′ 5″ – + screw in butt extension H26579 £82

SALMON DE-LUXE
3 piece + spare tip
14′ – £61, £88
9′ 6″ – with extension butt £143, £99
– without extension butt £99, £66

SALTWATER No 3
2 piece
7′ 2″ – No E38518 £82

SALTWATER No 4
2 piece, greenheart tip
6′ 6″ – No 22498E £82

SALTWATER No 5
with spanner and detachable butt
6′10″ – H11138 £88

SIDEWINDER No 5
7′ – 2 piece big game rod £33

SPECIAL
3 piece + spare tip
14′ 9″ – C7984 £44
14′ 7″ – E4111 £20, C19309 £44
10′10″ – 3 pc, No A81321 £33
8′ 6″ – E41734 £104

SPINNING ROD
2 piece
10′ 6″ – £16
8′ 8″ – £44

SPLICED JOINTED SALMON
16′ 4″ – split cane, 2 piece with bronzed joint keepers, £143

SUSSEX SPECIAL BROOK
2 piece
8′ – E30394 £75

TAUPO
3 piece + spare tip
10′ – H21968 £88
9′ 8″ – 3 piece, H46172 £44

TEAL
3 piece
10′ – £22

TEVIOT
3 piece
9′ – E26771 £71

TOURNAMENT
3 piece + spare tip
10′ 6″ – E66200 £27

TOURNEY
2 piece
9′ – H10903 £82
8′ 6″ – E74384 £77

TRAVELLERS ROD
Combination 4 pc Fly Rod and two piece spinning rod with detachable butt
5′ to 8′ 9″– £93, £253 No H2183

J J H TRIUMPH
8′ 9″ – £82, £61, £84

TRUECAST
3 piece whole cane
12′ – G25530 £33

UPSTREAM WORMING
3 piece. Whole cane and split cane top
12′ – G11865 £27

VIBRATION GREENHEART
14′ – G216584 £121

VICTORIA
3 piece
15′ – E11667 £55

VICTOR
2 piece
7′ – E31487 £44

WALLIS No 1 AVON
– £121

WALLIS No 2 AVON
– G23648 £187, £170

WANLESS
2 piece
10′ & 7′ – (two rods) £38
8′ – H2447 £55, No 48698 £22, E52730 £61
7′ – H21038 (Plus Altex) £66, E56052 £22, E66399 £44, £38, £28, £44, £36, £28, £46, £66

WANLESS LIGHT LINE
3 piece + spare tip
12′ 6″ – E83251 £44

THE COUNTY
8′ 7″ – 2 piece, H35174 £33

WEST COUNTRY SPINNING
9′ 4″ – 3 piece + spare tip, No H6250 £55
7′ – 2 piece E 60715 £38

WYE
3 piece + spare tip
13′ 6″ – H31786 £132, H3134 £110, E81010 £82, £121, E27583 £66, H55999 £181
12′ 6″ – Recent model £120, H23610 £82, H17520 £66, E29354 £60, H3167 £55, H17024 £55, H13720 £49, H68089 £165, H65405 £77, £93, £187, H29675 £154
11′ – 2 piece + spare tip H14772 £82
– 2 piece H7520 £71
– 3 piece + spare tip No C1849 £49, £187, £60 2 piece No E95622
10′ 6″ – 3 piece No E84727 £49

BRITISH REELS

Prices shown in italics denote amounts realised at auction during the last two years

ABU

AMBASSADEUR 9000 – *£49*

AMBASSADEUR 7000 – *£60*

AMBASSADEUR 6500 C – *£110* (sold with Intrepid reel)

AMBASSADEUR 6000 – £45, £49, £64, *£110, £77, £110* (with ABU Matic), *£154* (two), *£100* (with Ogden Smith reel)

AMBASSADEUR 5600 CDL, gold plated in wood box *£308*

AMBASSADEUR 5500 D – *£70, £88, £88*

AMBASSADEUR 5000 – £41, *5000 C with tools in case £121*

ABU – 3000 *£38* (with Mitchell reel)

ABU MATIC closed faced reel, an ABU 444 and a Cardinal 44 *£187*

ABU Cardinal 66 and an ABU 508 – *£66*

ALLAN

4½″ – Salmon reel £52
– Spinet reel £38, £27

ALLCOCK

VENTILATED ARIEL
3½″ – £44, £33, *£50*
4″ – £88 (with case), £33, £61, *£120*
4⅛″ – £36, *£110*
4⅝″ – £71, £27
5″ – 5″ MAHSEER £132

UNVENTILATED AERIAL
3″ – £95
3½″ – *£220*
3¾″ – *£110*
4½″ – *£95, £77, £200*

ARIEL POPULAR
3″ – *£30*
3½″ – *£20, £45, £80*
4¼″ – *£38*
4½″ – *£66*

AERIALITE
– (three) *£46*

COXON
(with wood backplate)
4¼″ – £154, £250
4¾″ – £99, *£170*

BELL SEA REEL
– £27

BLACK KNIGHT
– £8

COMMODORE
6″ – £33

DUPLEX
– £49

EASICAST
4″ – £19, £33

FELTON CROSSWIND
– £44, £33

IMPROVED FLICK-EM-MATCH
– £71

MARVEL
– £16, £38

MATCH AERIAL (1939) Model
– handle missing £275

LEVIATHAM BIG GAME
– £132

STANLEY REEL
– £13, £27, £20
– £33, £44

A & NCSL (Army & Navy)

ALLOY
3″ – *£58*
3¼″ – *£49, £38*
3½″ – £27, *£121* (in leather case)
4¼″ – £33
4½″ – £16

BRASS
2¼″ – *£41*
2½″ – £60
3½″ – £33
4″ – £60
4¼″ – £44
4½″ – *£121*

ANDERSON (Dunkeld)

4½″ – All brass salmon reel £71

J BERNARD & SON

3½″ – Nottingham type wood reel *£63*
3¾″ – Brass £44

Reels from left to right – Clamp foot winch 2⅛″ diameter, folding crank handle reel by Chevalier, Bowness & Son, multiplying reel by J C Conroy & Co, New York, multiplying reel in German silver by J C Conroy, NY, spike foot winch by Kelly of Dublin 1¾″ diameter, multiplying brass winch 2½″ diameter

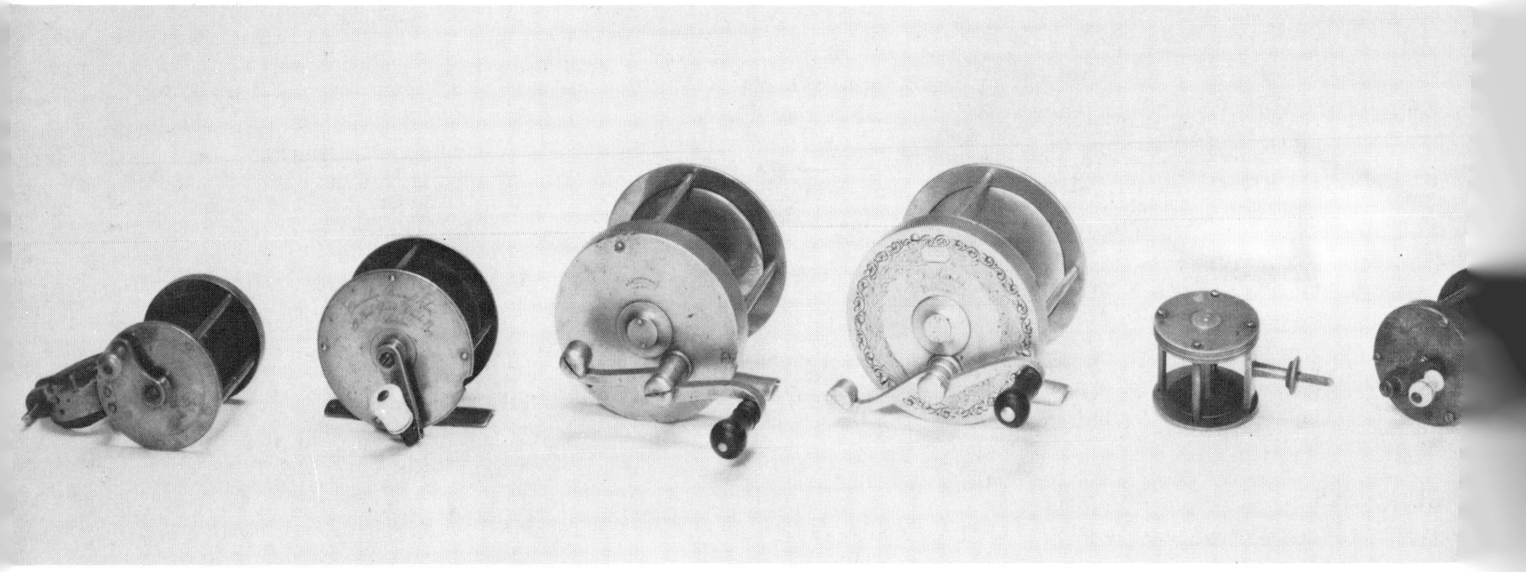

4¼″ – Alloy £27
5″ – Brass/ebonite £88
– Crank handled brass £71

BOWNESS AND BOWNESS

4″ – Brass plate reel £60

BRYSON (Perth)

5″ – Wood and brass *£77*

CARSWELL

Threadline casting reel £55

CARTER

Brass plate reel £38
Brass & ebonite with nickel silver rims, perforated drum and plate £66, £49, *£50, £89*

CHEVALIER, BOWNESS AND BOWNESS

2¼″ – Brass plate reel £44
3″ – Brass plate reel £121

CHEVALIER BOWNESS & SON

2¾″ – Crank handled brass reel with folding ivory knob and spring lock £165
3″ – Inscribed brass crank handled reel $220
3½″ – Brass with folding crank handle *£484*
3¾″ – Brass with folding crank handle *£230*
4″ – Crank handled with folding ivory knob *£77*

CRANK HANDLED UN-NAMED REELS

2⅜″ – Brass with turned rosewood knob on curved winding arm in deep anti-foul rim £49
2¾″ – Multiplier with raised gear housing to the face £120
2⅞″ – With folding ivory crank handle £77
3⅜″ – Brass with folding ivory knob with disc lock, stand off pillars £77
3¾″ – Brass with folding turned bone knob on straight arm, button lock £44
4″ – Brass with turned ivory folding knob with screw lock on straight arm with drum of horse hair line £104
1½″ – Brass winch, raised check housing and perforated foot *£84*

CUMMINS

2½″ – Pat. Centre Brake No 1″ £55

3″ – Brass/ebonite, nickel rims £44
3″ – Alloy trout reel *£38*

DINGLEY

4″ – Alloy salmon reel £71

DREADNOUGHT CASTING CO LTD

3⅛″ – The Meteor, alloy, bone handle £99
3¼″ – Alloy Impulse reel £55
4″ – Casting reel, ivorine handles £66
5″ – The Meteor £77

EATON AND DELLER

2½″ – Brass/ebonite plate reel £85
3¾″ – Salmon fly reel £71
4¼″ – Salmon fly reel £33
4¾″ – Large half wood reel. The drum, pillars, foot and moulded front plate of brass. The back plate and front rim of finely figured wood (probably ebony), with wooden knob £165

ENGRAVED REEL

2½″ – with fishing scene in raised relief on plates $247, *£110*

C FARLOW AND CO LTD

ALLOY SALMON REEL
4″ – £30

BARRETT
4″ – £27, £27

BILLIKEN MULTIPLIER
– Sold in 1984 £385

CRANK HANDLE BRASS
2¾″ – £48, one with raised check housing £77

CRANK HANDLED
3″ – £121, *£264* (folding handle)
4″ – £55

MYSTIC
3¾″ – Aluminium spinning reel £121

PATENT LEVER
4¼″ – £66, *£121*

PENNELL
4½″ – £77

PELICAN SEA REEL
6″ – £93

PLATE REEL
2½″ – £49
2¾″ – £71
4″ – £49
4¼″ – with case £88
4½″ – £49
4½″ – with case, £143, £88

PYTHON
4″ – £27, *£22*

REGAL
3″ – £93
3½″ – £77, £77
4″ – £77

TROLLING WINCH BRASS
Diameter 3½″, Wide 4″, £748

TURNTABLE
– Spring loaded £242, £400

BRASS SIDECASTER (Malloch Reel)
– £110

SCOTTISH TYPE
– Walnut/brass £237
– Walnut and brass plate reel with horn knob, inscribed 'John Hargreaves from F H 1874'. Diameter 4⅞″ £319

J K FARLOW

1⅞″ – Multiplying pole winch £275

FARSHURE

– A fixed spool threadline casting reel No 265 £121
– A similar reel No 64 – £286, *£154, £275*

FEATHERSTONE & HART

MULTIPLIER
– £880

FORREST & SONS

4¾″ – Salmon fly reel £44

FOSTERS

– Rare combination reel/butt mount 2⅜″ x 4¾″ £297
4½″ – Salmon fly reel *£82*

WILLIAM GARDEN

4½″ – Brass plate wind with horn handle *£84*

J GILLETT

3⅛″ – Brass/ebonite, nickel silver rims £55

GOW (DUNDEE)

3¼″ – 'Tayside' alloy fly reel *£35*

W B GOWLAND

– Multiplying brass pole winch with unpierced foot, ivory knob on curved crank arm £123

W H HAMLIN

3″ – Alloy trout reel *£44*

HARDINGS

– The 'Bercol' alloy threadline reel £55

HAYWOOD (BIRMINGHAM)

1⅝″ – Clamp foot with rim stop $176, *£500*
1¾″ – Clamp foot multiplying winch *£294*
1⅞″ – Clamp foot multiplying winch $275

HELLICAL CASTING CO

– Fixed spool reel in case *£50*

HOLBROW & CO

4″ – Crank handled brass winch with anti-foul rim £71

W F HOMER

4¼″ – 'Flick em' £66

HOLROYD

4″ – Brass and ebonite *£220*

HORWOOD (KILLIN)

5″ – Brass/ebonite trolling reel in case £110

ILLINGWORTH

NO 1 MODEL
Type 1 – £340, £242, *£395*
Type 2 – £330, £250, £231, £209, *£376, £528*

NO 2 MODEL
– £71, *£86, £78*

NO 3 MODEL
– £66, £49, *£99*

NO 4 MODEL
– £60, *£71, £66*

NO 5 MODEL
– £88, £82, *£141*

KELLY AND SON (DUBLIN)

1¾″ – Spike foot winch £132
5″ – Brass salmon reel £187, £93
2⅜″ – Spike foot winch £286

KEWELL & CO. (LONDON)

5″ – Half ebonite revolving plate reel £55

G LITTLE & CO

4½″ – Brass and ebonite salmon fly reel £121
4″ – Gun metal fly reel *£93*
3⅞″ – Half ebonite revolving plate reel £66
2¾″ – Alloy *£38*
2⅝″ – Brass *£93*
2″ – Crank handled patent brass reel with stand off pillars and 'H' frame bridge £132

MacPHERSON OF INVERNESS

2¼″ – Ebonite and brass plate winch with ivory handle and nickel rims *£68*

P D MALLOCK

BRASS PATENT SIDECASTER
2⅛″ – £120 (Phillips Chester)
2⅞″ – £66, *£55*
3⅜″ – £49
4″ – *£55, £60, £78*

ALLOY PATENT SIDECASTER
3¼″ – *£49, £44*
3¾″ – £33, *£44*
4″ – £30, £13, £19, £27, £38
4½″ – £30

SIDECASTER WITH GIBBS PATENT LEVER
3¾″ – £33, $110, £44

MULTIPLYING SIDECASTER
2¼″ – £80
3¼″ – £110

BRASS BIRMINGHAM
2¾″ – *£88*

EBONITE AND BRASS FLY REEL
4½″ – £55, $121

SUN AND PLANET TROLLING REEL
– £187, £143, *$300*

LARGE PLATE REEL
6″ – Brass with ivorine handle £198

ALEX MARTIN

3″ – Scotia alloy trout reel £16
3¾″ – Half-wood revolving plate reel, rosewood front rim and handle £44
4″ – Thistle salmon fly reel (sold with fly box and 118 flies) £60

M'CLEAY (INVERNESS)

5″ – Brass *£99*
4⅛″ – *£66*
3¾″ – *£82*

McGOWAN

3¾″ – Crank handled brass trolling reel with raised pillars £82, £190
4½″ – Crank wind with raised check housing and anti-foul rim *£300*

J E MILLER

CHIPPENDALE
Multiplying reel
– £154

THE REFITT MOORE 'RAPID' (PATENTED) MULTIPLYING REEL
– £176, £290

MARSTON-CROSSLE

4″ – *£65*

MILWARD

5½″ – 'African' wide drum Frogbag reel £49
4″ – Castover £44
3″ – Flymaster £16

MITCHELL

– 300 in case *£78*
– 710 Automatic *£22*

MONK (CHESTER)

3″ – Alloy fly reel £38

MOSCROP

'MANCHESTER' REEL
3″ – £49
4″ – £44, *£187* (two)
4½″ – £27, £60, *£104*
3″ & 4″ – (two) £99

NOTTINGHAM (UN-NAMED)

4″ – *£20*
3½″ – Good quality Sheffield pattern *£52*
High quality star-back in lovely cherrywood $71

OGDEN SMITH

3″ – Alloy fly reel £19
3″ – Exchequer $93
4¼″ – Exchequer £55
4½″ – Salmon fly reel with leather case £66, £57

PAPE

2″ – Brass and rosewood knob *£35, £55* (2 3/16″)

PATON (PERTH)

3¼" – Half-wood revolving plate reel. Backplate and rim of lignum vitae £93
5" – Rosewood and brass salmon fly reel *£126*

J PEEK & SON

4" – Salmon fly reel £24

PENN

SENATOR MULTIPLIER
– *£49, £49*
– Silver Beech No 99 £44
– Master Marina No 349 £44
– No 160 Model £33

PIRN

– Scottish trolling winch carved from hardwood. Diameter 2½". Width 4⅝" £418, *£825*

PLAYFAIR

4½" – Alloy salmon reel £27
4¾" – Alloy salmon reel *£121*
– No 3 salmon *£121*
– No 4 trout reel 3⅛" *£66*

POWNALL'S

– Patent Scarborough type sea reel *£66*

ROBERTSON (GLASGOW)

4" – Half-wood revolving plate reel £44

RYOBI

4" – Model 455 in box *£33*

SCOTTISH PATTERN

3⅞" – Brass and walnut £132, *£157*

SHARPE

3½" – Scottie alloy reel £30
The Gorden alloy reel £11, *£71* (two)
4" – Salmon *£71*

SHERRIFF (GLASGOW)

4¼" – Teak and brass plate reel £71

FRED SKINNER

– Archimedian Reel with an iron frame, brass drum and iron side-mounted foot marked 'Fred K Skinner's Archimedian Reel Sheffield' and No 1426 Registered on 25th April 1848. Two examples of this reel have turned up in recent years and the markings have fuelled speculation that it was the first reel to receive a British patent. However, the Patent Office report that there is no record of either a Skinner nor a patent of that number and they have no knowledge of a patent for the subject. One example sold in 1984/5 for £858.

SLATER

COMBINATION
4⅝" – £88
4½" – £71, £180

FLY FISHER'S S E J WINCH
– *£180, £100,* £190

WALLACE ZEPHYR model
3¾" – £66, *£50*
4½" – £71

ALBERT SMITH & CO

3" – Alloy trout fly reel *£33*
3½" – Alloy twin handled centrepin *£49*

C. STRATTON & CO

3¼" – Brass trout reel *£60*

TURNBULL

4" – Alloy salmon fly reel with fixed check, caged drum and brass foot *£77*

WADHAM

4" – Brass frame, foot and skeleton back plate with ventilated ebonite drum £143

WALKER

4¾" – Alloy salmon reel £44

From left to right: Top – Illingworth No 1, Featherstone and Hart Multiplier, Hardy Fortuna. Below – Hardy Starback Nottingham, Hardy Zane Grey, Hardy Barton

Bonham's

WALKER BAMPTON & CO

4¼″ – Fly reel *£71*
3¼″ – Wallace Watson No 3 £66
3½″ – Lennox salmon reel £27
3¾″ – Alloy salmon reel £33

WESTLEY RICHARDS

4″ – Rolo spinning reel £49
4¼″ – Rolo (Dingley's Pat. 20133) £33
4½″ – Rolo alloy Silex type reel £44, *£93, £60*
3¾″ – Alloy salmon reel *£77*

WILLIAMS

5″ – Brass Birmingham type reel £60

A G WILSON

3¼″ – Crank handled with circular screw lock, and ivory knob on straight crank £154
4″ – Rare nickel silver crank-handled reel with turned ivory knob and disc lock. Stamped 'A & G Wilson etc HRHPA' (Prince Albert) £363

WINCH WITH CRANK HANDLE

UNUSUAL
2″ – Multiplier with stand off pillars and foot and 'H' piece frame £209
1⅝″ – Brass winch with straight crank £132, *£187*
1¾″ – Multiplying pole winch with curved crank £165
1¾″ – Brass winch with straight crank £220, £143

WITHOUT PAD PERFORATIONS ON FOOT
1½″ – Brass pole winch, bone handle on curved arm £33
1$^{11}/_{16}$″ – Small pole winch, bone knob on curved arm, the pillars with sliding handle latch £88
3¾″ – 19th century brass winch, straight crank, ivory knob, screw lock, raised casing £88

WITH PAD PERFORATIONS
1⅞″ – Multiplying brass winch, ivory knob on curved crank arm £93, £170, £230
1⅝″ – Multiplying brass winch with drum lock on rim, and curved crank £88, £230
2¼″ – Multiplying winch *£105, £190, £290*

WINCH WITH CLAMP OR COLLAR FOOT

1½″ – £250
1½″ – With sliding pillar bar *£262*
1⅝″ – £198
1¾″ – *£440*
1⅞″ – £264, *£253*
– *£200, £375*

WINCH WITH CLAMP OR COLLAR FOOT

1½″ – £250
1½″ – With sliding pillar bar *£262*
1⅝″ – £198
1¾″ – *£440*
1⅞″ – £264, *£253*
– *£200, £375*

WINCH WITH SPIKE FOOT

1⅝″ – Brass winch with brass knob on curved winding arm and winged nut on the spike £319, *£198* (poor example)
1¼″ – Brass winch with turned ivory knob. Lovely patina £400

YOUNG

CONDEX
– *£18, £38* (two)

AMBIDEX
– Reel £14, *£16*

BEAUDEX
– £16, £33, £12, £27, *£38* (two)

FREEDEX
– £16

PRIDEX
– £24 (two), *£33* (two)

RAPIDEX
– £60 (three)

SELDEX
4″ – £42

TRUDEX
– £20

VALDEX
– Also a Pridex and Landex (three) *£66*

WINDEX
– £18

From left to right:
Top: Hardy Cascapedia, Hardy Birmingham Plate Reel, Hardy Fortuna Junior Fly Reel, Multiplying Collar Winch, Hardy Bronzed Crank Reel.

Below: Hardy Starback Nottingham, Hardy Bethune Line Drier and a Hardy Jock Scott prototype reel

A multiplying winch with perforated foot of 2¼″ diameter (top left), a brass winch with perforated foot and horse-hair line, 2⅝″ diameter (top centre), crank handled winch 4″ diameter (top right), large crank handled winch by Eaton & Deller 5½″ diameter (bottom left), trolling winch by Farlows 3½″ diameter and 4″ width (bottom right)

Sotheby's

BRITISH RODS

All rods split-cane unless otherwise stated

T ALDRED

RARE 3 STRIP-CANE VALISE ROD
– Ten piece with drop rings, mid 19th century £748

ALLCOCK

13′ 3″ – 3 piece + spare tip, spliced salmon rod £22

THE COLONEL
9′ – 2 piece, £27, £38, £22

THE CONQUEROR
9′ – 2 piece £13
– 3 piece £24

THE GLORIA
13′ – 3 piece £33
12′ 3″ – 3 piece £8

LIGHT CASTER
7′ – 2 piece £24, £27, £16, £33, £38
6′ 3″ – 2 piece + spare tip £44

MARVEL
8′ – 2 piece £27

THE POPULAR
9′ – 3 piece £11, £38

SAPPER
10′ 6″ – 3 piece £22

WALLIS WIZARD
11′ – 3 piece £44

A & NCSL (ARMY & NAVY)

16′ 2″ – Greenheart 3 piece + spare tip £27
15′ – 3 piece + spare tip £16
13′ 1″ – 3 piece + spare tip £22
12′ – 3 piece £33
9′ 4″ & 8′ 11″
– 3 piece 2 tops £30
7′ 3″ – 2 piece 'Dovey' £44

ANDERSON

16′ – 3 piece greenheart £49

BERNARD & SON

9′ – 2 piece greenheart £60

BIRD

– 3 piece £27

BLACKBURN

THE J H McGINN
10′ 2″ – 3 piece + spare butt £11

BOWNESS AND BOWNESS

14′ – Greenheart 3 piece + spare tip, brass fittings, drop rings £30

THE CHEVALIER
10′ – Greenheart travelling rod, 6 piece £60

CARTER & CO

15′ – 3 piece + spare tip No 1778, greenheart/ bamboo £16
14′ 3″ – 4 piece + 3 tops greenheart/bamboo £22
11′ – 3 piece + spare tip No 0335, split cane £27

CONSTABLE

R H WOOD'S CLASSIC
7′ 6″ – 2 piece No 470 £110

CHEVALIER

12′ – 4 piece greenheart £38

COGSWELL AND HARRISON

11′ – 3 piece + spare tip £38

CONSTABLE

SAWYER NYMPH
– 2 piece £77
9′ – 2 piece (almost new) £78

W J CUMMINS

HOTSPUR
13′ 10″ – 3 piece + spare tip No B1927 £16

ANGLO AMERICAN FLY ROD
– drop rings, nickel silver fittings £132

CUMMINS

CLARENCE
9′ – 2 piece + spare tips greenheart £38

DAWSON

WHARF ROD
10′ – 2 piece £16

DICKSON

WAVERLEY
9′ 7″ – 3 piece £16

EATON & DELLER

14′ to 11′ 3″
– 3 piece + 3 tops £49

EGGINGTON

6′ – 2 piece £71

ENWRIGHT

15′ 6″ – 3 piece + spare tip (warped) £42

C FARLOW

15′ 6″ – 4 piece greenheart and lancewood £33
15′ – 3 piece + spare tip The Fife £38
14′ 3″ – 3 piece + spare tip No 7000 £33
14′ – 3 piece bamboo rod £5
12′ – 3 piece + spare tip The Coombe Richards £35
10′ 6″ – Parabolic Grilse rod £88
10′ 3″ – Early greenheart with drop rings, marked Prize Medal 1862 £121
10′ – 3 piece + spare tip Special Tournament £51
9′ 3″ – 3 piece + spare tip No 6218 £22
9′ – 2 piece Edmund Drurie £27
8′ 6″ – 2 piece No 114 £22
8′ – 2 piece £44
6′ 9″ – 2 piece £27
5′ 11″ – One piece Lee Wulff Ultimate £297

T FORDHAM

ACCURIST
8′ 9″ – 2 piece £44

J FORREST

16′ – 3 piece + spare mid section + spare tip $137
12′ 6″ – Greenheart rods (15′ and 12′ 6″) 3 pc £33
10′ 6″ – 3 piece + spare tip £33, £38

FOSTER BROS

THE CHAMPION
9′ – 2 piece £38

THE ENGLAND FAVORITE
8′ 6″ – 2 piece £55

THE HOLDING ROD
7′ 6″ – 2 piece £19

AIR SPRITE
7′ – 2 piece $126

GLANVILLE

11′ 3″ – 3 piece £22

JOHN GODDARD

NYMPH
8′ 6″ – 2 piece £44, £77

A J GRAHAM & CO

14′ – 3 piece + spare tip £22

GREYS

THE SUPREME
9′ – 2 piece £24

HAMLIN OF CHELTENHAM

15′ – 3 piece + spare tip £68

W HANKEY & SON

16′ – 3 piece greenheart £20

HARDING

FORTY SPECIAL
8′ – 2 piece £27

FORTY SPECIAL MARK II
8′ – £55

HARRODS

13′ – 3 piece + spare tip £24

HATTON

12′ – 3 piece £25

J C HIGGINS

7′ 6″ – 2 piece £38

HOLBROW

THE HOLBROW BAIT CASTER
7′ – 3 piece £22

J C IVENS

RAVENSTHORPE
9′ 2″ – 2 piece £51

B JAMES & SON

RICHARD WALKER MARK IV
10′ 2″ – 2 piece £77, £88

FAYNE
9′ 6″ – 2 piece £110

THE GREBE
8′ 8″ – 2 piece £77

LEE

BLACK PRINCE
9′ – 2 piece £27

LIGHT CASTING CO

ILLINGWORTH
6′ 9″ – 2 piece £19

P D MALLOCH

17′ 9″ – Greenheart 3 piece + spare tip £84
15′ – Greenheart, 3 piece + spare tip. Three rods virtually unused £110
14′ – Greenheart 3 piece + spare tip £13
12′ 6″ – 3 piece + spare tip £71

A MARTIN

15′ – 3 piece £16
14′ – 3 piece + spare tip £19
10′ – 3 piece + spare tip £30
9′ 9″ – 3 piece £16
9′ 7″ – 3 piece £22

MARTINEZ & BIRD

10′ 6″ – 3 piece £22

McDONACK & CO

9′ – 3 piece £11

J McGOWAN

17′ – 3 piece + spare tip, greenheart and lancewood, brass fittings and drop rings £33

MILWARDS

THE HOLLAND
– Greenheart valise rod of two butts, eight middle sections and three tops £286
12′ 8″ – 3 piece £22
10′ 7″ – 3 piece £13, £27

FLYOVER
9′ 6″ – 2 piece £11, £16

SPINCRAFT
9′ 2″ – 2 piece £27, £16

SPINMASTER
9′ 2″ – 2 piece £27

FLYCRAFT
9′ – 3 piece £19

FLYMASTER
9′ – 3 piece + spare tip £30, £27
8′ 11″ – 3 piece + spare tip and Milward aluminium rod case £27
6′ – 3 piece £55
6′ – 3 piece £55

SPINVERSA
8′ 10″ – £30

7′ 7″ – 2 piece £77

FLYLITE
7′ 1″ – 2 piece £30

A H MOORE

12′ – 3 piece greenheart £22

OGDEN SMITH

14′ – 4 piece greenheart/bamboo with cane bound grip £55
12′ – 3 piece + spare tip £30, £22
11′ – 3 piece + spare tip £27

WARRIOR
10′ – 2 piece + spare tip £30
9′ 2″ – 3 piece spare tip £11, £84

ROYAL SOVEREIGN
9′ – 3 pc + spare tip £38

8′ 10″ – 3 piece £27
8′ – 3 piece + 2 extra tips $99, £66
7′ 6″ – 2 piece £55

OLIVER

13′ – 3 piece £44
11′ – 2 piece £22

KNEBWORTH
11′ – 2 piece £49

PARTRIDGE OF REDDITCH

8′ – 2 piece + spare tip inscribed ‘World Fly Fishing Championship 1987’, in case (only 20 made) £330

J PEEK & SON

THE GRAYS INN
9′ – 3 piece £33
7′ – 2 piece £38

PEZON ET MICHEL

PARABOLIC SALMON
12′ – 3 piece £82

PARABOLIC GRILSE
10′ 6″ – 2 piece £33, £55

PARABOLIC DRY FLY
9′ 7″ – 3 piece No 1511483G £16

SAWYER STILL WATER
9′ 6″ & 8′ 9″
– 2 piece + spare tip, 1960 £77

PARABOLIC SUPREME
9′ 2″ – 3 piece + spare tip £48

TELEBOLIC
8′ 9″ – 2 piece with two tops making 8′ 9″ and 8′ 3″, £33

PARABOLIC ROYALE
8′ 8″ – 2 piece £132

RITZ SUPER PARABOLIC FARIO CLUB
8′ 6″ – 2 piece + spare tip + rod tube £82

RITZ SUPER PARABOLIC
7′ 6″ – £38, £71
7′ 3″ – 2 piece £27

THE LUXOR ELITE
7′ – 2 piece £36

SUPREME
7′ – 2 pc + spare tip with parabolic action, very good, $440

PLAYFAIR

16′ & 12′ 9″
– Two greenheart rods, 3 piece + spare tips £13
13′ 6″ – Greenheart 3 piece + spare tips, in excellent condition $55

POOLE & SON

9′ – 3 piece £33

GEOFREY RIVAZ

7′ – 2 piece £33

ROACH POLE

– 11 piece, 4 tops, 4 hollow butt sections acting as receptacles for tops and 6 intermediate sections £61

A E RUDGE & SON

WYCO
13′ – 3 piece £27
12′ 7″ – 3 piece £11

DUCHESS
9′ 6″ – 3 piece £33

7′ – 2 pc £33

SEALEY
10′ – 2 piece £22
9′ – 2 piece £44, £22, £22
7′ 6″ & 6′ 11″
– 3 piece, 3 tops £19

J S SHARPE

CANE ROD WITH SPLICED JOINTS
13′ 3″ – £55

ABERDEEN
3 piece + spare tip
14′ 10″ – £66
14′ – £44
13′ 4″ – £44
13′ 1″ – £49
13′ – £60, £24, £44, £143, £157
12′ 6″ – £44, £143, £38
12′ – £60, £49, £44, £30, £33, £132
11′ – £66
10′ 6″ – £44
10′ – £33
9′ – £44

EIGHTY-EIGHT
2 piece
8′ 8″ – £60, £55, £51, £55

FARIO CLUB
2 piece
8′ 5″ – £71

FEATHERWEIGHT
2 piece
8′ 7″ – £22
7′ 6″ – £44, mint $187

J S SHARPE
2 piece
9′ – £61
8′ – £33, £77

SALMON FLY ROD
3 piece + spare tip
13′ – £55, £49, £82, £71
12′ – £143

SCOTTIE
3 piece + spare tip
14′4″ – £77, £66
13′ – £104
12′ 2″ – (only 3 piece) £38, £48
10′ 6″ – 2 piece £38
10′ 4″ – (only 3 piece) £33
10′ – (only 3 piece) £38, £22, £38
9′ – 2 piece £38, £45, £44
9′ – 2 piece £44, £38, £27
8′ 3″ – 2 piece £49
8′ – 2 piece £49
8′ – 2 piece + spare tip $55
7′ – 2 piece £55

SPECIALIST
3 piece, stand off rings
12′6″ – £22

SIMPSONS OF TURNFORD

7′ – 2 piece £95

ALBERT SMITH & CO

– 4 piece greenheart £33

E L SOWERBUTTS

ROACH POLE
Hollowed bamboo in 5 pieces
21′ – £132
19′ 9″ – £78
17′ 8″ – (repaired) £33
16′ 9″ – £121
– Whole cane rod, 4 piece with greenheart tip section £16

TROSSACH

McDONALD
9′ 6″ – 3 piece £38

VALISE ROD
6′ 3″ – 4 piece £126
– 10 piece hickory rod including 4 tops with brass fittings and porcelain lined rings £61

WILKINS

8′ 6″ – £24

WALKER BAMPTON

13′ 2″ – 3 piece + spare tip £66, 30925 £22
12′ – 3 piece + spare tip £24
11′ – 2 piece No 31421 £27, £16
10′ 6″ – No 34317 2 piece £19
9′ 6″ – 2 piece No 15744 (plus tip tube) £44, £18
9′ 3″ – 2 piece £27

WESTLEY RICHARDS

10′ – 3 piece £38

TRAVELLERS ROD
9′ 2″ – 4 piece £55

WILSON

INTERNATIONAL
8′ 3″ – 2 piece £44

MISCELLANEOUS TACKLE

BAIT CANS
Three old bait cans $55, £19

BAIT HORN
Ventilated cowhorn with cork bung 5¾" – c.1800 £99

BAIT KETTLE
Oblong galvanised bait kettle with convex and hinged recessed period lid 8⅛" x 4⅝" x 4½" £55

Similar with meshed lid £33

Galvanised with handle £19, £66 (three)

Copper fish kettle with braised seams and heavy brass handle. Inner fish tray with simple scrolled handles and interior tinned 38" x 10" x 7¼" £286

Bait kettle, kidney shaped by W J Cummins £121

BANK RUNNER
Turned from mahogany. Spool with laquered brass tackle cap. Unused 10¾" £99

CABINET
Westley Richards portable oak and leather cabinet with lift out tray with drawers and partitioned interior 19½" x 12½" x 9½" £462

Case in leather, divided into 8 compartments with brass corners 15" x 12" x 8" £275

CLEARING RINGS
- 2½" brass, hinged opposite its locking latch £88
- 2¼" brass, hinged opposite the closure (latch locking), c.1820, retaining its turned rosewood bobbin and line £110
- 2¼" brass, hinged at the base with simple locking latch £55
- 19th century brass clearing ring £82

CREEL LEATHER
- Pot bellied creel of leather in bulbous form with brass hinges and oval latch 15" x 7½" x 7" £462
- Similar 12½" x 6¾" x 4½" £825
- Similar 11¼" x 7" £682
- Similar with replaced hinges and damaged lid £520

CREEL WHICKER
- Unnamed creel £15, £31, £41

CURATE
- Combination tool including tweezers with gut cutters, handle hollowed as oil bottle and used as a priest. Brass and steel, knurled for match striking, 6½" £132

EELING FORKS
- Hardy's two rare Forks Nos 3 and 4. Length 12′ 4" with mahogany box £231

FLY BOX
- Army & Navy japanned (42 flies) £44
- Wheatley Silmalloy and 40 salmon flies £110, £99
- Wheatley Silmalloy (two) + 47 wet salmon lies £49
- Wheatley Silmalloy (three) + cast box £27, £44
- Wheatley Silmalloy (four) + 160 flies £99
- Wheatley Kilroy fly box £22

FURNISHER
- Cylindrical carved softwood cast Furnisher c.1820. Body with eight notched frames, the core sub-divided into four compartments. In paper-mâché drum case 6" x 2" £132
- Similar 5¾" x 2" £165
- Similar 5", four screwed together compartments with case £143

GAFF
- Vintage brass gaff £30
- Telescopic gaff with steel head, hickory inner shaft and brass caped mottled bamboo outer shaft, 64" extended £49

Sotheby's

- Full length gaff with scorched bamboo shaft, the steel point hinged to fold at the bend and locked by a blued iron spring 48¾″ c.1880, stamped Pat. 6516 £55
- Telescopic gaff with steel shaft and point, mahogany handle with iron end pieces and turned grip. Extended 25½″ £82
- Late 19th century folding gaff with polished wood shaft and brass mounts. The broad butt hollowed as a sheath for the hook £68 Telescopic gaff with turned wood handle £88, £110

KNIFE
- Pegley Davies angler's knife £36

LANDING NET
- Folding landing net with oval ash hoop, brass and steel locking hinge and scorched bamboo shaft 51″ £38
- Landing net with ash hoop, fine mesh net, brass socket and ash shaft 14½″ c.1870 £44
- Folding landing net with greenheart forks on brass head, with recessed iron spring latch, molted bamboo shaft 71″ c.1890 £38
- Farlow long handled landing net (sold with a telescopic gaff) £55
- G Little & Co, telescopic folding landing net with bamboo handle £143
- Ogden Smith Reversa landing net (sold with another folding landing net) £60
- Ogden Smith 3 piece brass and steel telescopic gaff with wooden handle £66

LINE DRIER
- Allcock's Windmill line winder £33
- Farlow early steel and brass table-edge line winder (sold with landing net) £82
- Malloch line winder, fully bronzed £30

LINE TWISTER
- A gut line twister of brass with turned bone knob on curved winding arm, iron twisters with hooked ends and turned iron mounting shaft, the casings secured with iron screws, 2″ diameter £165
- A gut line twister with three large steel hooks, and bone handled crank, mounted on small table clamp £110, £187
- Large gut line twister, the heavy brass plates with lined borders, iron shafts and large mounting screw, the backplate with cross mounted handle and multiplying gear and ivorine handle, 2⅝″ diameter £220, another £176 another £253

PRIEST
- A Priest of turned rosewood with turned ivory end caps and lead loaded head 8⅞″ £88
- A Priest with turned thin shaft and large lead filled head 8½″ £38
- Large Priest, curved in the form of a priest with glass eyes £104

RESERVOIR
- J Bernard & Son japanned fly reservoir containing six graded trays with about 177 salmon flies (23 doubles and some 84 gut eye) £297
- C Farlow & Co japanned fly reservoir. Six lift out trays with about 160 flies £133
- Farlow japanned cantilever fly case. The three trays and hinged lid containing about 120 flies 8″ x 4¾″ x 2″ £146

ROD CASE
- Farlow leather case 4′ 9″ £99
- Leather rod case 4′ 2″ £220
- Canvas and leather rod case 6′ 1″ £44
- Oak rod case with lock and key £33

HARDY TACKLE

ANGLER'S KNIFE
- £80, £100, £187

CABINET
- Roxburgh Salmon Fly Reservoir of polished teak with five lift out clipped trays and quantity of flies £528, £570
- Unique Salmon Fly Cabinet. Drop down front and ten drawers each with a selection of flies £638, £800

CLEARING KNIFE
- £82 (with Wardle magnifier)

CREEL
- Perfect model £88, £190

CURATE
- Combination tool £132

FLY BOX
- Girodon Pralon, japanned with 72 flies £61, £104 with reel case
- Multum-in-Parvo No 1 spinners box £110, £110
- Neroda fly box £60, £71

GUT AND LINE GAUGE
- Sold with 4 trade hook gauges £121

LANDING NET, GAFF ETC.
- Folding landing net with telescopic handle, sold with telescopic gaff £33
- Folding landing net £55, £61
- Hardy landing nets (two) £30
- Hardy longstaff, Hardy shortstaff and tailer (three) £99
- Improved Royde net and aluminium gaff £92
- Kelson gaff £33
- Orchy wading staff £49

LINE DRIER
- Compact line drier £44
- 1911 Model collapsible line winder £104
- 1897 Model with four numbered detachable 'T' frames and axle of gilt brass; also stand £77
- Jock Scott line winder £82
- Practical line drier £198
- Hotspur line winder £16

SPORTSMANS WALKING STICK SEAT
- £52, £110

TACKLE CASE
- Hold All leather tackle case 19″ x 12″ x 9″. Five compartments with lift out trays £462
- Leather tackle box, size 15″ x 10″ x 8″ with three compartments £231

THIRD ARM
- £165

TROPHIES

A carved and painted wood half-model salmon trophy, mounted on a painted pine backing. Size 37 lbs, 15″ x 50″. Sold at Christie's April 18th 1985, £345

TROPHIES BY UNKNOWN MAKERS (WOOD)

- Half block trophy of a cock salmon. Carved and painted wood. The back inscribed '45 lb Salmon killed on Aaro River Norway, etc.' Length 49″, Girth 27″, unmounted 47½″ £418

- A painted carved wood trophy 42″ of a 30½ lb fish killed by H G on the Wye 1905, mounted on a wood frame 51″ x 17¼″ £792

TROPHIES BY FARLOW (WOOD)

- A carved wood life-like salmon trophy. The 39½″ fish finely painted in bluish hues. Mounted on mahogany board and inscribed 'Upper Glen Tana April 12th 19*7'. Size 45¾″ x 15″ £528
- A large carved wood life-size salmon trophy. The 48½″ fish well painted in bluish hues and mounted on a board 56″ x 19″ £550

TROPHIES BY HARDY BROS (WOOD)

- A life-size trophy of a brown trout. The finely painted carved wood 21″ fish mounted on oak board 26½″ x 11¾″ £385
- A finely modelled and painted life-size sea-trout trophy A 37″, 19 lbs fish caught on the Laerdal, Norway, August 1927. Plaster and wood on dark board 42½″ x 14½″ £748

By 1987 there had been a dramatic rise in prices.

- A fine carved and painted wood Cock Salmon by Hardy Bros. Sold June 1989 £3300

- A fine Farlow carved wood trophy of a salmon mounted and inscribed 'Killed at Warnford Testwood March 31st 1897 by Col. Fereday'. Length 45″, girth 25″, weight 38 lbs,

A carved wood life-size salmon trophy by Farlow. The 45″ fish painted in bluish hues and mounted on a green painted board 51″ x 19½″ £572

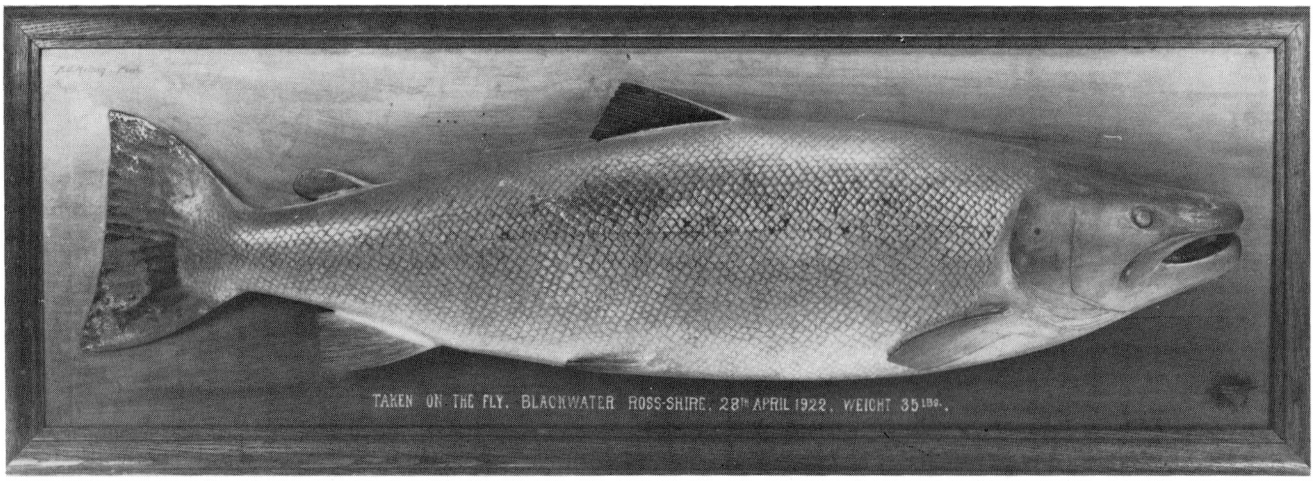
TAKEN ON THE FLY. BLACKWATER ROSS-SHIRE. 28TH APRIL 1922. WEIGHT 35 LBS.

Above: A carved and painted wood three-quarter model salmon trophy mounted on a painted pine backing with a fly hook in oak frame. Sold at Christie's April 18th 1985 £432

the reverse stamped C Farlow & Co, Fishing Rod Manufacturers, 191 Strand, London. Sold for £2200 (varnished finish)

- An unnamed fine carved wood trophy of a salmon, mounted and inscribed 'On a Lemon and Gray at Cumberlands Ford, River Spey, Fochabers, Oct 14th 1920, 30 lbs'. Sold for £3080.
- A fine plaster cast salmon painted in naturalistic colours by P D Malloch of Perth. Mounted in a mahogany and bowed glass display case with the inscription 'M. Coats's First Salmon, 21 lbs caught with fly, 29th Aug 1917', £1320
- Farlow carved wood trophy of a salmon mounted and inscribed 'F E Stansfield, Shevch Pool, Cultor, Aberdeenshire, Dee, October 24th 1896'; weight 14½ lbs (sold. Provincial sale 1989) £990
- Fine carved wood trophy of a salmon, length 47", girth 26", mounted on oak frame with affixed part label – 'Taxidermist Inverness'. Overall size 58" x 22" £1650

FISH TROPHIES

Best quality are the ones prepared by P D Malloch and J Cooper & Sons. Prices vary greatly depending on condition.

SOLD IN MARCH 1988

- Preserved pike (20 lbs 10 oz) in gilt bow fronted glass case by Cooper 1926 (44" x 16½") £550
- Preserved pike (27 lbs) in bow fronted glass case by Cooper, Caught by Lord Symes at Mote Park (46" x 164") £583
- Preserved chub (4 lb 3½ oz) in gilt lined bow fronted glass case by Cooper 1897 (25" x 14½") £286
- Preserved bronzed bream (5 lbs 2½ ozs) in gilt lined bow fronted glass case by Cooper 1951 (26" x 16") £374
- Preserved tench in bow fronted glass case by R Ward (22" x 12") £286
- Preserved pike (24 lbs) in glass fronted case (49" x 15") £385
- Preserved trout in bow fronted glass case by Spicer £363

WALLETS

ARMY & NAVY LEATHER WALLET
- Containing large cast winder £71

FINE 19TH CENTURY DUBBING WALLET
- In Morocco, unfolding to display 18 wallets with gold leaf lettering and border having brass catches with contents. Inscribed 'W M Middleton, B & I M Telegraph Co Liverpool'. Probably a presentation wallet. £1,210

RARE DATED FISHERMAN'S WALLET
- Embossed leather, concertina packets with marbled interiors and eleven pages of cloth envelopes, embossed with gilt letters, 'John Gorden, New Gallway 1772', 6½" x 4" £77

SCARCE 19TH CENTURY LEATHER FLY AND CAST WALLET
- The vellum leaves with finely hand painted flies, named and numbered after Ronalds. Good condition for age but some moisturized moth damage £157

Top opposite page: A Victorian carved wood salmon trophy painted in a naturalistic palette and mounted on a rectangular board inscribed, 'Killed by Earl Winterton in the Rock Pool, October 11th 1892, 50 lbs', length 4' 1½", girth 2' 4" in reeded frame 22½" x 57" overall. Sold on June 5th 1987 by Hy Duke & Son (Auctioneers), Dorchester for £2860

Centre opposite page: Carved wood salmon trophy painted and mounted on an oak rectangular board and inscribed, 'Caught on a Colly by G H Logan at Tobin's Hole, March 1st 1917,' length 3' 2". Sold for £1155

Bottom opposite page: A fine display of sea trout by J Cooper & Sons, each about 28", mounted one above the other against reeds and grasses in bow fronted case, 25½" x 44¾" x 9½". Sold by Sotheby's, 21st of January 1985, £418

CATALOGUES

BRITISH

ALLCOCK

1965/1968
– 6 catalogues £33

CUMMINS

1935-36 – 28th edition £38

FARLOW

1907 – £55
1915 – £44
1930 – £77

HARDY BROS

1911 – £242
1914 – £71
1915/1920
– £110
1917/1951
– £99
1923/1955
– £82
1924/1933/1935 (Supplements)
– £49
1925 – £41
1928 – £55
1930 – £44, £41, £35
1930/1937/1938 supplement – £71
1931 – £24, £33, £22
1951 – £13
1951/1952/1954 – £33
1951/1957 – £49
1960/62/63/64/65/66 – £61

AMERICAN

ABBEY & IMBRIE

1875 – NY Catalogue No. 157, condition very good $140
1911 – 174 pages, excellent $38
1926 – 128 pages, very good $33
1928 – No 200 (+ 3 South Bend Catalogues) $40

ABERCROMBIE & FITCH CO

1903 – 159 pages, staples rusted and moisture stains $121
1909 – 456 pages, in very good condition $38
1913 – and 1929. Two catalogues, staples rusted $27
1930 – 68 pages in prime condition $60

1910 – 45 pages (9″ x 12″) excellent $132
1937 – 31 pages, near mint $71
1938 – 27 pages, mint $143

BUEL

1913 – Rare J T Buel, Whitehall, NY with 30 pages (12″ x 9½″) of lures, spears and history $291

THOMAS J CONROY

1889 – Rare, 115 large pages (9″ x 12″). Aged cover otherwise condition good $198

CREEK CHUB

c.1916 – Sizes 8″ x 5″ rare, containing 6 pages of New Pinkie Minnow. Condition very good $137
1947 – 22 pages, full colour, condition excellent $27

CHUBB

1886 – Thos H Chubb, 51 pages, dealers copy $220
1891 – Thos H Chubb, 9th edition, 48 pages in colour and black and white, front cover loose, otherwise very good $71
1910 – T H Chubb Rod Co, 122 pages $60
1926 – T H Chubb Rod Co, 79 pages, staples rusted and pages discoloured $49

DIVINE

– Rare Fred D Divine Co, 27 pages $308

EDWARDS

c.1930 – E W Edwards & Sons, 16 pages $324

HAWES

– H W Hawes & Co, 26 pages, mint $126

HEDDON

1914 – No 12, 16 pages of large 10″ x 13½″ size. Fold crease otherwise condition very good $375
– No 14 catalogue (2nd edition revised), 16 pages 9″ x 9″, colour plug illustrations, condition very good $440
1931 – 40 pages 7″ x 10″ condition excellent $49
1932 – 31 pages, excellent $38
1937 – 40 pages with original order blank $60
1949 – 88 pages $27
1952 – 'Deluxe', 77 pages with brochures and coloured fish print, all mint $33
1953 – 'Deluxe', 76 pages $27
1955 – 'Deluxe' 76 pages $16
1956 – 'Deluxe' with original Heddon mailing envelope $11
1957 – 'Deluxe' 70 pages with original envelope $13

HERMAN H KIFFE

c.1870 – Tackle catalogue 8 pages, condition very good $27

HORTON M'F'G CO

1907 – 48 pages, cover edges rough, very good $110
1940 – Catalogue of rods and Meek reels, 27 large pages, condition mint $38

LOOMIS PLUMB & CO

1882 – Catalogue entitled *The Fisherman's Automatic Reel;* covers separated and stained $22

MEEK

1916 – B F Meek & Sons, 36 pages, staples rusted, otherwise in near mint condition $302

H H MICHAELSON, BROOKLYN NY

1912 – 208 pages, 4 colour pages of Heddon, condition good plus $115

WILLIAM MILLS & SON

Note: WILLIAM MILLS & SON catalogues are the standard reference for LEONARD rods and reels and also various types of tackle
1918 – (+ a 1936)
Covers and first page missing, sold with a 1936 (127 pages), mint $110
1922 – 157 pages, excellent condition $143
1931 – Two catalogues. Section one 80 pages, section two

140 pages, both excellent $55
1932 – (+ a 1935) A 1932 spring booklet of 78 pages, the 1935 with 142 pages, excellent $27
1936 – Excellent condition $11
1937 – (and 1938) Two catalogues of 80 and 88 pages, condition excellent and fair $99
1941 – No 141, 80 pages, condition mint $27
1950 – (and 1961) Two catalogues, 56 pages and 60 pages $60
1959 – (and 1962, 1966) $16
1963 – (and 1971) Two catalogues plus 5 various $22

ORVIS
c.1910 – Chas F Orvis, 113 pages $192

PAYNE
– Rare E F Payne Rod Co catalogue of split bamboo rods entitled Fishing $159
1951 – 46 pages. Writing on front otherwise excellent $88

PFLUEGER
1919 – 112 pages, condition excellent $38
1926 – No 146, 120 pages 5″ x 8″, excellent $49
1927 – (and a 1928). 1927 #247, 16 pages, mint plus a letter head and two letters. Catalogue 1928 #149, 128 pages, condition excellent $49
1919 – (and a 1931). 1919, 151 pages, coloured lines, cover faded. 1931, 136 pages, condition mint $49
1935 – No 55, 128 pages 5″ x 8″, mint $38
1935 – (and a 1936) 1935, with cover stain on corner, 128 pages, excellent $27
1938 – (and a 1940). 1938, 128 pages, lightly soiled. 1940, 244 pages, dealers catalogue, coloured illustrations, well used $27
1941 – Trade catalogue No 61, 244 pages $35
1941 – (also 1957, 1959, 1962) sold as one lot $66

READ
1912 – W'm Read & Sons, 94 pages, cover worn $49

SCHOVERLING, DALY & GALES
1913 – No 65, 162 pages, very good condition $121

SHAKESPEARE
c.1928 – 47 pages 8″ x 8½″, condition excellent $38

BOB SMITH, BOSTON
c.1920 – 96 pages, condition good $44

SOUTH BEND
1916 – No 22, 48 pages, 5½″ x 12″, covers tatty/ separated $88
1919 – 'Days of Real Sport', 60 pages 5½″ x 12″ plus price list $110
1922/3 – Dealers Trade Catalogue, 7 pages 8½″ x 10″, covers separated $132
1924 – (and a 1931). 1924, 68 pages, covers missing 1931, 80 pages, condition good $27
1926 – (and a 1931), 114 pages, 79 pages, both excellent $60
1931 – (and a 1933), 79 pages and 100 pages $38
1931 – (and a 1939), 79 pages and 127 pages, very good $27
1932 – (and a 1933), 84 pages and 100 pages, very good $27
1932 – (and a 1941), 83 pages and 13 pages, excellent $33
1932 – (and a 1942), 83 pages and 135 pages, very good $33
1934 – (and a 1936), 92 pages and 111 pages, very good $27
1934 – (and a 1939), 92 pages and 127 pages, excellent $33
1935 – (and a 1936), 107 pages and 111 pages $22
1935 – (and a 1937), 108 pages and 112 pages, very good $22
1936 – (and a 1937), both 112 pages $38
1945 – (and a 1947, 1950, 1951). All sold for $55

DAME STODDARD & CO
– 290 page catalogue, excellent condition $121

F E THOMAS
1955 – Catalogue and price list $49

EDWARD K TRYON CO
1913 – 120 large pages of Heddon Pflueger, Kingfisher, Paw Paw, Talbot, Meek, very good $110

EDWARD VOM HOFE
1907 – 138 pages. Store stamp on cover otherwise in excellent condition $275
1919 – 168 pages, excellent $181
1928 – 171 pages, good plus condition $60
1930 – 173 pages, very good condition $82
1934 – Prime condition $90
1936 – 173 pages, excellent $99
1973 – 177 pages, excellent $99
1939 – 175 pages, mint condition $80

JULIUS VOM HOFE
1911 – 22 pages, cover soiled otherwise excellent $962

VON LENGERKE & DETMOLD
1917 – 188 pages, back cover loose $60
1900 – 111 pages, cover worn and separated $77

WINCHESTER
1920s – Pocket catalogue, 32 pages, excellent $60

YOUNG
1934 – Paul H Young catalogue, 48 pages, staples rusted otherwise excellent condition $93
1937 – Paul H Young catalogue, 102 pages, excellent $55

ZWARG
– Catalogue of Otto Zwarg for custom built reels $181

LIMITED EDITION

A leather bound first edition of this book limited to fourteen numbered copies has been produced for the author.

A copy has been given to Kew Palace, the Kentucky Museum, Christine Turner, Paul Hicks and one to each of the author's three sons.

Six copies will be sold through selected auction houses in Britain and America at the discretion of the author.

'Billinghurst Patent, Rochester, N.Y., Aug. 9th, 1859' marked Birdcage trout reel. Sold for $1760

'T H Bate & Co, NY' New York ball handle multiplier. Sold for $385

Early Bogdan salmon reel with hard rubber plates. Made 1948-1950. Sold for $2090

AMERICAN REELS

AMERICAN REEL CO

2⅛″ – Ball handle bait caster marked 'American Reel Co, Indianapolis, Ind., Pat'd Jan 31 1882'. A multiplying reel with Terry 1871 (marked). Foot filed and gear tooth missing $330

ABBEY & IMBRIE

2⅜ – Small brass ball handle multiplier $154, $110

2⅞″ – 'Abbey & Imbrie NY', balance ball handle multiplier $165

2⅞″ – 'Abbey & Imbrie Pat Jan 17 '82', brass balance handle multiplier $49

3⅜″ – Brass click reel with half crank $55

BALLAN

– Special Bill Ballan presentation trout reel engraved 'RWO 2nd Annual High Rollers Auction' in new condition $440

T H BATE & CO

1⅞″ – New York ball handle multiplying reel marked 'T H Bate & Co., NY'. Condition excellent $385

BILLINGHURST

3″ – Rare Birdcage Trout Fly Reel marked 'Billinghurst Patent, Rochester, NY August 9 1859 and 1873.' America's first fly reel $1045

3¼″ – Rare Birdcage Trout Fly Reel. America's first fly reel, unused in original cardboard box $12,650

3½″ – First model 'Billinghurst patent, Rochester, NY August 9, 1859' marked Birdcage trout reel, excellent $1760

– Second Model 'Billinghurst Patent, Rochester NY, Aug 9, 1859 and 1878,' Birdcage trout reel $770

BLUE GRASS REELS

Sutcliffe & Partners c.1898 – 1915
Horton Manufacturing Co 1916 – 1945

No. 3 – 'Blue Grass (Horton M'f'g)' $99

No. 3 – 'B F Meek & Sons, Louisville, Ky. Blue Grass No. 3' reel $236, $375

No. 3 – 'Blue Grass Reel made by B F Meek & Sons, Louisville, Ky No. 3' $247

No. 3 – 'Blue Grass Reel Works, Louisville, Ky. No. 3', c.1901 $375, $935

No. 4 – Blue Grass (Horton M'f'g. Meek) $275, $374

No. 25 – 'B F Meek & Sons, Louisville, Ky No 25 Blue Grass Reel', on back, 'Carters Pat July 5, 04, Nov. 28, 05'. Made of German silver, no level-wind $99

No. 25 – 'B F Meek & Sons, Louisville, Ky, No 25, Blue Grass', $275

No. 33 – 'Blue Grass Reel, made by B F Meek & Sons, Louisville, Ky, No 33' $121, $220, $88

No. 33 – 'Blue Grass No 33 Simplex (Horton M'f'g)' $38, $90, $88

No. 34 – 'Blue Grass Simplex Free Spool No 24' $187

STAN BOGDAN

2⅝″ – Handmade narrow spool 'Baby' trout reel in new unused condition, $2200, $2420, $2650

– 2¾″ Handmade Baby, 4 oz reel in all black finish. Set for right hand wind. New unfished condition. $2860

2¾″ – Handmade 'Baby', right hand wind $2860

2¾″ – Handmade Baby trout reel (⅞″ wide), mint, in leather bag $1375

3⅛″ – Handmade standard size trout reel (¾″ wide spool), new, $2090

3⅛″ – Narrow drum trout reel $852

3⅛″ – Handmade No 0 multiplying salmon reel, excellent $1595

3¼″ – Trout reel with narrow ¾″ spool $1347

3¼″ – No 00 multiplying salmon reel in all black finish. Unused, in leather pouch $1650

3¼″ – Steelhead fly reel $990, $1925

3⅝″ – Multiplying reel with ⅞″ wide spool, stamped '73-6″ ' $1430

3⅝″ – Multiplying reel with 1″ wide spool in gold finish, silver foot $770

3⅝″ – Early multiplying salmon or tarpon reel (1¼″ wide spool). Sold by

Abercrombie & Fitch. Mint, in leather case $1320, $1265

3⅝″ – Handmade with narrow ⅞″ spool, mint $1155

– No 0 handmade multiplier. The gold and black anodized reel has German silver handle and foot, lever operated drag on back and click on/off switch $1870

– Early salmon reel with hard rubber side plates. This multiplying reel with traditional lever was accompanied by a makers letter stating made about 1948-1950 and one of the few times he used hard rubber for sideplates. Condition excellent $2090

BRADFORD

2″ – Tiny German silver trout click reel marked 'Bradford, Boston'. Made before Martin L Bradford formed the Bradford and Antony firm in 1856. Condition mint $990

2⅛″ – Ball balance handle multiplier marked 'Bradford Boston' $440

2¼″ – Rare New York ball balance handle reel marked 'Bradford, Boston'. This maker later formed a partnership with Antony $467

2¾″ – Early 'Bradford, Boston' marked brass fly reel with raised rear click housing and walnut handle $495

BRADFORD & ANTONY

2⅜″ – Brass trout fly reel marked 'Bradford & Antony, Boston' $1155

3⅜″ – Brass multiplier with balance ball handle marked 'Bradford & Antony Boston' $77

CARLTON MANUFACTURING CO

– A 9-1 multiple bait casting reel $104

CARPENTER & CASEY

2⅝″ – Model 1-N Serial No 6. Handmade by Walt Carpenter and Frank Casey in aluminium and German silver $605

– Trout fly reel Prototype Serial No 1. Mint $412

– Trout fly reel Prototype Serial No 2. Mint $412

CHAMBERLAIN, CARTRIDGE & TARGET CO

– Hunter reel marked 'Chamberlain, Cartridge & Target Co., Hunter Reel Patented' $297, $275

CHAPMAN

– Rare brass trout reel marked 'Chapman & Son, Theresa NY' and on foot with Terry's patent 'Pat. Nov. 14, 1871' with walnut handle $275

THOMAS H CHUBB

– Henshall-Van Antwerp Black Bass reel with the May 22 '83 and Sept 27 '87 on backplate, in case $1595

– Rare 'T H Chubb, Maker', marked trout reel, 2″ diameter with one piece cast foot and walnut handle $357

COATES

1⅞″ – Rare 'A Coates Pat. March 20th, 88 Watertown, NY' marked side mounted convertible single action or multiplying trout reel. Condition good plus $660

CONROY

2″ – Rare trout reel with balance handle, raised rear check housing and off-set foot $467

2⅛″ – Brass reel with off-set foot, raised rear check housing and black walnut knob on half crank handle, marked 'J C Conroy & Co NY' $330

2¼″ – Brass S-handle multiplying reel c.1870, marked 'Thomas J Conroy, Maker, NY' $412

2½″ – Fly reel No 3 marked 'Thos J Conroy NY' and on the back 'J V Hofe Pat Oct 8 '89', mint $550

2¾″ – Brass balance ball handle multiplier marked 'J Conroy, Maker'. Condition poor $242

2¾″ – Balance 'S' handle multiplier marked 'Conroy and Bisset NY' (Partnership lasted from 1881 to1883) $275

2¾″ – 'J C Conroy & Co., NY', c.1864 ball handle multiplying reel, very good $330

3″ – Early brass ball handle multiplying reel marked 'J Conroy, Maker' c.1835 $467

'Bradford Boston' marked early brass fly reel with raised click housing of 2¾″ diameter

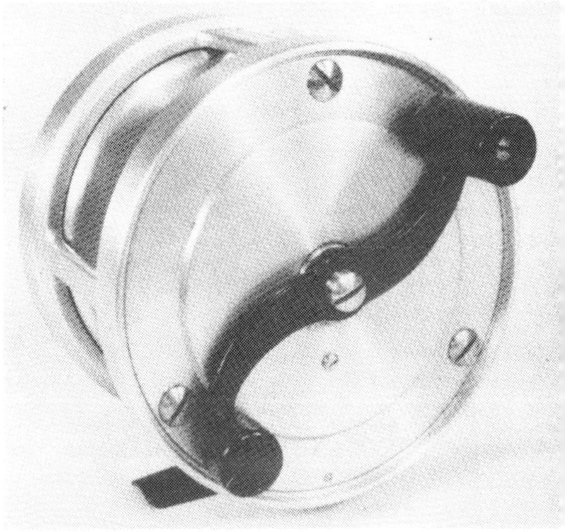

Stan Bogdan 300 multiplying reel marked '73-8'. Sold for $1265

Stan Bogdan handmade 'Baby' wide spool trout reel. Sold for $2090

Ball handle multiplier by 'J Conroy, Maker' of 3″ diameter. Sold for $467

J B Crook & Co, New York of 3″ diameter. Sold for $357

Early original Follett side mounted fly reel of 3⅝″ diameter. Sold for $550

3¼″ – Brass 'S' handle multiplier with rosewood knob marked 'J C Conroy & Co NY' $176

3⅜″ – Multiplying reel in German silver with turned wooden handle on serpentine counter balance winding arm. The end plates engraved with borders of scrolling foliage and inscribed 'J Conroy Maker' and 'Ed Hunter, Pelham' $1540

4½″ – Early 'Thos J Conroy, NY, Maker' salmon reel with classic bullet handle on heavy ornate balance crank $550

CONROY, BISSETT & MALLESON

1⅞″ – Tiny reel marked 'Conroy, Bissett & Malleson' $484

J B CROOK & CO, NEW YORK

2⅜″ – Balance handle multiplier marked 'J B Crook & Co., NY, Makers, Ouadruple' $33

2½″ – Multiplying reel in German silver with turned wooden handle on straight winding arm with counterbalance bell weight $286

3″ – Multiplying reel with heavy rectangular transition handle crank in German silver with rim mounted drag control and sliding bearing cap covers $357

DAME, STODDARD & KENDALL

2¼″ – Raised pillar multiplier with 'S' handle $27

2⅜″ – Size 3 J V Hofe type multiplier $27

J DEALLY

3½″ – Ultra rare 'J Deally, Louisville, KY, No. 10' marked, handmade in German silver with thumb lever brake on back. A tarpon or heavy duty bait casting reel by Kentucky reelsmith $4070

DREISER

– Combination rod and reel marked 'J Dreiser, Patent Aug. 14, 1883, NY.' Virtually unheard of maker $990

FOLLETT

3⅝″ – Side mounted trout fly reel with wooden handle $550, $220, $242

– Virtually unheard of Follett patent automatic trout fly reel marked 'The White-Ross, M'f'g Co., Olean, NY 19, 1889'. Follett's patent was assigned to White and Ross $1100

AL FOSS

– German silver bait casting reel marked 'Al Foss, Cleveland, O., Easy Control No. 3-25' with large metal spool abor, jewelled bearings and sliding click button $495

FOSTER

– New York balance ball handle multiplying reel marked 'W Foster, Maker' $88

A H FOWLER

First to make a reel from moulded hard rubber in c.1872

2¾″ – Fowler Gem trout reel marked 'Fowler's Patent, June 1872'. Dr Alonzo Fowler, a dentist from Ithaco, New York used the molding technology of his trade to design a hard-rubber reel. Near mint condition $15,400

2¾″ – Gem trout reel marked 'Fowler's Patent June 1872'. One of only six known examples. Foot ends broken off $4400

P M FOWLER

5¾″ – Multiplying big game alloy reel with counterbalance handle, star brake and brake collars. Stamped 1928 externally and 1929 inside (handle locking nut missing) $264

G W GAYLE & SON

2¼″ – Trout fly reel marked 'G W Gayle & Son, Frankfort, KY'. Lightweight aluminium reel with ivory handle. There are some 'dings' on the front plate and along rim edge, also two tiny abrasions on back plate. Apart from minor imperfections, in excellent condition $9350

4½″ – The 'Intrinsic' tarpon reel. Shown in Mill's catalogue of 1910. Made in polished German silver and hard rubber. Marked 'C M 1/0'. In case $990

GEORGE W GAREY

5″ – Rare big game reel with narrow spool, exposed rear spool rim, back mounted star drag. Made for F W Utz $550

5¾″ – Big game reel made for F W Utz with 2⅜″ wide spool and traditional front star mounted drag $907

HARRIS

– Harris rod handle reel. Early attempt to build the reel into the rod handle. Marked 'The Harris Reel, Gloversville, NY, Pat Sept 22 1903' $330

HARTILL

2¾″ – Ball balance handle multiplier marked 'A B Hartill NY' $253

HAWKS & OGILVY

– Brass ball handle multiplying reel $302

– 1/0 size (3″ diameter) brass ball handle multiplier $154

HORTON MANUFACTURING CO

– Meek No 2 (Horton Manufacturing Co) $412

– Meek No 3 (Horton Manufacturing Co) $330

– Meek No 3 (Horton Manufacturing Co) with double 'Tulip' handle $412

HEDDON

– Freestripping No 87 $25

– Little Rivers No 26 fly reel $38

– 3-35 level-winding bait caster $99, $60

– Pal-41-LW, lightweight Tournament model with level-wind, jewelled, with tag from factory marked 'Proto P41 L Walt Wilman etc'. Wilman was inventor of Pal model and this was a factory prototype $110

– 4-18 bait caster with windshield wiper, level-wind and front sliding click $330

KIFFE

– 'H H Kiffe & Co, New York'. Balance handle multiplier $55

E C KOENIG

2⅜″ – Trout fly reel marked 'E C Koenig, Newark, NJ' c.1880. Condition excellent $412

KOSMIC

2″ – Rare 'The Kosmic Reel'. Original c.1890 with raised pillars and not the later Montague trade reel. Excellent condition in leather case $2970

2¼″ – Multiplier with 3½:1 gear and marked 'The Kosmic Reel'. Early raised pillar model in case $880

– Multiplying Kosmic 2-1 reel with raised pillars in case $710

2½″ – Kosmic reel. Original c.1890 design with raised pillars $2860

4⅛″ – The Kosmic reel. Model 821, c.1890. Made of German silver and hard rubber with rotary drag control and removable bearing cap $715

– Later trade multiplier reel marked 'Kosmic Reel' without raised pillars $88

Presentation trout fly reel inscribed 'Greene Smith Presented by M James'. Sold for $2860

Presentation fly reel inscribed 'Col T J Hoyt, from J R R, May 18 '74'. Diameter 2¼″. Sold for $797

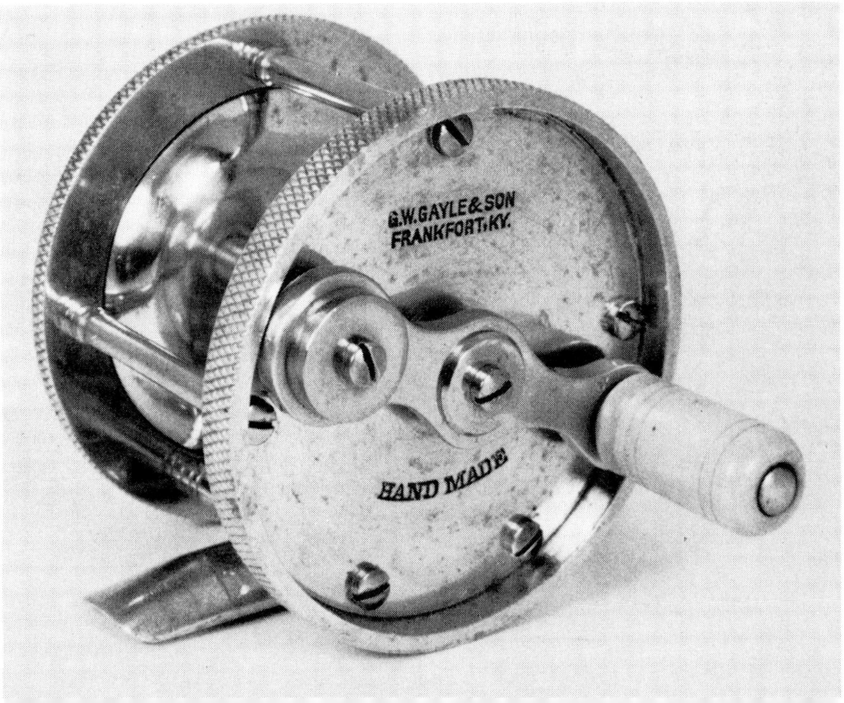

A reel by GW Gayle & Son which sold for $8500 at Richard Oliver Galleries on February 26th 1988

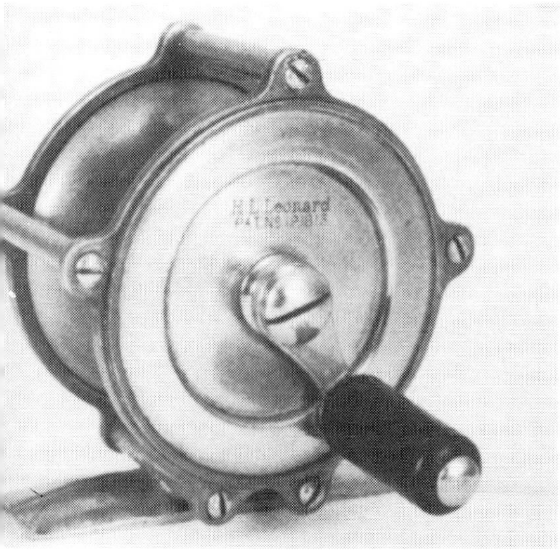

Rare 'H L Leonard Pat. No 191813' (the 1877 Philbrook & Payne patent number) in a 2⅛″ diameter size. Sold for $1540

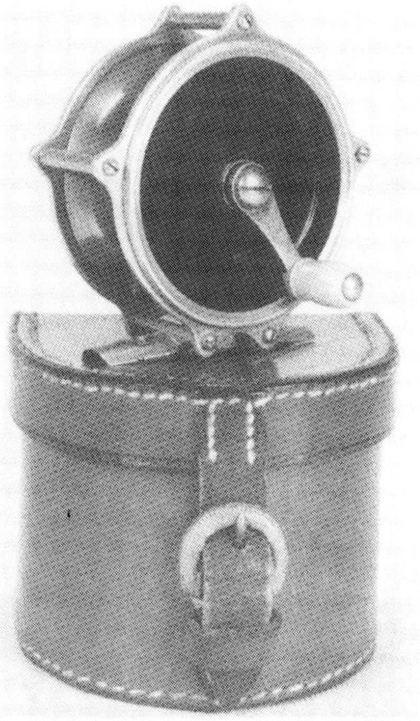

Early 'H L L Pat. No. 191813' and 'Mills New York'. Diameter 2¾″. Sold for $1100

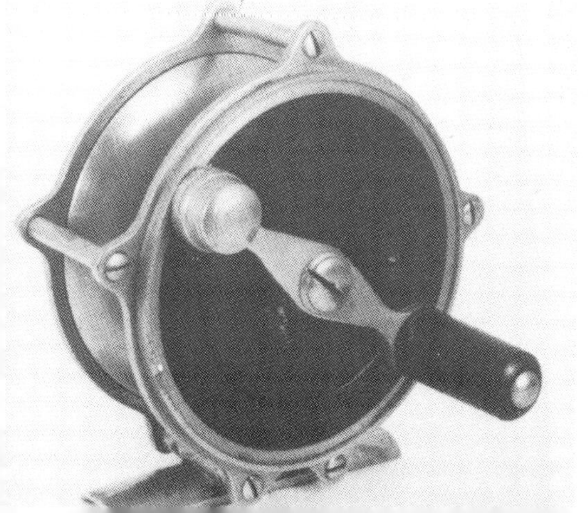

H L Leonard, Model 44 with patent number 191813, in 2¾″ size $825

LEONARD

2″ – Early Leonard-Mills raised pillar trout fly reel with balance handle, aluminium spool ends and plates, perforated foot and sliding click button $990

2″ – 'H L Leonard, Pat No 191813' marked 'Leonard Bi-metal trout reel', mint $1760

2⅛″ – Tiny German silver and bronze trout fly reel marked 'H L Leonard Pat No 191813' (the Philbrook & Payne patent number). Condition excellent $1540

2⅛″ – Tiny Leonard-Mills trout reel with raised aluminium pillars and hard rubber inserts $632

2⅛″ – 'Leonard-Mills' marked Midge reel with balance handle and raised pillars $605

2⅛″ – 'Leonard-Mills' Midge click reel with straight crank handle $825

2⅛″ – Tiny 'H L Leonard, Pat June 12, 1877' (Philbrook's patent). A bi-metal trout reel, German silver/brass $2750

2⅜″ – Unusual 'Leonard-Mills' wide spool (1⅛″ wide) raised pillar trout reel $522

2⅜″ – Rare 'H L Leonard Pat June 12th 1877' trout reel in bronze and German silver $1760, $2750

2⅜″ – 'Leonard-Mills' raised pillar trout fly reel with aluminium spool ends, handle and plates with rubber inserts, perforated foot and sliding click button $880

2⅜″ – 'H L Leonard, Pat June 12th, 1877' marked first model Bi-metal trout reel carrying the Philbrook & Payne patent date. Polished $1210

2⅝″ – Early 'Leonard-Mills' No 44A trout reel $55

2¾″ – Model 44 marked patent No 191813 $825

2¾″ – 'Leonard-Mills' trout click reel in aluminium, German silver and hard rubber $770

2¾″ – 'Leonard-Mills' trout click reel with untypical ivory handle $715

2¾″ – Early 'H L Leonard, Pat No 191813', marked 'Mills, New York' trout reel carrying the Philbrook & Payne patent. Raised pillar reel of aluminium, German silver and hard rubber $1100

2¾″ – 'Leonard-Mills' marked widespool trout reel with balance handle (1¼″ wide spool) and external pillars $825

2⅞″ – Aluminium raised pillar with hard rubber inserts $330

3″ – 'Leonard-Mills' raised pillar trout reel with polished aluminium spool ends and plates and rubber inserts $550

3⅜″ – 'H L Leonard' marked reel made just before the business finished $214

3½″ – H L Leonard dry fly salmon reel. Model 51A-D with rear mounted adjustable drag $605

3¾″ – Raised pillar salmon reel (inscribed W W from J C T 1898) £308

4″ – 'H L Leonard' marked salmon reel with sliding drag regulator and Philbrook & Payne 1877 'Pat No 191813'. Excellent in leather case $550, $440

F MALLESON

1⅞″ – Multiplying reel marked 'Patented by Fred'k Malleson, Sept. 4th, '83', with novel arrow head click indicator. Very good, $605

2⅝″ – Single action multiplier with raised pillars, balance handle and arrow head click indicator $412

McVICKAR & SON, TUXEDO, NY

3″ – Bushkill trout reel $330

J F & B F MEEK

– Extremely rare c.1845 'J F & B F Meek, Frankfort, KY' marked brass, three numbered screw bait casting reel with horn handle and front sliding click button. The logo marking used from 1838–1853 for a total of about 100 reels. It is the earliest for this maker. Size 2⅛″ diameter with 2″

wide spool, very good $11,550

MEEK & MILAM

- Scarce early Kentucky reel marked 'Meek & Milam, Frankfort, KY No 3' in German silver with half-crank $1430
- 'Meek & Milam, Frankfort, KY, No 4' marked bait casting reel $1320

B F MEEK

- Rare 'B F Meek, Louisville, KY' marked handmade tarpon or heavy duty reel. There is no size marking but 'N T Depauw' on back $2860
- Rare 'B F Meek, Louisville, KY' marked handmade narrow spool No 7 size Muskie Bait Casting reel. Serial No 303 and 'N T Depauw' engraved on back. Diameter 3″ $2750
- Similar to reel described above except Serial No 427 and is not engraved $2805

Rare B F Meek, Louisville, KY No 4 in German silver with ivory handle, click and drag buttons and early red jewelled bearing caps. Serial No 688. Early marking without '& Sons', was made for only a short time when Meek moved from Frankfort to Louisville, KY to build reels in competition with his old partner Milam $1925

Handmade 'B F Meek Louisville, KY' marked No 7. Sold for $2805

The 2¼″ diameter 'BF Meek & Sons, Louisville, KY No 44' sold for $18150

Meek No 2 (Horton M'f'g) handmade reel in German silver. Sold for $412

Above: Meek No 3 (Horton M'f'g Co) with double 'Tulip' grasp handle. Sold for $412

Below: Meek No 3 (Horton M'f'g Co), serial No 11580. Sold for $330

B F MEEK & SONS

– 'B F Meek & Sons, Louisville, KY No 3'. Serial No 491. Near mint condition, in case $412

– Rare 'Meek No 44, B F Meek & Sons, Louisville, KY'. Early flat back model with knurled rims, on/off click button and handle screw. In box with papers and bag $6600

2¼″ – Rare 'B F Meek & Sons, Louisville, KY No 44'. German silver trout reel with raised rear click housing $4400

2¼″ – Rare 'B F Meek & Sons, Louisville, KY No 44', custom made trout reel. Possibly made around 1898 by Benjamin Meek himself. This German silver reel has tusk ivory knob, a serpentine handle crank on one side and straight (in the style of his bait casting reels of that time) on the balance weight end. Front plate engraved with owner's name. Mint $18150

– Early 'B F Meek & Sons Louisville, KY No 4' marked bait casting reel with rare eary type non-removeable bearing caps. Serial No 926 and 'N T Depauw 1896' on back $935

– Rare 'B F Meek & Sons, Louisville, KY. Club Special', serial No 2103. Basically a No 2 size in German silver $1237

A F MEISSELBACH

3½″ – Early Neptune type salt water reel with knurled ring under the handle to engage free spool feature $154

3¼″ – Early Neptune variant reel with Rabbeth handle, drag marked 'Jan 14 02'. Take-apart featurc $160

– Okeh free spool level-winding reel No 620 with 1905 and 1907 patents. Novel dropping level-wind and take-apart feature $93

– Meisselbach–Catucci Newark N J Symploreel No 257 with level-wind and non-backlash $280

– Neptune-type salt water reel with Elyria address $27

– Neptune salt water reel marked 'Pat. Feb. 6 1912, others pending' $38
– Symploreel No 370, 3″ bakelite reel $38
– Amateur fly reel with thumb brake 3″ $27
– Expert 17 fly reel (wide model) $38
– Featherweight fly reels. Four sold together comprising of three 250s and one 290 models $60
– Tripart. Two sold together No 580 and No 581 $85
– Take-apart No 680. Scarce bait caster $82
– Symploreel. Non backlash, free spool non level-wind $16

B C MILAM

– Rare early all brass 'B C Milam, Frankfort, KY No 3'. Condition excellent $1210 $632
– Scarce c.1890 'B C Milam, Frankfort, KY No 4', in German silver with ivory handle and click and drag button. Foot ends shortened $990
– Early German silver 'B C Milam, Frankfort, KY No 3'. Serial No 7207 with ivory handle and click and drag switches, excellent $935
– Rare 'B C Milam & Son, Frankfort, KY, Rustic No 3' marked bait casting reel. Serial No 10050 $187

WILLIAM MILLS & SON N Y

– Early 'W'm Mills & Son, N Y', 1/0 size $275
– Multiplier with raised pillars and marked 'William Mills & Son, N Y', 2″ diameter $550
– Tiny 'Fairy' trout reel, 2″ diameter with external pillars, straight crank and intended for use with Leonard 'Baby' Catskill rod. Mint $1760
– Rare 'W'm Mills & Son, N Y Intrinsic' marked high quality bait casting reel made by famous George Gayle & Son, Frankfort KY. Shown in Mills catalogue as 2″ in diameter. Excellent condition $1320
– Multiplier with raised pillars, 2⅝″ diameter $154
– Multiplying salmon reel marked 'William Mills & Son N Y, Pat. June 25, 89'. A Leonard reel in German silver and hard rubber, 2¾″ diameter $935
– Multiplying salmon reel (Leonard) 2¾″ diameter, with raised pillars in aluminium, German silver and hard rubber. Shiny mint condition $440
– High quality 4″ diameter reel marked 'William Mills'. A Leonard pattern with sliding drag switch marked 'Pat. July 22, 90' (rare E F Payne). In German silver and hard rubber $550

MITCHEL HENRY

9″ – Big game centre pin reel. Full caged alloy construction with brass drum, 10″ handle bar with large grips.The back plate with leather and steel band brake with rim lever $990
– 9/0 salt water reel $495

OCEAN CITY

– Ike Walton Club Ocean City M'f'g $40
– Long Key Ocean City M'f'g $50

C F ORVIS

– 1874 Patent fly reel in original walnut case marked 'C F Orvis, Manchester, V T. Patented May 12th 1874' $660
– 1874 Patent fly reel in original walnut case $1870
2¾″ – A riveted version of the famous 'C F Orvis, Maker, Manchester, V T, Patented May 12th 1874' marked, narrow ventilated spool trout reel $1100, $1237, $605, $2420

PECK & SNYDER

2½″ – 'Peck & Snyder, NY', brass balance ball handle multiplier c.1879 $126

PENN

– Penn Squider No 140 (Pre 1960 reel) $25
– Penn Surfmaster 200M No 9 Star Drag $45

PENNELL

– 'The Tournament Reel'. Non level-wind and balance handle. Two sold together $44

Handmade 'B C Milam, Frankfort, KY, No 4' c.1890. Sold for $990

Early 1887 patent Pettingill Trout Reel with 'No 3 – Mohawk' marking on foot, 3″ diameter. Sold for $225

A PETTINGILL

2⅞″ – Early side mounted 1887 patent trout reel marked 'A Pettingill, Pat P'd'g No. 2' $425
2⅞″ – A No 3 trout reel marked 'A Pettingill, Pat. P'd'g' on front and 'Pat. P'd'g' on back $412, $357
3″ – Early 1887 patent Pettingill trout reel with rare 'No 3 – Mohawk' marking on foot. Some nickel wear and wooden handle does not rotate $225

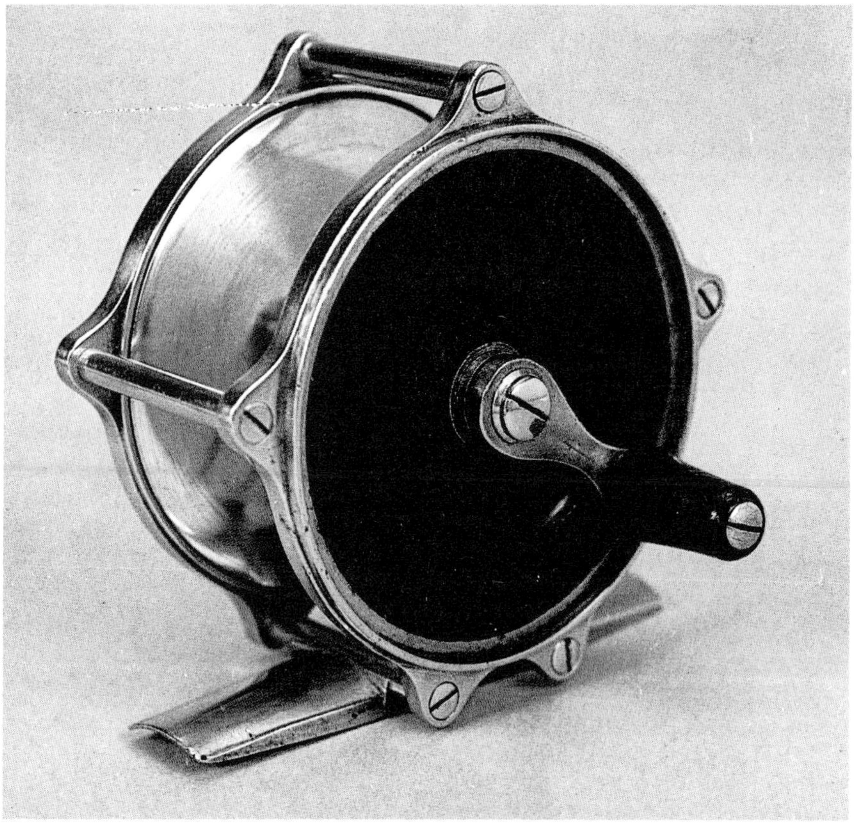

Philbrook & Payne reel. Sold for $20900

PFLUEGER

- Akron multiplier with level-wind $11, $26
- Autopla No 2479 $80
- Buckeye No 993, mint in box $176
- Capitol multiplier in box £19
- Everlaster with leather thumb drag $55
- Hawkeye trout reel 2⅜″ diameter $385
- Medalist No 1495, mint $60
- Medalist No 1592 with both right and left-hand line guides. Belong to Harry Darbee $296
- Progress £33
- Redifor No 1176 Patent 30th October 1808, $27, $88
- Rocket No 1355. Mint in box $60
- Rocket multiplier in box $25
- Summit. Three sold together $50
- Supreme with star drag $82, $80, £26
- Templar 1420. Half big game reel with leather thumb brake $66

PHILBROOK & PAYNE

2″ – Rare, tiny Philbrook & Payne marked 'H L Leonard. Maker'. At this time the makers were granted their reel patent in 1877 and assigned to Leonard. It is believed that these early reels were made by Ed Payne and marketed by Leonard. Most of these orange and black marblised plate reels are found unmarkėd and only more important examples are marked 'Philbrook & Payne, Patent Pending'. This tiny 2″ diameter reel of German silver and hard rubber has a black hard rubber handle and tiny oil hole in the rear bearing cap. Close to mint $12,650

2⅜″ – Fly reel in German silver with black and orange marblised hard rubber plates, rear bearing cap without hole and marblised handle. It was patented in 1877 and assigned to the H L Leonard Co. The reel is unmarked $8800

– Described as 'Perhaps the rarest and most historically important of all American fly reels'. Marked 'Philbrook & Payne Makers. Pat. Apld For'. Made before the granting of the 1877 Philrook patent and its subsequent assignment to the H L Leonard Rod Co who marketed the Leonard reel for a century. The diameter is 2⅜″ with click, orange and black side plates and made of German silver. Condition near mint $20,900

RITTER

- Side mounted in hard rubber and German silver marked 'G Ritter, New York, Pat'd 1886 – 209' and Serial No 192 $159, $247

ROCHESTER REEL CO

- Multiplier of 9-1 ratio marked '9 Multiple' $55

J L SAGE

- Tiny No 2 reel made of German silver with horn handle and sliding click and drag buttons. Size 1⅝″ diameter with 1⅜″ wide spool. Excellent $5500

SEAMASTER REELS

- Seamaster Dual Mode reel. The rarest of this make. Mint $1650
- Seamaster anti-reverse, hand-crafted, small left hand wind salmon reel. Size 3 3⁄16″ diameter. Mint $2035
- Seamaster anti-reverse, right hand wind salmon reel. Size 3 7⁄16″ diameter. Almost mint $1155
- Seamaster Mark IV tarpon or big game fly reel. Size 4½″ diameter and 13 oz. Unused $1375

SELLERS

- Side mounted fly reel marked 'Sellers, Kutztown, P A, US Patent 1947141' with agate line guide, wood folding handle and click on/off button $1100

SHAKESPEARE

- Level wind No 3, 60 yards style B, serial No 3170. The reel has the early novel level-wind

mechanism $132
– Hercules level winding No 1966 $27
– Alamo reel with bearing missing $80
– Five models – Criterion, Ideal 1963, Marhoff, Superior and Triumph; sold together $70
– Two Marhoff reels $44

A B SHIPLEY & SON

1¾″ – 'A B Shipley & Son, Philadelphia, PA' marked reel with external pillars, 'S' balance handle with walnut knob $154
2″ – Unmarked A B Shipley multiplying trout reel with click and drag levers on the back $27
2⅛″ – 'M A Shipley Phila' trout reel $104
2⅜″ – 'M A Shipley, Phila' trout reel $154
2⅞″ – 'A B Shipley & Son, Phila' marked reel $110

SOUTH BEND

– Multiplying reel No 350 Model C and similar model No 400. Sold together $60

SQUARE STAMPING CO

– Side mounted casting reel marked 'Waltonian Casting Reel, M'f'g. By Square Stamping Co., Inc., Barneveld, N Y, cap., 100 yards. Pat. pending' $440, $385

H C SQUIRES

– 'Henry C Squires, N Y' multiplier with 'S' balance handle, condition excellent $60

W M STUART

– Original patent model for the 1865 patent rod handle reel engraved 'W'm M Stuart, Newark, N J'. This was America's first patent for a rod handle reel (length 21″) $770

W H TALBOT

– Talbot special order reel made of coin silver with gold click and drag switches. Faceted diamond jewelled bearings, fishing scene engraved on back plate. Amber handle and front plate engraved 'Fred N Peet, Aug 16 1900' (Fred N Peet had the distinction of being the Champion accuracy bait caster of the World in 1897 and in 1909 was all-round champion of the United States) $7810
– High quality 'Talbot Reel & M'f'g Co., KC MO, USA Star' marked German silver handmade bait casting reel. Serial No 14740. Near mint $357
– Early 'W'm H Talbot, Nevada, MO No 2' marked bait casting reel. Serial No 304. Replaced handle screw $742
– Model No 31 marked 'Talbot Reel & M'f'g Co' Mint in original box marked 'Richardson Rod & Reel Co' $682 $990
– 'Niangua' marked 'Talbot Reel & M'f'g Co, KC, MO, USA'. New in original box marked 'Richardson Rod & Reel Co.' $632
– No 54 Talbot KC MO reel in German silver and ivory handle $1320
– 'W'm H Talbot, Nevada, MO No. 3'. Serial No 281 $715

ELI TERRY

1¾″ – Brass multiplier with rim stop latch. Foot marked 'Pat. Nov. 14, 1871' $82, similar 2″ $44

BENJAMIN THUMEZY

– Bait caster with complex thumb operated anti-backlash device $550

UNION HARDWARE

– Samson reel with unique hinged front plate which can be opened for cleaning and oiling $71

VALENTINE

– Fly reel model 375 £49

Spectacular one of a kind Talbot bait casting reel of coin silver with gold click and drag switches, faceted diamond jewelled bearings, fishing scene engraved back plate, amber handle and front plate engraved 'Fred N Peet, Aug. 16, 1900'. Sold for $7810

Benjamin Thumezy reel with complex thumb operated anti-backlash device, c.1916. Sold for $550

EDWARD VOM HOFE

- Perfection trout reel size 1/0 (3″ diameter) in hard rubber and German silver with aluminium foot, spool ends and handle crank. The back sliding click button engraved 'H F 12-25-40' (owner). Excellent plus in leather case $3850, $4015
- Perfection trout reel, size 1/0 (3″ diameter) with 1896 patent date and unusual acorn handle nut. Mint in case $1980
- Regal Black Bass Reel, size 1/0 with 1883 patent date. Condition excellent in case $330
- Restigouche, size 1/0 (3⅛″ diameter) with 1896 patent date, in case $1760, $1320
- Presentation No 1 (2⅞″ diameter) bass reel with leather thumb brake. Handle retaining nut missing $286
- Col Thompson size 1/0. A 3-1 multiplier $907, $770, $1540
- Size 1/0 salmon reel with ebonite and German silver fittings, and serpentine counter balance winding arm £286
- Universal No 1 size without model markings but stamped Serial No A674, 3″ size and 1896 patent markings and rear rim drag lever. Mint $550, $467
- Tobique Model 504, 2/0 size multiplier with scarce Philadelphia address and 1902 patent date $550, $1045
- Tobique Model 504, 2/0 size multiplying salmon. Originally belonged to C O V Keinbusch with 1902 patent date $2420
- Tobique Model 504, 2/0 size multiplier with 1896 patent date in leather case $907, $880
- Matecumbe Bonefish reel No 800, size 2/0 (2¾″

diameter) $550, $637, $330
- Perfection trout reel size No 1 (3″ diameter) with front mounted adjustable drag with pointer and red dots and 1896 patent marking. Shiny mint $3300
- Perfection 2½″ diameter with 1883 patent marking. Hairline crack on front plate. The reel has back sliding click button, front mounted adjustable drag with early arrow head pointer and red dots $2200
- Perfection trout reel 2/0 size (2¾″ diameter) in German silver and hard rubber. Crack on back plate and some dents $1815
- Special Star, 2/0 size in German silver and hard rubber $462
- Universal Star No. 621, size 2/0 with stylish detent hole star drag and 1896 patent dates $935
- Star surf casting reel, 2/0 size (2⅞″ diameter) with 'S' handle $310
- Early 1867 patent reel 3¼″ diameter. Marked only 'Edward Vom Hofe, Maker, Pat. Nov. 26, 67' $330
- Model 355 Peerless, size 3 trout reel with January 23, 1883 patent markings, 2½″ diameter $3025
- Salmon reel No 423 in 3/0 size with rare German silver rims which wrap around to protect the inner plate $1320
- Restigouche 423, 3/0 size with 1902 patent date and scarce Philadelphia address $360, $660
- Surf casting reel 3/0 size No 883 (3¾″ diameter) with 'S' handle and fresh water knob. Unused $275
- Universal Star Model 621, 3/0 size, hand made with 1902 patent date and leather thumb brake $192
- Surfcasting reel No 621, 3/0 size in German silver and hard rubber with 1902 patent date $467
- Tobique 3/0 size, model 504 $742
- Tobique 3/0 size multiplying reel No 504 in sparkling mint condition in original box $2750
- 3/0 size, marked 'Edw. Vom Hofe, Maker, Fulton St, NY, Pat. Jan 23 83'. Good, in case $330
- Star surfcasting reel No 550, 3/0 size with 2 rim controls, 1902 patent date and 'S' handle $100
- Restigouche Salmon Model 423, 4/0 size with scarce Philadelphia address $440, $440, $495, $825
- Salmon reel No 504 4/0 size, single action, click button, centre side plate drag (crack on side plate) $210
- Size 4/0 No 423 $250
- Size 4/0 multiplier of ebonite and German silver with 1883 patent date £170, £154
- Size 4/0 No 621 salt water reel with 2 rim controls, 1902 patent date, star-drag, hole locks, handle nut ratchet lock $125, $55
- Universal Star Model 621, 4/0 size $198, $110, $176, $132, $209
- Salmon reel No 423, 4/0 size with 'Pat. Jane. 23 1883' in German silver and hard rubber $175
- 4/0 salmon reel with 1879 patent drag and engraved 'Marvin Olcott, Camp Albany'. In leather case with silver plaque marked 'Marvin Olcott 1919' $1155
- Restigouche, 6/0 size with 1879 patent adjustable arrow head indicator drag on front plate $577, $495
- Restigouche, 6/0 size with 1883 patent date $770
- Restigouche, 6/0 size model No 504 with 1902 patent date. Needs cleaning and oiling $962
- 6/0 size Tarpon reel with Rabbeth handle drag and 1883 patent date $286
- 6/0 salmon reel (4¼″ diameter) £165, £143, £104
- 6/0 No 562 salt water reel with 02 patent date and 'S' handle $170
- 6/0 Salmon No 504. Single action with adjustable automatic tension $200
- 9/0 size, No 501 with star drag and 1896 patent date $120
- 9/0 size, No 621 with 2 rim control buttons, and star drag with hole locks (thumb drag missing) $70
- 9/0 size with leather thumb pad $187
- 12/0 size salt water reel with 2 rim control buttons $600
- Big Game Commander Ross Model 722 (6″) $550
- Commander Ross Model 732 $1760
- Big Game 14/0 size (7¼″) £528

FREDERICK VOM HOFE

2⅝″ – Brass ball handle multiplier $550

2⅝″ – Early 'F Vom Hofe & Son, Pat Nov 26, '67' in German silver and hard rubber (replacement handle) $495

2⅝″ – F Vom Hofe & Son, Maker with wood handle $495

'F Vom Hofe & Son, Maker' brass ball handle multiplier of 2⅝″ diameter. Sold for $550

Early fancy Julius Vom Hofe reel with sculptured plate rims and back plate with 1885 and 1889 patent dates. Diameter 2¼″. Sold for $286

JULIUS VOM HOFE

2″ – Tiny external pillared balance crank reel marked 'Abbey & Imbrie, NY Pat. Oct. 8, 1889' $385

2″ – Very early 'Julius Vom Hofe, Maker', marked trout reel with c.1880 square corner thick German silver raised pillar plates $605

2⅛″ – Rare quality raised pillar trout reel with aluminium spool ends and plates with rubber inserts. Condition mint $522

2¼″ – Type 3½″ with 1885 and 1889 patent dates $121

2¼″ – Scarce 'Pat Oct '89' in German silver and hard rubber $375

2¼″ – Plate trout reel marked 'Julius Vom Hofe, NY. Maker'. $165

2¼″ – Tiny trout reel marked 'Julius Vom Hofe, Maker, NY' with back sliding click button $165

2⅜″ – Type 2 in German silver and hard rubber with raised pillars $550

2⅜″ – Type 3 trout reel marked 'Julius Vom Hofe, Maker, NY' in hard rubber and shiny brass $192

2½″ – Small trout reel marked 'Julius Vom Hofe, Maker, NY' and 'Thos. J Conroy, NY'. Excellent $330

2⅝″ – 'Julius Vom Hofe, Pat. Dec. 20. 92 – President' marked reel $275

– 1/0 size reel with 1899 patent date $93

– 1/0 size 'Pat Oct 8 '89', raised pillar multiplier $11

– 1/0 size reel marked 1885 and 1889 patent dates $88

– 1/0 size (2¾″) in German silver and hard rubber $412

– 4/0 size salmon reel. High quality early reel having 191813 patent number of the 1877 Philrook patent $192

– 5/0 large Julius Vom Hofe 'Pat. Oct. 8 '89'; also marked 'Dame Stoddard & Co. Boston' on front $209, $357

– 5/0 multiplying sea reel with ebonite plates and nickel silver pillars, drum, counterbalance handle and handle plate. Adjustable brake with toddle catch $88

– 6/0 salmon reel with adjustable drag-lever, sliding click button and wear compensating cap on the back, 1889 and 1903 patents marked $187

– B-Ocean 6/0 size handmade 1911 patent reel with back sliding click button $187

– Big game reel 6/0 size with 1911 patent $99

– 6/0 size high quality salmon reel with adjustable drag lever and 1889/1903 patent dates. Two light back plate scratches, otherwise excellent $357

WALKER

2″ – 'A L Walker, NY, Maker' and 'M3' marked Midge trout reel with aluminium foot, spool ends, handle crank and back sliding click button $2750

2½″ – Midge or small trout fly reel marked 'A L Walker, Maker, NY', with 15/16″ wide pillars $2090

2¾″ – Walker TR2 in German silver, polished aluminium and hard rubber $687

'Wheeler & McGregor, Mikwaukee, Wis, Pat'd May 29 – June 26 1984. No 3.' First commercial level-wind. Sold for $825

3″ – Walker TR3 in German silver, polished aluminium and hard rubber $522, $935

3¼″ – A Walker, Maker, NY, with black bakelite plates, aluminium and German silver, left hand wind $525

WHEELER & McGREGOR

– First commercial level-wind reel marked 'Wheeler & McGregor, Milwaukee, Wis. Pat'd May 29, June 26-94 No. 3' $825

WILLSHER & DAMEREL

2¾″ – Brass ball balance handle multiplier marked 'Willsher & Damerel NY' c.1860s $77

WINCHESTER

– No 4253, non-level wind, balance handle $49

YAWMAN & ERBE

3⅜″ – Automatic fly reel with 1881 and 1891 patent dates $40, $99

OTTO ZWARG

– 1/0 Model 400 Laurentian custom built multiplier $990
– 2/0 Laurentian No 200 custom built multiplier $330
– 2/0 Maximo. Excellent, in case $412
– 3/0 Model 400 Laurentian, multiplier reel $440
– 3/0 Model 400. Serial No B17, 59 and Ex(experimental) with 2 extra drill holes in back $440
– 3/0 Model 400 multiplying salmon reel $412
– 4/0 Maximo Model 600 $352
– 4/0 Salmon Model 300 $330, $385
– 4/0 size Model 400 multiplying salmon reel $550
– 9/0 Maximo big game reel $552

Walker TR-3 trout reel with rare adjustable drag. Diameter 3″. Sold for $935

Otto Zwarg Model 300 in 4/0 size. Sold for $330

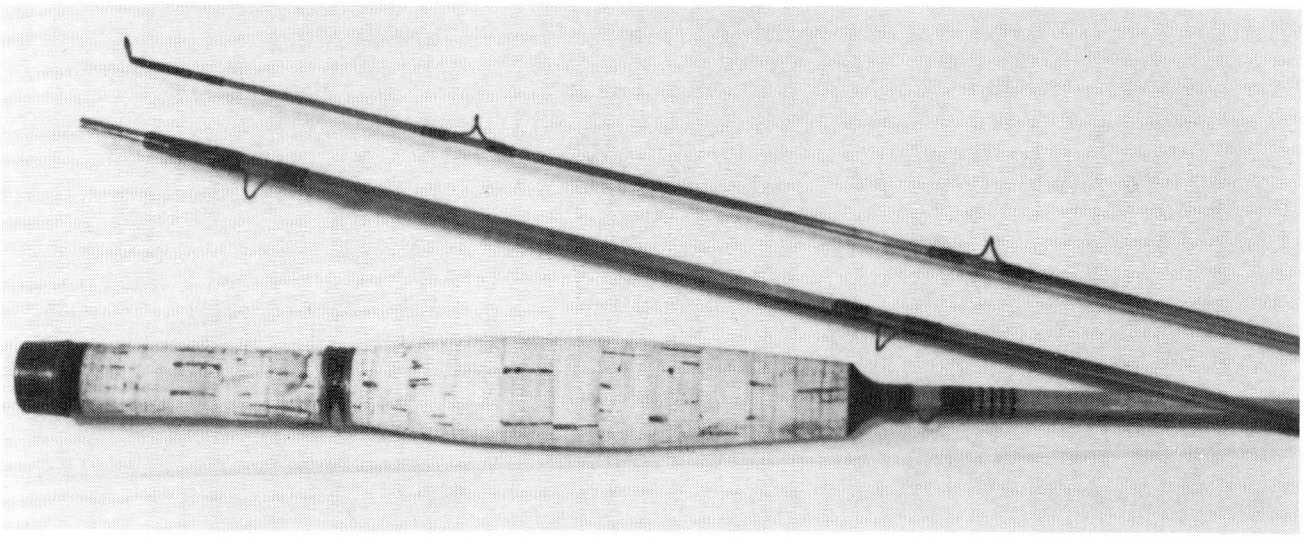

AMERICAN RODS

ABBEY & IMBRIE
11′ – 3 piece + spare tip, marked 'Abbey & Imbrie New York, Best' and 'Pat. December 13th 1881'. Excellent $121
9′ – 3 piece + spare tip, marked 'Abbey & Imbrie 100th Anniversary Rod 1820 – 1920' on the reel seat $66
8′ 6″ – 3 piece + spare mid-section + spare tip $165

ABERCROMBIE & FITCH
8′ 6″ – 3 piece + spare tip, 'Yellowstone Special' trout rod in wood-form cast and bag $192
7½′ – 2 piece + spare tip. G spiker fittings, morticed cork sliding band reel seat (needs a varnish) $385

C BAILLIE
14′ – 3 piece + spare tip + extra mid-section marked 'C Baillie Maker St John N B'. Spliced (no ferrules) and possibly greenheart with loose ring guides, wood butt and in original wood case $192
9′ – 2 piece + spare tip. 'C Baillie Maker St John N B'. Spliced lancewood, loose rings, brass fittings, wood butt and wood case $231

BARR
8′ – 2 piece + spare tip, Andy Barr 'The Windigo' five strip trout rod made in 1979, mint $154

BASSETT
9′ – 3 piece + spare tip, marked 'Bassett' with short swelled butt section inlaid with cedar strips. In original velvet lined wood box $110

SAM CARLSON
7′ 6″ – 3 piece 'Thomas Four No 6220 – 4753' marked quadrate section (four sided). Mint in labelled bag and leather case $3080
6′ 6″ – 2 piece + spare tip, rare four sided trout rod with an agate stripper guide and sliding band, over cork reel seat. It is signed 'Bill Rosgen, Winsted, Conn' (the retailer who sold many of Carlson's rods) $4950
5′ – One piece six sided trout rod marked 'Thomas Rod Co 1101' (marking used when Sam Carlson first aquired the F E Thomas Rod Co). Sold with a 5′ graphite rod. $6600

WALT CARPENTER
8′ – 3 piece + spare tip No 78180. This light Browntone rod was made while Walt was at the Payne Rod Co. Unused in bag and tube $990

Sam Carlson four sided 6½′ trout rod, 2 piece with spare tip. Sold for $4950

CHUBB
14′ – 3 piece + spare tip two handed salmon rod with varnish roughness in bag and wood case $385
10′ 6″ – 3 piece + spare tip (one damaged other short) with ash butt section. Varnish deterioration $27
6′ – 2 piece + spare tip, eight sided with reversible handle and gold leaf logo and made of Calcutta cane in wood case and tube $220
Various lengths – Outfit consists of handle and seven sections of various lengths with Chubb logo on handle and made of Calcutta cane with German silver fittings. Almost mint in form case $385

CONROY
11′ – 3 piece + spare tip (short) marked 'Conroy & Bissett', made of Calcutta cane with German silver fittings. One ferrule replaced, otherwise excellent $192
10′ – 3 piece + spare tip 'Thos J Conroy. Maker NY', c.1890s trout rod $357
8′ 6″ – 3 piece + spare tip, marked 'Thomas J Conroy, Maker, NY' and unique lever locking reel seat, swelled butt and handle extension. Good plus in wood form case and bag $126

J B CROOK & CO

9′ – 3 piece + spare tip 'J B Crook & Co. Makers NY'. Cedar reel seat, German silver fittings, moderate condition $88

DAME, STODDARD & KENDALL

10′ – 3 piece + spare tip (crack at end) marked 'Dame, Stoddard & Kendal, Boston, Never Break', c.1890. Cedar inlaid swelled butt, loose rings, German silver ferrules and sliding band reel seat, excellent in wood case $225

9′ – 3 piece + spare tip, marked 'Never Brake'. Cane wrap handle, German silver fittings with blue velvet lined case $280

DICKERSON

9′ – 2 piece + spare tip, marked '9' Special Salmon' with screw down-locking reel seat and half Wells grip. Very good plus condition $440

8′ 6″ – 3 piece + spare tip Model 861711 D trout rod with screw down-locking walnut reel seat. Usable $742

– 2 piece + spare tip, 8614-'47 trout fly rod with screw down-locking walnut reel seat, $935

8′ – 3 piece + spare tip (both ends about 4″ short) 'Dickerson 801510-D' rod in very good condition $335

8′ – 2 piece + spare tip, Model 8014 trout rod, marked 'Dickerson 8014 Guide '51' and presentation inscription to owner. The rod with screw down-locking over walnut reel seat. Mint in bag and tube $4675

7′ – 2 piece + spare tip, Model 7012, with screw down-locking reel seat with walnut spacer, traditional Dickerson brown tipped black wraps, blued ferrules and original owner's name with 1953 date in ink. Excellent plus condition in original bag and tube $9900

DIVINE

10′ 9″ – 5 piece or 8′ 8″ 4 piece. A rare combination rod made for President Grover, Cleveland in the 1880s $330

9′ 6″ – 3 piece + spare tip c.1910, marked 'The Divine Rod, Utica, NY' and serial No R448 on butt cap, with morticed cedar wood sliding band reel seat $330

7′ 4″ – 3 piece + spare tip, 2⅝oz, serial No H1610 with sliding band over cork reel seat, red wraps and intermediate winds. About excellent condition $990

E W EDWARDS

3 piece + spare tip

9′ – 'E W Edwards Autograph #70 – 9′' trout fly rod. Has screw up-locking reel seat of polished walnut. Made after Edwards business arrangement with Horton M'f'g of Bristol CT. Mint condition $632

9′ – 3 piece + spare tip. Some varnish roughness $192

– 3 piece + spare tip with screw down-locking reel seat. Condition excellent in bag $154

8′ – 3 piece + spare tip, 'Edwards Mt Carmel' trout rod with rare butt cap stamping 'E W Edwards & Sons, Makers, Bristol, Conn.', which was used for a short time by Bill and Gene Edwards, working together shortly after the death of their father Eustis. Some varnish roughness $550

8′ 6″ – Bristol F-7 trout fly rod, German silver ferrules and screw down-locking wood reel seat and red wraps. Near mint condition in bag and tube $110

– 3 piece + spare tip #50 quadruple section (four sided). Mint in labelled bag and leather case $770

– 3 piece + spare tip, 'Bill Blogette #3 Custom Built

239 Dickerson Model 7012 trout rod, 7′, 2 piece with spare tip. Sold for $9900

240 Dickerson Presentation 'Guide' Model 8014 trout, 8′, 2 piece with spare tip. Sold for $4675

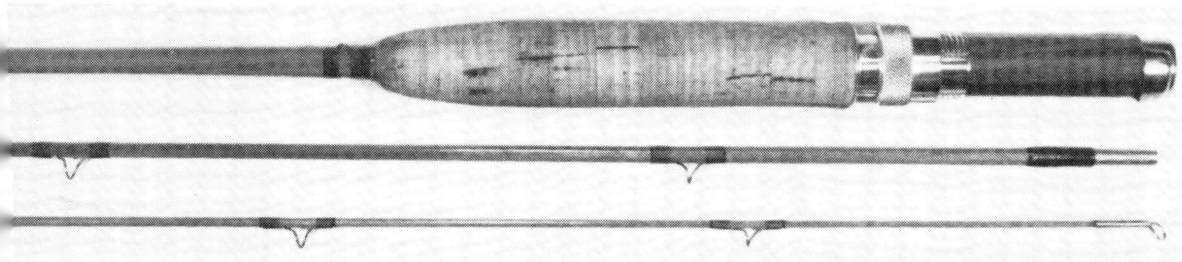

239.

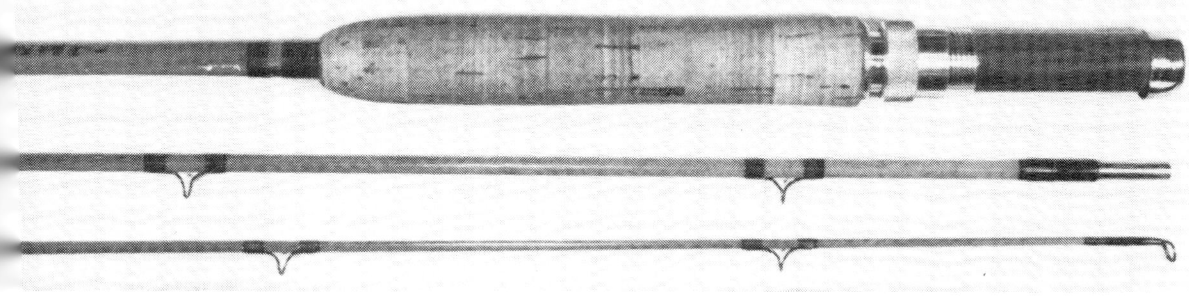

240.

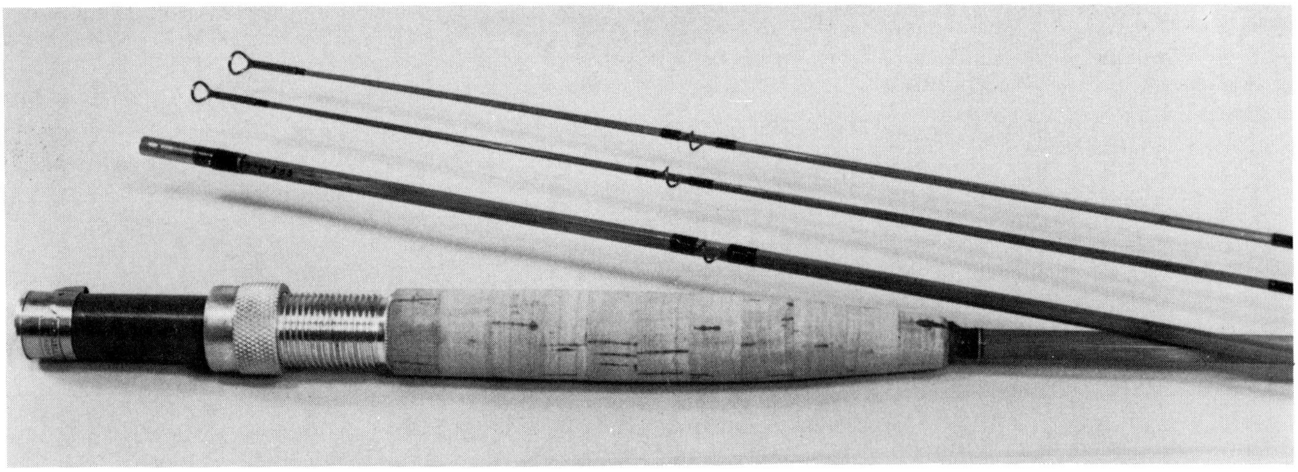

H S Gillum rod. Sold for $13200

by Gene Edwards'. Mint in bag and tube $220

– 3 piece + spare tip, $5\frac{5}{8}$oz, 'Bristol' trout rod with German silver sliding band reel seat. Mint in bag $165

7′ – 2 piece + spare tip, marked 'E W Edwards Deluxe' and with Abbey & Imbrie label. Some varnish roughness otherwise very good in bag and tube $495

– 2 piece, $4\frac{1}{4}$oz, Quadrate No 425 spinning rod. Near mint in bag and labelled tube $137

5′ 6″ – 'E W Edwards Autograph Mt Carmel $5\frac{1}{2}$ Med', 2 piece custom rod with straight grip. Mint condition in labelled bag and tube $302

GARRISON

All rods 2 piece + spare tip unless otherwise stated.

9′ – Light salmon rod #228 with German silver reel seat and fittings. Made 1942. Mint $3300

9′ – 3 piece + spare tip ($3\frac{1}{2}$″ short). Mint 218 light salmon rod with 5″ detachable extension butt $550

8′ 6″ – Model 220 trout rod made in 1962. Marked 'Garrison 220' and 'D-86-2'. A few varnish chips and one tip has a splinter removed requiring a 3″ repair wrap. In original bag and tube $880

8′ – Model 206 trout rod with copper sliding band cork reel seat and screw two piece copper butt cap, in leather hinged top wood case, c.1943 $1650

8′ – 2 piece + spare tip, serial No 0-8-11, for a #5 line. Made in 1945 and used condition $4950

8′ – 2 piece + spare tip, serial No F-8-1, for a #6 line. Cork reel seat shows some reel foot chafing and one tip repaired $1540

8′ – Model 221 FT (Fast Taper), serial No P-8-1 (1972), 2 piece, 2 tips, $4\frac{1}{4}$ oz with S-Z ferrules and a Garrison ferrule plug. Used a few times with minor varnish faults otherwise near mint $9075

7′ 9″ – Model 206 trout rod made in 1941 and unused. Sliding band cork reel seat $2200

7′ 9″ – Model 206 trout rod marked 'Garrison 206' and 'E-79-4'. It is the lightest 7′ 9″ model Garrison made and appears to have an old well done varnish overcoat. There is one

The Garrison Model 201 Trout Rod sold for $9900

guide wrap replacement otherwise good plus $3520

7′ 6″ – Model 204 trout rod. War time rod with copper sliding band cork reel seat $2200

7′ 6″ – Model 209 trout rod made in 1960. Marked 'Garrison 209' and 'B-76-2'. This model, for about a 5 weight line, has the fastest dry fly action of 7′ 6″ models. A few minor varnish chips. Condition excellent in original bag and tube $5500

7′ – Model 201 trout rod with sliding band cork reel seat with silver soldered butt cap and black oxidised ferrules. Mint 1945 $2420

7′ – Model 201 trout rod for a 4 weight line marked 'Garrison 201' and 'N-7-3'. This is the lightest model 7′ rod Garrison made. Constructed in 1944 at a time of war and material shortage. Garrison's compulsion to continue building fine rods led him to make the reel seat parts of copper rather than the compulsory German silver. It has some varnish age lines on butt otherwise in excellent plus condition. In original bag and replacement tube $9900

H S GILLUM

9′ 6″ – 3 piece + spare tip light salmon rod with famous aluminium conical extension butt. Condition excellent in bag and tube $1870

9′ 6″ – Salmon rod with his famous removable aluminium conical extension butt. 3 piece + spare tip (one a replacement). Reel seat stamped 'H S Gillum, Maker' $935

9′ – 3 piece + spare tip, 5¼ oz, serial No 1-724, trout rod with Super-Z type ferrules, screw up-locking reel seat with wood spacer and butt cap. Mint in bag and tube $1870

8′ 9″ – Fly rod for a 7 weight line. The reel seat is not stamped but it is accompanied by a letter of authentication from Mrs Gillum. Condition original almost mint $880

8′ 6″ – Light salmon fly rod stamped 'H S Gillum, Maker' on the ring of the screw unlocking reel seat. The rod has a removable

H S GILLUM RODS
43 9½′, 3 piece with spare tip. Sold for $1870
44 9′, 3 piece with spare tip. Sold for $1100
45 9′, 3 piece with spare tip (one shorter). Sold for $550

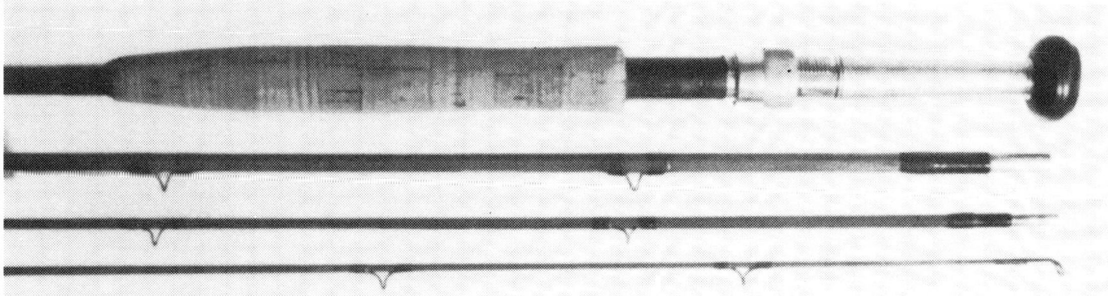
43.

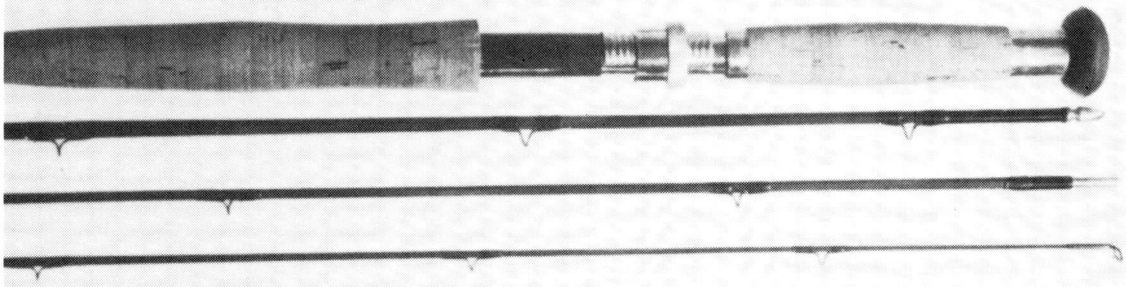
44.

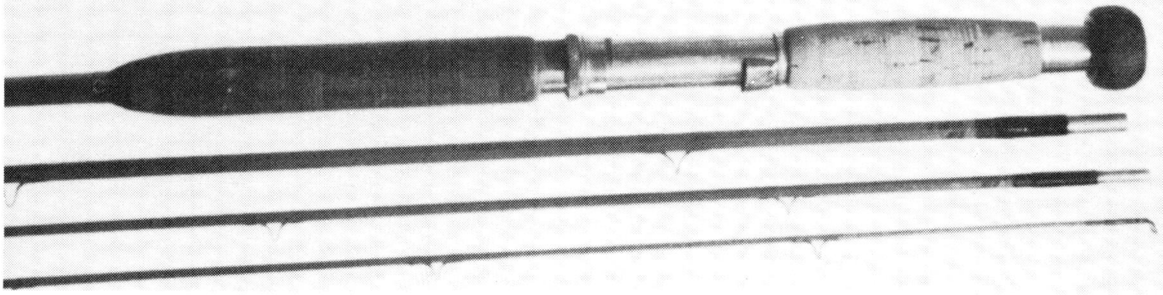
45.

butt. In used condition with hook digs in the cork at the end of the handle and one line guide has been lost otherwise in good plus original condition, with bag and tube $1100

8′ 6″ – 3 piece, serial No 601 with screw up-locking reel seat and marked 'Gillum Custom Built' on rod shaft. Professionally re-done $1540

8′ 6″ – 2 piece plus spare tip, 4⅜ oz trout rod marked 'H S Gillum Maker' on screw locking-up reel seat. Unused in original bag and tube $4950

8′ – 3 piece + spare tip, serial No 582, trout rod with wood up-locking reel seat $3850

6′ 9″ – 2 piece + spare tip, 3½ oz for a #5 line trout rod with down-locking reel seat over tiger striped mahogany spacer. The butt cap is marked 'H S Gillum, Maker'. $13200

6′ – 2 piece, 1¾ oz trout rod, serial No 1-715 with Super-Z ferrules, tiger striped mahogany reel seat and lightweight aluminium sliding band and butt cap. The wraps are black with white tags and blued ferrules. Condition is excellent with some varnish scratches. In bag and labelled tube $19,250

8′ – 3 piece, 2 tip, 5½ oz rod in new unassembled condition with original protective paper handle covering $8250

8′ – 2 piece, 2 tip rod with Super-Z ferrules, brown wraps with black tags and screw down-locking reel seat $4400

9′ – 3 piece, 2 tips, 6½ oz, light salmon rod with famous conical aluminium extension butt in new unassembled condition with original paper handle covering. It has Super-Z ferrules and serial No. 1922 $4675

9′ – 3 piece, 2 tips, 6⅜ oz with a screw up-locking, over walnut spacer reel seat, Super-Z ferrules. Mint $2200

9′ – 3 piece, 3 tips (one is non original) with screw up-locking reel seat. The rod has been re-done and the extension butt filler plug is missing otherwise excellent $1650

GRANGER

SPECIAL

9′ – 3 piece with German silver screw up-locking reel seat marked 'Made by Goodwin Granger Co Denver' and a 1938 patent date. Re-finished with a long invisible wrap in the mid-section $49

– 3 piece + spare tip with 1938 patent and German silver screw up-locking reel seat. Some varnish chips $126

GRANGER VICTORY

8′ – 3 piece + spare tip (1½″ short). The nickeled screw up-locking reel seat is marked 'Made by Goodwin Granger Co, Denver April 12th 1938'. Heavy overcoat of varnish $93

ARISTOCRAT

7′ 6″ – 3 piece + spare tip (shorter), 3¾ oz, trout rod with German silver screw up-locking reel seat $165

7′ – 2 piece + spare tip with German silver screw up-locking reel seat. $1155

DELUXE

7′ 6″ – 3 piece + spare tip, 3 oz, serial No. GD7630, with half-Wells grip, sliding band down-locking reel seat. Cork handle has been cleaned and some areas of roughness. Very good $962

HALSTEAD

8′ – 2 piece + spare tip. One tip is labelled 'Trout', the other 'Bass'. Few minor areas of bag sticking otherwise very good in bag and tube $1100

7′ 6″ – 2 piece + spare tip custom trout rod with a sliding band over cork reel seat and translucent tan wraps. The old varnish has been carefully removed and a new coat applied. Excellent plus condition $1760

581 George Halstead, 6′, 2 piece with spare tip. Sold for $8470
582 Orvis-Halstead, 7′, 2 piece with spare tip. An Orvis kit rod made up by George Halstead. Sold for $440

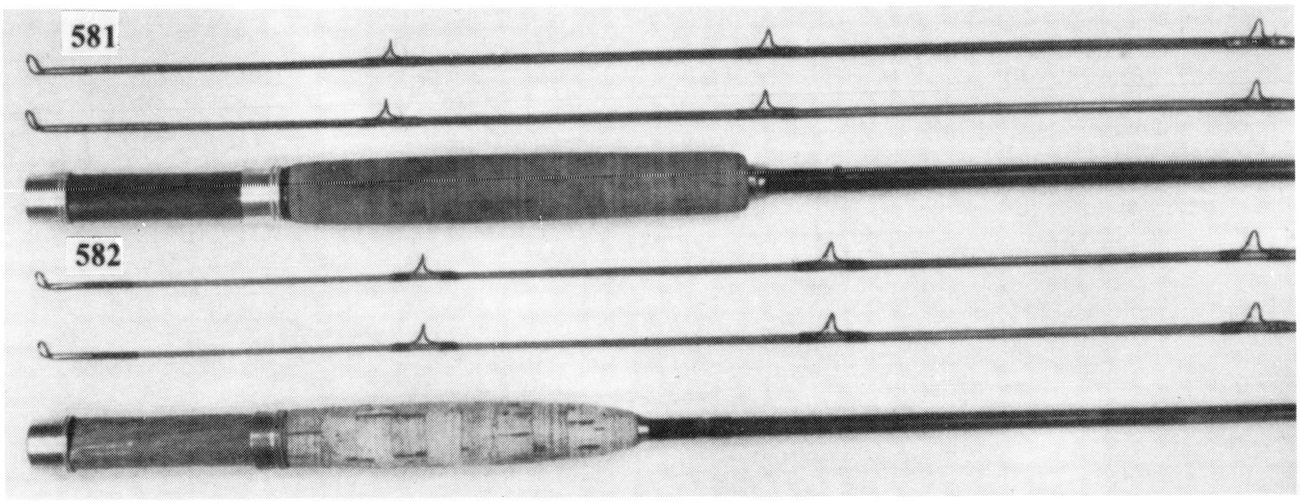

– 3 piece + spare tip custom trout rod with a screw down-locking over tiger striped reel seat and henna wraps. Re-finished by Walt Carpenter and retains paper handle covering $2530

6′ 2″ – 2 piece + spare tip, signed 'Halstead' and has Super-Z ferrules, tan wraps with black tags and lightweight aluminium sliding band and butt cap. Other than some soiling to the cork handle about mint $8800

6′ 2 piece + spare tip with German silver sliding band down-locking reel seat and brown wraps at butt $8470

H W HAWES & CO

9′ – 3 piece + spare tip + extra mid-section. Marked 'H W Hawes & Co., Abercrombie & Fitch Co. Sole Agents. New York USA A15'. $1320

9′ – 3 piece + spare tip (one tip a replacement) No A286. Very good in bag and tube $495

8′ 9″ – 3 piece + spare tip, without serial number, marked 'H W Hawes & Co., Makers, Canterbury, Conn.' Very good condition $1100

HEDDON

All rods 3 piece + spare tip unless stated otherwise

9′ – Early high grade trout rod, with walnut screw up-locking reel seat, gold wraps tipped black $231

– 3 piece + spare tip #14 trout rod with screw down-locking wood reel seat. Very good $49

8′ 6″ – Cane marked '#8½FT-2F-HDH or E'. Tenite screw down-locking seat. Mint $143

DELUX PRESIDENT NO. 50

– with wood seat and cork handle with plastic, German silver and aluminium hardware $210

THOROBRED

– Marked '14-8½-1¾ F-HDH or E'. Condition excellent $55

BILL STANLEY'S FAVORITE

– Model 20 $38

– 2 piece + spare tip, 4½ oz, trout rod with screw down-locking plastic reel seat $110

BLACK BEAUTY

– 3 piece + spare tip trout rod with down-locking plastic reel seat. Excellent $165

PEERLESS DELUXE

7′ 6″ – 3 piece #35 #4 weight line trout rod with patented down-locking reel seat with Circassian walnut spacer. Mint in labelled bag and tube $715

PAL

7′ – Hollow steel, cane finish, spinning rod #2770-7′-M', 2 piece $44

5′ 6″ – #3151-5½′-L'. Hollow steel bait caster with cane finish, offset detachable handle. Mint in original case $110

HEDDON RELIABLE

5′ 6″ – #451-5½′-L' with detachable offset handle $176

BILL VOGT

5′ 6″ – Two 5ft bait casting rods. A No 10 'Bill Vogt' two piece with metal reel seat. Also a 'Pal' No. 751 L steel casting rod. Sold together $126

GARY HOWELLS

9′ – 2 piece + spare tip, 5¼ oz, serial No 3873 (1972), with extension butt, screw up-locking, over fancy wood reel seat, palm and thumb handle depressions, brown wraps tipped gold and ferrule plug. Handle soiled otherwise near mint $1127

8′ – 2 piece + spare tip marked '8′, 4⅛ oz, #4620'. New condition in bag and tube $550

KAMP

8′ 6″ – 3 piece + spare tip 'Geo. Kamp & Co., Makers, Utica, NY' Calcutta cane, German silver fittings and swelled butt. Some missing winds and one tip top guide damaged $165

KOSMIC RODS

3 piece with spare tip

The Kosmic Rod was the fine quality product produced by three skilled rod makers in their combined venture after they had learned their trade while working for Hiram Leonard. This make of rod is very rare as the venture was short lived. The makers were Ed Payne, F E Thomas and Bill Edwards

9′ – Trolling rod with rattan handle and marked on the all German silver reel seat 'The Kosmic, US Net & Twine Co. – 2589'. $192

8′ 6″ – Bait or Black Bass rod with earliest marking 'The Kosmic, A G Spalding & Bros.' on the butt cap and 1890 dates on ferrules $302

8′ 3″ – 'The Kosmic' on butt cap and ferrules with 1890 patent dates $275

8′ – Cane trout fly rod marked 'The Kosmic, US Net & Twine Co.,' 2071 on German silver butt cap and on the ferrule 'Pat'd May 6th 1890, Pat'd May 27 1890'. Unusual size and weighing only 2½ oz. Fittings are in German silver and ivorine reel seat. Superb original condition in brass fitted bamboo case $2750

8′ – Described as the finest early Kosmic rod weighing only a mere 2½ oz. All the metal parts of the rod are gold or gold plated. Its tiny handle is made of cork rings ⅛″ wide. The reel seat is made of gold and ivory grain celluloid. The reel foot pocket is engraved in script 'D.A.H.' and the butt cap 'The Kosmic – A G Spalding & Bros.' Spalding was the first to market these rods. The Kosmic ferrule patent was granted in 1890. Condition near excellent in original tattered bag and leather case $8800

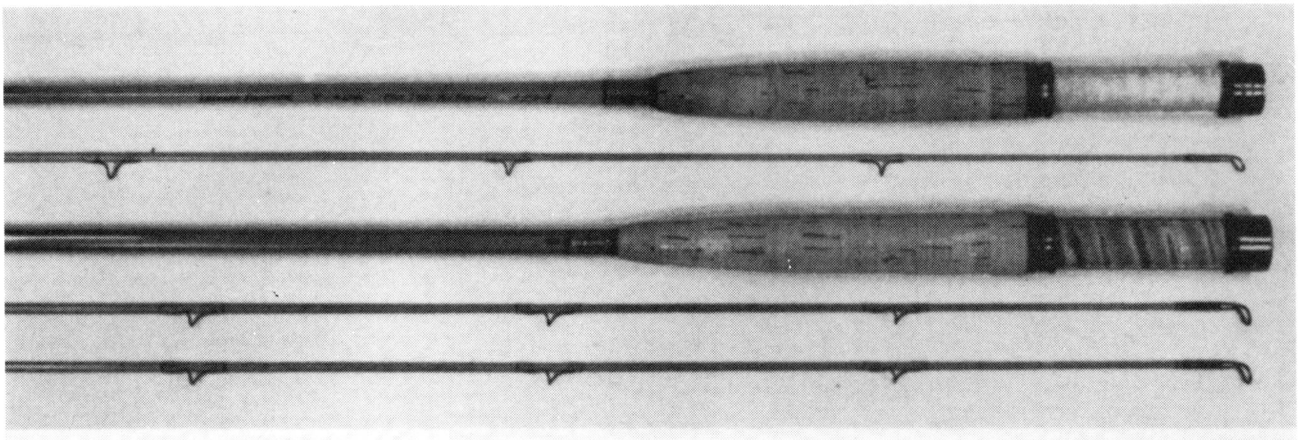

603
604

KREIDER

9′ – 3 piece + spare tip C M Kreider fly rod $577

LANDMAN

9′ 3″ – 3 piece + spare tip, marked 'J G Landman, Maker, Brooklyn, NY' and 'Pat. Aug. 19th 1890'. On reel seat band and butt cap 'Von Lengerke & Detmold, NY' (Predecessor of Abercrombie & Fitch). Almost mint with bag and tube $1210

H L LEONARD

15′ – 3 piece + spare tip with German silver fittings and cork grip (3 eyes missing) $110

13′ 6″ – 3 piece + spare tip with German silver fittings, interrupted screw down-locking reel seat. Varnish roughness $92

11′ 6″ – 3 piece + spare tip, Bangor made trout rod with rare short lived 'Abbey & Imbrie NY Sole Agents' marking. This pre-1878 rod has only the 1875 ferrule patent, condition good $577

11′ 4″ – Rare early 4 strip and round in cross section. Nickel silver mounts and sold with unmarked reel £680 (Sotheby's)

11′ – 3 piece + spare tip, early salmon rod marked 'Wm Mills, Sole Agent'. Re-finished $467

10′ – 3 piece + spare tip with extension butt $247

9′ 6″ – 3 piece + spare tip, 'The H L Leonard Rod' – Leonard and Mills with nickel silver fittings and patent ferrules £93 (Sotheby's)

9′ – Leonard and Mills 'Tournament' rod, 3 piece with German silver fittings £88 (Sotheby's)

– 'Leonard & Mills Co.' marked 3 piece with spare tip (repaired) weight 4⅝ ozs £66

– 3 piece + spare tip, 1875 and 1878 markings, with German silver sliding band reel seat, very good $198

– 3 piece + spare tip (tips shorter) with 1875 and 1878 markings. Only fair condition $77

8′ 10″ – 3 piece + spare tip 'Tournament' rod with metal reel fitting in alloy tube cases £132 (Pearsons)

8′ 6″ – 3 piece + spare tip 'Tournament' Model 50-½ DF trout fly rod. Professionally restored $412

– 3 piece + spare tip 'Tournament'. Re-finished $176

8′ 6″ – 3 piece + spare tip, 4⅛ oz Model 50½ dry fly trout rod with sliding band, over butternut reel seat, agate stripper and tip top guides. The ferrule 1875 and 1878 markings and 'Tournament' on the butt cap. Used condition in bag with tag and tube $1155

8′ – 2 piece 4½ ozs fly rod with a screw down-locking wood reel seat. Butt cap is marked 'The Leonard Rod, H L Leonard Rod Co. Makers, Reg. US Pat. Off'. Mint with original bag, tag, tube $495

– 2 piece + spare tip. Model 40L 'Letort' cane rod 2¼ oz. High quality in leather case $495

– 3 piece + spare tip, serial No 1042 with screw down-locking, over brilliant wood spacer reel seat. Unused in bag and tube $1155

– 3 piece + spare tip (one tip 2″ short), Leonard Pre-fire 'Tournament' trout rod. Fishable $495

– 3 piece + spare tip 'Pre-fire' Leonard Catskill Model 39 trout fly rod. It is olive wrapped, 2½ oz (one tip is ⅜″ shorter) and condition is excellent in bag and tube $660

– 3 piece + spare tip 'Tournament' marked trout fly rod. It is honey wrapped, agate stripper and tip top guides, also early patent marked ferrule. Professionally restored in original bag and tube $825

– 4 piece + spare tip Model 71 'Tournament' with 1875 and 1878 patent date ferrule markings and agate stripper guide.

603 Rare Maxwell-Leonard 'Pattern Stick' for 'Leonard Prototype 7′ – 4 line fast/dry fly action #38H-4' is written on this single tip rod. Sold for $1430

604 Leonard 'Esopus Special' – 3 of 6, 7½′ – 5 wt'. This rod is 7½′, 2 piece with spare tip. Sold for $2310

Re-finished in bag and tube $825
- 2 piece + spare tip 'Duracane' No 4581, impregnated, with red wrappings and plastic handle covering. Mint in bag and tube $577
- 4 piece + spare tip, Model 76 trout rod with sliding band over cork reel seat. Excellent with bag, tag and tube $825
- 3 piece + spare tip 'Fairy Catskill' trout rod with 1875 and 1878 ferrule patent markings and sliding band wood reel seat. Original condition $2420
- 3 piece + spare tip, 1875 and 1878 patent markings and sliding band over wood reel seat. Excellent $935
- 3 piece + spare tip with early patent markings with screw down-locking wood reel seat. Re-finished $247
- 3 piece + spare tip 'Tournament'. Restored $605
- 2 piece + spare tip, Model 807 Duracane, serial No 2459. Excellent in bag and tube $467

7′ 6″ – 3 piece + spare tip. Special Leonard Model #36 'Catskill' fly rod with sliding band cork reel seat and butt cap marked 'The Leonard Rod, HL Leonard Rod Co. Makers Reg. US Pat. Office'. Mint $990
- 2 piece + spare tip, 3⅛ oz Model 39L trout fly rod in mint condition $880

7′ 6″ – 3 piece + spare tip, Leonard Hunt 'Special' 49-4 trout rod, serial No 81225. Fitted with traditional 'Hunt' gun metaled German silver fittings, flamed medium brown cane and tiger striped reel seat. Mint in bag and tube $3850
- 3 piece + spare tip (one 1″ short). An old 'Pre-fire' trout rod which is structurally sound but with a moderate set, varnish blemishes and re-done. $770
- 2 piece + spare tip, serial No 1639 with red wraps, sliding band, over wood spacer reel seat. Some German silver tarnish otherwise mint, in bag and tube $1430
- 2 piece + spare tip, model 39L trout rod. The serial No 2568, red wrapped, 3⅜ oz, 4wt line Model, in mint condition with bag and tube $990
- 3 piece + spare tip 'Pre-fire' trout rod. Professionally restored $990
- 2 piece + spare tip, 'Esopus Special' 3 of 6, 7½′, 5 weight, serial No 3781, mint in bag and tube $2310
- 2 piece + spare tip, Model 39 H trout rod, 3¾ oz. Near mint in bag and tube $550

7′ 3″ – One piece fly rod 2⅝ oz with morticed wood reel seat and German silver sliding band. Butt cap marked 'The Leonard Rod, H L Leonard Rod Co. Makers Reg. US Pat. Office'. Mint $825

7′ – One piece fly rod, 2⅝ oz. A 'Pre-fire' example with morticed wood reel seat, German silver sliding band and butt cap marked 'The Leonard Rod, H L Leonard Rod Co. Makers Reg. US Pat. Office.' Mint condition with bag, tag and tube $715

7′ – 2 piece + spare tip unused model 38ACM 'Baby Catskill Fly Rod' with morticed wood reel seat, silver sliding band and the butt cap marked 'The Leonard Rod, H L Leonard Rod Co. Makers Reg. US Pat. Office'. Pristine condition with bag, tag and tube $1100
- 2 piece + spare tip 2¼ oz, early 'Baby Catskill 38H', marked 'The Leonard Rod, H L Leonard Rod Co. Makers' and the 1875 and 1878 ferrule patent markings, condition, very good $660
- 2 piece split cane rod by H L Leonard Rod Co $35
- 2 piece + spare rod 1¾ oz Model 36 trout fly rod, serial No 879. Apart from a tiny mark on wood reel seat, in mint condition $1155
- 2 piece + spare tip, serial No 1229, with red wraps and sliding band, over wood spacer down-locking reel seat. Some tarnishing otherwise mint in bag and tube $1540

7′ – 3 piece + spare tip 'Maxwell' Model 48 'Hunt' trout fly rod. The serial No 80100, deep maroon wrapped dark cane with tiger maple reel seat, agate stripper guide and all metal parts finished in black. Mint in bag and tube $1485
- 2 piece + spare tip, model 38ACM 'Baby Catskill' fly rod (sold in 1985 for $1100) $3630
- 3 piece Maxwell-Leonard 'Hunt' 48ff-3 fly rod, serial #352. Mint $3520

6′ 6″ – 2 piece + spare tip 'Maxwell' Model 38 trout fly rod marked 'Catskill, 38-4, 2116,' with traditional Leonard honey wraps, oversize guides and dark walnut sliding band reel seat. Mint in bag and tube $770
- 2 piece + spare tip, 'Ausable' Model 37H trout fly rod. The serial No 1122, red wraps, 4 weight line rod is in unused condition in bag and tube $825
- 2 piece + spare tip, serial No 1529, with sliding band over wood spacer, down-locking reel seat. Mint condition in original dirty bag $1540
- 2 piece + spare tip 'Maxwell Era', Leonard model 37-3 trout rod with turned and knurled sliding band down-locking over fancy wood reel seat and tan wraps. Mint with original protective handle covering $2750

6′ – 2 piece + spare tip 1¾ oz Model 36 trout fly rod, serial No 879. Apart from a tiny mark on wood reel seat in mint condition $1155
- 2 piece + spare tip, 15/16 oz, Model 37 'Baby Catskill Trout Rod', 'The World's Lightest Rod' with down-locking butternut reel set and red wraps. Mint in bag and tube $5225

– 2 piece + spare tip 'Hunt', Model 36 trout rod, serial No 642 with blued metal parts, sliding band over morticed tiger striped maple reel seat and red wraps. Mint $3410

– 2 piece + spare tip marked 'The World's Lightest Rod'. Weight $\frac{15}{16}$ oz with sliding band reel seat. Mint $4400

– 2 piece + spare tip 'Hunt' 36-4 trout rod in medium dark flamed cane and black (blued) metal fittings. Mint $3025

W MITCHELL & SON

10′ – 3 piece + 2 spare lancewood tips + 2 extra mid-sections signed 'W Mitchell & Son N-York' and the handle with his 1883 patent date. Rod not perfectly straight and ferrules need wraps, also one re-setting, otherwise good in bag with brass fitted bamboo case $550

MONTAGUE

9′ – 3 piece + spare tip 'Montague Flash', cane fly rod marked 'Genuine Tonkin', with a metal screw down-locking reel seat $22

8′ 6″ – 3 piece + spare tip 'Montague Sunbeam' trout cane fly rod $44, $22

7′ – 2 piece Montague Radidan 'Genuine Tonkin' cane spinning rod $44

MURPHY

10′ 6″ – Probably about a 12′ rod originally with red wraps and snake guides. Marked 'C F Murphy' with butt spike. Very good $550

NEEDHAM

NEEDHAM'S SPECIAL

8′ – 3 piece + spare tip, 4.75 oz, custom made by Omar H Needham, Manchester, Vermont, USA. Used condition $880

7′ 6″ – 2 piece + spare tip, marked 'Needham's Special', custom made by Omar Needham, Manchester, VT and #481, 7′ 6″ HEH'. Excellent $1127

B F NICHOLS & CO

12′ – 3 piece + spare tip marked 'B F Nichols & Co., Boston, Mass Makers', turn of the century cane rod with rattan handle, swelled butt, German silver fittings $275

ORVIS

10′ 6″ – 3 piece + spare tip with removable extension butt and German silver screw down-locking reel seat $88

– 3 piece + spare tip with removable extension butt. Near mint in bag and tube $302

– 2 piece + spare tip with all metal screw down-locking reel seat. Excellent in bag $126

– 3 piece + spare tip with plastic reel seat, mid-section set and shows much use $27

– 3 piece + spare tip and spare mid-section with 1882 patent reel in original wood case, serial No 726. Early trout rod in Calcutta cane. Mint in bag and wooden tube $1402

8′ 6″ – 2 piece + spare tip, $5\frac{3}{8}$ oz 'Light Salmon', of the older dark cane and 'shooting star' type guides and an extension butt $522

$8\frac{1}{2}$′ – 3 piece + spare tip, impregnated 'Battenkill' fly rod, serial No 11492 with all metal screw down-locking reel seat $330

– 2 piece + spare tip, $5\frac{1}{2}$ oz, serial No 21755, impregnated light salmon fly rod with all metal screw down-locking reel seat. Mint $550

– 2 piece + spare tip, $4\frac{1}{2}$ oz 'Limestone Special'. Mint in bag and tube $330

– 2 piece + spare tip, $5\frac{1}{8}$ oz 'Battenkill' fly rod. Mint in bag and tube $192

– 3 piece + spare tip (one shorter), experimental 'Bakelite Impregnated'. Some line guide rust $55

8′ – 2 piece + spare tip, $4\frac{3}{8}$ oz 'Wes Jordan', with screw down-locking wood reel seat and made from beautiful dark impregnated cane with dark brown wraps. Sold 20 years ago for $165. Mint $396, $550

8′ – 2 piece + spare tip trout rod 'Wes Jordan', serial No 55560, $4\frac{3}{8}$ oz, with screw down-locking over walnut reel seat. Mint $770

– 2 piece, $4\frac{3}{8}$ oz 'Orvis 99' trout rod with wood reel seat and down-locking ring. Impregnated cane with red wraps. Mint in bag and tube $302

– 3 piece + spare tip 'Charles F Orvis' trout rod with impregnated cane. Excellent condition $308

– 3 piece + spare tip trout rod marked 'Impregnated, Pat. Pend.' with cork reel seat. Mint in bag and tube $742

– 2 piece + spare tip, $4\frac{3}{8}$ oz, #7 line rod. Mint $220

– 2 piece + spare tip, $4\frac{1}{4}$ oz, with set in cane tip $137

7′ 6″ – 2 piece + spare tip ($1\frac{1}{2}$″ short) lightweight trout rod, brown wrapped impregnated rod $88

– 2 piece, $7\frac{1}{4}$ oz 'Heavy Spin', serial No 74441. New in case $160

7′ 6″ – 2 piece + spare tip, $3\frac{7}{8}$ oz, with screw down-locking over walnut reel seat. Near mint $495

– 2 piece + spare tip, $3\frac{7}{8}$ oz, Battenkill Trout Rod, excellent in bag and tube $220

– 2 piece + spare tip, fly rod with experimental era 'Bakelite Impregnated' marking, excellent $275

– 2 piece + spare tip, $3\frac{7}{8}$ oz, Battenkill Trout Rod. Serial No 47800, mint in bag and tube $220

– 2 piece + spare tip, $4\frac{1}{8}$ oz, 'Special' Trout Fly Rod. Re-wrapped in bag and tube $192

7′ 6″ – 3 piece + spare tip 'Rocky Mountain Special', near mint in leather case $990

7′ 6″ – 2 piece + spare tip, $3\frac{5}{8}$ oz 'Midge'. No 63147 trout rod with bag and tube $522

7′ 6″ – 3 piece + spare tip. No 13448 'Battenkill', trout rod with bag and tube $495

7′ – 2 piece + spare tip, $3\frac{3}{8}$ oz. No 46644 'Battenkill',

Orvis Rocky Mountain fly and spinning, two rod set which once belonged to Clarke Gable. Sold for $6050

trout rod with bag and tube $440

7′ – 2 piece, $4\frac{1}{2}$ oz. No 5829 marked 'Impregnated Pat Pend'. Mint $247

– 2 piece + spare tip, $2\frac{5}{8}$ oz, serial No 60908 with double sliding band over cork reel seat. Near excellent $495

6′ 6″ – 2 piece + spare tip, about $2\frac{1}{4}$ oz 'Orvis Impregnated De-Luxe', older cork reel seat and two sliding bands. Hook digs in handle otherwise excellent $363

6′ 6″ – 2 piece + spare tip, 2 oz 'Flea', mint in original bag and tube $440

6′ 6″ – Two rods once belonging to Clarke Gable in a green felt lined carrying case engraved 'C G'. One 3 piece + spare tip 'Rocky Mountain' trout fly rod. The other 3 piece 'Rocky Mountain' spinning rod. Both in mint condition with a letter of authenticity $6050

– 3 piece, $2\frac{3}{4}$ oz, serial No 48700 'Rocky Mountain', fly and spin trout rod. Soiled handle and one guide missing $440

JIM PAYNE

10′ 6″ – 3 piece + spare tip with removable extension butt (butt plug missing) *$275, $247*

10′ – 3 piece + spare tip salmon rod. It has a removable extension butt, down-locking reel seat and agate stripper guide. Butt cap stamped 'Sold by Abercrombie & Fitch Co, New York'. Sold with all accessories $990

10′ – 3 piece + spare tip with detachable extension butt. It has aluminium and German silver screw down-locking reel seat $440

9′ 6″ – 3 piece + spare tip with detachable extension butt. It has a screw up-locking wood reel seat and ferrule plugs. Excellent in bag, tube and case $1375

9′ – 3 piece + spare tip with screw up-locking wood reel seat. Needs re-finishing $192

– 3 piece + spare tip with screw up-locking wood reel seat, very good condition $220

– 3 piece + spare tip light salmon rod with extension butt. Mint condition with ferrule plugs, bag, tube (with perfect label) and canvas case for tube $1100

9′ – 2 piece + spare tip, Model 430 with detachable extension butt, ferrule plug and screw down-locking reel seat with owners' name. Near mint in bag, tag and tube *$3190*

– 3 piece + spare tip with a screw down-locking, over walnut spacer reel seat and agate stripper guide. Condition fair, in bag and tube *$770*

– 3 piece + spare tip, $6\frac{5}{8}$ oz 'Bass Bug', fly rod sold by Abercrombie & Fitch. About mint *$1540*

– 3 piece + spare tip + spare butt section. Custom built Model 400 with extension butt. In excellent condition, with ferrule plugs, bag and tube $5720

8′ 6″ – 3 piece + spare tip, $4\frac{5}{8}$ oz trout rod. One tip has moderate set and a tiny hook dig mark, also several guides have rust. In bag and tube $605

– 3 piece + spare tip, $4\frac{3}{4}$ oz, Model No 204. Professionally restored and little used. With bag, tag and replacement tube *$1045*

8′ – 2 piece + spare tip (one $4\frac{1}{2}$″ shorter) with screw up-locking wood reel seat and half-Wells handle. Excellent condition with tube and bag $302

8′ – 3 piece + spare tip (one $4\frac{3}{4}$″ shorter). Some patches of varnish roughness $550

8′ – 3 piece + spare tip, $3\frac{7}{8}$ oz, Model 202 trout rod with sliding band over walnut reel seat and agate stripper guide $330

8′ – 3 piece in excellent condition $550

8′ – 2 piece + spare tip trout rod with a sliding band cork reel seat and agate stripper guide. Some finish wear on butt and sliding band which is dented from reel foot otherwise mint with bag and tube $1650

8′ – 2 piece + spare tip (one 2″ short) and both have mild sets. In used condition with bag and tube *$660*

– 2 piece + spare tip. Professionally re-finished with hook digs in cork handle. Walnut reel seat is rough. Original bag and labelled tube *$1430*

– 2 piece + spare tip, 4 oz with sliding band over walnut reel seat. Near mint $2750

7′ 6″ – 2 piece + spare tip, 3⅞ oz with screw up-locking reel seat. Very good condition $1320

– 2 piece + spare tip (one for 6 weight line and one for 5 weight line). Excellent condition in original bag $660

7′ 6″ – 3 piece + spare tip, 4³⁄₁₆ oz, dark cane rod with screw up-locking, over walnut reel seat, stylish plugs. 'Sold by Abercrombie & Fitch, New York'. Sparkling new condition with original paper handle covering. In bag, tag and tube *$9075*

7′ 6″ – 2 piece + spare tip trout rod. Appears to have been professionally refinished $715

7′ 2″ – 2 piece + spare tip, 2⅝ oz. Model #97 with cork reel seat, brown wraps tipped gold. Butt cap marked 'Sold by Abercrombie Fitch Co NY'. Except for some oxide finish wear on reel seat band and butt cap, the rod is mint, with bag, tab and tube $1710

– 2 piece + spare tip, 2⅝ oz fly rod with morticed wood reel seat and down-locking slide band. Mint with bag, tag and tube $1705

7′ 1″ – 2 piece + spare tip, 3 oz, Parabolic trout rod with sliding band down-locking wood reel seat. Near mint $4950

7′ 1″ – 2 piece Parabolic trout rod with standard cork reel seat. The tip appears original but ¼″ shorter than butt section. Near mint in bag and tube $2090

7′ – 2 piece + spare tip, Model 98 trout rod with original c1930 Model 98 taper for a #3 line. It has a sliding band down-locking wood reel seat. Mint in bag and tube $5500

7′ – 2 piece + spare tip, 3 oz, Model 98 with sliding band over walnut spacer reel seat and ferrule plug. Mint in original bag, tag and tube *$7700*

6′ 6″ – 2 piece + spare tip, 2½ oz, Model 96 trout rod with morticed reel seat and sliding band. Butt cap marked 'Sold by Abercrombie & Fitch Co NY'. Pristine unused condition with bag, tag and tube $1760. Two

JIM PAYNE RODS
583 Rare tiny Payne Banty trout rod, 4′ 4″, 2 piece with spare tip, 1⅝ oz. Sold for $6600
584 Jim Payne Model 98 trout rod, 7′, 2 piece with spare tip. Sold for $5500
585 Payne 7′ 1″ Parabolic trout rod, 2 piece with spare tip, 3 oz. Sold for $4950
586 Payne 7′ 1″ Parabolic trout rod, 2 piece. Sold for $2090

583
584
585
586

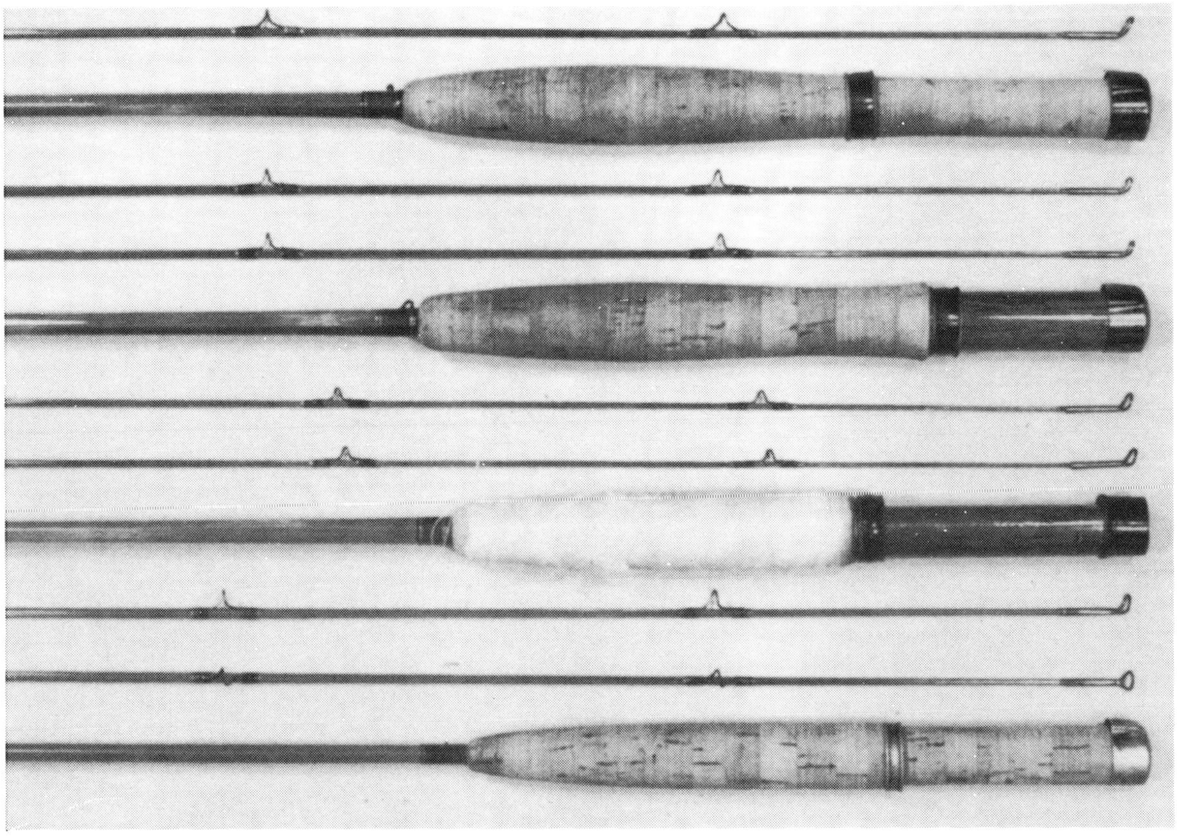

similar rods sold for $1760 and $2530

6′ 6″ – 2 piece trout rod authentically re-finished by Leonard. Some reel seat wear otherwise mint $880

6′ 6″ – 2 piece + spare tip, 2½ oz, Model No 96, marked on the butt cap 'Sold by Abercrombie & Fitch, New York'. Near mint in bag, tag and tube *$8250*

4′ 4″ – 2 piece + spare tip, 1⅝ oz with dainty sliding band down-locking cork reel seat and ferrule plug $6,600

4′ 4″ – 2 piece + spare tip, 1½ oz 'Banty', trout fly rod with dainty sliding band down-locking over cork reel seat and ferrule plug. Mint in original bag with tag and tube *$5500*

E F PAYNE

13′ 2″ – 3 piece + spare tip, with German silver fittings and cork grip stamped 'E F Payne, Sold by Abercrombie & Fitch' $100

6′ – 2 piece + spare tip, 1½ oz, assessed as Model 26. Marked on butt cap 'E F Payne Co Makers' and 'Sold by Abercrombie & Fitch Co New York'. Condition excellent except for a few chips to varnish $2970

E C POWELL

9′ 6″ – 3 piece + spare tip marked 'E C Powell Maker Marysville, Cal' and No 1932986. Condition good except cork handle chewed up $302

9′ 4″ – 2 piece + spare tip 'Hollow Built', condition good in original bag $187

WILLIAM READ & SONS, BOSTON

9′ 6″ – 3 piece + spare tip 'Imperial', with German silver fittings. Butt piece re-finished and some wraps missing $33

REED & GILDNER

10′ – 3 piece (tip is short), marked 'Reed & Gildner, Makers, 510, Girard Ave, Phila' $275

DAVE SCHOCH

7′ – One piece 'Nodeless' trout fly rod marked 'ZXZ' $495

D SCRIBNER & SON

15′ – 3 piece + 2 spare tips and extra mid-section marked 'D Scribner & Son, Makers, St John NB'. A two-handed light salmon rod in very good condition $247

15′ & 11′– 2 piece (11′) and 3 piece + spare tip (15′) greenheart spliced joint fly rods (two) $220

J F SEGER

8′ – 3 piece early greenheart wood surf casting rod marked 'J F Seger, Makers, Ashbury Park, NJ', with rattan handle and foregrip $60

SCHAER

8′ – 3 piece + spare tip with closely spaced intermediate windings, agate stripper guide and German silver fittings in fine wood box $605

SHAKESPEARE

6′ 6″ – 2 piece + spare tip with green wraps tipped red and German silver metal parts. The sliding band stamped 'Shakespeare 1233-B-6½, Made in USA, Pat 1,410906' (1924 patent year). Mint $550

BOB SMITH

14′ – 3 piece + spare tip (one 3″ shorter). A two-handed Calcutta cane rod marked 'Bob Smith Boston' and 'May 15 1906' patent $66

F E THOMAS

14′ – 3 piece + spare tip (one 2″ shorter) 'Browntone Special'. Very good condition with bag and tip tube $220

13′ 6″ – 3 piece + spare tip 'Special', with 'Pat Stamp June 19/13'. Condition very good, re-varnished $110

10′ – 3 piece + spare tip 'Special', with extension butt and 1913 patent. German silver locking reel seat $88

9′ 6″ – 3 piece + spare tip 'Special', with German silver locking sliding band reel seat in good original condition $154

– 3 piece + spare tip, fly rod with German silver reel seat. Very good condition, in bag and tube $187

– 3 piece + spare tip fly rod (one tip shorter, the other has spinning rod tip top guide. Re-finished $60

9′ 3″ – 3 piece + spare tip 'The Bangor Rod', with German silver butt cap, screw down-locking reel seat, excellent condition with bag and tube $275

– 3 piece + spare tip Bangor fly rod. Mint in bag and tube $192

9′ – 3 piece + spare tip 'Dirigo', with German silver sliding band reel seat. Except for ageing varnish and one missing guide, condition excellent $220

– Matched set of Dirigo trout fly rods, both stamped on butt cap serial No 31. Both 3 piece + spare tip and mint in bag and case $330

– 3 piece + spare tip. Some varnish roughness $66

– 3 piece + spare tip. Varnish roughness and butt re-finished $132

– 3 piece + 3 spare tips 'Dirigo', mid-section is one inch short but looks original. Condition good $165

– 3 piece + spare tip (one 1½″ shorter) 5⅝ oz. A 1944 dated Certificate of Registration signed by Leon Thomas accompanied the rod and states 'H 16 serial No'. Condition excellent with ferrule plugs, bag and tube $110

– 3 piece + spare tip (one 1¼″ shorter) 'Dirigo', one guide missing and a repair wrap, otherwise good $77

– 3 piece + spare tip, 'F E Thomas; Bangor Maine 9050', marked in ink on shaft and 'Browntone', on reel seat, condition excellent $110

– 3 piece + spare tip 'Special', mahogany rod with sliding cork reel seat, half-Wells grip and German silver fittings, condition very good with bag and tube $797

8′ 6″ – 3 piece + broken spare tip 'Special', with screw down-locking wood reel seat, heavy varnish overcoat, otherwise condition good $99

– 3 piece + 2 spare tips (both shorter) 'Special', with German silver reel seat and agate stripper guide. Very good $110

8′ – 3 piece + spare tip, fresh water trolling rod with a 1944 date Certificate of Registration signed by Leon Thomas serial No E26 and weight 7½ oz. Screw locking wood reel seat. Condition very good $132

– 3 piece + spare tip 'Special', trout rod with a screw down-locking reel seat. Excellent *$1155*

– 3 piece + spare tip 'Browntone Special', with a few replaced wraps otherwise excellent, in bag and tube $357

– 3 piece + 2 spare tips (different lengths), 'Dirigo' salmon and togue trolling rod $99

8′ – 3 piece + spare tip 'Browntone', trout fly rod, very good, in bag and tube $880

7′ – 2 piece 'Special' with pronounced swelled butt and signature wraps. The reel seat of morticed wood and sliding band. Condition mint in Leonard bag and tube $465

7′ – 2 piece + spare tip trout rod. Almost mint in original bag and labelled tube $2,475

7′ – 2 piece + spare tip, 3⅛ oz, 'Browntone Special' trout rod with sliding band over walnut reel seat and maroon wraps. About excellent *$825*

6′ 9″ – 2 piece + 2 spare tips (one ¾″ short, the other ½″ short). 'Special' trout rod with sliding band over walnut reel seat and agate stripper guide. Wraps suggest the tips have been re-wrapped and some varnish fine age craze lines *$1100*

6′ 8″ – 2 piece + spare tip, 2¼ oz, 'Special' trout rod with maple morticed reel seat and sliding band. Wrapped in red silk and straight and tight. Flaws – chips in varnish and hair line crack at base of the tip $99

THOMAS & THOMAS

7′ – 2 piece + spare tip, serial No 2173, custom made 'Paradigm'. Built to Leonard's Model 38H tapers at the owners request. Excellent used condition *$1155*

– One piece, 3 oz, 3 weight line rod marked 'Sans Pareil'. A beautiful dark wood reel seat spacer and tipped translucent tan wraps. Excellent plus condition *$1705*

TROWBRIDGE

11′ – 3 piece + spare tip (one shorter), 'Trowbridge Boston' black bass rod in Calcutta cane with moulded hard rubber handle $110

USLAN

8′ – 2 piece + spare tip, impregnated 5-sided trout rod,marked 'C3', with sliding band over cork locking reel seat $550

VARNEY

9′ 6″ – 3 piece + spare tip with Varney's 1890 ferrule patent and marked 'Geo. I. Varney, Montague City, Mass.' Mid-section re-finished and tip set $192

EDWARD VOM HOFE

16′ – Seven strip, two-handed salmon rod, 3 piece + spare tip (3″ short) and extra mid-section. German silver reel seat and fittings $312

7′ – No 6 salt water, cane wrap, with German silver fittings $75

C E WHEELER

10′ 6″ – 3 piece + spare tip (repaired), extra mid-section 'C E Wheeler Maker' marked on reel seat $198

R L WINSTON

8′ – 2 piece + spare tip marked '8′ 4 oz #1943'

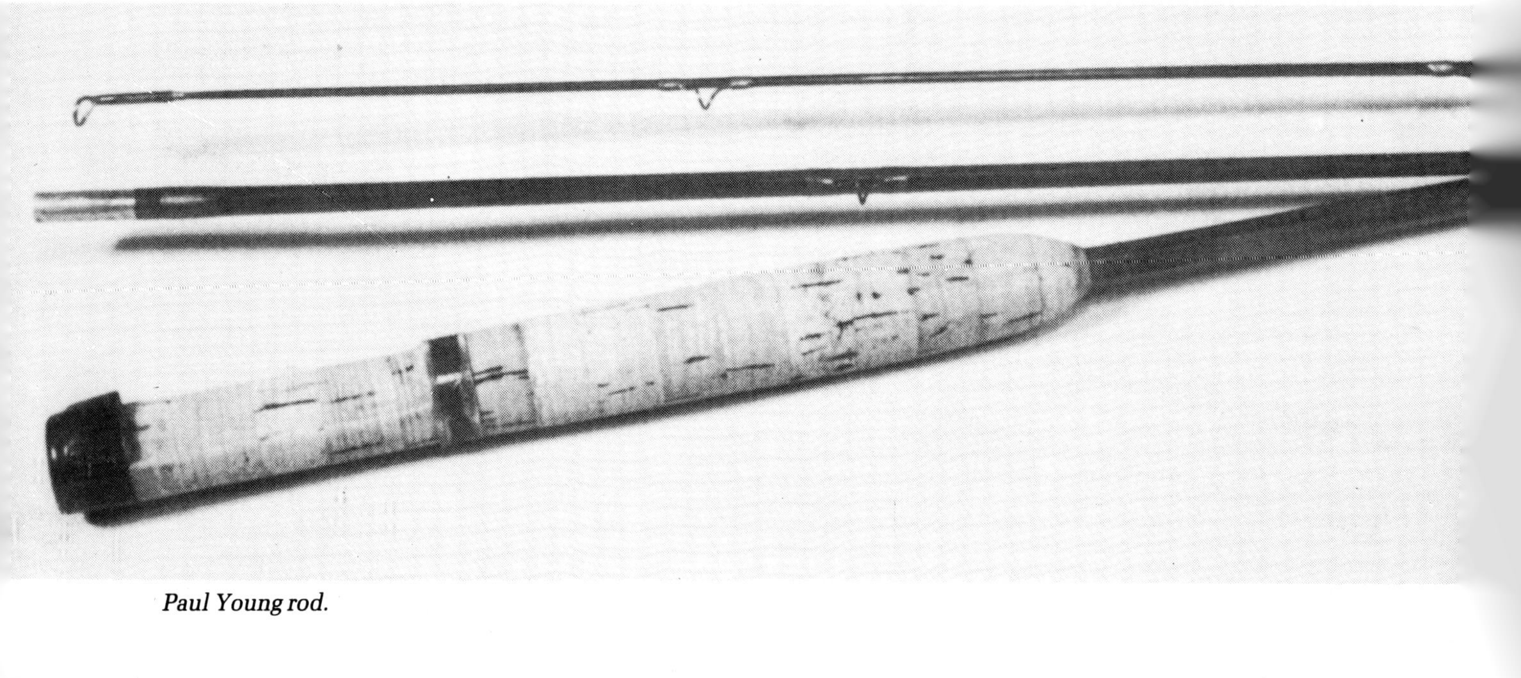

Paul Young rod.

with rosewood reel seat. New, in bag and tube $522

PAUL H YOUNG

9′ – 2 piece + spare tip, 6 oz, serial No 3927, 'Bobbie Doerr' with removable extension butt, Super-Z ferrules and screw down-locking reel seat. Excellent *$1650*

8′ 6″ – 3 piece + spare tip fly rod marked 'A Paul H Young Co Rod 'Parabolic' 17, 8′ 6″, 5½ oz' and Serial No 4596. Near mint, in bag and tube $550

8′ 3″ – 2 piece + 2 spare tips, 4.24 oz, experimental trout rod made for Harry Noll (marked on rod). It has screw down-locking cork reel seat. Condition excellent, in bag and tube $990

8′ – 2 piece + spare tip, 4 oz, 'Para 15' trout rod with wet and dry fly tips. The rod has Super-Z ferrules, screw down-locking cork reel seat and tan wraps. Cork handle soiling *$2200*

– 2 piece + spare tip, 3.85 oz, 'Parabolic 15' for 'HDH-HDG' line with an invisible wrap on one tip and the other tip which has an invisible wrap is broken in half *$522*

– 2 piece + spare tip (one 2″ short) 'Don West Dream' trout rod with black wraps. Re-done *$715*

7′ 6″ – 2 piece + spare tip, 2½ oz, Serial No 4373 'Perfectionist' with Super-Z ferules and tan wraps. Mint *$3850*

– 2 piece + spare tip, 2.79 oz, Serial No 4009, not with Super-Z ferrules but tan wraps. One tip broken otherwise in near mint condition *$1650*

7′ 6″ – 2 piece spare tip, 'Special' 7½′, 3½ oz, morticed cork sliding band reel seat with half-Wells handle. Except for a broken snake guide and need to re-set the butt section ferrule, condition excellent $181

7′ 6″ – 2 piece, 2.55 oz, 'Perfectionist' trout rod. Rod shaft marked in Young's writing 'HEH Paul H Young Co Detroit, Maker' and bears date 'Xmas 1954'. Mint condition in bag and tube $4070

7′ – 2 piece + spare tip, 2.72 oz, 'Little Giant' trout rod. Mint, in bag and tube $5170

7′ – 2 piece + spare tip, Serial No 3809 'Princess', 2.9 oz, with sliding band reel seat $7150

6′ 3″ – 2 piece + spare tip, 1¾ oz, 'Midge' trout fly rod. Mint, in bag and tube $3300

6′ 6″ – 2 piece rod, Serial No 2218, 'Little Giant 6′ 6″, 2.78 oz, HDH'. It has old gold wraps, blued Super-Z ferrules, cigar grip with thumb depression and a cork reel seat with blued nickel silver slide band. Only three of this model/size made in 1956. *$6600*

6′ 3″ – 2 piece + spare tip, 1.7 oz, Serial No 1990, 'Midge' trout rod. Re-finished by Bob Summers *$2750*

6′ 3″ – 2 piece + spare tip trout rod marked 'Midge 6′ 3″. 1¾ oz A Paul H Young Co Rod'. Condition mint in original bag $2860

The author, Graham Turner, pictured with part of his large collection of fishing tackle

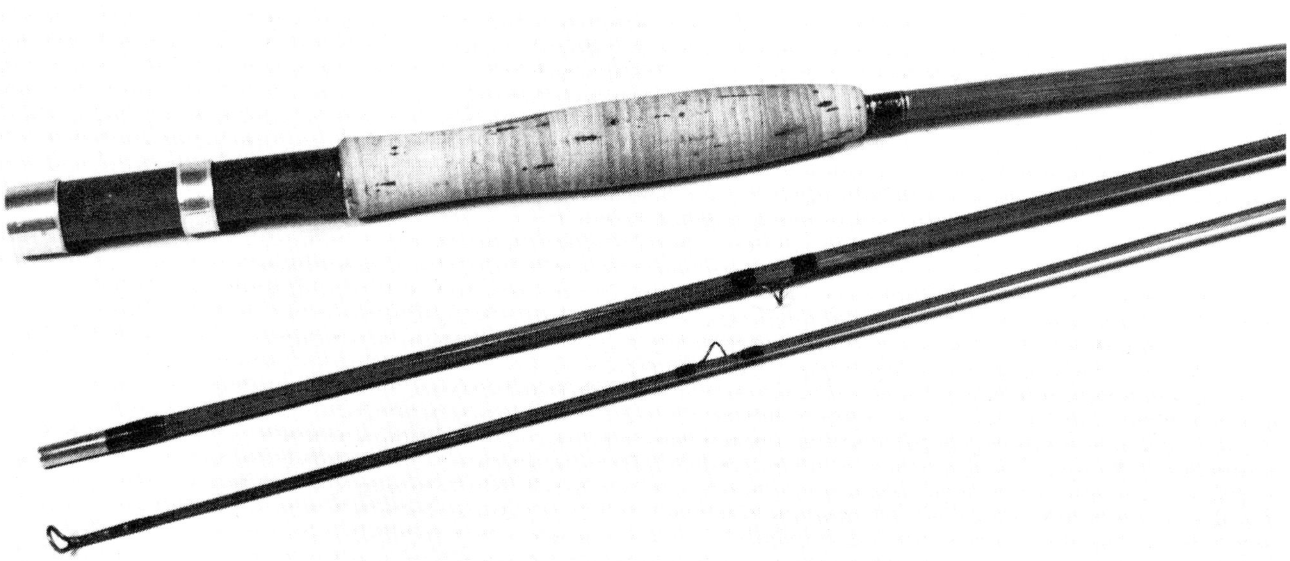

H S Gillum, 6′, 2 piece 1¾ oz Trout Rod. Sold for $19250

AMERICAN LURES

Names and descriptions of lures are taken from catalogues

ABBEY & IMBRIE
GLOWBOY MINNOW
- Luminous rod inside a glass tube $88
- New in early 'Patent Applied For' marked box c1920 $275

ARBOGAST
TIN LIZ SUNFISH
- Large, with glass eyes (one has lines), metal lure $198, $313, $385, $275

ARNTZ
MICHIGAN LIFE-LIKE MINNOW
- 3¾″ long in original box $770

T H BATES
SERPENTINE SPINNER
- Marked ' T H Bates Patent, June 12th 1855', also size '2'. This 2¼″ long hollow body lure with spiral wrapped fin is made of copper and in excellent condition $330
- Marked '3' is 2″ long and in excellent tarnished condition $385
- Marked '4' is 1½″ long and made of brass and silver. Excellent condition $407
- Marked 'T H Bates, Patent, June 12, 1855' and the size '3' $632

A F BINGENHEIMER
BINGS'S NON-WEEDLESS MINNOW
- Made around 1910. Metalized in gold marked 'Nemahbin Minnow'. Condition fine $450

BONAFIDE MANUFACTURING CO
BONAFIDE ALUMINIUM MINNOW
- Ultra-rare by Van De Car. The 1907 patent papers show Hiram H Passage which he assigned to George E Van De Car of the Bonafide Manufacturing Co $8800

HENRY C BRUSH
FLOATING TROLLING SPOON
- Brass, kidney shaped, red paint on underside. Condition fine $55
- Patent August 22-'76, Brush Mills, NY. Silver over brass, red float. Condition prime $65
- Floating bait marked 'H C Brush, Brush's Mills, NY. Float Pat. Aug. 22-'76', on the 2¼″ silver spoon $154
- Early 1876 patent spoon with flyer. Marked on its brass blade 'H C Brush, Brush Mills, NY. Float Pat. Aug. 22-'76'. Considered by many to be America's first wood body lure. Condition excellent with red body $330

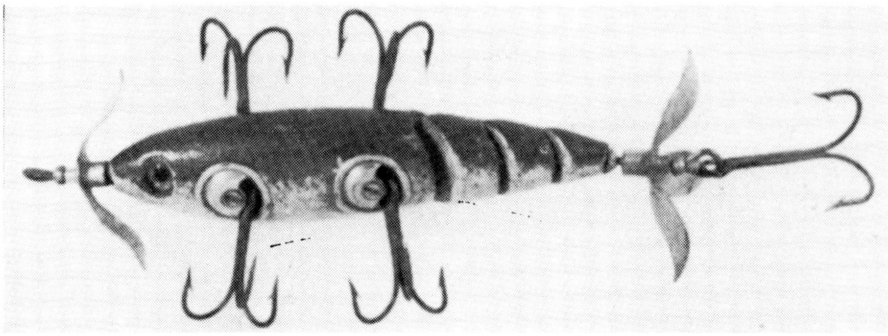

Arntz Mitchigan Life-Like Minnow. Sold for $770

J T BUEL
- 4½″ – Trolling squid with heavy double hooks, body revolves on shaft, with rusty hooks $70
- 4″ – Metal hollow squid marked 'Buel, Whitehall NY 3/0' $198
- 3½″ – No 1/0 arrowhead spinner in its original box $302
- 2½″ – Nation's first patented fishing lure marked 'J T Buel's Patent 1852, Whitehall NY, No 3' Excellent $121
- 2⅛″ – Earliest patented lure, hollow body with silver top and brass underside. Marked 'J T Buel's Patent 1852, J Warrin, NY. Sole Maker 3' $220
- 2⅛″ – Early Buel's spinners (two). Kidney shaped nickel silver over copper with red paint on underside. Stamped 'J T Buel Patent 1852 and April 22 1856, Whitehall NY'. The other 'J T Buel – No 2, Whitehall NY' $30
- Buel's spinners (three) including one marked 'No 1 J T Buel's Patent April 6th 1852, Whitehall NY' (no shaft or hook): another 'J T Buel's Patent 1852 – No 4' (treble hook missing): another 'No 5, J T Buel, Whitehall NY' $80
- Spoons (three) including a No 1, No 2, No 3 $50

CHAPMAN
ALLURE NO 1
- 2⅛″ – An open double scalloped wing. Very good $70
- 2″ – Metal lure marked 'Chapman & Son, Theresa, NY. Allure 1' with original swivel $159

ALLURE NO 2
- Similar to No 1 but not silver plated $75

NO 2 BASS
- Unusual shaped wing spinner $80

1000 ISLAND BAIT NO 7
- Artist's palette shaped spinner, silver plated over

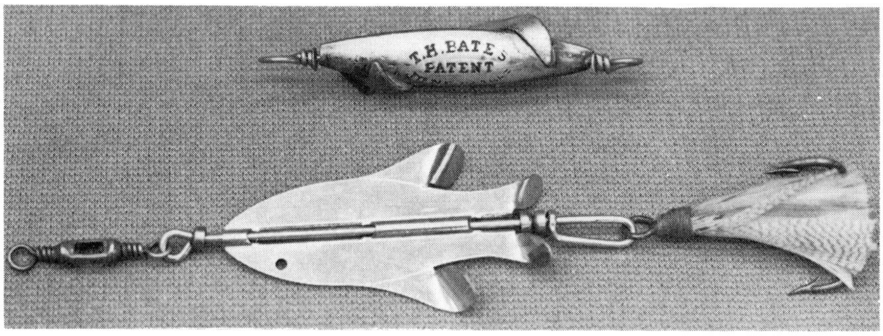

Bate's Patent Spinner (top) and Edgren Minnow

copper. Condition fine $60

PICKEREL
– Bait No 5 with silver top side and all its original red paint underside and a weedless feathered treble hook. Condition excellent $202

PROPELLER BAIT
2¾″ – Unusual brass lure in almost mint condition $440

HOLLOW BODY LURE
– Metal brass lure marked 'Chapman & Son, Theresa, NY'. Condition very good $126
– Winged hollow body lure marked 'Chapman & Son, Theresa, NY, 3' Pat May 4th 1870'. Silver plated on one side and the other brass. Condition good with early Chapman swivel $209
4″ – Long brass hollow Muskie bait marked 'W D Chapman, Theresa NY Patent May 4th 1870 1/0'. $412

SPINNERS
– Two spinners marked 'W D Chapman, Theresa, NY' also '3' and '4' the other $467
1⅝″ – Arrowhead shaped black bass spinner marked 'W D Chapman, Theresa, NY 4'. Nickel plated $159
1⅞″ – Kidney shaped spinner marked 'Chapman & Son, Theresa, NY 2'. A spoon with black outside and red inside $137

CLEWELL
SNAKER BAIT
4¼″ – New, in original box $990

EDWARD COLLINS
BUCK HAIR MOUSE
4¼″ – $88

COMSTOCK
COMSTOCK FLYING HELGRAMITE
– Rare, marked 'H Comstock, Fulton, NY Pat. Jan. 30, '83'. Signs of wear and finish wear on the nose, one hook slightly damaged and two of tiny glass wing beads are gone otherwise very good condition $9075

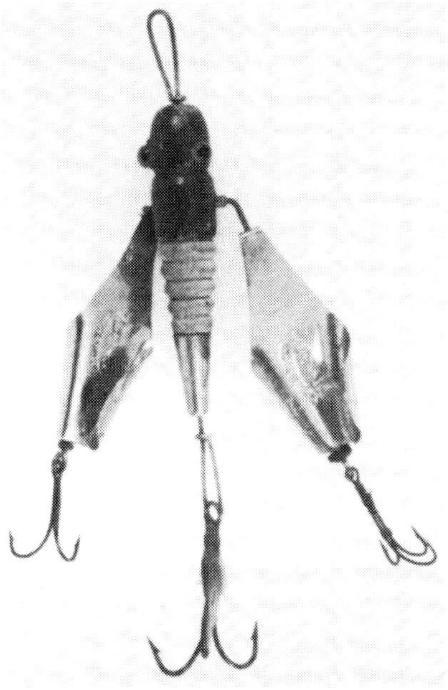

Rare Comstock Flying Helgramite marked 'H Comstock, Fulton, NY, Pat. Jan. 30 '83', length 2⅜″. Sold for $9075

COMSTOCK 1883
TYPE 1 FLYING HELGRAMITE
2⅞″ – Rare. This specimen has a body with a deep red mahogany finish. The lure has seen use with several bent or broken hook tips, light body scratches and evidence that the hook and lure tie 'snaps' have been opened. Some moth damage to treble hook feathers otherwise very good $3850

TYPE II FLYING HELGRAMITE
2⅜″ – Marked 'H Comstock, Fulton, NY, Pat Jan 30 '83'. The body with green front and natural wood rear section, metal tail cap and glass eyes. Some wear on nose otherwise excellent condition $6050

CREEK CHUB
BABY BEETLE
– #6000. Gold and black with black bead eyes. Condition excellent $38
– In yellow with green/black spots wings, flap lip. Condition very good $49

BASS BUG WIGGLER
1¼″ – #1100. Gold bug finish, painted eyes. Condition above excellent $99

BABY CHUB WIGGLER
– #200. A rare variation with two double belly hooks and tail treble hooks. Early chub scale with hand painted gills and glass eyes. Early flat cup rigs, plain lip and double line tie. Very good $44

BABY WIGGLERS
– (Two). Both have glass eyes, plain lip, flat cup rig, double line tie. Condition good $38

BEETLE
– In black with with red wings/yellow spots, bead eyes, improved lip. Condition very good $66, $49

BEETLE
– #3850. Orange and red with black spots, black bead eyes, flat lip. Condition mint $77, $104

BIG BOMBER
– #6700. Golden shiner scale. Big ding on back, otherwise very good plus $22

BIG BUG WIGGLER
– In red and white bug finish $220

BUG WIGGLER
– No 1400, in bug finish. Mint $137
– No 1400, in red and white $99
– In bug finish $88
1⅜″ – Fly Rod Lure in red and white bug finish. Almost mint $110

CHUB SUCKER
– #3900. Natural sucker scale finish and glass eyes. Condition good $132

CREEK BUG WIGGLER (1100)
1¼″ – Bug finish. Excellent $110

CREEK AND RIVER LURE
2¾″ – This glass-eyed, green back and red side scale finish plug has 3 double hooks. Condition very good $385

CRIPPLED MINNOW F90 FLY ROD
1¾″ – With flexible (fibre) fins and tail. Long wood body in silver flash finish. Almost mint $275

DARTERS
- (Four). One #2000 'S' spinnered Darter, one #4900 Jointed Darter, one #8000 Midget Darter, one #8000 D B Concave Belly Darter $33

FLY ROD CRAWDAD
- #F-50. Natural crab finish, squirrel hair claws are moth eaten otherwise excellent. Deluxe Wagtail Chub #800 in early chub scale finish glass eyes, hand painted gills, plain lip and tail, flat cup rig, double line tie and single removable hooks. Both sold as one lot for $49

DINGERS
- (Two) Both have glass eyes, one is #5600, the other #6100 Midget Dinger. Condition mint $27

DING BATS
- (Two) Both have glass eyes, one #5100 in pike scale, new in box, the other #5200 Midget Ding Bat in frog finish. Condition mint $27
- (Two) One #5400 Surface Ding Bat, the other a 1950s #5300P (plastic). Condition mint $16

FEATHER CASTING MINNOW
- #F-10, ⅝ oz, chub scale, painted eyes. Condition very good $88, $209, $143

FIN TAIL SHINER
- #2100. White with glass eyes and red cloth/rubber fins. Condition very good $77

FLIP FLAP
- #4400. White with red head, glass eyes. Mint condition in 1934 box $60
- (4402) White and red. Condition mint $71

GAR MINNOW
- #2900. Green gar scale, glass eyes. Has a gouge ⅜″ on left side otherwise excellent $115

5¼″ – No 2900, new in box. This classic in natural gar finish has glass eyes and 3 treble hooks $467
- In natural gar scale finish with glass eyes, chip on belly weight. Condition very good $93
- In natural gar scale finish and early metal nose cap and glass eyes. Condition very good $71
- No 2920 in green gar scale finish with weights in the side. Condition excellent in box $159

GIANT PIKIE
- (Three) All new in boxes, one #800, one #833 and a Giant #6001 $55
- (Three) All new in boxes, one #818, one #834 and one #6006 $55

HUSKIE DING BAT
- #5300. Pike scale with glass eyes and hook marks. Condition very good $27, $38, $93

HUSKIE DINGER
- #6100 with glass eyes and metal head plate in pikie finish $49
- #5700. Silver flash finish, glass eyes, metal head plate, early rigs. Very good $55

HUSKIE INJURED MINNOW
- #3500. Early perch scale, glass eyes, heavy duty screw eye rigs. Some hook digs otherwise very good condition $55

HUSKY MUSKY
- Jointed plugs (two) with glass eyes. One blue mullet scale finish. One rainbow finish $170
- No 600 in natural chub scale finish. Some varnish age lines $66
- #600. Early perch scale, glass eyes, pug nose, heavy duty screw-eye rig, name on lip, double line ties. Condition very good $27

HUSKIE PLUNKER
- #5800. Pike scale and glass eyes. New in box $55
- Blue mullet with glass eyes. Mint $60

JIGGER
- #4100. Dace scale finish, glass eyes. Condition very good $82
- In frog finish, glass eyes. Condition very good $82
- In black and white. Almost mint $121
- In red side scale finish with glass eyes. Condition very good $44

Rare unknown model, only 1″ long. Sold for $412

LUCKY MOUSE
- #3600. Grey with black bead eyes. Condition mint $77

MUSKY WIGGLE FISH
- Early perch scale, glass eyes, heavy duty screw eye rigs, flat lip and double line tie. Belly hook drag marks. Condition very good $88
- In gold scale finish with glass eyes. One eye broken and deep drags on belly $55

OPEN MOUTH SHINER
- #500. Early dace scale, flat cup rig and painted eyes. Condition very good. Sold together with Wig-L-Rind #S-10 in mint condition $38

PLUNKER BASS BUG
- with black body and yellow hair. Excellent in box $104

PLUNKING DINGER
- #6200. Pike scale with glass eyes. Mint $27

POLLY WIGGLE
- #1700. Spotted pollywog finish, and black bead eyes. Condition excellent $110
- In natural pollywog finish with weedguard and original cloth imitation pork rind $126
- With bead eyes in

pollywog finish without wire weedguard. Chipped at nose $49

POP-IT FLY ROD
– In brown bug finish $33, $55

RIVER RUSTLER
– #3700. Perch scale with glass eyes. Condition excellent $60

SALTWATER CHAMP
– #S-50. Chrome finish with one treble hook. Condition mint $27

SARASOTA
– #3300. Pike scale, glass eyes, 2 treble hooks. Condition good plus $143

SARASOTA 3314 SPECIAL
– Yellow with red and black spots, glass eyes. Condition mint $275

SILVERSIDES
– #1700. Silver flash finish, painted eyes, three treble hooks, cup rig. Condition very good $110

SKIPPER
– #4600. Pike scale finish with glass eyes. Sold together with Wiggle Fish #2405. Both in mint condition $27

SNOOK PLUNKER #7100
4¼″ – Blue mullet finish with glass eyes. Sold with similar lot. Condition very good $33
4¼″ – White with red head and glass eyes. Bucktail moth-eaten otherwise new in box $44

SUCKER #3900
– Grey sucker scale, glass eyes, early model. Condition very good $121
4¼″ – In natural sucker scale with glass eyes $165
– With glass eyes in natural blue sucker scale $154
– With glass eyes in natural yellow sucker scale $88

SURFSTER #7335
5¾″ – Old humpback style with glass eyes and purple eel finish. Condition excellent $27

SURFSTER #7234
4¼″ – Old brass humpback style in blue scale flash with glass eyes. Condition good $11

SURFSTER #7334
5¾″ – Pikie humpback with glass eyes. New in box $44

TINY TIM #6425
– In white scale finish with painted eyes. New in original box $22

UNDERWATER SPINNER MINNOW NO 1800
– In rainbow finish with glass eyes and 5 double hooks $330

WEED BUG
– #2800 in frog finish with glass eyes. Condition very good $88, another $66
– With yellow body, green wing and black spots and red bead eyes. Condition excellent $99

WEE DEE
– #4800 Green spotted frog with glass eyes. No wires otherwise very good condition $55
– In yellow with green wings and red front with glass eyes $154
– In frog finish in original box $209
– In frog finish with two chips $187

WIGGLER #100
– White/red head, no eyes, round nose, name on lip and double line tie. Very good $33
– Early perch scale finish, glass eyes and painted gills, pug nose, flat head, plain lip, washer hook, rig and double line tie. Condition very good $35
– Early red side scale, glass eyes, round nose and flat head. Name on lip, flat cup rig and double line tie. Condition excellent in box $71

POP DEAN

FROG MUSKIE LURE
8″ – With jointed legs, protruding eyes, leather feet and 4 hooks $880

MASTER BAIT
10″ – Double jointed large Muskie, with glass eyes and carved gill detail $330
6″ – Rainbow Trout Baby Master Bait. Reported to be the only one made. Mint $275

DECKER

DECKER-WOBBLE PLUG
2⅞″ – In aluminium paint with large brass prop, external washer-type lead tail weight, an internal weight, screw eye and conical washer hook hangers $550

ANS B DECKER UNDERWATER PLUG
3¼″ – Long wood body with heavy gauge brass props and grey enamel finish. Condition mint $691

ANS B DECKER TOP WATER BAIT
3¼″ – $104
3½″ – $66

WOODEN SPINNER BAIT
2⅝″ – Rare wooden spinner bait with props, marked 'Decker' $275

DETROIT BAIT CO

BASS CALLER PLUG
– New in box $38

Rare Ans. B Decker Underwater Plug, length 3¼″. Sold for $687

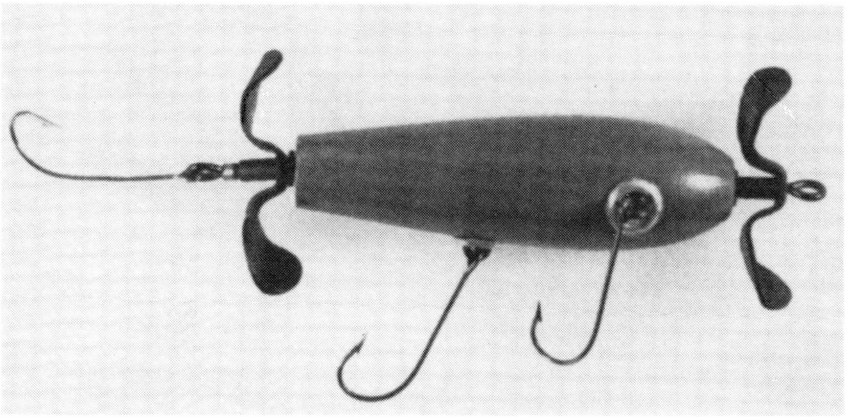

DETROIT GLASS MINNOW TUBE COMPANY
GLASS MINNOW TUBE
3¼" – $412, $467, $375

DICKENS
DUPLEX DARTER
3½" – With red wood body and white head in box $121

JOHN DINEENS
1911 SPINNING MINNOW
– A form of bent copper shaped like a fish with a weedless type feathered tail hook. Minor chippings in the paint. Condition fine $275
3½" – Spinning metal minnow c.1911, marked 'Pat. A'p'd For'. Nickel plated with red inside $49

JIM DONALY
CATCHUMMBIG BAIT
– (or Redfin Floater) White with red collar and anal fin marks and Jersey rigging. Condition very good $451, another $605

REDFIN FLOATER
2⅞" – In yellow with black markings. Condition very good $71

WOW
– With white body and red/black hand painted decorations. Condition excellent $104, another $88

REDFIN FLOATER COLLAR TYPE BAIT
4" – Rare. Only known example of this large size lure in white with red collar and screw eye hook hangers. Excellent condition $330
2⅜" – Rare, excellent $302

DARIUS DITTY, ELMROCK, PA (1912 to 1950s)
DUCK MUSKIE LURE
4" – Hand-made. Excellent $330

EDGREN
MINNOW
– Patent No 760028. A German silver fish shaped lure which spins on centre shaft. Mint $40

FROGS
– Six old rubber frogs. Conditions vary $209

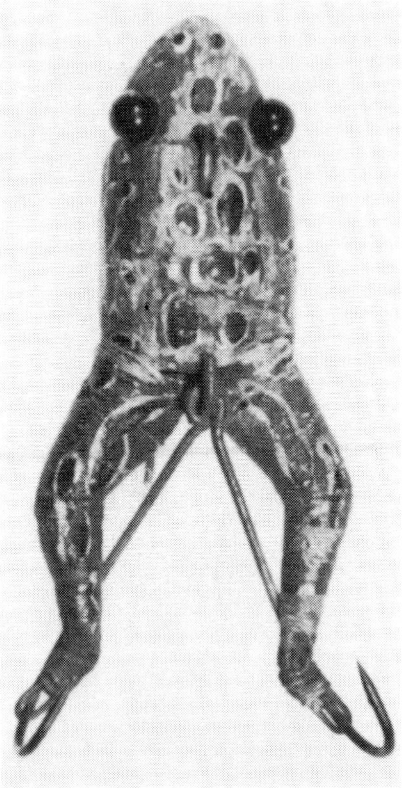

Harris Cork Frog, length 3". Sold for $1100

GEE WHIZ
GEE WHIZ FROG LURE
– Appears wood composition with rubber movable legs. Condition excellent $110, $71

GREEN
GREEN'S PATENT METAL BAIT
3¼" – Long brass lure retaining virtually all hand painted finish $33

GREGORY
– Metal lure marked 'Gregory' and patent stamp denoting April 18th 1879 with 3" hollow half-body and centre shaft with red painted weight and detail engraving $308

J HANSON
MUSKEGON SPOON JACK MINNOW
4¾" – Rare (c1910). A white minnow with large single spoon type front prop, glass eyes and 5 treble hooks. Enamel faults $302

HARKAUF
BUCKTAIL WOODEN MINNOW
2¾" – Prohibitively rare c1904, stamped 'The Harkauf' $990

C R HARRIS
FEATHERBONE MINNOW
– In original box marked 'Hand-Made C R Harris, 358, Ontario St, Chicago Ill' (hitherto unknown address). Only known specimen $1870

CORK FROG
3" – Patented in 1897 and hand made and painted life-like with large glass black eyes and painted eyelids. Condition excellent $1430, $1100

Featherbone Minnow by CR Harris, 358 Ontario St, Chicago, Ill., length 3¼". Sold for $1870

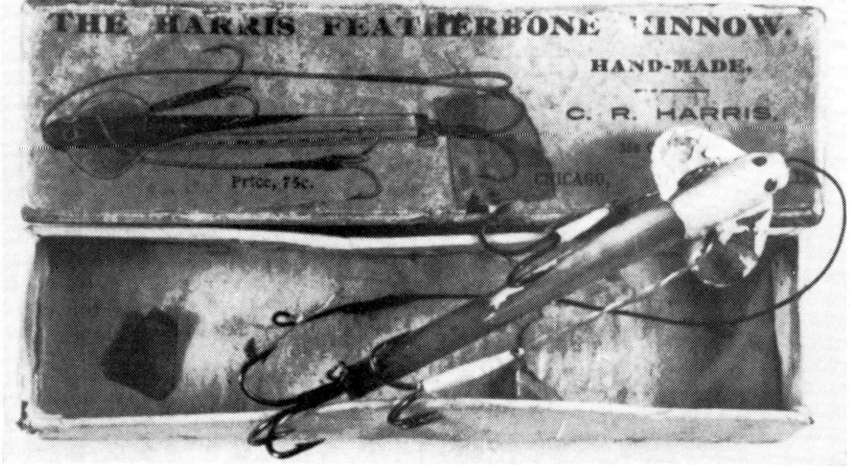

THE HASKELL MINNOW was made by Riley Haskell of Painesville Ohio and based on his patent of September 20th 1859 described as a 'trolling bait for catching fish'.

In July 1987 a Haskell Minnow was sold by Richard Oliver Gallery for $9240 and as a result of the publicity on television, radio and in the press, other examples were found and came to auction.

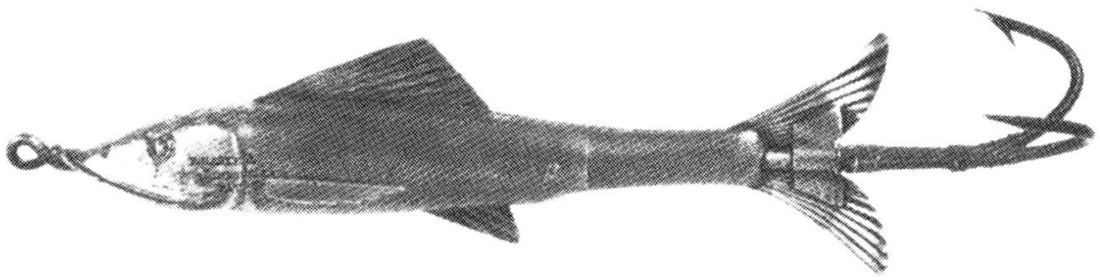

A 6″ example sold for $14,850 in February 1989

Extremeley rare and early Haskell Minnow marked 'R Haskell, Painesville, O. Pat'd Sep'd 20 1859'. Size 4½″ – Sold for $9240 (July 1987)

A 3⅜″ example sold for $22,000 in June 1988

A 3½″ example sold for $20,350 in February 1988

HAYNES

PEARL CASTING MINNOW

– c1907 with long mother of pearl body and German silver front wings $55

HEDDON

SAMPLE SET

– Important 1916 set, comprised of two cases containing 70 plugs. Many were mounted at the factory without hooks to save space. The Black Sucker was found loose which probably caused some varnish marks $13,750

ARTISTIC MINNOW No 50

– c1905. The sienna-yellow crackle back minnow has Heddon marked nickeled prop, glass eyes, hand painted gill marks and bucktail treble hook. Almost mint $187

1¾″ – With rare original wood casting weight. The sienna yellow crackle back plug has gold plated hardware and gill marks $82, $192

BABY VAMP #7400

– (Two) Both have glass eyes and L-rigs. One is shiner scale, the other pike scale. Condition very good $16

BASSER #8500

– (Five) With glass eyes and L-rigs. One frog scale, two shiner scale, one pike scale and one rainbow scale. Condition good to very good $77

– In rainbow finish with L-rigs and glass eyes. Condition excellent $16

BIG MARY

4″ – With glass eyes and L-rigs (two) $154

BLACK SUCKER #1300

– A very scarce Heddon classic. Some varnish chipping and a small gash on the left side, otherwise very good condition $550

– Some chipping and two hooks replaced. Condition very good $522

BUBBLING BUG FLY ROD LURE

1⅞″ – In original box, $176

1⅝″ – $176

CRAB WIGGLER

– (Three) Condition good $27

– (Four) Condition fair to very good $27

CRAZY CRAWLERS #2100

– (Two) Condition mint $38

– (Two) Condition mint and excellent $11

DARTING ZARA

3¾″ – Having the rare Creek Chub yellow with green and red spots finish. This glass eyed bait has Heddon two-piece hook hangers and plated hooks $154

DEEP DIVING WIGGLER #1600

– L-rigs, 4 slant head, pig tail line guide. White with red and green-spots. Condition generally good with varnish chips $27, another in good condition $99, another with chips $66

– In white with red head, L-rig, and inch-worm line tie. Condition very good $38, $44, $77

DEEP DIVING WIGGLER No 1609B

4¼″ – In original box $121

DOWAGIAC MINNOW

– With L-rig, red with black decorations and hand-painted gills. Condition very good $82

No 107

– In original 1902 patent marked wooden box. A fancy early sienna-yellow crackle back minnow with glass eyes, hand painted gill marks and early cup rig hook hangers. Mint $632

No 20

2⅛″ – In white with red eye shadow, has glass eyes and cup rig hook hangers $220

DUMMY DOUBLE #1500

– Early cup (football) rig, 3 hook model (2 hooks missing), white body with red and green spots. Condition very good $286

– In original box with papers. Some hook rust otherwise near excellent $495

3¼″ – With 'Football' hook hangers. In green crackle back and hand painted gill marks. This plug has tiny chip on nose tip otherwise excellent plus $522

EXPERT SLOPE NOSE MINNOW

– A little later than the #647, with fatter body, nickel plated cap and cup, blue head, white body, collar with traces of red and retained by two pins. Condition very good $275

– No 200 with brass tail cap and hook cup. Narrow body bait is white with blue head and red (possibly added) collar, secured by two pins. Body has several age lines but all its varnish. Head has 3 small chips and a collar rub. In original box (poor condition) $385

4¼″ – In box with flyer. This red, white and blue lure is an important forerunner of the generations of 'collar' baits. It has a collar held in place by two pins. Minor chipping $412

FLAP TAILS

– (Two) One No 7050 RH, white with red head, painted eyes, in box with pocket catalogue. One No 7110, ¾″, white with red head, two piece rigs and glass eyes. Condition excellent $49

– (Two) One No 7050 Giant in blue herring scale, painted eyes. One No 7000 in perch scale, 4⅜″, 2 piece rigs and large glass eyes. Both in excellent condition $27

FLIPPER BAIT #140

– With glass eyes, L-rig, three small spots of yellow primer showing otherwise excellent plus $302

4″ – L-rig, glass eyes, shiner scale finish. Tiny chip at end of tail otherwise in mint condition $154

FLOAT VAMP SPOOK

– Early plastic. Silver scale, worn off one side but shiny condition $49

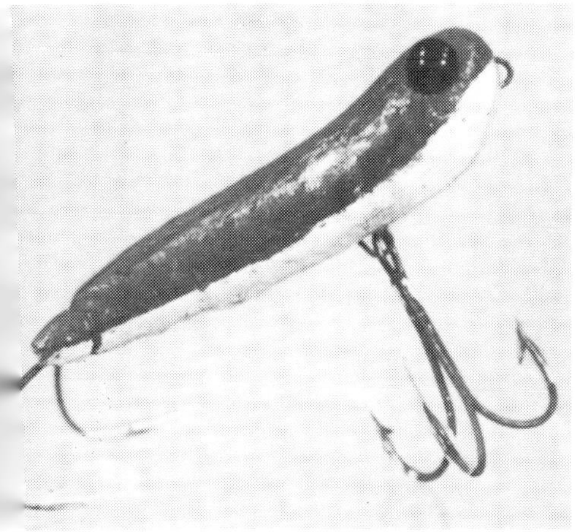

James Heddon Wooden Frog c1898

FROG

JAMES HEDDON WOODEN FROG c.1898
– Prior to forming the Heddon Tackle Company, James Heddon carved a few frogs for himself and friends. Only 8 authentic frog plugs are known to exist. This frog comes with authenticating papers from the Heddon factory. Other than some age wrinkles in the paint, the frog is in remarkably fine condition. It was sold by the Oliver Gallery on July 3rd 1985 for $5500

GAME FISHER PLUGS
– (Six) One large #5500, two are baby size #5400. Condition ranges from very good to excellent $55

GIANT JOINTED VAMP
7″ – In pike scale finish. The Muskie bait has heavy duty L-rigs and glass eyes $71

GIANT RUNT #7510
– With toilet seat rig, white bucktail, silver minnow with red eyes. Mint $220

GREAT VAMP No 7549
4¾″ – In Allen Stripley finish, glass eyes, and heavy duty toilet seat hook hangers. Condition very good $165

HEAVY CASTING MINNOW #175
– Rainbow with red hand painted gills. Heavy duty cups and trebles. Large unsigned props. Slight varnish flaking and ⅛″ of the paint is off the belly otherwise excellent $247

HUSKY FLAP TAIL
– In Allen Stripley finish, painted eyes, 'paper clip' hangers. Condition average plus $27

LIGHT CASTING MINNOW
2¾″ – No 10 with rare early long body. Moth damage to feathered single hook, hairline crack at tail and varnish chipping but original paint $302
2⅜″ – Glass eyes and hand painted gill marks. Chipped and some varnish flaking $231

LUCKY 13
4″ – Prototype from factory $99, $88

LUNY FROGS SERIES #3500
– (Three) Made of Pyralin and introduced in catalogue of 1927 $90

LUNY FROGS No 3509 BB
– With toilet seat rig. Mint $99
– New in box $66

MEADOW MOUSE #4000
– In grey mouse fur finish with bead eyes, leather tail and ears, two piece rigs. Condition excellent $38, another $28
– (Two) Condition very good $55
– (Four) Condition average $70

MINNOW No 0
3¼″ – In rare green spotted frog finish. This bait has L-rigs and glass eyes. Apart from a belly weight paint chip, in excellent condition $469

MINNOW No 100
– With fat body in frog finish, glass eyes and L-rigs. Hook rust and varnish chips $55
2⅝″ – With early sienna crackle back and red perch stripes $115
2⅝″ – In wooden box marked 105. The minnow is in near mint condition $181
2⅞″ – In wooden box. Some chips $209
2¾″ – In wooden box with flyer. In green crackle back finish with glass eyes, 2 cup belly weights and hand painted gill marks $330

MINNOW No 150
– 3 hooks, rare model $440
– Condition very good $49, $66
– (Four) Condition poor to very good $44
– (Two) Condition very good $38

MINNOW No 152
– Mint in original box with flyer $154

MOONLIGHT RADIANT PLUG
4″ – Rare plug with white glass eyes and deep nickel plated cup rigs. Unusual finish with tail hooks, drag mark. Condition excellent $660

No 500 MULTIPLE METAL MINNOW
2⅝″ – A production model of Heddon's second patent of 1907, nickel plated and copper eyelets. Condition excellent $660

MUSKOLLONGE MINNOW #700
4¾″ – 3 treble hook bait in rainbow finish with marked props, cup rigs, glass eyes and hand painted gill marks. Some varnish chipping $286

MUSKY FLAPTAIL
– (Two) One #7040 and one #7050. Condition fair $88

MUSKY MINNOW No 175
3½″ – Early one in green crackle back, in box. Excellent condition $550

MUSKY MINNOW No 700
– In fancy sienna back, yellow belly and red sides, three treble hooks, glass eyes and hand painted gill marks. One hook missing otherwise condition good $385

MUSKY SURFACE MINNOW #350
– With heavy duty toilet seat rig, no name on props. Green scale pike finish. Hook drag mark on chin otherwise excellent $286
– in unusual bronze/green

with black finish. One cracked glass eye and age lines otherwise new but may have been coated $165

4″ – In rare pike scale finish. This lure has large glass eyes, heavy duty toilet seat rigs and hooks, large unmarked props and red chin and eye shadows $357

MUSKIE VAMP
8″ – Made of layers of walnut, cedar and birch and in natural finish $93

NEAR SURFACE WIGGLER No 1700
– In white and red head, L-rig, glass eyes and inch-worm line tie. Has small rub on nose and age lines $99. Another sold for $49 and one with large chip on side realised only $11

PUNKIN SEEDS
– (Two) One wood No 740, a shore minnow in red and white, 2 piece rigs, line tie below mouth and one tiny plastic $38

RUSH TANGO
4⅜″ – Prototype plug. Very good $275

SALMON (DELUX) BASSER #8522
– Luminous with red eyes and tail, glass eyes. Mint, in box $55

SALTWATER SPECIAL
2⅛″ – White with silver glitter and pink chin and eye shadow plug with glass eyes and cup rig. Mint $247
3½″ – In red and white with glass eyes and toilet seat hook hanger. Condition excellent $192

SEA-RUNT
2½″ – No 61955 in box $66
2⅝″ – Wood plug $11

SIDE HOOK FLIPPER
4″ – Marked on props with retailer Abbey & Imbrie. The plug has glass eyes and L-rigs $330

S.O.S. MINNOW #170
– (Two) One in shiner scale and one in dace scale. Hook rust but otherwise excellent $66
– (Two) One #170, glass eyes L-rig, in red side dace finish. One #160, 2 piece rig in perch finish. Condition excellent $33

SPIN DIVER #3000
– L-rig, signed front prop, glass eyes and crab finish (perch). Condition very good. Sold for $110 and similar examples realised $121 and $93

SPOOK No 9100
– With glass eyes, toilet seat rigs, white with green and red, Pyralin plug c.1930 $55

SURFACE BAIT #200
– White/red nose, 2 piece rig, plain collar held on with three screws, marked 'Heddon 200 Surface' on belly. Shiny excellent condition $82
Similar example $66
– Cup-rig, unmarked, 2 pin flange collar, metal tail cap, frog finish. A few age lines otherwise mint $93
– White with blue head, marked 3 nail flanged nickel plated collar, tail cap and L-rigs. Some chips otherwise very good $38

SURFACE BAIT No 209F
– In frog finish and L-rig. Condition excellent in box $99

SURFACE MINNOW #300
3⅝″ – In white with red and green, L-rigs and glass eyes. Condition very good $77
3¾″ – Early cup rigs and hand painted gills, scarce sienna-yellow crackle back finish. Condition excellent $121, another $143
3¾″ – Fat body, glass eyes, two piece rigs, white with red and green spots. Rare 6 treble hook model. Condition good $110
3¾″ – In white and silver glitter. The fat body plug has glass eyes, hand painted gill marks, L-rig and double belly hook. Mint $302

SWIMMING MINNOW #800
3″ – Yellow body with green and red decorations. Tiny chip at the top of the tail otherwise excellent $605
2⅞″ – Factory prototype. The four-sided yellow plug has 4 belly weights, some original red hook paint and is marked in pencil. 'A Fine Darter'. Only 2 or 3 examples known. Condition excellent $522

SWIMMING MINNOW No 900
– White with green and red finish, belly double hook and treble tail hook. Condition good plus $187, another 4½″ $220

TAD POLLY #5000
– (Four) All have glass eyes, L-rigs. One is in frog finish, one early green scale, one later green scale and one in shiner scale. All conditions good or better $55

ZIG-WAG
– Shiner scale blue head (same as the blue used on the #200 Experts). Glass eyes, L-rig, 2 hooks. This the long body, short head, early model. Near mint, rare colour $82

HILDEBRANDT
2½″ – Wooden bait with red bucktail with white painted body and 'safetypin' hook hangers. Condition very good $38

HILL
SPRING LOADED SPINNER BAIT
2½″ – With large Muskie hook marked 'L S Hill, Gd Rapids, Mich., Pat. May 23, '76, Feb 4, '79 – 2½″' $82

HINCKLEY
PHANTOM FLOAT
3¼″ – Livingston S Hinckley marked 'Pat. Jan. 12. '97'. Hollow aluminium bait with its original box swivel. Condition excellent $27

J A HOLZAPFEL
MUSHROOM BASS BAIT
3¾″ – Rare J A Holzapfel 1908 Patent. This white lure has 3 treble hooks (one broken) $275

HOSMER
MECHANICAL FROGGIE
5" – Rare, only 4 known to exist. New, in original box $3850, another in good plus condition $990

HOWE
VACUUM BASS BAIT
– In original tin black enamel with gold paint and borders box. Near mint $385

IMMELL
CHIPPEWABAIT
3" – $99, $209
3½" – $385
4" – $154

W H JAMES
SPINNING SQUIDS
– Maker W H James, Brooklyn, New York. Marked with the maker and patent date and is a nickel plated spinner which revolves around the shaft of single hook. Condition fine $100

Provenance: The current owner of the 'Pickerel Boxes' has owned them since the early 1950s and they had been out of his house only twice since then. They were aquired from a man who got them from an estate in Lakeville, Massachusetts in 1950. The only information this man had was that the boxes were made by the owner's grandfather, being used in south eastern Massachusetts to ice fish for pickerel and pike. The owner was 75 when he died in 1950, thus he was born in 1875. It is estimated the grandfather made the boxes c1850 or possibly earlier. Sold for $13,200

JAMISON
NEMO
– Scarce Bass Bait with original hanging weight in red and white. Condition very good $242

COAXER
– No 1 Coaxer in good condition, in box $24
– (Five) Condition good to very good $33

CHICAGO WOBBLER
4" – In red and white $99

HUMDINGER
3¼" – In red and white $77

MUSKALLONGE MASCOT
– Mint in box $577

STRUGGLING MOUSE
2¼" – $231

WIG-WAG
– With glass eyes, in box $121
– With glass eyes $176

GEORGE JENNINGS
2⅞" – Hollow metal plug bait marked 'Geo. Jennings, Newark, NJ Patent Pending'. No 1 a feathered treble, some 'dents' and crack in blade $200

TORPEDO BAIT
2⅞" – Rare 'George Jennings, Newark, NJ Pat Pending' and 'Abbey & Imbrie, NY' marked metal bait. Early, without size markings, with original fixed box swivel in front. Condition excellent $385

JOHNSON
AUTOMATIC STRIKER
3" – With scale and green striped body, c1935. Condition excellent $110, similar $165, $154

KALAMAZOO FISHING TACKLE MANUFACTURERS

RHODES MECHANICAL FROG
– Mechanical swimming frog c.1910, in original wooden box. Nearly new condition $770

RHODES WOODEN MINNOW
3¾" – With front prop. marked 'Pats PNDG'. Only about 6 known to exist, c.1902 $3025
2¾' – In original box marked 'Kalamazoo Fishing Tackle Company', c.1904 $495
– With green and aluminium belly, 3 hand painted gill marks, white glass eyes, large props. and 2 belly weights $440

K & K MANUFACTURING CO
K & K ANIMATED MINNOW
– Believed to be the first American animated jointed wood bait. The Minoette model with 3" body and 3¾" overall length in silver shiner (green back and silver sides) finish with glass eyes. Three fixed double hooks. This rare 1907 bait is mint (except for some hook rust), in its original box (torn end flaps), with a great pocket catalogue $352, another with age flaking $165
– In green and silver scale finish, body measures 4¼" and overall length 5", glass eyes. Mint in original Patent 25 1907 marked box $605
– In rainbow finish, body measures 3¼", overall 3¾", glass eyes. Many

large chips, in poor condition $71
4¼″ – In rainbow finish with glass eyes $550

K & K JOINTED MINNOW
5⅜″ – This gold bait with green back and black slash lines has red faceted glass eyes, 3 double hooks and a metal tail. Excellent $412. Another similar 4⅜″ $275

K & K MOONLIGHT GHOST PLUG
2½″ – This wooden bait with glass eyes, lead head and trailing feathered treble hook $467

W M C MILES BAIT CO
BILLS PRIDE
3½″ – Jointed, white with red head, chamois tail and nickel plated spinner $33

MILLER
REVERSIBLE MINNOW
– C1916. Wooden body in white with red head and gold spots, Neverfail side hook hangers, one set of spinners marked 'Pat. Applied For', the other is nickelled. Condition very good $880
4¼″ – C1916 with Neverfail hook hangers, set of brass spinners in yellow with gold spots. Excellent $2420

REVERSIBLE SPINNERS
– In original box $302

WILLIAM MILLS
STORE LURE DISPLAY
– With 18 unusual baits $1265

MOONLIGHT
FLOATING BAIT
– With staggered cup rigs and metal tail cap with luminous white finish $55

JOINTED PIKAROON
4″ – In yellow and black spots and red nose with glass eyes $302

PAW PAW FISH SPEAR PLUG
4″ – In box $907

POLLY WOG
4″ – In excellent condition $132

POLLY WOG JUNIOR
3″ – $88

PARDEE
KENT CHAMPION FLOATER
– Early Pardee (Samuel Friend). Hand made and painted frog with wooden body in aluminium paint with brown top and sides and black lines and spots, yellow glass eyes $2,200

STRING-TIED MINNOW
4¼″ – Believed to be the Nation's earliest commercial underwater wooden minnow. This is a rare minnow. Fat body with 3 treble hooks and earliest thru-body string hook hangers, plated props and flat end tail. Forerunner of Pflueger Trory Minnow. Mint $5225

KENT DOUBLE SPINNER ARTIFICIAL MINNOW
3⅞″ – The body of this 5 treble hook plug is silver with black back and tail. Very good plus condition $2750

KENT CHAMPION FLOATER
2¼″ – This old turn-of-the-century hand-made and painted frog has yellow glass eyes and aluminium props. Near excellent $1540

PAYNE
WOGGLE BUG PLUG
3″ – $412

PEPPER
WONDERWOOD FISH SPINNER
2¼″ – Joseph E Pepper's 20th Century Wonder Wood Fish Spinner $236
– John Pepper Jr metal bait marked 'Pat. May 2, '93' $825

JIM PFEIFFER
TOP LURE #004
2¾″ – Open mouth shiner-type, painted eyes with aft spinner. Mint $22

LIVE BAIT HOLDER
4″ – Glass, with moulded acorn end, with 4 treble hooks. Mint condition in box $440
3¾″ – With marked metal cap and acorn tail. Crack in glass near front hook hanger $715

PFLUEGER
ALL-IN-ONE PLUG
– In green frog finish and faceted diamond eyes with lip #4. Condition excellent $154

INVINCIBLE
3″ – Hand painted rubber minnow with original hanging treble hooks on woven silk trace $110

KENT FROG
– A classic wooden plug with glass eyes, surface belly hook hanger and green back with yellow and black markings, yellow sides with red band and white belly $313

LIVE WIRE PLUG
– With celluloid dorsal fin, faceted red eyes and surface rig. Mint $66

CRYSTAL MINNOW
– Luminous c1885. A glass body lure with chipped tail (usual) and flake off the top fin, scarce $802

MAY BUG SPOON
1¾″ – With gold and green wings, maroon body and black details on top. The underside has gold wings with red stripes, a white luminous body and black legs. Condition unused with factory tag $4510

METALIZED MINNOW
3⅛″ – C1910. The minnow has a wood body plated with thick layers of copper (undercoating) and nickel. Also Neverfail hook hangers and glass eyes $302
3¾″ – With 5 hooks $137
3″ – With 3 hooks $82

NEVERFAIL MINNOW
3¾″ – Unusual green scale finish, glass eyes, Neverfail hangers, bulldog marked prop. Condition excellent $38
3⅝″ – In yellow with brown crackle back finish, glass eyes, hand painted gills and Neverfail hangers. Some age lines, condition good $55
3⅝″ – In luminous/gold spots with glass eyes, bulldog marking and Neverfail

hangers. Condition very good $49

3⅝″ – No 3170 Unused in box $110

3″ – In yellow perch, glass eyes and Neverfail hangers. Condition very good, in box $44

3″ – In rainbow finish, glass eyes, Neverfail hangers, bulldog marked prop. Condition excellent $33

PEERLESS MINNOW

– White/yellow stripe on back. Unplated brass early shaped prop in front, Neverfail hangers with no plate underneath, 3 treble hooks. In shiny mint condition $44

TOURNAMENT CASTING FROG

3″ – Rubber. This frog has about 80% of its original white luminous finish. Only two known examples. Condition good $330

WEEDLESS MEADOW FROG

– Of rubber in box $27

WIZARD MINNOW

– Green back, white belly, 2 hand painted gill marks, yellow glass eyes with black pupils, 5 hooker. Correct shaped early props, each marked only with an 'L', one lead belly weight. Some age lines but in average plus condition $77

WIZARD WIGGLER

3″ – Green spotted frog, red painted eyes, 1 piece Push-In hangers, 2 double hooks, signed tail. Moderate age lines, finish wear around lip otherwise condition excellent $27

1½″ – One dozen fly rod Pflueger Wizards on cards in factory box. Six colour patterns of scarce wooden baits $253

WIZARD WOODEN MINNOW

3½″ – With plain wired-through hook hangers $467

PONTIAC

PONTIAC MINNOW

2¾″ – Rare, in wooden box with illustrated paper label on top. In excellent condition $660

LOU RHEAD

MINNOW

2¾″ – Condition very good $71

– Scarce Lou Rhead Frog. Condition mint $638

GRASSHOPPER LURE

2″ – Handmade with tiny glass eyes, feathers on back and various shades of green and orange colouration. (c1916–1920s) $440

HELGRAMITE LURE

2¾″ – Handmade with multi-colour body with feathered back $550

STONECAT LURE

2″ – Handmade, unusual lure in green, black and brown with gold covered body, glass eyes, feather tail and legs $275

RODIGRASS

4″ – Hollow bait of copper, brass and German silver $60

– Four Rodigrass spoons $55

SHAKESPEARE

EVOLUTION RUBBER MINNOW

– With prop marked 'Pat Applied For'. Condition very good $132

– With pointed props $49

FROG SKIN BAIT

3¾″ – Condition very good $71

LITTLE JO

– In tangerine with black back and yellow spots and glass eyes. Condition very good plus $38

METALIZED MINNOW

– Actually a wood plug with a heavy plating of metal. Size 3″ with copper glass eyes, see through hangers, 3 treble hooks. Very minor dings and one short ⅜″ crack in metal, otherwise in excellent condition $132

MINNOW

– In white with centre wire hangers, hand painted gills, and glass eyes. Hook drag marks $22

3″ – Early Notched Prop Series 33 in original wooden box. The glass eyed, yellow perch minnow has flat plate see-through hook hanger $209

– Early Notched Prop Series 03 in box $363

– (Two) With glass eyes, hand painted gills and blended red backs. One 3″ (flat hangers), one 2¾″ (wire hangers). Condition very good $55

5¼″ – With three treble hooks, green crackle back, large glass eyes, flat plate see-through hook hangers and hand painted gill marks. Condition very good $385

REVOLUTION

3½″ – First wood production model. The plug marked 'Pat Appl'd For'. The side hooks are held to collar tabs by twisted wires. This lure was patented in 1901 but replaced by aluminium version in 1902. Condition very good $990

3¼″ – Hollow aluminium plug, 2 props in middle, acorn tail. Condition mint $176

3¼″ – With 'Pat Appl'd For' marking and rounded props. Condition excellent $121

– Marked 'Pat Appl'd For' with round headed props. Rear unit is rounded version painted red, front unit is painted yellow. Light yellow and red head, has no hooks (some paint chipping) $200

3¼″ – Marked 'Patented Feb 5 1901, April 9 1901', acorn cap. Condition excellent $121

– (Two) Round headed props on both. Flat back 'Acorn' rear end with the flap part on the inside next to props, and the earlier rounded version with body hook tie ¾″ back from nose. 'Acorn' type has its body hooks, the other has none. Condition very good $200

– With later pointed-style propellers. Good plus condition $99

3¼″ – With notched props, aluminium bait $209

SEA WITCH MIDGET

– (an uncatalogued version) with an unusual True-To-Nature scale finish and hand painted gill outline extending diagonally to the tail $275

STRIPED BASS WOBBLER
6″ – Natural green scale, pressed eyes, U wire hanger, keel, 2 treble hooks. Condition very good $60, another similar $55

UNDERWATER MINNOW
3⅝″ – In wooden box with early notched props and green back, salmon sides and white belly rainbow finish. This 5 hook bait has glass eyes, hand painted gills and flat see-through hook hangers. Almost mint $440

WAUKAZOO SURFACE SPINNER
– In frog finish. Mint $165

WHIRLWIND SPINNER
– With early notched props and red body. Condition excellent $165

WORDEN BUCKTAIL SPINNER
– A number sold in very good condition, $77, $99, $88 and $190 (two)

MALCOLM A SHIPLEY
CEDAR PROPELLER
3″ – With nickel plated props. Condition very good $82

SMITH
SMITH WOOD MINNOW
– With green and white body and glass eyes. Tail wire broken and part gone $2860

SOUTH BEND
BASS ORENO
– (Two) One early pink side scale, no eyes (2 chips of paint off near cup rigs). One white/red head, no eyes (light ageing lines). Condition shiny excellent $33

COAST ORENO
6¼″ – Blue mullet scale, rare colour, big single tarpon hook. Light age lines otherwise condition shiny excellent $121

COMBINATION MINNOW
2⅝″ – In rainbow finish, glass eyes. Bucktail dressed treble otherwise condition excellent $44

KING BASS ORENO
4¾″ – Luminous yellow/red head, black shadow wave, pressed eyes, 2 treble hooks on break-away wire leader. Condition mint $33

MINNOW
3⅝″ – In yellow and red finish with glass eyes. Condition very good $44

MIN-ORENO
4″ – Red and white, tack eyes, two treble hooks. Light age lines otherwise near mint $16

MUSH-ORENO
– Earliest version, green spotted frog, no eyes, 3 treble hooks, few small 'dings'. Condition shiny excellent $11
– Slightly later version, still 1920s, white/red head, no eyes, 3 treble hooks. Slight varnish 'flaking' otherwise shiny excellent $16

MUSKY MINI-ORENO
5¼″ – Red and white, tack eyes, two treble hooks. Age lines otherwise excellent $66

MUSKY WIGGINS-ORENO
– Metal trolling bait, 11″ overall, 3 nickel plated brass spinners, huge weighted lure, 1920s. Condition average plus $16

PANATELLA MINNOW
– (Three) with glass eyes. One red and white, one green crackle back, one green crackle back with pink scales $55

PIKE-ORENO
– (Two) One 4½″, green scale, glass eyes with eye shadow, 2 treble hooks. One Baby Pike-Oreno 3¼″, green scale, glass eyes with eye shadow, 2 treble hooks, light age lines. Condition excellent $22
5⅜″ – White and red head, glass eyes and black eye shadow, 2 big treble hooks, moderate age lines, ding in head otherwise excellent $33

WHIRL-ORENO
– White/red head, red and black hackle. Light age lines and light wear on edges $60

WIZ-ORENO
– Rainbow, glass eyes with black eye shadow. Condition mint $33

BASS ORENO
– (Three) One early #973 RSF, with glass eyes, red scale. One Pike Oreno #29565, silver flash with pressed eyes. One Fish Oreno, red/white with tack eyes. All mint or excellent $82

ZANE GREY TEASER
11″ – Red and white, pressed eyes. Few small dings but shiny excellent condition $55
11″ – Pearl-type finish, tack eyes. Several dings and showing primer $49

STALEY-JOHNSON
TWIN-MIN F105 PLUG
– New in box $82

BUD STEWART
– Two plugs. One 4″ and the other 1½″ long plunker with front hooks removed $71
11″– Older triple jointed Muskie plug $71

STREICH MANUFACTURING CO
STREICH'S FLEX-O-MINO
– With painted red and white metal head, glass eyes and white rubber body (with pocket catalogue). Condition excellent $27

U S ATHLETIC CO
KETCHALL WOBBLER F606
3¾″ – Rare, with white and red head, body and treble hooks (c1920s). New in colourful box $99

VAN CLAY
VAN CLAY MINNOW
4″ – Green spotted frog with red head, glass eyes, 3 treble hooks, unusual hangers, spring loaded head to facilitate removal from snags. Condition shiny mint $192

ED VOM HOFE
SPOONS
– (Two) No 6 and No 5 $40
4¾″ – Trolling spoon marked 'Edward Vom Hofe etc' $77

ARCHER WAKEMAN
– Archer Wakeman's lure April 13th 1886. A Devon type lure which held a minnow. Plated metal, fish-shaped body called Wakeman Skeleton Bait. Two blades protruding have white paint on the back side with red gill marks. Some later ones had a tear-shaped blade on the nose; this one does not. Condition – feathers are worn away from treble hook and body treble hook is detached $250

WALTON
SPEED BAIT
– Made by Walton Products, Rochester, New York c1931. No 2W bass size (1⅝″) with 16 tiny props each marked 'Pat. Appl'd' in silver finish. Condition very good $175

WELCH & GRAVES
GLASS MINNOW TUBE
4¼″ – Marked 'Welch & Graves, Natural Bridge, NY, Pat. Jan. 3, '93' $588
4¼″ – With 3 feathered treble hooks $990
4¼″ – Similar to patent drawings $495
4½″ – 'Welch & Graves Natural Bridge, NY, Pat. Jane 3, 93' is moulded into the early glass minnow tube lure. Condition excellent $632

WILSON
WILSON'S SIZZLER
3″ – Metal weedless/automatic hooking lure marked 'Pat'd Aug 24 1904'. Condition excellent $221

WILSON FROG BAIT
2⅛″ – With painted body, rubber legs and glass bead eyes. One foot pad missing $522

FISH DECOYS

ERNIE AAMOT
3″ – Rare, miniature white fish with typical fin/tail painting. Condition excellent $385

JERRY ADAMS
YELLOW-BELLY PERCH
9½″ – Markings in ink on belly, copper fins, glass eyes, carved head/tail. Condition mint $247

ROCK BASS
8″ – Markings in ink on belly. Condition mint $192

GEORGE AHO (Contemporary)
BLUEGILL
7″ – In grey with pink belly, blue gills, glass eyes, curved body. Signed/dated on belly. Condition new $99

SUNFISH
7″ – Grey and white, pink chin, glass eyes, curved body. Signed/dated. Condition new $88

WALLEYE DECOY
16″ – Grey and white, long curved body. Signed/dated. Condition new $220
6½″ – Grey and white, curved body. Signed/dated. Condition new $99

MEL. AASERUDE, CASS LAKE, MN
This carver has been ice fishing in the Bemidji area of Northern Minesota for about 20 years. His love for dark house spearing inspired him to carve his own decoys over the years.

CRAPPIE
5¾″ – With original jigging stick. It is black and white with glass eyes and carved head $286

CRAWDAD
4″ – With wood body, brass tail and claws. Unusual decoy has orange body, tack eyes, iron legs/feelers $198

FISH DECOY
8″ – Natural wood body, tack eyes, brass fins and tail and copper line tie $181

FROG DECOY
7½″ – With carved wood body, tack eyes and leather legs. The body is natural wood with burn design $121
5″ – With copper feet and rudder. The wood body is brown with white belly and black/red spots $154

SALAMANDER DECOYS
– Two with brass feet. One is 6″ in brown with red/yellow spots. The other is 5¾″ in black with yellow spots $440

TURTLE DECOY
3½″ – With wood body and brass head, feet and tail. Body is natural wood with carved detail and orange and yellow edging $330
5½″ – In mint condition with leather feet and tail $49

BOB BEEBE, SEYMOUR, TN (Contemporary)
BASS
10½″ – With curved body, copper fins, glass eyes. Marked 17 of a limited edition of 100. Condition new $198

BROWN TROUT
10″ – Carved after T Van den Bossche MI c1930s. Carved copper fins. Marked 22 of limited edition of 100 $137

MUSKIE
15″ – In the style of c.1910 PA carver with glass eyes and copper fins. Marked 19 of limited edition of 100 $231

STURGEON
11½″ – In the style of c.1940 MN carver with black/white spots and stripe and red head. No 41 of 100 made $27

KENNETH BRUNING, ROGER CITY, MI (1919–1974)
BROWN TROUT
6″ – C1950. His decoys are usually bright and colourful. This is dark mustard yellow along the back blending into a light orange on the sides which blends into a burgundy red along the bottom. Vermiculation along the back is in dark brown and red and yellow spots on side $550

BUCHMAN, MT CLEMENS, MI
BASS
11″ – With curved tail, glass eyes and red gill and mouth details. 'Alton 'Chub' Buchman' signed on belly $1100

BROWN TROUT
13½″ – Working decoy and carved jigging stick. New condition $302

RAINBOW TROUT
13″ – Working decoy $187

JOHN CROSS, LAC DU FLAMBEAU, WI
SUCKER
6½″ – Condition excellent $145

WILLIAM FLANAGAN, STAPLES, MINNESOTA (1917–1968)
DECOY
6½″ – In natural pine with burnt-in stripes and head details. The fins and tail are yellow with green and red. Unused $176
6″ – In natural pine with burn circles, carved open mouth, red head detail and fins and tail in red/white/blue. Unused $176

FRANK GENSLO, STOCKBRIDGE, WI
NATIVE INDIAN STURGEON
10½″ – Original cedar finish with tiny tack eyes and copper fins, c1940. Condition very good $385

CLEVER GILBERT, FRANKFORT, MI
SNOW GOOSE
– Fish decoy with stick and box containing interchangeable spinner blade feet $700

GOULETTE, NEW BALTIMORE AREA, MICH
PERCH
5¾″ – Fish with nice paint detail and form, tack eyes and carved gills. Minor paint touch up on bottom side of fins. Very good $825

GREENE
CRAPPIE FISH DECOY
6¼″ – Signed 'Greene 86, 486'. The glass eyed fish has superb paint and carving detail. Condition mint $200

HEDDON
FISH DECOY
– No 409L with glass eyes and perch finish. Very good $375
– No 409P with glass eyes and scale finish. It has seen much use $150

HANS JANNER
HERRING
13″ – With great form and paint detail, sign reflector glass eyes and saw-tooth dorsal fin. One tail tip has been glued $650

SHAD DECOY
12″ – Rare, of solid walnut with carved tail and copper fins $2530

M. KUHA, WOLF LAKE, MN
METAL CRAPPIE
– With over 150 rivets, copper eyes $1155

CHARLES LUNDGREN
PERCH DECOY
– In original condition, c1940s $522

JIM NELSON
BROOK TROUT
10½″ – Largest known Nelson decoy with carved mouth, gills, underside and up-turned sweeping tail $2200

OSCAR PETERSON (1887–1951), CADILLAC, MI
BROOK TROUT PLAQUE
18″ × 8½″
– An area of the fish's side has been professionally restored $2860

RAINBOW TROUT PLAQUE
36½″ × 11½″
– The background (not the fish) has been professionally restored $5500

SUNFISH PLAQUE
17″ × 10″
– The colourful glass eye plaque was pictured in the November and December 1982 issues of 'Natural Resources Magazine'. Condition excellent $9350

NATURAL SIDES
8″ – Decoy with hand drawn scale details. While this scale finish was found on one authenticated Peterson lure, this is the only known decoy with a scale finish. With flat tack eyes, copper fins and line tie, this honest old fish is in very good condition $4400

BASS SMALLMOUTH
8″ – Period III. Fat body with painted white gills and tack eyes. Condition very good $3000

BROOK TROUT
9″ – Period IV. Excellent condition $1210
8¾″ – Tack eyes, some finish off belly $2640
8″ – With large tack eyes, the back painted a golden tan blending down to a seldom seen gold on the sides, with exceptional black and red accents. The famous Peterson trademark of a black moustache outlines the upper lip and the lower is painted a lovely Indian yellow which continues across the body. Near mint condition $3190
7″ – Has use wear and touch up on fins and belly $770
7″ – With tack eyes and black spots. Chipping on belly weights and two fins and a bruise to tip of lower jaw, otherwise excellent $850
6½″ – Period IV fish with painted eyes. Paint loose on belly, chipping on fins otherwise very good plus $1750
5¾″ – Period IV. Near mint $880
5⅛″ – Only ¾″ high. Other than paint chipping on the belly weight areas and little on the fins, in mint condition $1100
5″ – Period III with fat body and raised tack eyes. Condition very good $900

BROWN TROUT
– Small fat body. Excellent except small spot touch up on right side and 3 pin holes in head area $550

NORTHERN PIKE
– With average wear $990

PERCH
9½″ – Rare early Period II (1920 – 1924) fat body fish with

brass top fins. Tail tips are chipped and one side of tail has finish wear and normal paint chipping on the metal fins otherwise in near excellent condition $3520

7″ – Period III with raised tack eyes. Very good $1750

7″ – With flaking on dorsal fin and tail $440

5⅛″ – Tack eyes. This little fish has a thin crack from the line tie to the tip of the jaw and paint is chipped off eye, otherwise in very good plus condition $935

5″ – With painted eyes. Paint chipped on belly weight and little on fins otherwise excellent $950

4½″ – Period III. Near mint $605

PIKE

8″ – Sleek lines and red painted tack eyes $880

7″ – Period III with raised tack eyes. Very good $450

7″ – Period III with tack eyes. Very good $400

PIKE MINIATURE

5″ – With flat tack eyes $700

4⅞″ – Only ⅝″ high. A miniature with painted eyes excellent condition $1430

SHINER

8″ – With tack eyes. It has a chipped tail, small spear point gouge and paint off belly weights, otherwise excellent $600

8″ – Period III with tack eyes $440

7¼″ – With red spots, tack eyes and tiny tail chip otherwise very good condition $715

SMELT

9″ – Period IV. Near mint $990

7″ – With silver sides, black back and tack eyes. One small chip otherwise mint $1045

SUCKER

9″ – Period V fish with large tack eyes, green back and yellow belly. Almost mint $1750

– Excellent original condition with some minor flaking on the bottom $2090

7½″ – Period III, c1920s, and non-typical. The dark back and light belly blend in perfect accord $1870

5⅞″ – With large domed tack eyes and somewhat fat body. Some belly rubs and fin edge chips otherwise mint $1045

TROUT

7¾″ – With tack eyes, natural unpainted sides, black back and white belly, copper fins and steel line tie. Paint chipping on belly weight areas and line tie, otherwise mint $1650

PFLUEGER

RUBBER FISH DECOY

5¾″ – C1898. It has much finish wear, crack at tail and the metal fin has become loosened in the body $400

FRANK FINNEY PUNGO, VA (Contemporary)

ANTIQUE STYLE

8½″ – Paint chipped, in green with lead fin weight. New $16

RED SALMON

42″ – With detailed carving including scales and glass eyes. Ring in mouth for vertical display. New $165

STURGEON

21″ – With lead weight fins. New $38

JESS RAMEY (1891–1963), CADILLAC, MI

TROUT

6½″ – In blended green, c1950s. Excellent $660

– In green with red/white/black, c1950s. In use paint wear $308

SIMMS, CADILLAC, MI

PIKE

11″ – C1940s, walnut with black marks, aluminium fins, tack eyes and curved tail. Very good $66

DECOY

8½″ – In gold with red/yellow/black spots, brass fins, tack eyes and curved tail. Condition excellent $121

TONY SMITH, HOLLAND MI (Contemporary)

FROG

– In brown and tan, glass eyes and multiple line tie $181

WALTER WERTSER, GRAND RAPIDS, MI

SUCKER

9″ – With carved tail and lead fins $577

UNNAMED DECOY

7¼″ – Spectacular and rare early Lake Chautauqua, NY fish decoy with leather tail, body thru-hole line tie and straight back edge metal fins. The delicate and very fine paint and carving detail makes this very special and one of the finest New York decoys. Other than some finish chipping on the leather tail, belly weight and tack eyes, the fish is near mint and with original jigging stick $6325

An unnamed decoy which sold for £6325

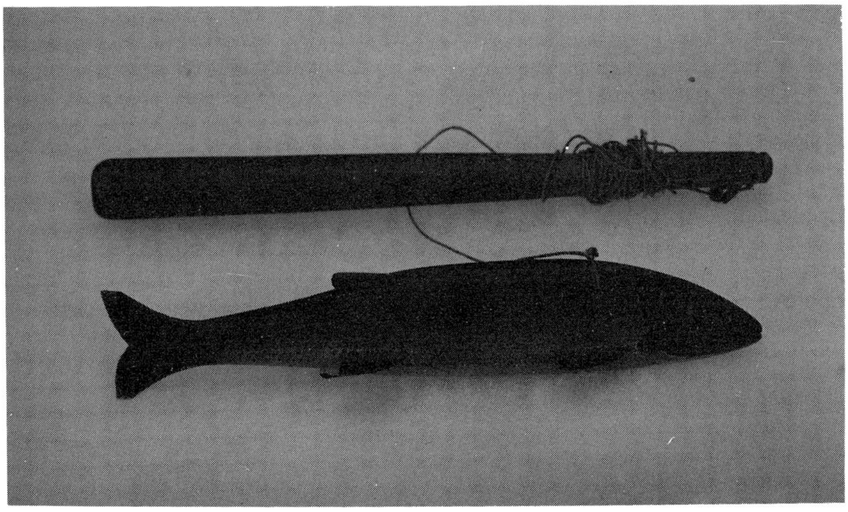

INDEX